LET THEM ALL TALK

THE
MUSIC
OF
ELVIS
COSTELLO

Design: David Houghton

Printed by: Redwood Books Limited

Published by: Sanctuary Publishing Limited, 82 Bishops Bridge Road, London W2 6BB

Copyright: Brian Hinton, 1999

Photographs: Redferns Music Picture Library, Pictorial Press (including back and front covers), All Action Pictures, London Features International, Lynn Goldsmith/Corbis and the *Surrey Comet*

ISBN: 1-86074-197-7

Coventry University

THE
MUSIC
OF
ELVIS
COSTELLO

brian hinton

"...the old poet stamps in off the cliffs, shaking rust from his beard by the wicket gate to encounter Charlton Heston, Koo Stark, David Bailey and (inevitably) Dr Brian Hinton."
Iain Sinclair, 'Nearly A Moon', from *The Ebbing Of The Kraft* (1997)

For Eileen Ann McManus. No relation, but the light of my life

reviews for brian hinton

Joni Mitchell – Both Sides Now
"Hinton is to be congratulated on his painstaking research, forming information from hundreds of sources into a coherent and intelligent analysis...a fine and readable book."
Shadows And Light, Joni Mitchell fanzine

"Intelligent, enthusiastic and surprisingly sympathetic. Hinton lends an academic rigour enlivened by speculative exploration of the huge grey areas left undefined by one of our most enigmatic artists. There's a genuine post absorption feeling that you've become more intimate with the imposing subject."
Folk On Tap magazine

Celtic Crossroads – The Art Of Van Morrison
"A delight from beginning to end. Written with what appears to be consummate ease by Brian Hinton...definitive, readable and ultimately enjoyable thanks to Brian's sheer skill as a writer; it comes as no surprise to know that he also has a background as a poet, as it is exactly that kind of gifted insight that leads to the subject in hand."
Ptolemaic Terrascope magazine

"Hinton has the confidence to locate Van in high culture. Revelations, speculations, insights...the book is full of them."
Wavelength, Van Morrison fanzine

acknowledgments

Particular thanks are due to Mark Perry, co-editor of *Beyond Belief*, a superb fanzine devoted solely to Elvis, which spans the Atlantic. The same to Richard Groothuizen, of the *Elvis Costello Information Service*, who single-handedly has put together two fact-packed books on Elvis, and a six-times-a-year magazine. Anyone who enjoys the cordial purveyed here, could do far worse than to go on to the "hard stuff" of their respective Costello tracking devices. (Contact *Beyond Belief* c/o Mark Perry, 6 Hillside Grove, Taunton, Somerset TA1 4LA or Mike Bodayle, 110 Granburg Circle, San Antonio, TX 78218, USA; email bb@perrys.prestel.co.uk; contact ECIS c/o Richard Groothuizen, Primulstraat 46, 1441 HC, Purmerend, Netherlands.)

I would also like to record my huge debt to Geoff Wall, who has read sections of this book as they appeared from off the word processor, and whose rock archives – at last being plundered by grateful record companies – have supplemented my own. Clive Whichelow of Backnumbers has ferreted out all kinds of interesting press cuttings.

I would like to convey my endless gratitude to Penny, Jeff, Eddy and Michelle of Sanctuary Publishing for their encouragement and support – it's a lonely job, writing! Thanks also to Arcy, Julian Bell, Emma Bradford, Brian at Island Computers, Ken Brooks, Arthur Brown, the Cunliffes, Andy Darlington, John Delaney, all at Dimbola, Aidan Dun, Graham Elwood, Dave Eyre, Jean Foister and all at Golden Hill Fort, David Harris for his surprise treat of an Elvis gig in

Cardiff, Amanda Hemingway, Jeff Lewis, Peter Loveless, Elli McCarthy, all at Ottakers bookshop, Neil Philip, James and Linda Sale, David Sellars, Adrian Smith, my fellow poet Deryk Soord and his wife Claire, and the peerless Martin Stone. Special thanks to my dad, who has given me *every* kind of support over the years, Sylvia at Ventnor Music Library, Bebe Buell and Muffin men everywhere.

contents

Elvis, a variant of "elfish", meaning man of superhuman powers...

introduction

Within days of the mysterious death of INXS lead singer Michael Hutchence, *The Guardian* carried an interview with Jacky Gerald, a rock 'n' roll therapist. As she told Peter Coleman, "You get situations where one person's behaviour might be so erratic that everyone's affected. Everyone's feeling crazy and they don't know why. You've got money being lost, people falling apart, and it can be absolutely horrific." On the other hand, some managers do not wish their charges to be made well, as they would be less easy to manipulate. "It's a very macho business," she says.

Elvis Costello has had his fair share of road madness; not least the 1977 Stiff tour, about which he wrote 'Pump It Up', on the nastiness of excess. He does exemplify, though, exactly the kind of therapy that Jacky Gerald tries to instil into her charges: "If people get to where they have a sense of self, it doesn't matter if, in the eyes of the world, one day they're great, and the next they're crap – because they know who they are." This kind of self-definition is par for the course with any good singer-songwriter who tends to delve into their own personal experience for material. In previous books for Sanctuary, I have followed the careers of Joni Mitchell and Van Morrison, and traced a similar sense of self-determination. Elvis is of a slightly later generation, missing the hippie daze through which the two others plunged like dolphins, but he shares much with them, and indeed is a friend of both. All three display a sense of musical craft, belief in the power of words without making the music which accompanies them a poor relation, integrity, and sheer bloody-mindedness when they see fit.

All three served a long apprenticeship before fame came knocking, and each has learnt how to deal with the aftermath of fame, recognising in Gerald's words that "success or failure in the business isn't the be-all and end-all of life". Costello has sought instead success in purely artistic terms, like another soul-mate, Neil Young. Indeed, the vanities and trap doors of fame have been one of his guiding subjects. If Joni's work centres on herself, from waif to superstar, and Van's deals with lost dreams and paranoia, then Costello is a colder eye, watching from the shadows. Not so much "Mr Angry" as hurt and ironic, a bruised romantic in tinted glasses, hiding from a cruel world.

In late 1997, Costello guested on Clive Anderson's BBC1 chat show (its theme tune: 'Let Them All Talk'), scruffy and unposed. He seemed affable, an ordinary bloke freed of all disguises, but not someone who even the politely waspish Clive would dare push too far. There is a hardness in Elvis's eyes which repel any attempt to dig too deep. Anderson joshed him about his name changes – Napoleon Dynamite, the Emotional Toothpaste – thus neatly opening up the central enigma, that this pose of the man next door was precisely that, a pose. One thought about the whole tradition of rock stars taking on new names, from Larry Parnes' gay transformations of ordinary lads into Vince Power or Billy Fury, of Bob Dylan redefining himself from a Jewish shopkeeper's son into an Okie sharecropper, of David Jones becoming David Bowie. From suburbia to exotica. A move repeated self-referentially in the punk years: Richard Hell and Tom Verlaine, Rat Scabies and Dee Generate, Wreckless Eric and Sting. A move which in the 1980s became corporate – Madonna, Prince – and then ended in the cartoon world of The Spice Girls. No wonder that Elvis wrote 'Puppet Girl' for one of their forebears, Wendy James.

Costello, christened Declan MacManus, has shrugged off each category (or stage name) with which management, critics and even himself have tried to shackle him. Here is a man who once declared, "My ultimate vocation in life is to be an irritant." He has subverted his "career" whenever it began to bore him. Too dangerous for live TV, social commitment has provided the continuing muscle which drives his art still. His particular mission statement was outlined in the title of his first album, and the shouted, pleading, endless chorus of

'Alison': "my aim is true" – as in purity of intention, or the steadiness with which he can fire off a lethal volley. There is something in Costello of the "watcher in the dark" of Richard Thompson's 'Shoot Out The Lights', a sniper whose words can kill.

The first Elvis needed others to write his songs for him. His namesake creates songs in which the personal and the political chafe against each other, endlessly scratching at the scab of "armed forces". *All This Useless Beauty*, his latest and in many ways his finest album at the time of writing – excluding compilations and guest appearances, which are endless – crystallises a kind of luxuriant decay, dealing with everything from global warming to the nature of failure, in songs originally written for others. A torrent of words and music, from a man who carefully retains his inner core of mystery. The first post-modern rock star.

So who exactly is he? Here are two snapshots, to prepare us for the home movie that is about to follow. The 1980s are dragging painfully to an end, in retrospect the final days of the reign of the Empress Margaret, but it sure doesn't feel like that at the time. The Thatcherite hegemony has been slow to assert itself, but after its defining moment, the Falklands war – whose militaristic chutzpah Costello predicted so witheringly in 'Oliver's Army' – and two successive General Election triumphs, it seems to be universal, and endless.

Big Sister is watching you, in just the kind of mixing up of the private and political which Elvis has made his own musical territory. Political opposition is divided and mealy-mouthed: the real action is out in the streets, with near riots over the naked unfairness of the poll tax, the rich robbing the poor. As workers at GCHQ have already found to their cost, to speak out is to risk your job, especially from a new generation of hatchet men busily infesting the former bastions of the welfare state. With the introduction of legislation like the notorious "Clause 27", outlawing the public championing of gay rights, the sentiments of 'Green Shirt' – which at the time had sounded needlessly paranoid – were bang up to date. Suddenly, there is "no such thing as society", while Norman Tebbit unleashes graveyard images – maggots infesting rotten corpses, that kind of thing – about the very idea of a wider public good.

Onto BBC2's minority segment arts programme *The Late Show*

(subsequently retitled *Later*), live and decidedly dangerous, barges Elvis Costello, already in self-imposed exile in Dublin, but here a prophet crying in the wilderness, a wild beast uncaged, full of sweaty intensity and foreboding. His short set culminates with his own twisted love song to Mrs Thatcher, 'Tramp The Dirt Down', an almost sorrowful declaration of how he will stamp on her grave when she is dead and gone. Soon, he hopes. The lyrics suggest its anti-heroine to be some kind of vampire figure, almost impossible to kill, and thus particularly important to guard from the dangers of resurrection. The song ends much like the final verse of Dylan's 'Masters Of War', but targeted not onto a generic hate group – arms manufacturers – but onto a real, living human being. It is an assassin's song to his next victim, and Elvis means every word.

Just like Kennedy's assassination, in fact, and I remember watching in awed delight, then endlessly running back my video, still half disbelieving, this healing torrent of spite, loathing and determination. Costello lit a fire in the dark that night, and its ramifications went far beyond music, or entertainment.

Fast forward. It is 1996, with John Major's mediocrity about to run out of time under a welter of sleaze and mismanagement, in a kind of puppet-play Thatcherism, its architect bitter, driven from power by her own side, and spitting poison from the wings. The British race has settled into a kind of cold determination, waiting for its long delayed chance to throw Thatcher's children into the dustbin of history.

Ironically, Costello too seems a relic of the previous decade, a musician who has somehow slipped out of focus in the public mind. Still hugely respected as a songwriter of undoubted genius, his early work is recycled on compilations of his greatest hits, as sure a grave as the one he wished Thatcher into seven years before. He has split with his comrades in arms, The Attractions – dropping them like Margaret humiliated Geoffrey Howe, and reaping the same bitter whirlwind, in the form of a novel by his former bass player which lays bare life on the road, and his own supposed aloofness. Elvis's image has blurred through frequent, tedious name changes and jolts in musical direction. No-one is quite sure who Elvis is anymore. Like Van Morrison, he is now the prisoner of a fanatical cult following, outside of which Costello is largely seen as a figure from the past, a musical jack-of-all-trades who commands cool respect rather than hot fanaticism.

Just as the Britpop skyrocket begins its slow burn-out, Costello appears on a *Later* Special, produced as before by British cultural svengali Mark Cooper. The impact is much the same as Dylan's appearance on MTV's *Unplugged*, or indeed Elvis Mark I back on TV after his years as a GI in Germany. Suddenly, here is a youthful looking Costello, sharp as a flick-knife, in total musical and visual control. The concert – since transferred to home video – opens with him reunited with The Attractions, the full clatter of a live rock band's grace and danger. Guest star on his own showcase, Costello moves through a carefully chosen mix of career highlights, and songs from his latest album, *All This Useless Beauty*. In come The Brodsky Quartet, supplemented with a full brass section, The White City Septet. Of all things, it is Elvis's interpretation of The Beach Boys' 'God Only Knows' which really has the hairs on the back of one's neck bristling, the sheer power of his voice soaring and cracking against a hymnal arrangement like a soul on its way to heaven. Costello's whole rich musical history is laid out before us, like a jeweller's display.

The only response is awe. That night, a star was reborn.

This book is a musical appreciation of one of the finest talents of our time. That's what it is. What it isn't, is a trawl through his personal life, a voyeuristic journal of titillation desperate to expose and humiliate. But a master songwriter will always put himself into his work to some extent, and to that same extent it has been my task to decipher the clues and, where possible, relate them to events in the singer's life, whether it be about his childhood, his family, his divorce or latest passion.

The challenge of finding meaning in songs written by one intent on maintaining his privacy is not to be undertaken lightly. And yet for those who persevere, there are very real rewards, since Elvis has never resorted yet to bubblegum lyrics. He usually writes about *something*; whether in anger or admiration, he always cares about his subject. Bebe Buell, Costello's former girlfriend, merely confirmed this to me in a transatlantic phone conversation. She revealed that, "Elvis is never going to write his own life story: he's like any rock star, they cover up their real lives like a smokescreen. But I really think that deep down he would like someone to tell the truth about all this. It really is about time." Despite his apparent desire for secrecy, she insisted, everything we needed to know is out there already, in his lyrics. The clues are there, if you know how to interpret them.

Let Them All Talk is, amongst other things, a biography of one of the world's greatest living songwriters. It is also an evolving study of a work in progress, the pursuit of a mystery trail where the final destination is unclear, but the clues are scattered to be found.

CHAPTER ONE

my name is true

In 1972, when Elvis Costello was seventeen, and went under another name, Revelation Records issued *Glastonbury Fayre*, a triple album so anachronistic that its boss, one Andrew Jakeman, was left with thousands of unsold copies, "stiffs" in industry slang. Five years later it was just the kind of music that the spiky haired revolutionary of *My Aim Is True*, was intent on sweeping into oblivion. A punk messiah, with short songs that never overstayed their welcome, bitter lyrics in which "love" was almost a dirty word, and where guitar solos – when present at all – were kept under strict control. Perversely, *Glastonbury Fayre* is as good a place as any to begin the long strange trip that must mark any proper investigation of Elvis's musical odyssey. Seemingly contrary to everything which he has achieved, this album – released just as Costello was beginning to work as a semi-pro musician, it is a seed bed of the forces that created and moulded him.

The music within is largely stale and well past its sell-by date, one disc of which in particular plunges the depths, with side-long, one-chord, twenty-minute jams by The Pink Fairies and Edgar Broughton. The kind of music which was steamrollered by glam rockers like Bolan and Bowie, both here represented, the former in his earlier, hippie incarnation. Seemingly in a different musical universe are a twenty-three-minute 'Dark Star', rich and stately, by Elvis's future musical heroes The Grateful Dead, taped at the Empire Pool, Wembley in 1972. The only home-grown band – here or anywhere –

to match its ambition and sense of mystery is the terminally obscure Mighty Baby, with a fifteen-minute instrumental 'A Blanket In My Muesli'. Martin Stone, a veteran of the blues boom with his own Stone's Masonry, and then a brief spell with Savoy Brown – until kicked out for excessive drug use – plays yearning, questing guitar, which floats over the most flexible and inventive heavy rock rhythm section England ever produced.

As The Action, they had been schooled in the kind of sweet soul music Elvis was himself to reinvigorate on *Get Happy*. By now followers of the Sufi faith, this musical act of devotion – an improvisation on John Coltrane's 'India' – was bootlegged on a portable cassette machine from a three-hour performance on "a tiny corrugated iron stage in a Glastonbury field at five am, 25 June, 1971. Drug credit: clear light sunshine and free porridge".

The source of this miraculous tape was the second Glastonbury festival, following on from a small-scale event held by farmer Michael Eavis on his Pilton farm the previous year, headlined by Marc Bolan, still in acoustic pixie mode. Nineteen-seventy-one saw the full monty, bands appearing on a specially constructed pyramid, free at the point of entry, and helmed by mad psychedelic pioneers, grown a little rancid and ragged in the four years since the summer of love. The whole sorry, idealistic mess, a melange of Gong, Arthur Brown and Melanie, was filmed by Nicholas Roeg, produced by David Puttnam, and hit the video racks only recently. There is a lot of full-frontal nudity, posh voices emerging from men like haystacks with the shakes, out of tune flutes, and people recreating the Garden of Eden on a stoned English hillside. All under the healing nipple of the ruined chapel atop Glastonbury Tor. A time which now seems as irrecoverable as the building of Stonehenge, or the epic upriver journey in the film *Aguirre, Wrath Of God*, though here the central task is the erection of a see-through pyramid. One which, against all the odds, and under the combined weight of myriad onstage idiot dancers, does not fall down.

From such amateurish fumblings grew the greatest annual music festival in the world, at which Elvis himself has since headlined. More to the immediate point, Mighty Baby soon split asunder, and Stone went on to found Chilli Willi and The Red Hot Peppers, with the lanky, pony-tailed Pete Thomas on drums and Andrew Jakeman, aka Jake Riviera, as their manager. A dry run for Elvis Costello And The Attractions, who inherited the Chillis' skewed take on American country-rock, laced with English irony.

In retrospect, *Glastonbury Fayre* is like the cast of *Hamlet* waiting for the arrival of the Prince (who would later cast them all aside). There is a studio take of Brinsley Schwarz, playing 'Love Song', written by their bassist Nick Lowe, and with thanks to manager Dave Robinson, who later co-founded Stiff. (Even) lesser known bands at Glastonbury that year included Help Yourself, one of whose songs Elvis would cover early in his career, and Quiver, with bassist Bruce Thomas. Jakeman is strangely absent from the credits, unless he is the Andrew Speedy Tweedy who provided photographs, but already in embryo here is his trademark, an independent release with superb packaging. A transparent plastic overlay comes complete with cartoon, and fits over the fold-out cardboard (and rubs off on albums adjacent in the rack!). Purchasers also found free inserts, including a cut-out dome and pyramid, an inventive label design, and a booklet packed with photos and graphics. All that is needed now is a dose of irony and business paranoia, though the idle boast that a live tape by Bowie will "remain in our vaults until the revolution" remains just that.

The album, like the Festival, derives from the communal idealism of the fading hippie dream – "All this music was given freely." The ornate, sci-fi-derived artwork comes courtesy of the American Barney Bubbles, a veteran of Woodstock, and a master at parodying any artwork put in front of him. At this point in time, he is still fixated with a melange of sex, drugs and rock 'n' roll, Aubrey Beardsley on acid, which he mastered on the extraordinary packaging of Hawkwind's *In Search Of Space*. The work here is like an issue of *Oz* magazine: there is even an Edward Barker cartoon. In Bubbles' weird mind, a naked young girl is girded with phallic guitars and a peace pipe: printed text is superimposed on photographs of marijuana plants.

Barney is also one of the signatories to the album's mission statement, itself printed over a photo of a pyramid. The recipients of half the proceeds, Solstice Capers, "intend to set up a non-profit ecological research foundation…into man's possibilities on this planet". In a foreshadowing of punk's attempts to demystify capitalism, "We have spent about £9,000 on records, packaging and purchase tax." This missive is signed with "love". Such idealism was to touch the young Elvis, much of whose cynicism is really a lament at its loss. After all, he did choose to perform The Beatles' 'All You Need Is Love' at Live Aid. *Glastonbury Fayre* is a kind of dry-run for Stiff records, without the bracing dash of cynicism, marketing flash and lyrical wit that was to mark that enterprise. What its music lacks – despite the presence of Bowie, Bolan and Pete Townshend – is Costello's knowingness, and his gritty individuality. That, and his sense of passion.

The man later to be known as Elvis Costello first saw the cold light of day at St Mary's Hospital, Paddington on 25 August, 1954, on the cusp of Leo and Virgo, under the defiantly Irish name of Declan Patrick MacManus. Elvis would later add the middle name Aloysius, tongue in cheek.

His grandfather, after whom he took his middle name, was himself a musician, a Catholic born in Birkenhead, "but his folks were from Ireland. They came over like everybody else." There is a family tradition that Patrick's father was murdered; certainly Patrick himself was brought up as an orphan, in a military school of music. As Costello told *Folk Roots*, "When war came he was sent to France and was shot, and wasn't fit to go back to the front. So he ended up in the British Army in Dublin in 1916 on the wrong side. I'm not saying that James Connolly came to him and said, 'Keep your head down', but some Scallies that he knew there said, 'You'd better watch out.'" 'Oliver's Army' – based on Cromwell's earlier savagery towards the native Irish – encapsulated his grandfather's quandary. The bitterness against British troops billeted in Dublin helped foment the Irish rebellion of 1916, mythologised in verse by WB Yeats. The savagery with which its leaders were dealt led directly to the founding of the Irish Free State.

Patrick later worked as a ship's musician, and spent some time in New York. As *NME* reported, in America "he became caught up on the fringe of the Prohibition era gang world. He went to stay with a boxer friend on the west side – and found himself sharing a house with Legs Diamond, the notorious gangster." Patrick MacManus is also credited with helping to bring the blues to Britain, and inspired many of his early grandson's early songs – as yet unheard in public – including 'My Friend' about those New York days. The *King Of America* album is partly a rich tribute to Patrick's memory. 'King's Shilling', from the later *Spike*, is directly based on his grandfather, written in an "early part of the century way of speaking".

Declan's grandmother later inspired another of his greatest songs, 'Veronica'. His father, Ronald "Ross" MacManus also joined the Irish diaspora, moving to Liverpool, where he married Lillian, a local girl from another transplanted Irish family, by the name of Costello. The couple later moved to Twickenham, in west London, while often returning to Merseyside for holidays and family reunions.

There, life was, literally, a ferry cross the Mersey, across the choppy waters from outside the Liver building to Birkenhead, on the south side of the river. As Elvis later said, "If the place in one of my songs isn't mentioned, it's usually in Birkenhead. That's where most of my songs are set in my mind." He also learnt rebellion early, from his father. "I was brought up with this *anti* attitude," he says. "My father got that from his father, who was anti-English. He passed that on to my dad and my dad passed it on to me."

It is interesting that, just as joining the EEC helped turn the Irish republic from a backward, priest-ridden country to a forward-looking nation, fully in tune with modern technology, confident and wealthy, so many of the most important musicians, post-punk, are of Irish extraction. It is no coincidence that what few good venues for live rock remain in England are under the control of Irishman Vince Power and his Mean Fiddler empire, nor indeed that Elvis himself now lives in Dublin. The Beatles were part of the Irish diaspora to Liverpool, while Van Morrison came roaring out of Protestant Belfast like a young bull, and Phil Lynott added poetry to heavy rock. The most genuine punk anger came from the likes of Stiff Little Fingers, The Radiators, and (even) The Boomtown Rats, though primarily, of course, from John Lydon. As Johnny Rotten, even his teeth were green.

Since that healing spite, U2 and Morrissey have led their different ways out of the emotional self-centredness of the Eighties, U2 by embracing the world, Morrissey by embracing himself. Irish folk, once the preserve of shamrock nationalists like The Dubliners, has broadened onto the world stage, whether purveyed by Christy Moore or Mary Black, Clannad or The Chieftains. An extreme version of the drunk poetic visionary, especially in the self-destruct stakes, Shane MacGowan seems to have swallowed the whole Irish bardic tradition, only to regurgitate it up in his own image. Costello has been touched by all of these, while staying true to his own, peculiarly twisted lyric muse, and taking more musical risks than all of them put together.

An only child, Declan grew up in the London suburbs, under the ever-present dominance of the Catholic faith, educated in church schools until the age of eleven – even being under the tutelage of nuns at one point – and forever imbued in that faith's odd combination of guilt and spiritual transcendence. As Elvis later said to Nick Kent, "I had to be Catholic or Jewish, now didn't I!" His first biographer Mick St Michael describes him as "a self-confessed loner", though this runs contrary to the childhood pictures on the cover of *Brutal Youth*. Declan – aged about five – poses on a wall with a girlfriend, and puts his arm protectively round a young West Indian playmate. As his father later told the *NME*, Declan's mother insisted on accepting the equality of others in a multi-racial area. "It wasn't just something on the side," he said. "It was a central issue."

Equally central to Elvis's life, from early childhood, was music. "I've always been a fan," he says. "That's where it all stems from, from this terrific *enthusiasm* for music." Even before he had learned to talk, his parents would subdue his questing nature, not with toys, but with the music of Frank Sinatra. Declan's future career was almost pre-ordained, and seems to curl back to his own Celtic roots. "I started with rock 'n' roll and you don't really think of it in a scholarly way," he says. "Then you start to take it apart like a child with a toy and you see that there's blues and there's country...then you go back from country into American music, and you go back from American folk music and you end up in Scotland or Ireland eventually."

Like so many rock stars, Declan was born into a musical family, a heritage he would at first seem to subvert, then embrace. His grandfather had achieved a musical education, courtesy of the British army, and worked the great liners as a ship's musician. One presumes that his own forbears brought with them to Liverpool the precious heritage of Irish folksong. Ross MacManus was a professional singer with the big dance bands which dominated popular music after the second world war. His own role models were the likes of Bing Crosby and Frank Sinatra, coming out of white jazz, using the human voice like another instrument in the ensemble. Ross's commercial breakthrough was to join Joe Loss's palais orchestra in 1955 as featured vocalist. Joe Loss himself would soon be an anachronism, all slicked-back and brilliantined hair with a patent leather grin, but his brand of latin smooch was ideal fodder for the dance halls of the time.

Loss's apogee had been during the war, when in one week alone his twelve-piece band played to 10,000 dancers in Glasgow. Their repertoire – and the band's image – remained forever stuck in the wartime era, providing chirpy cover versions of Glen Miller's 'In The Mood' and Woody Herman's 'Woodchopper's Ball'. This unchallenging, nostalgic image and musical librium played by men with neat haircuts and in dinner suits, was to deeply engrain itself into the young Declan's psyche, even if only as something against which to rebel; *Trust* includes a posed photo of Elvis as band leader, stage centre in front of a tuxedoed crew, with the featured singers sitting demurely on the far right. It is no coincidence that some of Costello's most memorable performances have been at Hammersmith Palais, where the Joe Loss Orchestra had virtually been the house band a generation before, or that his own image on stage has always been natty and stylish, however bug-eyed his stare, or deranged his lyrics.

Ross MacManus has since been parodied as some kind of musical hack, the high point of his career that of tenth place in the "Big Band Vocalist" section of the 1955 *NME* readers' poll, but except for a handful of mavericks, the rules of the music business for those determined enough to turn professional remain what they always were. Play rubbish well and you'll make a good living: play experimentally, and you'll starve. As Costello told Radio One, "Over the years the Joe Loss dance band, which was on the Glenn Miller model, outlasted its time amazingly. While a lot of other bands went to the wall, or stayed playing in a rather nostalgic way, they always moved with the times in a peculiar way." True pros, they absorbed whatever the pop music of the day was.

Elvis first became aware of his father's day job when "in the early Sixties, they were synthesising beat group music and arranging it for big bands". Joe Loss's unchallenging muse might even escape the most perverse of "easy" fans nowadays, but MacManus also worked with such certified jazz greats as Ronnie Scott, Tubby Hayes and Phil Seaman (all three as self-destructive as any punk). As Elvis later told Bill Flanagan, "My parents were a bit beatnik. My dad was a jazz musician, then he took a paying job as a band singer. He kind of sacrificed his artistic ambition in order to pay the rent."

Ross himself was to have a brief solo career. He had a hit single in Germany in 1969 with 'Patsy Girl', and the following year , under the name "Day Costello", he recorded 'The Long And Winding Road' from The Beatles' *Let It Be* for the Spark label. His son was later to adopt the same surname professionally, long before he ever met Jake Riviera. "It ran easier on the phone," he says. "There were too many hard consonants in the name MacManus." He changed the intonation, though, moving the emphasis so that Costello rhymes with Othello – not pedalo – and leaves the mouth like a bullet. Ross is now best known – albeit anonymously – as the voice on a TV advert for "I'm a secret lemonade drinker", sang fruitily, with his son providing guitar and backing vocals sometime in the early 1970s. It was Declan's first professional recording session, long before Stiff plucked him out of obscurity, and he even apparently appears briefly in one of the commercials. Mind you, the poignant, heartbroken voice of Linda Thompson once sang the praises of cornflakes, and the revolutionary forces of the Jefferson Airplane combined on an ad for Levi jeans. We've all got to eat!

Even more extraordinarily, Ross MacManus confesses to having released an LP called *Day Costello Sings Elvis Presley's Greatest Hits*, though *after* his son began to call himself Elvis. Though never formally trained, and unable to read musical notes – just like future collaborator Paul McCartney – young Declan began his musical career playing rhythm guitar in his father's showband. One guesses that this was drawn from friends and relations, as an antidote to the Joe Loss years.

While still a child, he received a precious educational opportunity through his father, almost by complete chance. The BBC was still dominated by an aggressive Musicians Union, in particular their demands for "needletime" restrictions, but one way of getting round this was the use of session musicians to provide cover versions, so Ross would often bring home advance demos by the likes of The Beatles, to learn and regurgitate them on air. "My first exposure to singles was having these demonstration records passed onto me by my dad," recalls Elvis. "Some of them are are very valuable – EMI 'A' labels on vinyl and even Dick James acetates. I always made a particular point of keeping The Beatles, as I was so interested in them. I used to really hope that we would be allotted my favourite single, as it would eventually come my way. I was very lucky, as I had far more records than pocket money would have afforded me."

If this was not valuable enough, through his father's day job Declan met the leading beat groups of the era, with the likes of The Merseybeats, Mojos or The Beatles, even the surly Rolling Stones, all fighting to appear on the Friday lunchtime *Joe Loss Show*, on BBC radio's Light Programme. Backstage, the young MacManus met them, if not on equal terms, then at least on the right side of that unspoken divide which exists between performers and audience. "Friday lunchtimes during the holidays were something that I really used to look forward to," Elvis says, "because I used to see bands rehearse. I would get there at nine in the morning, I'd see The Hollies, then Billy J Kramer, then Engelbert Humperdinck, or whoever it was."

Declan's mother ran the record department at Selfridge's department store in Oxford Street. Her own tastes stretched to the light jazz of Frank Sinatra and Ella Fitzgerald, crooners whose brand of relaxed sophistication Elvis was later to deconstruct in dawn raids like 'I Want You'. It also provided him with an early grab-bag of songs which became engrained into his psyche. As he told *Record Collector*, "Through my dad being a jazz musician and my mum selling records, I had very sophisticated tastes in music until I was about eleven, when I discovered The Beatles. Before that, I listened constantly to jazz and Ella and Sinatra and Mel Torme and Tony Bennett, so I knew all these songs. I mean I can sing you hundreds of them."

Was this why he recorded such apparently arcane songs – for a new wave rebel – as 'Love For Sale' or 'My Funny Valentine' early in his career? "They were all stuck in my head from when I was a kid," he says. "My mother says that I could work the record player before I could walk properly. And before I could talk properly, I would request certain records. 'I've Got You Under My Skin' was one of them. So it was ingrained, almost brainwashed." The first single he went out and bought with his own money, though, was 'Please Please Me', as fine a point as any on which to start. "And I got *With The Beatles* as a Christmas present." His first EP purchase was *Fame At Last* by Georgie Fame.

He soon plunged into the obsessive collecting which many children then take onto adult life. "All that stuff, all the childish stuff of music, was very exciting," he says. "I suppose that you graduate from having toy guns to toy guitars, which is a lot healthier, and make guitars out of cardboard boxes, or draw pictures of guitars."

As he told Greil Marcus in *Rolling Stone*, he had soon added John Leyton's 'The Folksinger' to his collection: "I was just into singles, whatever was on the radio – The Kinks, The Who, Motown. It was exciting. I was in The Beatles' fan club when I was eleven; I used to buy the magazines. The one kind of music that I *didn't* like was rock 'n' roll – as a distinct form." No wonder, by now the music was a parody of its former self, the preserve of greasy Teds in provincial transport cafes, the kind who would spit on The Beatles and their ilk as proto-Mods, and fight them on the beaches of Clacton. "The girl next door loved The Shadows and Cliff Richard – I thought that was really old hat," he says. "Someone who lived across the road from my grandmother liked Buddy Holly – I thought that was terribly old fashioned. I couldn't understand why anybody liked it. It never occurred to me that someone as *archaic* as Chuck Berry could have written 'Roll Over Beethoven' – because I was quite convinced that George Harrison had written it."

The Beatles turned the young Declan around, not only for their own songwriting, but for their creative archaeology, covering obscure rock numbers by the likes of Carl Perkins, and black girl groups. Indeed, a love for the moptops was only displaced by Declan's immersion in Motown, soul and even reggae, the kind of stuff which it was perfectly respectable in discos – which, indeed, DJs like Guy

Stevens turned into a cult in various music biz nightclubs – but which few then took seriously as art. More overt attempts to create an artform from rock music left the young MacManus cold.

"I didn't get into psychedelic records until I went to Liverpool in 1970, so I missed all of 1967," he says. "The only time I heard psychedelia was when my dad listened to it, when he became a sort of hippie. He was listening to The Incredible String Band, The Butterfield Blues Band, and The Grateful Dead and Jefferson Airplane. I played them, but didn't find a lot in them for me, because I was really into Marvin Gaye and those 'Return Of Django' records – the stuff we danced to at teenage parties." Declan was like the young Dylan, a kind of musical vacuum cleaner, taking it all in. "From the time I was eleven to sixteen – only five years but five pretty important years in your life – I concentrated on pop music, and the changing trends."

This was not a merely passive activity. By the age of twelve, Declan was playing guitar, and writing his own songs. The teenager cut his musical teeth as a floor singer in local folk clubs, a kind of free audition space, where a tolerant audience would endure all kinds of no-hopers in the spirit of communal tolerance. Not that this extended to folk's superstars. Declan's first public performance in his own right was at just such a folk club, the Crypt at St Elizabeth's, Richmond, in 1969, when he was a tender fifteen years old. The name guest that night was Ewan MacColl – Kirsty's father. As Costello later told Colin Irwin, "I got up with my little guitar, and he sat in the front, head bowed all the way through my set, and I'm sure he just nodded off."

As MacColl had reacted even less favourably to the young Bob Dylan seven years earlier, during his first visit to London, this was probably some kind of compliment, though it didn't feel that way at the time. "So I had a traumatic first appearance with this old bloke falling asleep, or *pretending* to fall asleep during my song – as you can imagine that was pretty crushing," he says. MacColl must have gone down in an early version of Elvis's notorious little black book, for Costello extracted revenge by having The Pogues "trash 'Dirty Old Town' and have it turned into a football chant, which I thought was a marvellous disembowelling".

As Elvis told *Record Collector*, "I knew I had a career when I was fourteen. It just took the rest of the world a little longer to work out how to do it." Ross, though, tried to convince him against entering the "industry of human happiness", as Andrew Loog Oldham's Immediate label once optimistically described the music biz (Immediate went bankrupt shortly afterwards). Such a move was "something you do in spite of your better judgement". Though, as Costello retorted, "When you're convinced that this is your vocation, you think it's inevitable that you will eventually have the chance to do it, even if you do other jobs to pay the rent."

The London folk clubs gave him a further musical education, seeing the likes of Noel Murphy, Mike Moran, Jo Ann Kelly, and the Sallyangie, featuring a young Mike Oldfield playing acoustic guitar. "This was all one summer – I had a great summer," he says. "I played when they let me and I made my first faltering steps – and then I moved to Liverpool" – just as he turned sixteen. Despite this, Elvis later recalled, " I hated folk music when I started out, simply because of the resistance I found."

Declan's formal education had continued in a Secondary Modern in Hounslow, and in Liverpool he went on to High School, leaving with a solitary "A" level in English. He did leave a more tangible mark in issue one of the school magazine, *The Campion*, published in July 1971. D MacManus of the Lower Sixth – also part of the editorial team – contributes an untitled poem, which rhymes and scans, and is beautifully crafted, the end of the third verse echoing and contradicting that of verse one.

Indeed, this might be the lyric for an early song. Heavily allegorical, it seems to presage his future career, even his name change to the King of Rock.

If you want to be the King.
Lying on a bed of gold.
Take the sceptre of the old,
Take the sword and wear the crown
You're in your robes and on the stairway,
Looking down.

This from a man who would, literally, wear a crown on the front cover of *King Of America*, trimmed with ermine and studded with jewels of the purest paste. In pre-Christian Ireland, the roles of poet, king and priest were interwoven, and Elvis, brought up a Roman Catholic, knew all about the continuing power of the priesthood.

In the second stanza, the religious life is another possibility, but again it is seen as something false, defined by outer show:

> But choke the collar at your throat,
> You'll not be telling why you're wearing
> Such a coloured coat.

A reference to Joseph, which shows that all that church attendance had not been in vain. Declan sees that one's public image means little in the end, even though he would transform himself through all kinds of names and personae, as the years passed by.

> Remember: when forsaking all your titles,
> You're on the staircase, going up.

The poem is prophetic. Elvis remains a public performer who is both oblivious to fashion, and yet continually shaped by it.

Quite why so obviously brilliant a man should have been failed by the education system remains a mystery. Secondary Moderns were, after all, the sink into which the three quarters of the population rejected by the grammar schools fell. His schooling left behind a song title from his most personal of albums, *Get Happy!!*, and a sense of under-achievement, against which Elvis's manic energy and desire for self-education ever since can be set. Here is a man forever with something to prove to himself, even after the rest of the world has been convinced. It might explain Elvis's ingrained tendency to overdo things.

Declan had by now moved to Birkenhead with his mother, following the breakdown of his parents' marriage. It was a crucial change of place. To this day, his speaking voice is more Scouse than Cockney, and judging from his own personal passions – Liverpool football club, *Brookside*, The Beatles – his heart lies near the Mersey rather than the Thames. Ross remained in the capital, and later remarried. His four sons by this second liaison – Kieran, Ronan, Rory and Liam – now gig in the London suburbs as Second Nature, including covers of songs by their step-brother in their act. As their proud father told the *NME* in 1977, "I'm not sure whether they're going to be altar boys or punk rockers."

Ross left Joe Loss in 1969, for a solo career, playing the northern club circuit as a singer doubling on trumpet and piano, a beloved entertainer in the unironic showbiz tradition. Eight years later, he would occasionally run into his son at a by now infamous service station on the M1 – Roy Harper was forced to remove a particularly scurrilous song about the "plate of crap" then purveyed – where London-based musicians would rendezvous after a gig up north, or vice versa. "The only time I see Elvis now is when we meet at Watford Gap at six o'clock in the morning, on the way home from our gigs," he says.

There is a proud sense of young Declan following in the family profession, whatever the differences of hairstyle, or musical label. Like most men, Elvis even looks – and acts – increasingly like his father as he grows older.

There was one musical path down which the teenage Declan refused to follow his father, at least at the time. It was a weird reversal of the generations, like a male version of *Absolutely Fabulous*, with the serious son disapproving of his dad's flirting with the avant-garde. To everyone's amazement, Ross had become a proto-hippie, "a bit psychedelic around the edges", and would give his son albums by the likes of The Grateful Dead or the Jefferson Airplane. It was the sort of music still largely confined to an underground cult, a world of *IT* and hippie clubs and open air festivals. John Peel had broadcast these West Coast delights to a national audience, first on Radio London, and then Radio One's *Top Gear* and the more arcane, late-night *Perfumed Garden*. Lorry drivers would phone in to complain that some madman was playing the records backwards. As such things go, the determinedly non-conformist Peel is now a national institution, and the only DJ to survive on Radio One from the original roster.

By 1970, such music was the *lingua franca* of kids of the time – me included – though Declan was just a few years too young to experience its full glory, and psychedelia had already lost its early bloom. He would keep his father's cast-off albums for a few weeks, then exchange them at the second hand shop for Marvin Gaye records. Liverpool was still into acid rock. "I used to *hide* my Otis Redding records when friends came around," he recalls. "I didn't want to be out of step. To the age of sixteen it's *really crucial* that you're *in* – and I tried hard to like The Grateful Dead or Spirit." The young Declan even eschewed the very drugs whose use such bands spent so much of their existence either singing about, or sedated by, and it would take Bebe Buell to turn him on to marijuana in the late Seventies.

Something must have rubbed off, though. As the Sixties ended, the best of the psychedelic bands were transforming themselves into something else entirely, purging their previous excess by delving into roots music. Thus Fairport abandoned their West Coast affinities for the traditional folk of *Liege and Lief*, The Grateful Dead turned from thirty-minute jams to harmony vocals and the semi-acoustic *American Beauty*, while The Byrds had already flown from 'Eight Miles High' to country rock. Most crucial of all were Dylan's Woodstock companions The Band, who had turned their back on the cataclysmic clatter of the 1966 world tour for songs which chronicled America's history. As well as setting Elton John's whole musical agenda at the time, their bassist Rick Danko's unique "downhome" singing style influenced Declan's own vocals, as did their lack of showbiz flash. "They didn't look pretty," he recalls. "It appealed to me that they looked really ugly."

As he later told *Record Collector*, Declan started to seriously listen to country music in 1970: "Groups like The Band, The Grateful Dead's records of the time and particularly The Byrds' *Sweetheart Of The Rodeo*" – the latter an album whose low sales figure belie its long-lasting appeal. Gram Parsons had already formed the first country rock hybrid, The International Submarine Band, while still a spoilt brat at Harvard. Hired initially as a piano player, Parsons enthused Roger McGuinn to record a themed album, combining his own songs with those of the Louvin Brothers and Merle Haggard. It was hardly fashionable, the diet of the retards in the film *Deliverance*, or the music of choice of those who were to blast away the two hippie bikers at the end of *Easy Rider*. Poor white trash, with short back and sides, minimal intellect, and a gun.

Parsons was only with The Byrds for a few months, going on to The Flying Burrito Brothers, hard drugs and taut nerves, an early death and a bizarre cremation. His vocals were even erased from *Sweetheart* for contractual reasons. His influence, though, lingers on, not least in Costello's own repertoire. "I got curious to find out who these country singers were that these bands were covering," he explains. It was the same process as white teenagers discovering Little Willie John through Fleetwood Mac, or Howling Wolf through The Rolling Stones, a band who Declan had first considered "ridiculous", as he had learnt the likes of 'Little Red Rooster' direct from the source. Country, though, had not informed the young Declan's listening tastes, before he found Gram Parsons as a pathfinder. "It was quite hard to find unless you were really a specialist country fan, you wouldn't know George Jones' stuff, or Merle Haggard's," he says. "Then it was a natural step to try and write something in that style. I liked the plainness of the chords, the churchy harmony."

Elsewhere, Elvis talks of the largely American influences on his early singing style: Lowell George from Little Feat, Van Morrison (Irish, but heavily influenced by R&B and soul) and Rick Danko. How hard was it to escape influences from across the Atlantic? "I didn't even worry," he claims, even if the later punk era was to place a premium on authenticity, so that John Lydon and Ian Dury exaggerated their original cockney, and Pete Shelley turned up his Mancunian accent. "But most singers had that transatlantic pop voice – even The Beatles did, although sometimes they accentuated the American and sometimes the Liverpool accent. It's all acting. I talk in a voice that's much lower than I sing. And I've never found any problem with it."

Elvis was once asked by the Norwegian writer Borre Haugstad why his voice sounded so much like that of David Accles, and agreed there might be some "reference point from way back that I've learnt". Accles' first album is one of his favourites, "Though I've never met anybody who's ever heard of him." Accles was a kind of American precursor to Elton John, with better lyrics and a less optimistic outlook. His rich melancholy infests two peerless Electra releases, the first of which Costello himself describes as "gothic-psychedelic", and 1972's more ambitious – though less emotionally piercing – *American Gothic*, whose centrepiece, 'Montana Song', does indeed prefigure the baroque elegance of Costello's grander effusions.

Meanwhile, as he told Greil Marcus, young Declan was already "writing my own songs – dreadful songs, performing them more or less religiously. I didn't think the songs were worth recording – but the only way you get better is to play what you write. Then you have the humiliation of being *crushed* – if you're obviously insubstantial. If you don't put them over, you quickly learn from experience." He further opened up to *Folk Roots*, "I don't have any tapes of those songs – they were probably pretty awful. Aren't everybody's first songs? People would tolerate you at the beginning of the night – somebody had to get up and sing first. That was a way of learning. You didn't think about it as ambition."

In Liverpool, the glory days had certainly gone: the beat boom years were well over, and it would be another five years or so until the new psychedelia hit town. Declan found only "a folk scene dominated by Jacqui & Bridie and sub-Spinners people and it was like running into a brick wall – it was horrendous. The contemporary/traditional paradox was at its strongest. Contemporary was a dirty world. A traditional singer could get up and be terrible and he could do 'Wild Rover' and do an encore and he'd come back and do 'The Holy Ground'! I hated those fucking songs."

This was especially frustrating, as Declan had already made a lifetime commitment to music as a career. Not fame or glory, indeed these were the things he was intent on avoiding at any cost. As he told Radio One, "I decided when I was about seventeen that I wanted to do it. You're much more idealistic about it, you cannot see commercial concerns and you're also at that age – at least I was – when you're very precious about it. I wasn't going to be tainted by anything as vulgar as electric guitars, at one point." Just like the young Robert Zimmerman, who shed his rock 'n' roll roots for an Okie disguise, a stage name and an acoustic guitar.

And just like Dylan, the lure of Fender's finest proved too great in the end, like a reformed alcoholic returning to strong drink. "I was dead against electric guitars, and then I went all on them."

Of crucial importance to Declan's future was a chance meeting with Allan Mayes at a New Year's party at the tail end of 1971. A fellow musician, Allan found common ground with young Declan in terms of musical heroes: Neil Young, Van Morrison and Bob Dylan. Aged eighteen, so MacManus's senior at a time when such differences matter, Mayes had already been playing in a band for two years.

The two had first met in 1969, presumably when Declan was up in Liverpool on a family visit. Allan was in a progressive rock band called Medium Theatre, named after *Medium*, a small press poetry magazine with which Ross MacManus was somehow associated. "I remember meeting Dec very briefly at a house where these guys lived," he says. "He said he played, I found out who his dad was, and then he disappeared." The chance encounter at the New Year's party was almost like the start of a love affair. "We both took our guitars and sat in a bedroom while everybody else was drinking and chasing women. It was like the typical John Lennon and Paul McCartney thing: 'You know all that stuff, let's play together.' So we just sat on the beds for three hours and played all these songs and just had a great time. So we possibly exchanged phone numbers."

Costello seemed to almost mimic his new friend, to take over his persona. Even now, "After all these years, he and I sound alike," Mayes admits. "Our accents, our vocal tones, the way we speak sounds so alike. We are very similar individuals really…he and I play the same guitar style. We are the only two in the world who do this. We play our barre chords with the little finger above the ring finger. Our right-handed style is very similar. We have a similar stance with our hands. Neither of us taught the other. I guess we just picked it up at a time when we were both very susceptible to learning stuff and what you learned at seventeen as a guitar player you're stuck with for life." They even look alike still, short hair and glasses, though Mayes has the warmer smile. "He used to dress kind of geeky, though," Mayes recalls. "He used to wear these big plaid jackets and big red shoes. He used to call them 'clown clothes' and he didn't exactly go out of his way to look rock 'n' roll."

Declan soon joined Mayes' group Rusty, featuring Allan on vocals and guitar, Declan on vocals and guitar, singer Dave Jago and bassist Alan Brown. On Friday, 21 January, 1972 the band played its first paid gig since Declan's arrival. Headlining at the Lamplight Folk Club in

Wallasey, Rusty performed original songs, including 'The Lady Holds Out Her Hand', 'Wisdom In The Basement' and 'She's Almost Human'. They also played their own versions of Neil Young's 'Dance Dance Dance', Dylan's 'The Mighty Quinn' and 'I've Been Working' by Van Morrison. Declan even brought into the set his own latest song, 'Warm House'.

Talking to Greil Marcus, Costello recalls that he first joined a band having left just left college. He had taken a job working in a bank as a computer operator, the first thing he could get, and "comparatively well paid" for work which consisted of putting tapes on machines, and feeding cards in and out. "I stuck out the first computer job for about six months," he says. "At the same time I got into a group in Liverpool, a sort of folk group – we'd do a few rock 'n' roll tunes, and songs of our own, but we weren't getting anywhere."

George Gimarc's *Punk Diary* prints a photo of a chubby long-haired Elvis in jeans and cradling a guitar, and a ticket for Rusty in concert with Medium Theatre at Lynwood Hall, Rice Lane, 12 February, tickets 25p. By springtime, Rusty has been trimmed to a duo: Mayes and MacManus. As the latter commented to Radio One, "I was in a group that went from a four-piece to a two-piece. By now you're talking about 1972 and everybody wanted to hear Slade songs, and we're standing there with two acoustic guitars and they want to hear 'Cum On Feel The Noize'; we're in Widnes or somewhere, where if you don't play it, they'll fill you in. That's how I got to sing so loud over disinterested people, just to stun them to be silent because I could sing louder than they could talk."

He later added in an interview with Colin Irwin, "The others went off to college and there were just the two of us left. We used to do anything to get gigs. We used to gatecrash poetry nights and they'd let us sing if we didn't do anything too poppy." Allen Ginsberg had recently declared Liverpool to be the poetic centre of the universe, and Roger McGough, Adrian Henri and Brian Patten had gone on to international fame, leaving a flourishing poetry scene in their wake. "And some nights we'd go out to somewhere like Widnes and play anything that was in the charts that we could play on two guitars – people just wanted a good sing-song."

On 6 June, 1972, the duo were booked to provide weekly folk club concerts at the Temple Bar, on Dale Street in central Liverpool, sometimes themselves booking other guests, and operating an open mic policy. The Tuesday night bookings ran weekly through to the end of December, and the duo split half of the door money between them, as well as each playing a short solo set. "Back in Liverpool it was really down to running your own club if you wanted to do anything," he explains. "We'd get about five people along." This would lead the landlord to call a halt to proceedings. "The people who came didn't drink anyway. It wasn't the carousing crowd – it was the sensitive types in greatcoats. That's what we were anyway."

Sensitive, but hardly quiet. "You'd get some really hostile reactions from organisers. You'd go somewhere that supposedly had an open policy and you'd get shoved on at the worst possible time – after the raffle, or something. I think why I ended up in rock 'n' roll was that my voice got so loud from shouting people down."

Onstage at the Edmonton Folk Festival in 1995, Costello recollected how "me and my partner used to play this 'Lonely Hearts Club' cause it was the worst gig you could possibly have. Early in the evening, all the ladies sat on one side of the room and all the men on the other and completely ignored each other and anybody was singing. And once they had about fifteen gin and tonics, they'd just talk to each other and ignore us. So it was a great gig." Like a scene from an Alan Bleasdale drama.

Beyond Belief, the invaluable Costello fanzine, succeeded in tracking Allan Mayes down to a gig at an uptown shopping mall in Austin, Texas, where he now lives. He introduced one song as something he had written "with a fellow who went on to become Elvis Costello. It's all about dealing with fame. It's funny that now, years later, one of us is famous."

At the time, the two discovered an affinity for harmony vocals – a lost art these days, outside the likes of the High Llamas – which they displayed on virtuoso performances like CSN&Y's 'Wooden Ships', making their two voices sound like four. "More by luck or instinct, we both used to go in the right direction for the harmonies," Costello says. Original songs would only make up about a quarter of the set, though the two rarely collaborated when writing their own material: one such, 'Maureen And Sam' later became Elvis's 'Ghost Train'. As to the rest of their repertoire, Allan had introduced Declan to albums by Brinsley Schwarz, which along with Neil Young's solo work – 'Heart Of Gold', 'Everyone Knows This Is Nowhere' etc – formed the bulk of the set.

As Mayes later pointed out, "Forget all that stuff about Hank Williams being his roots. He was just as into wimpy acoustic music as the rest of us: David Crosby, Van Morrison, The Band." Mayes bought the first Brinsley Schwarz album in a junk shop, but it left the young Declan unimpressed, labelling them a poor man's CSN&Y. "But when *Silver Pistol* came out it really hit him, and we hammered those songs to death."

Other classics redeemed included The Turtles' 'Happy Together', 'Old Kentucky Home' by Randy Newman, and Simon And Garfunkel's 'Cecilia' – hardly a threatening set list, and a contemporary photograph shows a long-haired Declan bent over his guitar, playing to an audience comprised almost entirely of old age pensioners.

On a good night, they would be paid £8 each. "Declan didn't have a car and never drove," Mayes says. He did not share Declan's Grateful Dead fixation, or his love for Jesse Winchester, of whom MacManus declared, "This is the way to go. Gloom and doom, this is so dark." Just wait till he got to hear Richard Thompson! Declan also revered David Accles, as already mentioned, the early Flying Burrito Brothers – with Gram Parsons – and The Nitty Gritty Dirt Band's extraordinary triple album *Will The Circle Be Unbroken*, a meeting of three generations of country musicians. As to their aspirations, it was that of becoming superstars, though they rarely talked about it. "That was all we cared about," Mayes says. "When can we stop doing this shit and do things properly, the way we want." Such fame was never going to happen in Liverpool, "Although we had little local managers chasing us a couple of times."

Rusty managed to temporarily escape the Liverpool-Walton-Wallasey axis, when they are booked as opening act for three London concerts, supporting Ralph McTell and Bridget St John. The headliners both had their own solid (and polite) audience, to whom Rusty's repertoire would appeal. McTell began as a ragtime guitarist when he left the army, then began to sing gentle parables, songs of innocence betrayed. One of these, 'The Streets Of London', became so famous that it disabled McTell's whole later career, as his shows have ever after been exercises in nostalgia. Costello loved ragtime music, and its champions. "John James," he singles out. "I sometimes wonder whatever happened to him. Tremendous guitar player. I was fascinated by that – transposing those rags onto guitar. I always wanted to play like that but I could never get the co-ordination together."

Bridget St John, a one time protegee of the John Peel roadshow and signed up by Peel's Dandelion label, was a kind of New Zealand-born earth mother. Best noted for her collaborations with Kevin Ayers, her deep and sensual vocals were best heard when combined with Ron Geesin's inventive arrangements on 1971's *Songs For The Gentle Man*. The follow-up, 1972's *Thank You For* featured sensitive bass playing from one Bruce Thomas. Both McTell and St John represented the kind of music to which Rusty aspired: melodic, unostentatious, in thrall to beauty. Not much room for anger or jealousy here. Rusty stayed in London to play some small-scale gigs in their own right. On Thursday, 13 July, they guested at New Bards Folk Club, the next day the New Moon in Putney and then on to the Troubadour in South Kensington.

If fame was the spur, it was yet to descend on Declan's head just yet, especially when one short-term manager temporarily changed Rusty's name to Procyon. It did not stick, and neither did Declan. In early 1973 he told Allan that he was moving down to London to live with his father: his musical partner had a steady job with the council, and remained in Liverpool. There were a few gigs yet to fulfil, the final one of which – at Warwick University on 24 June, 1973, supporting Cockney Rebel – marked Rusty's last stand. "He travelled from London north and I travelled from Liverpool south," Elvis explains. "We both went back our separate ways and we were now living 200 miles apart."

Beyond Belief reproduces the set list, including 'Your Eyes Are Looking Down' by Help Yourself, and eight Brinsley Schwarz numbers, including four written by Nick Lowe. Other covers include The Band's 'Up On Cripple Creek' and 'The Weight', rock classic 'Willie And The Hand Jive', Loudon Wainwright's 'Dead Skunk', Leadbelly's 'Cotton Fields' and – somewhat out of character – Rod

Stewart's 'Gasoline Alley'. Although only three appear on the final set list, during his time with Rusty, Declan composed – and sang – over a dozen songs, including 'For Miles I See', 'Dull Echoes', 'Sweet Convincer', 'Daybreaks', 'Goodbye Florence', 'Morning Changes', 'Are You Afraid Of Your Children', 'Two Days Rain', 'The Show Must Go On', 'Sleeper At The Wheel' and 'Sunflower Lancers'. If any tapes exist from this time, they have never reached the public domain, not even the shadowlands inhabited by bootleggers, which might be just as well.

Allan Mayes was later startled to see the change of image which the record label Stiff imposed on his old friend, once a "hefty, long-haired hippie, with *Easy Rider*-type glasses". When he phoned Stiff, about an article which a Liverpool music magazine was about to run on Elvis's lost years, Mayes says, "Declan phoned me and said, 'I've spoken to Jake' – and this is a quote – 'and if anything like that goes in print, legs will be broken.' We laugh now." Not me. Having had much the same threat from a leading rock lyricist, if I did not pay him in full for an open air festival gig which I had helped organise. At the time, these things are not funny at all!

Mayes met the man now named Elvis Costello at a soundcheck for a 1977 gig at Eric's, and once again a year or two later. He still remembers his old friend's ability to write in any style which appealed to him at the time. "He was the same with anybody," he says. "Like, 'I need a Robbie Robertson song' and the song would appear. The Nick Lowe songs, The Beatles' songs, he'd just throw them together. It was staggering." As to having missed out on fame himself, while seeing Declan go on to world stardom, "Everything that's happened to him, I would have killed for. The only saving grace is that he's so good."

Allan can still remember that extraordinary will to succeed and "the intensity when he used to show me those songs. He would say, 'Here's a new song', play it, and finish with his eyes bulging and a wild look in his eye, then switch straight off again and say, 'I wonder what's on TV tonight?'" The difference between honest talent and pure inspiration.

Allan Mayes cannot remember Declan having a steady girlfriend while he was in Liverpool, but after he had moved back to London,

Declan came back to see his mother bringing a fiancée, Mary Burgoyne. Elsewhere, Mary is described as Declan's childhood sweetheart, so this might not have been quite so sudden an occurrence as Mayes suggests. "She by coincidence came up to do college in Liverpool, probably within a year of him moving down there," he explains. Declan was by now in Flip City, and playing London club gigs. "Then she moved back, and Matthew was born."

It was towards the end of his time in Birkenhead that Declan first met Nick Lowe, already one of his musical heroes. With fitting symmetry, this was at the original Cavern club, soon after demolished to make way for a car park. That's the trouble with Heritage Britain; it always preserves the wrong bits!

Brinsley Schwarz played on "the famous 'Beatles-stage' you see in all the old footage", and if history was repeating itself, it certainly had a comic twist. Apparently washed up, except in the ears of John Peel and a few hard core fans – I plead guilty! – the Brinsleys' music was simplifying itself, like The Beatles in reverse, hard back to the moptops' first album with all those covers of girl-groups and American soul. Nick Lowe was undoubtedly the leader on stage, and he and his band-mates were now dressing as spivs rather than country hicks, and even cutting their hair to pre-Beatles styles. I remember seeing Brinsley Schwarz around this time, and being most startled by the band's near short back and sides, that and the shortness of their songs. No guitar breaks for longer than twenty seconds, just like George Harrison ten years before. As their friends Chilli Willi sang, "This ain't no psychedelic show." And yet there was a knowingness here, the kind of ironic back-pedalling that Stiff would turn into a whole lifestyle. The band chatted to Declan and Allan after the gig, obviously impressed that two young fans knew all their songs.

As Costello told Greil Marcus, Lowe "was still with Brinsley Schwarz; it was the *autumn* of their career. We'd do a few of their numbers in our set; we had a show at a little club – they were playing at the Cavern – and we went along and met in the bar and started chatting." Here was Declan's dream, that of making a living from music, made flesh in the later Jesus of Cool. "He was in a real proper group that recorded records! That was the first time I'd ever spoken to anybody that was in a group – and his attitude *even then* has been reflected in the way he's been since."

The usually unreliable Krista Reese adds that Declan began to stay on the floor of Lowe's London apartment, while making trips down from Liverpool. Lowe also claims that MacManus roadied for the Brinsleys, as a general gofer and dogsbody. This would tie in with the whoop of joy which Greil Marcus, surely our foremost cultural critic, draws from him on the subject of what is now derided as "pub-rock", and the musical vistas it exposed. "I was already playing – coming back to London, seeing a lot of groups, Nick Lowe and the Brinsleys, pub-rock groups. I discovered that all the music I liked secretly, that I'd been hiding from my friends – that was what was great fun in a bar: Lee Dorsey songs! Suddenly it was all right to *like it*; that was when I saw the light. There was nothing wrong with it."

On 18 April, 1973, Declan went solo, and got a gig at the Barmy Arms pub in Twickenham, close to that venue of musical legend, Eel Pie Island. He performed a mixture of cover versions and his own songs, under his new stage name of Declan Costello, his grandmother's maiden surname. Support act were the New State Ramblers. The surname MacManus was consigned to musical history, at least for the time being.

As he told Colin Irwin, the singer "came back to London after two years because I realised there wasn't any scene in Liverpool to get into. It was completely dead in the early Seventies. So I came down and did that for a while, and then I got into a group and when that hit a dead end I went solo again. All semi-pro."

In summer 1973, Declan met bassist Michael "Mich" Kent by chance at a Brinsley Schwarz concert – where else? – at St Pancras Town Hall. The two decided to put a band together, teaming up with drummer Malcolm Dennis, an old school friend of Mich's. Under the punning name "Mothertruckers", they played tiny South London venues, such as Wimbledon's Southlands College. They soon changed their name to The Bizario Brothers, and then Flip City, a name provided by Mary Burgoyne. She took it from one of her favourite albums, Joni Mitchell's *Court And Spark*, from the comic interplay between Cheech and Chong on the Annie Ross song 'Twisted'. Elvis has always been a firm admirer of Mitchell's music, which has moved from folk to jazz to rock and back again, and later bought her favourite acoustic guitar. The name Flip City, heavily American in its use of slang, did not convince everyone at first, until the London listing magazine *Time Out* printed their publicity shot, a parody of a Barefoot Jerry album cover to those in the know. Soon, Charlie Gillett was name-checking them on his Radio London show *Honky Tonk*, and the title stuck. It was no worse than, say, Dire Straits, a band who came out of exactly the same scene, to rather more immediate effect.

Flip City soon expanded to a five-piece, adding Steve Hazelhurst on lead guitar and Dickie Faulkner on congas and percussion, as well as backing vocals. Hazelhurst was rejected after his first audition, but the guitarist chosen proved to be a "dopehead", so Steve was in. He would perform a brief solo set, to take some of the strain off Declan, who took all lead vocals, and wrote extensively for the band, in the same musical vein as the American country-rock they were covering onstage. As Laura Marcus told St Michael, there was no resentment at Costello's creative dominance. "It wasn't his band but he was always the dominating factor, the driving force," she recalls. "He also did the least amount of humping gear, due to his 'bad back' – but I guess that's what they call artistic temperament. He was totally, utterly and unquestioningly dedicated. He had no doubt that he was going to make it. It was a dream to the others, but for him it was a definite ambition."

To pay the rent, Costello found a new job as a computer operator, at Elizabeth Arden cosmetics in Acton, later immortalised as the "vanity factory" in 'I'm Not Angry'. As he later told Greil Marcus, his chosen profession "was a total bluff really. I knew nothing about it, but I knew enough of the jargon. It was ideal: waiting for the machine to do the work, there's a lot free time for writing and reading." I can only concur, having worked as a computer clerk for IBM at the same time! The kind of memory which today lurks in a desktop PC then filled a room, and was a dumb, if noisy, beast, needing an army of operatives to tend its every whim round the clock.

One of Declan's best songs for his new band, 'Sweet Revival' contained the words, "I get the weekend, they get the rest". The young songwriter would often come home with new lyrics written on spare computer paper. "Shift work was never allowed to interfere with rehearsals or gigs."

As to Flip City, they were also very much of their time, *clunky* in both music and dress. As Mick St Michael noted, they were "a bunch of scruffy-looking American music fanatics, primarily *enthusiasts* and it came over in their music. Stage presence, stage clothes and other such niceties were for the birds." There was a large circuit crying out for cheap, semi-pro bands, £20 all in for two forty-five minute sets.

Those prototype English hippies Traffic had started the trend for "getting it together in the country", following the example of the likes of Quicksilver or Grateful Dead who had escaped San Francisco for farmhouses somewhere in the hills, out of the prying eyes of the police or unwelcome fans. It became a lifestyle, so that later bands like Gong or the stoned aristocrats of The Global Village Trucking Company, lived the communal experience to the hilt, in all its true horror. Bands would split, on major issues like whose turn it was to do the washing up next, or empty the outdoor privy. The film *Withnail And I*, in which two actors retreat to a cottage in the Lake District, captured perfectly the squalor and cold, yet also the crazy sense of freedom, which such sudden immersion in country air could bring.

It was even more vital for bands which espoused the countryside in their songs to escape from the city between gigs. There is a touching note of English provincialism in the attempts of the likes of Help Yourself and label mates Brinsley Schwarz to get their music together in the rural wilds. Even further down the rock pecking order, the members of Flip City agreed to join their sound mixer Mike Whelan at 3 Stag Lane, Roehampton Vale. All were in work, and without – as yet – family ties, and the rent of £32 a month was eminently affordable.

Here was Declan's variant on going away to university, roughing it with mates far from the clutches of the family home. As well as the small profit on gigs, Malcolm Dennis worked at the Fender soundhouse in central London, Steve Hazelhurst drove a van, Mich was a tool maker and Dickie Faulkner a maintenance man. As Mick St Michael writes, there was nothing to indicate that "Declan was anything less than 'one of the lads'. Although he wasn't a heavy drinker and was never known to take drugs, he knew how to enjoy himself – and with four young men in their early twenties living together there were always plenty of practical jokes of the toothpaste-on-door handle variety."

Laura Marcus recalls him being deliberately perverse in band discussions, taking the contrary view just for "the hell of it. All night debates were not uncommon, with Elvis's left-of-centre political views well to the fore." His religious upbringing meant that he opposed abortion – as did fellow lapsed Catholic Johnny Rotten in the scabrous song 'Bodies', extreme even for The Sex Pistols. Nevertheless, he declared himself a supporter of feminism, though his most fervent alliance was to the Liverpool football team.

He was also keen to introduce his musical enthusiasms to the rest of the household. The band played the kind of post-psychedelic rock music championed by magazines like *Zigzag* and *Dark Star*, who later were both to transfer their allegiances to the new wave. Stage favourites included Bob Dylan's 'Knocking On Heaven's Door', Little Feat's 'Willin'' and 'Cold, Cold, Cold', and Hunter-Garcia songs from *American Beauty* and the eponymous *Grateful Dead*. 'Third Rate Romance' was a song associated with Jesse Winchester, who covered it on his 1974 album *Learn To Love It*. Van Morrison had been a long time influence on Declan, and the band's arrangement of Sam Cooke's 'Bring It On Home To Me' was close to that played by Morrison live in London in 1973, and captured on the *It's Too Late To Stop Now* album. Flip City often played it back to back with Cooke's 'Another Saturday Night'.

Declan was the musical mastermind as Laura Marcus recalls. "It wasn't so much he imposed the ideas," she says, "he was the one who *had* the ideas. The others went along with them." Talking to Radio One years later, he downplays this part of his career as a kind of training ground, a way to pass the time. "A group of us got a house together, and it just happened that enough of us were different instrumentalists to form a group, on the periphery of the dying embers of the pub scene," he insists. This reverses history, though the details are accurate enough. "We played for peanuts. The most we ever made was £25, on a Saturday night. We just copied the blueprint of the pub groups, most especially the Brinsleys. You had to have one R&B song, one country song, a few songs you had written yourself, a Dylan song: just a regular bar band."

Costello reveals that "what lay behind all of this was The Band. They were the holy grail of that scene, in my opinion. That was the music we aspired to play, they were the ultimate rock 'n' roll band." As if to prove the point, the radio documentary he is speaking on then plays a rare BBC session take of 'On Exile's Road', written and sung by Declan, and striving for just that kind of ego-less warmth which is The Band's most valuable gift to rock music. There is a bite and spite to the lyrics, though, which place its author somewhere else entirely.

Another influence was Bruce Springsteen, especially his debut album *Greetings From Asbury Park NJ* with its dense poetic lyrics, long before his music was widely known in Britain, through the hype surrounding *Born To Run*. Unfortunately, Flip City could hardly match Springsteen's towering stage performances of this time. If they shared his burning belief in the healing power of rock music, they were unable to fully express it in their music.

The release of Springsteen's second album *The Wild, The Innocent And The E-Street Shuffle* was an obvious influence on 'Radio Soul', written by Declan in early 1974. As St Michael comments, "It bore the unmistakable Springsteen stamp, with a clipped rhythm guitar intro and celebratory release in the lyrics. A visitor to the house hearing the new material commented, 'It's like "Greetings From Stag Lane" here.'"

The band were gradually learning to let themselves go on stage, using good time songs like Hank Williams' 'You Win Again' and Dylan's 'It Takes A Train To Laugh', to will the audience to dance along.

Steve Hazelhurst sang lead vocal on the latter, with Costello's stumbling attempts at lead guitar failing to convince. The band were ferried round in a battered Ford transit van, purchased for £20, and St Michael itemises some of their more bizarre bookings. These ranged from an American college near Maidenhead to the Howff, a folk club in St John's Wood. A gig at the Gun, in south London, turned out to be at a lair of bikers, in full leathers and ready for action. Laura Marcus recalls her own terror, but also the natural diplomacy emanating from Costello. "Dec just started chatting to some guy who said he could play harmonica and invited him to come up and have a blow," he says. "The result was the audience all loved him. That was an example of his common touch."

A piano player called Nick joined for a while, having answered a music press advert which named The Grateful Dead, Little Feat and The Band as reference points. Pub-rock was suddenly the coming thing, emerging from key pubs like the Kensington, which Flip City played in July 1974.

Two key events happened that winter. The first was musical. Ace – the epitome of pub bands, with Alan "Bam" King once of Mighty Baby on rhythm guitar and Paul Carrack, later to join Squeeze, on keyboards – stormed the charts with the plaintive 'How Long', a song about an errant bassist which defined the sorrow one felt at betrayal, of any kind. The second was highly personal.

In November 1974, Declan left Stag Lane, to marry Mary, who since leaving Liverpool, had been working as a ground hostess at Heathrow airport. They moved to a flat in Twickenham, below Ross MacManus and his second wife Sarah, where their son Matthew was born in January 1975. The young family later relocated to Whitton, in Middlesex. With this added responsibility, Declan would have to either make music more than an ill-paid hobby, or abandon it.

Flip City were also going through changes. Malcolm Dennis had been replaced on drums by Ian Powell, and in March those band members still living in Stag Lane moved to East Molesey. They continued to gig widely around Greater London: at smaller venues, Declan would go on first, with a short solo set. As St Michael reports, he could already give as good as he got when faced with a rowdy audience. "He'd be so rude; he'd just *glare* at them."

The band would usually open with Costello's own song 'Pay It Back', which was to reappear in altered form on *My Aim Is True*. Flip City was widening its sphere of influences. They reworked Marvin Gaye's hit version of the Smokey Robinson song 'One More Heartache' into a "bluebeat shuffle". Another of Declan's songs, 'Flatfoot Hotel', contained a new note of lyrical mystery, with lines like "You start as a good guy and end as a thief", Costello compounding the enigma by confiding that "the point of this song is that there *is* no point". For the record, Mick St Michael guesses that the hotel of the title was Kingston's Royal Charter, "commonly known as 'The Fishes' and a mecca for south London hippies of the time".

Flip City were a natural support act, reliable without that defining spark which separates the memorable from the merely pleasant. They became a regular fixture at the legendary Marquee, opening for Dr Feelgood in 1975. Their lead singer, the gravel-voiced Lee Brilleaux, was later to play a material part in Elvis's future, by bankrolling Stiff records, but their flash and sweaty commitment was light years removed from Flip City's home counties' cosiness. Nick Kent, the wildman of rock journalism, was so intent on interviewing Wilko Johnson backstage that he ignored Flip City completely.

Costello was himself becoming disillusioned with his band. As he told Greil Marcus, "There was no focus to it; it was aimless. We could get through the usual bar-band repertoire – but I remember Pete Thomas, now The Attractions drummer and *then* a drummer in a quite successful pub-rock band, Chilli Willi, coming to see us – he was a *celebrity* to us – and he walked out after about thirty seconds. I think he came to see our worst-ever gig – but with no offence to the guys, we weren't very good."

Flip City did record some demos at Dave Robinson's Hope and Anchor Studios in 1975, on a (unique) seven-track console originally bought for Eamonn Andrews' Irish TV chat show. One track, Costello's 'Imagination Is A Powerful Deceiver', surfaced officially on the CD re-release of his first solo album. Costello's voice is already in place, luxuriantly licking at each syllable, menacing and sour, with lots of natural vibrato and cracking with emotion at one point. The problem is twofold. The band, who sound zonked on valium, provide a cushion rather than a trampolene to their lead singer. Particularly awful is the mock Chinese riff. The lyrics are callow, self-pitying, about a former girlfriend who is avoiding the singer, though they already show traces of masochism – "if you want to dance on my face" – and of verbal trickery, "I go out of my mind, if I'm losing your touch".

The tapes have survived to be circulated on the collector's market, with three takes of the above song, all much the same, and some in-the-studio chat. "At last," shouts Declan, after a second run-through, in a thick Liverpool accent, and another band member whoops in triumph.

'Third Rate Romance' is a weary plod, as compared to Jesse Winchester's earlier version. It throws into contrast the later song by Racing Cars, 1977's 'Weekend Rendezvous', on which Morty emotes a genuine sense of loss and hurt. The Welsh band were one of the saddest casualties of rock history, with all the right credentials, then punk happened, they looked old and shabby, and that was that. Lost in the rush along with the likes of The "O" Band and Peaches – who only got to do one John Peel session, transcendent all the same. The stubbed-out fag ends of the past, which could have lit a forest fire if things had worked out differently. Flip City, by contrast, sound like eternal losers, albeit with a singer who is giving it all that he can.

The tune to 'Third Rate Romance' was later incorporated into 'No Dancing', with infinitely better words. It's theme seems a perennial one for Costello, which is presumably why he chose to cover it. Sub Dylan's 'Positively Fourth Street' it sounds like a "let's be nasty to a ex-girlfriend" moment: "You're already looking for another fool like me". 'Radio Soul' is an early version of 'Radio Radio', with Dylanesque vocals, and lyrics which praise AM culture – as Lou Reed did in 'Rock And Roll', and Van Morrison in 'Domino' – rather than coming to bury it, as the rewritten song will. Costello/MacManus sounds bored by his own song, as it drags its weary way to a conclusion.

'Pay It Back' has more of a swing to it, sounding very much like Graham Parker and a tranquillised Rumour, promising revenge. What sounds like a saxophone livens the pace, and there is almost a reggae lope to the proceedings, even if the chorus of voices behind Costello is amateurish in the extreme. Another vocalist, presumably Steve Hazelhurst, takes over on the second cover, of 'Knocking On Heaven's Door', and it becomes less a lament than a dirge. My own reaction as I listen to the tape is to shoot the bugger again, so that he stops singing. A wonderfully out of tune guitar solo, to boot, though not as funny as Neil Innes' intentional self-parody of a bad plectrum abuser on the Bonzos' 'Canyons Of Your Mind'. This is barely youth club standard, and Costello is notable by his near absence.

The tape ends with two more of his songs, the first 'I'm Packing Up' which after two false starts and lots of Elvis-like echo settles into a polite moan. There is a trace of 'Mystery Dance' in the chorus, and the ghost of 'Roadrunner'. Barely competent guitar, again, fiddly where it should be self-assured, the best bit is in the middle, where Elvis sings without the band, and sounds Fifties rather than Sixties, as does a Jordanaires type vocal chorus after the song restarts. 'Don't Stop The Band' is hardly a plea which many paying audiences would have echoed if this tape is representative of live concerts. A touch of Captain Beefheart in the riff – probably more through incompetence rather than in tribute – and Costello comes in like a terrier. The words "lost my faith in a promised land/put all my faith in a backstreet band" are, if true, misplaced, though a little bit of verbal venom seeps into the song as it proceeds, a sign of things to come. At this stage of Costello's career, though, the demo is nothing special, pleasant background music at best. The writing was on the wall, and all of Flip City knew it. In mitigation, the BBC demo of 'Exile's Road' sounds far more assured, and in tune!

To put this in context, compare the work of Help Yourself, who also rose little further than the rock clubs, and whose four albums are now collectors' items, and just released on CD. They continue to entrance a small cult following, who speak their name with awe. Lead singer and songwriter Malcolm Morley affects an American accent – like Costello – while the band work very much in the shadow of Neil Young, but there comparisons end. Morley's songs are dark chronicles of a bleak world, sung with passion and a total lack of irony. The first album carries paeons to lost love, distance – "baby stay away from me, you've been on your own too long" – and in 'Old Man' to a man about to die, performed with total conviction. White man's blues, and effortlessly emotional. "We tried to love you too hard, we tried but you know nothing is easy, my friend, living ain't easy." Almost whispered, to a fretwork of country guitars.

The loose theme is that of life in the countryside, but unsentimentalised, "water falls on the mountainside, and it winds its way to sea". The album plunges back into urban reality with 'Street Songs', about the death (or worse) of an ex-girlfriend. "Everybody laid her, she was easy meat. Now they came and took her, I cried myself to sleep." Morley is totally confident of his role, observing and chronicling a circle of acquaintance, and allowing himself a full-blown romanticism which Costello has never quite dared: "Deborah, your hair is turning grey, and you still wear the ring your father gave."

As against the pedestrian plod of Flip City, a tight but floating rhythm section here act as a setting for the chill tone of Richard Treece's lead guitar work. The band were very much a collective, swapping personnel and instruments, while Morley and bassist Ken Whaley later joined Man. Just passing through was Sean Tyla, later to emerge during the early days of the new wave, while Morley played with Wreckless Eric, and sung on and off with Plummet Airlines until ill health drove him out of the business. In another coincidence, Help Yourself were signed to Liberty by Andrew Lauder, who later became involved with Radar and F-Beat.

In comparison, Flip City sound one-dimensional, schoolboyish. Mind you, so do The Eagles. Help Yourself did not long survive the disastrous 'Happy Daze' tour, while Flip City's swansong was a four-night residency at the Red Cow, Hammersmith, on succeeding Sundays. The same venue was later to act as a launch-pad for new wave Mods The Jam and AC/DC, whose lead guitarist literally was a schoolboy (if a rather superannuated one) and who John Peel in one of his more laconic asides suggested should be hung from the neck by his satchel. Opportunity did not knock for Flip City. The last of these gigs, on 30 November, 1975, saw original drummer Malcolm Dennis return to play on the 'Long Dead Train', and his replacement Ian Powell play guitar along with Declan and Steve on what they called their Blue Oyster Cult impression, with multiple "plank spankers". Such jokiness, though, sat uneasily with the intensity of Declan's own material.

'Imagination Is A Powerful Deceiver' was particularly striking, a kind of dry run for 'Alison'. Mick St Michael remembers how Costello howled "Turn out the light so you can tell me the truth" over and over, as if in agony, "and for one moment the Red Cow stood hushed and attentive. It was a sign of things to come." Words that do not appear on the recorded version. Maybe he misheard: more likely, Costello had a sudden spurt of pure imagination.

Flip City played their last ever gig the following month, playing support to the fading delights of The Climax Blues Band (now well on the way to becoming flaccid) at Ewell Technical College. It was almost a metaphor for their career, or lack of it, and the tension which should have fuelled their music was finally unleashed. "Everyone was rowing and fighting," Elvis recalls. Some of the band continued to live at the communal house in East Molesey, and Steve Hazelhurst recorded a demo tape, which drew myriad polite notes of rejection. "I frame all mine," was Declan's response, and he recommenced the solo career he had first attempted in the folk clubs of London and Liverpool, but now under the stage name of DP Costello.

Talking to Colin Irwin in *Folk Roots*, Costello remembered that, "At this point I was getting the odd gig for a tenner. I was resident at the Half Moon in Putney for a while – I used to get 50p and a plate of sandwiches." By now, people had to listen to him "because I was so fucking loud they didn't have any option. I'd abandoned all attempts at playing subtle guitar." His early love of ragtime had been abandoned too: "I could never get the co-ordination together. And I was never happy playing with nails so I just had to go to a flat-pick. And from a flat-pick I got into rhythm because rhythm gave me more cover. So the style came from having to cover myself in noisy clubs."

Thus was born Elvis's driving guitar style, the "little hands of concrete" he later satirised himself as possessing, which proved so effective with The Attractions. Playing textures, rather than solos. Costello hated open tuning, because "it would always end up in some kind of Chinese tuning". Gigging without a band proved to be far from an easy option, though. As Costello later told Greil Marcus, "There's no real platform for solo singing, unless you sing traditional music and *recognised blues*, doing re-creations – you know how *reverent* Europeans are." He found it difficult to develop his own individual style.

"I have no idea who it was I might have been imitating, whether consciously or unconsciously," he says. "Playing alone did build up an edge. I did the odd show just to keep up, to keep trying to *improve* the ability to play. You'd soon know if you were dying in a club. Playing on your own you'd have the tension – you could increase the tension at will, not relying on anybody to pick up the beat." More important for Costello now was that somebody should pick up on *him*.

In February 1976, an unsuperstitious DP Costello began a weekly residency at the Half Moon, Putney, opening on 13 Friday. The pub was well known for its associations with folk rock; Fairport would often run through their set for the Cropredy festival in front of a hundred or so rabid supporters. Costello as yet had no such fan base. The advert for the first gig headlines the invitation "Singers Welcome", with Costello's name in tiny print beneath, like an afterthought.

Something was gathering in the wings of a stagnant music scene, though, a new hideous energy pulsing out from the pubs and outer venues of London, like the first stirrings of an alien invasion force. George Gimarc's invaluable *Punk Diary 1970-1979* (the very title a rewriting of conventional rock history) lists for that same night gigs by Ian Dury's Kilburn And The High Roads at the Nags Head, Joe Strummer's 101ers at Hampstead Town Hall, and The Stranglers at the Red Cow. All three were groups on the cusp between pub-rock and new wave, (relatively) old men who would spearhead a youth revolution.

Costello himself was still only twenty-one, even if his material and stance did seem stolen from a slightly older generation. The sets he played between floor acts at the Half Moon were fascinating, sloughing off his previous repertoire and airing new songs which entered darker, more personal territory. There was something newly dangerous about Costello onstage: perhaps it was desperation.

This spilled over into his unsettling habit of making day visits to A&R men in their offices, armed not with the usual demo tape but with a guitar and attitude. Like a pedlar with his wares, trying to make a doorstep sale. There was nothing worse in the Tin Pan Alley days than having to audition in front of a bored and jaded executive – why does Mickie Most suddenly come to mind? – who would listen impassively then never return your calls. Or worse, in my own case, then arrange matching suits and a gig in a gay club in Portsmouth! Declan, though, gave as good as he got. "I used to make embarrassing scenes," he recalls. "I used to get a guitar and say, 'What do you think of this song?' I actually did force a few people to be bored for twenty minutes. It was particularly embarrassing when you're in the middle of a song and you really think you're convincing the guy and suddenly the phone goes off and he says, 'Yes, darling, we'll have supper at eight.'" Nick Lowe remembers the embarrassment cutting both ways. "It's the most intimidating and awe-inspiring thing to happen," he says, "because he's extremely loud, as if he's singing through a great PA to thousands of people and he's only three feet away from you. You don't know how to react."

For someone so genuinely politically radical, it is ironic that what Costello was embarking on was testing himself against precisely those market forces which Thatcherism was to endorse, and have the whole of society follow. Any musician, painter, actor or writer who wishes to live by the fruits of their own individual talent, rather than make it a mere hobby, or abandon it as a childish whim, has to thus learn to market their abilities – and thus in some ways themselves – to any bidder they can. The likes of fame and popular success seem unthinkable at such a juncture, and of little importance. Everything depends on that first break, and self-sufficiency is the main issue, nothing else. The wider public will only hear about the winners, years down the line.

With a wife and child to support, and having turned his back on any conventional career path, Declan was ploughing a lonely furrow, without reviews or any great public reaction. Even fans of Flip City were beginning to wonder if he had been right to split up that band, which at least had some kind of localised following, and provided company onstage. Now he was on his own, in more ways than one. As Laura Marcus told Mick St Michael, "We used to drive him to gigs, because he'd never learned to drive. It was really nickel and dime stuff." A look at Costello's sparse gig sheet confirms this, tiny folk haunts like the Grail Folk Club, Hounslow, London's Centrefolk and the Troubadour. Wouldn't they love to rebook him, now! "I used to feel for him," she continues. "It's like seeing someone on the stage in a show that's not doing very well. They didn't understand or appreciate him. People would say, 'Oh this guy's ripping off Graham Parker,' and we'd say, 'No – he's really good. Just listen.'"

If Costello was noticed at all, it was indeed as a kind of copycat version of ex-petrol pump attendant Graham Parker, then busy burning up London stages with his band The Rumour, largely drawn from Brinsley Schwarz, but newly tough and snotty. Parker did indeed share similar influences though – Springsteen, Dylan, Van Morrison –

and he was really an old hippie off the Katmandu trail (as was Wilko Johnson, for that matter) but one who had cut his hair and learnt how to portray hatred onstage. The love years were over. Though hampered by a musicality and professionalism that would damn him a year or so later, like an aristocrat exposed by the mob, he was at the moment a kind of John the Baptist to punk, setting out its parameters. Parker's venom was to seem small beer when punk really got going, and blew him away. A series of albums which leeched away energy and inspiration didn't help. For the time being, though, with songs like 'Howlin' Wind' and 'Don't Ask Me Questions' and a sparkling production on his first album by Nick Lowe, Parker was the most spiteful thing on the block. It can have done Costello's short term success little harm to be seen as an acoustic variant to this new wave of anger.

It certainly helped bring Declan to the notice of Charlie Gillett, whom he had been pestering for months for free plugs for his solo gigs on Gillett's Capital Radio show *Honky Tonk*. Finally, on 15 August, Gillett bowed to the inevitable and, performing his own new songs, Costello made his radio debut as a solo artist. The shock waves are still reverberating.

Strangely intimate, as if Costello is standing close – too close – to you and whispering directly into your ear, the demo tape features quiet vocals and jazzy acoustic guitar. Costello's voice has undergone a quantum leap since the Flip City demos, and the sparse backing releases him – just like the young Dylan – to express a whole gamut of feelings: cheeky, threatening, witty, passionate, laconic. It is a voice both obviously fake – the American accent is emphasised, a roomful of echoes of other singers – and yet melded with Costello's own psyche, so that there is something visceral and exciting here, a man hot-wired direct into his own unconscious. No wonder that what emerges is closer to Hitchcock than James Taylor. The results are both shocking and somehow cleansing, with this young unknown singing about the great unmentionables, things previously beyond the romantic themes of love and death which rock music espoused. Sexual failure, violence and dissatisfaction.

The set was widely bootlegged, and eventually reached a legitimate release on the augmented *My Aim Is True* CD. 'Blame It

On Cain' is set to a jaunty guitar, and sung with brio. Along with 'Mystery Dance' it was to be recycled on Costello's debut album, the latter with a extra, concluding verse:

> I'm going to walk right up to heaven dodging lightning rods,
> I'm going to have this very personal conversation with God,
> I'll say you've got the information, why don't you say so
> He'll say well I've been around and I still don't know.

The chorus follows on, this time as if spoken by God himself. If even the Father of Creation doesn't understand sex, then we really *are* in trouble.

'Cheap Reward' combines lyrics eventually rewritten as 'Lip Service' with a country tune and sense of misery that was later to grace 'Stranger In The House': "I might be horizontal by the time the music ceases, so I think I'll get acquainted with the floor." He even greets the floorboards, as old friends. 'Jump Up' begins jauntily, like a campfire tune by Burl Ives, with a trace of the ragtime guitar which Declan once idolised, then turns slower and into a minor mode. The words are something else entirely: a first person narrative of neglect and abjectness and poverty, like The Kinks' 'Dead End Street' ten years on, and now a cul-de-sac:

> When I'm locked up in a room about half the size of a matchbox,
> Got holes in my socks
> That match the ones that I got on my feet.
> I put my feet in the holes in the street
> And somebody paved me over.

Positively surrealistic. There is an odd comparison with that emotionally decadent – and poet laureate – Alfred Lord Tennyson's *Maud*, of all things.

> And my bones are shaken with pain,
> For into a shallow grave they are thrust,
> Only a yard beneath the street,
> And the hooves of the horses beat, beat…

Beat into my scalp and my brain.

The same weird atmosphere seeps into another Costello demo, 'Poison Moon', one minute and fifty three seconds of mental breakdown, sung with the wired intensity of, say, Norman Bates in *Psycho*.

And these bones, they don't look so good to me…
One day soon, I will laugh right in the face of the poison moon.

No wonder the narrator – which sounds suspiciously close to Costello himself, is "cut loose in a nightmare".

There is something peculiarly brave in the way that late Sixties troubadours – some now nearing their late sixties! – like Roy Harper or Jackie Leven or Robin Williamson can still hold the attention span of an audience over a couple of hours with just their voice and a guitar (or in Williamson's case a Celtic harp). It is a kind of throwback to the bardic tradition, with a round of rhymed short stories, but there is also something vulnerable in which the personality of the singer is exposed, and their songs inevitably given a personal dimension. Perhaps because of this, sensitive souls – I mean those two words literally – like Nick Drake or Sandy Denny found the intensity of such public self-revelation too much. Costello is equally able to hold an audience in the palm of his hand, for a whole evening, but he has never released an album without backing musicians, and perhaps these songs show why. There is something almost too personal in their delivery, a sense of someone you just don't want in your life invading your brain.

This reaches its apogee with the jaw-dropping 'Wave A White Flag':

When I hit the bottle
There's no telling what I'll do,
'Cause something deep inside me
Wants to turn you black and blue.

Though Lou Reed had written about sexual violence in *Berlin*, it was strictly through a mask. Even if John Cale boasted in interviews about beating up his wife, it was Richard Thompson of all people who put these dark thoughts into song. His unrecorded 'Dragging The River' was merely one among many songs which exuded a cheery misogyny, promising his lover that the police would soon be getting out their dragnets. The later song 'I'll Regret It All In The Morning' dealt with a loveless encounter, at the end of which he might "beat you black and blue", to his shame when sober. This from a teetotaller, and someone projecting the black thoughts one sometimes feels in any relationship into a fictional situation. Costello went further. The way he sings "to take your pretty neck and see which way it bends" sounds something positively to be relished. Such domestic violence is mutual:

Beat me in the kitchen,
And I'll beat you in the hall.
There's nothing I like better
Than a free-for-all.

The love object is no longer an angel – "take off your shoes, hang up your wings". The performance owes much to the kind of sick irony of Randy Newman or Tom Lehrer, sung with relish, and leaving a sour aftertaste. "Hope you don't murder me," Costello concludes, and it seems far from rhetorical. While definitely not politically correct, it is merely the first of a series of such portraits of domestic disharmony which thread through Costello's later career. "Emotional fascism" come early. Jamie Kitman describes the song as "self-incriminating…an aberration, a joke, or it represents Elvis's thinking at an early moment, what William Burroughs calls the larval stage of development."

As Elvis told *Record Collector*, by the age of twenty-two he had made several false starts "at getting bands together, some of them documented, some of them so fleeting that no one knows about them". The *Honky Tonk* songs were from a demo tape recorded in his bedroom, on a Revox borrowed from a friend. Before that, Costello had relied on an old Grundig, and in sending out twenty songs at a time, in the forlorn hope that anyone would listen beyond track one. "I had a pretty good idea from bitter experience that you had to make a *presentation* just like putting on a show," he reflects. "I'd been playing solo a lot, so I was much better at presenting my songs to hostile audiences, and winning them over. So I made a little show reel of six songs, and sent it off to various people."

On a later broadcast, Gillett replayed with pride some of the demos by (then) unknowns first aired on his daytime show "on Radio London, 206 on the medium wave and 94.9 VHF. Here's a group who were crucial to the whole live music thing back in 1972 when I started *Honky Tonk* off. I was mainly interested in playing records. I didn't think about live music, and then somebody sent me a little tape. The band were Bees Make Honey." He plays the album track 'Kentucky Chicken Fry', as a prime example of pub rock, just the kind of stuff that Flip City purveyed.

Indeed, Gillett seems to be referring to Costello's formative days in his dedication of this special programme to "all those people who entertain us nightly in London, playing live, and anyone who isn't involved in it would never have any idea how hard it is for those bands to get together, get the PAs, and do it all for the £30 they get paid by most of the pubs they play in. It's also to all the people who send in tapes and one way or another have been connected to the programme."

As to Costello, the demo came "in a raw form, and if you hear it now, you'll see why". He plays 'Wave A White Flag'. "And one of the differences between various companies in this country is that when CBS heard the tape, they sent a letter back to DP Costello saying not bad, promising, 'Come back in a year and we'll see what we can do.' Stiff heard it and took him in a studio and three weeks later Elvis had an album, and a new name too." Not *quite* the real time-scale, as we shall see.

Just before playing 'Lip Service', Gillett adds that he found Costello's original letter which accompanied the tape. "It said, 'Here's a tape and I hope that one day it'll be worth auctioning off.' Well, I'm not going to do that. I'm going to keep it."

Costello writes in the sleeve notes to the CD that, despite the presence of titles and lyrics recycled on later songs, they present a radically different style to what surfaced on his subsequent debut album. With hindsight, he "must confess that I am uneasy with my blatant imitation of certain American singers and songwriters". He does admit to having learned a great deal "from trying (and failing) to copy such artists as Randy Newman, Hoagy Carmichael, Lowell George, John Prine and The Band". Many of these names became unfashionable in the years of punk. Costello hopes that the listener will be "amused, one way or another, by these steps in my apprenticeship".

It is interesting that Costello name-checks Lowell George, whose band Little Feat took boogie into hitherto unimaginable areas, and in live concert cold slip into an almost supernatural looseness. Lowell died young, of pure excess, but his lazy brilliance is very much the antithesis of Costello's sweaty determination, and Little Feat could slip and slide through precisely the kind of funk which Elvis always made sound stiff and cerebral. Of the others on his list, Newman was also from a family steeped in music, and fused a sneaky, unmelodic voice to songs which seemed at first to promote racism, or attacks on short or fat people – his early albums had to be literally given away by his record company – and with deliberately lush backings. John Prine, very much a Dylan clone at first, developed his own brand of laconic, throwaway singing, semi-spoken. Every singer on this list is quirkily humorous, another and sometimes overlooked attribute of Costello himself.

The *Honky Tonk* broadcast really "got things going". Such obvious talent really could not be ignored, even by the media. "I had several different people after my signature then," Elvis says, "none of them aware of the others' existence." Gillett himself – a rock 'n' roll professor, whose *The Sound Of The City* remains the definitive guide to black music – had plans to sign Costello up to his own label, Oval. Instead, Costello turned down "a really pitiful deal – even then I knew enough to laugh at it" from Virgin, in favour of Stiff, "who had the initiative to say, 'Let's do it now.' It seemed almost magical after two or three years of getting really indifferent, or completely bewildered, responses to all the tapes I'd created." Wait long enough, and the world catches up.

Stiff was founded in July 1976, by manic control-freak and prankster Jake Riviera and genial Irishman Dave Robinson. Robinson had been tour manager for Jimi Hendrix, then managed Eire Apparent, as their name suggests also hailing from Ireland, and discovered by Hendrix. Their lead singer Ernie Graham, shorn of about a ton of hair, and sporting a skinny tie, rather than a well worn tie-die, was later to record for Stiff as a solo artist.

Robinson went on to found the public relations firm Famepushers, whose most notorious scam was flying a plane load of journalists over to New York to see his charges Brinsley Schwarz make a disastrous debut at the Fillmore East. Having pushed no-one to fame, Dave went back into management with Kilburn And The High Roads, as bizarre (and wonderful) a band as I have ever seen on a public stage. He also ran the small seven-track recording studio in the basement of the Hope and Anchor, where Flip City had their half hour of immortality, and many more besides from the early days of pub-rock: Bees Like Honey, Ducks Deluxe and Eggs Over Easy, an American band who supposedly developed the genre in the first place. Ironically, the Flip City tapes are among the few full sessions to yet emerge, albeit surreptitiously, and one wonders what aural marvels still lurk in the Robinson archives.

Jake Riviera, born under the more prosaic name of Andrew Jakeman, was a former advertising man who had been manager of Chilli Willi and The Red Hot Peppers, and packaged them and their records with just the kind of zany wit that he was to employ with Stiff, as well a kind of weird competence. As Andy Childs reported for *Zigzag*, "Jake was the only person exhibiting signs of life, hand on the steering wheel, eyes fixed on the road, singing and talking, trying to stay awake." Revelation's second and final release – after *Glastonbury Fayre* – was the Chilli Willi debut, *Kings Of The Robot Rhythm*. An apt title, as their singer Phil Lithman reinvented himself as Snakefinger, and became involved with The Residents, American West Coast conceptualists and pranksters. Jakeman specialised, even then, in acting as a kind of male dominatrix, subjecting Chilli Willi to periodic truth attacks, which put everyone in their place. Everyone, of course, except himself.

Bert Muirhead got him just about in his book *Stiff: The Story Of A Record Label*. "His was a curious blend of the innocence and enthusiasm of the pop fan, translated (via the nimble brain of the rock professional who had seen all the big company dirty tricks and shady deals) into a 1970s hybrid," he suggests. "The push hustler who knows where he is going and he is going to get there without the aid of corporation lawyers, teams of accountants, committees etc."

Jakeman's big invention was the 1975 Naughty Rhythms tour, based on the Stax soul revue, with Chilli Willi, Kokomo and Dr Feelgood alternating as headliners, and cheap tickets subsidised by the three record companies involved. The problem with such apparent democracy was that, as with the later Stiff tour modelled on this event, that winners and losers soon emerged. Chilli Willi were going nowhere in particular, and Kokomo – whose swooning music, combining the rhythm section of the Grease band and the rich harmonies of Arrival has matured with age – were too smooth for a rock audience. Dr Feelgood's psychotic stage show, combined with simple, pounding three-chord rock, won the day.

Jake subsequently became tour manager for the Feelgoods during their first US tour – Nick Lowe, refreshed by a publishing deal, was along for the ride – but quit in San Diego during a dispute about a lost wah-wah pedal. Riviera took refuge with Pete Thomas, formerly Chilli Willi's drummer, who had come over to play with John Stewart, once lead singer with The Kingston Trio, and since the release of the deeply sentimental and patriotic *American Bloodlines*, subject of a minor cult. Stewart even had a fanzine devoted to him, *Omaho Rainbow*, but his music was becoming increasingly smug, and Thomas correspondingly homesick.

Meanwhile, the Feelgoods called Jake back into the fold: presumably the wah-wah pedal had been found. It was subsequently a loan of £400 from Lee Brilleaux which helped set up Stiff in a damp basement at 32 Alexandra Street in London's Notting Hill. The label later moved to a larger building just up the road, once it had signed a distribution deal with Island, and took on rock scribe Pete Frame as its press officer. There had been a council of war, held at the Bricklayers Arms, in which the likes of Muirhead and John Tobler agreed help to distribute and publicise the new label's product. Jake and Dave had listed eight bands – all drawn from the pub rock scene and – including the Brinsleys and Chilli Willi – who were unfairly neglected.

Stiff was based on small US independents like Flat Out and Beserkeley, and named after the American slang for the kinds of discs which end up in bargain bins. The secondary meanings of "stiff" – a dead person, an excited part of the male anatomy – were all part of the joke, especially in the days before political correctness, leading to double-entendre slogans like "if it's not Stiff it's not worth a fuck".

Jake's marketing expertise came into operation, flooding the world with coded messages like 'Jupp Jupp And Away', 'Elvis Is King', and 'I'm Drinking For Nick Lowe'. All very childish, and none the worse for that, and a kind of inversion of the star system. No wonder that they proudly boasted they were the "world's most flexible record label". Such processes, a kind of deconstruction of the mystique in which pop records were promoted and sold, ensured that the label grabbed the attention of record collectors from the very start, a process aided by their policy of rapid deletions, and putting singles in picture sleeves, or onto coloured vinyl.

Perversely, the high values once put on this early product have dropped away with the years: the whole enterprise was a little too calculated, and lacked the mystery of what eventually become holy grails for collectors to slaver and fight over, and boast about, whether obscure rockabilly, or the product of tiny labels like Oak or Holyground or Les Disques de Crepescules, or ephemeral new wave. Stiff's instant rarities were – in hindsight – a little too manufactured. At the time, though, it was huge fun, especially for those who had previously thought themselves too grown up to indulge in such baubles. This was music for the jaded palate.

The new offices reminded Mick St Michael of a "cross between the Battle of Britain operations room and a student squat. Posters festooned the walls, a blackboard proclaimed the day to day movements of Stiff artists, and great piles of records threatened a vinyl avalanche." The first Stiff single was also Nick Lowe's solo debut – after long stints with the pop-psych band Kippington Lodge and the Brinsleys. 'So It Goes'/'Heart Of The City', a double A-side, was recorded at North London's tiny (and cheap) Pathway studio for £45, and went on to sell 10,000 copies. The wit of early Stiff was right there on the label, "mono enhanced stereo", with "three-chord trick, yeah" engraved on the matrix.

Vinyl Mogul's press release announced that Stiff "favours sound over technique and feeling over style". Both songs "are under three minutes, use less than three musicians and less than three chords", and light years removed from Lowe's country epics with the Brinsleys, mainly in praise of fresh air and eager girls. 'Heart Of The City' is pure rock, with a Velvet Underground rush, and bizarre words, alligators running loose in the sewers. 'So It Goes' sounds like a Thin Lizzy outtake, and deals with the seamier side of the rock biz, and the way it is entering anarchy: "They've got 50,000 watts and a big acoustic tower, security's so tight tonight, they're ready for a tussle, better keep your backstage passes, 'cause the promoter hired the muscle." There is a guitar solo straight out of The Shadows, all reverb, and short as a slow intake of breath. Lowe sang, wrote both songs, and played all the instruments other than the drums – provided by Steve Goulding – as well as co-producing the single with Riviera. A new wave, one man band.

Since the Brinsleys' split, Lowe had been in low spirits. "I didn't have anything going for me at all," he admits. "I teamed up with Jake Riviera because I used to sleep on his couch when I had nowhere to go – I stayed for about a year." The four-CD *Stiff Records Box Set* – a quarter genius, three quarters filler, much now barely listenable – resurrects the Lowe/Riviera composition, 'I Love My Label', credited to Lowe and L Profile.

Pathway became Lowe's second home. He would clock in, and wait "to see who Jake had sent up there. They'd sing their song, I'd knock it into some sort of musical shape and we'd make a record. Almost anyone who had a bit of front would get a try out." Like future multi-millionaire Chris Blackwell, when his label Island was purely an outlet for ska and Jamaican reggae, Jake marketed his records himself, carrying them in the boot of his car to record shops. If he objected to the owners' haircuts, he would refuse to provide stock. Perhaps accordingly, his main problem was satisfying the demand from hip customers. Punk was to make buying singles fashionable again, and the earliest mass-market example, 'New Rose' by The Damned, came out on Stiff as their sixth single release. A few months later, The Adverts' archetypal 'One Chord Wonders' emerged as Stiff Buy 13.

After all, such jerky, hyper-charged music was best over a two and a half minute stretch, maximum. Most bands' sets now lasted less than both sides of an album, anyway. Stiff also helped pioneer the cult of the picture sleeve, a continental idea previously restricted in Britain to odd and extremely collectable releases by Dylan, The Beatles and Hendrix. It now became *de rigueur* to have a colour cover, with new wave graphics, part of the collecting craze which Riviera so assiduously fostered.

Stiff was largely a hippie affair, even if the protagonists now had new haircuts (or simply no hair). Early single releases featured the likes of The Pink Fairies, Martin Stone, Sean Tyla – once a member of Help Yourself – and Motörhead (a single deleted before release, and only available as a forty-five on a limited edition box set, extreme marketing even by Stiff's standards). Motörhead's bassist Lemmy had previously been a Rockin' Vicar, a member of Sam Gopal Dream, and a founder member of Hawkwind, who played on 'Silver Machine'. *Glastonbury Fayre* revisited, once again with graphics care of Barney Bubbles and Edward Barker (both now passed over to the great open air rock festival of eternity, with Hendrix, Jim Morrison, Janis Joplin, Jerry Garcia and John Lennon jamming onstage, forever). Not that this was unusual in a punk scene where everyone rewrote their personal history.

Thus did John Peel exchange The Perfumed Garden for Sniffing Glue, Caroline Coon her sterling work in the drug tents of innumerable free festivals to co-manage The Clash, and Malcolm McLaren transform his late Sixties situationism into hip capitalism. It was all part of the spectacle. Virgin dropped most of their original, late-hippie acts for The Sex Pistols, and more of their ilk. This was not simple opportunism: punk offered the same kind of anarchic freedom as had the communitarian ideals of the Summer of Love, before both were steamrollered by commercialism, and rigid dress codes. It was just ironic to find old hippies telling you not to trust an old hippie.

The Damned, whose bassist Captain Sensible was a fan of the early Soft Machine, and a skilled guitarist who had to de-learn his instrument, gave Stiff their first sizeable hit with the swaying menace of 'New Rose'. It was produced by Nick Lowe who speeded up the band in the studio, and claimed it as the first – some still say the best – punk single to be made available nationwide. Under the surface menace, and Rat Scabies' clattering dustbin-like drums, it was a love song, no more, no less.

As Costello told Greil Marcus, "The Damned were the best punk group, because there was no art behind them; they were just enjoying themselves. There was no art behind them that *I* could see. They were just – *nasty*. I loved them from the start. I liked the Pistols as well – but you could see the concern behind it. It's dishonest to say, 'Oh yes, we were just *wild*.' They weren't just wild. It was *considered* and *calculated*. Very art. The Clash as well." It was ironic that not only was Costello considerably younger than the people behind Stiff, but than many of the bands claiming to be young punks. There was a great deal of professional forgetfulness going on, with the likes of The Police or 999 or The UK Subs or The Stranglers taking years off their CVs. Just like after any revolution, which the punk ethos certainly was, people could reinvent themselves, in whatever image they saw fit.

Stiff Records were looking to build a new empire, so were keenly on the lookout for new talent. A small ad in the music papers drew the eagle-eyed attention of DP Costello. History was about to be made. In August 1976, on the very day that Stiff Records released its debut single, Costello delivered a four-song reel-to-reel demo tape by hand to the label's office.

Like Stanley recalling his meeting with Dr Livingstone, Nick Lowe told Radio One's Nicky Campbell that he had met Costello "on Royal Oak tube station, and he had his guitar with him and I said, 'How are you doing,' blah blah blah. He had just been up to Stiff to buy a copy of 'And So It Goes', and to leave a tape with Jake Riviera. We shook hands and I wished him luck, and I went up to Stiff Records, and Jake was extremely excited, he said this geeky specs guy has left this tape and it's really cool." Another account has Lowe suggesting that Costello try Stiff, and the singer replying, "That's just where I've been."

It was the first tape that Riviera had listened to, and he immediately grabbed the worth of the songs. In particular, 'Mystery Dance' stood out, and seemed ideal material for Dave Edmunds. "Jake was saying, 'This tape is fantastic,'" Lowe recalls, "but he was going to sign him as a writer. We listened to the tape a bit more and he decided to sign him as an actual artist." Costello was summoned over a few days later, and offered a recording contract.

"I was the house producer," Lowe explains of the Stiff set-up, "basically because I'd spent more time in the studio than the other two people involved with Stiff. So it was my job to cut his first records." Lowe later confessed to Nicky Campbell that, as a songwriter, he thought Elvis "was pretty ropy to start off with, to be honest, 'cause he was far too wordy. His first stuff, it was like there were five songs in one song…He was Declan then. It took years to get used to calling him Elvis. It was during the making of *My Aim Is True* that I began to realise this guy is a bit special. With his early stuff, I used to help him a lot." The first two tracks they cut together were 'Mystery Dance' and 'Radio Sweetheart'.

CHAPTER TWO

please to see the king

Riviera's first decision, once he had signed Costello, was to persuade him to call himself Elvis. "Changing my name stopped people dead in their tracks, and made them say, 'He can't be called that. He *is* called that!'" Costello remembers. "By that time he'd noticed me more than the bloke called Joe Smith." Both Riviera and Robinson would come on at Costello like "good cop, bad cop, everything was heavily fuelled. A lot of Strongbow cider was being imbibed there after hours" – brainstorming, in management parlance, although the playfulness of Stiff would send any consultant for an early bath. "All these mad plans would be hatched and then they'd be all off the next day. Jake said we're going to call you Elvis, ha ha ha, and I thought it was just another of these things that would pass off, and it didn't. Then it got to be a matter of honour, to carry it off."

Jake decided to accentuate his new charge's geeky charm. Elvis's first press release, under his new name, read "baggy suited and bespectacled, a Buddy Holly on acid". Stiff was interested from the start in something that punk was to temporarily render unfashionable, the art of songwriting. In Costello, and Ian Dury, and even Wreckless Eric, they were to hit paydirt. Robinson declared that the new label was on the lookout for acts "involved in a kind of fairly basic song/band structure where there were lots and lots of songs, and that's what I've always been interested in". A passion which would reap millions when he later signed Madness.

In an interview with *Record Collector* Costello confirmed that he was the first performer under contract to Stiff. "Nick Lowe was the first artist *on* the label, but he wasn't actually signed," he explains. "Despite that, I ended up with the eleventh release on the label. All those records came through from people like The Damned and Richard Hell, which were very much tied to the moment, so their timing was crucial. It was frustrating for me, because I wanted to get on with it." When his break came, he grabbed it with both hands. "I was writing very fast and one day I went to Pathway Studios where Nick Lowe was producing a Wreckless Eric record. Wreckless was very nervous, so Nick took him for a drink to loosen him up a little bit, and I recorded eight songs while they were gone, just guitar and voice. That was the bulk of the demos for *My Aim Is True*."

Up to the point, Stiff had thought of splitting a debut album between Eric and Elvis, one side each like the classic Berry/Diddley LP *Chuck Meets Bo*. "They didn't really think either of us could sustain a whole album, in terms of the audience's tolerance for two such unusual singers," Elvis says. "Then it became apparent that I had five times more songs than him, and they needed a full album with me."

In late 1976, Stiff funded Costello's first professional sessions at Pathway, a small eight-track studio in Islington, with the American band Clover recruited as his temporary backing group. Clover already had a small cult following in Britain, with magazines like *Zigzag* singing their praises. Allan Mayes recalls that what most impressed him with *My Aim Is True* was that "my all time favourite band, Clover, had been his backing band. We used to do some Clover songs. That's another weird twist." Costello already possessed their second Fantasy album *Forty Niner*, released in 1971, and Alex Call's song 'Mister Moon' was a firm stage favourite with Flip City. It was later covered by Carlene Carter. Clover had also already worked with Nick Lowe – Carlene's husband for a while – who had demoed material for their album *Available*, while the Brinsleys had also covered some of the band's material in live performance.

Clover were formed out of an archetypal, second division Californian band from the Summer of Love, The Tiny Hearing Aid Company. In 1969, they changed their name, and played the dying San Francisco scene: the Fillmore, Avalon and Haight Ashbury's Straight

Theatre. It was Creedence Clearwater Revival who recommended Clover to Fantasy, and their first two albums are minor classics, though spoilt by the kind of rough recording quality which used to make you keep on getting up to remove imaginary fluff from the needle. There was always something good-timey and unserious about them, with their most famous crowd pleaser the comic 'Chicken Butt': in comparison, another early influence on Costello, Barefoot Jerry, have a steeliness and musical backbone, as well as a lyrical toughness, which Clover could never match. Nevertheless, early publicity photos of Flip City, slightly seedy and unkempt, in denim and leathers, and set in the countryside, seemed modelled on the Clover image.

It was music whose time was just about to pass forever, which was unfortunate for Riviera and Robinson, who had just signed the band to a management contract, and brought them over to England. As lead singer Huey Lewis recalls, "Jake and Dave were partners on Clover and then started Stiff three or four weeks later." Less than a month, the fault line between old wave and new. By the time they arrived, Clover were already an anachronism, playing exactly the kind of music that punk rock set out to destroy: tuneful, laid back, vaguely hippie in spirit, and praising the USA. Just the kind of sacrificial victims which Johnny Rotten would sink his decaying and bored teeth into.

When Elvis Costello appeared as if from nowhere, Riviera detected his country roots, and decided on the spot that "Clover are American – we'll have them back you up." As he told Radio One's Nicky Campbell, "Clover were signed to Phonogram, and couldn't get arrested, and they had the time, they didn't have anything to do, so they were living at Headley Grange. I sent him down and they learned all his songs, and we cut the *My Aim Is True* album in four three-hour sessions. Two days in the studio, it cost a thousand pounds." A slight under-exaggeration. The more down to earth Costello reckons double those figures, twenty-four hours' studio time and a cost of £2,000. A startling bargain, all the same, especially as one presumes that the band were paid basic union rates.

There were some adventures along the way, as Elvis relates. "As I still had my 'day-job', these sessions had to take place on 'sick days' and holidays during late 1976 and early 1977," he says. "The musicians could not be credited at the time due to contractual reasons. They were at a loose end, they'd arrived in London at just about the worst time they could have possibly done, because the thing that was starting to happen was punk, which was absolutely nothing whatsoever to do with being able to play your instruments, it was down to attitude and style and the directness of the whole thing. American hippies, which is what they looked like, just didn't fit in, and the fact that they could play and cared whether they played rather than what they wanted to put over, left them in the wrong time. So I got suddenly to rehearse with these guys who were not legendary, but had a mystique about them, because people that I knew had talked about them."

He joined them at Headley Grange, so they could learn his material. It was not as romantic a setting as it might first have sounded. "I used to sleep in the rehearsal room with all the gear, because if you put the lights off the rats came out," he recalls. "One night, Dave Robinson stumbled in a little the worse for wear from the pub, and put the light off and I woke up to this roomful of rats, which was one of the worst things about making the record." Pity The Stranglers weren't in residence. Elvis then returned to Pathway, with Nick Lowe again at the controls. He took up the story, for Radio One. "Punk rock was just starting, and I'd got this dodgy reputation as a producer, and the people I was working with were very young," he says. "I was only in my twenties, twenty-six or twenty-seven, but to the people I was working with I was a real old guy, people who were in their teens or very early twenties. I was this experienced old cove, but I didn't really know anything about anything, except that Elvis gave off something, you could tell that here was somebody different. He didn't buy all my dodgy old jokes, with which I used to cover up that I didn't really know what he was doing. As young as he was then to be so clear and in control showed a maturity beyond his years.

"I was cutting The Damned records about this time, which were great records, but in a different kind of way, reckless and full of abandon. But here was a guy who was the same age as those guys but he was very mature, not a worn out kind of thing, unsettling and very soulful, soulful beyond his years."

Costello was shrewd enough to appreciate that the energy of punk rock would help him make an impact, and ensured that he was part of the new musical zeitgeist.

"What it came down to was ignoring swing, which was something I had to relearn when I wanted to go into a different kind of music," he says. "The difference being, like Chuck Berry music the drummer is playing a swing feel, and he's playing that 'dinka dunka' which really shifts along , but if you play it all in eighth notes, down strokes, dunk dunk dunk dunk, you get a really rigid pulse which sounds kind of Nazi. A lot of punk has that slightly fascistic sound to it, really gets in your face. That's really what we did, but the songs had a bit more tune. A lot of the things off the album have that grafted onto what would otherwise be much nicer songs, underneath them they're nastied up by this attitude thing. We weren't really emulating anything it was all happening too quickly."

At Pathway, Mickey Shine played drums and John Ciambotti bass, with John McFee on lead guitar, supplying sleazy slide licks on 'Waiting for the End of the World'. Keyboards were provided by Sean Hopper, with Stan Shaw of The Hitmen on 'Less Than Zero'. It was not that different a sound from Flip City, just a bit smoother and livelier, and with a lead singer transformed almost out of recognition, in terms of the energy and spitefulness he now imbued into his delivery. The one odd track out was 'Mystery Dance', a pared down sound with Elvis on piano and Nick Lowe on bass and "drumstick", presumably, a relic from their first session together. Lowe added backing vocals, though Clover's own singer, Huey Lewis, was notable by his absence. "I took a vacation," he explains. "I could have sung a bit or played a bit of harmonica, but we'd been on the road since 1970." He later fronted The News, and had a US Number One hit single in his own right. McFee was to make a name for himself as a hot session guitarist, and returned to guest on *Almost Blue*.

Some of Costello's more technically adventurous songs, like 'Hoover Factory', 'Dr Luther's Assistant' and 'Ghost Train', were recorded at this time, but omitted from the first album, and appeared almost surreptitiously on stray EPs and singles. Despite their surface brilliance, they would have confused Elvis's new public image of a straight talking psychopath. He confirmed to *Record Collector*, "Yes, I did have these slightly baroque songs. I performed 'Hoover Factory' when I first appeared in London, before my record came out. I did a guest appearance with The Rumour, at the Nashville Rooms." Costello used to travel past the Hoover factory every day on the bus to work: with a wife and son to support, he still needed his weekly wage from Elizabeth Arden, as Stiff were not yet in a position to promise him a living wage.

Elvis realised that it was the most direct and aggressive songs which seemed to hit home. "The rhythm of the times was like that," he says. "I seemed to get across to people with those ones, both when I played in clubs and when I was sending the demos in. A lot of those other songs didn't get recorded until later, when we needed B-sides. By then I had an audience, so I could record other kinds of songs, without running the risk I would have done earlier of showing that I knew more than three chords." Although it was among the first songs to be recorded, had Elvis released the country-styled 'Stranger In The House' at the time, it "would have put me back on the other side of the style wars that were going on. At that stage of my career, I could have been killed by that sort of thing."

Punk had rewritten musical history to a narrow spectrum of The Stooges, The MC5, The Velvet Underground, New York new wave, and dub reggae. Later, the accepted canon would allow experimental music by the likes of Can or Ornette Coleman. Even if the likes of The Ramones and The New York Dolls came to their full, seedy magnificence at New York's downtown club CBGBs – which opened in 1971 under its full name "Country, Bluegrass, Blues and Other Musics for Uplifting Gourmandizers" – country music, and bands like Clover did not fit the brave new world of 1977.

Sniffing glue and being sick had replaced rural weekends, tower blocks were suddenly more romantic than a bluebell wood, and anger and amphetamine seemed infinitely preferable to drifting away on a dope-fuelled reverie. The new audience didn't sit back like junior league Bob Harrises and wait to be cosmically enlightened. They were there at the front of the stage, pogoing and spitting right in the musicians' faces. I remember my own first live sighting of The Ramones, and the blood and broken bottles on the floor, the snorting of various brain-damaging chemicals in the gents. Punk was city-based, and the dungareed lead singer of Flip City had transformed himself into a streetwise town crier, in a collar and skinny tie. The denims he wears on the cover of *My Aim Is True* are resolutely unflared.

The days of early punk were heady ones indeed, with a huge sense of playfulness and joyous anarchy. All kinds of icons were being smashed, and there was the brief, ecstatic sense of freedom which characterises the start of any revolution. "Punk rock" had originally been a term of abuse, a description of brutish, mid Sixties American garage bands like The Standells or The Chocolate Watch Band, which suggested music made by – and for – cretins and hooligans. The likes of The Ramones gloried in recreating such apparent idiocy, playing up the dumbness. Punk, second time round, was a meeting place for the dispossessed and the marginalised.

While punk was starting up in London, I remember staying with my friend, the painter Julian Bell in a squat opposite Covent Garden Tube, and watching kids on their way to the Roxy, myself taking in gigs at the Hope and Anchor and the 100 Club, and revelling in just that sense of anarchy, where people could dress, and act, and look, just how they wanted to. There was none of the fashion fascism that came later: you could wear a safety pin *and* long hair. Early fanzines like Mark Perry's *Sniffing Glue* were deliberately rough and ready, photocopied and stapled, badly spelt bollocks, but with a huge love of music and the new bands coursing through them, like body heat.

Stiff's genius lay in marketing this new sense of fun and hierarchies tumbling, reinventing itself day by day. The renaming of Costello was a master stroke, both cheeky and a sacrilege, making an American icon suburban Irish. Photographs of the new "Elvis" as a nine-stone weakling with glasses and pigeon toes only compounded the outrage. Costello's image was one among many oddballs – Ian Dury on crutches, Larry Wallis as a superannuated hippie, Nick Lowe as the Jesus of Cool – which tied in with the rough democracy of the new order. Anyone could make it, suddenly. The Ramones sang "gabba gabba hey", the chant of the circus freaks in Tod Browning's weird movie, as a gesture of solidarity. Stiff too was like a benevolent freakshow: all of its artists were as far removed as possible from the rock 'n' roll ideal. Only a twisted teenager would pin photos of any of them up on his bedroom wall.

Stiff inhabited its own universe of pranksterism and self-parody, which for a short while made it the coolest record label in the world, and which in turn has dated its product severely to that brief time, when the Sixties were finally dead – after almost a decade of aftermath – and the Eighties had yet to begin. The marketing of Elvis's early work was partly fuelled by the singer's own ideas. As he told *Record Collector*, "I actually made up some of the Stiff slogans. I used to go there on the train after work which made me feel as if I was involved in the music business full-time. I hadn't actually turned professional yet and I was making *My Aim Is True* in stages, using sick days and holidays off work. I had to keep working because I had a wife and child to support."

On Friday, 25 March, 1977, Costello made his public debut on Stiff Buy 11 with 'Less Than Zero' – a crunchy anthem to nothingness. It was fuelled by Elvis watching blackshirt leader Oswald Mosley appear on TV, unrepentant and calling for the imposition of order on striking public sector workers. A political programme to be followed a few years later by Mrs Thatcher, whose rise Elvis predicts here: "There's a vacancy waiting in the English voodoo." Even before her ascension into power, Costello was waiting for a showdown, and the psychic battle between the two could almost define the next decade.

Appropriately, the B-side is the startling 'Radio Sweetheart', its jaunty, supercharged tune undercut by lyrics about love in a fascist state. One which would come as close as anytime this century in the mid Eighties, when Margaret and her supporters seemed to be running (and ruining) everything. Costello is already there in his imagination, "goose step dancing" in the disco, part of a world where "you and I have been sold". The packaging was less intimidating, recorded in "reasonable stereo", while covert messages scratched in the inner vinyl read "Elvis is King" and "Elvis is King on this side too", insolent references to Presley, currently rotting in Vegas. The whole thing was like a bomb ticking, with Elvis a dangerous conspirator, as serious as your life.

Charles Shaar Murray – an old hippie, who once contributed to *Schoolkid's Oz* – wrote in the super-cool *NME* that "it's a great record. Doesn't have a snowball's chance in hell. What a bleedin' shame." He compared Elvis's music with Graham Parker, Bruce Springsteen, Phil Lynott and even Billy Swann's remake of the original Elvis's 'Don't Be Cruel'. Murray mistitled the forty-five 'Half Past Zero'. The annoyingly (mis) named Jonh Ingham in *Sounds* was more spiteful: "It's spot the rip-off time as a cross between Graham Parker and Brinsley Schwarz (the group) takes a wander through the pop history book in search of suitable riffs...why bother when there's B Schwarz albums that do it far better." With records like this, "Stiff is going forward into the past." The single indeed failed to chart. As Elvis commented, "Not that it changed my life when 'Less Than Zero' came out. In fact, the first three singles did nothing."

On 30 March, Stiff issued its second album – following *Damned Damned Damned* – the compilation *A Bunch Of Stiffs*, subtitled "undertakers to the industry: if they're dead – we'll sign 'em". Elvis appears with a different mix of 'Less Than Zero', alongside (Martin) Stone's Masonry, stoned Roundhouse veteran Magic Michael, and an uncredited 'Back To Schooldays' by Graham Parker and The Rumour. Dave Edmunds guests both as himself and as "Jill Read".

In late April, *Sounds* carried the first interview with this "mystery man", as Chas de Whalley's piece was subbed. The "brash" young star was photographed leaving a phone booth, as if through a spy camera, and declared "no pictures. I want to keep my own face. I don't want people to know what I look like." Why put a full length photo on your first picture bag, then? De Whalley finds a "slippery customer", a man "proud and protective of his privacy", in his mid twenties, "about five feet ten, clean featured, poor-sighted and unfashionably dressed". He is not fooled, and lists Costello's previous incarnations, though the singer wants the slate of the past wiped clean. He also attacks those who have slagged off his first single: "They ought to see a mortician." Costello denies that he is a Graham Parker: "I'm just as influenced by Charlie Parker or Hank Williams." As to the new single, "Use your imagination. Work it out for yourself."

People were starting to wonder quite why this new enigma never gave concerts. Indeed, he was to make his solo debut – under his new name – on Friday, 27 May at London's Nashville – he would be playing the real thing a few years later – playing solo electric guitar, as support act to The Rumour, *sans* Parker. That same night, American new wave hit the Birmingham Odeon, with Television and Blondie (I was there!).

With The Rumour promoting their "solo" album *Max*, Mick St Michael reported that "standing alone, with his antiquated sunburst

Fender Jazzmaster, he left the place in breathless pandemonium". Costello was wearing a polka dot shirt – cue Dylan 1966 – and Allan Jones recalls, "There was a cursory introduction then he ran out, plugged in and launched into his set without a word. In the context of The Clash and Pistols, it was remarkable to see one bloke achieve the same sort of impact. He rattled on, barely waited for applause, did virtually the whole of the first album, then he was gone and we were all stunned. Who was that man?" The previous Friday, Stiff Buy 14 had been released, Elvis's second single, 'Alison' backed with 'Welcome To The Working Week'. Two of its competitors in the marketplace, issued on the same day, were The Clash's 'Remote Control' and 'God Save The Queen', by The Sex Pistols. Exciting times.

On the picture bag, Elvis crouched in a corner, in dark shades, like a wild cat about to spring at the viewer and tear out his or her throat. The rear sleeve announced Stiff's policy of "pre-planned deletions", and indeed the single again failed to chart. A stiff by any other name, and a startling A-side, despite its lack of immediate success: the chorus alone acted as a taster for Elvis's forthcoming album, and the song reinforced an already exploding reputation. In *The Heart Of Rock & Soul*, Dave Marsh finds Costello's performance "uncommonly redemptive, because it lets you feel the intensity with which Costello fights his own jealousy". The singer himself told Nicky Campbell that the song drew on Philly soul, as had some of the pub-rock bands. "It was my Detroit Spinners' song," he says, "the whole chorus line is taken from 'Ghetto Child', that kind of staccato thing. Emotionally, it was something else entirely. I can't go into that."

Sung with a softness and grace completely contrary to the punk bark, 'Alison' was pure emotion, moving from respect, to jealousy, to regret, to anger, to tenderness, all in three and a half minutes. The record fades on Costello whispering the chorus over and over, as if to himself. As Nick Lowe later said, "The day we cut 'Alison' was the day when I thought this is something really happening. A fantastic recording, a major artist, and I remember it it was a pretty awe-inspiring moment, actually. I don't mind admitting, I wept, but I like weeping sometimes, it cheers me up! When we did that I thought, 'This really is something. I believe this.'"

'Welcome To The Working Week', one minute and twenty-two

seconds, with a punk beat and hand claps. The lyric is more complex than it first sounds, and seems as much about the rock lifestyle as the daily grind of most mortals, then. The title was certainly ironic, as Elvis was about to leave the conventional nine-to-five forever. The song seems to be more deeply centred on a lack of self-belief, pushing away a would-be friend "when I feel like a juggler running out of hands". This time round, the two sides were labelled as "Would-Have-Been-Stereo" and "Forty-Year-Old-Stereo". One of the run out grooves had scratched on it the odd message "Elvis Joins The FBI", a reference to Presley's willingness to act as a drugs informer to the US Government, while himself chucking down his throat a whole chemist's shop of (legal) pharmaceuticals. Except that this wasn't really common knowledge until long after his death.

Punk rock was already hardening into a series of cliches: a vaseline-haired singer shouting in cockney, drums like clattering dustbin lids and square on the beat, three-note bass, guitar like a switchblade. Costello steered clear both of the image, and the reality. As he told Nicky Campbell, "I started to take a more conscious decision about where I was in relation to what everything else was. There's no point in trying to pass myself off as part of this rebellion scene, which I always deeply suspected was scripted by Malcolm McLaren. Things were informing other groups very quickly, the smarter ones were able to come up with their own version of it, like The Clash. The dumber ones just copied it and looked ridiculous. I thought the best thing to do was to stay where I was, in the suburbs, and take an outside look at everything."

Battle lines were now being drawn. Every revolution ends with public executions and Robespierre emerging from behind the barricades, and the unlikely style fascists were the *NME*'s two young turks, Tony Parsons and Julie Burchill, the latter particularly fitted to sit knitting in front of the guillotine. One now writes for the *Daily Mirror*, the other continues to prattle ill-informed dogma for Saturday's *Guardian*, for vast sums. Long live the Revolution! These were only two among many careerists waiting in the wings, alongside the pure idealism of the likes of *Sniffing Glue*'s Mark Perry, still broke, ever hopeful. Elvis was right to be suspicious. Parsons and Burchill published their *The Boy Looked At Johnny*, a joint "obituary of rock and roll" in 1978, but it encapsulated a view programmed from the start. Thus, Stiff was a label "erected on the momentum of the resentment that chases inadequacy".

The deadly duo predict – wrongly – that the careers of Costello, Dury and Lowe are already over. Lowe is a "middle-aged, multi-chinned senile cynic" – how can one be both middle-aged and senile? – "with a split ends basin-cut and sweaty armpits". Costello is pushing a "contrived, calculated image", but wasn't that all part of the fun? They do acknowledge that his first album disguises "whining...by catchy couplets", but complain that he has spent too long slobbering over his "insignificant ego deficiencies".

If that was the accepted punk view, then Elvis needed to escape that ghetto fast. With Clover already signed to Phonogram, and projecting *exactly* the wrong image, Elvis needed his own band to promote his forthcoming album, and one which broke the prevailing mould. The two-month delay while Stiff sorted out a distribution deal with Island gave Jake Riviera time to select a backing band for his new star. He advertised in *Melody Maker* for a "rocking pop combo" which "must be broad-minded, young or old", and hit paydirt.

The Feelgood's guitarist Wilko Johnson was auditioning for a new band, and flew over Pete Thomas from California, along with his former colleague from Chilli Willi, Paul "Bassman" Riley. Within a week Thomas had decamped to Costello, with Wilko having picked up the cost of the airfare. Born in Sheffield in 1954, the tall and gangly Thomas spent his youth in local bands in the Sussex area, first appearing at the age of nine with The Surfriders, and moving on to Grobs. Two years in Chilli Willi led to his immersion in American music for real with John Stewart. As he told Radio One, his first concern was to get his new image right.

"I had clocked enough of what was going on to know that it was basically shiny suits and skinny ties, and when I was a kid I would watch *The Saint* all the time, and it seemed like a golden opportunity to do a Roger Moore, so that's what I went for," Thomas says. "I went straight out to Pasadena where you could get all those fantastic old suits, and got my hair cut so that by the time I came back to England I had all the gear." This rather disconcerted Riviera, who had wanted Pete to keep his long hair and die it blonde – shades of The Police –

while calling himself Pete Bond. Now that a first class drummer was safely on board, Jake advertised for a bass player and an organist/synthesiser player, both of whom could sing.

The Rumour's rhythm section Andrew Bodnar and Steve Goulding filled in during auditions, but were already otherwise committed. Perhaps they should have jumped ship, as their boss was already going up the down escalator, whereas Elvis was set for the top. Bassist Bruce Thomas "rang up the ad in *Melody Maker* to do the audition. I had half an idea who it was for. I heard what I presume was Elvis's voice in the background asking who he likes, and the secretary who was organising the auditions who I subsequently married, so it was quite an auspicious phone call. I said I like Steely Dan and Graham Parker, so this voice said, 'Dump him', so I went out and bought Elvis's two singles and spent a couple of days learning them so I pretended to learn them at the audition very quickly. I more or less muddled through it."

Thomas had the longest musical pedigree of any of The Attractions. Born on 9 August, 1954 in Sheffield, he first jumped onstage to play harmonica with a school band called The Tremors. Still resident in the north east, he later joined The Roadrunners in spring 1967: their lead singer was no less than Paul Rodgers, later of Free. Thomas first recorded with organist Pete Bardens in Village, then played in Bodast with Steve Howe. (Howe went from hip respectability in Tomorrow, alongside 'Teenage Opera' singer Keith West and the manic Twink, to later massive fame in Yes.) Thomas told *Zigzag*, "I went through the whole acid head change thing and it did me in eventually." He was also a fund of stories, with tales of getting his stand-up bass stuck in a bus at Salford, and of his group's van being used "by a bloke who whizzed round the country picking up wellington boots for retreading." A taste for anecdote which would inform his later novel about life on the road.

Thomas went on to record two albums with Cambridge-based country rockers Quiver, not that far removed from being an English Clover, though with more bite. Quiver were a tight little combo on a good night, with twin lead guitars, courtesy of Tim Renwick and the Canadian emigre Cal Batchelor. On the Hipgnosis sleeve of their first album, Bruce's face, complete with John Lennon glasses is superimposed on a leaf; on the second he has shoulder length hair, and a pigeon-toed stance close to that of his later master, though presumably not self-parodic. Quiver recorded Bruce's first song to reach the public domain, the rocky 'Back On The Road', about being glad to be just that, and about the joys of "good time music". It leads into a spirited jam. His songwriting is notable by its absence on the band's second album. Quiver then committed artistic suicide by joining forces with soft-rockers The Sutherland Brothers – authors of 'Sailing' – until Thomas could stand no more, and left in 1973 after the album *Dream Kid*.

Thomas also became a prolific session bassist, "scratching a living in the armpit of popular music", as he memorably put it. He played on albums by Marc Ellington – a mysterious figure who now lives in a castle in Scotland, and retains tight links with the Fairport mafia – Jonathan Kelly, Ian Matthews, Bridget St John and Al Stewart, spanning soft-rock and folk. Prior to joining The Attractions, he gigged with Moonrider, alongside Keith West and ex-Family guitarist John Weider. In 1977, Bruce again attempted songwriting, this time producing a theme song for Queens Park Rangers, his local football team.

Before his premature expulsion from that institution, Steve Nason had studied piano and classical composition at the Royal College of Music. When he phoned Stiff, he was told, "We've got this Elvis Presley impersonator," but turned up anyway! An ingenue in the world of popular music, "The only rock albums I owned were by T Rex and Alice Cooper," he says. "The only concert I ever saw was Alice Cooper. That was great, that was." As for Elvis's debut album, he told Mick St Michael that he "couldn't stand it". He later changed his stage name to Steve Naive, among others, and finally settled on Steve Nieve, in homage to the punk idea of inventing your own surname: Rotten, Strummer, Scabies, that kind of thing. Unlike the other two Attractions, by now cynical musos, to his new boss's delight, "one week he discovers Booker T And The MGs, the next week he'll say, 'Have you ever heard this album?' and it's *Hard Day's Night*. He's that bit younger than the rest of the old cronies in the band."

The lack of a proper guitarist placed more emphasis on keyboards and bass, with Costello chopping out rhythm and fractured riffs, but rarely a solo. In retrospect, this gave the band its own sound, although the addition of, say, Martin Stone on lead guitar would have been interesting. As Costello insists, "I didn't want a lead guitar player. The Pistols had one, The Clash had one, all the groups had someone who soloed and I didn't want anyone who soloed. I made four records before I had a guitar solo. There were guitar solos on the first record, but I didn't play any of them. The idea was that I would just make a noise on the guitar. We had a thing that nobody else had, we had a really good piano player, and a bass player who could play melody, and a drummer who wanted to be Keith Moon."

It seemed a good balance of "ages and experience and inexperience and naivety and cynicism". The new band were christened The Attractions, a kind of pun on their personal desirability, and their role as tonight's star players, at wherever they happened to be playing. The sound of this stripped-down band was short and snappy, like Clover on speed, justifying Elvis's comment to *Melody Maker* that, "I hate anything with extended solos or bands that are concerned with any kind of musical virtuosity. I get bored. That's why I write short songs. You can't cover up songs like that by dragging in banks of synthesisers and choirs of angels. I've written hundreds of songs. They're not all classics."

In early July, Stiff rush-released Costello's third single, bringing it out in such a hurry that there was no time to print a picture bag. '(The Angels Wanna Wear My) Red Shoes', backed with 'Mystery Dance' again failed to trouble the charts, though the matrix this time around read "Help Us Hype Elvis" and "Larger Than Life And More Fun Than People". Costello later admitted, "I remember it being very demoralising, feeling that my only contact with the world was those singles, and those people who I didn't know or I'd never met had the make or break of it…that was very depressing." The A-side was Elvis's jauntiest offering so far, stuffed with melody, and starting with a near joke: "I used to be disgusted, but now I try to be amused." A harder take on 'Alison', the song flirts with the notion of early death, suicide perhaps. Costello puns on "sentence", both as a spell in prison and as the words of the song, which is itself like a chance collision between the original Elvis's version of 'Blue Suede Shoes' and Richard Thompson's equally morbid 'The Angels Took My Racehorse Away'.

Undeterred by the lack of chart action, Costello gave in his notice at Elizabeth Arden, to devote himself to his new career. "I'd amassed enough material to make up an album, which was when Jake Riviera and Dave Robinson asked me to turn pro," he recalls. "I said, 'Only if I can earn as much money doing this as I do in my job, because I have my responsibilities.' So they promised me they'd pay me the same as my job – which wasn't a fortune, so it wasn't too difficult. I turned professional the week the album came out." Riviera recalls, "Once he'd made the album, I thought it was the dog's breakfast, and I said, 'You've got to promote this. Do you fancy chucking your job in, I think this is really happening,' and he was ready to do that. As soon as he got the chance, he left the vanity factory."

Now a free man, Costello could take his new band down to a cottage in Davidstowe in Cornwall, to knock off any rough edges. As money was in short supply, the band paid no rent, but agreed to play at the cottage owner's wedding the following June.

On 14 July, The Attractions made their public debut, as support act to Wayne County at the Garden, Penzance. Labelmate, and merry prankster, Captain Sensible attempted to invade the stage. A *Record Mirror* journalist along for the ride described the band as "machine-like…every song is rattled out effectively and efficiently".

The following evening, Costello and The (unbilled) Attractions played their first headlining gig at the Woods Leisure Centre in Plymouth. The press advert that the following Tuesday was "New Wave Night" with X Ray Spec (sic) and Punk DJ Handy Razor. Chris Rushton of *Record Mirror* compared Elvis and troops as the kind of group who would have played the Cavern ten years earlier, with "ties, starched collars and stylised haircuts", a roughened up Gerry And The Pacemakers. Elvis himself looked like "a slightly stroppy creep of a school prefect", but held the audience's attention through the power of his lyrics and his voice, "without ever resorting to clever tricks or smooth talking between numbers". For the *Observer*, Mark Kidel reported that Costello, "understandably nervous", stood almost totally immobile at the mic stand. The club itself was a "bizarre meat market…terylened troupes of office boys and girls eyed each other like plastic-wrapped steaks." Meanwhile, back in London…

The *Melody Maker* for 23 July, 1977 announced: "At last – Elvis to tour", an ironic reference to Presley's refusal to materialise in person for his British fans. The new Elvis would be less elusive. Unlike *NME*, the staider *MM* was still in two minds about this new music, carrying Allan Jones' highly favourable review of *My Aim Is True*, while also announcing an essay competition for its readers, on the theme "The new wave has nothing to do with music – discuss". Stiff paid for a two-page advert showing a third of Elvis. "To collect your free dramatic action pic of Elvis, cut this out and stick it on the bedroom wall", so punters had to buy *NME* and *Record Mirror* that week too. Rumours surfaced that Stiff was on the verge of bankruptcy as a result of its publicity campaigns.

Melody Maker had earlier printed Allan Jones' in-depth piece "The Elvis (Costello, that is) interview", which began with its subject surly and aggressive. "'I don't,' he said, adjusting his shades impatiently, 'really think that the *past – my past –* is all that interesting.'" As to his early years in the musical shadows, "Nobody showed any interest in me *then*. If you weren't there you missed it and that's that." He does give the first insight into his incredible hunger to create. "I've written hundreds of songs. I write at least a song a week. That doesn't necessarily mean I keep them all. They're not all classics." As to his one-time role model, "Bruce Springsteen's always romanticising the fucking street. I'm bored with people who romanticise the fucking street. I live near Hounslow. It's a very *boring* area. It's a terrible place. Awful. Nowhere. Nothing happens."

Costello believes in his own talent, despite the rejections. "No, it didn't make me bitter," he says. "I was *already* bitter. It was always the same response. 'We can't hear the words.' 'It isn't commercial enough.' 'There aren't any singles.' You just have to look at them to tell they're fucking idiots. I couldn't give a shit about the music business." His own project is to rescue rock music from "fucking synthesisers and crowds of angels". Music has to "get to people, in the heart, in the head. I don't care where, as long as it fucking gets them." His mission is to revive the power of good songwriting: "Songs are just so fucking effective. People seem to have forgotten that." You can live your life by them, though Elvis himself writes only "about the things *I* feel, I'm not an arbitrator of public taste. I don't have a following of people who are waiting for my next word." That said, is there anyone he would like to see becoming famous. "Yeah, *me*."

My Aim Is True was finally released on 22 July. The first pressing contained a "Help Us Hype Elvis" flyer, as asking purchasers to send in a twenty-five word description of why they liked the "English" Elvis. The first 1,000 replies would have a copy of the album sent free to a friend of their choice, though it is easy to imagine some loved ones taking this gift the wrong way, as a coded goodbye. The idea had originated with Warner Brothers' desperate attempt to break Van Dyke Parks, Brian Wilson's collaborator on *Smile*, and the composer of dense song cycles. At least Elvis, unlike Van Dyke, could carry a tune.

The album was produced by Lowe for Keepitasahobby Productions, and came in a choice of four colours, all of them hideous. Here was the very opposite of star appeal, despite the endless motto "Elvis is King" printed on the chequer-board surround. A parody of Brigid Riley's swinging Sixties op-art paintings, the black and white columns of letters seem to sway and shimmer as you look. Keith Morris was already a veteran of the late Sixties underground – with some particularly striking photos of Mighty Baby in *International Times* – but had carved out a new reputation as a chronicler of the new wave.

On the front cover, Elvis hunches in monochrome, pipecleaner legs and pigeon-toed, with a worrying smirk, hedgehog hair and heavy rimmed glasses. He throws a long shadow. On the back cover, he is a grey cutout on a ground of pure colour, looking slightly crippled with an over-large head, and an early candidate for "care in the community". A fashion-free zone, apart from the Fender he holds so cack-handedly, as if "figure one" from a guitar tutor manual. David Gouldstone compares him to "a demented version of Brains from *Thunderbirds*, to Woody Allen, and to Piggy, the sacrificial victim of William Golding's novel *Lord Of The Flies*. No Sean Connery, then.

As Mick St Michael commented, "This fellow looked like he'd find it hard to aim a paper aeroplane." The hand of Barney Bubbles is omnipresent, if uncredited, from the way both artist and title are almost subliminal, to the deliberately unrestful typography and inks used. The whole package seems to scream of weakness, of a vengeful imposter.

Perhaps this was truer than they intended. Allan Mayes remembers Costello phoning him up, and arranging a meeting that night at his mother's house, to which he brought an advance copy of *My Aim Is True*. "I said, 'Where'd the glasses come from; where'd the bow-legs or knock-kneed-look come from?' I immediately thought, 'This is a package deal.' They've taken what are potentially some very good songs. They've looked at the market at the time, and the Pistols and The Clash are all breaking. We've got a guy here who could either be Stephen Stills and die, or adapt him enough to be heard."

Mayles was reminded of the TV show *A Star Is Born* where a man playing in the street goes through a conveyer belt…"hat goes on, glitter, new guitar and in the end comes out this shining star, all animated. When I saw Dec's picture, that's immediately what I thought of. They'd taken this hefty, long-haired hippie, with *Easy Rider*-type glasses and thought, 'I'm sorry, we need a name, an image and a mystique.' I would have imagined because he and I thought so alike he'd have gone, 'You cannot be serious. I wanna go in a lumberjack shirt, hiking boots and blue jeans.' But he must have gone with it either by choice or because he knew he was onto something. Either way, it worked."

The music inside the packaging is something else entirely. I still remember being startled on first hearing by the sheer tunefulness, the novelty of the bruised romantic portrayed within, and the sheer self-confidence which radiates throughout. New wave for old farts. As the opening track, 'Welcome To The Working Week' takes on an extra resonance: after all it is Elvis whose picture is now in the paper – and on the cover – being "rhythmically admired".

Of the new songs, 'Miracle Man' and 'No Dancing' sound lively and upbeat, until the words seep through, about men subservient to tough and domineering women. It is almost like a manifesto for the "men's movement", spearheaded around this time by American poet Robert Bly, an attempt to claw back the political initiative from feminism. Costello lacks that perspective, though, or any need to play drums in the woods, or get back in contact with his lost father. This is a more specific series of hurts. As David Brown punned, "It's sheer El before zero stuff."

Dancing is a metaphor for sex, and the male of the species – this one anyway – isn't getting any. The very antidote to the macho braggadocio of soul, with its one-man love machines. Technically, 'No

Dancing' is unsettling for two reasons, its unexpected jolt from the key of D major to D minor, and the way the verses get longer as the song goes on, delaying the chorus. 'Sneaky Feelings' comes over as playful, with a jovial chorus: you can almost hear the musicians smile. The words barely add up, except as an exercise in non-communication for a couple somewhere in between lust and love. As Dave Gouldstone points out, Elvis's world is a "hostile and dangerous place".

The closest comparison I can make is *Fighting Terms*, the debut poetry collection by Thom Gunn, who subsequently came out as a gay man and wrote the most piercing of all elegies to those stricken by Aids. His too is a world prey to "armed forces" – Gunn was part of the Fifties generation who had to undergo military conscription – in which love is an arrangement, brief, bloody and cynical. "You know I know you know I know you know I know."

Gunn's generation were later characterised as "angry young men", with a rage against the stuffiness of post-war austerity culture, which often boiled down to a simple dislike of women. One thinks of Jimmy Porter, in John Osborne's play *Look Back In Anger*, first performed in 1956, or of Colin Wilson, author of *The Outsider* – a primer of existential thought – who also wrote seedy murder fantasies. They were men (and, very occasionally, women) alone, walking a tightrope over the abyss of a meaningless universe: as Beckett pointed out in *Waiting For Godot*, we give birth above an open grave. The whole movement was wonderfully sent up by the likes of Tony Hancock in his film *The Rebel* – about pretentious artists – and one of his finest half hours, *The Poetry Society*, but it did flow from genuine frustration and rage, England's loss of empire and failure to find a new role. The early Costello has the same mix of seriousness and aggression, of tightly wound feelings which can strike back in the listener's face, like a whip.

Thom Gunn has spent most of his time since living in California, writing poetry with more of an American "accent", and coming to celebrate how the individual can fulfil himself through others. Costello has made much the same journey, if not geographically then emotionally, away from the cold anger of 'Mystery Dance', memorably described by Mick St Michael as underlining "the sad plight of an overgrown adolescent who's thumbed through every dirty magazine in the shop".

The tone is bitter, and if in Lou Reed's *New York* Romeo and Juliet represent a way out of the city, a brief act of love, here they are merely two more victims, trapped like insects in a jar. Costello will return to Juliet, as a kind of wayside saint, much later in his career. Meanwhile, clattering drums and a breathless rush of words and beats – like a souped up E Presley, with a staccato guitar break to match – mimic hurried and bad sex. The same theme of fumbling innocence informs Richard Thompson's song 'Read About Love', but it lacks the querulous rage of Costello's vocals. The song ends unexpectedly, missing its climax, so to speak.

Straight into the jangling piano of 'Pay It Back', a deeply cynical song, like the dark side of the classical romantic ballad: "I love you more than anything in the world/I don't expect that will last." The promised payback is both financial and vengeful, though Clover tinkle hereabouts where The Attractions will storm. 'I'm Not Angry', and that's a lie from the start, is like 'Alison' written for voyeurs. Peeping Elvis waits downstairs and listens to the "stutter of ignition", surely one of the nastiest ever metaphors for the start of lovemaking. Someone else's of course.

The opening song in this claustrophobic album talked of crazed workers who would "bury me alive", and in its last, 'Waiting For The End Of The World', Costello is stuck between stations on the London underground, in the dark. He sounds like Mick Jagger at his most threatening, relishing each syllable, with John McFee copying Ry Cooder at his nastiest on slide guitar, queasy and distraught. The song is half Dylanesque ramble, with stock figures like "the legendary hitchhiker" – while sharing the weird dream-like logic of 'The Last Trip to Tulsa', Neil Young's exercise in Zimmerman-inspired whimsy – half a Bunuel fantasy, with a whole wedding party suddenly boarding the train.

The sadistic touches, about pulling the hands off the TV personality, and what comes close to rape in the darkened carriage, are part of a territory which Costello had laid claim to, simply by releasing this album. There is the same sense of Apocalypse approaching as in Dylan's own 'All Along The Watchtower', and Elvis's performance is close to glee. The sagas of love and work gone wrong which comprise *My Aim Is True* lead up to this view of a decaying world, watching people drown but refusing to throw them a lifeline. "You" here could either be the singer, or God, or the listener. Certainly the stoned hippie of the middle verse will be no help at all.

Anyone could question – and many critics have – what right Costello has to impose his cynical and potentially destructive world view onto us. Nick Kent is supposedly the "man from the television" on the final song, and he gives a valid answer. The album "hits you on so many levels that even if you happened to be repelled by the more extreme aspects (and I've met many who find Costello's revenge/guilt fetish persona totally unappealing) you couldn't help but be impressed by some other area of the man's astonishing talent...a needle-sharp sensibility for strong musical backdrops."

There is something exhilarating about the man's sheer intelligence, much as one felt of David Bowie around *Hunky Dory*, otherwise about as far removed from Costello's self-presentation as humanly possible. On the evidence of *My Aim Is True*, it is Elvis who is the truer bug-eyed alien, viewing humankind as if from another planet.

There were many great debut albums released in the mid to late Seventies, and many were never bettered by their creators: *Horses*, *Marquee Moon*, *The Ramones*, *Never Mind the Bollocks*. *My Aim Is true* was, in retrospect, merely the sound of Costello clearing his throat, but it caused immediate impact.

Chas de Whalley of *Sounds* jumped the gun in early June, when the album was first projected for release, but says he has not yet got to grips with the songs: "Like a flower, Elvis's debut album is opening up into something of metallic beauty." The *NME*'s Roy Carr found "sexual psychoanalysis set to a dozen superb juke joint anthems...a Seventies interpretation of Sixties rhythm and roll." Costello's songs "spill over with emotional torture and melodrama". A man whose heart has been well and truly broken, and should he ever give up songwriting, he "can always answer readers' letters for *Forum*". In *Melody Maker*, Allan Jones found that "hell, you can dance to it, swoon and romance with it, smooch and romance to it". Jones also identified in its accounts of "suburban perversions", a "mordant, Ortonesque humour", referring to Joe Orton, in whose plays unspeakable desires are acted out in limpid prose. Truer, perhaps, of Morrissey.

Costello lacks exactly that kind of cultivated coolness: his wordplay is part of a passionate engagement with raw emotion, the chronicle of his own heartbreak. As David Gouldstone notes in his book *A Man Out Of Time*, which analyses his work song by song, "Costello's very direct vocal delivery means that it is impossible to listen to the album with disinterest – he continually grabs us by the shirtfront and harangues us, and we are sucked into the vortex."

Elvis's own particular trick is to ally this kind of emotional upfrontness to songs, where some of the connecting links seem to have been omitted. In previous books for Sanctuary on Joni Mitchell and Van Morrison, I have tried to show that their best work is highly personal, impressionistic, truly poetic, but capable of analysis. Costello's work is far less linear, and as Gouldstone's book itself shows by its ultimate failure, is not fully explicable. One can only – to quote Dylan – shovel glimpses into the pit of which each one means.

One description of *My Aim Is True* is that it was like a collection of songwriter's demos, rather like the first solo album by Elton John. Exciting as both still sound, they present a young songwriter's work in embryo, and if Bernie Taupin's lyrics always struggled for sense, Costello's words have since grown ever craftier and more allusive.

The painter and art critic Julian Bell caught exactly this point in a letter. Elvis's work "relies very heavily on being *between* emotions, between sensations, ideas, informations. I am feeling this, but I am also feeling that. I love you and I'm indifferent to you. All this between-ness makes it an art of nuance and complexity rather than classic simple statement. His sensibility is terribly thickly informed (musically, poetically) and each line, each bridge, each musical embellishment can seem almost to snarl up and choke on this overdetermination. As a result one remembers much of his stuff in terms of these little particles, rather than smooth-running whole songs."

The history of the street singer – subject of one of Malcolm Morley's finest songs – is a long and honourable one. The likes of Homer and West Indian calypso singers unite over the millennia, wandering bards with their feet on the street, and their repertoire firmly in their heads. London had long provided a marketplace, human nature being what it is, for pedlars selling contemporary ballads about gruesome murders or the saucy histories of highwaymen taking the one-way trip to Tyburn tree. The gutter press of their day, literally sold in the gutter. The hippie daze gave new legitimacy to the Street Singer. One, David Lannon, was even recorded, under that very title, with the front cover showing him at work. Here was a censorship-free zone, where John Lennon's cult favourite David Peel could sing songs of dope and liberation, Wild Man Fischer could invent his mad little sagas in a cracked scream, and Ted Hawkins on Venice Beach conquered inner demons to resume his career.

Punk planned to overturn the rock biz, subverting it from the inside, though as in Orwell's *Animal Farm*, the new masters soon began to look very much like the old. It took Stiff records to turn the streets into a career opportunity, and one that succeeded beyond even their twisted dreams. It was an everyday Tuesday in late July, and mighty Columbia Records was holding a convention for its staff, world-wide. This was the company which had broken Bob Dylan, through the faith of one man, John Hammond Snr, who kept faith with a man nicknamed "Hammonds' folly", and was later to do exactly the same with a New Jersey no-hoper called Bruce Springsteen. Hammond was now retired, his son a semi-successful white blues singer, and his corporate successors were gathering at London's Hilton Hotel. They arrived to witness an event which entered rock legend, as had been consciously intended.

Outside on the pavement, a skinny man in glasses, with a Vox practice amp strung over one shoulder, was playing guitar and singing in a voice that could not be silenced; a most superior form of street entertainer. Back at Stiff headquarters, Jake Riviera had already deeply insulted an American journalist of oriental extraction by christening her Pearl Harbour. He now disbursed roadies Kosmo Vinyl and Alphonse to stand outside the Hilton with placards reading "see Elvis on your doorstep", much to the amazement of those who had never heard of Presley's namesake. They would now.

Costello arrived by cab, dressed in a smart sports jacket, two-tone shoes and check trousers "with a crease you could cut your throat on". He began his alfresco performance with – ironically enough – 'Welcome To The Working Week'. A crowd of "suits" began to gather as he launched into 'Waiting For The End Of The World', at full volume to a gaggle of bemused Japanese tourists, then 'Less Than Zero'. Allan

Jones notes that at this point an "emphatically smarmy" city slicker asks if the singer knows any Neil Diamond songs. Paul Conroy, Stiff's general manager, quips back, "Listen mate, Neil Diamond doesn't do any of Elvis's songs, so Elvis isn't going to do any of his."

Hotel security were nonplussed by this unbilled attraction messing up their sidewalk, and the uniformed concierge almost coming to verbal blows with Jake Riviera, obviously the lead prankster. Jake is well out of control. "If you think *we* look suspicious, what about those fucking people wandering about with masks on?" This while pointing to a group of Arab businessmen, their wives in yashmaks, just entering the hotel. What a charmer! Like Malcolm McLaren's equally bold stroke of having the Pistols sign a record deal outside Buckingham Palace – 'God Save The Queen' being an unwelcome royal anthem – there was sound business sense behind the stunt Riviera has just devised. Stiff records were looking for an international distributor. Who better than Columbia, and who more appealing as bait than Stiff's new star.

Elvis was almost hidden from view by a circle of record company executives, people who would earlier have ejected him from the office, clapping and singing along to 'Mystery Dance'. All it needed for the genuine whiff of teen spirit was a brush with the law. As if on cue a police officer arrived, and Riviera stoked the fire further: "He's not busking, he's just singing in the street. You can't stop people from singing." He was quite wrong in this, as it happens. The constable requested that, having no licence for public entertainment, Elvis should move on. He took one step to the left, and continued singing. The result was immediate arrest, with Costello taken to Vine Street station where he was charged with obstruction; fined £5 the next morning, he had to ask the magistrate for time to pay.

"I fought the law, and the law won." Mind you, Bobby Fuller covered this Crickets' song and was later murdered for his pains, and The Clash, who re-recorded the same tune, were arrested and charged after a particularly despicable stunt, shooting pigeons on a London roof. Meanwhile, back at Stiff, Kosmo goes off to the pub with Lee Brilleaux of Dr Feelgood, and adds animal cruelty "jokes" to Riviera's racism. He describes how on Canvey Island he would murder crabs by ripping off their legs, and sticking needles in their eyes. The level of intellect on display is suggested by the following conversation. "'Ere, Lee, I wish crabs had ears." "Why's that?" "So I could tear 'em off."

Equally unrepentant, Elvis was released in time to deliver a set that evening at Dingwalls, on Camden Lock. Word had spread, and the gig was heaving with CBS personnel, who did indeed sign the band up, the prelude to two years' heavy duty touring across the States. It was the London debut of Elvis with The Attractions. They had warmed up with gigs at Manchester's Rafter's Club – supported by The Lurkers – and at Island Records' Video Room, playing a private gig for the salesmen who were going to get their "product" around the country. Nick Kent sneaked in, and reported that Elvis was only a year older than Johnny Rotten: "He's not too flashy, plays great sparse guitar, and the band is really hot." The organist now calls himself Stephen Young, and plays "in a particularly Doors-like way, both understated and very, very sinister", as were Costello's songs. The new ones were best, with Elvis's "sudden, stuttering, one-note guitar break" in 'Lipstick Vogue' a stand out. Elvis had also just made his first television appearance, solo on Granada, playing 'Alison'.

At Dingwalls, the terrifying Julie Burchill held her thumbs aloft: "This is bedsit-room, singles-bar, phone-in agony from which the venom oozes over into that rarity, luxurious rock 'n' roll. The guilty secret, the useless anticipation, the unrequited ache all unite to dambust through into bitterness, betrayal and disgust." She admires Elvis's sense of nuance, though misquotes 'I'm Not Angry' as "the stutter of admission", even filthier than the real words. Ms Burchill also admires Steven Young on organ, "and *what* an organ". The band play "nirvana dancing music", which leaves her so entranced that she "barely applauded".

At the same gig, Allan Jones notices, "You couldn't squeeze in a greased monkey after ten pm." The sense of anticipation is "choking", and Elvis's self-confidence unassailable. It is "the most startling set since Television pinned me to the deck in Glasgow". And British, too. "This combo is so damned hot, that it could reduce the Post Office Tower to a mess of molten metal in sixty seconds flat."

The sound is "naked and aggressive", while like Kent he describes Costello's guitar sound as "spare", "somewhere between the effect Lennon achieved on 'I Found Out' and Neil Young's classic apocalyptic raunch". The evening ended with Jake Riviera on the receiving end of someone's fist. "The rest of us just got absolutely legless." Daring to hope that lightning would strike twice in a row, Jones saw the band again the following night, at the Hope and Anchor, and, "I'm still shaking." Over the next two months, they zigzagged the country, from the Rock Garden, Middlesbrough to JB's in Dudley, Huddersfield Poly to Falkirk's Mannequin Ballroom, with continental jaunts to the Bilzen Pop Festival in Belgium, Marseilles, and Sweden. Live on Swedish TV, with a pick up rhythm section, Costello refuses to describe his music style: "I just play it, and other people can say what it is."

The real sign of rock acceptability, though, is to pass the test of John Peel's one good ear – a true barometer of musical freshness. Elvis and The Attractions made their radio debut on 1 August, on the great man's Radio One show, just then passing through one of its periodic golden seasons: this old hippie had been the first person to play 'Anarchy In The UK' on the BBC, and I still remember my acute disappointment after all the hype. Was this it, speeded up Hawkwind riffs, and Harold Steptoe's brother on vocals? I also remember the sheer zest, tunefulness and spite of The Attractions' debut, recorded a week earlier, and making a mental note to buy the album. All four songs were taken from *My Aim Is True*, with new enhanced backing, an extravaganza of mad organ, tight drumming, and aggressive bass. To virgin ears, it sounded like The Stranglers – a band now almost written out of rock history – but with better tunes: the misogyny was shared, as were The Doors' riffs, and the general impression of speed, in every sense.

I have just dug out the tape I made at the time, a melange of sessions and new wave singles, with John Peel (as much a pseudonym as that adopted by Declan or Mason) shedding his somnambulant scouse for something a bit livelier. Punk had woken him up, and he proved – as always – a reliable guide to a new, still dangerous musical form. "I'll tell you who they are. There's Peter Thomas on drums, Bruce Thomas on bass and Steve Mason on piano and organ. And the first is a song that is already on its way to becoming a contemporary classic, I think. It's called 'Red Shoes'." Nieve plays a keyboard figure straight out of the 'Moonlight Sonata'. Crunchy drums drive the whole thing along, taken slightly slower than the recorded version, with a definite swing. The call and response between Elvis and the backing chorus – rough and laddish – is repeated over and over.

As Peel comments, "A very spiritual kind of dude, that Elvis Costello." On 'Less Than Zero', which should "have been played a great deal more by my colleagues than it actually was", Elvis's voice is heavy with echo, backed by a mysterioso organ, like Alan Price's wonderful break on 'The House Of The Rising Sun'. Costello will revisit another Animals single, nine years later. The keyboards turn psychedelic, weaving around the singer's "hey-hey"s. The take is relaxed, rather than angry. "Oh, very tasty indeed," comments Peel. 'Blame It On Cain' boasts an aggressive guitar riff from Elvis, and two short and spiky lead breaks, one at the end. The whole thing has a driving beat, like a new wave version of The Band, with Steve Nieve embroidering honky-tonk style, staccato piano, like Dylan at around the time of *Highway 61*.

'Mystery Dance' opens with just Elvis's voice and Pete Thomas's driving tom-toms, then the rest crash in. The organ is again like a time trip to the mid Sixties, leading a spirited charge at the end. The whole thing is supercharged, with the pace of punk, but far more sophisticated bass playing, and a more knowing kind of singer. "Well, I would say that 1977 has got to be the best year ever for British music," comments an awed Peel.

The following Sunday saw the new band play the Nashville Rooms, with four times the venue's capacity milling outside in the street. Even Bonnie Raitt was turned away. Two songs from this first gig later appeared as the flip-side of the 'Watching The Detectives' single. By now, Steve Mason – or Nason or Young – had adopted the stage name of Steve A'dore. Maybe Morrissey should have followed suit.

Good luck rides its own freight train, and it was a godsend for Costello, though no fun for Presley, that Elvis's namesake died of a heart attack on 16 August, 1977, sitting on the loo, and reading *The Scientific Search For The Face Of Jesus*. A sad end for the man who started it all, but his own media resurrection was set to outdistance anything since those early, wild gigs, and the sound of Sun. Whatever Costello's private sadness on Presley's demise, in career terms it was a huge bonus, forcing press attention on him by reflection, just as his first album hit the provinces. Conversely, those rock 'n' roll bibles the

Daily Express and the *Daily Mail* cancelled planned pieces on Costello, out of some kind of twisted respect for his namesake.

By 20 August, *My Aim Is True* had reached Number Fourteen in the UK album charts. The following day, Costello and The Attractions made their third Sunday night appearance at the Nashville Rooms. Despite the ticket restrictions, at least a thousand people, drawn by the buzz, were outside. There is something hypnotically enticing about a rock act just on the cusp of breaking nationwide, a sense of being on to something as an insider, before the common herd follow. A weird energy pervades such gigs, something that can never be recaptured, though some musicians spend a lifetime trying.

Staff at West Kensington tube station were not so enamoured by the crush, and phoned the police. Twelve officers soon arrived, and began to shoo away the desperate majority outside the sold-out gig. Things steadily got uglier, and eight people had their evening further ruined by being arrested for "wilful obstruction". Five were journalists, sent to cover the event. Punk and new wave had stormed the capital, during this "summer of hate", and less crowded gigs that night included 999 at the Sundown, future Elvis collaborators Squeeze at the Other Cinema and Eddie And The Hot Rods at the Marquee.

Tim Lott finally got to talk to Costello, after three failed attempts, and seems not in the best of moods as a result. "Elvis Costello looks like a creep, a weed," he wrote. "The paste-on glasses, the skinny face, the pinstripe suits and executive tie. The sort of face that begs to have sand kicked into it." That's just for starters. "He didn't enjoy Dingwalls the previous night, and here he is dressed in his wedding suit, following his court appearance. He doesn't like interviews, which he distrusts. 'I don't care about a *lot* of things. Making records, writing songs, performing is about all. All I want is to pay the next bill. Wanting a lot of money is a sickness.'"

A far more illuminating interview, the most important of Costello's whole career was conducted a few weeks later by Nick Kent for the *NME*. Along with his music, it has forever fixed Elvis's image in the public imagination. Kent, later to be stomped by Sid Vicious, had himself long lived the rock 'n' roll lifestyle, hanging out with Keith Richards – who, beside Nick, looked positively healthy and plump – and all kinds of interesting bohemian lowlife. A chance sighting in the

Tube led to Costello writing him into 'Waiting For The End Of The World', as mentioned above, as "the man from the television", a fact its subject records with pride.

Kent's article is snappily entitled "DP Costello of Whitton, Middlesex, it is your turn to be The Future of Rock and Roll". Elvis apparently carries with him at all times a little black book, filled with the names of those who have hindered his career. "'The only two things that matter to me, the only motivation for me writing all these songs,' opines Costello with a perverse leer, 'are *revenge* and *guilt*. Those are the only emotions I know about. Love? I dunno what it means, really, and it doesn't exist in my songs.'" He does recall that Kent once visited the Marquee, when Flip City were playing a residency as support, and ignored them for the headliners Dr Feelgood. "I really resented you for that . You were almost down there on my list."

A chance encounter with a record company bimbette, who leaves in anger, provokes Costello to soundlessly produce a huge, bent steel nail, his chosen weapon of self defence. But back to music. His favourite album, a brave choice for 1977, is *GP* by Gram Parsons. He praises Parsons for not sticking around: "He made his best work, and then he died." Ironically in retrospect, Elvis declares, "I'm never ever going to stick around long enough to churn out a load of mediocre crap like all those guys from the Sixties. I'd rather kill myself. I'm not going to be around to witness my artistic decline." He then reveals that he has 400 unrecorded songs. He also hates drugs, though alcohol is different. "Let's say I went through my phase of drinking heavily. Really heavily," he says. At Elizabeth Arden, he was seen as the factory "freak", though he has worn the same hairstyle, clothes, and bifocal glasses for years, or so he claims. Ask Allan Mayes.

He also reveals that BBC2 were approached to make a TV programme about his move from the computer factory to showbiz, but the concept was soon dropped. As to other musicians, Springsteen is a "lousy lyricist", Elvis claims never to have heard Van Morrison's *Astral Weeks*, but does admire Pete Townshend's early work with The Who. "'Substitute' is a perfect song, but he blew it by being too bright for his own good, too analytical," he reckons. He personally scythed the guest list for the Dingwall's concert, of at least half its names, doubtless using his little black book as a reference source. One particular casualty was Island's A&R man Richard Williams – who became the cinema critic of *The Guardian* – because he had failed to recognise the young Declan's talent. Costello comes over as a control freak, even checking the guest list for each gig, so that anyone who does not show up is struck off. He also appears paranoid, though with every justification. The National Front are dogging his steps, after 'Less Than Zero'. He will not allow any other guitar player on stage with him. The weirdness piles up. Riviera and Lowe look on, and both "think he's loopy, but a genius to boot", with which Nick Kent silently concurs.

On 10 September, Elvis and The Attractions played the annual Crystal Palace Garden Party, organised by Harvey Goldsmith. The young pretenders were second headliners to Santana, once vibrant Latin rockers, but now a backing band with a flashy guitarist. The rest of the lineup was an equally cogent argument for the new wave, with mainstream rock music of the time shagged out by the likes of the bands featured here: Crawler (lacking Paul Kossoff, killed by drugs), and the arid jazz rock of Brand X. Even Southside Johnny, best known by association with Bruce Springsteen, had seen better days. Costello was the token new waver, and despite having at first demanded a "ludicrous" amount of money to put the promoters off, they called his bluff by offering enough to cover a recent bill for new equipment.

To add to Costello's unease, the stage was fronted by a lake, beyond which lounged an audience of around 20,000 defiant old-wavers, displaying "the biggest exhibition of natural apathy I can ever recall seeing at a rock concert". After one song, only two people clapped Elvis, both of them in the press enclosure. It was a sunny autumn day, and a stiff breeze carried Elvis's words back to him: the audience could barely hear him. Clad in an ill-fitting and shiny black suit, he stormed off after a short set which culminated with 'Mystery Dance', having rushed to his amp and yanked out the lead in disgust, leaving a storm of feedback in his wake. At least the instruments that caused it were now paid for.

If the fossilised audience hardly noticed his set, one undoubtedly impressed participant was Jon Savage, who later wrote *England's Dreaming*, the definitive history of English punk. "So intense, so bitter. He refused to pander. His gestures accentuate the biting lyrics, fast high-pressure sound: stabbing, pointing fingers, hurriedly declaimed announcements, shoulders hunched like a ball. Dylan anger." As to The Attractions, they mesh perfectly in both sound and vision, "short, undyed hair, drainpipes. And? And The Mysterions' best two-note organ." As Savage implies, punk rock on the original model.

Stiff well understood the collectors' market, and just as audience demand caught up with the label, and it gained distribution through Island, it deleted its first ten singles. A new album, *Stiff's Greatest Stiffs* gathered together one track from each, including Costello's 'Radio Sweetheart'. As *NME* commented, in suitably barrow-boy language, "There's something a bit pony about this deal" with a full price album mainly consisting of B-sides. Neil Spencer did admire the inner sleeve, recommending records on other labels, from Lee Dorsey to *Trout Mask Replica*, and Elvis's contribution, "a fresh intriguing melody and long distance love lyric, with steely flashes of Elvis's Gram Parsons country leanings. Quietly brilliant." Despite such hype, Stiff was in financial trouble, with record sales failing to cover its outlay in publicity, so Riviera – like a reckless military commander – made a preemptive strike by arranging the first Stiff package tour.

He recycled his Naughty Rhythms brainwave, keeping ticket prices low, alternating the headliners, and offering five bands for half an hour each, each night: Costello and The Attractions, Ian Dury And The Blockheads, Nick Lowe with The Last Chicken In The Shop band, featuring Dave Edmunds and Man's drummer Terry Williams. Much the same line up recombined as The Psychedelic Rowdies, backing Larry Wallis, while Wreckless Eric was joined by The Blockheads' Davey Payne on saxophone, Ian Dury on drums and Denise Roudette on bass. The comperes were Kosmo Vinyl and Les Prior, of Alberto Y Lost Trios Paranoias. It was like a series of quick change acts, though rehearsals at Manticore studios established that the two acts with real fire in their creative bellies were Dury and Costello, whose rivalry for the top spot would intensify as the tour unwound.

Never one to take the easy option, Jake programmed in twenty-four dates in a month, with the eighteen musicians transported by coach, immediately commandeered by the "Twenty-Four-Hour Club" of all night ravers, including two of The Attractions. The plan of campaign made the front page of *Melody Maker*, with a photo of the mainmen, in which Elvis looks like a young Robin Day on a trip – eyes like black pinholes – and Wreckless Eric like a ventriloquist's doll, in a tartan jacket. The tour motto for this weird bunch was "Dumping Music On The People".

The Stiffs Greatest Stiffs Live Tour kicked off in High Wycombe, on the same night that avant-garde punks Wire played the Hope and Anchor, and psychedelic veterans The Only Ones the Vortex. Vivien Goldman for *Sounds* greatly preferred the "demented fairground barker" aspect of Dury to Costello's lack of flash: "It's just like the geezer next door had splashed out on some leathers, charisma or no charisma." She also disliked "Elvis's totally self-absorbed way of lecturing the audience like a parrot in NHS specs, holding a warning finger in the air, while cocking his head pensively on one side".

Twenty years on, *Mojo* carried a magnificent chronicle of the whole episode, with participants looking back as if on a war zone. That night Costello, uncomfortable in a shiny black bomber jacket, annoyed the audience by playing none of the songs from the new album – his set would change every night, and tonight he was previewing *This Year's Model*. To make matters worse, legendary publicist BP Fallon threw hundreds of Stiff badges out to the baying crowd, mid set. In the Stiff equivalent of being taken out and shot, Riviera took him backstage to give Fallon the "full corgi", an instant (and one-sided) job appraisal interview, complete with intimidatory hand signals.

As the tour lurched across Britain playing a mixture of universities and civic halls, the music papers printed dispatches from the front line, with various journalists trying to join in with the all-out excess of the Twenty-Four-Hour Club. It was no coincidence that each evening's entertainment concluded with a massed version of Ian Dury's song 'Sex And Drugs And Rock 'N' Roll', like The Gang Show on acid. Casualties occurred, as they do in any war. Dave Edmunds left the tour for a spell, following a drunken prank involving "blood and chocolate", the victim of which ended up in hospital, and inspired a later Costello album title. Wreckless Eric missed Manchester, thanks to laryngitis (though his voice was hardly that of a nightingale, even when fit). Dury and Costello filled in with extra songs, including Elvis's own tribute to the absent eccentric, covering Eric's 'Whole Wide World'.

Bruce Thomas moved to a second drum kit, Davey Payne played sax, and Denise Roudette bass.

Costello had learnt, after High Wycombe, to include more familiar songs, and be less confrontational onstage. Offstage, he kept well out of the action, sitting alone on the tour bus and hiding behind dark glasses, taking solace in the odd bottle. Charles Shaar Murray described "a potato face carved out of granite and surmounted by a pair of massive horn-rims. Costello looks like Clark Kent the day after he decides to stop coming on like a wimp." His reading material that day is *The Essential Lenny Bruce*. Meanwhile, Steve Nieve discovers a bottle of green slime at a coach stop, and spreads it around liberally. Elvis's pleasures are a little less messy, walking fifteen minutes to the nearest Woolworth's, and finding *two* copies of 'Anarchy In The UK' in a bargain bin, 32p each. "Who's the greatest scorers of records that ever lived?" he gloats. I feel jealous, even at this point in time.

At Leicester University, he and his band resembled "the kind of kids at school who hated rock 'n' roll and got to be prefects before anybody else, served as school librarians, and were astonishingly officious if you returned a book late". They were also "the hottest little teen combo that ever got the kids sobbing while they frugged at the end of term dance". Costello joins in Nick Lowe's set, on rhythm guitar.

NME's Tony Parsons attended the Croydon gig, a week before. He resorts to cockney rhyming slang to describe Elvis: "a midget Japanese Kamikaze Pilot who wants to look like Buddy Holly and dresses down to clerk-chic of conservative two-piece tonic mohair whistle 'n' flute, dark peckham-rye and shoes like dead men's noses." As to his music, it is like a "Modern World Torch Jukebox. Elvis never misses, Mister." Parsons predicts that Costello will be making classic love albums long after the new wave, a view he changed radically by the time of *The Boy Looked At Johnny*. He was right first time round.

At Leicester, Dave Robinson badly injured his hand, intercepting a pint glass hurled mid-gig towards Costello. This was particularly ironic, as the singer was "never big on communal drinking over long hours, but I did have a little blue sandwich case with my notebook, a half bottle of gin, and a few lemons for my throat". He also spent the long hours in the coach composing new songs, including 'Sunday's Best', for Ian Dury. Costello's own response to his surroundings was 'Pump

It Up', about pointless excess. Written on a hotel fire escape, it was a response to the "get off your face and be an asshole" side of the tour, though Elvis himself admitted, "It's impossible to look into the mind of someone who was out of their mind on vodka and amphetamines."

Two performances by Elvis later appeared on *Stiff's Live Stiffs*. These were 'Miracle Man', recorded at Leicester University, and an agonised cover of Bacharach and David's 'I Just Don't Know What To Do With Myself' from the UEA gig, dedicated to Dusty Springfield, for whom he later wrote 'Just A Memory'. The Bacharach connection was also destined to last. Other songs covered by Costello onstage were The Everly Brothers' 'Price Of Love', The Merseybeats' 'Really Mystified', and the rather different 'Love Comes In Spurts', while its author Richard Hell watched from the wings.

Dury won the right to headline the biggest gig of the tour at London's Lyceum, though a jaundiced Pete Silverton found the rest of the proceedings "little more than a narrow celebration of mutual hipness, the warmth forced and the fun doubtful". Costello resembled a puppet pulling his own strings, and his attempts to converse with the audience seemed either embarrassing or laughable. Silverton did note how Elvis had worked on his onstage stance, learning from Joe Strummer how to kneel down with his guitar.

Despite losing around £11,000, the tour helped bring the Stiff front line to a wider audience. Nick Abson filmed the tour, as yet seen only by chosen participants, and unlikely to ever see public release. Elvis yawns as Farrah Fawcett-Minor, the "tour nurse", had her breasts forcibly revealed for the camera. More edifying is the onstage footage, with Costello crouching among the amps, like a psycho, as he sings 'Watching The Detectives'. On the 'Sex And Drugs And Rock 'N' Roll' finale at the Lyceum, Elvis is motionless and deadpan. "I was usually somewhere else when the finale was going on, but I had my arm twisted at the Lyceum," he told *Mojo*. "I was extremely drunk. It was a bunch of mad people on the road. There was a lot of staying up late and a lot of badness. We were young, we were free. Just like Cliff! But it was hardly Summer Holiday."

My own memories of the Birmingham gig were of the strange contrast between the ornate Town Hall, and the motley crew who combined and recombined onstage in different combinations. An evening full of the unexpected, with an emphasis on songs, rather than pointless jams, Ian Dury emerged as a great showman, with The Blockheads full of colour and good humour, but the monochrome, grim-faced Elvis stole the show with a set literally frightening in its intensity. He seemed superhuman – if hardly friendly – that night, with his band a blur of manic energy. The whole thing reminded me of the package tours of the mid Sixties, when acts as disparate as The Walker Brothers, Jimi Hendrix and Engelbert Humperdinck would share the same stage and equipment, and it reignited that same breathless anticipation of what was going to happen next. In retrospect, it also shared an affinity with Dylan's Rolling Thunder Revue of the year before, a travelling show celebrating a kind of post-hippie togetherness, but in which the real dramas seemed to be going on offstage.

On Radio One, Pete Thomas explained that the whole thing was like a sudden release of pent-up energy. "Everyone had been playing in these funny little groups, or in their bedroom, or out in the woods," is his view. "That was what you did when you got famous – take loads of drugs and cavort about, carrying on alarmingly." Costello adds, "On the package tour, everything went on backstage or back at the hotel. What was odd about it was that all of these people were on *Top Of The Pops*. In the next six months, we all became some sort of pop star, not rock 'n' roll animal-looking people but we all looked kind of innocuous." Not *quite* the way I would myself describe Larry Wallis, or Wreckless Eric, or Dury, or even Elvis himself, but there you go. "It was all going on behind the scenes," he continues. "I don't want to glamorise it. On one hand it was kind of fascinating, and on the other slightly repellent." Pete Thomas remembers that The Attractions were, from the very start, "a pretty rocking unit. We were never going to take any prisoners, the whole thing was to blow everybody out, we're great, you're not. And he's got such a strong thing going. And he's so determined."

But at the hour of their greatest triumph, Stiff Records was splitting in two. Nine days before the tour started, Paul Conroy returned from a football match to find broken bottles littering the pavement outside, and the office carpeted with shards of glass. Perhaps this was the inspiration of Nick Lowe's hit single 'I Love The Sound Of Breaking

Glass'. Riviera had finally, himself, cracked. The record label he had helped mastermind was "doing Jake's head in", added to the pressure of co-managing Graham Parker, Nick Lowe, Clover and The Damned.

Lowe further confused matters, by joining Rockpile along with Dave Edmunds, Billy Bremner and Terry Williams. The band signed to Led Zeppelin's Swansong label, and Riviera was almost immediately elbowed aside by the intimidating figure of Peter Grant, who as a manager did for real what Jake always pretended to: frighten people. Grant sent the band on a disastrous US tour, made worse by their demeaning position, opening for Bad Company. Elvis wrote 'Hand In Hand' about the empty vanity of Zeppelin and their ilk on the road, ripe for excess and humiliation. "The main figure is the sort of inhuman monster type I could become if I let myself go *that* far," he revealed. Compared to such Viking-style raids on America, the Stiff Tour was innocence personified. The only people to get hurt were participating musicians, and their tour manager, not hapless groupies penetrated by fish heads. Led Zeppelin represented a darker brand of wickedness, doubtless fuelled by the wilder thoughts of Aleister Crowley. Stiff was more like the Bash Street Kids.

Back at Stiff HQ, the two bosses walked round the block, and agreed that Robinson should continue alone, while Riviera took Costello and Lowe with him to a new, as yet unnamed label.

Riviera was gradually freeing himself from all that, concentrating on his main assets as any management consultant would advise. The new label was soon revealed as Radar, with offices in Parker Street in London's West End. The logo was based on a radar wave, a form of tracking aircraft developed during the Second World War. The name was part of a new wave taste for industrial imagery – Factory was to come along later, though Cleveland bands like Pere Ubu were already adding industrial noise to heavy rock. David Lynch's film *Eraserhead*, released the following year, was also set in a heavily industrial world, with weird mutants living some kind of life in its crevices. The new label was to be run by two former stalwarts of the British wing of United Artists, managing director Martin Davis and A&R man Andrew Lauder. At UA, they had signed many of the best British communal bands: Man, Help Yourself, and Brinsley Schwarz, as well as Riviera's old friends Dr Feelgood. They also licensed for British release many of the country rock stars who had so impressed Flip City. By joining Radar, Elvis was in some ways coming home.

Having escaped the world of corporate rock, Lauder saw Radar emulating Stiff and Chiswick, run by "fans who not only wanted to do it with the right attitude", while adding some vital business know-how: "We have even more experience and expertise." In truth, Radar was not to last long in the marketplace, but its releases remain a benchmark for excellence, and are increasingly collectable, not least its re-release programme by the obscure likes of The Thirteenth Floor Elevators, a tradition which F-Beat and Edsel records carry on to this day, run by much the same people. Radar had the distribution muscle of corporate giants WEA behind them, worldwide except in the US, Canada and parts of Scandinavia, where the deal with Columbia continued.

Elvis was now set to become an international star, with a tour schedule to boot. The chance of British fans to see him on a regular basis was about to end, barely after it had begun. Meanwhile, Pete Frame, the Edward Gibbon of rock history, had as usual slipped in a deliberate error into his latest "family tree", largely to see who would first steal it. The ludicrous error this time around centred on the nerdish guitarist "Wally", unceremoniously dropped from The Sex Pistols for being too boring, when they were still known as The "Swankers" (ignore the initial "s"). In a characteristic flash of wit, Frame – later to serve briefly as Stiff's press officer – named this reject as a young Elvis Costello, a calumny repeated open-mouthed by *Time Out*, as if rock gospel.

Elvis Costello had written 'Watching The Detectives' in May, during auditions for his new band: producer Nick Lowe captured the raw thunder of a band live in the studio. Clover were toytown, in comparison. The pick-up rhythm section were bassist Andrew Bodnar and drummer Steve Goulding from The Rumour, which is why the results are credited only to "Elvis Costello", though Steve Nieve later overdubbed keyboards. Had contractual commitments not intervened, this could have been an alternative Attractions; in a parallel universe, they probably are. Costello later credited the inspiration behind the sound, vicious as a flick-knife, to The Clash's cover of Lee Perry's 'Police And Thieves' on their first album. Mick St

Michael describes perfectly the frightening sound as, in the white heat of inspiration, "Elvis scattered shards of splintering, reverbed guitar across the bleakest of aural landscapes."

The UK single was issued on 14 October, as BUY 20, a contractual farewell to Stiff. It shot into the Top Twenty, the first Stiff single to do so, peaking at Number Fifteen just before Christmas. On the picture bag, Elvis leans toward the viewer, his hands foreshortened and held together, as if with invisible handcuffs. He has the aggressive air of a man on a police photograph. The single was also issued in a now rare "telephone directory" bag, listing all the "Stiffs" in the London telephone directory, over and over. The B-side, this time credited to "Elvis Costello And The Attractions", contains two songs live from the Nashville, supercharged versions of 'Blame It On Cain' and 'Mystery Dance'.

The disc became *NME*'s single of the week, and a strong contender for single of the year. Of the decade, one could now add. If Elvis had recorded nothing else, he would be remembered just for this, an endlessly fascinating slice of white reggae. The words wind back on themselves like one of Escher's drawings – defying perspective – or another rock surrealist, Kevin Ayers, in sinister epics like 'Lady Rachel'.

Roy Carr describes how "drums rattle like a stack of half-filled oil drums being kicked over in an underground car park, and all four musicians are transmogrified into a sinister dub maelstrom. Against the throb of the bass the organ pipes and guitar deviates from a chucka-chucka and James Bondian twang", while the drummer delivers the same "hefty clout" as Bowie achieved on 'Sound And Vision'. As to the production, "Instruments and voices zoom in and out of focus and reappear without warning as, with menace in his heart, Costello narrates a bizarre narrative."

Nothing is clear, in a song structured like an avant-garde movie, as it itself acknowledges: "long shot", "close-up". Whole academic theses in media studies could be written on this song, about how the signifier and signified dance around each other, and fail to quite cohere. She becomes him becomes you becomes I.

There is something dreamlike about the whole thing, and yet it also contains scenes of extreme torture – "she pulls the eyes out with a face like a magnet". In this aural film noir, a boy watches his (ideal) girlfriend as she watches a cop show on the TV, then a murder occurs, and the couple are in the midst of the action. "Someone's scratching on the window." Scary stuff. The song contains a beating, a search for the body, and tearful relatives viewing the corpse. As in Talking Heads' 'Psycho Killer', the song's narrator is gradually revealed as a killer. Costello's voice enters new worlds on this song, relishing and polishing each word. He repeats "shoot" like gunfire, sounds scratchy and exuberant and threatening and resigned, then replays the chorus endlessly, as if to himself, as the music fades away.

CHAPTER THREE

trampling across america

M*y Aim Is True* had become the biggest selling import album in US history, and reached Thirty-Two in the US charts when released in a revised form by Columbia. Ever perverse, Riviera talked of importing back copies of Elvis's records into Britain, until the Radar deal was finalised. The Damned, The Jam and The Clash – despite their professed boredom with the USA – had already set off for America, to take punk to a bigger marketplace. Now Costello and The Attractions began their first US tour, opening in mid-November with three gigs in two days at the Old Waldorf in San Francisco.

In *Beyond Belief*, Patrick Hannigan remembered queueing outside the nightclub for tickets, and grabbing a front row seat. Disliking his relaxed slouch, with legs resting on the small stage, Costello addressed him at the end of the gig with an unjovial "fuck you". Support acts are meant to mirror the main act, and here were American new wavers Leila And The Snakes, featuring Pearly Gates, later of Pearl Harbour And The Explosions. A name as confrontational to patriotic Americans as The Dead Kennedys! The highlight of the act was Gates licking the centre out of a chocolate bar. When Costello appeared, there was no dancing. Not only had pogoing or slam dancing yet to evolve in the States, but tables and chairs were packed so close together that the 300 strong audience found it difficult to move, or even breathe. Costello and band "ripped through a GREAT set of tunes, really smoking," according to Hannigan. The set lasted barely forty-five minutes, with no encore. The press were told that Elvis was booked for a recording session at SF's Beserkeley Records, the American counterpart to Stiff. After two nights at LA's Whiskey, a place of rock legend with "girls in bin liners, who thought we'd be really impressed", the band circled the States, gigging at small scale venues.

Jeds in New Orleans, the Capri Theatre Atlanta, Bunky's in Madison, and New Haven's Oxford Ale House were all blessed with visits from the hottest act in the West. I'm sure that every reader of this book has been there at least once, standing in a small club watching a band about to go nuclear. Sylvie Simmons captured the feeling for *Sounds*, reporting on the Hollywood gig. She was at first disappointed that "the man who stepped quietly behind the mic, shoulders hunched with the weight of a big black guitar, looked quite harmless, more like a bank teller than a psychopath, like Popeye before he had his spinach". Even his haircut looked like "a barber's nasty accident".

Once he started, though, the joke was on his detractors, with surprisingly strong vocals, and a good backbeat from The Attractions. 'Alison' was introduced as a song about someone he used to care about, and Costello grasped the microphone with passion, "the whole emotional outburst aided by some very pretty organ sounds (a cross between Stevie Winwood and Southend Pier)". 'You Belong To Me' was louder and brasher, with sweat running down Elvis's face. Costello wagged a finger at the audience, in warning. "That, and the contemptuous dropping of the lower lip being the only sight betrayals of punkish tendencies." Eleven songs, no encore, and a long queue for the second set, which Jake Riviera promised would be an entirely different choice of songs.

The best tour recordings came from the Riviera Theatre, Chicago – captured on *Armed And Dangerous* – and the Agora, Cleveland, where Elvis shared the bill with Eddie Money. The second album of *50,000 Elvis Fans Can't Be Wrong* captures the latter gig. Another three tracks from that record are taken from the Four Ackers Club, Utica.

Bootlegs are notoriously lax with their information, and although the bulk of the first album is credited as "Radar demos", it is in fact a mixture of radio and TV broadcasts, and two official UK B-sides. There are solo performances from Capital Radio – including a particularly spiteful 'Radio, Radio' and a fascinating acoustic take on 'Hoover

Factory' – and a brief snippet of 'Alison', from Granada TV. *Top Of The Pops* provides a slower, reggaematic 'Watching The Detectives', with The Attractions still feeling their way, and Elvis sounding as if he needs a throat pastille. Maybe it's just the quality of the original tape. The way he drops his voice on the final 'Detectives' is masterly, and Nieve injects a queasy, supper club quality into his final organ flourish.

'Lip Service' and another, equally laid-back 'Detectives', are taken from the TV show *So It Goes*, broadcast in early August, and feature the band coalescing as you listen, with Costello already learning how to break his voice on cue, as if with emotion. The rinky-tink keyboards of Steve Nieve are decorative, but as yet a little lacking in confidence.

Nieve is more upfront on the Four Ackers tapes, where the drums lead, bass provides the melody, organ fills in the gaps, and Elvis strums rhythm guitar. Ian Dury's 'Roadette Song' – mistitled as 'I Wrote This Song' – is quite different to The Kilburns' version now, with cockleshell organ, just like 'God Only Knows' or a precursor of Orchestral Manoeuvres In The Dark (kind of *bouncy*), and Elvis sounding at the edge of his tether. 'Living In Paradise' drives along, and Costello outdoes his namesake by *singing* with a pout, and sounding almost bored. He plays a rare, atonal guitar break to end 'Little Triggers', sung close to the mike for extra intimacy. The Attractions have already learnt the art of the slow burn, musical or Chinese. Elvis is like the school bully, with his three cohorts carrying out his orders, with due intent. The performance is understated, soft as snow falling, yet menacing as a knife held against your throat.

The Agora set, taken from a radio broadcast, is more rough hewn, with the instruments less differentiated, a blur of voltage. The whole thing sounds as if it was played at high volume, with ragged backing vocals to Elvis's sore-throated croon, and an excited audience shouting the musicians on. In 'Welcome To The Working Week', Costello's voice sounds an octave lower than usual, and the band rush between songs. It is as if they are taking a leaf out of The Ramones' textbook, speeding up their set like a road race, running against the clock.

Nieve is now dominant instrumentally, with the same rhythmic thrust as Dave Greenfield of The Stranglers – and the same Sixties psyche roots – though he doesn't so much solo as repeat the riff, with variations. It's like the young Them, with a surly lead singer, thin and swinging keyboards and a thuggish rhythm section. Unlike Van, Costello greets the audience with some kind of welcome: "It's a really bad night, we really appreciate you being here."

There are two kinds of touring bands, those who attempt an assault on the unknown every night, and those who have in their mind a perfect set, and attempt each time to reach it. The first can be exhilarating, and in the case of mid-period Can, or the four-piece King Crimson, each night is an event, a raid on the collective unconscious. At the other extreme, such a high wire act can easily fall to earth, and either disintegrate musically or – even worse – descend into dullness. Costello and The Attractions are of the latter type, so that tapes from different performances on the same tour differ only in terms of how the venue and audience and band's mood have affected them. Fascinating all the same, but lacking the element of danger which, had Nieve been an improvising genius like Dave Sinclair or Mike Ratledge, he could have injected into each gig.

Armed And Dangerous, a vinyl bootleg with a vertigo swirl on its centre, is taken from the Chicago gig, and has a cleaner sound with Elvis's voice upfront. The funniest thing is the backing vocal(s), seemingly from only one of The Attractions, which sounds as if a member of the audience has climbed onstage to undertake a musical dialogue. The version of 'Waiting For The End Of The World' is a huge improvement on the Clover-backed original, with Nieve holding long notes behind Elvis's determined vocal. He is relatively chatty between songs – "This next song is called 'The Beat': we've just been out, looking at the beat." Nieve pours organ notes over Costello's voice, like maple syrup over a savoury pancake. The sweet and the sour, a combination which always makes life interesting.

The album cover is a black and white shot of Elvis – lit from below – holding both his hands in the air, like a juggler running out of hands, or as if accepting arrest. My own copy is signed by all four musicians – unusual for a bootleg – and no, you don't know where I live. The same set also appears as record one of the *Exit* double, with a woman boxer on the front (perhaps ready to give Elvis a good pounding), and a bondage shot on the back.

The month-long tour culminated on the east coast, with four shows at the Bottom Line – supported by The Tuff Darts – and two at Asbury

Park's Stone Pony, with The Shots. A press advert announced that people had followed the tour around the country, and some had flown in from Boston and Los Angeles for the final show. The Bottom Line was packed with rock industry types, about which Costello changed the words of one song to "watching the defectives". He played a ten-song, fifty-minute set the first night. One local review noted how how "he often laminates a workman-like rock 'n' roll sheen over lyrics that are intellectually sophisticated, even bordering on the surreal", and how eagerly awaited the show was in hip New York circles.

As Stanley Mieses reported for *Melody Maker*, "He means business. He never smiles. It is this severity of demeanour that provides a cutting edge for his romantic vision." Costello's set was largely that of material already available on record. 'Less Than Zero' was a highlight, "performed with knife-point sharpness". The seated audience at the Bottom Line proved a barrier to the production of great rock music, as a seated venue always does. You have to be able to move and dance, even if only with yourself. Ask Elvis's dad. Columbia Records slotted in an extra New York gig at the Ukrainian National Home, a ballroom with lots of room in front of the bandstand for people "to stand, dance, jump or what-have-you" and the electricity of all those bodies must have had some some effect. Costello played a rocking set, "chock full of double-time boogie numbers. He opened with 'Radio, Radio' and proceeded to burn his way through an hour's worth of short, punchy, dynamic numbers." Most of the material was new, drawn from his forthcoming album.

It was announced that Costello had a new album about to be released, the first to feature The Attractions, and provisionally titled *The King Of Belgium*, supposedly after Elvis's physical resemblance to King Albert.

He was about to risk his crown, though. On 17 December the band deputised for The Sex Pistols – then trashing Holland – on NBC TV's *Saturday Night Live*. In fraternal greetings, Pete Thomas sported a "Thanks Malc" T-shirt, and the resulting fracas owed much to the Pistols' notorious swear-in with Bill Grundy. There is nothing like live TV for stoking up instant public controversy. Costello opened with the new single, 'Watching The Detectives', as programmed. He came back and began 'Less Than Zero', again as scheduled, only to break off midway, just as Jimi Hendrix had once done on *The Lulu Show*. "I'm sorry ladies and gentlemen…there's no reason for me to do this song here." Oswald Mosley was not exactly a well known figure in the States.

Elvis launched instead into a new song, 'Radio, Radio', dealing with the kind of compromises that American culture imposed on creative artists. Just what the doctor didn't order, and the producer tried to bring the performance to a rapid end, which only served to heighten Costello's anger. It burnt up to a final crescendo, after which he gave a brief, ironic bow to the invisible audience, jerked his guitar lead out of the amp, and stormed offstage, just like at the Crystal Palace Garden Party.

It was as dramatic a spectacle as his frequent declarations about retiring from showbiz, and almost as regularly repeated. Doubtless Elvis did both in full sincerity, but there was a whiff of Violet Bott in the *Just William* books, threatening to "scream and scream until she was sick". There was an immediate embargo on unleashing Elvis on live TV, not broken until 1981.

The American tour had staggered Elvis with the country's resistance to change. As he told Nicky Campbell, "We were having a really hard job. The reviews we got were really funny, we 'sounded like we formed on the plane'." One particular favourite was that the band suffered from "cymbal crashing ineptitude". 'Radio, Radio' was (re)written on the road. "Everywhere you went, you heard the same records," he says. "Driving down the freeways of America, and turning the dial, there were different parts of the same track on different stations. That's how blanket the acceptance was of The Eagles, Linda Ronstadt, Fleetwood Mac, Journey, Boston, Foreigner, and between that you had 'Stairway To Heaven', which by this point had been out for five years, was played every day on some stations, and it's about two and a half hours long!" It was proving intensely difficult for Elvis and The Attractions to get their own, somewhat fresher music on the radio, "so inevitably we took against it".The English pop media were more sinister, with everyone knowing their place. With 'Radio, Radio', "we stated the bloody obvious, as far as I could see".

Costello and The Attractions returned home to play a three-night residency – concluding on Christmas Eve – back at the Nashville Rooms. Tickets were priced at a modest £1.75, and limited to four per punter: it was announced that recordings from the Nashville would emerge as a double album, for American release only. No sign as yet, a mere twenty years on, so we'll just have to wait for a Costello box set, sometime in the new millennia. *MM*'s Allan Jones reported that the band's equipment had been mislaid somewhere over the Atlantic, so The Attractions played on gear that Jake reckoned was "more suitable for a skiffle group", and the sound balance was hardly perfect. Even so, the self-confidence of the unit conquered all. "The gig was remarkable for the songs they didn't play: he omitted a whole sackful of songs that most songwriters would sacrifice their lives for, and still managed to include more great tunes than you'd find on your local jukebox." 'Mystery Dance' was "brief to the point of impertinence", while 'The Beat' proved that the Thomases were maturing into "the best white rhythm section this side of nobody". Jones concludes, "If it ain't Elvis, it ain't rock 'n' roll."

Punk was already being marketed as a new career opportunity, while the less threatening term New Wave was a catch-all title under which all kinds of older musicians could reinvent themselves. Thus did members of Stackridge become The Corgis, Alan Hull's Lindisfarne reinvent themselves as Radiator, and even Peter Noone of Herman's Hermits become lead singer of power poppers The Tremblers. Whereas Noone once spotted the potential of the young Bowie, and covered 'Oh You Pretty Things', he was now quick to pounce on Costello's 'Green Shirt', shearing off the menace of the original like a true pro. Linda Ronstadt was also to use Elvis's songs as a mark of her new wave sensibilities.

Elvis remained about it all, a man whose blazing talent would have come to the fore, whatever the musical atmosphere. That said, the sheer rapidity of his rise to fame – after years in the shadows – was undoubtedly helped by the cracks in the smooth edifice of rock which those brief months had ruptured.

He later told *Record Collector* about how he positioned himself in those strange times. "Some people thought that singing with a proletarian delivery, and a certain kind of regional accent, whether that was London or Manchester or Bristol, was some sort of badge of authenticity," he reckoned. One thinks of Johnny Moped, like a tone deaf version of the younger Steptoe, or Eddie "Tenpole" Tudor, or of Sid Vicious's self parody, 'My Way'. "That's bollocks. It's what in your heart that matters. I don't hear any geography in good singing." He had not really cared whether or not his music was labelled punk. "It just gave my career a degree of propulsion. In retrospect, it's been seen as calculated and there are always these style wars that go on all the time but they only exist in the music business, not the real world."

Interestingly, when Bern Scott wrote to *Melody Maker* in November 1977, predicting that punk rockers will "in their naivety and weakness, sell out their ideals", it was accompanied by a cartoon of Elvis as a representative figure, squint-eyed, and spiky-haired. Most of those who created punk rock were, like Costello not from the fabled inner-city tower blocks, or the Westway, but deeply suburban.

Much the same had applied to English R&B, largely from the Home Counties, or psychedelia, with its three leading bands from Cambridge, Canterbury, and Seattle. It was money and success that brought the likes of Hendrix or Paul McCartney or Van Morrison, to live in central London. Early punk saw the "Bromley contingent" follow the early Sex Pistols, bare breasted Siouxsie Sioux *et al*, and having escaped to the big cities, they themselves had become style fascists. Suddenly every young punkette looked like Siouxsie, every punk like Sid Vicious. "When you went down to Plymouth and there were just three kids with safety pins stuck in their lapels rather than wearing bin liners, they were having a hard job living up to what they had been taught to think was groovy," Elvis says. "I hated that kind of tyranny. It's so insignificant, it goes by in the bat of the eyelid."

Elvis himself had missed out on the original wave of punk bands, having neither the money nor opportunity to go to the Roxy, in Covent Garden. As he told Greil Marcus, you needed a taxi to get there from the suburbs – the bands played long after the Tubes had closed for the night. "I don't know who went to the bloody gigs – I can only guess they were rich people with cars and loads of drugs." He was up at seven, and off to work, to support his wife and son.

Costello came to know about punk, like the rest of the general public, from reviews in the pop weeklies, the occasional TV appearance and from records and Peel sessions. It was an incestuous scene, with bands and journalists feeding off one another. As Julian Bell, then freelancing for the *Record Mirror* put it later, in *Three Odes*.

Back in the close warren, in Covent Garden's canyons,

the evening sparks and roars.
From dormer town and highrise
Young punks converge into the Roxy's jaws.
Your gang of hacks and music business minions
swagger and opine
brains primed for wipe-out in the sweaty White Lion.

A poem which ends with the coming of Thatcher, in 1979, and a wasted expedition to check out a gig that turns out to be cancelled.

Costello did respond, though, to that first rush of excitement. "I suddenly started thinking, 'Hang on – this is something a little bit different.'" He had indoctrinated himself with the first album by The Clash, listening to it through headphones for thirty-six hours non-stop, then writing 'Watching The Detectives'. The Clash's angry rant, shorn of melody or musical subtlety, "was quite influential in its spirit rather than its music, because I didn't think any of them could play to save their lives".

As to the Pistols, he liked the way their records were produced, without believing that the band itself had a lot to do with the end product. The social scene masterminded by Malcolm McLaren was "completely fake". Fifteen years on, Costello could still listen with pleasure to The Buzzcocks – a "pop group who played fast" – but much of the music of that time had dated badly. "A lot of the other groups were pretty awful," he says. It was the attitude of those fractured times, rather than the soundtrack, which proved appealing to the young MacManus. He told Greil Marcus at the time that he admired the Anti-Nowhere League because "they're just *animals*, they drive around in a van that says 'WE'RE THE ANTI-NOWHERE LEAGUE AND YOU'RE NOT!' I mean, that's great."

Barry Lazell's near definitive *Punk: An A-Z* puts things succinctly, with the benefit of hindsight. Elvis was "never part of the core punk movement", though inextricably linked with it. He appeared on the scene at the same time, and his part in what was perceived as the new wave "served as a catalyst and role model" for those escaping punk for wider frontiers. The first album was touched by the anger of punk, its short sharp songs, and his own short sharp image. "He proved early on that you could be halfway to mainstream appeal, and still have attitude.

Psychologically, that was extremely important to punk as a whole."

In retrospect, punk provided the spur – or more likely camouflage – for the last great wave of British songwriters. With the single back in vogue, and the musical floodgates open, all kinds of weirdness and pop invention was allowed. You could become exactly what you wanted, English Mods or Syd Barrett, or white Jamaicans. With Costello at their head, a whole generation of songwriters who would previously have been judged too unusual for the rock pantheon suddenly broke through. The results are still enriching British rock, with Shane MacGowan, Paul Weller, Sting, Chrissie Hynde, Jackie Leven and Robyn Hitchcock now established as among our finest creative sparks.

If one adds the likes of Andy Partridge, Green from Scritti Politti, Kirsty MacColl, John Lydon, Hugh Cornwell, Pete Shelley, Joe Strummer, Martin Newell, Pete Perrett and Captain Sensible, all of whom came out of the punk dungeons of 1977 (some, like Elvis, conveniently forgetting earlier musical exploits), a whole generation of quirky singer-songwriters emerged, as if from nowhere. It was the renaissance, and last flowering, of great British guitar pop, though as far removed from it in image terms as could be imagined.

The CBGB's scene was just the same, with The Ramones and Blondie providing two radically different parodies of early pop, and Talking Heads giving Sixties soul a twisted neck. No wonder the likes of Pete Townshend, Dick Taylor and Ray Davies embraced the new wave when many of their contemporaries were decrying it as the work of Satan. Even The Sex Pistols were pussy cats compared to The Pretty Things, put on a plane in New Zealand and banned from that country for life, The Kinks – who virtually saw an onstage, inter-band murder – or The Who. Musicians, if not journalists, realised this from the start, with the Pistols' wonderful version of 'I'm Not Your Stepping Stone' by The Monkees, The Jam recycling The Who on Immediate, and The Pretenders reliving Ray Davies, before he even *thought of* concept LPs.

The sledgehammer of identikit punk soon put an end to all that, standardising snotty rebellion, and cutting out inventiveness. As far as Elvis was concerned, the phrase "new wave" became simply a slogan with which the likes of Polygram used "to sell a bunch of crap American records like The Runaways, and stick 'em all on a compilation with a Boomtown Rats track and something by The Dead Boys. It wasn't fast enough to sound like punk. And the name stuck."

The only slogans he himself employed were deliberately ironic, like his own phrase "surfing on the new wave". It was typically arrogant. If there was such a thing as a new wave, then, "I'm right on top of it." And he was.

The new year saw Elvis and The Attractions escape from intensive work in the studio, to unwind with a free gig at the Roundhouse – home to all kind of Sixties madness – on 20 January, 1978. Elvis came hotfoot from a TV interview on *Today*, where he was quizzed about the break up of The Sex Pistols. The two support acts spanned the new musical landscape, Whirlwind's retro-rock 'n' roll, and a fresh take on psychedelia from The Soft Boys, through lead singer Robyn Hitchcock's twisted acid visions. As to Elvis, Jon Savage found that playing America had given him "access to a lot more authority and intensity". Onstage, with a tight band behind him, he commanded the stage: "His movements are angular, full of jerky, awkward grace as he hunches over, leans his arms over his guitar, cajoling, threatening." He had learnt to excite the crowd by out-staring them, "as he delays singing the verses they want, standing motionless." He challenges a "rabid" 300 or so punks at the front – who keep their distance – and works himself into a frenzy during 'Watching The Detectives', "pacing the stage like a caged tiger, doubling over, exploding with tension". Costello has the knack of turning pop cliches on their head, "veering towards quality rather than throwaway".

The Attractions added a new, harder edge to Costello's sound, with high register Vox organ echoing around the old railway shed, so that a song like 'Waiting For The End Of The World' is now just that, a blast from the apocalypse. It starts, as Mick St Michael describes, with Costello playing a guitar riff, straight out of The Sex Pistols: "Nieve forsook his customary stabbing organ style for some swirling Ray Manzarek-style fills, piling on the pressure and inspiring Elvis to harangue the unsuspecting spectators as if the very spirit of Jim Morrison was wracking his puny body. 'I been waiting…for so long. For *sooooo* long.' He gasped as if his – and everybody's else's – life depended on it. The consequences were nothing less than frightening."

'Less Than Zero' was also transformed. The Oswald referred to was now Lee Harvey, and the setting no longer English fascism but the shooting of JFK in Dallas. The whole thing is watched on TV by a woman who looks up from "giving head". It is implied that her husband, riding on the President's limousine, is somehow implicated, which gives new meaning to the line "I hear that South America is coming into style", and would explain why "she's got rubies on her fingers". The past is again put away, as Oswald lies shot in a basement and the police ask half-heartedly for home movies of the event: "They've got a thousand variations, every witness in a file." The song now has the same kind of hall of mirrors quality of 'Watching The Detectives', with an incident of sexual violence somewhere in the middle: "Her lover throws her on the bed to teach her she's alive." The whole thing is translated into American, for a Stateside audience. It is an exercise either in cynicism or transformation, depending on how much you believed Costello's passion on the original.

Costello refused a second encore when, "having faced a torrent of gobbing throughout the set, he found a specimen of said mucous in the glass he was drinking out of to quench his thirst on stage and stormed off in disgust". Within the week, he and his band were playing a CBS convention in New Orleans, alongside Talking Heads. David Byrne had his own wired vision of the world, acting out the extraordinary tension of 'Psycho Killer', so the combination must have hit the audience like twin punches to the head. Furthermore, both bands were fuelled by the same kind of jerky violence, with relentless rhythm sections that did not so much swing, as rock like a piston.

Elvis confined his public statements to brief comments, barked between songs. During six weeks in America, travelling in a customised, luxury Greyhound bus, he granted only two short press interviews. His songs could speak for themselves. The tour, with various support acts as before, wound around the States. One support act was Billy Connolly, then in the transition from folk musician to comedy superstar: that must have been *some* night. The main attraction played bigger venues this time around, big city theatres and universities.

The best tour document is contained in the *Crawling Through The USA* bootleg CD, a radio broadcast from the CW Post College, Greenvale. The sound is richer and less rough 'n' ready than on the first US tour. Nieve's keyboards are fuller in tone and more swirling, in the Garth Hudson mould. Bass and drums mesh into solid bedrock of sound. The Attractions now fit Costello like a good pair of shoes: a band in their own right, no longer a lead singer with backing musicians. In 'Radio, Radio', for example, every note is spot on to the microsecond, and the band croon "listen, listen" almost subliminally. Elvis talks, even, though cockney has replaced scouse, for the time being. "Can you 'ear us all right? You'll have to bear with us, 'cause we just got here, and we didn't have a chance to check the sound, so we'll have to hope it gets better as we go along. We should explain that we got hit by a car on the way here, and that was why we was held up, and the door fell off our bus. So we're just about as cold as everybody outside."

'Less Than Zero' has stabbing organ, like a burst of gunfire, and 'Waiting For The End Of The World' a rocking riff from Bruce Thomas. '(I Don't Want To Go To) Chelsea' breaks off in the middle for a weird, dub-like passage, bass and drums. Then the organ climbs, as if to heaven. 'Pump It Up' boasts a shout of "oi" from the rest of the band, and is insistent as a toothache. Nieve plays counterpoint on 'You Belong To Me' on what sounds like a celeste, with high bass notes and thunderous percussion from the rhythm section. "Not very lively are you. Is anybody out there?" barks Costello.

'Last Of The Lipstick Vogue', as it is introduced here, would wake the dead. There is a storming middle section, where The Attractions take off like Sonic Youth, with weird electronics – the audience can be heard to gasp – then piercing organ notes seem to split the listener's skull. Elvis sings softly over Nieve's doomy chords, the calm in the eye of the hurricane, until the rest of the band crash in, shouting hoarse background vocals, like a bunch of ruffians. Straight into a crunchy 'Watching The Detectives', without a pause for breath, spiky guitar and churchy organ – as gothic as Procol Harum at their spookiest – then Elvis casts it away to sing direct and untrammelled, slowing things right down. As Charles Shaar Murray once wrote, "Things always get weird and dangerous when Costello performs without his guitar."

A final 'I'm Not Angry', sung more like in sadness – and Elvis can now see people "standing...up...no I see you much better". The song almost marches, and Costello plays a guitar solo, one note undulating, against rich organ chords, then picks at his strings like a madman, so that the whole crests to a Doors-like crescendo, with Elvis coming on like Jim Morrison, singing in a deep voice, as if to himself. Nieve imitates a police siren, and drums thunder to a conclusion. Cut to a curt "goodnight", and riotous applause.

For *NME*, Murray flew in with Nick Lowe and guitarist Martin Belmont to link up with Costello in frozen, upstate Buffalo. Outside, it is forty degrees below zero: inside the band are crammed onto a tiny stage, with a ceiling so low Belmont – who dwarfs Elvis – looks as if he would hit his head if he stood up straight. He joins The Attractions on their final song, 'Pump It Up', using a miked-up thirty-watt practice amp. He prowls the stage, "rearing and jerking like Herman Munster under electro-shock, mouth working furiously, slashing and wrenching at his brand new Gibson L-6 as if he was ready to rip the neck off the sucker". Lowe now appears, cradling a borrowed Telecaster, and plugs into Elvis's amp to play a short medley of four songs, with Elvis now relegated to backing musician. He occasionally wanders up to the mic to sing "spot-on vocal harmonies", while playing "rock solid second lead guitar between Belmont's compulsive solos and Lowe's scratchy, spiky rhythm".

Back in Britain, *Live Stiffs* emerged in mid February, seemingly already part of ancient history. *NME*'s Neil Spencer found a "zany British rock update on the great Stax/Volt and Motown Revues in the Sixties". Elvis steals the album with his poignant reading of a virtually *a cappella* 'I Just Don't Really Know What To Do With Myself'. "The screaming, intense version of 'Miracle Man' will have Costello freaks panting for more…an almost arrogant affirmation that the man is one of the most compelling live performers we have, as well as one of the very best songwriters,"

Meanwhile, Radar records announced its first batch of singles: Nick Lowe's ironic comment on Bowie's Berlin recordings – and the Stiff bust up – 'I Hate The Sound Of Breaking Glass', Iggy Pop's vicious 'Kill City', and Costello's slyly comic '(I Don't Want To Go To) Chelsea'. Released in early March as a taster for the new album, just getting the nod over 'Radio, Radio', it reached Sixteen in the UK hit parade. Charles Shaar Murray had given Elvis his first good review, picking up on his debut single, and considered the new one so good that "the very act of releasing it amounts to bragging on a colossal scale". It was "a nightmare vision of the Swinging London of the mid Sixties – and, by extension, now", complete with "mordant, insinuating vocal".

Across the Atlantic, the North American tour concluded on 6 March with Elvis and his band playing two nights at Toronto's El Mocambo. A small club, with only capacity for 500 people, it provided an antidote to playing the arena circuit, and had been used by the Stones to record tracks for their *Love You Live* album. A thousand people were turned away, and forced to listen to the live broadcast on CHUM FM instead, combining songs old and new. The general effect was like a blowtorch, a musical torrent of drums and spite, fiery and unstoppable, exhilarating from a distance, terrifying close up. One of those bands who you avoided eye contact with, at all times.

The magnificent results, a British new wave band who could actually play – and how! – were pressed up on vinyl in a limited edition of 500 for radio station broadcast, and bootlegged almost immediately. Riviera was not over happy to have unreleased songs available over the airwaves, but as a snapshot of the band in full slash and burn mode, it is invaluable. There is something of the guerrilla, take-no-prisoners, sound of Dylan or The Band touring England in spring 1966, but Elvis raises a cheer, not boos or cries of "Judas" when he shouts to the crowd, "We've come to ask for the country back."

The results are finally available commercially on CD. The inner sleeve reprints a review from *Fanfare*, which fills in the visual details. "He's wearing a sloppy grey jacket, sloppy tie. His hair has been clipped close to the scalp." White shoes, too. "He's wearing glasses, black horn-rims. Elvis has a sharpness about him that makes you think he emerged from the womb with a shaving kit and a tube of Clearasil. He's always been an adolescent. A nasty one." At the end, Nick Lowe comes on to sing 'Breaking Glass', while "Costello stands off to the side, twitching in his jerky, mechanical fashion, slapping a hand to the top of his head and holding it there for a double beat." Someone shouts "Elvis", as if to a new deity. He acknowledges obeisance "by slowly running his tongue across his bottom lip in a movement at once invitingly erotic and repellently hostile". No wonder Jay Scott's piece is headlined "Elvis's aim is pure rock 'n' roll".

NME dubbed the night a "holocaust in microcosm", with Chalkie Davies' *cinema verite* photos of Elvis having his face wiped by an adoring female fan – maybe she later sold the sweat – being embraced by another, and posed with one leg in the air, mid chord. Charles Shaar

Murray noted the punky thrash of the Stiff tour has yielded to a more measured set, "a raw nerve striking back". This was not to all tastes. Susan Hill in *MM* was worried by their moving beyond "the classic three minutes of bleak staccato." For Murray, though, the band are moving "with almost ludicrous ease" into a musical landscape of their own unique creation. Steve Nieve might be "an all-purpose mutant" offstage, but he inserts "surreal washes, robotic bleeps and outrageous quotes", while Costello "throws tortured, splay-footed, knock-kneed shapes and makes a Fender Jazzmaster do things that the maker never intended.

The recorded evidence bears him out, though the audience only catch fire at the start of 'Lipstick Vogue' – as Elvis barks out, "These guys have got the right idea, they're standing up" – from which point proceedings become ragged and exciting in roughly equal measures. The song breaks into something close to a drum solo, the kind patented by John Bonham that emphasises strength rather than facility.

'Watching The Detectives' has lost some of its nagging quality for a new musical intensity, with piercing lead guitar, and Nieve playing a Hammer Horror soundtrack on his keyboards. Elvis croons with even more of a sneer than usual, like a malevolent shadow of his dad. The "taking off her clothes/we never close" rhyme is intoned with cold contempt. Quite what did those girls who rushed the stage think they were kissing?

'Miracle Man' comes complete with Stax riffs on organ, and Elvis breaks off to hoarsely introduce the band: Nieve is "in a very sophisticated mood indeed". Costello can barely sing the first verse of 'You Belong To Me' for laughing, though whether he is amused by the audience, his band or the sheer brilliance of his own lyrics is unclear. Bruce Thomas's bass rises high through the thrash like the Loch Ness monster briefly surfacing for air.

Pounding drums, then Martin Belmont is introduced as the "Empire State of the E chord", and events conclude with 'Pump It Up', on which Belmont plays Mike Bloomfield to Costello's Dylan. Roars for more, and the tape fades out, as if knackered.

If Elvis's characteristic response to the media at this time was hostile, bordering on paranoia, then he was in surprisingly affable mood on Capital Radio's *Your Mother Wouldn't Like It* following his return from America. Probably because rather than failing to answer personal questions, he was given the freedom to play some favourite records, by the likes of Dylan, Bowie, Graham Parker, George Jones and – less expectedly – T Rex and Fleetwood Mac. Confirming that he preferred the music to do the talking, he said, "What I like to do on days off is to go to radio stations and do DJ shows, because I think you give away more of what you're about. You give away what makes your world tick the same way as you go to somebody's house and look at the bookshelf."

Days off were few and far between, though. On 16 March, the band had hardly had time to shake off their jet lag before they began a month long UK tour, opening on foreign soil at the Stella Cinema, Dublin. The support act was new Stiff signing Mickey Jupp, a veteran of the Southend band Legend when they had influenced Dr Feelgood, so hardly a teenager now. The following night, they played Belfast, and Elvis took great pleasure in reciting *Sounds'* Pete Silverton's bad review of the Stiff tour back to him, word for word. Being anywhere with Elvis ensures "a highly charged atmosphere" and in the photo opposite, Costello accompanies a St Patrick's Day procession, looking like the Yorkshire Ripper with glasses. As to the gig, the band were so wired that "it was like watching some kind of high intensity encounter group therapy". Mass hypnosis, without the usual risks.

There is something messianic about him onstage, especially when he hands his guitar to a roadie during 'Watching The Detectives' and wraps himself around the mic, "tearing his throat into the anguish of it all, like a matinee idol trying to come on real for once, and succeeding by the sheer power of his belief". His band then turn his songs into "widescreen epics".

The tour took in mainly Top Rank ballrooms and the larger clubs: Rafters in Manchester, Birmingham's Barbarellas, and Erics in Liverpool. There would certainly be dancing this time around. At Edinburgh's Tiffanys, the Elvis gig was sandwiched between The Skids – "catch them while they're still a cult" – and The Monos. Punk was entering its second phase at just this time, with a whole new generation of bands coming through. That same night saw Adam And The Ants and Billy Idol's Generation X play Manchester's Rafters, Australians Radio Birdman at the Nashville, and Siouxsie And The Banshees at London's Alexandra Palace.

The following day, Radar released *This Year's Model*, Costello's first album with The Attractions. The inside groove of the record had a secret message scratched into the vinyl, like something out of Enid Blyton: "Special pressing number 003, ring Moira on 434-3232 for your special prize." The first 5,000 purchasers eagle-eyed (or obsessive) enough to notice such things won a bonus Costello single coupling 'Stranger In The House' with his cover version of former label mates The Damned's 'Neat Neat Neat'.

This drawing of musical influences from others – a constant motif in Elvis's career, along with a matching curiosity for new models to inhabit – has marked Costello from the start. *This Year's Model* hints at, in its title, temporary music, made up from the latest mix of sources. Postmodern, just like Barney Bubbles' artwork, a rich soup of others' visions. "Barney Bubbles had a mind like an art encyclopedia," Costello says. "He would borrow from different periods quite shamelessly in a very witty way – he did a poster for 'Watching The Detectives' that was a blatant take on Warhol." Elvis spoke illuminatingly about this trait in his own work in an interview with *Record Collector*.

"We never made any bones about the fact that we ripped stuff off from other things. Sometimes it was done very consciously, and sometimes it was simply me thinking about it and not telling the rest of the band. I usually ripped off things that I didn't like very much. I was quite a long way into my career before I did anything too overtly. They were usually quite subtle, like there's a sixth chord at the end of 'Lip Service', like there is at the end of 'She Loves You'. That's a fairly off-the-wall one. There's maybe a suggestion of 'I Want You (She's So Heavy)' at the end of 'Party Girl'. The Beatles were my main influence, but there weren't really Beatles references until we got to the stage where we were pretty confident."

The same process, without Costello's sense of irony, informed Brit Pop, and Oasis's recycling of the Lennon-McCartney songbook. Elvis took the whole thing more seriously, and eventually went the whole hog by actually collaborating with McCartney direct, a new and even more bitter slice of Lennon to give just the right flavour of stringency to leaven Paul's musical sweetness. What separates him from the aridness of most post-modernists was his obvious love and respect for the sources he was recycling.

"I could look back affectionately. I knew all The Small Faces' records backwards when I was thirteen, but I didn't have the ability or the platform to use what I'd learned from them until I was twenty-three. So when we did 'You Belong To Me' and it sounded like 'What'cha Gonna Do About It' crossed with The Rolling Stones' 'The Last Time'. I didn't really think about it, because the references were so fleeting. It was more that the whole spirit of *This Year's Model* was related to the Stones' *Aftermath* because it was about the same kind of moment in somebody's life, updated for the late Seventies."

Pete Thomas also looks back with wonder to those days, lived in fast forward. "Everyone was just chucking things in thick and fast," he says. "I remember we were in this little rooming house, and of course we got drunk all the time on cider, and one night I remember him saying that he wanted the new album to sound like *Aftermath*, which was my favourite album, all the songs on it were great, a bit sexist but great. I can remember getting out of bed and punching the wall. It just all seemed to be coming right. It all seemed to be just falling into place. I guess it all was special, the chemistry of it."

The packaging of *This Year's Model* was a deliberate attempt to reflect this. "We wanted to catch people's eyes," Costello says. "If they said, 'Why is it printed off register?' as the initial pressing was, it was because we wanted people to ask exactly that. It meant they'd pause just that little bit longer in front of our sleeve." The title was deliberately ironic, with Elvis behind the camera. "And I've no idea what's happening on the back of the record, where I'm flying through the window or what the washing machines or dummies are about. Or the Sinclair TV, which didn't exist at the time. There *weren't* any colour TV's of that size. Even the things that appeared to be fashionable were actually fantasy. As to me having a fashionable image, well my suit cost me two dollars from a thrift store. It was hardly the height of fashion."

Nevertheless, as Nick Lowe told Radio One, "Elvis definitely had the final say, absolutely all down the line. Even though he would always listen to what anybody had to say, even in the face of massive objections, in some cases. I remember him having ideas for strange backing harmonies, and I would say, 'Go ahead,' and I would think he'll never remember, when I come to mix it. I'd try this on a couple of times, and he'd say where's that funny backing vocal. He'd insist on it being there. And he'd be right. I started backing out of my heavy-handed producer role. I'd basically just sit there while he did the record, and would either approve or raise an eyebrow, or give him a sideways look if it wasn't going to work. I made sure that the music was speaking to everybody right. I was waving my arms in the air, making jokes, a very important part of the process."

Pete Thomas remembers Elvis as being "like a whirlwind in the studio. And Nick would just work it up into a frenzy through the day, when you were playing stuff that you never thought you could play, and Elvis was singing stuff that he never thought he could sing. You'd come and listen to it the next day, and you wouldn't even think it was you. Nick would be waving his arms in the air, and he'd turn the volume up full. We'd be pinned against the wall. He'd wait five minutes, and then say, 'You can do better than that, you bastards.' Very, very exciting. 'Come and hear it,' that was his big line. Fantastic."

The results, as heard on *This Year's Model* were startling, light years away from the plodding moments of *My Aim Is True*, like moving from a grainy home movie to Hollywood technicolour.

Recording began at Eden studios at the tail-end of 1977, and completed early in 1978, after eleven days in the studio fitted in around the first American tour. By this point, Elvis "had lost track of time". The album was butchered for American consumption, with 'Night Rally' and '(I Don't Want to Go To) Chelsea' omitted in favour of 'Radio, Radio', and the sequence for the British release buggered up. For the remastered CD reissue, Costello restored the original running order, so it seems fair enough for us to take that as the authorised version.

The album crackles with self confidence. Tim Lott in *Record Mirror* worried for "his ego, and us all" if Elvis reached the musical perfection for which he seemed to be reaching. The songs are less vicious than on his debut, but Costello remains an "Aladdin's cave of anti-matter". His voice is "insubstantial but wiry" and the music he produces "clever in its very lack of detail". Lott compares the organ-heavy sound here with Blondie, a Sixties' sound "trapped for ten years on atmospherics".

In *Melody Maker*, Allan Jones found a "prodigious talent" only superficially exposed on his debut. Elvis explores infidelity and humiliation, while The Attractions, "with razor-blade cool, slice across the mix". Steve Nieve's icy keyboards are a crazed hybrid of Garth

Hudson and Can's Irwin Schmidt: they "shiver nervously behind Elvis's alarm-central lyrics. The penetration of the language matches the vaulting hysteria of the performance." *NME*'s Nick Kent was almost beyond speech. The album is so ridiculously good that "one's immediate inclinations are to clamber effusively over the top, superlative peaking superlative to the point where well meaning enthusiasm turns an unattractive tint of bloated sycophancy".

Kent, the least sycophantic of reviewers, traces Elvis's rapid rise from being seen as little more than "another Stiff crazy gang product, a touch heavy on the old Graham Parker, Van Morrison etc influences" to this "joyous event". The Attractions attain what Dylan was seeking for in *Blonde On Blonde*, "metallic and bright gold...a wild mercury sound". They interlock "taut as a clenched fist, getting tighter and tighter until the veins bulge out like railroad tracks". Uneasy listening, but Costello is currently the best, as Kent was as a critic, and the *NME* as a magazine. This review – proved true with time – is itself a summation of the finest flowering of rock journalism, anywhere. "There's no-one within spitting distance of him. He has his finger on the pulse of this desperate era and his perceptions are so disquieting because all too often they're too damn real to be strenuously ignored."

Jon Savage, writing in *Sounds* is part of a new generation of cooler, varsity educated writing – cue Barney Hoskyns and John Rogan – which has since spread into the posh Sundays and the media mainstream, followed by an unspeakable raft of dry academics, from Simon Frith downward. Here he finds Elvis "less than loveable", and The Attractions "spare yet full". It is an "excellent, soon-to-be popular *album*". In turn, this is the kind of writing you admire rather than love, and the likes of Kent – and Paul Williams and Allan Jones and Pete Frame and Mark Williams and Steve Burgess – will always remain closer to my own heart. Enthusiasts all, yet with a wonderful sense of irony. Just like Costello's music, in fact. There was surprisingly little criticism of Elvis's misogyny at this point: indeed Savage remarks that "Elvis has the grace to make clear that it's a two way process and *he's* at fault. Just wanna be your victim..."

Like the songs it contains, the album sleeve is deliberately off-centre, so that the title becomes "His Year's Model", with a minimum of verbal information. On the front cover, Elvis takes the viewer's picture, while someone takes his: in a careful reconstruction of a still of David Hemmings from Michelangelo Antonioni's *Blow Up*. The movie is set in the "Swinging Sixties", but deals with a (possible) murder, captured on a roll of film. We are all under surveillance. He crouches forward on the US cover with both hands on the camera, like a gun: on the British version, he stands back a little, with his hands opening like flowers. Elvis is alert and predatory as a weasel, pencil thin, dressed in dark suit and polka dot shirt. His eyes are black holes, reflecting nothing, allowing in nothing.

The back cover is like an outtake from *The X Files*, with a curtain billowing inwards, and the four boys in the band reacting with mock horror. Three have black ties, worn at half mast, while Nieve sports a V-neck pullover, mighty like a wasp. The room is deeply hideous, a vomit of beige and brown with curtain drapes and matching bedspread like an LSD trip gone wrong. The whole thing screams "cheap American hotel room", and is deeply claustrophobic. There doesn't appear to be any door. On the inner sleeve, which seems misplaced from a Kraftwerk album, a robotic hand, perhaps a cybernaut from *The Avengers* grips a mini TV on which Elvis is playing, standing on one leg. On the other side, four colour-coded and dismembered showroom dummies model string vests in a launderette: Costello and his musical chums have seemingly turned to marble. Twenty years on, it would probably win the Turner prize, it's *that* vacuous.

The album was placed at Number Eleven in *Rolling Stone*'s all-time poll held in 1987, for the way Elvis surveyed "the modern romantic terrain with keen cynicism, caustic wit and furious energy". Remastered on CD, it still bristles with an extraordinary self-belief. Light years advanced from *My Aim Is True*, an album which could have been produced by the (twisted) boy next door, it creates a paranoid universe, where everyone is being watched. The same world view, led by conspiracy theory, which informs the films of Alan J Pakula, or *The Prisoner*, or a whole library of science fiction dystopias. Come in Philip K Dick, and tell William Gibson the good news.

The songs bristle with references to the technology of mass control: corporate logos, video surveillance, vigilantes, torturers, warders and night rallies. "They're putting all your names in the forbidden book." Costello comes on as a liberal bleating against all this, but there is a sense of secret complicity: on the cover he looks like a secret policeman, himself. Elvis too has been known to keep his little black book containing lists of his enemies.

In 'No Action', Elvis is a telephone pest, seeking complete control in a rather different way to The Clash. The chorus "I just wanna put you down" is both metaphorical and literal, dropping the receiver. The album opens on Costello's voice – solo, intimate and threatening – before The Attractions crash in. The jealousy just about controlled in 'Alison' has turned psychotic – "the things in my head start hurting my mind" – and the song ends with solo drum taps, like gunfire.

'This Year's Girl' deals with fashion, and how the media bring images which real people then imitate, or (impotently) desire. One thinks of the thousands of Siouxsie Sioux clones who suddenly emerged at about this time. The song opens with a drum pattern, around which bass and Farfisa organ create baroque patterns. As Allan Jones described it, "Elvis flicks off taut guitar sequences over Steve Nieve's swirling keyboard shrouds and a central percussion motif that exaggerates the mounting tension." The vengeful words are sung with cloying sweetness, and one couplet exposes the uglier side of male fantasy – "you want her broken with her mouth wide open" – with a neatness close to genius.

The song's intro is a direct cop from 'Dr Robert', while the middle section is also pure Beatles. The next song, 'The Beat', is a kind of musical perversion of Cliff Richard's bouncy and innocent song 'n' film *Summer Holiday*, and opens with the same first line. The only shadows here are psychological, though. Set to swirly organ, a tango beat and vibrato guitar, the heart of the song is a sordid and unfulfilled sex act: about the closest the album gets to romantic love. The most companionable thing here is the male chorus; the only unalloyed humour Bruce's nudge and wink bass pattern after the words "I don't want to lick them". And we're not talking about postage stamps.

'Pump It Up' comes in all brash and boisterous, with Costello singing on one note, Bob Dylan-style. The song is (im)pure Chuck Berry, via 'Subterranean Homesick Blues'. Drums pump like pistons, or the obsessive sexual desire which fuels the lyrics, and the whole thing is claustrophobic and unending: it fades out as if the needle is stuck. After that, 'Little Triggers' is a particular delight, opening with delicate piano, and mutating from soft soul to Burt Bacharach. The closest thing to a love song here, though the singer wants *not* to be "hung up, strung up" on desire. The lyrics are an exercise in chain rhyming, a technical *tour de force*, but the sheer desperation of Elvis's vocal delivery – and the crooning backing voices – sidestep Brian Ferry-type smoothness for something far more affecting.

If the whole album is a kind of shadowplay, mimicking the mid-sixties Rolling Stones, then 'You Belong To Me' – similar to a title previously used by Dylan – directly quotes the title of 'Under My Thumb', and the tune of 'The Last Time'. The plucked guitar at the start is pure Brian Jones, while the downward bass run near the end echoes Wyman. Costello's voice, though, avoids Jagger's braggart sneer for something far nastier, with lots of sexual innuendo, gone rancid. The album's coupling of fashion and military control centres here on the line "no uniform is gonna keep you warm", with its internal rhyme. The Stones would never have written with such irony, so that the singer's repeated pledge that he will allow no-one to say "you belong to me", becomes exactly the opposite, a statement of sexual master.

'Hand In Hand' opens with Hendrix-like feedback, and backward vocals, then settles into a rock shuffle, with Costello coming on as a minor league gangster. Adam and Eve were expelled from Eden, hand in hand, but the well matched "lovers" here are walking straight down into hell. Elvis sings with a tender relish. The whole thing sounds like an episode from *EastEnders*, and indeed the woman here sees life as a soap opera, with herself as a starring player.

By that token, the next song, '(I Don't Want To Go To) Chelsea' is a British film from the Swinging Sixties: *Alfie* – referred to now as one of the "warders" – or *Smashing Time*. Chelsea was, of course, the centre of hip London back then, with the Kings Road an endless fashion parade. "Sixty six" could be the year, or the highway. 'This Year's Girl' is now twelve months out of time, and little more than a prostitute. There is a wonderful discontinuity between the herky-jerky backing and Elvis's urgent but disdainful vocals, as if a quarter of a century separates them. Costello sounds half-mad, and the action ends in a mental ward, just like *Morgan, A Suitable Case For Treatment*, or so many "survivors" from those strange times. Costello really should have more compassion!

'Lip Service' is a pun linking subservience with oral sex, set to handclaps and a tuneful chorus – counterpointed by a pretty bass pattern – just like something by The Hollies. Ringing guitars, and a perky vocal twang, which almost sounds like Forrest Gump, signal 'Living In Paradise', which was often introduced on stage as a song about America, but written years before he first visited. It certainly purveys a different version of the American dream to Tom Hanks' film. The song has been largely rewritten, and sharpened in focus. Elvis is at the keyhole, and watching a live video of his erring girlfriend's latest liaison. Since Flip City, Costello's delivery has grown far more confident, as has his guitar technique. In the magazine *Trouser Press*, that testament to all things power pop, Ira Robbins notes, "Elvis has developed a very effective style of strumming just one chord and letting it ring, creating a less-is-more hole where other guitarists would keep right on banging away." Alternatively, Allan Jones saw the song as "set against a neurotic calypso backdrop, with Elvis phrasing his lyrics with a flippant, disquieting glee, his voice twitching and kicking over the jerking rhythm".

'Lipstick Vogue' shows that Gary Numan was not the first singer to deal with alienation! The way that Elvis sings about "almost" feeling like a human being is deeply upsetting, as his delivery here is far from ironic, but driven and desperate, as if singing through clenched teeth. A crooner from the suicide ward. The drums begin everything, and interact with bubbling bass: the way that things slow right down in the middle, then come up to the boil again, is brilliant, as is the central pun. Mouths that wear lipstick can also speak out words "they don't allow to be spoken".

'Night Rally' opens quietly, and is granted luxurious sound, like Procol Harum in their *Grand Hotel* period, with Costello's voice taking on Gary Brooker's sense of stoned pomposity. Then the words kick in, and we're in a nightmare of state control and worse. The reference to the gas chambers would be inexcusable in "pop" music any less allusive or serious as this. One thinks of Siouxsie And The Banshees' early live lyric about "too many Jews for my liking", and shudders. Costello avoids the whole thing becoming an over-the-top paeon to paranoia by a quick joke – "get that chicken out of here" – and an obscure reference to 3D cinema, a short-lived craze in which the whole audience had to don special glasses. Just when you think it's safe to leave, a song which opened as if the singer was simply lovelorn ends with the title repeated over and over while, in Nick Kent's words, "the organ motif rings out like a siren, leaving one disorientated and not a little scared". Then it all suddenly cuts off dead.

In *This Year's Model*, Costello's lyrics are strongly visual, as befits the voyeurism which fuels many of the songs. The cover shot also seems to refer to Michael Powell's movie *Peeping Tom*, once vilified but now revered, in which the young hero murders women with a blade concealed in his camera tripod, using a mirror to allow his victims to watch their own deaths. The augmented CD adds 'Big Tears', Elvis's "favourite outtake", featuring Mick Jones of The Clash, and opening with a sniper taking aim. "When you're lying in your coffin/tell me who's been taken in." Certainly not Elvis, on the evidence of this paranoid, terrifying, ecstatic album.

There are also solo demos of two songs from the *next* album. 'Big Boys' was "my attempt to write a song in one chord". 'Greenshirt' contains an extra, concluding verse: there are wires on walls, windows, your face...Of course, Elvis knows all about computers. Hearing this mesmeric song with just voice and guitar takes me back to Portsmouth Guildhall a few months later, where Elvis also performed it solo, and a thrill of unease ran through the audience, and up and down my own spine. I remember the stage lights shining back from his glasses, like binoculars trained on the audience.

Otherwise, 'Crawling To The USA' – the title is obviously double-edged – was obviously influenced by the brutal rudeness of New York customs. Wires again, leading under the Atlantic, and having been body-searched, Elvis appears to be having sex with the Statue of Liberty. The otherwise unreleased 'Out Of Angels' sounds "as if I was making it up as I went along, which I probably was".

CHAPTER FOUR

mystery girl

As to last year's model, in March 1978 the US issue of *My Aim Is True* – with several changes in the UK running order, and the addition of 'Watching The Detectives' – had climbed steadily to Number Thirty-Two after thirty-six weeks in the American album charts. On 1 April, the new album hit Number Four in the UK, just as his fourteen-date British tour hit the mainland at that rock 'n' roll shrine, the Bracknell Sports Centre. The atmosphere of violence within the tour party rebounded when Bruce Thomas cut his hand badly backstage at Manchester's Rafters club. The cause was his macho demonstration of how to smash a bottle to make it into an offensive weapon. So what happened to the peace and love of Glastonbury Fayre then, Bruce. Nick Lowe and Thin Lizzy's Phil Lynott filled in.

Lowe's second gig was Portsmouth Guildhall, and he was late back from London, forcing Costello to go on first, solo with electric guitar, playing five songs thus and five with a bassless Attractions, before Nick Lowe hove into view. Those present were aware that they were attending something special: I was and the sheer intensity of Elvis's solo set is still burned into my soul. More prosaically, Barbara Charone of *Sounds*, noted that the errant Lowe was "dressed in black, sporting the cleanest hair I've seen since Jackson Browne graced British stages". Aggro broke out down at the front – well, it *was* Portsmouth – and Elvis barked at them, "You wanna fucking fight, then you go home and fucking fight." It was part of the general air of mayhem. "The kids acted like they were watching Status Quo, or at least a football match, heaving tiers of chairs in the direction of the security guards. Elvis just looked at the chairs, and proceeded to play."

On 15 April, the tour – with Lowe still a temporary Attraction – culminated with two consecutive nights at the Roundhouse, captured on the bootleg ironically titled *Accidents Will Happen*. Like REM a few years later, Costello had taken up the habit of occasionally throwing in a cover version of a favourite song, seemingly unrehearsed, treats that included The Damned's 'Neat Neat Neat', Ian Dury's 'Roadette Song', 'Love Comes In Spurts' by Richard Hell and 'Six O'Clock' by The Lovin' Spoonful. The *NME* reported that Steve Nieve looked like "some giant insect", while Elvis seemed more relaxed than a few months before: he was now singing *to*, rather than *at* the audience. Phil Lynott took over the bass for 'Mystery Dance', obliging with "one clenched-fist salute as he left the stage".

'(I Don't Want To Go To) Chelsea' was only descending down the Top Thirty when Radar released a new single, 'Pump It Up', to keep up the sense of endless rush. An advert in *NME* had a spectacularly weird full page photo of the band crowding out the light, all now with shorn hair, and Elvis in a shiny suit. Bruce Thomas looks like a Kray extra, in giant shades, but Nieve's are bigger still, and round, with a circle of light reflected in each lens. He looks like an extra from a sci-fi movie.

In March, Nick Kent had returned to interview Costello a second time. The band are about to appear on *Top Of The Pops*, and Elvis considers attaching a sticker for his new album – "warning: this is not this year's model" – to one of the Legs And Co dance troupe. He also reveals that the new LP was originally to have been called *Little Hitler*, before Nick Lowe nicked the title: Costello's later song 'Two Little Hitlers' is his riposte. The change of title was probably for the best, especially when you consider the storm of protest when Joy Division appropriated various Nazi trademarks.

Kent also interviews The Attractions, finding Nieve "easily the weirdest guy I've ever, *ever*, interviewed". This is saying something, as the *NME* ex-hippie has interviewed everyone from Syd Barrett to Keith Richards, his own role model. Steve – who despite his expulsion took, and failed, his final exam in composition at the Royal College of Music – questions why "we're not as big as The Bay City Rollers. It seems very slow, this pop music thing." His favourite musician is Michel Legrand, and he hopes to eventually write the music for Hammer Horror movies, and *Love Story*! Elvis's music is best when it gets "weird and spooky".

So are his interviews, and this is a case in point. Costello is still angry and bitter. "The music biz – the crassness of it all – still actively disgusts me," he fumes, "and any degree of success I will attain will not weigh against all that crap I went through initially. Even if I got to be as big as Fleetwood Mac, I still wouldn't feel any different." This is particularly ironic given Costello's problems with WEA almost twenty years later: things don't change. Kent comes in hard, quoting Ian Dury to the effect that Costello is not a mature or fulfilled human being – heavy stuff for a rock interview. Elvis agrees, though he doesn't think that musical success will make him a nicer human being.

"Christ, when I was eighteen – five years ago – I felt thirty," he explains. "I was really deadly, deadly cynical, and it's only been in the last six months that I've been feeling much younger, much less serious." Elvis laughs, about becoming fashionable. "That's the last thing I ever wanted. There was never any airbrush stuff. I could never imagine a lot of people wanting this ugly geek in glasses ramming his songs down their throats. And that's *exactly* what I'm in it for, to disrupt people's lives."

His ultimate vocation is to be an "irritant, someone who disrupts the daily drag of life just enough to leave the victim thinking there's maybe more to it all than the mere hum-drum quality of existence". As from the very start, Elvis wants to be successful, rather than famous. The idea of being a rock star is something that still appals him. 'Hand In Hand', for example, draws on Nick Lowe's Swansong dealings with Jimmy Page: "Just the sort of unhuman monster type I could become if I let myself go *that* far."

His own personal breakthrough came with the "fragmented style" of songwriting first seen in 'Watching The Detectives', non-linear and impersonal. It was a way of escaping his own obsessions, and he now projects himself though other people, which does not diminish the seriousness of his mission. "Rock 'n' roll as such *is* my life," he proclaims. "It's all I do, so these songs *are* me. That's why people whose songs you admire are usually so disappointing when you meet them. Because their songs are their lives, and they don't have a life outside their songs. And often I feel exactly the same way."

In *Melody Maker*, Allan Jones writes a fine career overview, in lieu of the interview with Elvis he has *not* been granted. He recalls two incidents on the Stiff tour, Elvis brandishing a flick knife on the tour bus, and baiting a neanderthal security guard in Glasgow – of all places – armed only with a can of fruit juice which he has customised into a blade. "He was prepared to push himself past the point where there existed any possibility of retreat."

He recalls watching Elvis's first solo gig under that name, supporting The Rumour, and legendary publicist BP Fallon drawing comparisons with the young Dylan. Here was somebody who could sound "as rapidly angry as a barracuda and yet still not lose sight of an articulate perspective". I would concur here: both have the ability onstage to set their own agenda, creating their own time and space. I can only compare it to watching a great actor like Ian McKellan, a mesmeric intensity which can only be experienced face to face – *not* though film or video – and which transmits at a level far beyond the verbal or explicable.

On their first face-to-face meeting, when Costello was still working at Elizabeth Arden, Allan Jones was amazed by this young unknown's "forthright determination. He *knew* how good he was, so what was to be gained from adopting any self-effacing, ingratiating stance." As for today, "Elvis Costello is the only one of us who knows for sure how far he's willing to take it, and he knows the risks."

The new single soon climbed to a slightly disappointing twenty-fourth place in the UK Top Thirty. There was no relief, though, from Elvis's hectic tour schedule. He was almost immediately back in the States for his third US tour in six months. Clover's John Ciambotti played bass for the first gig, before Bruce Thomas was fit to rejoin the band: a rare and unplanned vacation. As Elvis later told Radio One, "From the Stiff tour, we didn't stop touring for two and a half years. The only time we stopped is when we went to the studio. We didn't take anything like a holiday. That was for the wimps."

Pete Thomas adds, "We were really confident. Just travelling in a station wagon, and it was all fuelled on vodka and five or six hundred mile drives every day. Get to the gig, get drunk, go mad, hammer through the set, refuse to do encores, then people would riot. Proper job." Bruce Thomas is more downbeat. "The physical workload was pretty devastating," he admits. "You had to get through it in whatever way you can. You peak at eleven o'clock at night, it takes you half the night to wind down, you sleep while you're travelling, so you get into this very peculiar cycle. The curse of the mini-bar. Everybody has drunk two tia marias, two bourbons, two gins...It's those nights when things get a bit wild. The first couple of years I was at home a handful of nights. Jake went over the top with the gig list. We'd be in the middle of a 138 day tour, and he'd be wheeling in the gigs for a few months ahead. I'll never forgive him for that."

Elvis's third US tour was a thirty-nine-gig, ten-week grind, opening in Minneapolis in late April, and concluding at San Francisco's Winterland in early June. At that same venue, The Sex Pistols had played their final, blood-soaked gig, back in January. Punk was already dead in the water. Elvis was headlining over two bands who purveyed a kind of new wave R&B, against which The Attractions' visceral energy would shine. Nick Lowe's Rockpile were old friends, Mink DeVille a part of the New York CBGB's scene and already with a hit single, 'Spanish Stroll'. Their mainman Willy DeVille had first recorded at the same tiny studio beneath the Hope and Anchor as Flip City. He soon let it be known that he had no great sympathy for this bespectacled nerd, or his insulting use of a genuine rocker's first name: like medieval monarchs, affairs were sorted out by a pitched battle between their respective road crews.

In a false display of harmony, Columbia issued an EP in trendy orange-coloured vinyl of the three acts. Elvis was now big business: *Billboard* lists the New York Palladium gig as the fourth biggest money spinner that week, with gross receipts of $54,000. The 3,000 seat Santa Monica Civic sold out within hours, though Elvis's set was still confined to sixteen songs, with no encore. In May, the US version of *This Year's Model*, augmented with 'Radio Radio', reached Number Thirty in the American album charts. It was the highest placing so far either for Costello or any "new wave" music.

Three tracks from LA's Hollywood High came as a freebie EP with the next album. 'Accidents Will Happen' is slow as a funeral lament, with florid cocktail-bar piano over which Costello mimics grand passion. In 'Alison' – by now rarely performed – his tender vocal elongates and almost cracks on the final chorus. 'Watching The Detectives' opens with feedback and twangy guitar, almost like surf king Dick Dale. The pace is laid-back compared to earlier blitzkriegs, but things get spooky in the middle. Then Elvis comes back in, altering the tune as he goes, and ends howling like a wolf.

Costello briefly returned to Britain, to play a Cambridge May Ball: held, just to confuse the lower orders, in June. He also took in a Dingwall's gig by George Thorogood And The Destroyers, but this was a rare evening off. Elvis and band plunged straight into a nineteen-concert European tour, with hardly a break. To increase the alienation effect, the support act were the two-man US band Suicide, who married avant-garde poetry to synthesiser drones.

Audiences were unused to forty-five-minute sets and no encores, leading to riots at the Hague's Congresgebouw – a concert attended by Bob Dylan – and in Scandinavia. The Paris L'Olympia gig is regarded by cognoscenti as one of Elvis's finest ever. Rock fans – and MTV – are forever grateful to the German TV show *Rockpalast*, which captured full length concerts on video and stereo tape by many bands whose work would otherwise remain unchronicled. Elvis and The Attractions visited the Cologne studios on 21 June. The aural results have been much recycled since on bootleg CD, most recently *The Rise And Rise Of Declan MacManus* and *Superlative Live*, though both misdate the proceedings.

On the thirteen songs recorded, the band is superbly tight, with Elvis sounding urgent and desperate, as if trying to rush through the set as rapidly as possible. There is one new song, 'Two Little Hitlers'. 'The Beat' has an almost psychedelic middle section, with a rare lead guitar break over sustained organ chords. 'Night Rally' opens like Tubeway Army, robotic and threatening, and Elvis can hardly force the words out, supposedly with fear. '(I Don't Want To Go To) Chelsea' has a particularly weird, atonal break. Elvis comes back in, from a whisper to a shout, and at the end guitar and keyboards swirl up to heaven. They repeat the trick in 'Lipstick Vogue', which sounds close at times to early Pink Floyd, melodic bass over fairground organ. Elvis drags things away from Syd-like whimsy, but his voice is peculiarly deep here, and it is echoed by cossack whoops from the boys in the band. The music moves straight into 'Watching The Detectives', crossed with the 'Teddy Bear's Picnic' on organ! The break this time is even further out, like Mike Ratledge in the early Soft Machine. After that, Elvis makes rare contact with the audience – "This song is called 'Pump it Up'" – and it's back to punkish thrash.

Back on planet earth, George Jones had invited Elvis to duet on Costello's own song 'Stranger In The House'. While his band took a short break, Elvis flew over to Nashville, and – due to Jones' "incapacity" – played solo in local bars. He broke his journey back in New York, where he joined Delbert McClinton at the Lone Star Cafe, singing Chuck Berry's 'Don't Lie To Me' and Hank Williams' 'You Win Again'. August saw Elvis and The Attractions reunited at Eden Studios, where they laid down tracks for the next album with their usual speed, completing seventeen songs in six weeks.

One of the brightest aspects of the new dispensation was its multi-culturalism, with dub reggae as the black music of choice for young white punks, though The Clash's 'White Man In Hammersmith Palais' dealt with some of the tensions inherent in this. All the same, it is hard to imagine a singer like Poly Styrene gaining a hit single before 1977. Post-punk, a whole generation of mixed race bands was just about to break into the mainstream, through the Two-Tone label and the ska revival.

The formation of Rock Against Racism was part of this process, and Costello – as an early adherent – agreed to take part in an open-air gig at Brixton's Brockwell Park on 24 September, in support of the new movement, putting aside his dire memories of the Crystal Palace debacle. The previous night, he had played a warm-up date at the mistitled Grand Hotel, New Brighton, south of the Mersey and thus close to his spiritual home of Birkenhead. A fracas ensued, and – par for the course – Jake Riviera was directly involved.

In what the *NME* wittily nicknamed "Rock Against Journalism", Mike Simpson, a reporter from the *Birkenhead News* who also worked for *Record Mirror*, asked one too many questions. He was bundled down a flight of stairs, receiving a broken wrist for his pains, and needing five stitches in a head wound. Riviera explained, "Elvis isn't doing interviews with anyone at the moment. Plus he was trying to talk to his mum at the time." When the journalist demanded a further reason why he should leave, "I said, 'I don't like people with long hair.' He said that wasn't a valid reason. So I said, 'Here's a valid reason,' and hit him." Elvis joined in the resulting fracas, and Riviera himself claimed to have been punched in the mouth four times. Simpson further quoted Riviera to the effect that he couldn't stand people with "long hair, velvet jackets, flared jeans...or hippies wearing plimsols". Funny, but that sounds just like Chilli Willi, the band who Riviera had managed, and their audience of the time, not to mention Jake himself.

Costello's PR team further fuelled the flames. "If he walked in my office, I'd smash him in the fucking eye myself," Riviera continued. "I'd smash anybody that worked for *Record Mirror* just if they were walking down the street. Journalists are all dogs. They treat anyone with a bit of talent like a piece of meat." So what exactly *is* funny about peace, love and understanding?

Elvis and entourage were in more peace-loving mood the next afternoon, at Brockwell Park. The Anti-Nazi League Carnival had marched from Hyde Park, over Vauxhall Bridge, and down into Brixton. Garry Bushell of *Sounds* – and now *The Sun* – later came out as a proponent of the right wing "Oi" bands, so it is ironic that he should cover this left-wing event in such glowing terms. Elvis's set was his own particular highlight. He stood there, "red drape, black collar, check shirt, black cords and belted through sixteen songs", starting with 'Night Rally' and ending with 'Radio, Radio', both appropriate in the circumstances. "Welcome to the black and white minstrel show, 'ow about jumping up and down against racism," he told the crowd. This concert saw the public debut of 'Oliver's Army', a song which Bushell gave his immediate approval to. It would make a fine anthem to be sung on football terraces!

Politically, sociology professor Simon Frith is about as far removed from Bushell as chalk from cheese. Both put a political world view before the music, in my view, but each has his eager constituency, of dunces and pseuds. Frith reported for *NME* that the sound balance ruined the set, rendering the guitars inaudible, and making Elvis's voice "so upfront that it seemed almost eerily disembodied from any musical foundation". 'Watching The Detectives' featured a "melodramatic talkover section in the last verse that didn't work at all", but was a highlight all the same. When Elvis quit the arena, so did a large proportion of the audience.

'Radio Radio' was finally issued as a single in the UK that October. Its B-side was 'Tiny Steps', an outtake from the sessions for Costello's forthcoming album, provisionally titled *Emotional Fascism*. The single was more a picture of musical fascism, and Paul Gambaccini bravely made it his single of the week on Radio One. The less enlightened Tony Blackburn described Elvis as a "silly little man" when the playlist forced him to spin these seven inches of protest at everything that the likes of Blackburn stood for. Doubtless "our Tone" was immediately entered in Costello's notorious little black book, and an appearance on TV's *Top Of The Pops* gave him a perfect opportunity in front of a nationwide audience. Over a pre-recorded backing track, he changed the lyrics to "silly little men" controlling the airwaves, waving contemptuously at the programme's compere, none other than Tony Blackburn himself. "One mustn't take these things personally," was the DJ's embarrassed response on air. But Tony, you should! With little airplay – but what did Elvis *expect*? – the single only reached Twenty-Nine in the charts.

Elvis's cause wasn't helped by another Tony, the one surnamed Parsons who came on as a punk terrorist for the *NME* and who had certainly changed his mind on Elvis in the past year. "All you need to know about 'Radio Radio' is that what The Clash did on 'Capital Radio' with an abundance of vitality, originality and venom, Costello does with forced fury, catchy commerciality and his mandatory Angry Little Man whine." When Joe Strummer had wandered into CBS's New York office to see posters of Elvis plastered everywhere, he pantomimed retching. "I can't stand him," he told Parsons, who in turn urged his readers to stick with their free Clash EP. "Kids, to me Costello is in tune with nothing at all."

Also in late October, the second Stiff tour set off around Britain, this time by train, with Lene Lovich, Mickey Jupp, Rachel Sweet, Jona Lewie, and Wreckless Eric, still failing to recoup his advance, and Mark Williams – Britain's greatest lost rock journalist – as compere. Without Riviera's madcap visions, or the musical fireworks of 1977, the thrill had gone. Stiff had become just another record label, and with next year's signings Madness an extremely rich one. Meanwhile, Radar were failing to increase their own artist base. They attempted to sign The Tourists – a prequel to The Eurythmics, with Dave Stewart and Annie Lennox – but failed. Meanwhile, their main effort continued to be that of breaking Elvis worldwide, and for the rest of 1978 he extended his tour itinerary to Canada, Hawaii, Japan and Australia.

Before the tour got underway, Elvis joined Richard Hell onstage at CBGB's. In Vancouver's Stanley Park, he filmed what was to become the promo film of '(What's So Funny 'Bout) Peace, Love And Understanding'. Japanese fans on Tokyo's Ginza Street were amazed to see Costello and The Attractions playing a free concert from the back of an open-topped truck.

It was like a street level version of The Beatles playing on the roof of Apple Corps, or of the Hilton revisited, this time with a band. *NME* reported, half tongue in cheek, that he "hammered out a free and furious set of venomous rock 'n' roll. Featured classics naturally included 'Ripstick Vogue' and 'Ladio, Ladio'." Extending the parallel with the Hilton performance, Elvis almost immediately drew the attention of a passing policeman. He was arrested and fined 4,000 yen on the spot, roughly equivalent to £10. Doubtless Elvis could afford to pay immediately nowadays.

Elvis was resolutely refusing to be interviewed or have his photo taken: "If Bob Dylan did it, then I can do it too," was the logic behind it. Despite this, *NME* showed a photo of Elvis under arrest, himself looking half-Japanese with slit eyes behind thick glasses, and dressed in a high collared dark suit. A large sign on the side of the truck bore the message – in Japanese – that "Elvis Costello is now touring Japan". He played five dates in Tokyo and Osaka, and was the first Western star to play local rock clubs, rather than prestige gigs like the Budokan. It was like his first tour of the States, starting from the bottom. As such, he introduced the new wave to a whole new audience (though God only knows what they made of his lyrics).

In Australia, he provoked a near riot after a fifty-minute set which saw him near to exhaustion: the audience, disappointed by his brusque attitude, and failure to return for an encore, showered the stage with lager cans and bits of stray furniture. Elvis later commented that their reaction had been "too mechanical".

In turn, the crowd chanted "Elvis loves his money" and "Costello is a capitalist". At Sydney airport, Costello screamed, "Who the fucking hell do you think you are?" at a press photographer, and journalists were advised that they attempted to talk to the new superstar at their own risk. Audiences, as in the USA, expected warmth and humility from their stars – onstage, at least – and more music for their money. A radio interview on Sydney's Double Jay station led to death threats, on air.

Reports also surfaced of a backstage fracas, which saw Costello and Riviera roughing up a photographer. Richard Wood, the aggrieved party, turned out to be *NME*'s house punk, Tony Parsons' cousin, and this might well have been Elvis's reaction to his dire review of 'Radio Radio'. Even so, Tony was not the best person to upset, as Parsons and his co-writer and fellow hyena Julie Burchill now declared open season on Costello. Like the grubby Sundays, rock journalism conformed to the philosophy of "first make 'em, and then break 'em".

Elvis had – and has – tried to keep his personal life under wraps; no kiss and show TV biogs *à la* Sir Elton John. This was bad enough while he was living quietly in Middlesex with wife and young son, but writing and performing songs which attacked the vanities of the media world – "I want to bite the hand that feeds me" – meant he would have to learn that they would not hesitate to bite back.

In an extraordinary act of media defiance, Costello turned up for an open air Sunday afternoon Hyde park concert starring punk poet John Cooper Clarke. He was just part of the crowd, looking slightly shifty in a pork-pie hat. Hardly startling in itself, but he was accompanied by Bebe Buell, a model previously romantically linked with Todd Rundgren, Rod Stewart and other flashy rock stars. Whatever her inner qualities, in photographs she looked like a glossy fantasy figure, tailored to satisfy the basest male desires. The kind of glamorous starlet whom one would least associate with the puritan author of songs like 'This Year's Girl', but that is just what she was, made flesh.

It was like throwing raw steak to a bunch of polecats, and hacks with cameras followed every move the new couple made. News soon leaked out that Costello had abandoned his wife, child and suburban home, to set up a love nest in a Kensington flat. Elvis would be reunited with Mary within the year, but his image as a love-starved loner was blown forever.

In an interview with Mat Snow of *Mojo*, Bebe gave her side of the story. She had first seen Elvis in 1976, in an extraordinary twist of fate. She was doing a fashion shoot, and an Elizabeth Arden factotum came over to deliver some papers. It was the young Declan MacManus. "Bebe asked who was the weedy youth in the overalls and glasses. Name of Declan, came the answer, married with a kid, plays in a pub band called Flip City she probably wouldn't like – 'folky and boring'." In an interview for *Please Kill Me*, an oral history of punk, she declares, "I fell in love with him the second I saw him. I didn't even know what his name was." She couldn't get him out of her mind, though.

Eighteen months later, a friend took her to a gig at Hollywood High. "I think once or twice in your life you have moments that are just totally magical and you really feel like God is at work," she suggests. She could hardly believe this was the same man. "It was just like an Elvis Presley movie – he looked right at me and sang to me the whole night. It was just too much, I thought I was gonna die." Elvis was now the hottest thing in town. "When the lights first hit Elvis it was extremely provocative. They lit him from underneath, so that he would look almost frightening – the shadow of his glasses was extremely pronounced. He was the most handsome thing I had ever seen. And I thought it hysterical that he wore a powder blue suit with a tie in the middle of summer. Elvis looked thirty-five when he was twenty-four. And he had this non-ability on the guitar that made these fabulous screeching noises."

Her girlfriend was unaware of the seismic changes going on in Bebe's psyche, and tried instead to fix her up with Elvis's manager. "He combs his hair like a gangster, and he wears shiny suits just like Johnny Thunders," was the reasoning. Jake had no chance, though, when the two went on to the Whiskey to see The Runaways, and who should walk in but Elvis. She approached his table, and "immediately knocked his glasses off by mistake," Bebe recalls. "I apologised – he had a great sense of humour about it, he told me he didn't need his face anyway – and we were sweating and shaking and totally scared of each other. You don't feel that kind of purity too often in your life."

The next day, they met at the Tropicana hotel, Elvis still in suit and tie, and Bebe borrowed her girlfriend's car. "At that time he had never used any drugs and I got him to smoke pot with me. So all we did was drive around all day, you know, laughing." The cultural shock on Elvis of all this is incalculable. They cruised Sunset Boulevard, playing tapes of The Beatles and Cheap Trick – "he knew every lyric" – and presenting a copy of *This Year's Model* to a hapless member of The Bay City Rollers, standing at a bus stop. Less happily, they were crawling around a recording studio on their hands and knees – it must have been powerful grass – when they literally bumped into the President of CBS records. "I'm sure they thought I was a horrible influence on him, because at that point there was only one person badder than me, and that was Anita Pallenberg. It was like the Punk and the Model – Beauty and the Beast. And the Press pulverised us."

Elvis had to take off to his next gig, but though – or because – they had not yet made love, he bombarded her with postcards, letters and poems. The first of these began on a note of doubt: "See us dancing cheek to cheek, but you won't remember me Wednesday week." As Bebe reveals, with the voice of experience, "He really knew how to pen a letter to a lady. Made me wonder if he hadn't done it before." By August, she had succumbed, and moved to London without her one-year-old daughter Liv (the result of a liaison with Aerosmith's Steve Tyler and now a world-famous actress). "I was like a mail order bride," Bebe recalls.

But Bebe was hardly the sort of girl to stay at home, and darn his socks. She ended up one night at Denny Laine's mansion, with new punk on the block Billy Idol. Someone spiked her drink, and she ended up sleeping on the pool table, but Elvis refused to believe her story. After another hard day recording *Armed Forces*, he got blind drunk. Bebe does not so much draw a veil over subsequent proceedings as illuminate them with a 100-watt bulb. "He hung his head over the side of the bed and threw up all over my shoes," she says. "That's when he confessed how much he loved me: 'I'll never be able to keep you the way you're accustomed.' Between puking, I was getting Shakespearean speeches. The next day, he would hardly speak to me."

A reconciliation with Todd Rundgren and even accusations that she was having sex with John Cooper Clarke led to further ructions, fuelled by Elvis's management, who saw her as a complication in Elvis's life. The pair finally broke up at Easter 1979, shortly after the brawl with Stephen Stills (See Chapter Five). Costello flew home to London, and out of her life, at least for the time being. "I was inconsolable," Bebe admits. "My parents had to come and get me, and moved me up to Maine. I had an emotional breakdown."

Costello's new (half) single was hidden on the flipside of Nick Lowe's 'American Squirm'. Listed under the name Nick Lowe And His Sound, it was a cover of Lowe's '(What's So Funny 'Bout) Peace, Love And Understanding', a song originally performed with Brinsley Schwarz in the mid Seventies. Some reviewers even commented about how Lowe was starting to sound like Costello! It was a brave, and deeply unfashionable song to sing. Elvis, a man previously associated only with fear and revenge now had a rock 'n' roll girlfriend, and seemed to be espousing the philosophy of Glastonbury Fayre.

The song was taken – as rumour had it – from the forthcoming album *Emotional Fascism*, or *Cornered On Plastic*: rumours differed. The choice of single led to predictions that the new record would consist solely of cover versions. Had Costello run out of songs already, or was this just some kind of ironic game? After all, the rear of the pic sleeve has a photo of Lowe standing in front of a window with a reflection of Elvis from the *This Year's Model* photo session near the bottom. All was not what it seemed.

Lowe's original is an exercise in irony and cynicism. Elvis's take on the song, though, transforms it to – in the words of Dave Marsh – "joyous acceptance and thinly veiled remorse". It is Costello's most openly emotive record: "Even on his soul reworkings, he's never left himself this uncovered." With Nieve's organ part "that sounds like it was developed on the field of battle", and The Attractions as good as any rock band in the world, Elvis comes over as passionate, angry, choking on tears of rage. When he sings 'each time I feel like this inside/it just makes me want to cry' you not only feel he might, but that you've cracked the code of his most obtuse songs as well."

In mid December, Elvis returned to a British stage, playing seven consecutive nights at London's cavernous, 2,000 seat Dominion Theatre (temporarily replacing the film *Star Wars*). It was the start of a nationwide tour, and all seven nights sold out. As an indication of Costello's position in rock's pecking order, this was a pre-emptive strike. Due, doubtless to Riviera's powers of persuasion, Costello and his band were the first rock act to play here. Among the small number of pop singers to previously appear here were Judy Garland and David Essex. A bizarre trio indeed, and it is difficult to think of three more different performers: torch songs with a death wish, twinkly-eyed pop with gypsy curls, and a sour faced bruiser, singing songs of hate and retribution.

Those attending found a free single of 'Talking In The Dark'/'Wednesday Week', on their seats. There were two support acts, both designed to annoy. Richard Hell, once of Television, and inventor of the whole ripped T-shirt, and short, vaselined hairdo look, led his band The Voidoids through some New York punk music, already feeling its age. Dylan sixty-six lookalike John Cooper Clarke, wrote motormouth poetry, which he carried around on scraps of paper, in an old plastic bag, and read aloud in an impossibly bored Manchester accent. It was a torrent of words too far, and Clarke was booed when I caught the tour at Southampton Gaumont.

At the Dominion, Nigel Cross of the wonderfully titled fanzine *Bucketful Of Brains* (named after a Flaming Groovies tune), reported audience reaction to Clarke as that of "stuffed dummies. I loved it, but the poseurs all headed for the bar." He found Costello's own performance "tired, sterile and boring", and left before the end. Richard Williams for the *MM* found Hell "simply and irredeemably awful", and Costello sloppy, not yet a "very reliable performer". In 'Pump It Up', "the drums finished a half bar ahead of Elvis. This led to recriminatory scowls all round, and Bruce Thomas appeared to kick his mic-stand into the photographers' pit." Costello used his introduction to 'Watching The Detectives' – lit to appear as if he was at home, watching the TV – to attack the audience; never the best of ideas.

Two letters to the *New Musical Express* the following week put the singer right. One is merely ironic: "We were so ungrateful, we took the free records and badges, we bought the T-shirts and programmes but we didn't go mad when you hit the stage." The other is a little more direct. "Listen, myopic one. The Ramones, The Undertones and The Rezillos don't need to tell me to dance – why should you?"

That (rightly) said, the faded, velvety grandeur of the Dominion was hardly the place to dance on one's seat, or even rip it up. It is far better suited to music which relied on nuance rather than brute strength to stretch out across the footlights, and this was not the kind of material which Elvis was offering. The Brodsky Quartet would be ideal for this setting. Ideal, too, for the likes of Richard Thompson, whom I saw play two extraordinary concerts there, one with Linda, one very much without.

Elvis would not appear here again until 1984, when his music had itself undergone a radical change. Meanwhile, 1978 ended on a brighter note, when *Melody Maker* made *This Year's Model* their album of the year. "Much of the excitement and exhilaration of the next year will be derived from watching him try" to produce something even better.

The title of Elvis's third LP, released early in January 1979, was changed at the last moment from "Emotional Fascism" to the slightly less contentious "Armed Forces", which meant much the same. The album had been recorded in "what we regarded as a very extravagant six weeks" at Eden studios, again with Nick Lowe at the controls, and early copies included a free EP with three songs recorded at Hollywood High School in California in June 1978. The UK version first emerged as a limited edition that includes an unusual fold out sleeve – designed by Barney Bubbles – and four colour postcards, marked "don't join".

On one, Bruce Thomas is blindfold, and plugged into his stereo. The cover boasts a stylised painting of African elephants, with birds circling overhead and mountains – or ice floes – behind. The ground is obscured by mist, from which emerges an oversize human ear. The album title appears underneath, in the kind of fussy typeface found in the cheaper kind of gift shop. The whole thing is like a fairground prize. The back sleeve shows various patterns, from which emerge colour sketches of soldiers on the march, their eyes hidden beneath red triangles, and tanks on manoeuvre. These in turn flap open to reveal a drawing of three sailors loading a huge gun. There are further geometric patterns – parodying op art, pop art, hard edge abstraction and abstract expressionism – over which the album title is again scrawled, this time in a style halfway between Jackson Pollock and Ralph Steadman.

The inner sleeve carries two photographs: the four "boys" stand on a suburban drive, with a tieless Elvis indicating that all this is his. Overleaf, a white-socked, fully clothed Elvis lies prone across a diving board, as if dead, with a black rubber ring floating on the pool surface below. Beneath, another body lies submerged. The sides are labelled "my place...or yours", with the motto "emotional fascism". Like an artist's palette, a series of boxes are labelled with all the colours of the rainbow. Each one is exactly the same shade of yellow.

As Elvis told *Record Collector*, the ideal vehicle for this information, "The *Armed Forces* sleeve was very involved. I loved it, it was very funny. We wanted to make it as impractical and ghastly as possible. There were kitsch elements of pop art in it, of trash art that you can buy from Woolworth's, of postcards that are disposable and you lose them. It was never supposed to live forever, so it's ironic that we've ended up reissuing the thing." The CD does not even attempt to mimic the open-out flaps though, something probably even beyond Hipgnosis! "That's why we put the first reissue package out in a cardboard box that falls apart after six months, and it's in horrible colours. We weren't trying to make it leather-bound and gold-embossed just because we were reissuing it. We wanted to make it as cheap and horrible as it was when it was issued originally." The CD inner booklet comes in the shape of a cross.

Record Collector, whose trainspotting name belies its cultural seriousness, digs deeper. Could not the working title of 'Emotional Fascism' have been the subtitle of his early career. Elvis at first seems not to follow the question. "It would have frightened the hell out of American record companies if we'd used it," he begins. "By that point, we were in a bubble, travelling very fast – we did three American tours in quick succession." The less personal nature of the lyrics reflected Elvis's own change in circumstances, with the successful artist plucked out as if with giant tweezers from his previous lifestyle.

This is a common occurrence, usually leading to a drastic decline in quality control with any newly breaking act rapidly using up its stockpile of material, and forced to write more in odd moments on the road. For Elvis, though, it became something of a liberation. "The period of your life where you're going to work and writing the songs on the train goes away and instead you're on a bus, looking out the window at a country you've never been to but have only read about, listened to and absorbed through your imagination and suddenly it's out there and it's something different to what you thought. You've got strange people offering you this, that and the other. It all gets mixed up."

So too do the influences which moulded the album, even more "post-modern" than its predecessor in its deliberate cultural mix of signifiers and all that jazz. "*Armed Forces* is a very modern record of its time – self consciously modernist," Costello explains. "We borrowed sounds from some records that we listened to constantly, almost obsessively, at the time. We were into strange behaviour! If you're sitting in a station wagon driving from Atlanta to Madison, Wisconsin and listening to Bowie's *Low* and *Heroes* and Iggy Pop's *The Idiot* and Abba's *Greatest Hits* over and over again, that's the kind of record you'll make. We'd be driving through the Appalachians listening to some ghastly synthesiser music made in Berlin. It was bound to mess you up. The reference points were bound to get unglued. In the end, we got terribly arrogant and confident, and that's why the record sounds like that."

Endless touring led to a road movie in words. Thus the Quisling Clinic was a real place, glimpsed in a trice and quickly written down. "It just sounds good," he says, "something out of a Forties Nazi film." Such references are like little bombs thrown into the listener's imagination. Many of the phrases in *Armed Forces* sound like song titles in their own right. "You get a lifeboat mentality when you tour…who shall we eat first! You can only write what's in your head, and I had these jumbled images, filtered through travel, drink, drugs, whatever…."

The reviews reflected how good a job he had done in putting these images back together again, in a new and unsettling pattern. In *Record Mirror*, Sheila Prophet found the "bitter bite" of earlier albums exchanged for "depth and subtlety and new textures". A shame, then, that the review was called "Swell El". Janet Maslin in

Rolling Stone described Elvis's new songs as "short, blunt compositions that don't demand to be taken seriously", and therefore could be. Tony Rayns' review in *Melody Maker* was titled "Elvis: A Compulsive Confusion", and he found no guiding concept, but a "more relaxed display of energy and precision". In *NME*, Charles Shaar Murray did. His piece was titled with a brilliant pun, worthy of its subject: "OUT GO: The Politics Of Impotence. IN COMES: The Impotence Of Politics".

Costello's early persona of angry wimp was long gone. "The majority of the songs here are aimed at institutionalised violence, but the theme underlying the entire collection is totalitarianism," Murray says. The album expresses compassion for the victims, "as well as terror and rage towards the criminals". The only problem is that Elvis himself – and his management team – are using this very LP as a bid for rock domination, and perhaps more besides. "Nick Lowe as Minister of Culture?" Murray might seem a little paranoid, though immersion in the album is enough to do just that. He does, however, put his finger on the tendency which led to journalists being beaten up, and racist remarks made in a motel bar. The Attractions too were an armed force.

Simon Frith contributed a piece to the "Consuming Passion" section of *Melody Maker*, which also deals with this change of attack. Subbed "Elvis switches targets", he compared him with Randy Newman, both serious songwriters, one nasty, the other weary. "Elvis reaches us via more production companies than the average American film (though it's all the same old Warner Communications in the end). Elvis commissions pompous sleeves and wants to be alone. Elvis swats cameramen and draws the press as moths to a flame. Elvis doesn't think his audience appreciate him, and I think Elvis is a creep."

For all that, the new album reveals him as a consummate writer. "His punning sets up resonances, ripples of verbal possibility", using running analogies "like a soul singer". His best songs "pull the comfort out of cliches". Here, he is using war words for domestic strife: the album should be retitled "Home Front", or "Behind The Wahing Line". Most heartening is the way that "the words rhyme with more compassion" here.

'Accidents Will Happen', the opening track on *Armed Forces*, opens with two words sung by Elvis intimate and solo – "Oh, I" – then the band power in. It was described by Charles Shaar Murray as "an ornate, melodic and exquisitely danceable pop song designed to lull American record executives into a state of false security", with chiming guitars and harmonies, like a cross between The Byrds and The Beatles. It is addressed to a Bebe Buell figure, bruised in love, who is first the tease and then the victim. The final verse seems to switch around again: surely only a man can be "well hung". There is a wonderful description of sex, rising up "in the sweat and smoke like mercury", and a final refrain of "I know" repeated, like a mantra.

The real subject of the song seems to be Costello himself, confused by the new range of sexual possibilities which fame has brought him. Elvis's voice is richer than before, possibly double-tracked, with odd intonations. 'People' sounds like Michael Howard used to pronounce it while Home Secretary, a comparison which neither would welcome.

'Senior Service' has a tune which spirals upward like cigarette smoke, making Elvis's voice sound like a chuckle. The central pun links the brand of untipped fags of that name with Her Majesty's Navy, but the song is really about office politics.

'Oliver's Army' works on all kinds of levels, but became a hit because everything coheres: the brilliant tune, and the way the bass intersects with the drums with the keyboards with the vocal chorus. Its jauntiness belies the underlying rage. The Irish, "white niggers" for whom Elvis talks as an angry representative, suffered the first of their many massacres at English hands under Oliver Cromwell. Cromwell is the nearest English equivalent to Napoleon: both men worked their way up through army ranks to become dictator, ruling with "armed forces". Ironically, neither left a proper successor, and their popularist regimes yielded to a return of the monarchy.

'Big Boys' is Elvis Costello by numbers, a song about what Murray describes as "sexual fascism". The opening sounds like OMD, then martial drums come in, and Elvis's voice grows whiney. Parts of the song sound as if the needle has stuck.

I will never forget hearing Costello sing an acoustic version of 'Green Shirt', shortly after it was written, and wondering quite what he was on to think up songs this bleak and scary. The sheer *jouissance* of Elvis's vocal, here and then, suggests some kind of complicity in the world depicted here, straight out of *1984*, or a Britain where Hitler won the Battle of Britain. Oswald Mosley would be less of a joke, in such a society.

The song opens with harpsichord – Stones, circa 1966 – and a different keyboard later sounds just like the pizzicato trumpet in 'Penny Lane'. The song predicts the growth of chat/sex lines, and was apparently inspired by newscaster Angela Rippon, whose stern features – like those of a dominatrice – fuelled many a teenage fantasy. She was in this sense a kind of Joan the Baptist for Mrs Thatcher. Murray describes the song as "a muted claustrophobic essay in paranoid crystal-gazing" which exactly captures the sealed nature of the sound.

'Party Girl' is the nearest to a love song that Elvis has come to since 'Alison' and in many ways more tender. Circumstantial evidence would suppose it to be about Bebe Buell, although she herself denies it. Where, therefore, are all the songs of devotion to Mary Costello, the artist's wife, and mother of his son? Elvis's vocal is wistful, with almost subliminal background chorus, and an echo of *Abbey Road* at the end. The middle section is beautiful, like a Hollywood tear-jerker. Charles Shaar Murray challenges Linda Ronstadt to record this song. I'd prefer Rod Stewart myself, shot away now as a songwriter, but still the best interpreter of a tender lyric going.

'Goon Squad' has an intro straight out of the Thin Lizzy school of romantic raunch. After all, Lynott did fill in on bass a year before. Murray describes the song, memorably as "a noisy howl of political disgust which bears an unfortunate resemblance to what might conceivably occur if Status Quo and ELP were forced to drink gin and snort speed for forty-eight consecutive hours and then jam at the bottom of a very large oil drum". They don't write 'em like that any more! As to the song, the lyrics flirt the boundaries of bad taste – "no-one's going to make a lampshade out of me" – while parodying Allan Sherman's parody 'Hello Mother, Hello Father', about a spell at boys' camp. For the final verse, Costello's voice sounds as if barked through a megaphone, which both fits the song – he is, after all, supposed to be a military policeman – while recalling John Lennon on 'Tomorrow

Never Knows'. Who said that Oasis were the first band to creatively rip off The Beatles. The band seem to explode, literally, during the chorus, and Nieve's organ goes berserk at the end, into atonality.

'Busy Bodies' mates the riff from Roy Orbison's 'Oh Pretty Woman' with half the tune of 'A Whiter Shade Of Pale', to present a jaundiced view of the mating game. The ending evokes 'Heroes And Villains'. There are lots of double-entendres, and no heart, which is the point.

'Sunday's Best' has been compared with John Cooper Clarke's 'You'll Never See A Nipple In The Daily Express', as fellow desecrations of the news media. Both writers have a great nose for the sordid: "readers' wives". Playing waltz time in strict tempo, the band sound like a merry-go-round, while Costello sings cheerily with a "deft acerbity which one applauds even as it chills", or so Murray reckons. It is like a rehearsal for the Falklands conflict, with its fatuous "Gotcha" headlines. The chorus refers to a medical check up, presumably for newly conscripted youth, from a nation about to go to war.

'Moods For Moderns' is a pastiche of Booker T, overlaid with what Murray describes as "an oddly disturbing ghost of a song". New wave, by numbers, though the chorus is again Beatleish in the extreme. The lyrics are opaque, possibly a farewell to a long-suffering wife.

A great track to dance to, all the same. 'Chemistry Class' is a more meditative take on the same theme, about the chemical attraction between two people, and how it can then fall apart. There are some odd sound affects, as if the smooth reception of the music is subject suddenly to a spot of interference. One reviewer describes this song as being about "dark fun", and there is a perverse sense of enjoyment through mutual pain. The "final solution" is of lovers parting, but a darker meaning obtains, with images of butchers' knives and human garbage. Here, the penultimate track, is a reply to the first, 'Accidents Will Happen'. Falling apart is a natural conclusion to falling in love. Otherwise, "some would never ever learn".

The final song in *Armed Forces* is the hardest of all. It is a picture of two long-time lovers, like beasts engaged in a fight to the death, as in Edwin Muir's savage and unresolved poem 'The Struggle'. Murray suggests some musical forbears. "Alex Harvey played this stunt as ghastly burlesque with his live 'Framed', Bob Geldof played it for light crisp irony in 'I Never Loved Eva Braun', but Costello plays it as pure, icy horror." Elvis again sounds smooth and triumphant, leering into the microphone, while his band exude self-confidence. Nieve plays bar-room piano, like a new wave Elton John.

The album's theme of public and private worlds melting into one – a lack of due privacy – comes to a head. There are bitter puns on wanting "to join the party" and "members", and a final verse set in a dating agency come concentration camp. The chorus, like a U2 anthem gone wrong, is one of dogged defiance. "I will return, I will not burn." Saint Paul considered that it was better to marry than to burn, but the marriage here is far from made in heaven. It is a song from hell.

The idea for the album's new name supposedly came from Pete Thomas. The songs are a hotline to the unconscious, capturing the disjunction of a band on the road. As Nick Lowe told Radio One, "There was nothing more fantastic than to be in an outfit like that: spoiled rotten. To be successful and yet also to be an outsider. You felt you were still an underdog, though you weren't. You were staying in good hotels, playing in big places. People would get outraged if you only played for half an hour, they'd start ripping the place up. Nowadays, people would be relieved." He also remembers Elvis appearing in his hotel room in Tucson, Arizona with two songs that he had just written that day, 'Party Girl' and 'Accidents Will Happen'. "I couldn't believe it – in the midst of this mayhem – he seemed to be getting better and better. I was staggered…"

Elvis himself remembers being stuck in a traffic jam in LA, in the middle of an eight-line highway, and "these archetypal blondes" in an open-topped convertible, shouting their recognition. "There was no real hit single. It just seemed to happen from the album as a whole. It wasn't concentrated on the one song."

Here, too, was a whole civilisation rapidly losing its bearings. The album was literally ahead of its time, a prelude to the 1980s and beyond, where all the old certainties were up for grabs, and up for sale. For the army, read the market economy, and the whole incoming cult of "management". The sort of people who would be sent off to luxury hotels and then paint-ball each other, or split into teams to erect a canoe. Elvis was certainly *not* into self-control. "Taking stock wasn't what it was about, even if we had time. We made as good and as bad a job as anybody could have done, in terms of fucking it up."

As a full page advert in *Rolling Stone* put it, apocalyptically, "Where were you during the big one? World Elvis Costello Album Three." The new superstar poses in the studio, in leather jacket and closed eyes behind dark glasses, electric guitar slung around his neck. It could be Dylan circa 1965. On the wall behind, someone has scrawled "scabs", strike-breakers or scars healing. The matching advert in *NME* offered £1.20 off the album to shoppers visiting Our Price. In *Melody Maker*, Elvis holds a machine gun, not a guitar, with the barrel in his mouth, as if about to blow his own head off. By his side, a hand grenade is missing its pin. "Pay Attention" and "Be Mercenary", captions advise, "Get Armed Forces".

Various outtakes and alternative tracks later emerged. Costello's gruff-voiced cover version of '(What's So Funny 'Bout) Peace, Love And Understanding' replaced 'Sunday's Best' on the US pressing, as did his intimate take on Rodgers and Hart's 'My Funny Valentine', supplanting 'Oliver's Army'. Both sides of the single given away free at the Dominion were studio outtakes. 'Talking In The Dark' ticks like a clock, then moves into a 'Penny Lane' pastiche. The words are fairly direct – "when the barking and the biting is through". 'Wednesday Week' sounds like The Animals, reedy organ riffs, curt guitar and Elvis a second Eric Burdon, spitting aggression. The song is another front line despatch from the sex war. There is nothing as common as a tune, until the slow middle section, which seems to be from another, better, song.

'Tiny Steps' first appeared as the B-side of 'Radio, Radio'. A film crew had wanted to record the new sound, and Elvis launched into this song, in which "for reasons I cannot explain we elected to sound as much like our *last* record as possible. Not without justification, they made their escape, and the film was never completed." It is one of Costello's more bizarre lyrics – which is really saying something – about desire turning infantile,with a tune that grips and twists like a cobra. The mood changes border on the sinister. 'Clean Money' – with Dave Edmunds on backing vocals – is one minute and fifty-seven seconds of mayhem and cossack shouts which did not surface publicly until 1980. Its chorus of "love for tender" was recycled as a different song on the next album.

'Oliver's Army' was itself almost left off the British pressing too. As Elvis later reveals, "We had the rhythm track, but no-one was holding it together, and Steve said, 'What about if I do the piano from Abba's 'Dancing Queen'. That was the thing that made it." The power of octaves. As Dave Marsh wrote in *The Heart Of Rock And Soul*, the single works on all levels, as a "grand melodic pop song, as a quirky political comment on imperialism and as a series of not quite opaque puns". The speaker could be either a man trying to recruit unemployed kids into the British army, or a banker "offering an oligarch prosperity at the price of independence".

Before January was out, *Armed Forces* had hit the Number Two spot in the UK album listings, and was also racing up the US charts. As Nick Lowe observed, "A lot of Americans found punk hard to identify with. I think with myself or Elvis or Parker or Dury the approach is a lot easier for Americans to understand. There is almost an over reaction – they like us too much, because they've been dying to get cracking but can't relate to The Damned."

On a rare day off during his UK tour, Elvis rejoined Nicky Horne at Capital Radio, to play some more of his favourite records. His choice was a mixture of the weird and wonderful, ranging from the Left Banke's heartbroken 'Walk Away Renee' – its baroque string section a pointer to his own future – to the derided Bay City Rollers. He chose their cover version of Will Birch's warm-hearted 'Rock And Roll Love Letter'. The Records' original was better musically, but Elvis was making a point, that you should never pigeonhole or dismiss any musicians, just because of the hype surrounding them.

He also chose songs by The Jackson Five and The Jam, whose lead singers would both later go on to glorious solo careers, thus proving his credentials as a pop prophet. He also delved into the past, with choice Sixties Britpop like Sandie Shaw's 'Girl Don't Come' – long before Morrissey "rediscovered" her. A record which looked past and forward simultaneously was *NME* journalist Chrissie Hynde's band, The Pretenders, giving a dramatic retread to The Kinks' 'Stop Your Sobbing'. Nick Lowe had produced the session, with Costello paying for the studio time out of his own pocket.

Between records, Elvis admitted to Horne that the Dominion

residency had been a mistake. "Bored" with rock venues like the Hammersmith Odeon and Rainbow, he had tried for an upmarket venue, but then found its plushness too constricting.

A review by Paul Rambali in the *NME* of one of those gigs chimes with my own memories of the tour as a whole, with Elvis saying to his restrained audience, "I feel like I ought to do my shirt and tie up," which he did. Gone were the nights of him playing virtually a whole show of new songs. "There's scant sense of a person bursting with his muse," rather that muse had now become "just a package, an addition". Two bad signs were Elvis bating his audience, and those same fans applauding the stage lights, "oh so cleverly orchestrated washes of pop art", like a series of Warhol's Marilyn Monroe silkscreens.

The last date on his tour, at the tail end of January, found Costello at the far more congenial – and unseated – Hammersmith Palais, a former haunt of his father with Joe Loss, and a place where band and audience could properly let themselves go. For Penny Valentine, appearing an hour later than expected, but playing for a full seventy-five minutes, with three encores, Elvis seemed now to want his audience to like him. "He still can't manage to smile, though – thank God." She noted his loud checked coat, and kipper tie, and the way "he still uses his left hand to express whatever it is his face quite obviously doesn't/can't". But Elvis has lost something: "He's stopped writhing on the floor."

Charles Shaar Murray felt much the same. "The set was chilled and despairing. The response was warm but damp." He puts much of this down to sheer exhaustion. "Elvis and his boys are completely dead on their feet. Shagged out, wiped out, drained. Trying to be dynamic, but the starter won't start. There's only so far you can pump it up." Dave Edmunds came onstage for a final 'Mystery Dance'.

Nick Kent had joined the tour earlier, at Sheffield, and found the band "magnificent", with their cover version of 'I Stand Accused' a particular highlight. After the gig, Elvis refused him an interview, attacking the *NME* as having become "cheap and offensive", particularly in the revelations it had made about Bebe Buell. Kent tries instead a four-way conversation, with Richard Hell and John Cooper Clark, but both soon leave, and he has only asked Elvis one question when a courtier informs Kent that it's time to depart, with a degree of menace. "I look at Costello, who sits there smiling inscrutably, and I realise that I've been set up. The whole thing has been a performance impeccably acted out, with Costello the likely instigator. He'll probably get a song out of it."

Being like all journalists at heart a truffle hound, Kent does nevertheless discover some scraps of information from others in the party. Costello has all the songs for his next album written, and material for another three LPs already prepared. Bruce Thomas, with whom he rooms – maybe the reason they have since fallen out, familiarity breeding contempt – confides that Costello is "an insomniac who spends the sleepless nights feverishly composing. He is a workaholic. "The only thing I'm worried about is him having a heart attack at twenty-six," he says. "He's driving himself insanely hard." If not, the band are planning a feature film, along the lines of *Help!*, for which the desert island video of 'Oliver's Army' is a tester. A script is already written. Twenty years on, the world still waits, though Elvis *was* to appear in *Spice World*, based on much the same idea!

Early February saw the release of 'Oliver's Army' as a single, climbing within a month to Number Two in the charts. This proved to be a mixed blessing. As Elvis told Radio One, "The tour that gave me the heebie jeebies was when 'Oliver's Army' was a hit." It was as if a barrier had been erected between him and the audience. "Before, we were all in it together, then suddenly this celebrity has been visited on us. You'd play some places and people would look dumbstruck that you were actually there – previously they'd been throwing stuff, gobbing on you, suddenly we were in showbiz. I was ready to pack it in, to be honest. Pete Thomas talked me out of it."

The laid-back drummer confirmed this, without overdue concern. "He was always going to pack it in, about three times a week, since the word go," he recalls. "I said once, 'You can't give up, because all people will have then is The Boomtown Rats!" That certainly hit home: Bob Geldof's combo were nothing more – or less – than Sixties R&B, updated, with Geldof playing Jagger. It certainly brought Elvis to his senses. "He owed it to people. He's got an incredible power of bouncing back. He'll apologise to everyone, say, 'Right, let's get on with it.' He's capable of getting out." Absent or not, Costello had already been accorded the sincerest form of flattery – imitation. Joe Jackson, with the fundamentally amiable but lyrically sharp 'Is She Really Going Out With Him?', which reached Number Thirteen in the summer, was merely the first of many who would seek to adopt – and tame – Elvis's aggression.

Over in the USA, the Grammy awards set the pattern for rejecting Elvis's work – he should worry – by picking the subsequently unknown A Taste Of Honey as Best New Artist at the twenty-first annual awards, with Costello to choose from. Unbloodied, The Attractions had already set off for their fourth tour of the States, unaware of the nemesis that lay in wait, somewhere out on those endless highways.

CHAPTER FIVE

motel matches

The Armed Funk US tour, his fourth American circuit,was Costello's most exhausting yet. The support act for the tour was Ray Campi And The Rockabilly Rebels, a retro act signed to Radar. They name-checked heroes like Carl Perkins and the original Elvis, while mocking modern Nashville in lyrics like "sounds like they've had too much rehearsal/now it's time for the big reversal". Just the sort of thing that would be also said of *Almost Blue*, a few years down the line.

Opening on 6 February in Seattle and concluding at Dallion gym, Princetown in mid April, the itinerary took in the usual mixture of universities, civic theatres, arenas and opera houses, with most gigs sold out well in advance. Elvis played a standard fifty-minute set, ten minutes less if it suited him, with no encores. The standout show was at the Palomino Club – a country and western club in North Hollywood – where John McFee made a guest appearance on steel guitar, and Elvis tailored his set accordingly. As Paul Green reported, he covered Jim Reeves' 'He'll Have To Go', and "a version of a macabre novelty by Leon Payne, 'Psycho', about a twisted individual with a penchant for killing". Elvis censored himself, replacing the final line "Mama, why don't you wake up" – he's killed her, too – with the less offensive "mama, better let them lock me up". Even this set lasted no more than an hour, with one encore.

Something was about to give. Elvis went down with a stomach bug in Dallas – perhaps its cause was partly psychological, his body declaring UDI before the predicted heart attack had a chance to strike him down. To Jake's fury, a whole week's engagements had to be cancelled.

Stoking up the pressure still further, Columbia had arranged that each gig be unofficially sponsored by a local radio station – even if it was one which had not shown any prior interest in Elvis – and then broadcast exclusively by them (a bootlegger's gift). Corporate rock in all its monopolistic glory. It was an accident waiting to happen, given the sentiments of 'Radio, Radio'. On 6 March, in St Louis, Missouri, and during a rendition of that very song, Elvis made an unflattering remark about KSHE, the sponsor of that night's concert. He had already dedicated 'Accidents Will Happen' to "all the boys at radio station KADI", a rival channel which had given far more airtime to the new album, and had tipped him off to what was going down.

Now he dedicated his final number to "all the local bastard radio stations that don't play our songs – and to KSHE". *Billboard* described it as "one of the biggest slams ever hurled by a performer at a concert host". A KSHE executive declared himself "upset and shocked that a performer would behave in such an unprofessional manner", as if talking about an errant employee. That was Elvis off the KSHE playlist, for starters, and the news soon spread.

Rumours also began that Elvis was short-changing his audiences. With a tour schedule of fifty-three gigs in sixty-nine days, the band played short sets. They caused a near riot in Seattle, where ear-bleeding white noise had to be played through the house PA to clear the hall. Feedback as an aggressive act was first employed by The Who and The Velvet Underground. Hendrix tinkered with it, The Jesus And Mary Chain made it a career. Neil Young used it as a kind of catharsis for the Gulf War, sculpting a whole album, *Arc*, while Lou Reed put a scratchy drone onto four sides of vinyl and called it *Metal Machine Music*.

The Seattle manoeuvre was not art, in any of those senses, but sheer aural terrorism, worthy of *Clockwork Orange*. The undertow of violence – *Armed Forces* for real – spilled over to the road crew, dressed in army-surplus chic, who would beat up anyone trying to illegally capture the gig on tape or camera, or excited enough to invade the stage. No wonder Elvis was so obsessed with fascism in his current lyrics: his tour party seemed to exemplify it.

There was also the suspicion that Columbia was not fully behind its new star, especially when they refused Riviera the upfront cash to book Shea Stadium – forever associated with The Beatles, and thus a challenge for each new pretender to their crown. He had received 25,000 applications for free tickets at a New York venue, shades of Altamont, and where better? Jake's response was to dispatch a vanload of shovels to the executives concerned, with the curt message that "if you *really* want to bury my act I thought you could do with some help". This, of course, only made matters worse.

On 15 March, the shit really hit the fan, a PR nightmare that every spin-doctor's shovel in the world could not have buried. As Riviera later told Nicky Campbell, these things always happen when the manager is away, and unable to give advice. Netherthless, it was an accident waiting to happen (and Jake's own comments suggest exactly why).

"He was resented, people were hoping for something," he says. "Because they don't have access they resent his talent and his driven workload, so they're waiting to knock him off his pedestal. It's the same with anyone who won't put up with the bullshit of the music industry.

"We didn't do encores, we didn't do interviews, we just came and played and left your town. There wasn't any" (here he adopts a greasy, American accent) "gee great to see you, you're fantastic, love you baby. The trouble is that when you say to journalists that my artist is too talented to talk to you – instead of talking to you and the *Columbus Gazette* he could be writing a song, which is more important in the great scheme of things? – they don't like it. In fact, they hate it."

The band had played a return gig at the Agora Club in Columbus, Ohio. Afterwards, they checked into a nearby Holiday Inn, to find another tour bus parked outside. It turned out to belong to Woodstock veteran Stephen Stills and band, exactly the kind of act which punk had aimed to do away with. Stills had formed Buffalo Springfield with Neil Young in the mid Sixties, where their duelling twin lead guitars helped set the agenda for late Sixties rock. Stills' precise picking, and Young's wild flourishes, formed a musical dialogue which proved influential to everyone from Moby Grape to

Thin White Rope. Stills wrote one of the greatest protest songs in rock, 'For What It's Worth', about the riots on Sunset Strip. He and Young had been rivals since teenage days in Canada, and their clashing personalities were carried into Crosby, Stills, Nash And Young, for a while the biggest band in the world, and the short-lived Stills-Young band. Neil Young bailed out of both.

After the break-up of his band Manassas, Stills was on the skids creatively, with his songwriting gifts atrophied. He also had a notorious taste for illicit substances, which he carried around in a customised briefcase; "Old tin nose," as Elvis supposedly called him that night. Among his current band was Bonnie Bramlett, who had once sung in The Ikettes, with Ike and Tina Turner, and had just emerged from a clinic for recovering alcoholics. Her partnership with husband Delaney in the late Sixties produced good-time, egoless music which had inspired Eric Clapton enough – after he left Cream – to join for a while as rhythm guitarist. The kind of communal music, in fact, that had also inspired the likes of Flip City. Both musicians had seen better days, and their music – once, briefly, as fiery as Elvis's – was now slipping down the one-way slope into "adult orientated rock".

As Pete Thomas reminisced for Radio One, "There was this Holiday Inn in the middle of nowhere. I can remember seeing this other bus, and the general feeling was "another group". It was as if sailors came into harbour and saw another boat there. And then, woah, 'It's Stephen Stills!' The old school sort of thing. It's only schoolboy sport. It didn't seem that unreasonable." There was a little more to it than that. Fred Schruers was reporting on the tour for *Rolling Stone*. "A mixture of paranoia and arrogance made the Armed Forces tour party as mean and as squirrelly as any platoon of marines trapped behind enemy lines." Roadies were dressed in combat fatigues, and Jake had even labelled the tour bus "Destination: Camp Lejune", in letters a foot high. This was the Marine Corps training camp, as commemorated in Stanley Kubrick's film *Full Metal Jacket*, and memories of the Vietnam defeat were still tender. "By turns petulant and rabid", Elvis and his cohorts "did not seem equal to the grand military metaphors" of Riviera's campaign. "They seemed, rather, to be conducting a messy police action."

Bruce Thomas understood better how confrontational Elvis and his party could appear. "We were still doing our myth building and being objectionable and new wave," he explains. Greil Marcus had encountered the same pig-headedness after the Berkeley gig, from which Costello and Bebe Buell had to be given a backstage escort past rioting fans. Marcus had filed the best report back from Altamont, so knew about intimidation. He therefore committed to Riviera offering him bodily injury, after Costello had refused to talk to him. "Jake's just a little thug," he concludes. "The concert was meant as an insult and performed as such, and people caught on."

Back at the motel, Costello accepted Stills' good natured offer to join him for a drink, but tension soon set in. As Bruce Thomas recalled, "Good natured banter gradually got an edge to it, and that edge became sharper: 'We're over here for your women. The Byrds ripped off The Beatles, Jimi Hendrix had to come to England, The Beatles had to sell you Tamla Motown.'" Of course, it could be said in turn that the new wave started with The Stooges and The New York Dolls, or that Declan MacManus's early repertoire was almost entirely American, as was the singing voice which he had adopted. These things are about kindred spirits, not geography. The most heartfelt punks were The Saints, "stranded" in Australia.

This was not, though, a debate in the Oxford Union, or even back in Stag Lane. Allan Jones wrote a brilliant report of what ensued, appropriately enough for *Uncut* magazine. A local fan had asked Costello what he thought of the American race, and Elvis did not prove himself to be a natural diplomat. "We hate you. We just come here for the money. We're the original white boys and you're the colonials." He went on to describe the land of the free as being a nation of "flea-bitten greasers and niggers". According to *Rolling Stone*, he now turned to Stills' fine percussionist Joe Lala, and called him a "greaser spic." Stills himself now grabbed Costello and gave him a good shaking, before storming out of the bar.

The argument now moved back to music, with Bonnie Bramlett accusing Elvis of stealing from the rich treasure house of black American music, to which the creator of next year's *Get Happy!!* would have to plead guilty as charged. Instead, Costello allegedly dismissed James Brown as a "jive-ass nigger" and Ray Charles as

LET THEM ALL TALK – THE MUSIC OF ELVIS COSTELLO

"nothing but an ignorant, blind nigger". Bramlett, herself white but steeped in the blues and soul, could take no more, and Bruce Thomas watched her take a swing at Elvis, knocking "him off his stool, succeeding in dislocating his shoulder. She gave him quite a good wack." Elvis disputes this, saying that she missed, and five of her road crew did the damage.

A drunken pushing match ensued, with beer bottles smashed and flourished, and punches thrown. The newly aggressive Bruce Thomas was in the centre of the action. Elvis picked himself up off the floor, "shaken but not stirred", and stumbled off to bed. Whoever swung the punch, Costello turned up at a concert in Cleveland the next day with his arm in a sling, which he joked was the result of a bust-up with Bonnie Bramlett. He and his entourage thought that the matter was concluded, though he was genuinely remorseful once he had sobered up.

"I was completely drunk, and I tried to outrage them by racist remarks, trying to shock them by criticising people so beyond criticism," Costello confesses. "Unfortunately, Americans do not share my irony. My words were way off, no excuse. They had the desired effect, to start a fight. I didn't think anything more about it, and certain members of that entourage took it upon themselves to inform the American liberal press, that I was a covert racist and we were in deep trouble." His later comment that Bramlett had "made one reputation off of one EC" – Eric Clapton – "and she's fucking well not going to get more publicity off another one", was not exactly the most gracious of apologies. It was also counter-productive. Bramlett had called up virtually every newspaper, wire service and magazine on the East Coast, giving her version of the events, and calling for retribution. Her wish was soon granted.

Armed Forces had jumped into the *Billboard* Top Ten, the day after the brawl, but as news of the incident spread, it plunged down the charts. Many radio stations were now boycotting Elvis's records, and he was picketed by Rock Against Racism, handing out leaflets in which, had they bothered to look, included a photo of Elvis at his free gig in Brockwell Park. Costello half-admitted to Radio One that it was an accident in waiting. "I was pretty wound up, we were really in a blinkered mentality. I wasn't in the best of shape. I had a degree of arrogance about it. There were elements of the liberal press in New York that was waiting for this kind of thing. They proceeded to get the wrong end of the stick and beat me about the head with it."

By April, when the Costello show finally reached New York, the singer had received over 150 death threats, no joke in a city which would see John Lennon blown away the following year, by a fan with a grudge. Indeed, the furore was much like that following Lennon's comments that The Beatles were more popular than Jesus. Americans are a race whose emotional directness render them immune to irony, and Scouse wit (with its underlying bitterness) was, literally, a foreign language to them.

As he later said, in a form of apology, "I'm sure everybody's had occasion to go to absolute extremes – even to say things you don't believe. Ask Lenny Bruce." The trouble was that you couldn't. Bruce died a self-inflicted death, but one brought on by the way his extreme form of plain speaking led to penury, threats and cancelled live appearances. Phil Ochs was even more brutally honest, and finally hung himself after his career nosedived and a mysterious beating up wrecked his vocal cords. Free speech costs.

Ray Charles himself was sweetness and light, further twisting the knife. "Anyone could get drunk at least once in his life. Drunken talk isn't meant to be printed in the paper, and people should judge Mr Costello by his songs rather than his stupid bar talk." Even Fred Schruers, who covered all this for *Rolling Stone*, and thus broadcast it to the world, conceded that "one could forgive a lot from this knock-kneed, squinty-eyed wonder, who wrote songs that took our own sins, from imperialism to narcissism, and paraded them before us in all their shabby selfishness. The guy was clawing his own flesh." By now, though, no-one was listening.

Columbia called a press conference on the fourteenth floor of their New York office block, to try to clear the air, though the fact it was held at two hours' notice suggests that panic was beginning to set in. Elvis might just have saved things by grovelling.

A good PR would have had him announce a programme of good works in Harlem – with picture opportunities of Costello holding a basketball, surrounded by smiling black kids – or had him very publicly booking into the Betty Ford clinic, or would have flown over

Elvis's wife and son, and had him hug them on live TV, in contrite tears. Instead, he made things worse. "It was necessary for me to outrage these people with the most obnoxious and offensive words I could muster to bring the argument to a swift conclusion and rid myself of their presence," he recalls. "It worked pretty good; it started a fight." Proof of the old adage that if you are standing in a whole, it is best to stop digging.

Elvis is visibly shaking, and wears a dark jacket, white shirt, dark tie, as if for a courtroom appearance. He also sports a lapel badge which reads "desire me". Not many takers, that particular day. His manner is so disarmingly droll as to lull his questioners to sleep, but they are made of sterner stuff.

Robert Christgau asks if he cannot properly apologise, because "it's not your style". Chet Flippo asks how Elvis would have reacted had someone called *him* a "sawed-off limey poseur". He replies that someone just did. One insistent voice quotes back the "white niggers" line from *Armed Forces*, gratuitously misreading the song. Costello replies that if quoted out of context, it can make one look like anything from "an angel to...you know...*Adolf Hitler*". Another tormentor asks, "Were you crazed when you made this statement?" "I think I'm crazed all the time." There is one last assault. Richard Goldstein of the *Village Voice* yelps, "You made yourself unavailable. We couldn't reach you. You can't blame it on the press. It was you! It was *you!*" Costello loses his cool, and seems to be squaring up for a fight. "TAKE ME." Suddenly he is like a wounded stag, turning on the hounds which pursue him, damaged, dangerous and defiant.

Despite facing down his critics, Elvis's career in America has never fully recovered. The States wanted a new wave act with good tunes, and having found Costello too bitter a pill to swallow, embraced instead The Police, who were just then embarking on the same kind of intensive touring schedule, but with a more conventionally handsome lead singer, more upbeat lyrics (the later 'Every Breath You Take' was an aberration, genuinely threatening) and an image carefully "policed" by Miles Copeland, son of a former CIA operative. *Armed Forces*, for real.

Back home in England, the reports that did filter through seemed merely surrealistic, given Costello's passionate, and well-known anti-racism, not just in songs like 'Less Than Zero', but in his practical support during the early days of Rock Against Racism.

Even Ross MacManus broke silence – like Joe Strummer's dad being a career diplomat, singing for Joe Loss was not exactly rebel chic – to phone *NME*. "Elvis is no racist. His mother and I were always very strict on that point. The race issue was always very important in our house. It wasn't just something on the side, it was a central issue." He illustrates the point graphically. "Elvis's mother is a Liverpool lady who'd beat the fucking tar out of him if she thought he was turning racist." When younger, one of her best friends had been a Chinese girl who she would help out at work. "It never bothered her that she was writing Chinese laundry labels, she just accepted it."

Ross now works the cabaret circuit, and hears "all the Irish jokes and the Pakistani jokes, and I still think it's wrong". His nose was once broken during an argument he had with a trumpet player who made some racist remarks. The *NME* merely adds, rather tartly, that maybe Elvis "should be as careful about what he says when out drinking as he is about giving interviews".

Ross MacManus, Twickenham, also wrote to *Rolling Stone*, along much the same lines. "My grandfather was an Ulster Catholic, and as a child I lived in an area where bigotry was rife. So we are those white niggers." Adverts for furnished accommodation would often state "no blacks, no Irish". "I am passionately opposed to any form of prejudice. And El's mother and I were both branded as hotheads and Marxists or anarchists. So you can see that we don't have any chic, white liberal attitudes (and El has publicly despised the latter many times). This is the water that Elvis has been born and bred in."

The Armed Funk tour continued bloodied, but unbowed. Costello played two shows at New York's Palladium, supported by power poppers, The Rubinoos. As if in apology, his set opened with 'Peace, Love And Understanding', to which The Attractions added a rich, almost orchestral tone. Next up was the savage 'Two Little Hitlers', with an extra verse, but the *NME*'s Richard Grabel noticed that Elvis's stage persona was newly user-friendly. "Tonight he was actually smiling at the audience, and friendly." He even joked with them: "You're not going to be a boring, early show audience, are you?" There were other changes. 'No Dancing' had a disco beat,

'Alison' new words. His mask of amiability only cracked during 'Big Boys', when he broke off singing to snarl "everything is so provocative", then dancing to the front of the stage, using his guitar like a weapon. Since previous tours, the band had tightened up to become "a powerhouse in their own right", with Nieve soaring and jabbing organ fills in any musical gap that dared to appear.

Another reviewer compared Costello's stinging guitar work to The Voidoids' Bob Quine, whose piercing style later fuelled Lou Reed's live renaissance, and the magnificent *Girlfriend* album by Matthew Sweet. Elvis has more hair, but both guitarists certainly have the kind of visceral edge in which even a wrong note can sound right. The band now shared a sense of dynamics, slowing down to a temporary halt on 'Radio Radio', with Costello matching the audience's lethargy, until "the crowd's enthusiasm literally powered the concert into its feverish climax". All great gigs are a chemical balance between those playing and those played to, and Elvis was learning to trust his own fans, metaphorically throwing himself onto them – as Iggy Pop did literally – and waiting for a reaction.

The following evening, 1 April, Costello played three New York clubs on the same night, at four-hour intervals. The publicity gimmick was named "The April Fool's Day Marathon". Well, at least it wasn't a massacre. Band and roadies dashed between country hang-out the Lone Star, industry hang-out the Bottom Line, and Great Gildersleeve's, a "red light showcase on the Bowery, just a block from CBGB's". At the Lone Star, Elvis declared, "This idea of playing three clubs in one night is somebody's idea of an April Fool, and I know who that fool is."

At the Bottom Line, protesters outside the gig brandished placards that read "Kick him again, Bonn" and "Send Elvis back to computer school". Onstage, Elvis "shook himself like a snake's warning rattle, shook streams of sweat off his face. He grimaced and menaced." At Great Gildersleeve's, Roy Trakin found the intensity almost too much to bear: "Tensions were running high, and the small room could barely contain the energy." Among the highlights were a cover of The Merseybeats' 'I Stand Accused', sung with feeling, and a new reggae arrangement of Ian Dury's 'Roadette Song'. White reggae, of course.

Fred Schruers' attention was taken by Elvis's tour manager, Des

Brown, "snake hipped, expressionless", built like a steeplechaser,and on the look out for hidden cameras or tape recorders. "He is playing his nightly game of Search and Destroy the Film", and giving every indication that he could go crazy in the blink of an eye. Two Hell's Angels flank him as he pops open cameras and rips tape out of cassettes. Quite why the fans' natural desire for personal memorabilia should be treated with such undue savagery is not explained. There is still a climate of fear and intimidation.

"Two club bouncers thud past, bulldogging a thickset, grunting teenager out the door. The teenager's face has been severely beaten. Blood trails from his scalp and out of one ear." Fred asked him if the bouncers were responsible for beating him up. "He shakes his head no, eyes fixed on the door. 'About eleven guys,' he says." Just about the number of Elvis's road crew, some in green fatigues, some in plain clothes, all distinguishable by their "nose-picker boots". In the words of Ziggy Stardust, is this rock 'n' roll, or genocide?

The following night, Jake expresses concern about a forthcoming gig at the Tower Theatre, Philadelphia, within range of the Three Mile Island nuclear reactor. "I suppose they'll clear the Yanks out first, wot?" Elvis and his camp are sitting in an Indian restaurant, refusing to say much, though Bruce Thomas does call the three gigs in one night scam "more a matter of stamina than creativity". Steve Nieve is with his new girlfriend Farrah Fuck-it Minor. Elvis dines with Bebe Buell, while David Bowie sits at another table, leaving each other alone. Later, Fred stops Costello, flanked by two bodyguards, one "so unprepossessing that I am sure he can break bricks with his hand". Elvis's closing word in a short exchange is "asshole".

After playing small venues in New England, Costello flew home a wiser and older man, and would not attempt to tour the States until after an eighteen-month cooling off period. His last working duty in the USA was to film a brief cameo appearance in *Americathon* as Earl Manchester. It was originally intended that the soundtrack would be split between Elvis – with rare delights like 'Hoover Factory', 'Clean Money' and 'Dr Luther's Assistant' – and Meat Loaf (an odd combination, brain and brawn), but only two Costello tracks survive onto the final cut.

'Accidents Will Happen', newly ironic, emerged as a single in May, and soon grazed the Top Thirty. Its packaging reflected the latest brainwave from Barney Bubbles' twisted mind. Befitting the title, early copies of the sleeve, with its geometric, cartoon-like design, were manufactured inside-out. No loss, artistically. A different and better cover later replaced both, with a roughly dressed Elvis and band posing in front of a closed fish shop in Chicago. In hideous yellow, its facia reads in huge letters, "Get smart…FISH IS BRAIN FOOD".

The British press were, as ever, less interested in racism than the private lives of the stars, and it was rapidly reported that Elvis was reunited with Mary. They were photographed together at Dave Edmunds' wedding reception, where Jake Riviera was best man, and at the Hammersmith Odeon for a J Geils gig. Elvis seemed relaxed and friendly, keen to shake hands with fans, and sign autographs. The two-month respite from constant touring was obviously doing him good. As Mick St Michael commented, "The couple's recent trip to Paris might well have been a second honeymoon – even though, as Costello confessed to a well wisher, they'd seen The J Geils Band twice there too."

This new, relaxed Elvis even went home to Liverpool to see his mum, and played unbilled at a Radar reception, held on board the Royal Iris Ferry, 'cross the Mersey. A crowd of 400 saw Elvis and The Attractions act as bottom of the bill to local signings The Yachts – some of whose members later became The Christians – and Elvis's later musical collaborator and producer Clive Langer, a bill advertised as "The Cruise of the Century". Gone was the old aggression, to be replaced with friendly charm. "Hi there. We're a little nervous because we haven't played for a while, but we thought we'd come and surprise you."

NME's Kevin Fitzgerald notes that in the grey, afternoon light, the band look anaemic and unhealthy. It was probably the first time they had played in daylight since Brockwell Park. "Togged up like a teddy boy on the African Queen in a baggy white suit and crepes, Costello grins." They open with a Merseybeat classic, 'I Stand Accused', accompanied by lots of smiles and "sweaty foreheads". Costello reveals his Liverpudlian accent on his minimal chat between songs, "rolled 'r's sticking out like broken bottles in a sandpit". The ship is rolling too, and some of the audience are about to see their lunches again.

Onstage, Elvis is receiving respectful applause rather than wild abandon, even for '(I Don't Want To Go To) Chelsea', in its new dub version: "the drums are ringing, spidery and epileptic" intersecting with taut guitar. Elvis's bottom teeth are showing, in a mock grimace. Suddenly the drums tumble like "oil drums dropped down a lift shaft", and lead guitar leads the melody home. He announces that he and his band "are getting into another boat because we're entering dangerous waters". 'Accidents Will Happen' concludes the set, and Elvis shouts out, "Thanks...see you in the bar."

Nick Kent was sitting in a first class compartment in a train bound for Lime Street, reading in *Rolling Stone* about how Elvis has sidestepped yet another journalist – leaving him with three quotes, "fuck off", "piss off" and "stick it" – when the lad himself puts his hand on his shoulder, in greeting. He is dressed like Bob Dylan, and seems amiable and relaxed. Kent meets Mary, "an extremely attractive bright girl with sandy coloured hair", and their son Matthew, his face almost hidden by a Fidel Castro hat. The name Bebe is not mentioned once during the three-hour journey, by anyone.

Costello reveals that the couple have been following The J Geils Band around Europe – he is mixing their latest album, *Sanctuary* – great name! – and even gives a brief Robert de Niro impersonation, for no apparent reason. They talk about *Americathon*. 'Hoover Factory' was taped two years before in a "make-shift four-track studio in Cornwall", when Elvis was first rehearsing with The Attractions. They briefly discuss the Ohio incident – "it was more like slapstick than anything" – and Elvis reveals that he has turned down front cover appearances on both *Rolling Stone* and *Newsweek*. "Why make life easy for yourself?"

Costello also found time to produce the first album by The Specials, a multi-racial band heavily influenced by ska and blue-beat, for Two-Tone. His production methods have been learnt at the feet of Nick Lowe – gimmick-free, just bash it down as live as possible – and the album still sounds fresh twenty years on. Dave Edmunds had asked Elvis to write a new song for *Repeat When Necessary*, his fifth solo LP. "He was in the studio at the time, and he whacked out 'Girls Talk' at a million miles an hour," Edmunds recalls. "It was a good song but it wasn't anything like the way it turned out. There are lots of different ways of doing it. I heard a supermarket version that was absolutely hilarious." Edmunds took the original demo, duetting on vocal with Nick Lowe over a rich bed of strummed acoustic guitars like a revamped Everly Brothers. Released as a single, by July this sweetened cover version was nestling at Number Four in the Top Twenty. Ironically, the B-side was Huey Lewis's 'Bad Is Bad', so that Costello was at last united with Clover's lead singer, on someone else's vinyl. Costello later reclaimed 'Girls Talk' for himself, using it to open his 1984 solo concerts. The *NME*'s Max Bell saw the song as "one on the nose for Bebe Buell".

The end of June saw Elvis and The Attractions embark on their next foreign jaunt, a five-date TV promotion mini-tour. They recorded a TV concert for the *Countdown* show in Amersfoort in Holland. The audience of sixty were the winners of a competition on Dutch radio. Fans were invited to send in an item which they thought Costello would like, and entries ranged from bike chains to imitation glasses.

The audience were told to react "enthusiastically", and each song was taped twice, just in case. Two days later, Elvis played a concert at the Theatre de L'Empire, broadcast in two parts on the TV series *Chorus*, then on to Madrid for a TV special, and back to Holland for the Pink Pop Festival. This was an open air show, compered by John Peel, for which Elvis donned a pink suit, but a sudden cloudburst left him, The Attractions and the 40,000 audience soaked through, with thunder crackling during 'Lipstick Vogue'. Other participants included The Police, Rush and Peter Tosh, a mixed bag indeed. The band then moved on to Brussels to appear on Belgian TV, headlining over exotica like Umberto Tozzi, Downtrip, The Misters, Doly Dots and Capital Letters.

Later in July, Riviera left Radar, in effect a distribution arm of WEA, to set up his new label, F-Beat (one can mentally add the missing "uck"), and ran straight into legal problems with WEA. Lacking a label to release any new product, Elvis made the most of his enforced holiday, attending concerts by Gang Of Four – a bunch of uptight Marxists, who somehow made that tension musically exhilarating – and Ian Dury And The Blockheads. He spent most of the next two months ensconced in the studio with The Specials.

At the tail-end of August, Costello and band set out for a five-dates

-in-five-nights tour of Scandinavia. In September, he appeared on Radio One's *Star Special*, as guest DJ. *MM*'s Richard Williams thought Elvis sounded "just like Elton John's more cynical younger brother", and – after alcohol had mellowed him – "like Elton John after a draw in the first-round away leg of the League Cup". Both come from the unfashionable outskirts of London, and served their apprenticeship on the rock circuit, even if Elton was a flamboyantly gay and Elvis a tortured straight, Elton an industry hack and Elvis an industry outsider. Elton imported Bernie Taupin to write his lyrics: Elvis wrote his own, and then some. After the news of Presley's death, though, Jake Riviera seriously considered changing his client's stage name to Elton Costello!

Williams identified in Elvis "a rock critic's mentality; he examines records carefully, cherishes ingenuity and originality, and feels a sense of sharp personal hurt when he's let down by people he admires, expressing his disappointment in sarcasm." Elvis had the same knack as a DJ as fellow mavericks John Peel and Andy Kershaw, mixing and matching, bringing together different modes of music. Thus, he played The Clash and Betty Wright, The Heptones and Jerry Lee Lewis, Robert Johnson and The Spencer Davis Group. His comments between tracks were terse. "The less said about Fleetwood Mac's fate, the better." "From the days when Nick Lowe would admit to knowing more than five chords." Soul music was a particular favourite: choosing tracks from *Dusty In Memphis*, and Otis Redding's 'Try A Little Tenderness' and Al Green's 'Tired Of Being Alone'.

Costello had earlier visited the Rock On shop in Camden Town, and invested £50 in a clutch of sweet soul music. Fuelled by these short bursts of emotion, he crossed back to Holland that October with The Attractions, producer Nick Lowe and engineer Roger Bechirian. The ensemble began recording sessions at a studio in Wisseloord, laying down a kind of rock 'n' roll encyclopedia.

There were two distinct recording sessions. The first, known to collectors as the "Get Happy" demos, feature eight songs of which only one has been released officially. 'Black And White World' appeared later on the US compilation *Taking Liberties*. Band and producer realised that these tracks were too much like what had gone before, "superior Jags", so struck off in a new direction. The second batch of "Get Happy" material includes the album as released, twenty hits of energy, and nine songs as yet unreleased, including cover versions of 'Slowdown' and 'First I Look At The Purse'.

Costello could have made retreads of *Armed Forces*, with diminishing artistic returns, but hefty commercial ones, for the rest of his career. *Get Happy!!* was the first of innumerable sideways moves and fresh challenges that Elvis was to set himself, and his admirers. It was a brave decision. As Jake Riviera told Nicky Campbell, "They chose to do that album in Holland, so I chose to go over for just one day. By this point, Elvis and The Attractions had decided that they were The Beatles, and they were going to do what they goddam pleased, just like they should do. It's their career at the end of the day. It's their prerogative to make as many mistakes as forward moves. Your job as a manager is to make sure that the artist gets paid their fee. If they then choose to have a bonfire in the lounge, that's totally up to them."

Nick Lowe recalls the studios as being just outside Amsterdam. "I remember the studio we were using was very Euro," he says. "It was difficult to make a record when what seemed like the Eurovision Song Contest was going on all around you. There were other studios in use. The other acts seemed so clean cut, with footballer haircuts: they all looked like Abba." They would poke their heads round the door, "fair dos, they knew something was going on, there was something in that room which they didn't care for. It was a strange atmosphere. We ran through about five engineers on that record: they got very upset about the way we were carrying on. It was pretty wild."

Nick cannot now remember – or chooses not to – much of what happened. Nothing could touch them. "It was like you had your foot flat down on the accelerator, it seemed like there weren't enough hours in the day. When we weren't recording an album we were touring, and behaving in the same irresponsible manner on the road. Swallowing life down. Guzzling life down. It was tremendous." By the same token, it was a time that could not possibly last for long. "Everyone was pretty fried when were making that record. It was like a snowball rolling down the side of a snow-covered hill."

Bruce Thomas recalls being "pretty far gone on Peruvian hay fever powder, and the rest of it. Pete and I used to stay up for nights on end and we'd turn up to the studio just gone. The worst thing was Steve

Nieve collapsed in a heap over his keyboards one morning. 'I can't play this monkey music any more, it's an insult to jazz.' I was worried at the time because I was seeing insects." Bruce had began seeing imaginary beetles – rather than Beatles – on the studio floor.

Pete Thomas puts all this down to the Nick Lowe school of most possible excitement in the studio, "which can only be taken to a certain level if sober, then gets a lot more interesting, if more erratic, when one introduces 'substances', or things to drink".

It would be some months before the results of this studio mayhem were unleashed. Meanwhile, cinema patrons that autumn had the mixed blessing of seeing Elvis make a cameo appearance, and singing 'Crawling To The USA' in *Americathon*, a comedy set in America two hundred years in the future, where a bankrupt state holds a telethon to pay off the national debt. The soundtrack also included '(I Don't Want To Go To) Chelsea' – not then released in America – along with songs by Nick Lowe, Eddie Money and The Beach Boys.

In early December, Elvis and The Attractions undertook a short tour of South West Europe, playing gigs in Cannes, Montpellier and Barcelona. They recorded promo clips for two forthcoming singles. The *NME* ran a special Christmas contest in which readers who successfully answered "trivial pursuit"-type questions about Costello would receive "the ultimate collector's item". It was a cassette entitled *Elvis At Home*, featuring the demo tapes young DP Costello recorded for *Honky Tonk* way back in August 1976, with the overall winner receiving the actual reel to reel tape. After strong managerial pressure, this prize was withdrawn, and substituted with the less exciting prospect of two days in the studio with Nick Lowe. Any reader who answered all eight questions correctly was instead sent a copy of the 'Talking In The Dark'/'Wednesday Week' single, along with a brace of tickets for a January 1980 gig at the Clarendon Hotel, Hammersmith. This was to be taped for a possible live album.

Get Happy!! was still being held up by legal shenanigans. The Specials tried to repay their debt to Costello by releasing his latest single, a cover version of Sam And Dave's 'I Can't Stand Up For Falling Down', on their own Two-Tone label. Thirteen-thousand copies were pressed up, and Capital Radio began giving the song massive radio exposure – no complaints from Elvis this time – until WEA issued another writ, and the records stayed firmly locked up in the warehouse. It was the first of Elvis's A-sides not to have been written by the singer, though the flip side presented his own version of 'Girls Talk'. From soul to country. Elvis also appeared on George Jones' album *My Very Special Guests*. He duetted with Jones – in separate studios – on 'Stranger In The House', and a director's chair with his name stencilled on the back appears on the record cover, alongside others labelled Waylon, Tammy, Emmylou, Linda, Paycheck, Willie (Nelson) and James Taylor.

CHAPTER SIX

trust me

Old wave met new wave at the tail-end of 1979, during the four Concerts for Kampuchea held at Hammersmith Odeon, as Queen and The Clash, The Specials and The Who, Wings and The Attractions, joined together for famine relief. Despite the rumours, The Beatles did not reform for the last night, but Costello had much of the sparkiness of the missing John Lennon, childminding in New York. "You've probably been eating turkey all week. So we've brought you a few more." Then straight into a set which half comprised new and unknown songs, and half new versions of old material. "The familiar shiny vinyl organ has been replaced by Steve Nieve pumping a Booker T croak from his Hammond, while the firm of B and T Thomas match the moods with appropriate Stax and Motown rhythms." Roy Carr's only complaint was that the lyrics to songs like 'High Fidelity' and 'Possession' were hard to decipher, but *that* never hurt Mick Jagger. After Wings' disappointing set, the night concluded with a giant "Rockestra", with Bruce Thomas on bass joining the likes of McCartney, Pete Townshend and Led Zeppelin, on an endless riff.

On 18 January, 1980, Elvis and The Attractions played a low key gig, just down the road, at an upstairs room at Hammersmith's Clarendon Hotel. A hand-picked audience of 300 *NME* competition winners were treated to free drinks and a buffet, the Wild Wax disco, and a set largely comprising new songs from the as yet unreleased *Get Happy!!*. Costello prefaced 'Accidents Will Happen' with the comment,

"Welcome to the Paul McCartney is innocent party." His future musical collaborator had just been thrown in jail in Japan on a cannabis charge. He also joked that 'Love For Tender' was a famous Elvis Presley song.

Afterwards, Elvis appeared among the select throng, signing autographs on "books, sleeves and limbs". The *NME* proudly reported, "The gig had a refreshing atmosphere, far from the taint of the music biz, with El fans from all areas of the country and all ages and shades of the rock audience spectrum." Why, though, were so many wearing glasses? The Attractions became more compulsive as the gig progressed, playing new songs "with an engaging precision and intricacy". Elvis modestly quipped, "I bet the *NME* never had a band this good before." At one point he asked how many of those attending had got all the questions right, so probably everyone who wrote in was invited. Those who could not attend the gig were sent a copy of the US promo forty-five of 'My Funny Valentine', on red vinyl.

The concert has yet to be released, though some tracks have surfaced on bootleg. Elvis later told *Record Collector* that at least one date from each of his tours had been professionally recorded, though for "one of those documentary live albums rather than any specific gig". He objects to bootlegs of complete shows, "Not because I don't get any royalties for it but I can judge for myself what is suitable for a larger audience." Of course, some of that audience might perversely want exactly what is *not* deemed suitable for them, false starts, bum notes and cracked vocals. Just like life.

As America was still virtually out of bounds, the new contrite Costello jetted off to New Zealand to play the Sweetwater Festival, then announced a month-long British tour, with ticket prices held at £3, playing only venues he had never visited before. Advertising was to be restricted to local newspapers. The gigs were standing room only – always the best way to respond to rock music – and the support act Clive Langer And The Boxes. The object was to "save fans having to travel great distances to see bands playing on the same old tired circuit".

Meanwhile, two Rockpile gigs in early February had as support not only US blues merchants The Fabulous Thunderbirds, but the previously unknown Horace Barlow Experience. This latter band turned out to look suspiciously like Elvis and The Attractions, and played a mixture of the old – 'Less Than Zero' and new. "This is for my great friends The Jags – it's called 'The Imposter'." He also joked about watching *Top Of The Pops*: "dancing away to The Nolan Sisters in my hotel room...and The Buggles...and Gary Numan...c'mon, let's hear it for Lena Martell."

Under his own (stage) name, Elvis appeared, in February 1980, on Chris Tarrant's children's TV show *Tiswas*, and seemed at ease among the mayhem, though he neatly avoided being drenched in cold water or warm gunk, like many less wary guests. He also participated in Radio One's *Round Table*, a pop version of Radio Three's *The Critics*.

With the tables turned, Elvis tore into Linda Ronstadt's album *Mad Love*. Her token "new wave" album, it featured three Costello numbers – which he and his management *must* have authorised, along with material by the rather less known Mark Goldenburg of The Cretones. Elvis was not exactly respectful. "I never want to hear that sheer torture again. She should stop making 'Top Of The Pops' records that sell at Woolworth's. The backing tracks sound exactly like ours and the dreadful vocals...a waste of vinyl." He gave generous praise to Squeeze and The Specials – "F Beat is the Stax to Two-Tone's Motown" – but not to The Police. "Somebody should clip Sting around the head and tell him to stop singing in that ridiculous Jamaican accent. They make great records, they can play, they're all pretty, and I can't stand them."

F-Beat Records had finally sorted things out with WEA, so that in a mirror image of the Radar deal the new label would handle "all marketing, promotion and advertising", while the conglomerate would deal with the nuts and bolts, pressing and distributing the records. Radar would continue as a wholly-owned conglomerate of WEA, but the parent company lost managerial control of Costello and Lowe – previously under contract through Riviera Global Productions – to F-Beat, run jointly by Riviera and Andrew Lauder. Also on the staff were Andy Childs, onetime fanzine editor and latterly involved with EMI's Harvest label, a home for old hippies, Stiff executive Kellogs and Judith Riley from Radar.

Radarscope had already successfully taken out an injunction against CBS, Costello, Riviera, Riviera Global and Lauder, preventing the January release of 'I Can't Stand Up' on Two-Tone as a single. *NME* made this "single of the week", while admitting, "It seems unlikely that it will become commercially available quite yet (and certainly *not* on Two-Tone). You're probably just as confused as we are by the legal shenanigans that place artist and audience in an equally invidious position." The same paper, the previous week, had announced that the disc would appear on the "Off Beat" label. *Melody Maker* claimed that the Two-Tone pressing was already fetching £75.

Costello had become a pawn in a power struggle, proving his earlier paranoia to be justified. "Warners claimed rightful possession to the artists, whilst the artists themselves insisted that their association with Radar was a strictly verbal release by release arrangement," the *NME* explained. Warners had already served a writ on Capital Radio, who had been playing an acetate of the single. Costello himself "had no intention of signing with Warners and attempts to persuade him to do so are unlikely to make him change his decision". He was quite prepared to quit the industry, forthwith.

Much of the new album refers to the singer's feelings of betrayal and being bought and sold. Once peace had broken out, WEA quoted Lauder as being "more than pleased to be able to finally get a record in the shops without further delay and after all is said and done, business is business".

The real winners in all this were the lawyers: "I've been cited so many times I'm beginning to think I'm a UFO," Lauder joked, little realising that this would be nothing to his later long running dispute with The Stone Roses, when they deserted Silvertone. As to the F-Beat/WEA shotgun wedding, it was like many of the deals which sanctioned the twin explosions of new bands at the end of the Sixties and the Seventies: new hip, radical labels were a kind of smokescreen for big business, while small record companies who tried to go it alone without proper distribution – like Holyground or Virgin or Rough Trade – had to evolve their own networks. In the case of the last two, empires were formed as a result.

Riviera also resolved the Rockpile situation, so that they could record under that name, rather than alternating as Edmunds' and Lowe's backing bands, but the resulting album *Seconds Of Pleasure* was correctly named, and Rockpile crumbled into sand. Nick Lowe joined F-Beat as a solo artist.

In February, F-Beat were now able to rush release Costello's new – much delayed – single. *NME*'s Max Bell pointed out that this cover of an old Sam And Dave B-side was "of greater vintage than many of the man's fans". It also "eschews the usual quota of instant hooks and crystal frequency in favour of a dense, propelling steady soulfulness. The singer is mixed back alongside clicking guitars, a jumping pulse of a rhythm and a counterpoint in smooth organ playing that reminds me of early J Geils." The following week saw the release of the matching album, with its stern injunction to *Get Happy!!*. It rose to Number Two in the UK album charts, and Number Eleven in the USA, helped along both by the buzz of expectation and by saturation coverage on soul stations. Just like in the glory days of Stiff, the music press was equally saturated with two-page ads, shouting that the new album was a "record to stand you on your feet".

This new style had much the same effect on its creator. As he told *Record Collector* fifteen years later, "We were still quite smitten with Bowie's music. We tried to play 'High Fidelity' like 'Station To Station' throughout one US tour – quite successfully – in this ponderous, heavy metal style. But we never had loud guitars at that point, so it was hard to deliver the clout that Bowie had, with his multi-tracked guitars. It always sounded punier and more poppy when we did it." Edgy times, and the album was largely written on the road. "The arrangements weren't bedded down in any sort of rhythm. They sort of rattled away, and the words flew by, and you couldn't understand them. Some of the songs needed to be slowed down and got into a groove." Elvis was listening again to the kinds of music he had loved (almost privately) in his teens. "A lot of Motown and Stax and Atlantic. I was digging out singles and trying to find odd tracks that had funny sounds on, for inspiration really." This new enthusiasm also communicated itself to the tour bus, as it lurched from gig to gig, the soundtrack to a seemingly endless silent movie.

The sound of the new album, denser and more compressed than anything that had gone before, as if heard through gauze, was the result of a false start in the studio. After a couple of days wasted on playing the arrangements they had roughed out on the road, "We went to the pub and said, 'Why don't we try playing slower?'" Replacing their usual "tricky, nervy kind of backing", the band hit a more rhythmic groove, and everything "just fell into place".

'Temptation' was one of the first songs to be recorded in this way, with Elvis developing new strategies on the hoof. The recording studio as a laboratory bench. "It was like sampling," Costello says. "We just took the riff from Booker T's 'Time Is Tight' and put the song over it – stretched it over this frame, like making a boat. Quite a lot of the songs were like that. 'Opportunity' was an Al Green song in our minds, though it doesn't sound anything *like* Al Green. 'Clowntime Is Over' was Curtis Mayfield. They all had an association, but we didn't want to go out of our way to model them any more than that. 'High Fidelity' has a quote from The Supremes, but that was there in the original song. The influence of the soul stuff had been lurking there all along." Truly post-modern, taking a whole bundle of cultural references, throwing them up in the air, and creating a whole new pattern. On *Get Happy!!*, Elvis would invest soul sources with an introspection and bitterness previously alien to the genre.

As Costello told Radio One, "We just changed direction completely. I said, 'Let's just play these songs as if we were a soul band, Booker T And The MGs,' so we had a particular time frame in terms of arrangements. It was based on Stax and Motown around 1965 to 1968, but played by these maniacs who had just been flying around the world for two years, and going nuts. *Get Happy!!* blew away the whole idea of us having to conform to some 1977-derived musical idea, which was only a means to an end anyway." Elvis was on creative overload, writing new songs in the gaps between recording. As with 'Possession'. "We went for a cup of coffee in Hilversum. I fell in love with the waitress and wrote the song in ten minutes. It was a total lust song, it had nothing to do with any art concept. I wrote it, then insisted on learning it on the way back to the studio. We were quite drunk, as it happens! I wasn't very serious."

Occasionally, Elvis would drop his Otis Redding mask. "'Riot Act' says exactly what I'd meant it to say. It was very truthful. I had to write it. It's the one song on the album – alongside 'Man Called Uncle' – which doesn't use any R&B disguise. I prefer the demo on the CD, because by the time we came to record it we were pretty wasted, we were out there. The vocal is much better on the demo, and the guitar sounds more evil." Indeed, the song – which ends the album – was meant to function as a kind of musical last word and testament. The line "It doesn't look like I'm going to be around much anymore" was for real. The pressures of the last three years were finally proving to be too much, and Elvis even admitted to a brief flirtation with drugs, not a mode of relaxation usually associated with him. "Any is too many", as he later warned.

Get Happy!! contains enough songs for a double album, but that would have destroyed the point entirely. The songs deal with claustrophobia – in love, in career, in life – and their being crammed ten onto each side is part of the message. So is the way that side one on the sleeve becomes side two on the actual record – and vice versa – and the title on the spine is reversed. The sleeve is a symphony of clashing colours, patterned like a Sixties Stax product, geometric in design with three identical photos of Costello viewed from the sky, hands in the pocket of a buttoned-up coat, his face almost deformed. Original pressings came with a fake coffee mug stain on the front, and a larger circle on the back, where the vinyl was supposedly wearing through the cardboard. On the inner sleeve, humankind is reduced to four diagrams, colour coded.

The songs here are packed with words, which are half swallowed by their creator. The lack of a lyric sheet makes them all the more hard to reckon, bearing out Julian Bell's theory on how Costello's best lyrics work as a series of brilliant fragments, unconnected except by a thread of logic to which the writer does not allow us access. The music, and Costello's tone, often provide better clues than the actual words. The CD makes the correct running order clear at last. One of the original reviewers who shall remain nameless – Dave McCullough – praised the way the album rose to a climax, but got the two sides in the wrong order! McCullough is a perceptive critic all the same, and I will use his comments as a guide through the musical maze which lies before us.

'Love For Tender' quotes musically from The Supremes song, and puns on the title of one of Presley's greatest hits, though the first Elvis never sounded this desperate, or vocally clotted. It is set in a dark underworld, a place described by Dave Gouldstone as "lacking in sincerity and loyalty", thus setting the tone for the whole album, and (unintentionally) its fiscal imagery the *lingua franca* for the 1980s. 'Clean Money', which first surfaced on *Taking Liberties*, sets much the same set of words to a new tune.

'Opportunity' sounds as if Elvis is singing through a megaphone, and seems to be autobiographical, born as part of the 1950s baby boom. There is a filagree of organ, and a solid rhythm, over which Elvis alternates tight vowels and the occasional, freeing whoop, just like Marvin Gaye. It ends bizarrely at a corporate health centre – get fit!! – thus neatly uniting two themes of the Eighties, the freedom to make a fortune and muscle toning. The chorus is about surveillance, a world like the novels of Iain Sinclair where everyone is under investigation, if only from the narrator.

'The Imposter' starts at a fast lick, with punk drumming square on the beat, and fairground organ, then slows down and takes on a ska lope. The title was later to give Costello a whole new persona. "Seething dynamics", with the singer's rival a kind of Arthur Daley figure, a spiv on heat. The subject is close to that of Neil Young's chilling and dismissive song 'The Loner', ironically – or not – a song supposedly about Stephen Stills.

'Secondary Modern' is set to a slower soul groove, and deals not so much with Elvis's schooling – though "second place in the human race" could reveal a chip on the great man's shoulder about his Eleven Plus failure – as with failure in love, as do virtually all the songs here. He dashes down from high romance to contraception. "Is it pleasure or business or a packet of three." Elvis's voice climbs to a poignant falsetto on the "blue to blue" line: who said that Otis Redding was dead?

'King Horse' has the same anthemic quality as 'Oliver's Army', and uses the "guitar figure" from The Four Tops' 'Reach Out (I'll Be There)' to underlie a song of "glorious self realisation". In folklore, horses are linked to kingship – the reason why blue blood still chases the joys of the turf – though I always took the song as some kind of heroin reference, though the lyrics don't really comply. So what. Dave Gouldstone finally realises, "The narrators of these songs are little better than the people whom they are attacking." It's called irony.

'Possession' is "velvety and moving with a wonderful loose and unfussed feeling", and was previously performed live as 'Idle Hands'. The opening line, and the basic chords, are a near quote from 'From Me To You', while the organ riff is straight out of Procol Harum. Both appropriate really, as The Beatles were one of the first white bands to popularise Tamla, and Procol had previously been The Paramounts, a Southend soul combo. There is a kind of joyless stiffness here, though, which the black originals – or even their Sixties white covers – totally lack. This is music which resolutely refuses to swing, being more like an uptempo funeral march, with Elvis intoning threats. He sings the title over and over again, like a man literally "possessed". Money is again the root of all evil here, and the narrator leaves just before violence sets in, presumably from his own fists.

There is more churchy organ – more Harum than harem – on 'Man Called Uncle', a reference to the cult spy TV series. The male figure here, though, is not so much affable old buffer Leonard Carroll, as a dirty old man, semi-impotent to boot. For McCullough, though, "the whole, invigorating spontaneity" of the album as a whole is "summed up in the closing drum clatter". It sounds to me more like a volley of suicide bullets.

'Clowntime Is Over' has that "familiar feeling of aggressive assurity, relayed in a sudden jerk at the end of every verse". A kind of de- and re-construction of 'We Can Work It Out', like a less coherent version of 'Watching The Detectives', but a gorgeous melody. The demo appears on the augmented CD, with a ghostly vocal, slowed right down over delicate organ. The extra space and time available transforms the song into something deeply felt, and communicated onwards to the listener.

'New Amsterdam' is in waltz time, with a wonderful bass counterpart to Costello's heartfelt singing over a bed of strummed guitars, all instruments played by the entertainer himself. The "double duchess" line was viciously singled out by Shane MacGowan as an example of Costello's word play at its most berserk, but every word here is carefully meditated, in a song good enough on its own to make sure of its writer's long-term fame. Without being presumptuous, the lyric seems to refer fairly directly to Bebe Buell, and Elvis's abject return home, where "they'll take you to heart". This is one song that doesn't sound like a persona talking, and Costello revisits docksides in London and Liverpool as if touching base with the places of his heart, feeling sympathy with people living a life "that is almost like suicide". The people on "the other side" could almost be ghosts themselves.

In sharp contrast, the bouncy beat and rhythmic piano of 'High Fidelity' is a deliberate echo of Tamla fun girls, The Supremes. Elvis seems to have a sore throat as he powers out the words. There are links with the previous song, a "tunnel" between the two sides of the river, and a central pun linking faithfulness to aural perfection. McCullough is entranced by a "rising chorus and a shimmying, irresistible rhythm track". I find instead the sound of a man in pain, sweaty with desire, and a matching joylessness to the music which surrounds him, as if the needle is stuck.

'I Can't Stand Up For Falling Down' is genuine soul, via Sam And Dave, and the lyrics do the job intended, not drawing attention to their own cleverness – except in the central verbal joke – but rather to the singer's pain. The performance here seems to pretend to exuberance, rather than body it forth. The Attractions join in vocally, as if offering moral support. 'Black And White World' is "hard and shaky", its semi-acoustic demo on the CD almost a different song, slower, more thoughtful, with chatty guitar. One of eight demos recorded at the tiny Archipelago Studios in Pimlico – of which only 'New Amsterdam' survives intact on the eventual LP, Costello still felt it had some quality "missing from that album version". Compassion, perhaps.

Apart from its clever/aggravating title, '5ive Gears In Reverse' is dirty-minded, sung lustfully rather than lustily. It doubles as a *raison d'etre* for the album, backwards into the future, "another fashionable first/like walking down the road to ruin". A John and Beverley Martyn album title, and Elvis howls like a wolf, or John at his most extreme, on the fade-out. 'B Movie' is "a quivering skeleton of a song", led by melodic bass which zooms all over the shop, a song about at Atlantic crossing whose lyrics seem to be addressed to Bebe Buell. There is real pain in the final line, "when I find you're finally making me cry."

The melancholy mood carries over into 'Motel Matches' where emotion overtakes cleverness. McCullough reckons it "moves silkily towards Gram Parsons at his most helplessly bitter". Another future classic, with The Attractions again playing at being Procol Harum. 'Human Touch' begins with a drum rattle, then into a ska-based, Specials-linked, stomp, with a tune heavily dependent on 'Lip Service'. Here is Elvis's equivalent to The Beatles' 'Ob La Di, Ob La Da', with a sudden descent into need halfway through, as if from another song. The first line (almost) repeats the title of an old Animals song, but domestic violence seems to be the real subject, not economic deprivation.

'Beaten To The Punch' opens like 'Taxman', and continues with a parody of the same bass line. Elvis grows hoarse on the final chorus, screaming quietly, as if he has suddenly lost self-control. Maybe he is just punch drunk. Emotionally at least, it is the woman who bruises her knuckles here. 'Temptation' is based on Booker T And The MGs' 'Time Is Tight', a song based on "alcoholism and defencelessness". The kid described, in his air-conditioned limo, could just be Elvis himself. The events of the past few months would be enough to turn anyone to drink. The line about going from "claws to clause" is surely about Costello, from Bebe Buell to WEA. It only works when written down.

'I Stand Accused' the Merseybeats cover, is certainly autobiographical, despite being written by Colton/Smith, two English musicians who were involved in a great, lost album by Poet And The One Man Band. I've got it, and I'm not selling!

On finally, in this breathless rush through a breathless rush of an album to 'Riot Act' "a silky lounge-lizard melodrama". It is the first genuinely relaxed song on the whole LP. "Costello and Lowe are having their own party, at last." Elvis's voice cracks as if with emotion here for the first time. It is a trick that he will repeat many times in the future. The drums are pure BJ Wilson, the organ perfect Matthew Fisher, the bass in the unique, plodding style of David Knights, and even Costello's voice a dead ringer for the ironic wistfulness of Gary Brooker, but Procol Harum were so terminally unfashionable at this point – and ever since – that Booker T was a far cooler name to drop. The lyrics even share some of Keith Reid's irony, though with added nastiness. The narrator here is out of control, and the violence of the sentiments seems like the prelude to a beating.

The demo version which concludes the CD – apart from an uncredited version of 'Love For Tender', which cuts off half way through – is quieter, more tense. Also recorded, but as yet unreleased, were cover versions of 'First I Look At The Purse' written by Smokey Robinson, and Larry Williams' 'Slow Down'.

The overall feeling left behind by *Get Happy!!* is that of a private diary, or words half-translated out of an unknown foreign tongue. David Gouldstone's book *A Man Out Of Time* has gamely tried to dissect Costello's work song by song, as I myself did in earlier books on Joni Mitchell and Van Morrison – far more linear wordsmiths, both. With Costello from *Get Happy!!* onwards, such an attempt to "shovel a glimpse into what each one means" is doomed from the start. Like Dylan, half the fun is that these songs are literally meaningless, though their urgency and self-belief connect on some deeper level altogether, as do the instruments – and instrumentalists – chosen to carry them. Again like Dylan, Elvis will also write in his earlier, more direct style, when the political or emotional need arises – 'Hurricane' or 'Tread The Dirt Down', 'Love Sick' or 'I Want You'.

Reviews of *Get Happy!!* were mixed, particularly in America. For *Rolling Stone*, the album failed, although it is a tribute to his temperament that "we experience both his quest and his failure as our own". Chris Brazier in *Melody Maker* reckoned that "twenty-track avalanches are difficult to absorb" and found that "its overall effect can be brittle, making you wonder if he really cares as much about the substance as the style". Other critics were more awed. In *NME* Paul Rambali found an album "crammed to the teeth", with few overdubs and no solos, except for one small guitar flourish at the end of '5ive Gears In Reverse'. The vocals are "more a part of the mix than its highlight", while the lyrics come "either from a period of sleepless nights in the US of A, or from later, more conciliatory times back home". There is more autobiographical honesty, and less contrivance. Dave McCullough of *Sounds* compares the plaintiveness of 'New Amsterdam' with Van Morrison's *Moondance*. Elvis has shrugged off the dangers of sterile perfectionism, and opened up his heart. "For the first time, Costello is relaxed and unfettered by external demands. It feels good to listen to."

Time has proved these last two reviews closer to the mark. *Melody Maker* looked back on "a gruelling exercise in self-laceration, songs vivid as headlines and full of bad news". The album was a *Blood On The Tracks* "for the desperate Eighties". *Rolling Stone* put it at Number Sixty-Seven in their all-time Top 100 albums, "a breathless outpouring of diabolical wordplay".

It also quotes Elvis on his most bitter creation. "It was very maniacal and emotional. But somewhere in the heart of the better songs is some sort of purity. Sometimes when you're throwing away things like that, you'll write something really true to your secret feelings in spite of yourself." Even if it sounds at first like the kind of printed notice that would be hung on the walls of the Quisling Clinic, *Get Happy!!* is, after all, an injunction to stop being miserable.

Part of the reason for *Get Happy!!*'s change of musical direction was Elvis's desire to be able to watch *Top Of The Pops* without feeling that he was looking in the mirror. During the years spent touring the States and beyond, a whole slew of British Elvis (Mk II) impersonators had risen up, just as Dylan's low profile in the late Sixties led to endless "new Dylans". Joe Jackson was briefly ironic, before going on to be a musical jack of all trades, while Danny Adler of Roogalator – managed by Robin Scott of M fame – wore glasses, played a Jazzmaster guitar, and sang about sex and the single girl in a (genuine) American whine. An Irish folkie called Clive Culbertson even hyped himself, unsuccessfully, as a total loser: "He's two stone overweight and he's never had a woman in his life." Or a hit. The appallingly wimplike Moon Martin had an "Elvis soundalike" label literally stuck to his album *Escape From Domination*, though didn't make it clear which one. Meanwhile, a young Ian Broudie was among those guilty men who recorded The Original Mirrors' debut LP, a 1980 effort which aped Barney Bubbles' sleeve designs to no great effect.

As none of these fitted the bill for the next king of rock, Allan Jones made a complete prat of himself writing a front page article on a pub act called Any Trouble, recently signed by Stiff. Clive Gregson – now with Plainsong – remains to this day a great musical craftsman, and supervised his young band like a favourite uncle, but he was already portly and bald, and his songs have a cuddliness which the real Elvis would attack with razor wire. The difference between talent and genius, and the well-meaning hype destroyed the band early. Gregson went on to make some heart-breaking albums with the terrifying Christine Collister, so all was not lost. A far less honourable cod-Elvis And The Attractions were The Jags, a London foursome who had a minor hit with 'Back Of My Hand', not so much a tribute as straight plagiarism. Once the real Elvis emerged back on the British scene, they vanished like the morning dew.

The Get Happy Tour opened on 1 March at Cromer Pavilion, and closed at Nottingham's Sherwood Rooms exactly a month later. As promised, it took in all kinds of weird and wonderful (and small) venues, from Lincoln's Drill Hall to Fishguard's Frenchman's Motel. Ian Penman of *NME* and as usual took about fifty paragraphs to get to the point – sample bullshit: "in the immediacy of a solipsism's aspersion are hidden doubt, debt, weak defences, dead emotion: 'insecurity' isn't so much a dirty word as a line of worn connections – after all, even cliches get insecure."

Having explained structuralist theory to teenagers, Penman deigns to notice some "confident but agitated, spiked but not arrogant" sounds, well mixed. The music is more sensual than before, "the difference between being left numb and having succumbed". The band remain anonymous, but are "rhythmically centrifugal". Elvis is a one-man antithesis to Sting, "cluttered cool, melancholy's violence, a sweaty statue". The songs are largely drawn from the new album, though James Truman of *MM* finds the Motown pastiche "largely lost in the lightning rush of a live sound, making the songs snappier and more forceful". He also notes a tendency for Costello to load in too many words, so that the audience wonder if they are being entertained, or "given an impromptu course in the correct use of the English epigram within the perfect pop song." Support act Clive Langer gives what Elvis can't: "Sweat in place of smirks, humour in place of tension."

There was plenty of tension on the door, with Riviera refusing press passes for the opening gig, so that journalists had to buy their own tickets from the local youth, and smuggle in cameras hidden up their jumpers. If as much as a lens cap was discovered, out they went. As a result, the pictures which appeared next week were wonderfully hole in the wall. Well, if *you* were risking being beaten up...Like all media workers, they stored these memories up for future vengeance.

It was too early to strike as yet, as a week later 'I Can't Stand Up For Falling Down' hit the UK Top Ten at Number Four. Elvis, though, was having one of his periodic bouts of depression about fame, and the demands for conformity that followed in its wake. "A lot of people came to hear 'Oliver's Army' and 'I Can't Stand Up'," he moans. "I just felt that I hadn't really got the bulk of songs over to a lot of people. I didn't want to be one of those one-or-two-number singers like Gene Pitney or somebody." A little ungracious to his own father, for whom one hit record would still be a bonus.

That notwithstanding, in April Costello "decided I didn't want to go on anymore and left the group. I just didn't see any point to it." This despite 'Hi Fidelity', the second single to be taken off the new album, reaching the UK Top Thirty that same month. It was Elvis's first single to be also released on the newly fashionable twelve-inch format – now, ironically, the mainstay of vinyl, in a club rather than a home context. The sleeve design is wonderful, a geometric design in purple and circling white lines, from which gradually a robot's head emerges. The yellow and red label appears through a die-cut hole. On the B-side is a *Get Happy!!* outtake, Van McCoy's 'Getting Mighty Crowded', learnt from "the great Betty Everett record".

Three more stray songs emerged on the mysterious 'New Amsterdam' EP, a classic of that limited genre, which made the Top Forty in June, but again failed to chart in the USA. To rub things in, Nick Lowe – notable by his absence as producer here – had just himself entered the US hit parade with 'Cruel To Be Kind'. The EP came both in a picture sleeve, parodying a hard line abstract of the New York school, with Elvis's tiny face superimposed as if he was wearing a party hat, and as a startling picture disc on which Elvis – looking like Michael Caine – buries his face in an armful of tulips. Oddly psychotic.

Of the "new" songs, 'Dr Luther's Assistant', about a sinister home movie, sounds like a slice of vintage psychedelia – with sitar, or backwards guitar at the end – but was written three years before, then re-recorded at Ampro studios. Elvis croons suggestively, and plays everything but drums, overdubbed later. 'Ghost Train' had been brewing since the early duo with Allan Mayes. Few songs begin with a line like "Maureen and Stan were looking for a job" and survive, but Costello – like Ray Davies, or Madness, or Squeeze – has the ability to talk about "common people" without patronising them. An uncle of The Specials' more focused 'Ghost Town', this song about struggling musicians was originally a kind of twisted self-portrait. Here, with what sounds like xylophone, and Elvis playing a fairground barker on the chorus, it is a pure delight. At least one non "pretty one" has made it through. The dreamy 'Just A Memory', eventually recorded by Dusty Springfield, was laid down at TW Studios in Fulham, with Nieve the only Attraction in sight. Was Elvis's threat to go solo already a reality?

Steve Nieve decided to use this temporary (or perhaps permanent) hiatus to fly to America for a holiday, but was almost immediately involved in a serious car crash in Los Angeles, in which a female passenger was killed. It brought Elvis to his senses: "I realised I was being a bit spoilt." The band were already contracted to a European tour, beginning in mid April, whatever Costello's plans afterwards. Nieve would be in no fit state to take part now, thus losing Elvis his unique live sound. An emergency replacement was drafted in from The Rumour, with whom Elvis had maintained links, but rather than simply swap keyboard players by using Bob Andrews, Costello asked lead guitarist Martin Belmont to cross the tracks. This gave a tougher sound to the ensemble – along with The Attractions' crashing rhythm section, the new wave Led Zeppelin – and took pressure off Elvis himself as sole guitarist. Costello himself played organ on 'Watching The Detectives'.

Initial reports of gigs in Holland and Germany were far from favourable. Belmont was enthusiastic, but tended to drown the band in a wall of noise. Without Nieve, they were growing sloppy and unsubtle, a fact born out by two much televised tracks, taken from the Rock Over Europe Festival in Belgium. By the time the tour reached France in May, Costello seemed to be reinvigorated onstage, and he added cover versions of 'Help Me' by Sonny Boy Williamson (also recorded by Eric Burdon and The Animals), 'One More Heartache' – as performed by Marvin Gaye – and Presley's 'Little Sister'. Frazer Clarke took in a gig at the Bataclan Club in Paris – a sweaty, Marquee-like hole which has seen premium live performances transferred to disc by everyone from Gong to Jeff Buckley.

Clarke found the twin guitar attack "a less sophisticated but funkier mix than before", closer to James Brown than Smokey Robinson. Even if Costello the songwriter remains bitter and twisted by life, the man on stage seems reborn, joyful and chatty with the audience, even if his voice sounds strained. The band seem happier on faster numbers, like 'Waiting For The End Of The World', now announced as "a message from the Ayatollah". The contrast between the two guitarists is fascinating, with Elvis "blitzing through to the bone", like a cleaver through meat, and Belmont earthier, more sustained.

The only problem is visual, with the tall and thickset Belmont wandering "into Elvis's mid-stage territory". The Attractions know their place better. Nieve had always remained behind his keyboards, with the odd (very odd) onstage leap, and the two Thomases remain phlegmatic, especially Pete, whose "trousers would have to be on fire before he'd be disturbed". Things were certainly settled musically by the time that the band hit London, disguised under the name Factory Act, to play a gig at the Hope and Anchor. "Thank you, we're not used to big city crowds," the singer quipped.

The results appeared as a radio broadcast, and reveal a top notch pub-rock band, without the icy particularity which Nieve brings, but playing with sweaty excitement. Some of Elvis's verbal subtlety is lost, but the crunchier sound seems to release something in his voice, so that 'Lipstick Vogue' takes off like the early Floyd, and 'Help Me' makes even the later Van Morrison version seem a little stiff. Elvis has never sounded so emotionally convincing, and verbally lubricated.

Belmont reckoned, "I just think I'm really lucky to have been asked to play with the most talented guys around." He had been even tempted to give up his day job with Graham Parker, though no job offer ever materialised from Elvis, other than some session work for *Trust*. Martin later joined Nick Lowe's Cowboy Outfit, as the next best thing.

Jools Holland took over Steve Nieve's keyboard role for an Italian TV gig in June, though apparently the band were only miming to the original record. By mid July, Nieve was back, in full flight, to rejoin The Attractions for the French Orange Pop Festival, and fourteenth Montreux Jazz Festival, headlining a special F-Beat night on the shores of Lake Geneva. Eight songs have surfaced on bootleg CD, an exuberant set, with Nieve boogying as well as adding embellishment, and Costello in full vocal flow. New songs like 'Clubland' and 'From A Whisper To A Scream' – "you can shake your body about if you want to" – draw a strong reaction, in particular 'Lovers' Walk' with its Bo Diddley beat. On 'I Can't Stand Up', Nieve attacks his keyboards like a young Jerry Lee Lewis.

That inveterate Elvis watcher Allan Jones is banned from the press gallery during a soundcheck, but holds no grudges. Costello might look a little out of condition, but he declares war on Montreux "with a virulence that would've shocked even his most longstanding admirers". Here is a man who unleashes on his audience "the darkest possible realities". Live shows are some kind of personal catharsis, and their drama lies in the way you never know how far he will dare go.

The set unfolds at a "violent pace" – it sounds quite restrained to my ears on the cold plastic of CD – and The Attractions' collective performance on an extended 'Watching The Detectives' rivals "the extraordinary dementia of, say, Neil Young's 'Last Dance', one of the all-time great moments in rock music". The band end on an "incendiary" 'Pump It Up', and Jones is left feeling "like an emotional corkscrew, all wound up and nowhere to go".

Into a bottle, I would have thought.

Squeeze were saying one of many farewells to their boogie pianist supreme Jools Holland on home turf, at Deptford's tiny Albany Empire. The festivities stretched over three evenings in August, all of which involved Elvis. He joined Squeeze onstage for encores which included 'Watching The Detectives', '(I Don't Want To Go To) Chelsea' and 'Pump It Up', as well as playing support with a band known as Otis Westinghouse And The Lifts, who looked remarkably like The Attractions. Introduced by John Cooper Clarke, they played a relaxed set largely drawn from *Get Happy!!*, to everyone's delight apart from "the braying of a collection of minor-league Deptford gangsters obviously worried by any kind of musical adventure". They covered Larry Williams' 'Slow Down' – as did The Beatles – and Elvis introduced 'New Amsterdam' with the words, "This one takes just a little less time to perform than it takes time to read Dexy Midnight Runners' press statements!"

On the third night, a (then) virtually unknown Alexei Sayle opened the evening with a satire on inarticulate rock stars. Hardly Elvis, though he seemed more wound up tonight, playing his greatest hits, "one after the other", as Glenn Tilbrook noticed. As professional cockney Danny Baker noted, "If he was doing this for fun and a favour, you'd never have guessed, no time for smiles, no breaks between songs, no musical gags, nothing was relaxed." He worried that Elvis was now wound so tight that this "austere veneer" was stretching him like a piano wire, which the slightest relaxation could snap. Backstage, he was handed a party hat, "but as soon as the person who gave it to him went off, he crumpled it up and threw it away." Onstage, he joined Tilbrook for 'Private Number', playing William Bell to Glenn's Judy Clay, "the highlight of the three days".

There was a secret agenda. Riviera approached Squeeze with a management offer which they were easily able to refuse. Jools Holland went on to host BBC2's *Later* – on which Elvis became a regular attraction – and later poached Squeeze's drummer for his own big band. That November, Elvis and Squeeze reunited at the Top Rank, Swansea, to play a benefit gig for local boxer Johnny Owen. Tilbrook and Elvis have remained in close contact ever since, as a mutual admiration society, and joint purveyors of quality, literate pop.

Three days after appearing as two brands of lift manufacturers, Elvis and The Attractions were billed as themselves at the Playhouse House Theatre, Edinburgh. Dave Conway found him flawless, and compared him to Ravel, of all people: "An entire concert is precisely orchestrated to achieve maximum effect." The Attractions did *not* play 'Bolero'. Costello opened the set "with a humble yet self-assured casualness", and with a startling version of 'Shot With His Own Gun', confined to his voice and Nieve's piano.

Sounds' Johnny Waller drew attention to Elvis's guitar work, his "flurry-attack gloriously intense", and Nieve's "precise empathy" to Costello's every change of mood. Elvis forgot the words to 'Pump It Up' in his hurry to introduce the band. For 'Lipstick Vogue', Waller draws particular attention to the lighting effects. "Shafts of penetrating green dazzle through the drumkit, bathing the band in a ghostly glow until dispelled by a sudden flood of yellow." Elvis alone remains unmarked, held in a white spotlight throughout. These things can make or break a concert, especially in such a huge arena. Support acts were The Rumour, and a real collectors' item, the short-lived Subterraneans, with Nick Kent on lead vocals.

Conway makes an interesting point about Elvis's voice, "with a twang like Duane Eddy's guitar". Much of his success comes from his evocation of "distant but living voices from the infancy of rock 'n' roll – Buddy Holly, Eddie Cochran, The Everly Brothers, Elvis the First, and the ghosts of many others booming hollowly from the Dansette past". He has learnt much from his father, as a "trouper in the great tradition, an ace performer who knows all the tricks", but is this really what Sid Vicious "lived, fought and died for". No, that was merely an extreme form of self indulgence.

Within the week Elvis was in Canada, topping the bill at Toronto's 'Heatwave Festival', over The Pretenders, The B52s, Talking Heads, and The Rumour, with Martin Belmont back in harness. Richard Grabel of the *NME* found The Attractions' wall of sound "keeps getting higher, thicker, more solid", even after the augmented, nine-piece Talking Heads – at their symphonic peak this year, and a hard act to follow. As to Elvis, the "spite and venom seem to be going out of him", with more emotional shadings to his songs, and voice. Unlike everyone else on the bill, he makes no attempt to ingratiate his audience, though. "He just lays it out, take it or leave it." Which is not to say that he doesn't care, and his final encore is '(What's So Funny 'Bout) Peace, Love and Understanding'.

At the end of September, Elvis and band were back in London, playing a fiftieth birthday tribute at the Rainbow, with "special guests" the refried rockabilly of The Stray Cats. It is their first big gig in the capital this year, and free copies of the Two-Tone single (no longer fetching £80) are given away free at the door. That factual fanatic Patrick Humphries finds "a pugnacious figure at stage centre, convinced of his own convictions", but records the set list with his usual accuracy. There are lots of songs from the forthcoming album. 'From A Whisper To A Scream' has a riff relentless as a headache, while 'Luxembourg' and 'The Beat' have the place "moving like a Glasgow hogmanay". Despite a poor sound balance, the band play for a full seventy-five minutes, ending with a "scorching 'Pump It Up', with more searchlights than the Blitz".

In *NME*, Charles Shaar Murray – a *great* writer – returns to the fray, and finds a genial figure replacing the 1977 model, "the one with the stone face and the reptile glare and the tracks of toad-sweat down forehead and cheeks". That menace has long gone, and here is a sequenced programme of songs old and new ("one for one, most of the time"), from a man who introduces each song, smiles occasionally, and is dressed in baggy khaki trousers and pink leather jacket. He cues in his band with hand signals, just like Frank Zappa. *Get Happy!!* has largely been dropped from the set list, to make way for both the new songs and reinvigorated retreads of the like of 'Green Shirt', 'Alison' and 'You Belong To Me'.

The Attractions were still trying – like Crazy Horse with Neil Young – to establish that they did not wholly belong to their quixotic master. The trouble is that both bands only come fully alive when plucked back by their lead singer, both of whom at the time of writing have sworn to a divorce, forever. Nieve had appeared on Twist's disposable 1979 album – well, I did – *This Is Your Life*, and Howard Werth's *Six Of One*, a cod reference to *The Prisoner*. The Attractions too wanted to be free men, at least temporarily, and while in Holland cut an album in their own right. Roger Bechirian – Nick Lowe's engineer – produced, and 'Single Girl' emerged in July as a seven inch, followed by the full album *Mad About The Wrong Boy*, a month later, with a bonus EP, 'Theme Music From The Film Outline Of A Hairdo', featuring Nieve playing mood piano.

Four "songs" are credited to Thomas P and Thomas B: the rest either to "Brain and Hart" – Nieve and his partner Fay Hart – or to Nieve direct. The cover is gratuitously awful; a dog sits on a formica table, on a red fluffy rug and looks down on a meal of chops and sausage. On the back the three men pose on a ladder, Pete Thomas in a jacket about three sizes too small, Bruce showing a paunch in growth, with Nieve on his knees and in paisley and a skinny tie.

The whole album has the feeling of a time-warp to a band circa 1967 when pop was turning into rock, mutedly psychedelic around the edges. Exactly the sort the thing The Rumour were also attempting at the same time, mutating backwards into Kippington Lodge. It sank without trace, except for 'Sad About Girls', which they would occasionally play onstage while Elvis took a rest. Listening again after many years' absence from my dusty turntable, the album is astoundingly weak, with weedy vocals and over-polite playing. "Don't wanna be a Numan, I'm too fast a human", they sing, but give me Gary's early synthesiser dystopias any day. One clever touch: "wrong" is spelt "rwong" on the back sleeve.

Charles Shaar Murray discerned "a slick, glossy album with a smirk on its chops", facile cynicism that tries to be 10cc, and fails. The band "prod the surfaces of their subjects with a long stick". The lack of any defined lead singer is the central flaw, that and the songs, all "slick misogyny and smug pokes at conformity". The lyrics are certainly poor Costello pastiche, on the level of "the way is all uphill she's so inclined". Bruce Thomas helped produce that gem, perhaps putting his later spite towards his former leader into context. Jealousy!

The band recorded a second album, but it never appeared. A later album and twelve-inch single on F-Beat by Blanket Of Secrecy is supposedly by The Attractions, or so I was told when paying over the odds. They turned out to be the kinds of record you forget even while they are still playing. Songs are credited to Tinker, Tailor, Sailor and Soldier. Nieve's own solo output has been of more interest, a weird succession of keyboard solos with weird titles, and exploring his own world of cocktail psychedelics and smoochy arpeggios.

Elvis's career was still on hold, and as usually happens at such times, his record company filled the gap with old product. This was no mere retread of greatest career moments, though. The US-only compilation *Taking Liberties* gathered twenty outtakes, demos and unreleased UK forty-fives, and got up to Number Twenty-Eight in the album chart. Elvis stands, splay toed, in an open American phone box. The phone is off the hook, and Elvis has himself become a piece of equipment, with one hand cupped to his ear, and the other transmitting the album's title. The whole thing is oddly out of kilter, and then you notice that the letters on the phone box are the wrong way round. The whole image has been deliberately reversed, another liberty taken on the purchaser, another outtake. Nevertheless, Columbia's Gregg Geller gives a corporate blessing in his liner notes to "the most versatile young singer-entertainer of the day...one change of pace after another".

Nick Kent found the album showing up the *Armed Forces* period as "far too busy and over convoluted", bearing out Elvis's fear of self-parody, while the earlier material had actually strengthened with time. The new, self-produced, songs show that he "hasn't lost a thing". 'Hoover Factory' is released for the first time, and this paeon to an art deco building which Elvis used to pass on the bus to work, now demolished, centres on the "tinge of sadness" which underlies all his best work. Under the headline "Elvis Holds A Rummage Sale", *Rolling*

Stone found that "by ceremoniously gift-wrapping his trash, the artist treats himself with an archivist's reverence, usually reserved for the dead". Here is a "panorama" of different styles, of which the most oddly satisfying tracks "can't possibly be passed off as anything but let's-fuck-around-in-the-studio memorabilia". For the Anglophile *Trouser Press*, this was as good as any of the preplanned albums "and certainly more consistent than *Get Happy!!*'s twenty maybes".

The record faced an import ban in Britain, though many copies got in under the net. A similar album, featuring a different track list and a detailed history of each recording, was released in the UK, at first in cassette format only, as *Ten Bloody Mary's And Ten How's Your Fathers*, an ironic and possibly sacrilegious reference to Costello's Roman Catholic upbringing. Elvis plays a double bass, in shades, on a sleeve designed by the great Phil Smee, whose Bam Caruso label later resurrected all kinds of psychedelic treats, old and new.

Both albums gave an insight into Elvis's molten inner core of creativity. There are more ideas and melodies on each song here than on The Attractions' complete solo output. They did represent past glories, however, and Elvis now retreated into the studio to put together a new album which drew together all the best strands of his work so far.

In late December, the single 'Clubland', a taster for *Trust*, peaked at UK Number Sixty. The cover features the same shot of Elvis playing double bass, with 'Clean Money' and 'Hoover Factory' reprised on the flip side. Paul Morley found himself unable "to make my mind up" about Costello. When has this ever stopped the most loquacious – and passionate – of rock critics. He found the A-side lacking transcendence, but also singled out the lost gem of 'Hoover Factory' as something that made pop music "a matter of life or death".

1980 drew to a close with a seven-date tour of Scandinavia, and a gig supported by Rockpile and UB40 at the National Exhibition Centre, Birmingham two days after Christmas. Playing material largely from *Get Happy!!* – as if saying goodbye to it – "the vastness of this dreadful venue did little to help the band's sound". Paulo Hewitt was verbally roughed up by Riviera backstage: "If you could use words like Elvis you wouldn't be a hack, would you." In fact, Hewitt is one of the best writers in rock, as a string of passionate Mod histories has since proved. Riviera spoke of Elvis and himself as a twosome – "we realise we're minimising our career" – in a rather worrying way. Onstage, Hewitt found the only worrying thing about Elvis was his burgeoning weight, as he entranced a full house. "Watching Costello is half the fun of it. His movements are so awkward, his jerky guitar playing never looks so in sync with the music; head bobbing constantly, it seems impossible for him to be actually playing." Paolo was also bemused how Elvis could get so worked up delivering "some of his more obscure lyrics". All part of the act.

The year had seen more record releases and fewer live gigs than in any twelve-month period since Elvis had changed his name from Declan. More fruitfully, Elvis met Johnny Cash at the home of his future (step)son-in-law, Nick Lowe, and duetted – as had Dylan – with this early Sun rocker-turned-country singer extraordinaire. A pointer to the future.

Rolling Stone's comment about Elvis taking himself perhaps a little too seriously can also be viewed as a record collector's approach to his own career. Nick Lowe told Radio One, "Elvis can come across as someone who's very conceited and pleased with himself, and that's not true, he's a very soulful and good man. It's just that he's fascinated by himself, by how gifted he is. He almost stands back, so he's interested in talking about this gift, it's rather a charming and childlike thing."

As if to confirm his own views on his musical worth, Costello now received that milestone in rock credibility, an article all to himself in *Record Collector*. It ends by declaring, "There is no reason why he should not still be a major rock figure" when the magazine celebrates its tenth birthday, some eight years hence. Elvis, himself a fanatical collector, guested on Mike Read's Radio One show, and chatted about who chose what to release as a single – himself – his liking for some disco, Donna Summer's 'The Wanderer' and Robert Palmer's 'Johnny And Mary', and his new-found passion for jazz. He also reveals his latest musical addiction: Frank Sinatra.

"He's my favourite singer," he admits, "because at his greatest he can reach beyond himself; he makes contact with whatever it is." Costello was also discovering an appetite for the kind of classic songwriters who Sinatra interprets – Cole Porter, Rodgers and Hart, Sammy Caine – and admits that his own father is a major influence on his musical taste. All of these factors are to feed into his forthcoming album, *Trust*.

For Elvis, the album was one about which he still feels ambivalent. "It was the low point physically," he recalls. "It was the most dissolute record that I personally made, so I wasn't in great humour at the end of it. I did a lot of things which made my first marriage untenable, and therefore it was a very fraught time for everybody. When I got over my association with the bad time" – for which one can, perhaps, read the Ohio incident or, less likely, Bebe Buell – "the record itself was surprisingly coherent."

As Nick Lowe told Radio One, "We realised that we had got a little over-excited, that we had to pull over to the hard shoulder, and that was hard, because we'd got used to steaming through these records, being out of control almost, a glorious chaos. We had to take ourselves into hand. I remember a lot of rows. Bruce Thomas had this lovely salmon pink Fender bass, and we used to talk about albums as a 'two flight' or a 'three flight' album, which referred to its flight across the studio, launched by Bruce Thomas usually towards the head of Pete Thomas. *Trust* was a six or a seven flight album." Bruce concurs, and adds that Fenders being among "the most robustly constructed instruments ever made", the bass is still in one piece, unlike the band. Costello adds that the sessions were "often frantic, swinging from elation to despair for which I must take most of the blame". After grappling with recording an accordion backwards – which he now acknowledges does not sound much different from an accordion forwards – "I went down for a little lie down in a cool dark room." Chilling out.

Trust was recorded at DJM studios, Holborn at the tail end of 1980, and completed back at Eden. Again produced by Nick Lowe, it appeared in January 1981, and debuted at Number Nine in the UK. In his witty sleeve notes to the augmented CD, Costello relates how first "self-induced fatigue" led him to quit showbusiness for a month or two, then Steve Nieve's injury forced him to emulate Jimi Hendrix, and buy "a Marshall stack and 300 effects pedals and fuzz boxes". The three-piece band "was a disaster which very few of the traumatised Channel Islanders, who were subjected to it, are willing to talk about".

Martin Belmont again came to the rescue, and guests here, as does

Glenn Tilbrook of Squeeze, who like Nieve, "came from the mysterious lands of South East London". Elvis is also collaborating on songwriting with Chris Difford. Some of the songs on *Trust* feed back directly into Costello's past. He wrote 'Different Finger' when twenty-one, "and trying to write a Tammy Wynette song". 'Watch Your Step' and 'New Lace Sleeves' were written even earlier. "Even the tune was old," he recalls. "I just hid it away for years. It was one of the flukey, more sophisticated songs I wrote when I was messing around with trickier chord sequences than most of the early stuff. It's still one of my favourites."

Trust was an attempt to capture the same rhythmic approach as *Get Happy!!*, but freed of any obvious influence, though 'Strict Time' alluded to The Meters, that same "scratchy guitar sound". Indeed, it attempts to foreground the most positive aspects of the two previous albums. As he told *Record Collector*, "The songs have tunes like those on *Armed Forces* but not what was seen at the time as the rather shiny production. I remember sitting in Jersey, talking to Nick Lowe about producing the record and saying that I wanted to cross the two approaches – more overt pop melodies and still keep the rhythmic element. And some of it works, like 'You'll Never Be A Man', which has a big chorus, but is still basically a soul groove." There is more sense of space than in *Get Happy!!*, and a greater sense of pastiche leading on to something new, less a K-Tel update and more like *Young Americans*, Bowie's own take on much the same source material. Plastic soul.

Elvis is uncharacteristically open about another, non-musical source of information, a territory more closely associated in the public mind with the likes of Bowie or Lou Reed. "I was taking a lot of drugs when I wrote some of these songs," he admits. "Some of them are pretty affected by that. That's not to say that I don't remember what they're about, but the logic is quite deliberately fractured. It's like short bursts of attention span, gathered together into songs." Thus, 'You'll Never Be A Man' is about a girl "who wants to play the sexual power game the way that men usually do. It just doesn't all make sense logically like a Sunday school parable."

The album sees a great distaste for the media, most directly in 'Fish And Chip Papers', about the gutter press. "I don't think I was attacking the press in relation to my career, just generally," he says. "It was starting to go bad then. It's got much worse since. The whole album was about sour and rotten doings in different areas. We used to spend a lot of time in quite seedy hotels, so I got quite a good look at the bastards who were carving up England with their guard down. We were trying to seduce their daughters while they were putting up their next multi-storey car park. There were always these bastards at these ghastly local functions. There would usually be some sort of altercation."

Record Collector points out the extreme use of wordplay throughout, a dance of puns and metaphors. Elvis argues, "All good pop lyrics try to work on that basis, unless they're really trying to be Esperanto and not use any words they won't understand in Taiwan – like 'I Will Always Love You'. You could play that to a Martian if you pointed enough. I took my cue from Smokey Robinson, and songs like 'I Second That Emotion', which are based on wordplay." The influence of Cole Porter would descend later, "Though that stuff was always at the back of my mind," he adds.

The front cover shot of *Trust* is peculiarly unreadable, with Elvis in suit and tinted glasses – his eyebrows arched – looking up impishly as if to heaven, like an altar boy seeing God. His name does not appear, just the album title, underlined. It is like a Victorian morality painting, or the picture of a man being cured of some dread disease by divine intervention. "The picture doesn't go with the title – the person on the cover looks completely untrustworthy, and that's the joke," he explains. The original cover shot was far more sinister, with Elvis looking like Guy Fawkes, lighting a cigarette. Trust is spelt with a Latin "v".

The back cover is deliberately skew-wiff, a shot of the band playing a cocktail bar, which turns out to be a stage set, presented as a promo card for a non existent film. Elvis is described as "looking Italian", and Pete Thomas as "the boy most likely to". Inside is an extravagant, posed shot of The Attractions and friends all dressed up as a Joe Loss-style big band, originally to have been the back cover, with the caption "The Soundtrack Of Life". They even have "EC" emblazoned on the drum kit and stage monitors. A tuxedoed Nick Lowe mimes playing saxophone. For all their efforts, the dance floor is empty. Overleaf is the shot originally planned for the cover (hardly user-friendly!) with Elvis frozen – in dark coat, glasses and fedora – in an uncomfortable pose, straight out of film noir.

Mixed signals, and reviews centred on the idea of "trust", and quite how the album embodied it. Some now saw Elvis as Britain's answer to Tom Waits, wearily chronicling low-life out of a kind of lapsed romanticism. *Rolling Stone*, though, took the title ironically. "The distance he maintains from his fans, his deadpan demeanour, the clever opacity of his lyrics, the jittery but artful leaps of musical style – all of these combine to form the persona of a man you can't trust."

It was such ambiguity which kept him interesting. In *Record Mirror*, Mike Gardner saw Costello cleverly keeping his "formula" from growing stale. His songwriting was now "more considered, less frantic", his twisting melody lines bolder, and his vocal style richer. "Elvis insists on experimenting with tone in an almost three-dimensional sense, developing his sandpaper rasp as much as the sweeter gears of his larynx." Sandy Robertson's piece for *Sounds* is entitled "All trussed up (and nowhere to go)". Elvis's main theme is now the "brutal pleasures of the one night stand", and *Trust* has "much of what made Costello famous, and little of what endeared him to me in the first place". For Allan Jones, the album arrives "like a flurry of punches, pinning back your ears as it pins you to the ropes". Elvis has replaced malice with compassion, though still "too acerbic for comfortable popular consumption". He is increasingly that rare thing, an "investigative songwriter".

NME's Ian Penman takes about seven paragraphs to get to the point, so I will attempt to translate his (fascinating) review into English. Unlike the fake mannerisms of the new romantics – Duran Duran and all that crew – he genuinely slices through the "negative codes of male and female sexuality". Most of the villains here are men. His voice is part of this loosening process, "judging with syllables to humorous, dangerous, languorous effect". Costello deals with "the resuscitation of words, ideas, meanings that are in danger of being neglected or crushed. This music respects *everybody's* intelligence."

It is no coincidence that the album is reviewed opposite new records from Sheena Easton and Spandau Ballet. Costello was by now estranged from the pop mainstream. As a retrospective piece in

Melody Maker puts it, "While the rest of pop was becoming increasingly simplistic, gaudy and escapist, *Trust* was angry, complex, a confrontation." It could be seen both as an assault on Eighties pop, and "a poignant anticipation of the bleak years ahead". Ironically, Costello's next project would itself be a retreat into simplicity, given a preview here on 'Different Finger' complete with clipped guitar break and lachrymose piano.

Trust opens with 'Clubland', the hit single that never was, and a song oddly prophetic of Thatcher's revolution. "The right to work is traded in/for the right to refuse admission." The criminal allure of nightclubbing – caught in the swoon of the music, and Elvis's luxuriant vocal – is laid out here before it became fashionable. Costello plays morse code guitar, and Nieve exuberant piano. The tempo is upped for 'Lovers' Walk', set to a Bo Diddley swagger, and with an insistent chorus. 'You'll Never Be A Man' has a Meters-style bounce, and sour words. The mix makes Pete Thomas's drums the lead instrument.

There is a far greater sense of space on this album, and 'Pretty Words' boasts a relaxed, almost bored vocal, and a tune which twists like a snake. Like the previous two songs, the meaning is private, and presumably personal, all about the shame of being in love. 'Strict Time' pulls off a trick denied to the songs of *Get Happy!!*, supple and taut all at once. Weekend courting in the suburbs.

'Luxembourg' could be the original Elvis, rockabilly style, with machine gun drums and heavy echo on the vocal track, even the odd feral shout, and a Fifties drawn out "well". The lyrics are strictly meaningless. 'Watch Your Step' is like a day trip back to the paranoia of *Armed Forces*, with the same kind of insinuating vocal, sung with relish to a Bach-like organ riff. 'New Lace Sleeves' is something new, with Elvis's voice close to the mic, and The Attractions note perfect on a lope through sexual infidelity. Elvis's voice seems to be pitched lower on this album, more confiding. He has Dylan's trick of half-laughing at one point, sounding slurred at another, but the way he is echoed by his band on the word "lies" – harmonies from heaven – is deeply poignant yet controlled in a way that a non-singer like Dylan could never reach.

The Costello who opens 'From A Whisper To A Scream' is a different man, playing the bit of rough to Tilbrook's angelic counterpoint. The two duet like a white Sam And Dave, on a song of seduction and drunkenness. 'White Knuckles' is an ambivalent song about domestic violence, and given The Stranglers' more brutal take on life, it is perhaps no coincidence that Bruce Thomas's bass sounds particularly like Jean Jacques Burnel. Nieve's keyboards are joyless, and the tune queasy: Pete Thomas's drums sound like a body being thumped. Apart from his wordless "oohed" interjections – by turn exulting, sexually triumphant, and sad – Elvis's voice is oddly distant, and uncommitted, but then he is playing a part (one hopes).

It is unclear quite who "just gives in", the man to his worst impulses or the woman to her punishment. The song turns round at the end, with the man abandoned, and the woman's family triumphant. A rightly dangerous subject, as The Prodigy found with their supposedly ironic 'Smack Your Bitch Up', a Home Counties take on the rancid woman-hatred which seeps out of some gangster rap. Thom Gunn, whose early style is so close to the young Costello, later wrote 'The Beaters', a piece never collected in book form, which attempted to locate tenderness and desire in sado-masochism, from both parties. There is an element of that in this contentious song, of love denied by a macho culture.

'Shot With His Own Gun' is sung to classical-style piano, and is either spookily dramatic or emptily rhetorical, depending on your taste for light opera. This could be Queen, with better words, and a pun per line. Live, the song seems emotionally stripped, the nearest Costello will ever get to a public apology for the whole Bebe Buell incident – exposed by the press but a self-inflicted wound. On record, the song sounds more distant, and finessed. 'Fish And Chip Paper' is jauntier, but more self-revelatory: it is like a sourer Squeeze, a laddish tale of London life and media betrayal, with local references – the Hammersmith Hotel where Elvis played his "secret" gig for *NME* – and the gutter press as the villains. The most telling words again are wordless, a prolonged "ooh ooh" like something out of Max Miller, suggesting the guilty thrill of reading the "news of the screws" on Sunday. Elvis seemingly sings the chorus through a megaphone, just like 'Yellow Submarine'.

'Big Sister's Clothes' was a production "Nick Lowe wasn't to blame for", with all instruments by Elvis. The theme of the previous song is told from the male victim's point of view, "sheep to the slaughter". It is unclear who is the little sister, Elvis lusting after a rock stars' plaything, perhaps. The spot of backwards accordion at the end is genuinely scary, like a musical shiver.

The augmented CD adds some interesting outtakes, and comments. 'Big Sister' uses "a figure borrowed from The Rolling Stones' 'Under My Thumb'", and the words were later amended to the song just discussed. Lost in the transition is the ska-like rhythm, and the line "Big Sister will be watching over you".

Among the other delights are a real collector's item, with Costello breathing life and meaning into Steve Nieve's 'Sad About Girls', the only time he deigns to notice The Attractions as creative songwriters. The world awaits *Elvis Sings The Songs Of Bruce Thomas*. Also present is the "rather bizarre" reading of the Cole Porter song 'Love For Sale', recorded shortly after *Trust* and sung solo to Billy Bremner's Spanish guitar. Proof that Costello has the gift of making the songs of others sound like his own. 'Weeper's Dream' is another first, a short guitar instrumental with lots of jazz inflections, and a melancholy feeling.

No-one can accuse Elvis of holding back on personal details here, except that they are not the kinds of secrets that anyone other than trainspotters really need to know. Entertaining, all the same. Thus, 'Gloomy Sunday', a 1930s song from Hungary about planning to kill oneself, which its writer later did, was recorded "to pass the time at September Sound Studio, Huddersfield during the Trust tour". From the passion in Elvis's voice, that sounds like only half the story.

In early January 1981, Elvis and The Attractions took their lives in their hands, and undertook the "English Mugs" month-long tour of America – "With Their Old Chinas" – with Squeeze in support. Glenn Tilbrook joined Costello occasionally for 'From A Whisper To A Scream'. After the previous disastrous US tour – too long, too hectic, too unsupervised – Riviera now programmed in proper rest periods. The gig list took in such stately venues as the Fox Warfield in San Francisco, Philadelphia's Tower Theatre, and Boston's Orpheum. As Tilbrook commented, "The venues were well-chosen, the itinerary was well worked out and both bands complemented each other well." Everything seemed improved. As one fan said, "I always liked his music, but now I like *him* too."

Martin Belmont played rhythm guitar some nights, as Steve Nieve's wife was heavily pregnant, and both men were on different kinds of emergency call. In fact, Steve's daughter did not emerge until Valentine's Day. The band covered lots of obscure R&B songs, but little country, except in Nashville – where the band made a trial recording with Billy Sherrill, and John McFee appeared for some country tunes as part of their gig at Vanderbilt University. In Austin, Joe Ely joined Elvis onstage for a Hank Williams tribute: 'Mind Your Own Business', 'Honky Tonkin'' and 'Move It On Over'.

Richard Grabel caught the tour in New York, and found that Costello had returned as someone different. The previous stage show used lots of red and green lights, "psychologically provocative". It applied the principles of Leni Riefenstahl's Nazi film *Triumph Of The Will* to a rock show, with Costello "a most unaccommodating and nasty Little Hitler". The same technique, incidentally, which The Residents applied to The Beatles on *Third Reich 'N' Roll*. The new Elvis actually smiles on stage, and sings to his audience rather than at them. Visually he is now matched by Nieve, bouncing on red high-top sneakers, a "bundle of nerves". He throws in a version of the Patsy Cline song 'She's Got You' – with gender reversed – and alludes to Bob Marley's 'Jammin'' in the middle of 'Watching The Detectives'. Where once his concerts were an ordeal, like surviving a battle, now, "He made me feel the pace of his heart and mind, which are both ticking very, very fast".

A detailed description of the band's last night at the Palladium opens Krista Reese's book. There is lots of junk merchandise out on the street – unofficial badges and T-shirts, while the adjacent pizza palace plays Elvis's music non stop. Tickets are being sold at four times their marked price. Inside, an official mug is for sale, as is the Two-Tone single for $3. The audience is young, white, and neatly dressed, while attendant celebrities include Richard Gere, Tim Curry, Peter Frampton and The Ramones, refused free backstage tickets. Elvis gets off the tour bus to a "rash of flashes", recoiling as if he has just been shot. When he comes onstage, everyone jumps to their feet, and he opens his set with 'Gloomy Sunday', of all things.

Elvis looks slick, "like Ronald Reagan" one fan comments, though the general consensus is that with more weight and a slightly receding hairline – and of course those dark glasses – he could be Roy Orbison.

He hardly moves, except to take the occasional drink from a cup on the organ. A couple kiss passionately during 'Watch Your Step'. Nieve is the stage standout: "In pants so snug they look like tights, he sways back and forth across the keyboard, as if waltzing." The lights come up, the audience disperses past a local radio station giving out free *Trust* adhesive patches, and coupons good for $2 off any Elvis album.

Reese's book is subtitled "a completely false biography based on rumour, innuendo and lies", which makes it sound more exciting than it actually is. The best chapter considers the career of obscure new-waver Jo Marshall, who Riviera brought over to London to record a demo tape. Elvis writes two songs for her, 'Mighty Man' and 'True Love', and teaches them to her in her kitchen. His famous black book is not just the index of slights of legend, but a working notebook, just like the one Lou Reed kept while slumming at Andy Warhol's Factory. "He carried it with him all the time," Marshall says. "He'd write down all kinds of things – dialogue, conversations and use it to write songs." He also passes out in her hotel room one night, through drink, "just like a little kid". Away from the media's prying attention, the F-Beat crowd are "really nice, really funny, and real drinkers".

Mary Costello is "very pretty, dark hair, beautiful skin…very English". One night at the Mudd club, Bebe Buell asks after Elvis; their nine-month liaison has finished that Spring. Supposedly she and Elvis collaborated on some songs together, yet to see the light of day. One night she talks about life on the road to Elvis: "I wouldn't care if my husband slept with the Dallas cowgirls. I've got his clothes, I know he'd have to come back." Elvis commends this attitude, and wistfully adds, "I wish you'd speak to my wife." Riviera is unable to fix up a deal for Marshall, and they part amicably, though he asks her not to record the two Elvis songs. No-one else has, unless they were retitled.

As proof of his new-found affability, Elvis even appeared on an NBC chat show, playing 'New Lace Sleeves' and 'Watch Your Step' – rush released on single as a result. He talked with Tom Snyder in a relaxed fashion, to the host's obvious relief. Elvis reveals that he was a humble computer operator, never a programmer, just a button pusher who cannot even operate a pocket calculator. He admires his dad, who "plays more dates a year than I do, he works very hard", and who warned him against getting involved with the music business. "I used to play with him sometimes, but I could never get in tune."

On their return, Elvis acted as producer on Squeeze's pop masterpiece *East Side Story*, assisted by Roger Bechirian, and the album proved an instant critical favourite, the *NME* describing it as "state of the art pop music". On the Tamla Motown influenced 'Tempted', Elvis sang backing vocals behind that master of aggrieved sadness, Paul Carrack. Carrack had left Ace – and 'How Long' – to replace Jools Holland, but in turn left Squeeze to join Carlene Carter, another F-Beat attraction. Squeeze soldiered on with Don Snow, and Costello again provided vocals for a later single, 'Black Coffee In Bed'.

Meanwhile, *Trust* reached Number Twenty-Eight in the US album charts, though the second UK single drawn from the LP, 'From A Whisper To A Scream', failed to chart. Jake did attempt some showbiz hype, arranging for the band to appear on Jimmy Saville's TV show *Jim'll Fix It*, in which Saville mimicked God, granting his young viewers' wishes like Santa Claus on Christmas morning. One boy wanted to become a roadie for a day, and did for the benefit of the cameras. On air at least, he missed out on an occupational hazard, Jake Riviera's notorious "truth attacks" on his staff. Elvis himself was under attack: a letter to *Melody Maker* from Karen Lubich, an Essex girl, who opined that he had got too big for his boots, while his "whining little voice murders any merit the song might have". As for 'Clubland' it was a flop because "it's no good and the paying public knows it". The authentic voice of the Eighties, market forces and all, already massed for the attack.

In March, Elvis and his band played a string of British gigs, under the generic title of "A Tour To Trust". The support act was Dave And The Mistakes, a band whom Elvis had first encountered in Stockholm. With a comic, overweight lead singer and songs halfway between Meat Loaf and Cheap Trick, they warmed up the audience nicely, without posing any kind of threat. Paulo Hewitt caught the opening gig at the St Austell Coliseum, Cornwall's answer to Las Vegas. 'Clubland' come to life, and two menacing bouncers deny access to the soundcheck. Once let in, the audience pogo enthusiastically, and Elvis "smiles and relaxes down to his silver shoes". 'Watching The Detectives' now quotes from Stevie Wonder's 'Masterblaster'. The way he screams 'Clowntime Is Over' sends "icy shivers down the spine".

At the Hammersmith Odeon, Costello opens with 'Shot With His Own Gun', dressed in a gumshoe's overcoat, smoking a cigarette, cradling his guitar with its plectrum still wedged in its strings. Adam Sweeting finds him "confident, relaxed and relishing his complete control of his music and his audience". In a packed hour, he ranges from the electric ferocity of 'I Can't Stand Up' – now quoting Wilson Pickett's '634-5789' – to a silky version of Randy Crawford's 'One Day I'll Fly Away'. "A timeless evening." Max Bell in *NME* saw the previous night's performance, which went more stickily, with Elvis at one point urging the audience to "cheer up". He revived 'The Beat' for "all of those who were with us in the Nashville days", and introduced one new song, 'Human Hands'.

The crowd at Birmingham Odeon were less mannerly, and unappreciative of the set list, largely drawn from *Get Happy!!* and *Trust*. They wanted the hits which Elvis promised them a medley of at the end of the concert, to which they impatiently concurred. There was no encore.

Costello told *The Observer* that "journalists hound me, which is why I haven't given an interview for years", but this didn't stop Mike Nicholls of *Record Mirror* getting backstage, and slipping past the dragon which is Jake Riviera. With a microphone under his coat – this is *Trust*, come to life – he gets chatting to an affable Elvis, relaxing in his dressing room after the Manchester gig, and hugging a girl who has just told him that he is a genius. He tells Nicholls, thinking him a fan, that he has a large stockpile of material, which helps him vary his live set every night. One evening on the current tour, he was called back eight times for encores. The recent US tour went well, "considering". The Columbus occurrence is skated over: "I was working and touring so much that it wasn't easy to stay in control."

The "interview" comes over as what it really is, Elvis letting his hair down and his mind wander, as he would with a real fan. No wonder that one feels Nicholls is skating on very thin ice here. As to current bands, Costello likes Julian Cope's The Teardrop Explodes, but not Echo And The Bunnymen. He still cannot understand why Graham Parker has not really made it: "He's got one of the greatest voices ever." As a lyric writer, "Chris Difford is really the business."

The ensemble move to the bar, where a clearly pissed Elvis buys his

215

supposed fan a tequila, then suddenly grows suspicious. "You're from *Record Mirror*. You're too suss." Suddenly Jake Riviera appears, tipped off by Mancunian Clive Gregson, an old friend of Costello's. "You're coming outside," Riviera menaces, and Nicholls is about to reply when "a viciously executed forearm smash caught the side of my cranium". A foot aimed at his groin connects with his knee, and he responds in kind, but protects his tape recorder. He exits, with dignity and interview intact, and bearing Elvis no ill will.

Riviera is a different matter: had I been that journalist, he would have been facing police action, or a private prosecution. This is the same man who threatened Krista Reese when she wrote informing him that she was writing a book on his charge that, "I would like to notify you that I will do everything in my power to prevent you. If this matter goes any further I shall pop in for a visit when I am next in New York." Maybe he did, but the book still came out.

On 5 May, Elvis showed his compassionate side, performing a solo concert to patients at the MENCAP Rural Training Centre, Lufton Manor. He played five songs including 'Little Sister' that were filmed to be screened at the "Year Of The Disabled" gig. At the month's close, he joined Pete Thomas, Nick Lowe and John Hiatt on guitar to guest on the George Jones TV special in LA's Country Club. Costello and Jones shared vocals on 'Stranger In The House', and flew down to Nashville to cut some tracks, in preparation for the full Attractions' sessions, a month later.

CHAPTER SEVEN

a country shade of blue

Costello had lost the large fan base he had acquired around the time of *Armed Forces*, when "new wave" music was still new, fresh and threatening. Now, the Top Forty was dominated by the narcissistic bleatings of the New Romantics, all puff sleeves and homo-eroticism, and the bleeps and whirrings of synthesiser bands. Even Costello's musical settings were starting to sound antique: real drums, how quaint! As ever in such circumstances, he did the unexpected, not attempting to catch up with technology, but instead plunging deep into the unfashionable waters of country music, seen in Britain as the resort of the terminally dim and unhip. Eddie Grundy in *The Archers* was a typical devotee, with his hat surmounted with cow horns, and his nostalgic songs to his favourite pig. A parody, but not that wide of the mark. By the same token, Elvis found in country a kind of blues for and by white trash, honest sentimentality and ponderous wordplay, but with a good heart. Exactly the mirror image of his own muse, in fact.

To add insult to injury to long-time fans, this renowned songwriter, the greatest of his generation, went full ahead by recording an album of cover versions of other people's songs. Elvis had played a form of country-rock with Flip City, specialising in the marijuana-fuelled, downhome style of the likes of Barefoot Jerry. His finest collaboration with the countryish Clover, 'Radio Sweetheart', was tucked away as the B-side of his first single. He had worked in Nashville as early as July

1978, duetting with long-time hero George Jones on his own song 'Stranger In The House', in itself some kind of cultural breakthrough. Nashville was not known to be over-impressed by foreign imitators, let alone from Great Britain, and certainly not from punk-rockers.

As Costello told *Record Collector*, "There we were, walking around Nashville. Someone had heard the outtake version of 'Stranger In The House'. George was doing this duets album and they figured they ought to cover all the markets. Truthfully I'd rather hear George Jones sing the song all the way through than me singing on it, but it was still a thrill to go there. The record company paid for me to go down there, took me out to see Bruce Springsteen and then George Jones didn't show, which was a bit disappointing. The producer, Billy Sherrill, said I might as well play a solo on it. I'd never played a guitar solo in my life, so the first one I put on record was this acoustic one."

He returned to Nashville in early 1979 on the Armed Funk tour. "We had a day off, and I went and made that record with Jones," he says. In real time, this time round. "Around that time, we recorded a couple of tracks, like 'He's Got You' as a try out, with Pete Drake on steel, working in the old Columbia Studio B, which was where *Blonde On Blonde* had been recorded. When we returned we were somewhat dismayed to find that they'd started renovating it, so we ended up in Studio A, which could have been anywhere. It wasn't so much what went on in the studio that coloured 'Almost Blue', it was more what didn't go on. Or what I got up to for the rest of the time."

George Jones had been introduced to Elvis by Greg Geller, who had signed Costello to Columbia, and it was during this session that he first met the legendary Billy Sherrill, Jones' own producer. Not known as an easy touch, he was immediately taken with Elvis – whose very name must have been like a loaded weapon in Presley's old musical haunts. Thus was the die cast. Costello had determined, "If we are going to do a record of ballads and country music, I want to do it properly and go to the heart of it and do it with Billy Sherrill."

There was one even greater spur to creativity, the deep fried emotion of Gram Parsons, already long dead, and a man whose brief but startling musical career had revolutionised the way that country music was perceived by the mass audience. As Elvis told Nick Kent, also no stranger to excess and, like Parsons, a man who hung out with

The Rolling Stones until burnt by their radiance, and expensive habits, "Gram had it all sussed. He didn't stick around – he made his best work and then he died. That's the way I want to do it." Not (fortunately) that Costello has yet been found overdosed in a seedy motel room. Indeed, for history to repeat itself, Jake Riviera would have to have then kidnapped the body, and cremated it in the desert, like a bizarre barbecue.

Costello neither shared Gram Parsons' privileged lifestyle, with huge personal wealth from the cradle, or his fundamental restlessness, leading to his rapid departure from first The Byrds, and then The Flying Burrito Brothers, and eventually from Emmylou Harris and his own company. Neither has Elvis approached quite the quality of heartbreak in Parsons' songs and voice. To be truly like that, you have to live it as well, as Nick Drake, Ian Curtis and Jeff Buckley all sadly attest. Not waving, but drowning. In any respect, the kind of nobility that Costello was trying to locate in country music, largely through Parsons, was a long way from the cheery banalities of Flip City, or the "funky country music all night long" which Bruce Thomas wrote about in Quiver. This was music for grown ups, with the lights full on.

On 18 May, Costello and The Attractions took up residence in CBS Studio A, Nashville, with Billy Sherrill at the mixing desk. John McFee was back, on steel guitar. Elvis needed someone he could trust as the musical mainstay for these uncharted waters, as bold in their way as Fairport Convention inviting fiddler Dave Swarbrick to mike up his violin, and rock up traditional folk. "We wanted the sound," Elvis says, "but we didn't necessarily want the main instrumental line which usually comes from the steel in country to be somebody we'd never heard before."

McFee was now a member of The Doobie Brothers. In February 1979, he had joined The Attractions at LA's Palomino Club, woodshedding country standards like 'He'll Have To Go' by Jim Reeves – a less glamorous fatality than Parsons – Eddie Noakes' 'Psycho' and '(If I Could Put Them All Together) I'd Have You' by George Jones. Costello was determined to choose and arrange the material for *Almost Blue*, and working with his old friend McFee, "We could do the arrangements properly before we got to Nashville." As Bruce Thomas was again indisposed, Paul "Bassman" Riley who had played with Pete Thomas in Chilli Willi helped during the rehearsal, where over forty country songs were demoed.

Costello had decided to take a break from songwriting, and express his "current feelings" through the words of others. As he told Nicky Campbell, "As much as I wanted to escape the limitations of just being a pop singer, known for only one song, it seemed there wasn't an obvious audience for what we did. *Get Happy!!* sold half of what *Armed Forces* did, and *Trust* didn't do as well as that. Maybe I could just get away from my own self for a while, and throw the light on the emotional side of what I do." He did not want this to be totally divorced from the other things he did, especially his work with The Attractions.

"Not all the band were that keen to do it, but I didn't want to go off on my own," he says, "and grab the Nashville rhythm section. Then it would be just like going to the funfair and sticking your head through one of those little cut-out things and having your picture taken. I thought it could be a good emotional record. It was something that was very real to me when I did it."

The original intention had been to record an album of melancholy songs, not a purely C&W project. He had already made trial recordings of 'Love For Sale' and 'Gloomy Sunday' – both now collected on the *Trust* CD – and live sets of the time included 'Two Steps From The Blues' and 'I'll Take Care Of You', both ironically enough by Bobby "Blue" Bland. Even the eventual album cover drew liberally from the sleeve of jazzman Kenny Burrell's *Midnight Blue* LP.

Over in Nashville, it was time to meet Sherrill, who had already infiltrated one of his own compositions, 'Too Far Gone', into the index of possibilities. His main job would be to keep things cooking in the studio – though he often seemed disinterested, and more concerned with buying a new speedboat – and arranging the overdubbing of strings and backing vocals onto the raw first takes. It was just this kind of smoothness that Sherrill was paid to provide, a master chef (over) sweetening the basic ingredients. It was just this kind of thing, conversely, that was most dedicated to alienating the target audience. If even Dylan had been tamed during the sessions for his anodyne *Nashville Skyline*, on which he disastrously tried to sing properly, what would become of Elvis. On the other hand, Dylan's richest album, *Blonde On Blonde*, was also a Nashville project.

The Attractions made a statement of intent at the outset, with a breathless gallop through 'Why Don't You Love Me (Like You Used To Do)'. All eyes swivelled towards the silent Sherrill. "We were expecting him to walk out." Instead, his voice issued – like God – from the control room intercom. "Elvis, we got Hank Williams on the phone." At first, it seemed plain sailing. From an initial list of thirty country classics, Elvis and The Attractions rattled through twenty-five in five days, working the afternoon shift, two till eight. Just like the vanity factory, in fact, though shorter and later hours. As Elvis explained, "The best way to work was not to labour over it too long. If it didn't come in one or two takes we'd go on to another song."

Sherrill knew all the songs, apart from those written by Gram Parsons – still a Nashville outsider, even after his death – and considered most of them "worn out", as viewed by contemporary Nashville. Sherrill offered instead a box of cassettes of material he thought more appropriate, including 'Heartbreak Hotel' and a Willie Nelson murder ballad, containing the lines "the flesh around your neck is pale/indented by my finger nail". Elvis was startled after one take to find Sherrill and engineer Ron "Snake" Reynolds comparing handguns behind the mixing console. "These Nashville people, they talk to one another all the time in this unbelievable code," he recalls. "They put each other on – 'Gee, I don't know how you get that sound on that fiddle, Toad.' They're always hitching up their tackle, so you don't think they're queer. It's all that flexing, and shuffling, and hitching...they are the kings of their castle, there. He'd be cleaning his gun in the studio. 'Have you seen my gun? This is the pocket model.' And I'd be going, 'Oh my God.'"

Elvis too, though, knew how to stick to his guns. Sherrill "found it quite hard to adjust to why all these mad English people were so enthusiastic about those songs which were old hat to him". Many others have wondered the same, since.

Perhaps it was all a way of overcoming the implications of the Holiday Inn fracas, showing Costello's musical catholicism. As he himself said, "I used to be quite a bigot, but I tried to find things in all kinds of music that I like." It was also a way of expunging the hurt of the Bebe Buell affair, and the damage that it did to his marriage. Like

John Lennon's 'Help!', it is easy to overlook the cry of desperation here, which is clear enough in the sleeve and song lyrics, if you regard the song as less an exercise in irony than an outpouring of personal feeling. It is probably both.

The album was recorded and mixed in two weeks. To celebrate, Elvis and band were invited to join Johnny Cash and his family for dinner, with Sherrill arriving by speedboat. This caused consternation in Nashville – where it was like a summons to Buckingham Palace – and back at the small hotel where Elvis and The Attractions were staying, and attempting to drink dry. "They had previously believed that we were only in town to rid the world of alcohol."

Pete Thomas was incredulous at what they found. "First of all there's June Carter's Railway Station Gift Shop, then you turn in, and pull into this extraordinary house on the side of a lake, and he came to greet us with no shoes on, and he said, 'How you like to see my Rooshian hogs?' We said, 'Yes, of course.' He's got his own game park." They arrive there by van, and Jake Riviera has a close encounter with an ostrich, which fixed itself onto his nose, and then ran off. The biter bit, one feels. "Then Johnny Cash threw himself over this fence, into this muddy spinney, with a bag of fruit, and a mango in his hand, the size of a baby's head. Then there's just this blur, and an enormous hog with tusks came out of the bushes, flew through the air, took half of the mango and vanished again. We're all just standing there. He says, 'Yeah, I brought those little dudes back from Rooshia under the seat of my Lear jet.'"

In September, 'A Good Year For The Roses', written by Jerry Chestnut and originally recorded by George Jones, was released as a single. It obtained heavy airplay spanning the pop muzak of Radio One and the easy listening of Radio Two, rising to Number Six in the UK charts, and proving its singer's contention that it "would probably reach a lot of people that don't buy our records normally", and even those who rarely listened to country records.

"We had this one very big hit out of the blue in England, nowhere else, maybe in Holland," Elvis recalls. "And suddenly, I'd be in the supermarket, and what were older women to me then were suddenly coming on to me in the fish fingers, because they'd been taken with this record, it was so romantic. It was like I was Julio Iglesias."

Almost Blue appeared in October, and rose to Seven in the album charts, and the edges of the US Top Fifty, though Costello complained that the Americans were unsure how to market it. Two years later, he felt the album was far too miserable. "I thank God I was never *this* depressed."

Although the album has not worn well, and regularly hits the bottom of fans' polls of their favourite Elvis records, it was well received at the time, not least for its bravery.

The album sleeve comes in a range of colours: in Keith Morris's dramatic photo, Elvis has removed his spectacles and covers his face with one hand – an ornate ring on its stubby middle finger – as if hiding tears. The "l" of "Blue" is like a strip torn down the middle of the photo. A removable sticker reads "Warning: this album contains country & western music and may produce radical reaction in narrow minded people." On the back cover the band grin faintly like psychos, and John McFee looks goofy in a stetson. "No spoiler signal", reads a logo.

Most reviewers agreed. Paul Du Noyer in *NME* found the album "a richly satisfying sidestep", respectful but never slavish. Elvis plays things straight, rather than "exploiting the coy, camp and kitsch angles" which country music lends itself to. Not to worry, Paul. Acts like the Arizona Smoke Review and hippie gynaecologist Dr Sam Hutt – under his alias of Hank Wangford – would do just that, to great comic effect.

Before *Almost Blue*, English country bands had usually been slavishly derivative of their American models, and captive to a small genre following. The one band to break out of this self-imposed ghetto was Matthews Southern Comfort, who had a Number One hit with their sweet and hopeful take on Joni Mitchell's song 'Woodstock'. Iain Matthews had used his own matchless taste for a good song to infiltrate material by Johnny Cash and Gene Clark into Fairport's live set. Southern Comfort were led musically by Gordon Huntley – a relatively old man often clad in sandals – whose use of steel guitar was at that time almost unique among English bands. American expatriate Glen Campbell (*not* the Nashville singer) had used steel with The Misunderstood, but to create psychedelic sound patterns, a different thing entirely.

Back, then, to the reviews. Long time Elvis fan Allan Jones saw his hero as already drawn to the "maudlin regret that invariably follows a surrender to sudden whims of self-destructive passion. Here he immerses himself in the sound of breaking hearts, and his voice has never sounded so expressive and relaxed. The poignancy of some of these songs should have you on the couch with a cushion in your mouth." The album is an affront to the "synthetic posturing of most current pop".

Country music is a defiantly American phenomenon, and *Rolling Stone* was more muted, though it found The Attractions doing a "decent job" as a country band, and praised the first Costello album on which you could decipher all the words. *Boston Rock* found Costello settling for love rather than passion, while *Trouser Press* asked, "Why *shouldn't* Elvis make a country album?" Back in England, Mark Ellen found "a dozen old songs with all the colour pumped back into them, served up as a cool classic country beat overlayed with swooning country guitars". Mouth watering!

For promo purposes, F-Beat released an interview album – subtitled "Elvis Introduces His Favorite Country Songs", note the American spelling – to selected journalists and DJs. It is now a collectors' item. "I tried to ask myself the questions, and I found it so embarrassing that I drank about three bottles of wine and by the end of it I sounded like Dean Martin." His comments are full of good sense, as are those on the CD reissue, and I will intersperse them with my own less sensible views of each track.

Hank Williams' 'Why Don't You Love Me (Like You Used To Do)' was a particular example of "some songs that didn't belong to me, but meant a lot to me." It opens at a gallop, with honky-tonk piano from Nieve, and a rockabilly vocal, and closes on a scream and two crashing chords. "For some strange reason, the entire performance was double-tracked in a bizarre double dare showdown," Elvis says. Don Gibson's 'Sweet Dreams' is a piano tour-de-force, with slowed down, melancholy vocal. A song covered by Patsy Cline and Loretta Lynn, "in whose fan club we were all given complimentary memberships while out walking in Nashville one day".

Steve Nieve found 'Success' on an obscure album by Loretta during the search for material. "We must have gone through

Elvis in "psychotic bank clerk" mode

Pete Thomas towers over the other Attractions: (l-r) Bruce Thomas, Elvis and Steve Nieve

Ross MacManus with Mary Costello, his daughter-in-law, 1985

On the road, thirsty for fame

With Jake Riviera, manager and managed

The Attractions in Chicago, posing amusingly

The bow-tied crooner

Bebe Buell – and one of her own Attractions – denies being this year's model

These men have come to repossess
your house

Human hands

With the legendary Chet Baker, cool as
a snake

With Ricky Skaggs, star of "new
country"

With Van Morrison at the Royal Albert Hall in 1987

Cait O'Riordan bites fellow Pogue Shane MacGowan

Live Aid, 1985, singing an old Northern folk song: 'All You Need Is Love'

The "beard years" begin

Elvis as Jerry Garcia's long lost son

With Sam Moore: blues brothers

With long time musical ally, Nick Lowe

With Burt Bacharach

With The Brodsky Quartet, the Theatre Royal,
Brighton, 28 May, 1993

Back to basics

With Debbie Harry of The Jazz Passengers

Quizzical Elvis, March 1994

At the Royal Albert Hall, 28 November, 1994

Elvis in 1995 – so just who was that angry, young sod?

With Bob Dylan at the Brixton Academy,
31 March 1995

At the 1995 Ivor Novello awards,
clutching his prize

Appearing on Channel 4's short-lived
The White Room

With Cait O'Riordan: his aim is true

hundreds of albums, trying to find that one song that we could make our own," he recalls. Another weepie, with Elvis curiously unmannered and Nieve's double-handed piano (the sign of a real player) by turn stirring and tinkly. 'I'm Your Toy' was originally called 'Hot Burrito #2' when recorded by The Flying Burrito Brothers on *The Gilded Palace Of Sin*. "It was written by a man called Gram Parsons and it has always been one of my favourite songs and it's been an ambition of mine to record it," Elvis says. He sounds genuinely moved as he sings this, and there is more beef to the rhythm section, otherwise largely mixed out of existence.

Parsons' work with the Burritos and on The Byrds' *Sweetheart Of The Rodeo* "provided [Elvis's] first sustained interest in country music" – same here – and led him to the likes of Merle Haggard. 'Tonight The Bottle Let Me Down' is "for panic drinkers anywhere", and Nieve is suitably inspired, running his fingers up and down the keyboard. Side One ends with 'Brown To Blue', written by Johnny Mathis and sung better by George Jones, whose version Elvis unearthed among a batch of ex-jukebox singles sent over from the States. Zal Yanovsky of The Lovin' Spoonful also cut it, for his bizarre *Alive And Living In Argentina* solo album, closer to Martin Mull than Johnny Cash in spirit, ie satirical.

Side Two opens with 'A Good Year For The Roses', also associated with George Jones who had a hit with it in 1971. The version is Nashville silk at its best, with a deep-voiced Elvis – breaking into emotion on the chorus – and a magical combination of subdued organ, steel guitar and strings. Pete Thomas is as laid back as he will ever get, laying brushes on his drums like a man breathing.

Charlie Rich's song 'Sittin' And Thinkin'' "was one of the songs that I almost left off the album". It was originally recorded for Sun, with a young engineer called Billy Sherrill at the controls. There is more force to the drums here, and Elvis sounds drunk, as the lyrics demand. The vocal chorus whoops in sympathy. 'Colour Of The Blues' "proves that Sherrill can still produce the simple honky-tonk", thus disproving some people's worries that Elvis might be swamped by the Nashville sound. The song was originally recorded by George Jones, "for both the Starday and Musicor labels", Elvis adds authoritatively. He leers the lyric, though the steel guitar is a little too syrupy here.

'Too Far Gone' was written by Sherrill, and "really got the Nashville treatment. Billy made sure that I sang his original melody, as the one I'd learnt came from various other interpretations." Elvis had first heard the version by Tammy Wynette. He almost speaks the words at times, while Nieve plays expressively, and the arrangement seems to ascend to heaven. Elvis could almost be Jim Reeves, here.

"We didn't just come to Nashville to record slow, quiet country songs. We also came to Nashville to record 'Honey Hush'." It began life as an R&B song, written by Big Joe Turner, although, "Our version owes more to The Johnny Burnette Trio record." The magic of early Sun records was just this, grafting white country onto black R&B. Costello sounds most like himself here, with a crack to his voice, and The Attractions hit a groove, like Dylan circa 1965, on the reinvigorated blues of 'From A Buick Six'. Costello almost barks at the end, though politely.

Allan Jones comments that this "brief, almost cursory flurry-like balling in the dark is good sweaty fun, but a bit fumbled"! I thought that country music kept that kind of thing firmly locked behind closed doors. Mind you, a rather suspect survey once claimed that country fans were both more loyal to one partner and more sexually active than adherents of other genres.

'How Much I Lied' comes from *GP*, Gram Parsons' first solo album. "We started doing the song of which we had no real formal arrangement. And yet we did it in one take." Elvis sounds confidential, and Nieve plays the lead instrument, as so often here.

With time, the album sounds a little over-polite, and it is shockingly short by Elvis's standards. The CD, almost double the length, is far more satisfying, with the live tracks recorded in Aberdeen in particular possessing a snap and crackle lacking on the Nashville takes. The Royal Albert Hall taping of 'I'm Your Toy', with full orchestra, pulls dimensions out of Costello's voice barely hinted at in the studio version: urgency, passion and danger.

Perhaps Elvis should have instead recorded a tribute solely to Gram Parsons, or a thematically more ambitious history of country music. The songs chosen may well reflect what is going on in the singer's own life – loss, despair, a love affair on the rocks – but they lack the nimble word play of his own lyrics, or indeed the self-revelation of *Blue*, Joni Mitchell's near namesake to this album, a *ménage à trois* (at least).

The album's success in the UK was helped by a documentary aired as part of Melvyn Bragg's ITV arts series, *The South Bank Show*, about the making of the album, and with generous in-the-studio footage. *MM*'s Adam Sweeting reckoned that Elvis came over as lucid and articulate: "Despite Riviera's efforts to persuade everybody otherwise, Costello is palpably human, almost academic in his knowledge of the history of country music, and even capable of nervousness when confronted with Billy Sherrill." The duel between the two men is at the heart of the film, arguing about whether Elvis should sing "drunk" or "loaded" – Billy wins – trading enigmas:"You sure know how to make a man feel old," the Nashville veteran comments, though he also later confides that, "I loved it. I might become an Elvis Costello fan after all."

Elvis talks about Gram Parsons' particular brand of self-destructiveness, "Which I don't subscribe to – yet." Both in the studio and live in Aberdeen, he sings Parsons' 'I'm Your Toy' "guitarless at the microphone and wringing the lyric out of himself with clumsy, almost spastic gestures, with his two clenched fists".

Years later, Costello told *Record Collector* that the documentary was well put together, but, "It made Sherrill the villain, and it exaggerated it a little bit. He showed more interest some days." Making the album had been a deliberate attempt to change his image, as popularly conceived. "It's obviously a blessing to have such a powerful image from your first few records, but limiting. And when your own record company defines you in those terms then it becomes difficult, because they're not even helping to promote the new image. The country record was one attempt to escape."

Such tensions surfaced when Elvis and The Attractions played the Grand Ol' Opry in Nashville, a foolhardy move indeed. Opening with three Hank Williams songs straight off didn't help. "The kids who came to see us in Nashville didn't want us to be country: they wanted us to be even more punk than we were perceived to be in the rest of America." Even there, they were accepted as the real thing. "The Pistols did one short US tour, The Damned did a tour before that and The Clash came afterwards, so we were the first group that many people in America saw that was anything like a punk band."

Costello had perhaps attempted his country excursion too young. "I feel it was like a young Shakespearean actor playing Hamlet before he should. I was begging the tragedy to come upon me before I was really ready to wear that grey beard." But isn't Hamlet a young man's role? The album is more like Hamlet attempting to play King Lear.

In June's *Hot Press*, Elvis was asked to name his favourite album. The list is fascinating, and concentrates on great singers and songwriters, often combined in one person. After listing everything from The Impressions' *Big Sixteen* to Billie Holiday to The Ronettes and The Supremes, to *Pet Sounds* and Richard and Linda Thompson, to Ella Fitzgerald and Joni Mitchell and the cream of the punk bands – with even a token nod to *Mad About The Wrong Boy* – he settles not on Hank Williams or George Jones but on Frank Sinatra. His album *Sings For Only The Lonely* gives few great lyrical insights into the human condition – "these songs date from an era of more stylised emotions" – but the voice "says it all". "The mood is extremely melancholic", romantic but never sentimental, and the singing has a "personal sounding sadness". Almost blue, in fact.

Despite their country excursion, The Attractions were still a rock band, one at the height of their powers, and business continued as usual. On 1 June, Elvis appeared at London's Apollo Theatre in aid of the mental health charity Mencap. The evening was punningly called "Fund-a-mental Frolics", and featured a mixture of musicians and comics: Ian Dury, Rowan Atkinson, Alan Price and Alexei Sale. Elvis appeared solo with acoustic guitar, singing 'Psycho' and 'Gloomy Sunday'.

The following month, reunited with The Attractions, he played the Macroom Festival in County Cork. An oddly violent crowd surged forwards during his set and during 'Watch Your Step' beer cans showered the stage. It was hardly an auspicious return to his roots. The band settled into the intro to 'The Beat', and kept it going. "We've been playing this riff for a long time now," he shouted back, "and we can play it for a whole *lot longer*." More cans rained down. "As if we weren't in *enough* trouble, assholes," he glared. He somehow continued through 'New Lace Sleeves', seguing into a brittle 'Lovers' Walk', then a heartbreaking version of 'Alison'. "Well, I was hoping this was going to be a *cheerful* occasion, but it looks like some of you fuckers have got other ideas." Even Pete Thomas expressed his admiration later. "I was proud to be backing my frontman," he admits. "I thought he gave it a damn good hiding." The ever faithful Allan Jones – to whom Elvis chatted amicably on this occasion – described the gig as "rock music that affected every moment of your life, a guerrilla attack".

Elvis and troops then set off for gigs in Belgium, Holland and Sweden, though Elvis was plagued with a sore throat, which led to the cancellation of some gigs. He looked ill and overweight, a pasty dead-ringer for Gram Parsons, as captured in a film of his concert at the Werchter Festival. Nevertheless, a Swedish paper headlined its review "Toppen, Elvis", and wrote of his "gott humor". He even performed Max Romeo's 'Wet Dream', an exercise in reggae smut. When the record was banned by the BBC, Romeo described its chorus of "push it up" as being about the erection of a garden shed. He was *not* convincing.

On 30 July The Attractions – joined by John McFee – filmed a concert in a C&W club in Aberdeen, for *The South Bank Show*, and to an audience in stetsons, Brylcreem, fancy shirts and cowboy boots. *NME* reported that the band at first sounded rusty, but Elvis soon began to "create more buzz than a queen bee". The highlight was a Merle Haggard song, 'Tonight The Bottle Let Me Down'.

On 29 August the band played at the Rock On The Tyne Festival at Gateshead International Stadium, along with rising superstars U2, the passionate attack of Doll By Doll and blues veteran Rory Gallagher. Costello represented "new" music, which indicated the mind-set of the organisers. U2 preceded Elvis on the Saturday afternoon, though *MM*'s Patrick Humphries found them unable to "communicate that passion either lyrically or musically" and the incendiary menace of Doll By Doll "unremarkable". He *did* like Costello's set, the songs "awesome in their power". Humphries points out that Costello stands "fists clenched, right leg slightly bent, at the confessional of the microphone stand", suggesting that young Declan's Catholic training has fed into his urge to reveal every sneaky passion. Is there really no such thing as original sin?

Paul Morley, as different a rock critic from Humphries' careful fact-finding as could be imagined, found that watching Elvis in such circumstances was like "trying to read Dostoyevsky in a cold waiting room in Crewe surrounded by bored United fans". He wrote down the set list, then lost the piece of paper – "the sort of thing that makes my editor sick"! For the record, Costello's set eschewed Nashville for previously unheard songs from the forthcoming record. 'Man Out Of Time', 'Tears Before Bedtime', 'Town Crier' and the 'Long Honeymoon' were all debuted, along with future outtakes like 'Town Where Time Stood Still' and 'Goody Two Shoes'. 'Why Don't You Love Me (Like You Used To Do)' was the only country tune in sight.

That autumn, Elvis and band rehearsed in a friend's cottage in Devon – eight-track recordings made at the time suggest an album very similar to *Trust* – then moved up to George Martin's AIR Studios. This time there was no Nick Lowe. The album was credited as "produced by Geoff Emerick from an original idea by Elvis Costello", though in practice the two collaborated as equal partners. Emerick had long experience as George Martin's engineer, and Costello was also rewriting song in the studio as he went, which adds to the freshness of the resulting album, still reckoned by many as Elvis's best. It was certainly the most luxuriant, produced with the same aural richness as Chris Thomas's early work for Procol Harum.

Elvis was far more affable these days, and visited Radio One's Andy Peebles to play his all time favourite records. Opening with The 101-ers, cut before Joe Strummer "discovered he could make money out of social consciousness", he worked his way through Little Richard, Mel And Tim – an obscure soul side he bought in Leeds – The Expressos and Chet Baker. He admits to finding synthesisers wearing, but admires the way that the likes of Soft Cell can now make records at home. Conversely, he has never been that keen on going to see live gigs: "I think records are the real test." His final choice is Nick Kent's sole single with The Subterraneans.

Elvis also undertook a "Blind Date Review" for *Melody Maker*. His comments are pithy: Simple Minds are "very wet in more than one sense", The Go-Go's "weak-kneed LA new wave", and Joan Armatrading is "under attack from a Steve Lillywhite production". Genesis are "neat muso-rock" and Freddie Mercury a "prancing megalomaniac." He *does* like The Fun Boy Three, ABC and Tammy Wynette.

Meanwhile, the Almost Blue Tour spanned late December and early January, taking in London, Los Angeles, New York, Nashville, Paris,

Dublin – and the Civic Hall, Guildford. The set list was divided almost equally between old favourites, new and as yet unrecorded material, and the country songs, which sounded "more alive" without the Nashville sweetening.

On 7 January, Elvis materialised before a sell-out audience at the Royal Albert Hall, and fronting the ninety-two piece Royal Philharmonic Orchestra, "added Attractions", after the interval. He had confessed in advance that he was nervous about the gig. "The orchestra's costing me a fortune, and I'm only getting one shot at it." The evening was scored by Robert Kirby, whose intricate musical settings for Nick Drake, Sandy Denny and The Strawbs were a benchmark in how *not* to swamp the singer. It was Elvis's first dip in the cool waters of orchestral sound, and a prediction of things to come.

The set list mixed songs from *Almost Blue* with some Elvis originals. Costello messed up the opening verse of the first song with full orchestra, 'Shot With His Own Gun'. "We'd done one rehearsal the day before, and I hadn't heard the arrangements before that," he explains. Given the full monty were orchestrally augmented versions of 'Alison' and 'Watching The Detectives', and new songs like 'Town Crier'. He encored with 'Peace Love And Understanding' then called Nick Lowe up from the audience to take a bow. The show was professionally filmed, though no footage or the projected live album have yet to emerge, though the evening must have been planned with exactly that in mind. The sound balance was crystal clear, and for the ever-faithful Allan Jones, "Costello's voice raided every emotional avenue on its way to the heart." Graham Lock saw the ghost of Billie Holiday behind the "long held hushes, as Elvis wrung intensity out of silence".

In April, the live take of Gram Parsons' 'I'm Your Toy' appeared as a single, with a cover photograph taken from the RAH gig, Elvis in bow tie and suit, like a younger version of his father fronting a big (ger) band. Different formats of the single came with outtakes from the Nashville recording session, some collected on the augmented *Almost Blue* CD, with a second take on Elvis's own song 'Tears Before Bedtime'. "The concept was to record some of the best country songs – mine don't belong to those. People might have presumed that I thought I was as good a songwriter as Don Gibson if I put my songs next to 'Sweet Dreams'. I know where my limits lie."

But could Don Gibson have ever written a song as powerful or vicious as 'I Want You', say. Elvis's cover of 'Psycho', a song as extreme as country gets, appeared on the flip side of 'Sweet Dreams', which rose to Forty-Two in the UK charts that January. It is an astonishing performance, with Elvis close to the mic, conveying psychosis "by entering an imperturbable calm", in the words of Dave Marsh, who rightly puts this among the 1,000 greatest all time tracks.

No-one else could so fully encompass "the singer's dissociation from his own actions and his absolute engulfment in self pity". It is the kind of inner deadness which crime writer Ruth Rendell is so good at evoking, hypnotically. As Marsh notes, "Costello has actually become the kind of guy whose life Bruce Springsteen took notes upon for *Nebraska*."

The country excursion was over, though.

CHAPTER EIGHT

imperial blue

Elvis set out for a short European tour in April, supported by the Dutch band Oh Boy – with a Costello clone on lead vocals – and a tape played though the PA of some of his favourite tracks, ranging from calypso to Patsy Cline. Red spotlights lit the opening song, 'New Amsterdam', during which a fan offered Elvis a bouquet of red and yellow tulips, then straight into ninety minutes of passionate singing. The sound system had been drastically upgraded for the tour, and Costello continued his habit of throwing in rare cover versions. This time around, these included 'All These Things' – a 1966 hit for The Uniques – and Sonny Boy Williamson's 'One Way Out'.

The only sour note of the tour occurred half way through a gig at Zwolle. A heckler near the front shouted out for "something up-tempo" during 'Almost Blue', then the ultimate post-punk insult, "You sound like Pink Floyd." Bruce Thomas threw a glass of water over the interloper, which made him swear all the louder, until Elvis hit him full in the face with the microphone stand, then carried on with the song as if nothing had happened. After finishing the song, he unplugged his guitar and walked offstage, to the mystification of everyone, closely followed by The Attractions. They returned, but tore up the original set list to play the minimum songs necessary to fulfil their contract, and at maximum speed. A forty-five-minute set, and no encores.

Later that spring, Elvis and band set off for a tour of Australia and New Zealand, supported by local bands Pel Mel and The Reels. Gone was the surly and brutish new wave star who provoked riots on his previous tour, back in 1978. Costello was affability itself, popping into local radio stations to spin some favourite sounds, allowing selected concerts to be broadcast and even talking to the press. There was even a special, Australian-only, LP release. *Almost New* gathered together rare B-sides and live tracks. A review of the Brisbane show, by Peter Mudd, noticed that his suit was of a "finer cut", while his guitar playing, "while still basic pluck/strum/thrash contributes more than it did a few years ago". There were few pauses between songs, and the set really rocked towards the end.

In June 1982, 'You Little Fool', failed to reach the Top Fifty. With a cover like a teenage magazine, scribbled over by Barney Bubbles in red and green felt-tip, it was the wrong choice as a taster of the new album, a "good pop construction", but the "track most reminiscent of what we had done before". As a sign of the name changes to come, the B-side contained 'The Stamping Ground', credited to The Emotional Toothpaste. When released in July, though, *Imperial Bedroom* came straight in at Number Six in the UK album charts.

Originally planned as a double, but squeezed onto one album, it was packed with songs and new sounds, like a more user-friendly version of *Get Happy!!*. The working title had been "Revolution Of The Mind", like something from the late Sixties, and a long distant echo of *Revolver*. This was later changed to "PS I Love You", shared with an early Beatles track, but that idea was ruined by the release of a compilation LP of the same title. This contained silly love songs a million miles from the twisted emotions that lurked here. The new title had, for Costello, "just the right combination of splendour and sleaze to fit all the tracks on the album".

The US promotional campaign centred on the word "Masterpiece?". The question mark particularly annoyed Elvis, but it worked, and American critics compared the record to *Sergeant Pepper*, in its range and majesty, a defining moment in rock history. As if to publicly acknowledge this new status, *Rolling Stone* carried a major interview between Elvis and Greil Marcus, headlined "Elvis Costello Repents". It was meant to be a once-only confession, for as Elvis himself said, with more hope than judgement, "I can't go on right through my life explaining that incident." Elvis wears red shoes for the interview, and the two talk for five hours, the morning after a sell-out, two-hour concert at Berkeley. If nothing else, Costello possesses extraordinary energy.

So does Marcus. *In The Fascist Bathroom*, which collects his writings on punk, is obsessive in its tracking of Costello's persona. As early as 1977, Greil notes an emotional coldness to the singer: "He never cracked a sneer, let alone a smile." Elvis combines this arrogance with "the fear of the imposter who's sure he'll be shot before he gets through the third number". Marcus went on to devote a book to Costello's namesake, in *Dead Elvis; A Chronicle Of A Cultural Obsession*, which includes a prose piece by Elvis II, about cannibalism. "The nose they say is served separately, or the tongue." He also provides a quote on the back jacket of *The Dustbin Of History*, which could describe either Marcus or himself: "But once you have enough words in circulation, somebody will come along to use them to trip you up."

The interview, though, is an attempt to set Elvis back on his feet. They talk first about Elvis's course of study at high school: "second half of the century working-class British literature – *Saturday Night And Sunday Morning, The Loneliness Of The Long Distance Runner*, and *Billy Liar*". Costello's latter-day lyrics mine much the same territory, kitchen sink drama which encompasses both realism and a dreamed escape.

Elvis learnt his craft by trial and error, in public. "Then you have the humiliation of being *crushed*." The Ohio incident was fuelled by the "musical dishonesty" which Stills and his ilk represented. Its impact remains, though. He had met Michael Jackson in the studio, with Paul McCartney, and all was fine until someone introduced Bruce Thomas as his bass player. "Oh God, I don't dig that guy," was Jackson's immediate response, not realising that Elvis was in the room. He had heard about the incident, third hand, from Quincy Jones. "It depressed me that I wouldn't be able to go up and shake his hand, because he wouldn't want to shake my hand. *Or* James Brown, for that matter. What could I say? How could you explain such a thing? But there's nothing I'd like more."

Costello's early image as an angry young misfit soon made it "a problem for me to incorporate the wider, more compassionate point of view that I felt". He feels corralled into a musical ghetto, with his own cult following. He had recently seen Randy Newman in concert, and was sickened by the smugness of the audience, faced by such savage and emotional songs. "I couldn't watch him for the audience." The only way out is to control the means of production. "We were comfortably contained within the business, instead of having some dramatic effect on the structure of the business." This is a conflict which continues up to the time of writing, with Costello signing a new contract which gives him exactly that freedom, to release what he wants, in whatever musical genre.

With the release of *Imperial Bedroom*, Costello made just such a breakthrough, to a non-rock audience, drawing fulsome tributes from the likes of *Newsweek, The New York Times* – which compared Costello to the Gershwin brothers – and *The Los Angeles Times*. Others reported Pete Thomas less than happy with his drums relegated to a subordinate role. One commentator even claimed that he had been "banned from the studio".

Pete Doggett for *Record Collector* asked why Elvis had at last agreed to have his lyrics printed on the inner sleeve, then deliberately scrambled them, as if to repel interest. "I've never been terribly comfortable with having these little poems on the sleeve," he explains. "I think it makes too much claim on the words. I intended them to be *heard*. So I thought I'd make them like a telegram where somebody forgot the punctuation. It makes for quite interesting reading. You can make up your own lines, starting in the middle of one song and into the next one." Or you could do a William Burroughs, and cut and paste them into something else entirely.

With a relaxed recording schedule, over twelve weeks, the band "wanted to try a few different options in the studio. We started working on all the songs that we were planning to record, and the tape of the rehearsal sounds just like *Trust*. But once we started to push them out a little bit and I started to mess around with the arrangements, they started to change in character." Geoff Emerick's experience helped here, and after supervising The Beatles at the height of psychedelia, he was "used to being thrown an incomprehensible garble of sounds and musical directions, and making some sense of it. He was used to innovation, and to the direction being a bit berserk."

Emerick was also working on Paul McCartney's *Tug Of War*, in an adjacent studio, a fortuitous coincidence. Steve Nieve came to the fore as an arranger on an album which Elvis saw as set apart by its "vocal and instrumental additions". Nieve wrote the charts for a trio of French horns, supposedly Wagnerian, on 'Long Honeymoon', a brass and woodwind section on 'Pidgin English', Philly soul violins on 'Town Crier' and a full orchestral score for 'And In Every Home'. George Martin himself cast his eye over this, as it contained various allusions to his own work with The Beatles. Nieve conducted the forty-piece orchestra himself.

The band themselves added new instruments to the mix. A twelve-string Martin guitar was run through a Leslie speaker, while a National Steel Dobro imitated a sitar, and a Danelecto sitar-guitar an electric harp. Harpsichord, vibraphone and accordion were added as required, while in post-production Elvis lowered his voice by an octave in 'Kid About It', sung falsetto – something he cannot sustain in concert – and overdubbed a whole choir. As he writes in the CD liner notes, making this record was a "do-it-yourself education in using the studio like blank manuscript paper. Enormous fun."

The cover painting had at first taken Elvis aback. He had written what he thought was his most optimistic album to date, then found Barney Bubbles had responded to "the more violent and carnal aspects of the songs". He had commissioned Bubbles to paint a series of abstracts, as a change from the usual mug shot, and now the artwork proudly hangs in Costello's music room, as a fond memory of the artist. The pastiche of Picasso's "Three Musicians" is underlined by the letters half concealed on the heads of the maggot-like creatures on the top right. They spell out "Pablo Si".

The work is credited to one "Sal Forlenza", dated 1942, and titled "Snakecharmer And Reclining Octopus". A violent exercise in harsh red and blues, a giant ear extends from a pipe played by the multi-planed human figure, with a pompadour and cuban boots, just like the original Elvis. Indeed, before his premature death in 1983, Bubbles was supposedly responsible for an extraordinary album distributed by F-Beat. *Ersatz* by The Imperial Pompadours, on the Pompadour label, is full of hate and mental distress. There is an injunction on the back sleeve to "play it loud you turkeynecks" and sample titles include 'See You Soon Baboon', 'There's A Fungus Among Us', 'I Want To Come Back From The World Of LSD', and the side-long 'Insolence Across The Nation'. It sounds like a slice of heroin hell, a suicide note on vinyl.

Imperial Bedroom was anything but, an album of astonishing vitality and musical optimism. For *NME*, beneath a wonderfully moody Anton Corbijn shot in which Elvis crouches behind the prison-like bars of a hotel window – shoot out the lights! – Richard Cook found him "cleansed", although still centred on impotence and defeat. Elvis's vacation in a "Nashville sob story" has not softened his outlook one iota. He writes "from a defence constructed from ambiguities, and therein exists the fantastic web of layers and shafts and resonances. If the acid remarks seem untouchably cold, then it may be that their heat is twice removed. Ice can burn too."

Simon Hills found the slower songs "wandering lounge style affairs", but Geoff Emerick's production rich enough to hide the weaker material. *MM*'s Adam Sweeting identified "more cleverness than soul, more artifice than art", and was disappointed that he should "straighten the pictures on the wall, instead of redecorating". *The Face* was a magazine which believed in decorating one's own looks and personality, traits which made it the perfect read for the style-obsessed Eighties. In their view, Costello *had* made a major shift, into irony. "Instead of standing at the centre of a song and firing in every direction, he's stepped sideways and become part of the arrangement...which allows for fury, ambiguity, laughs and smart window dressing. The balance is brilliant and lets Costello get away with blue murder." For *Sounds*, here was a "Tolstoy among these flea-bitten little rags of half talent".

As the new Tolstoy himself told Nicky Campbell, Geoff Emerick had the ability to sort out the "sonic soup" the band were blending, live in the studio. "My co-production consisted of abandoning the arrangements that we had carefully worked out," which now sounded forced. Anything went, in the search for new sounds. Pete Thomas recalled that one morning he came in having been up all night drinking, with fellow hellraiser Larry Wallis. "I just came in absolutely howling, and said, 'I can jam, I can play a bit of tambourine, but I'm sorry lads, I'm completely gone.'" Ninety-nine per cent of people would either have fired him on the spot, or sent him home, but Costello announced instead that he had a new, as yet unheard, song, 'Beyond Belief'.

"We went into the studio and literally jammed it," Thomas continues. "If you listen to it, it's just one take, everybody's tagging along, following what's coming into the headphones. And then he said, 'Right Pete, you can go home now.' I did a good day's work, before I went to bed." Years later, Britt Eckland came up to him, and told him the drumming on 'Beyond Belief' was the most fantastic drumming she had ever heard. "It just goes to show, there aren't any rules."

Bruce Thomas considers that *Imperial Bedroom* was the best album they ever did. "We were all throwing in musical ideas," he says. "That wasn't without its teething troubles. I remember Pete and Steve having a fight in the pub around the corner from AIR, which ended up with one of them lying on the floor at Paul Weller's feet, and he said, 'Well, you boys really take it seriously, don't you.'"

F-Beat released a double promo LP, now hugely collectable, in which tracks from the album are interspersed with Costello's apt comments. The (uncredited) cover photo is the same as that of the 'Man Out Of Time ' twelve-inch, a black and white shot in which Elvis in half moon spectacles and clean white cuffs rests his chin on a freckled fist, and glares at the viewer with eyes dark and cold as ebony. If not taken by David Bailey – responsible for the inner shots of *Imperial Bedroom* – then it should have been. The album works in artistic as well as commercial terms, splitting up the sometimes over-rich album, like a series of verses and choruses. Maybe Jethro Tull were right, and life is a long song, after all.

Nick Kent was amazed by the lowly sales of *Imperial Bedroom*, for an album that "should be Number One throughout the charts of the Western World". He reported back the promo album to *NME* readers as an hour of "good natured banter". It is more than that, a rare device in which the artist partly explains his creations, with no loss of mystery or any attempts to constrain the listener's imagination. I shall take it in conjunction with the songs it describes.

He begins with the overall game plan, or rather the lack of one: "We'd made a kind of pact in the band that we were going to try and treat each song individually rather than on previous albums where we'd had an overall production idea, which we'd thrashed out with Nick."

Costello and Geoff Emerick were agreed in their suspicion of contemporary productions. "The bass drum had got louder and louder on records, until it got ridiculous," Elvis says. "The voice has got quieter and quieter and more and more effects on it. He's really suspicious about a lot of digital effects. If you're going to have an effect it should leap out of the speaker and grab you by the throat. I wanted the voice up loud so you could hear the words." Most of the songs had been written after *Almost Blue*, when "there was something of a change of attitude generally in my writing". He then started to rewrite the arrangements they had already thrashed out in the Devon cottage.

The opening song, 'Beyond Belief', was in its raw state a "frantic" kind of track, but this soon changed. In a song about drunkenness and cruelty – just like Ray Davies' 'Sunny Afternoon' – Costello seems to sing with two new voices, one almost Paul Robeson deep, the other strangely confidential, and soaring to heaven. At times they intersect, over a wonderfully fluid backing, and Pete Thomas's drums are indeed superb, turning the beat around. "I thought that the original lyric was garbled, it was twice the speed, the lyric went at the same rate as the backing track, so I halved the amount of lyrics and sang them at half speed which makes for a very disconcerting effect because it sounds kind of calm when there's this sort of rattling sound going on." He even renamed the song, though from what is unclear.

'Tears Before Bedtime' started life as a country song, then took on a rock 'n' roll arrangement, like Fats Domino. Costello changed it to a "funny sort of rhythm", in the New Orleans style, with lots of falsetto overdubs, like The Coasters. "The theme is not light but I thought to treat it with this resigned way of singing. People can have enough of pain and misery – particularly on *our* records – so I thought it was maybe a good idea to throw it away a bit more. I think the backing track says the nastiness of it." It certainly expresses jauntiness, and I would have thought the real discontinuity was between the sound of the thing, which is a kind of joyful whoop, and its meaning. It is a song about how love turns to hate when trust is laid aside. "I know the name on the tip of your tongue", and an obvious biographical interpretation could be made, but I won't.

Costello was on tour when he saw an old music hall poster, framed in the lobby, which announced one act as "just a Shabby Doll". Whether because of her stage costume or her songs is left unclear, and Costello admits that most listeners at first think he is singing 'Shaggy Dog', which is far more misanthropic. "It's one of those songs where the title needs to be repeated as many times as possible." Maybe, like Dylan, he has the ability to sing two sentences at once.

The song shares its happenstance source of antique inspiration with John Lennon's 'Being For The Benefit of Mr Kite', but where that was good natured, this is sinister. One of Costello's most complex lyrics, it first sets up a scene close to prostitution, but then shifts its focus from the girl – a groupie, any possible identification would be libellous – to the "boy that I used to be". In what seems closer to self-revelation than scene setting, this male figure embraces maturity, and the sympathy for others that it entails. Even the puns are more subtle: "There's a girl in this dress, there's always a girl in distress," sung with exasperated tenderness. Ironically, it is the man who is now the "tired toy that everyone's enjoyed", and he in turn becomes the shabby doll. The smooth backing is overlaid with screaming at the end, whether from Costello's vocal cords or electronic is unclear, and the bass line rears up like a bucking bronco.

'Long Honeymoon' is "a very serious sad song". The tune had been offered to Broadway lyricist Sammy Cahn, but he sent it back, which made Elvis all the more determined to write his own words. It again deals with marital infidelity, told from the woman's viewpoint as she waits at home for her errant husband, with only her baby for comfort. "There is no money-back guarantee on happiness", and if he's out on a date, then "her life's in ruins". This is not the kind of book to point any fingers, but why should Costello the songwriter centre on such subject material – given the public knowledge of his private life in this area – if not to expiate guilt? He certainly sings with resigned sadness, and a Hawaiian guitar shivers, providing a whole template for David Lynch soundtracks. A brass arrangement comes in at the end, to accentuate the sense of melancholy, finishing on an unresolved chord.

'Man Out Of Time' opens with a scream and brutal guitar, to fade into a stately tune, backed by rich organ chords and clunking piano straight out of 'Like A Rolling Stone'. The original song had been worked up in two arrangements, one a folk version with acoustic

241

guitars, and the other speeded up with the riff, on the chord of E, which ends the new version. "We did a show in this country and western club in Aberdeen, and we stayed in this country house, and it seemed a bit sinister. It suggested these ideas of sinister goings on in aristocratic homes. Something like a Profumo scandal, that's what I had in mind, how people after a while crave notoriety rather than trying to hide it."

Elvis's sad reportage is studded with some of his finest wordplay. All three victims – an errant politician, the press baron who has lost touch with his family, a businessman set to retire – are men out of time. They could each be a version of the singer, craving a love he does not deserve, having killed it of his own volition. *Trust* has nothing on this as some kind of personal testimony, however fantastically disguised.

'Almost Blue' was "an attempt to write in a classic form". The lyrics would not have been out of place in the 1940s: "I could hear this muted trumpet but I thought people would think it was a parody." He wanted simplicity, not pastiche. The songs of the previous album of the same name – written by others – are encapsulated here, a Sinatra-like brand of tough regret, emoted in solitude by one half of an "unhappy couple". "There is part of me that is almost true," sounds like 'Alison' revisited, with caution, in the light of a truer self-knowledge.

'…And In Every Home' was a song about losing one's job, which started life as a rocker, though "it had slightly too many chords for it to be effective". He slowed things down, added a few more chords, then instructed Nieve to "go mad, write a really eccentric arrangement". Costello rarely sounded closer to the David Accles of *American Gothic* here, with the same combination of ironic, world weary singing and a full orchestra. There are some "cheeky" quotes from 'Eleanor Rigby' and the '1812 Overture' and 'Rhapsody In Blue'. It adds a comic element to a theme which is far from humorous. "It was meant to say that a person is of more worth than a job."

The song opens with a picture of wasted days – and lives – spent lying in bed, in which a "young blade becomes a has been", another fine example of a pun used sympathetically rather than to show off. The words then twist into yet another portrait of a failed marriage, in which the man is in prison, and his wife in terror lest he catch her "running with his mates". Lying in bed assumes a different meaning.

'The Loved Ones' is an attack on junkie chic, "the needle and no thread" which led to the untimely deaths of the likes of Gram Parsons, or Sid Vicious. "It's better to live than to die young in what people foolishly regard as a romantic way." Neil Young made much the same point in the album – and wracked tour – *Tonight's The Night*, in which he acted out a self-destructive drug user. The irony of how Kurt Cobain was a virtual dead ringer for Crazy Horse's Danny Whitten, and ended in much the same way – there are different routes to suicide – was not lost on Young, either. "Every junkie musician or alcoholic writer who dies in this blaze of phoney glory has a mum or dad or sister that's crying their eyes out. They're the ones who have to bury the sod."

The lyric is sung with a forced zest – his voice almost cracks at one point – and a sickly chorus of clashing voices, with piano arpeggios to make it all sound the more artificial. Elvis puts a cheerful tune to a "morbid idea", but one which is really about wanting to live – "that's why it ends up PS I Love You. The voice from beyond the grave."

'Human Hands' is "just a straightforward love song as far as I can see. It's a simple song." One with resonances though. Many took it as laying out some highly personal clues that Bebe Buell was still missed. Indeed, they recommenced their highly illicit affair. "I would meet him in hotels," she says. "We had pseudo names for each other. I was Jane or Candy" – both characters from Lou Reed songs – "he was Henry. He'd leave me his key at the front desk. And it culminated with me becoming pregnant."

She arranged a termination, and when he asked, some time later, if she had had the baby, "I could see that he was a little curious. I told him I abused myself so much when I was pregnant that I had a miscarriage. I just lied through my teeth. I wanted to say whatever I could to hurt him. And he put the phone down and never spoke to me again." I've been there myself, and I can only sympathise. Indeed, the whole incident shows Elvis as the wounded party. One wonders if the first time that he knew of the abortion – which to even a lapsed Catholic has a certain horror – was in the *Mojo* interview, in which case God help him.

We will return later to Buell's list of secret codes. One reviewer described the song as "an old stage favourite, too familiar to get excited about", and Costello would hardly sing it every night, just in case his old amour was by chance in the audience. Back to the song, then, which is set to an almost military beat, with a Motown-like riff following its chorus. Its lyrics – and the kind of voice Elvis chooses to sing it in – are far from straightforward, except the line "I've never said it like this before" and the directness of the need expressed. Whatever the cause or meaning, this marks an emotional honesty which Costello has been able before to declare only through the words of others.

'Kid About It' is the closest thing to a solo performance, though The Attractions rhythm section is present and correct. The organ and vibes are played by Elvis himself. From the start, "The song had a defined mood and even a chord that everybody said was completely wrong, but I held out." The lyric is about "lying", "about running away really, hence the bridge bit". 'The Leaving Of Liverpool' takes Costello back to his days in the folk clubs, and living in Birkenhead. "Turning into Americans" works on all kinds of levels – it is the basic plot of Elvis's career, and the *King Of America* album in particular. It could also refer to a change in partners, either musical or sexual. Costello's echoed voice certainly exudes poignancy, as he duets with himself.

"'Little Savage' was a slow song to begin with, and then it had a 1950s kind of rhythm, and then we ended by pounding it into the ground." The twin vocal lines are deliberately arranged, "a suggestion of a split personality, though the voices are both me". They trace two distinct lines of thought. Costello is deliberately trying to write songs that aren't "starry eyed", for "people in the middle". The songwriter is certainly not "Mr Average", but the opening words, about finally making "love out of something other than spite", bring a new spirit of joy into his work, even if the song is actually about a couple splitting up.

The backing track of 'Boy With A Problem' was recorded without Elvis at all. It started as an instrumental, and Squeeze's Chris Difford wrote the words – "he's such a craftsman in terms of meter and rhythm, much more so than I am" – from Elvis's piano demo. Costello "hummed along where I thought the tune should go." He later changed a couple of lines "because I felt more comfortable in singing them." It echoes the previous song, but here the errant lover has been forgiven, despite his resort to domestic violence. Both speakers are drunk, with booze and with self-pity. Freed from his guitar, Elvis hits the high register, and thus sounds a little like Freddie Mercury, of all people. Nieve is similarly at his most Semprini-like, full of pianistic flourishes. The track was added to the album at the last moment.

'Pidgin English' is "almost a political song", about the way that papers like *The Sun* and *The Daily Star* are taking the English language to pieces; "They're turning everything to jargon." The greatest danger is of "being manipulated by people who've taken away your ability to say anything different". A process which continues. The track was "done in segments", with the band adding odd sounds like xylophone and even a mellotron, an instrument forever associated with The Moody Blues. In the middle, Costello played "this ludicrously loud nylon string guitar solo". The overall effect was deliberately "bilious", fitting the subject matter.

It was the first song to be completed: "It's an experimental track, that's why it sounds slightly stilted." In rehearsal, the arrangement was too "new wave", like something by The Jags. The basic scenario, old man and young woman, stretches back in English literary history to Chaucer's 'Merchant's Tale', though Costello adds the relish of fisticuffs. The word play descends into near "gibberish", sung without feeling – which is the whole point of the song – except for the final, tender "PPS I Love You", repeated from 'The Loved Ones'. These simple words are the only ones that really make sense.

'You Little Fool' deals with "a young girl who is worth a lot more than the lot she is getting". Even in interviews, Costello cannot resist a pun! He sings as if with a split personality, so that "the guy in the chorus sounds like a real horrible person". The way that two lyrics clash was first explored by The Velvet Underground in their terrifying 'The Murder Mystery'. This is more 'Mother's Little Helper', written when The Rolling Stones "were still a good group", and with the kind of tinkling harpsichord Brian Jones first patented, and a touch of psychedelic phasing at the end.

Costello spent a good deal of time getting the running order exactly right. 'Town Crier' was placed last; "It's like riding off into the distance." Another take was recorded late at night, fast and drunk, "like The Attractions go to Rio". The lyrics are an antidote to the "whingeing" of *Almost Blue*. "I wanted a proud song to end with, and it is about giving up feeling sorry for yourself." Costello had The Impressions in mind here: the vocal arrangement is "my tribute to Curtis Mayfield".

It certainly brings out Costello's finest vocal to conclude an album in which he shows off all his voices – "let them all talk"! Here he is ironic, wistful, sad, passionate and determined, all at once. His leap upwards on "teddy boy tender" is exhilarating, and everything here is just about perfect, the subtle use of double tracking, the way the orchestration serves as a rich tapestry behind him, Nieve's piano as it echoes the main plot, even the touch of trilling organ, just like Mike Ratledge out of Soft Machine. The brass-heavy final riff seems to go on forever, just like 'Hey Jude'. Of course, one should never identify the singer with the character he portrays, but there does seem to be a large dose of self-identification here, "a little boy lost in a big man's shirt" – at least it's not green – and on one level it is a plea for forgiveness and compassion, from his audience, from his lovers, from himself.

Though unjustly downgraded by some fanatical Elvis followers, perhaps because of its surface attractiveness, *Imperial Bedroom* remains perhaps his most perfect achievement, and possesses an aural richness to which he will return in *All This Useless Beauty*. Timeless music. It is difficult to augment (near) perfection, but the CD version adds four tracks recorded at Matrix Studios, and produced by Paul "Bassman" Riley, which look back to Sixties Merseybeat, and various other oddities.

There are a couple of solo demos for the album: the unreleased 'Stamping Ground' sounds like a one-man-band: one can imagine Elvis with a big drum on his back. 'Shabby Doll' is more insistent and menacing than what eventually surfaced in public: Elvis's voice drags hypnotically. As with 'Almost Blue', the title song of *Imperial Bedroom* was recorded after the album's release. Costello sings partly in "rotten" French and to a bouncy beat with handclaps, and learns to programme a Linn drum machine. The song is extremely McCartney musically, and Lennon verbally, and about an adulterous coupling between bride and best man, revisiting a posh hotel's bridal suite, where she spent her honeymoon. "Life turns out like a TV serial." It is a lightly comic take on the "combination of splendour and sleaze" which made Elvis choose the same title for an album which mines far darker strata of the human condition.

This song and 'Seconds Of Pleasure' – a much rewritten saga of lovers failing to cohere – were sent to Frida of Abba, for her solo album. Costello now knows that "her producer, a certain Mr P Collins, didn't think much of any of them as I heard from his own lips". The mind boggles at how Frida would have wrapped her Swedish tonsils around these two tongue-twisters, and what she would have made of their manifest subtleties. Nevertheless, another name for the little black book. Phil should be so lucky as to be able to put together as varied and bold an album himself. *Imperial Bedroom* sure beats middle-aged melancholy, any day. If Frida's own reaction to these songs is not on record, Costello's admiration for Abba *is*. Their own lyrics are so nonsensical – a kind of polyglot good feeling – as to be almost surrealistic.

Despite all the rave reviews, and the originality of *Imperial Bedroom*, its sales were unspectacular. Perhaps it was too allusive and ambiguous for mass market acceptance. Costello's record company still hoped for *Armed Forces*, part two. "They hankered after that," he says. "I'm talking mainly about America. We had more control here. In America we were put under more pressure, particularly after we moved into the era when videos appeared. Back in the Seventies, we'd make videos for about two bob, and they looked appealingly like Charlie Chaplin films. The later ones started to get quite sophisticated."

Like the Ancient Mariner with his albatross, the dead weight of *Armed Forces* continues to this day to hang around Elvis's neck, as the kind of album he is always expected to make next, and never quite does.

In June, Elvis had joined David "Kid" Jensen, with a white label copy of the new album, and some favourite records: The Teardrop Explodes, Echo and the Bunnymen, ABC, and even 'Valley Girl' by Frank Zappa, not usually so favoured. Costello is Mr Affability, chatting about everything from the twin girls on the 'Good Year For The Roses' video – they had lent their violin to Steve to mime on, and were too photogenic to let go – to The Mandrell Sisters ("uggh"). Costello recalls seeing Willie Nelson, a new hero, at Caesar's Palace in Las Vegas. More surprisingly, he likes Hot Chocolate's version of 'Green Shirt'. This being radio, Jensen comments on his appearance; floral shirt, boater and rimless glasses. "It's my James Joyce look. Maybe when I'm old I'll go and live in the South of France and write books." Meanwhile, "I go through a certain amount of beating my head against the wall, up in the middle of the night writing." But inspiration is not really a problem, "It just seems to come when it does, it's there and then."

Mid July saw the start of a two-month summer tour of the United States, as the new album powered towards the American Top Thirty. Costello had not yet entered the goldmine of stadium rock – just as well, for the continued health of his music – and the biggest gig this tour was the 12,000 seat Forest Hills tennis stadium. In Minneapolis, he played the Great Northern Picnic, supporting Blondie, and blowing them off the stage. It's the same bind: play the small, intimate venues, build up a following, and then there's not enough room for everyone to see you. Not to worry, all musicians come back to the smaller venues, given time.

Elvis's onstage demeanour was now more user-friendly. Goodbye to the bodyguard's angry stare, hello to the occasional smile and hand signals during the most passionate songs. One review describes him as looking "seriously clerical, like Robert De Niro in *True Confessions*". To celebrate his birthday, in Merryweather Post, Columbia, Elvis appeared in a gorilla suit for the encores, sticking the microphone deep into the head. Jake had first warned the audience that a dangerous animal had escaped from a nearby children's zoo.

An anonymous review of the tour reckoned that the "mean little weasel" of earlier tours was gone forever. The set was more carefully formatted than before, running for over two hours, with encores, and Elvis driving the crowd wild by waving a towel around his head. New songs mingled with old, and he was beginning to run one song into another, 'Beyond Belief' into 'Clubland', 'Pidgin English' into 'Hand In Hand'. This was a technique already par for the course for the likes of James Brown, a sweaty exactness. Costello was taking more risks on guitar, and 'Shabby Doll' drives him to new heights, which the record barely hints at. Nieve had added synthesiser to his ranks of keyboards, and Pete Thomas worked as hard as ever behind his kit, though Bruce Thomas seemed subdued. Among a host of surprise covers were Percy Mayfield's 'Danger Zone', Bobby Bland's 'Two Steps From The Blues', and a "rocked out" version of Hank Williams' 'Why Don't You Love Me?'.

Where anybody would have rested on the laurels of the new LP, Elvis continued to drive forward, and the most moving of the new songs on view was 'Shipbuilding', an oblique response to the Falklands dispute, which had drawn to a bloody end in June. The most startling thing was his vocals, which would change on the same song, from night to night. Indeed, "The songs seem at time mere frameworks, and they occasionally touch base with them." It is the essence of any great *live* band, from Led Zeppelin to The Spin Doctors, different every time, just like life.

It is the sort of form that makes some madmen collect tapes of every date on the tour, for such rare delights as an "incredible jazzy vocal rendition of 'Almost Blue'", or to trace the growing vocal similarity to Dylan, "almost atonal". Back at home, the release on forty-five of 'Man Out Of Time', Elvis's own choice, flopped badly, reaching only Number Fifty-Eight in August. Perhaps the triumphalist mood of the country was out of kilter with a bitter song about spreading corruption. "It flopped, and they said, 'Well, we told you it wasn't a good record,'" to Costello's fury.

Scottish band The Bluebells were the support act on the British tour that autumn. Their May 1984 hit 'I'm Falling' was heavily influenced by Costello, who later produced an album for them. Even now, it has yet to fully surface, dribbling out instead as odd singles. Described on one ticket stub as "The Bedrooms of Britain Tour" – and unofficially as the "Bail Jake Riviera and F-Beat Out Of The Shit Tour" – the opening show in Southampton unveiled "a tight, efficient musical unit, with Costello singing with amazing power for two hours, ten minutes". There were forty songs, seventeen of them encores. Nieve's keyboard dexterity "seemed to suffer little from the hour or so he spent in the pub before the gig". Even Elvis, presumably stone cold sober, joked, and pulled faces.

Allan Jones was still doubtful about the new album – "more artful than heartfelt" – but cast aside critical detachment to declare that, live, "Costello continues to defy every expectation, leap tall buildings in a single bound…" Songs from his whole career were "re-shaped, reorganised, re-defined and resurrected". The kind of thing that Dylan has done for decades, and Jones' packed sentences capture the band's – and Band's – "manic aplomb". Thus, "a slow sultry blues was inserted into a compelling 'Watching The Detectives'; one of the best ever live versions of 'King Horse' was prefaced by a violent rendition of The O'Jays' 'Backstabbers'; 'Beyond Belief' was transformed into a barnstorming, psychotic rock 'n' roll avalanche; 'Clubland' was dispatched with such infuriated rage that it might have been played as an overture to the end of civilisation as some of us knew it." Just the kind of apocalyptic firestorm that burned through Dylan and The Hawks in 1966. Another witness, as he drove all the way home with a smile on his face, simply could not believe that the band could "conceivably keep up at such a crippling pace night after night". They did.

At the Bingley Hall, Birmingham, a "modest" sized crowd greeted each song with rapturous applause. Elvis was grinningly expressive: he "sang as much with his hands as he did with his mouth" – a mere thirteen encores tonight – and though clearly exhausted he jovially signed autographs afterwards, "giving kisses to all the girls who dared to ask". *NME*'s Graham Smith found him "*so* hard, *so* passionate, a prisoner of a cult audience who put out at the Apollo Theatre, Oxford the best concert I've seen in years". Why then could "the country's foremost songwriter and performer no longer sell records in any great number"? Once the initial nervous rush was over, the band settled into a "sensuously intimate" groove, with Costello playing an Epiphone guitar borrowed from The Bluebells, and the Thomases "breaking the rules of drums and bass". So *that's* where Goldie came from! "The whole notion of melody has been torn apart and reassembled, with little regard for formal 'pop' constraints."

For an anonymous reviewer at Glasgow, "only Springsteen can beat this", although again the venue was not full. *The Brighton Argus* found "no frills, no fancy lights, no videos, not even much movement", with "the brush-haired singer's latent energy" quite enough to fill the stage. At the final concert, live at Leeds, Costello opened with a cover of 'I

Got You', and by the third song his grey suit was ringing with sweat. "He sang the words to the songs and *meant* them – you could tell just by looking at his face."

In Anton Corbijn's shots which accompany Costello's first British interview for years, for *NME*, Elvis gloomily cups this same face between his hands, like a meditative angel, then covers his mouth with stubby fingers, as if stifling a scream. Neil Spencer finds "a more measured, more humble, more appealing type of fellow. "We were left with a warehouseful of *Get Happy!!*," he reveals, going on to tell that 'Man Out Of Time' is about "unemployment – and the person unemployed is me." The problem is where to position himself after the punk years, one that continues to this day, but he is physically in good form, far slimmer than a year before, dressed in black leather jacket, black slacks, white socks, Doc Martens and a straw porkpie hat he bought in New York; "I made the taxi stop when I saw it in a shop window."

Elvis now is consciously in the great tradition of songwriting, though they come "when you least expect or want it, when you're trying to sleep, or walking down the street". He uses craft almost unconsciously: "An American magazine picked up on internal rhyming in my songs, I'd never even heard of it," he admits. He does have a thing about shoes, and guns – "It's the most repellent image" – and likes using expressions he hears people use, like "tuppenny ha'penny" and "bone orchard", which he then checked in a dictionary, as it sounded so bizarre. 'Sunday's Best' used entirely phrases from the *News Of The World*. He would like to do more acting, but "the camera doesn't like me; every time we've appeared on *Top Of The Pops* the record's gone down the following week." He would also like to do more writing, not "poems or short stories" but "sketch things". Like, one presumes, the surrealistic snippet reprinted in Greil Marcus's *Dead Elvis*, much like the Kerouac-fuelled prose which Dylan used to provide as sleeve notes on his albums. Elvis would not use his stage name, however: "Even in this business I've got doubts about the name." Doubts that would intensify.

Back in September, Elvis issued another soul cover as a single. 'From Head To Toe' only reached Forty-Three in the UK, despite the slightly dubious practice of WEA giving away free copies of the *Get Happy!!* album to anyone who bought the single at chart return shops. The single is garnished with a typically inventive Barney Bubbles sleeve, a pair of eyes and huge spectacles superimposed on a giant foot. The back sleeve advertised dates on the Imperial Bedroom tour of the UK.

The song had originally appeared on The Miracles' *Going To A Go-Go*, but Costello took his version from obscure Liverpool beat boomers The Escorts. They released it as a single in 1966: its B-side, 'Night Time', was also given the Costello treatment, and surfaced the following year on the twelve-inch version of 'Everyday I Write The Book'. The Escorts released their first album – almost twenty years after the fact – courtesy of the new Edsel label, set up by Riviera and Elvis, and named after the most disastrous car ever to issue from the Ford motor company, which by the logic of such things is now itself a collectors' item.

Edsel specialised in rediscovering old soul and British beat classics, well annotated and coolly designed. Alongside similar trademarks of quality like Reckless and Bam Caruso, it predated the reissue mania which CDs so unexpectedly brought, a few years later. Costello's own keen instincts as a record collector, and catholic tastes, were now employed in passing on these cult passions to a wider audience. Suddenly, through Edsel, the entire back catalogue of Al Green was available, as were fascinating obscurities by the likes of The Action and The Birds. It was a whole secret history of rock, brought to light. The label later began to license contemporary acts, in particular the American Zippo catalogue, of updated psychedelia and cow-punk.

The Attractions entered the studios in their own right, to issue a second album without their leader, as yet unreleased. More fruitfully, Rough Trade released Robert Wyatt's version of 'Shipbuilding', as yet unrecorded by Elvis, and specifically tailored to fit Wyatt's principled dignity, and defiantly English vowels. As Elvis explained, "The melody was written by Clive with Robert in mind, so the tune really suggested Robert's voice. I just hoped the words were the sort of sentiments that he would be able to sing." It broke into the UK Top Forty just as Greenham Common began to welcome its first contingent of Cruise missiles.

The single was hand-tooled by the Costello team, with contributions from Steve Nieve on piano, Madness's Mark Bedford on bass, and Martin Hughes, the drummer from Clive Langer's band, The Boxes. Langer played organ, with Elvis on backing vocals and Alan Winstanley helping out on the console; thus the tongue-twisting credit, "A Clangwinstello Production". Much the same team were to produce Costello's next two albums.

As 1982 drew to a close, Elvis's latest single, 'Party, Party', taken from the soundtrack of the movie of the same name, a teenage adventure – subtitled "the night before the morning after" – grazed the UK Top Fifty. As Costello admitted, "The song was written in ten minutes and to be honest it sounds like it." The sleeve design looks just the same. Other musical participants included Madness, Sting and Midge Ure, and the single – and soundtrack album – appeared not on F-Beat but A&M, stressing Elvis's subsidiary role. The film itself resides in the celluloid graveyard, still hoping for a cult following to revive it, though Costello considered that its forty-minute pilot version was "very funny. It would have made a great TV play."

More notably, this was the first time that Costello sang along with a brass section, just like his dad, with Annie Whitehead on trombone, Gary Barnacle on sax, and the uncredited Neil King on trumpet making up the Royal Guards Horns. Elvis's 'Losing You', appeared on Dusty Springfield's *White Heat* album, also released in December. He had added an extra verse to the earlier 'Just A Memory', written with Dusty in mind. Once a member of The Springfields, and with a public image of ambiguous sexuality, Dusty remains an underrated singer. Her album *Dusty In Memphis* contains some of the greatest white soul ever recorded, certainly by an English singer.

Here was more wish-fulfilment, with Costello musically interrelating with a long-time musical heroine: the best side-effect of fame. "I was actually on the phone, she was transatlantic, singing the new verse, and I've got the phone at arms' length incredulous that I've got Dusty Springfield singing my new verse back to me."

December ended with an experimental gig at the Royal Court Theatre, Liverpool, which had played host to a local renaissance of playwrights like Willy Russell and Alan Bleasdale, with whose TV career Elvis was to be so closely associated. London's Royal Court had been home in the Fifties of the kind of kitchen sink drama – Jimmy Porter and all that jazz – which had so influenced the teenage Elvis. The no longer quite so angry young man emerged with an acoustic guitar, and played 'New Amsterdam' and a new song, 'The World And His Wife', before being joined by his band. The set list was much as the autumn tour, with two more new songs, 'Mouth Almighty' and 'Everyday I Write The Book': it was the second encore that brought the real experiment. What was almost a second set saw the onstage addition of the four-piece "Imperial Horns". One listener found this new addition "out of place and much too boisterous", but he was almost alone.

Two shows, on either side of Christmas, saw Elvis and The Attractions again filling the Royal Albert Hall. The audience rapidly quit the bar when they heard a new Elvis song on the PA – 'Pills And Soap' – and during his solo intro he also tried out 'The Comedians'. Steve Nieve was now sporting a skinhead haircut, and the audience finally climbed to its feet for an encore which saw Elvis and Nieve duetting, then nine songs with the brass section. "If any man deserved to be driven off in a Rolls Royce (as Elvis was after the concert) it was Mr Costello." A typical Riviera touch.

The two leading pop weeklies divided straight down the middle on the shows. *MM*'s Colin Irwin found the hall's notorious echo made the words hard to follow. Visually, he was "blending into the pomp in his bow tie...everything was subtly geared to the idea of Costello as the all-round family entertainer." Everything was too controlled: what next, "*The Morecambe and Wise Show, Celebrity Squares*, Princess Diana's birthday party?" The blind adulation of his fans allowed Elvis to get away with "epic overblown arrangements" of new songs. Irwin has to admit that it is easy to get caught up in "the emotional frenzy of it all", but his voice "sounded shot, and he simply tries too hard". Any more shows like this, and "he'll have dug his own grave".

NME also identified the sense that Costello's career was at some kind of crossroads, but found instead a performer at the height of his powers, putting out a "glorified 'best of'", together with obscure B-sides, unreleased songs, and classic covers. "The fact that it all hangs together with cohesion and clarity is an indication of the man's ability to *pace* a show." One particular triumph was the use of the same brass section which "once coloured Kevin Rowland's new soul dreams".

1983 would see this experiment pushed to its logical conclusion, resulting in more heart-stopping concerts, but with a whole new Elvis.

CHAPTER NINE

the pop years

On 27 January, Elvis and The Attractions re-entered AIR studios, this time with Clive Langer and Alan Winstanley as producers. "It was our chance to get reacquainted with the wonderful world of pop music, and still maintain a sense of humour," Langer says. The new producers had a string of hit singles with Madness, Dexy's Midnight Runners and The Teardrop Explodes. They provided an immediate contrast to Nick Lowe – who bashed it down live – Billy Sherrill's Nashville recipe, sweeten everything with strings, or Geoff Emerick, who used the studio like an aural paintbox. "We don't have any morals when it comes to studio craft," Langer explains. "We always mix in sections, then stick it together afterwards." Their bright and uncluttered sound was ideal for basic pop music, and all of a piece with the Eighties, but many saw it as over-slick, especially after the rich invention of *Imperial Bedroom*. This was more like a cheap motel.

Why had Costello chosen to plunge into the banal. "Well, that's what's life's like," he says. "I liked Clive Langer's records, and he was the hottest guy around on the English scene. We had a floating audience in America that only bought our records occasionally. We'd made two albums in succession that to some degree had lost ground. If you allow that contact with the mainstream audience to be severed for too long, you may lose the freedom to do what you want." Elvis first met Langer as a fellow producer at Two-Tone: with his band The Boxes, Clive had even opened for The Attractions during the Get Happy!! tour, and Elvis had in turn produced part of his album *Splash*. The sound of the album, its aural sugar coating, was part of a technique for survival among "the passionless fads of that charmless time".

As Elvis told Radio One, "Clive's brief was to be harder on my songwriting from a structural point of view. His job was to look for hooks. He got me to write a couple more rhythmic songs." For Langer, "The idea was to make Elvis popular again, and to make some pop records, after he'd done the wild ones, and I think we did well." For all that it was a clash of opposites. "I've got different ears to Nick Lowe, I was brought up a few years later, I was more into pop music than American country stuff, and that's what came out. Alan is a very disciplined engineer, very strict, which they weren't used to. When we were going for a backing track we were happy just to listen to the drums, and we wouldn't indulge in the pleasure and excitement of hearing the whole band playing." The Nick Lowe method would have everybody jumping at the time, but "a few days later you'd find a tom tom mike had fallen off". So what, one could retort; on some of the songs of Dylan's *Blood On The Tracks*, you can hear the buttons of his sleeve jangling as he strums the guitar, which merely adds intimacy.

What Elvis most resented was the loss of control. "I have been pretty hard on them," he says, "because it's the only time I've given myself over to a production sound, rather than working in collaboration with the producer. They were real pop producers so obviously the records date to the time they were made in. With all due respect that sound hasn't dated all that well." This, especially on the harsher medium of CD, is incontrovertible; the album sounds unpleasantly squashed, and never quite loud enough, no matter what volume you play it at.

On the other hand, this more formal approach did have its occasional triumphs. As Elvis told *Record Collector*, "'Shipbuilding' is a beautiful piece, and 'King Of Thieves' was one of those long, unwieldy, allegorical songs which were made listenable by Clive's production style. To balance them, we had a thing like 'Everyday I Write The Book' that anybody could whistle, and that was written in ten minutes as a spoof. Originally I tried to do it as a lover's rock song, and then we grafted on this kind of modern rhythmic treatment. It always begged to be done in some kind of pop style." He had no intention of being exiled to the sidelines. "There is something subversive about having 'Everyday I Write The Book' on the same album as 'Shipbuilding' and 'Pills And Soap'."

Costello had always been a political writer, whether in the anti-fascism of 'Less Than Zero', the anti-imperialism of 'Oliver's Army' or his reports from the sexual battlefront. With this album, his political viewpoint had become more urgent and specific, as befitted the reign of Queen Margaret. As he points out in the expansive CD notes, "Between 1979 and 1983 something strange happened. The British government mutated into a hostile regime contemptuous of anyone who would not serve or would not yield to its purpose." And Elvis would become, in his own mind at least, public enemy number one.

It was particularly ironic that such messages should be coded into what Elvis himself calls "a bauble", so that bitter lyrics are partially disguised by their pop sheen, like a sharp needle in a fluffy toy. Green did much the same thing in Scritti Politti, turning them from a loose and atonal collective to a swooning soul ensemble, with doubt at its heart. Not everything was so rigidly controlled. Afrodiziak improvised their vocal counterpoint live in the studio, while the TKO horns "employed some of the rude, unison sound they had fashioned in Dexy's", playing refrains scat-sung by Elvis on his original demos. String arrangements were by David Bedford, whose work had ranged from the avant-garde to the orchestral *Tubular Bells*, having starred with Mike Oldfield in Kevin Ayers' anarchic troupe The Whole World, where he played keyboards with a brick.

Whereas most of *Imperial Bedroom* had been written at the piano, a recipe for "melancholy ballads", Langer persuaded Costello to pick up the guitar, to write some "more lively material", arguing that he was becoming known for "only the most cynical and disillusioned songs". In turn, Elvis "remained allergic to the happy ending". For all that it is a quizzical, almost smiling Elvis who confronts us on the front cover, a Phil Smee classic of coloured typography. He wears a black cap, a dark coat with its collar up, and large steel-framed glasses, and looks much like the young John Lennon as he scratches his left ear. *Hot Press* describes this, rather unfairly, as "dressed in the glamour of commerce with ugly Elvis gazing out all soft-focus and cute".

The band look glummer on the back sleeve, hands in pockets with Bruce Thomas apparently playing pocket billiards. The title of 'The Invisible Man' has its middle word shading off into blankness. The inner sleeve features a lyric sheet, in jarring typeface, with sideways-on photos. Afrodiziak appear in turbans and the horn section in suits and ties, like a quartet of hit men. Nieve has had a drastic haircut, while Elvis has grown a scrubby beard. Chet Baker, his eyes closed in contemplation, has the pallor of a corpse.

The CD booklet contains Barney Bubbles' original artwork, which would have presented a far less user-friendly image. Elvis's face emerges in cartoon form from a cartoon which draws heavily on Russian constructivism; a metal hand offers him a screwdriver. In an even more disturbing montage, a photo of Elvis and his band has been corrupted so that The Attractions' heads are replaced with symbols; a pill capsule for Nieve, a question mark for Pete, a circle of black cogs for Bruce. What *could* he have meant?

MM's Adam Sweeting commented, "You don't *review* records like this, you just let them hit you like a fire-hose." Elvis's voice is further back in the mix, used as another instrument. For *Record Mirror*, it "probably represents the best collection of Elvis's songs on one album". The *Hot Press* found him "boxing clever...hitting back for hits". Graham Lock in the *NME* also finds Costello sick of being "a pop star who isn't really popular", so he has deliberately made his "brightest, bounciest" album since *Armed Forces*. Elvis continues as the finest songwriter in Britain, and one of the few white artists to use pop as a serious medium: his lyrics are no longer filled with rage, but "calmness and compassion". Elvis now blames politics, not people.

For all that, there is a "faintly manic air to some of the music", and as *Creem* reported, "This is adjudged a major let-down by Elvis's acolytes." Edwin Pouncey, aka the cartoonist "Savage Pencil", found the same "wild, witty, lyrical jigsaw puzzles, teaming with cunningly distorted cliches and interlocked double meanings". The cover might make him look "like the author of an arty beatnik novel", but Pouncey – previously unconvinced – found the album a joy to listen to.

'Let Them All Talk' provides the title for this book, in which a whole panoply of musicians, producers, fans and critics – as well as Elvis himself – comment on his career. Costello has always provoked strong reactions. Originally a "beat-group tune", this is a song to get the feet – and the album – moving.

"Have we come this far to find a soul cliche?" the song asks, and there is an ease in the music here, driven by the horn section, which was lacking in the joyless *Get Happy!!*. The words are something else. No critic ever seems to have properly looked this album full in the face: David Gouldstone, as usual barking up completely the wrong tree, finds it all "too abstract and uninvolving". In fact, the songs – whatever impetus caused them to be written, and whatever relevance, or not, they might have to their author's own life – add up to a terrifying world picture.

Far more frightening than the fantasies of *Armed Forces*, this is an everyday place where love grows stale, work palls and time is rapidly ebbing away. In a reversal of *Get Happy!!* the words are claustrophobic and the music enhancing, even if notably lacking in tunes. The Gang Of Four, with their piously Marxist analysis of family life in songs like 'At Home He's A Tourist', were never *this* bleak. Costello spies early the hidden project of the New Right – Thatcher in Britain, Reagan in the States – in which humanity is reduced to an economic transaction. Citizens become customers. Love is just another example of market forces: we all work longer hours, consume more, and feel more unhappy!

In 'Let Them All Talk', the narrator has lost his girlfriend and his days of hope. The radio plays cliches, "talk" which is cheap and meaningless, and the brass section echoes this mindless repetition, fading away into silence. The "fa-fa-fa" refrain – as well as a pun on "far" – echoes Talking Heads' 'Psycho Killer', and there is the same impulse to violence, which the rest of the album reflects. Costello has rarely sung before with such brisk sympathy.

'Everyday I Write The Book' was written in "about half an hour in an hotel room in Derby". For Pete Thomas, "It was this real English whiteboy attempt at some kind of funk beat." Without Langer's guiding hand, "We would have done it like The Merseybeats, that was how Elvis wrote it." Langer's rigorous methods also draw from Elvis his most sensual and relaxed vocal so far. Punctuated with percussive piano, like a typewriter, the song is about a relationship breaking down, but the author recasting it in his own mind. Here she is "captured", and he is working on a sequel in which he wins her back. The video had Charles and Diana lookalikes rowing with each other in a small, claustrophobic flat, and would doubtless now be banned.

"'The Greatest Thing' contained a reference to my dad's years with the Joe Loss orchestra by way of a quote from 'In The Mood'." The song is far from the straightforward love song which many reviewers discerned, as Costello's doubtful tone indicates. Love is a fantasy, described here in antique language, albeit one which keeps the worker punching the clock at the start of his shift. A failed marriage does not stop him from searching for a new girl "who takes my breath away" – an ambiguous image – thus starting the process all over again.

'The Element Within Her' has swooning, Beatle-like harmonies, and a "la la" chorus which at first suggests romance, but by the end of the song forms a wordless comment on the speaker's failure at love. The title is a weird sexual pun on his girlfriend's electric heater: the man is the frigid partner here. 'Love Went Mad' sounds optimistic, with Nieve tickling the ivories, but the roles are reversed here: it is the woman who fails to respond. Home becomes a battlefield, and the man is reduced in scale to "a big cheese in the workhouse".

The song is full of brilliant images, but doesn't quite cohere. By contrast, 'Shipbuilding' is as direct as an arrow straight through the heart. Clive Langer had written the melody in Nick Lowe's front room, influenced by Robert Wyatt's singing of 'Strange Fruit'. Elvis is on record saying, "I don't believe my version, vocally, is worth a carrot next to him." This is to underplay it. He lacks Wyatt's little boy lost tone, but is even sadder, more resigned. Costello was in Australia during the Falklands crisis, and foresaw a long war of attrition. "More ships would soon be needed, so welcome back to the discarded men of Cammell Laird, Harland and Wolff and Swan Hunter. Boys are being lost. We need more boys. Your sons will do…just as soon as the ships are ready." There is an extra resonance: the first of these shipyards is in Birkenhead, so Elvis would have grown up seeing the shipyards in decline.

The song is infinitely tender and understated, with the son's "they're going to take me to task" a reference to the "task force", and the wonderful "filled in/killed in" rhyme. Bruce Thomas considers this, "The pinnacle of our ensemble playing, with the catalyst as Chet

Baker. It's the way he follows the bassline through the solo, he's really, really listening, and even though he was a wreck of a carcass of a human being, he was the finest musician that we ever worked with." Both Elvis's father and grandfather had been trumpeters, and here – like Miles Davis at his most melancholic – Chet Baker brings out the haunting tones of an instrument which usually brags and blusters. Within five years, he was dead, falling from an upstairs window, which with bitter irony was also the cause of Robert Wyatt's incarceration in a wheelchair. "Diving for dear life," indeed.

'TKO (Boxing Day)' is not so much about violence as bullying, both in the workplace and the bedroom: "You need a back to break or a back to stab." Gouldstone called it "a wife beater's manifesto", but this is a drastic misreading. Costello sings with distaste in his voice, and while the exuberant punning removes any menace, the song is hardly celebratory. The final verse is about love grown stale, and the cruelty here is purely mental. There is something tinny about the musical arrangement, which is doubtless intended.

'Charm School' is far nastier, albeit with a prettier tune. As in 'Clubland' life is a cheesy nightclub, but the pain here is real, a marriage coming apart at the seams: "Nothing but a farce." Nieve plays keyboards like a xylophone. 'The Invisible Man' begins like a Madness outtake, full of bouncy charm, but Elvis comes in with passion rather than cocky cheek. The song gathers verses from three earlier songs, chronicled on the CD re-releases, and the title comes from HG Wells. Maybe the film on show stars Ronald Reagan: certainly someone is rewriting history, and busy dumbing things down.

The desire to escape, just like Harry Houdini, seems to have personal relevance to Costello himself, and this is – ironically – one of his most self-revelatory songs. Ditto 'Mouth Almighty', about a man who can't control his tongue, and drives his lover away. He ends like an image of his father onstage, with "crooner cufflinks" and not a hair out of place. Not a melody in sight either, unfortunately.

'The King Of Thieves' now sounds so listless as to be virtually unlistenable, with queazy harmonies and aggravating keyboards. A shame, as what Elvis himself describes as "a tricky tune about the trials of a blacklisted songwriter" is cunningly written. Scriptwriters whom the McCarthy hearings identified as "proto communists" – Elvis would have failed their test – were forced to emigrate, or work under pseudonyms. One even wrote the TV show *Robin Hood* which I watched as an innocent child, not realising that here was a Marxist collective, humiliating that arch-capitalist the Sheriff of Nottingham.

'Pills And Soap' features Nieve on piano, and Costello on drum machine and vocals. It could be the first step towards his resumption of a solo career. There were two sources of inspiration, *The Animals Film* which turned Elvis into a vegetarian, and Grandmaster Flash's 'The Message', a milestone in rap. Costello told the BBC it was a song about abuse of animals, "A strictly truthful but slippery explanation worthy of a Tory cabinet minister." It is a society being controlled by new masters, who can dispense with huge swathes of the population as surplus to requirement. The song is almost worthy of Swift, who used similar plausibility to recommend the eating of Irish infants. Elvis sings with the same kind of relish, making you half-believe he is serious.

'The World And His Wife', was "re-written from a solemn folk song about a drunken family gathering into a bilious knees-up", and it provides just the kind of musical uplift the album needs with which to conclude. The lyrics gather up the themes of this uniquely depressing record; boredom, family breakdown, drunken sex, a taste for violence. At least Elvis sings with a smile, and the horns intersect with Bruce Thomas's bass runs to leave the listener exhilarated, if a little puzzled. These are songs which would reach their full metier when taken on the road, with a hot brass section, just like Costello's favourites The Band when Allen Touissant programmed in horns for the concerts captured on *Rock Of Ages*. The words are best appreciated subliminally.

The CD adds 'Heathen Town', written as a response to Gram Parsons' 'Sin City', and the somnolent 'Flirting Kind', with "more than a tip of the hat to Burt Bacharach". Both were initially considered for inclusion on the album: the former is a lost masterpiece, a surrealistic tale of excess with "a girl dressed as a rabbit", a haunting melody and strange mechanical laughter at the end, like The Bonzo Dog Band on a bad trip.

'Shatterproof' is taken from a home demo. The song is Elvis's "unsubtle revenge on the landlord who swindled me out of my last penny when I was a twenty-one year old 'newly wed'". Not a word is wasted, and the violence here is exemplary.

By now, Madness had long replaced Costello as Stiff's main commercial entity. Costello added guest vocals to an alternative take of 'Tomorrow's Just Another Day'. Lead singer Suggs later reckoned, with Cockney relish, that Elvis was "as good as I've heard him. Mind you, he *was* singing a good song for a change." Costello made some surprise guest appearances with Madness in London and Brighton, as well as a slot on Swedish TV.

There was a brief hiatus, while F-Beat negotiated a change of worldwide distributor (excepting the USA) from WEA to RCA, under its new managing director David Betteridge. There was a certain poetic irony here, as RCA had signed up the first Elvis from Sun, a small and struggling independent label, just like early Stiff.

In May, Costello issued 'Pills And Soap' under the name of The Imposter, from his earlier song of that title, creating the IMP label as part of Demon. The 15,000 copies – four times that number were eventually sold – came in a plain sleeve, with an "extended version" of the same song on the flipside. Recorded on a Wednesday, acetates were sent to the press and radio the day after, and the finished single was in the shops by the following Friday. Elvis distributed copies to the music press in person, in a slimline metal briefcase. "I wanted it out quickly, because the record company lawyers were still arguing. It couldn't wait the month or two that it would take to finalise legal matters."

Elvis took a startled Assistant Editor of *Melody Maker*, and told him that, "Literally, at three o'clock yesterday afternoon, I decided to put *this* out." He phoned Andrew Lauder, who told him he could get it into the shops within the week. He was true to his word, and a week later it was in the UK charts, rising to Number Sixteen. "It was a hit, albeit with a bit of a con trick on the retailers and the BBC, when we threatened to delete it in a week, which helped catapult it into the charts. But in effect it was a broadside, a protest song."

In political terms, the single was a failure, as the Conservatives were re-elected on 9 June, with a crushing majority. The single *was* (supposedly) deleted on the eve of the General Election, and plans for a celebratory release in red vinyl on twelve-inch evaporated with

Thatcher's second victory. "It didn't change anything, but I felt that there were other people who felt as depressed about the inevitability of it as I did, and if there was a song which had some sympathy with that feeling, it was better than there being no song. You can't delude yourself, it was just a little bit of salve or something."

On General Election day, Costello recorded his latest session for the John Peel programme. The producer remembers, "Elvis was not in the best of health, but it was wonderful." The songs were carefully chosen, with 'Pills And Soap' – overdubbed with ghostly organ – 'Shipbuilding' and his cover of Percy Mayfield's 'Danger Zone', a slow burn. A passionate 'Big Sister's Clothes' segued into his insistent version of The Beat's 'Stand Down Margaret'. It was a cry of anguish, rather than a political pamphlet, and by the time the session was broadcast, on 21 June, the lady in question was back in Downing Street.

Elvis and band were midway through a six-date summer tour, playing Belfast and Dublin to make up for previous cancellations, and headlining a charity gig at Dingwalls. Concerts featured the TKO Horns – in which Jeff Blythe had replaced Brian Maurice – but not Afrodysiak. In Belfast, the 2,000 capacity Mayfield Leisure Centre was only a third full, but a relaxed show really kicked in with the TKO Horns – "Southside Johnny, eat your heart out." 'Shipbuilding' was dedicated to Harland & Wolff, with Europe's largest dry dock a mile down road. Barry McIlheney found Elvis "smiling and staring all the while, like some demented Eric Morecambe with a hammer up his sleeve". Sets were running at around the two-hour mark, despite Elvis developing a sore throat during the tour – no wonder – and ballads were largely dropped for faster material. Pete was introduced as "Red Hot" Thomas.

The Dingwalls gig was in the aid of Capital Radio's "Help A London Child", and also marked the tenth anniversary of the dancehall. On the poster, Elvis appears as a bespectacled penguin! Don Watson in *NME* heard "a sound of brutal sway, revealing once more Elvis the pub rocker". He sweats his way through, "*forcing* the energy". A tape of the night sounds like a noose gradually being tightened, with what Allan Jones described as "stabbing brass flourishes". Costello scats along with the horn section, like a young Van Morrison.

July saw the release of a forty-five rpm version of 'Everyday I Write

The Book', which edged the UK Top Thirty, and reached Number Thirty-Six in the USA. The band's photo is relegated to the back of the picture sleeve, where they pose around a lifeboat. Symbolic, anyone, bailing out from Thatcher's Britain? *Punch The Clock* followed in early August, and rose to UK Number Three and US Number Twenty-Four, eventually receiving a gold disc for sales of half a million copies, his best sales figures since *Get Happy!!*.

By the time of the Clocking In Across America tour, the band was sizzling. This time around, the word Coliseum, Stadium, Arena or Amphitheatre featured in most of the gig titles. Playing support were Aztec Camera, of whose mainman Roddy Frame, Elvis said, "*I* wasn't that good when I was nineteen." Reviewers mostly noted how the TKO Horns had revitalised Elvis's set, as did the more elaborate lighting, with panels lighting up with solid colours and bright patterns, in time to the music. There were incidental delights, Elvis dropping to his knees during 'Clowntime Is Over' screaming, "I'm so weak", then, The OJs' 'Backstabbers' segued into 'King Horse', Steve Nieve wearing a turban onstage at Merryweather. Material was largely drawn from Costello's Eighties output, with one-off cover versions thrown in when least expected: Presley's 'His Latest Flame', Laura Nyro's 'The Bells', the beat desperation of The Easybeats' 'Friday On My Mind'.

Costello joined Tony Bennett and the Count Basie Orchestra at a televised gig at New York nightclub Le Parrot. He sang 'It Don't Mean A Thing (If It Ain't Got That Swing)' in front of "a thousand posers in full Forties swag". Elvis had his bow tie undone, and Bennett's arm around his shoulder. One can only imagine Ross MacManus's pride, with perhaps a tinge of jealousy. A gig cancellation enabled Elvis to visit Allen Touissant's studio in New Orleans to record 'Walking On Thin Ice' – her tribute to John Lennon – for a Yoko Ono tribute album. As he later admitted, Ono's albums were not frequent visitors to his turntable, but Yoko did play him a rough mix of Lennon's last recording session, with the slaughtered Beatle's voice eerily echoing around the room, as he cracked jokes between songs. A weird rumour even surfaced that Elvis and Yoko were looking to set up home together!

All was not well on the home front. As Elvis dutifully battled through the gamut of radio interviews which his younger self had so wilfully refused, Bruce Thomas chatted to a fan, Jon Burks, who was staying at the same hotel. After the gig, Elvis went upstairs to write, and watch TV, but Thomas stayed at the bar, and the usual joshing here seems to have an edge. One that would soon cut The Attractions off from their front man. Here is a sample, drawn from the excellent *ECIS*.

JB: "You told us earlier that Elvis's nose and feet smell, what did you mean?"

BT: "That's probably not fair, he's a very hygienic chap these days. It's the 'paddy' in him. No, seriously, he did have a problem but he took my advice and bought all the stuff you need."

JB: "So tell me about Billy Sherrill."

BT: "He has the biggest asshole I ever met. The engineer [Ron "Snake" Reynolds] was a wise guy, he tells sick jokes all the time about nuns with daggers in their heads. He said, 'Hell, I voted for Reagan,' he's a real red-neck I suppose. Maybe it's like Dave downstairs playing the trumpet. I mean he's a real musician union type of guy. He goes to sessions with a copy of *Caravanning Weekly*...off the new album Elvis can't play 'Love Went Mad'. He reckons he doesn't want to do it, but it's because he can't. By the way the two versions of 'Pills And Soap' are identical in actual fact."

JB: "Who else in the band is drug free?"

BT: "Elvis, we cleaned up our acts at the same time."

Thomas reveals that he intends to stay with The Attractions for a further two years, maximum. He now needs to get to bed, as he has to battle Elvis on the tennis court the following morning.

Costello was no less unbuttoned when he talked to Barney Hoskyns for the *NME*. As to the New Romantics, "It does happen periodically that you do get a load of people pretending to be homosexuals in shorts." On 'The Greatest Thing', "We tweaked the vocal up so it's slightly higher, younger sounding. They do that on Michael Jackson records." The song is an answer to Wham's 'Young Guns': George Michael and friend irritate him because "they're making people feel small for what they believe in". Conversely, he likes Culture Club, as they are attempting a "soul music that brings people together". He saw Levon Helm and Rick Danko of The Band, at the Lone Star cafe, and Danko's 'It Made No Difference' had him "practically in tears". Elvis and Hoskyns – a noted expert – talk about deep soul, and how the *Get Happy!!* songs blossom in live performance. In the accompanying photos, Costello cradles a (tiny) sound system to his ear.

In September, 'Let Them All Talk', a new single taken from the LP, had only reached Number Fifty-Nine in the UK. The twelve-inch featured a fashionable "extended remix" and – in a flash of the old Stiff wit – an "extended sleeve". Elvis was back in fashion. The Clocking In Across The UK tour was sold out before it even started, and added Afrodiziak to the sound palette. It was booked into ballroom venues, apt considering the nature of the music purveyed, rhythmic and eminently danceable. I remember a sweaty gig at Cardiff Top Rank, and the strong physicality of the evening, with the TKO Horns seeming to punch holes in my chest.

He broke off after five gigs to fly to Essen to record a two-hour extravaganza for *Rockpalast*, a show which now regularly surfaces on satellite TV. It is awesome, both for its musical punch – Nieve is the star, dancing behind his keyboards, and stretching the tentacles of his fingers across them like a spider on speed – and for Costello's sheer energy level. Song follows song without a break – there is a sly moment when Elvis sings straight-faced about a "German sense of humour" – and the choice of titles ranges across his whole career, making new connections, so that 'Alison' follows on from 'The World And His Wife'. Elvis is like a driven man, barely in control of his feelings.

The tour recommenced, with gigs opening either with a short acoustic set by Elvis, or his duet with Nieve on 'Pills And Soap', lit in eerie green light, then brassy mayhem for the rest of the evening. He introduced 'Alison' under a different title every night, usually a song by someone else with the same sentiments. The sound mix was poor at some gigs, and the only new song to be unveiled was 'The Great Unknown', another Langer/Costello collaboration.

There were so many incidental delights. A chatty Elvis prefaced 'Everyday I Write The Book' as "a well known Harold Robbins hit", and dedicated 'The World And His Wife' to disgraced Tory chairman Cecil Parkinson. Alan Bleasdale was at the Liverpool gig, as was young Matthew Costello, beating the seat in front in exact time with Pete

Thomas. Elvis introduced 'Alison' as his "Joan Of Arc". Mat Snow first warmed to the support act, US country rockers Rank And File, then thrilled to the main attraction as "the closest Hitsville UK will get to the Sixties sock-it-to-me soul revue". Elvis's urgency "stripped the distancing ambiguity from the heart of his songs".

For Penny Kiley in *MM*, it was a "thinking man's party", grown up music which could inspire hope as well as anger. London gigs were spread across the compass, with Hammersmith Palais in the west, Streatham's Cat's Whiskers in the south, and Tottenham Mayfair in the north, on consecutive nights. The Hammersmith gig has surfaced on bootleg CD, and while not the best of the tour, it captures the ragged excitement of a brass section tearing through Elvis's back catalogues. Jackie Collins has now been added to Harold Robbins, as a co-author of 'Everyday I Write The Book'. Airport fiction. There were rumours that Costello was finding it hard to hit the high notes, but the sore-throated renditions here make up in passion what they lose in finesse. 'Man Out Of Time', say, might have lost its majesty here, but it has the force of a curse. 'Alison' is now brass-enhanced, and is a tender interlude, boiling to a climax with Elvis almost screaming "I love you", over and over.

Where anybody else would have taken a rest, the ensemble plunged straight into a major European tour. Costello's throat was still playing up, as was the sound balance, but in the two-hour sets, "Each song was sung and played as if it was their last ever." In Copenhagen, Elvis previewed 'Peace In Our Time', accompanied solo on electric guitar.

The Attractions were starting to spread their wings too, perhaps aware that a break was imminent. The intensity of the 1983 gigs had reached a plateau which no band could sustain forever. Steve Nieve was to be found playing jazz piano at Soho's L'Escargot, backing singer Chrysta Jones. In a notably odd interview in *The Evening Standard*, he revealed that he had a gold Cadillac in a garage in Florida, and that at home he cooked cauliflower cheese and mustard sauce. He collects human skulls, and "liquor bottles from the American prohibition shaped like skeletons".

He rents a "two-bedroomed, fifth floor flat in central London with a good view of the WRNS dormitories". This despite being happily unmarried, to a woman who "changes the colour of her hair every other week", with two young children. He has a massive toy train set, and listens to "some pretty weird music like the album soundtrack from *Psycho*". There are professional eccentrics, and then there are piano players. One thinks of Ron Geesin kicking tin cans around the stage, or Jools Holland with his offices in a faked up railway station, life-size in his case. Maybe it's ivory poisoning.

In December, Nieve left playing with his skull collection long enough to perform his first official solo concert at the Duke Of York, playing material from his solo album *Keyboard Jungle*, released by Demon. Holland was called onstage to play some boogie, as was a member of the audience to play four notes at the piano, from which Nieve demonstrated how many hit singles had been written using them. As well as his own tunes, Nieve performed virtuoso versions of everything from 'Life On Mars' to 'Imagine', before calling up four more members of the audience, ordering each to play a note, and then leaving them stranded onstage for at least five minutes while he sat in the audience, alongside Costello and his two fellow Attractions. Meanwhile, Pete Thomas played a reunion gig with Chilli Willi at Dingwalls. Grown men stood on chairs and shouted, "Martin Stone," as the shy genius unleashed another devastating guitar break while seemingly asleep.

On 18 December, Elvis appeared with Nieve at "The Big One", an anti-Cruise missile charity show. "They say familiarity breeds contempt, but in the case of songs I think familiarity breeds mediocrity." He examples James Taylor's 'You've Got A Friend' and 'Danny Boy'. "Let's go out and drown the bastard." Instead, Costello previews 'The Great Unknown' and 'Peace In Our Time', a peculiarly appropriate song in the circumstances. He also duetted with Paul Weller on 'My Ever Changing Moods', and made his public acting debut, as a bespectacled Prussian officer, revealed as Susannah York's fantasy lover. *I* should be so lucky.

As Christmas loomed, Elvis headlined three shows at the Hammersmith Odeon, with Costello at last giving a London audience a peek at both his light show and his gorilla suit. It was a leave taking of the TKO Horns and Afrodyziak, and began with Costello singing some songs from the forthcoming album, solo. Encores included

'Alison', introduced by Costello – now clad in a gold jacket – as a Barry Manilow song, and comedian Lenny Henry with a cardboard guitar doing Elvis (Mark I) impressions while Elvis (Mark II) got into his monkey costume.

By the end of 1983, Costello was back on a creative and popular high. If past behaviour was anything to go by, this was exactly the kind of thing to bore him, and make him look for new challenges. An interview with Timothy White earlier that year begins, symbolically, with a lorry splashing his red shoes with muddy water. "I don't have many friends, period – let's put it this way, I don't choose to have many." He remains a man in a hurry. "What useful things you find out in this world, you invariably find out on foot, on the move. You can't *wait*."

During January, The Attractions took a holiday, while Elvis "decided to stop rushing into songs as soon as a single idea sprang into my head". He applied himself to "an intensive period of writing", working business hours at F-Beat's recently abandoned offices in Acton, just like Randy Newman, who also composes at his office, in the time honoured tradition of Tin Pan Alley. "A burst of songwriting like that can sometimes get a sort of tension into it that perhaps was lacking on the last album," he explains. He took an electric piano and guitars as creative tools, as well as an easel and oil paints, for light relief. One of the resulting self portraits, "Pat And Mike" – an old fashioned microphone is crudely painted in on a swirl of blue and ghostly white – under the punning pseudonym of "Eamonn Singer" was reproduced on the new album. It is interesting that even Elvis's art is self-referential. He then rushed the new songs into Sarm West Studios, and roughed them out with the help, again, of Langer and Winstanley.

The Attractions road-tested these new songs on a hastily arranged six-gig French tour that February. They shot the photos for the album sleeve in Montpellier, and brought the songs back to the studio, to complete recording. Richard Thompson was pencilled in as a session guitarist, but could not comply, due to a US tour. Costello also spent some time in the studio with The Special AKA, producing the 'Free Nelson Mandela' single. When their singer Stan Campbell walked out just before a live appearance on Channel 4's *The Tube*, Costello took over on lead vocals. At the same time, Billy Bremner released

Costello's song 'Shatterproof' as a single – "musical polyfiller", wrote the *NME* – as did Tracie with his song 'I Love You (When You Sleep)', which Elvis himself later reworked as 'Joe Porterhouse'.

February also saw IMP's vinyl release of *Ten Bloody Mary's & Ten How's Your Fathers*, "indispensable if you want to be a *serious* Costello bore" in the view of *MM*'s Adam Sweeting. Here were Elvis's *Basement Tapes*, full of "claustrophobic clutter". Over at *NME*, Ian Penman – who never uses one word when a thousand will convey less – thought it sounded like a "lost and found, slightly dazed, slightly hurried, slightly hurt, fan-made cassette. And that can only be a *multiverse* better than something like a 'The Craft Of Elvis Costello'." It reflects a marvellously out-of-control "career", from "Spy to Socialite to Socialist". Penman now goes so far over the top that any attempts to reprint the following paragraph would cause illness in the reader. Suffice it to say that he likes the album. Or not. Or maybe perhaps. Well, *you* can translate into sense phrases like the following; "slipping into the stream of alliteration that often follows a repeated rehearsing of the Costello resonant rehandling of the everyday pun". Quite.

In April, The Imposter resurfaced – on IMP TRUCE 1 – with the single 'Peace In Our Time', again in a plain cover. It entered the UK Top Fifty at Number Forty-Eight. "I don't think I have to explain the politics of the song this time," Elvis said at the time. "It's just a song I wanted out right now for reasons I think will be obvious when you hear it." Colin Irwin made it the *Melody Maker* single of the week: "Over an arrangement so simple it hurts, Costello delivers his festering time bomb with agonising deliberation and sings – really *sings* – in a manner I've never heard before. A carefully weighted, considered performance."

Elvis subsequently took the song into the heart of Reagan's America, singing it live on the Johnny Carson show. As he told *Record Collector*, "What actually happened was that they couldn't physically hear what I was singing. It didn't have the musical equipment to get the message over in the way that 'Shipbuilding' and 'Pills And Soap' had. It had a pretty melody – I lifted it, but I'm not gonna tell you where from in case I get sued." The B-side was even more miserable, a "thoroughly depressing" version of Richard Thompson's 'Withered And Died' – a song of lost hope. Costello played another, equally bleak, Thompson song, 'End Of The Rainbow', in solo concerts that year.

Elvis revisited his early days as a folk singer (no disgrace in that, Rod Stewart and Hawkwind's Dave Brock both began busking in the streets), in an interview with the German magazine *TIP*. A tape has survived from his folk period, but, "These recordings should be left in oblivion." As DP Costello, he played lots of songs by Jesse Winchester, although Clive Gregson sounds more like him – and "the perfect pop voice" of Cliff Richard circa 1962! – than Elvis ever did. From the start, he resisted the kind of nasal "folk" voice which the likes of Peter Bellamy took to glorious excess (adding an unsettling chuckle in mid song), and found a lot of folk clubs hostile to his talents. "I often played in an atmosphere of impatience and intolerance." He now would like to play the Cambridge Folk Festival, at Cherry Hinton. "That has brought folk in touch with a larger public. It can be a springboard for songwriters who don't have their roots in folk music."

Two very different attractions were emerging from Elvis's band. Steve Nieve abandoned keyboards for a Gretsch guitar, and played a solo set at the Captain's Cabin, singing "ten or so very ordinary songs about sex and life", whose titles were often the best thing about them. 'Rubbing Legs', anyone? Meanwhile, Costello visited America in April for a three-week, sixteen-date, solo tour, sold out in advance. "I still don't know what I'll be playing. It will be a change and a challenge, which is the whole point of doing it."

"I made *Goodbye Cruel World* and I was having a miserable time – I was getting divorced – and I basically ran away to sea and went off on a solo tour. I had a ball. It was my first time as a professional, but I'd done it a lot in my apprenticeship as it were. I always enjoyed it. I did songs one night and then never again. The American leg was particularly great."

Costello alternated between electric organ, grand piano and guitar. He introduced himself as "Mr Costello and his guitar army", and 'Riot Act' was a splurge of electric guitar reverb. Audiences could suddenly hear his lyrics, and he played both the more obscure items from his own back catalogue, like 'Motel Matches' – introduced as "a Billy Joel song" – or 'Man Called Uncle', and favourites by others. Highlights were Jack Nitzsche's 'I Love Her Too', Philip Chevron's 'Captains And

Kings', and 'Girlfriend', by The Specials. Joe Tex's 'The Love You Save Might Be Your Own' was shoehorned into 'Alison'. Songs well known in their electric incarnation, like a slowed down 'Green Shirt' – with its lyrics changed to "I hope *all* of them are mine" – became suddenly intimate, as if breathed into the audience's ear.

He introduced 'Stranger In The House' as "a song I wrote when I was some other guy". There were particular cheers for the line, "There's already one spaceman in the White House", though Costello's most heartfelt performance was on Dylan's 'I Threw It All Away', for reasons that were to become all too clear.

Support act was the Texan T-Bone Burnett, soon to sign for Demon, and already a veteran of the Rolling Thunder Revue – in which Dylan revisited his own folk roots, with old chums from Greenwich Village. "We started having fun with the Coward Brothers thing, which became one of my devices to stop the tour being the sensitive singer-songwriter thing, which I'd been dead against," he says. "I was always anxious to avoid the protest singer element. It's fine writing those songs but if you adopt the posture you're a sitting duck." He even announced that his next album was to be called "Goodbye, President Reagan", and read out a spoof magazine article in which The Attractions revealed their sexual preferences.

Elvis would end proceedings with 'Pump it Up', improvising over a pre-recorded tape loop. "It was a lot of noise, and it ended the concert with the cacophony that people were used to hearing at the end. But before that, I basically presented two hours of ballads, and a few rhythmic things. And the thing with T-Bone also balanced the sombreness of some of the songs." Reviewers agreed. For Joel Selvin, "Costello never sounded so warm, so human and genuine", while *Record Mirror* saw him following in the footsteps of Billy Bragg: "Costello simply took a group of people and made them his." The shows were an important influence in the move towards acoustic music. In a role reversal, Bruce Springsteen attended the Warfield gig and gave Elvis credit for his own later decision to play solo.

Costello had joined Equity the previous year, and June saw his TV debut, in the second episode of *Scully*, a children's TV drama written by the young Alan Bleasdale. Elvis threw away his glasses, and played the hero's brother, mentally retarded and unable to speak, but sharing one trait with the actor playing him, fanaticism. Henry wears a British rail peaked cap, and an oversize pair of headphones, through which he plays the sounds of locomotives, from a cassette player which he lovingly polishes.

Elvis, Bleasdale and the fictional Scully are all obsessed with Liverpool FC, and Kenny Dalglish, perhaps the finest player ever to grace its turf, makes a cameo appearance, playing himself. For Elvis, "There was only one team for me." You can always tell where someone's heart really lies, by his – or her – choice of football team. Otherwise, we would all support Manchester United! *Scully*'s theme tune, 'Turning The Town Red' was a pun on the Liverpool strip, and appeared on the flip side of 'I Wanna Be Loved', which reached Number Twenty-Five in the UK charts. Featuring the voice of Green from Scritti Politti, the A-side had first been recorded in 1959 by Ricky Nelson, and later covered by Teachers Edition. For Elvis it was either a dip into muzak, or a cry of pain.

He flew straight to Fiji for a brief holiday, and then on to New Zealand for a tour of the Far East, beginning in mid May. In Adelaide, Jon Forsythe saw a "definite continuity" in songs which traced contemporary history – one can hear the Aussie chuckle – "as Britain sinks, suffocated by its self-importance and myth". For an acoustic gig, it was an angry and violent affair: "Costello walked off after the second encore of 'Pump It Up', whacked his guitar against the amp and flung his plectrum into the crowd." Meanwhile, Elvis had deep forebodings about the new album.

Goodbye Cruel World was released that same month, and reached Number Ten in the UK and Thirty-Five in the USA. As Elvis told *Record Collector*, he hated the final mix when he returned from his solo tour. "I knew I'd got most of it wrong. But we were locked into releasing it, or else I would have gone bankrupt at the exact time when I couldn't afford to go bankrupt, because I was getting divorced. I couldn't scrap the record, so I let it come out, warts and all." Years on, he could hear some passionate performances, buried under the arrangements. "But it was no fault of Clive and Alan. I feel apologetic to anyone whose favourite record it is, but I can't lie and say that I think it's a good record – particularly the pop songs that were put on there with an even more calculating ear for the nuances of the charts."

He reveals more in the extensive and contrite notes to the CD. The album's failure was hardly Alan Langer's fault: "I didn't need a producer, I needed a nurse (or maybe a priest). 'Pop music' was among the many things about which I was depressed and demoralised. That I thought of approaching Richard Thompson to add guitar is a clue to the dark tone I was really after. Like so many of my notions of the time, it came to nothing." Rather unfair on Richard, who writes the bleakest songs on the planet, but whose spine-tingling guitar ranges the emotional spectrum, and has graced records by everyone from Robert Plant to Suzanne Vega. For Elvis, "There isn't much rock 'n' roll on this record. Once you get over that, it makes a lot more sense."

After two weeks in the studio, "We called a truce." Langer remained involved "more as a friend than as a professional. I agreed to let them work their magic on a few cuts and give the record company some commercial focus while the rest of the tunes went fairly unadorned. It was a happy, if fatal, compromise." There is a "detached, almost sedated quality" to the rest of the songs. Although many of the stories are dense and obscure, they can't disguise the fears, doubts and desires…the product of my gloomiest and least inspired days."

At the last moment, he changed the title of 'Goody Two Shoes' to 'Inch By Inch', so as not to cause confusion with an Adam Ant hit of the same name. Costello later described the LP as, "The worst record of the best songs that I've written."

The title sounds like a suicide note in vinyl. It was originally to have been called "Pat And Mike", after his painting. "Congratulations," he tells purchasers of the augmented CD, "you have just purchased our worst album. At least that is the impression that I have given over the years. Many very private and personal concerns influenced the fate of these songs. Suffice it to say that I began the year as a married man, and after a fraught and futile period, during which I caused much unhappiness, I found myself living alone by the time this record was released. 'Mea culpa' as we used to say in church without being *really* sure what it meant. I was about to find out."

The album sleeve was photographed by Brian Griffin, who also took the inner shots for *Armed Forces*. It certainly hints at the tensions it enwraps. On what looks like the surface of the moon, everything is doubled – two trees, two men in white and two in black. Nieve is dressed as a fencer, and Elvis looks ready for a fist fight. The photo is slightly off-centre, and has an unsettling background of pure sky, as if the whole hillock is ascending to heaven. Perhaps all four are dead, and on their way to the afterworld. On the back, the musicians literally melt into the background, like dying souls. Bruce Thomas is not there at all, and Elvis is stripped even of his glasses. On the inner sleeve, his self-portrait shatters into a jigsaw, half of whose pieces have flown away. Needless to say, the background to all this is the purest black.

The album title was taken from the obscure Sixties single written by James Darlin, and has added resonance here. Costello had already announced to Langer that, "It was the last record I would ever make. I decided to quit for all kinds of reasons. Sometimes the best conclusion is to shut up. Bruce Thomas thinks, "It would have been a rotten album to end on…Side Two is completely forgettable." Pete thought they should instead have taken a holiday: "The whole feeling was so down." Langer at times felt like a passenger, and was certainly the wrong choice of producer. Whatever else they were, these were *not* cheery pop songs.

"I probably wanted to make a kind of "folk rock" record, but instead of an open ringing sound we ended up with a muted background against which events were supposed to occur," Elvis reflects. He considered abandoning these sessions, and replacing them with a solo, acoustic set, *Unplugged* years before the fact. Instead, he should instead have called in Joe Boyd, master of studio dynamics, who REM went to for *their* most troubled album, *Fables Of The Reconstruction*. Like Nick Lowe, Boyd knew all about capturing the shards of live music on tape, as he did so spectacularly on Richard and Linda Thompson's *Shoot Out The Lights*, a last minute replacement for an album's worth of over-smooth versions of the same songs. It too was about an impending divorce. In an odd twist of fate, Richard was flown over to a hotel in Swiss Cottage, but was completely forgotten, and flew back after a week. His angular, probing guitar would have intersected with these songs to wondrous effect.

Reviewers picked up on the inherent misery. *NME*'s Mat Snow asks why Elvis sings the line "why must I be so lonely" with more conviction and passion than "the rest of his new album in its entirety". The record "perspires, grafts and contrives" but never soars. *Melody Maker* found instead a "very-taking-care-of-business air about it, a grave, serious urgency". *Sounds* could not decide whether it is a wedding or a wake, but praised the album's "poignancy". For *Record Mirror* it was a "bitter sweet album", though one laced with humour. "Sad, depressing, but brilliant."

American critics were meaner. Don Shewey heard "as murky an album, musically and lyrically" as Elvis had ever made, while Robert and Ricky Fary were jointly bitter; Costello was metaphorically taking a dive into the river of commercialism. "The one song when Elvis definitely dons his swimming trunks is called 'I Wanna Be Loved'. It seems that Elvis might have been skinny dipping with Boy George when he wrote this." Except he didn't. The album comes in at Number Forty-Four in Jimmy Guterman's *Slipped Discs: The Worst Rock 'N' Roll Records Of All Time*. Elvis is imagined talking to The Attractions: "If we are lazy enough, we can make these powerful songs impotent." Like Dylan, "He wanted to put out his own album-length rant of self loathing, his own *Self-Portrait*. All you can hear on this record is distance between Costello and his band, Costello and his material, Costello and his audience."

'The Only Flame In Town' opens with a blast of Gary Barnacle's sax, like a man screaming for help, but then leads into some classic AOR with Daryl Hall, king of that genre. Elvis had got "tired of hearing my own voice harmonising with myself". In the video, the two of them serenade girls in a restaurant. Originally straightforward R&B, "until Clive persuaded me to get a more interesting rhythm going", the lyrics are far sadder than the music, about the fires of passion ebbing, as they do.

'Home Truth' opens with a wallop of drums, but the band seem to be playing in the next room. "It was the saddest song that I had ever written but it struggled to seem so in the sterile studio sound." Elvis's voice sounds under strain, and The Attractions tranquillised. Langer advised him to leave it off the album, "But I'm not the only person in the world who's watched his relationship go downhill." Maybe Clive was right after all, as the song is so personal and self-accusing – "the lies that I tell you" – that it hurts to listen to.

As Costello admits, "Meanwhile the bewildered tales of adulterous life fared much better, which I suppose was fitting." 'Room With No Number' is straight out of *The Avengers* – playing tricks with reality – and perkily sung. The Attractions regain some of their primal power here: there is even a drum solo at the end. The adulterous lovers are uneasy and being watched. 'Inch By Inch' also inhabits a secret-service world, "invisible ink" and all. Its chorus was an attempt to cross Henry Mancini with The Impressions, and Elvis sings with menace, and a spring in his step.

'Worthless Thing' was introduced onstage thus: "About thirty years ago, there was a kind of music that was very popular with people who put lots of grease in their hair. Nowadays we have wires that come into our living rooms and bring this music into our homes." The song is about media sickness, and specifically MTV, which "catches lightning, and turns it into a museum piece", and more to the point has boycotted Costello's videos. "Most of all it was about the lack of surprises. It is a pity that self-loathing wasn't more fashionable at the time." There is a slighting reference to "vintage Elvis Presley wine", not a drink that the dead singer was much associated with.

The song has the same bitter energy as Scorsese's movie *King Of Comedy*. Fame is the sickness of the late twentieth century. The injunction to "keep your bloody hands off my life" has been followed in the present book. Maybe Elvis will one day write his own life story, despite Bebe Buell's earlier prediction that it could never happen.

Elvis wanted 'Love Field' to sound like a Serge Gainsbourg production, a nocturnal version of 'Je T'Aime'. "I even tried to make the words sound as if they had been badly translated from another language," he admits. Never has alfresco sex sounded so unenticing. *Melody Maker* found the song "at once sad and bitter, aches with a frozen pain and a poignancy that somehow recalls Gram Parsons", and I can't improve on that. It leads on naturally to 'I Wanna Be Loved', where as in *Almost Blue* Elvis lets another songwriter do his talking for him. Here the master of ambiguity is stripped naked, letting his voice run free, and unleash what is almost a cry for help. Green's girlish harmonies add smoothness. Barnacle's sleazy sax leads into silence, as Costello moans the chorus.

In 'The Comedians' Costello "trivialised the drama by my wilful decision to rearrange it in 5/4 time". The song is about someone who is a fake: "It refers to a specific incident. Something to do with making friendships under the influence of drugs. Especially the people who use cocaine." Elvis sings with no emotion whatsoever, and his band play by numbers. 'Joe Porterhouse' was "about the funeral of a family strong man". Elvis wanted "a name that would sound strong, a name with muscles, something to do with meat". The setting seems to be back in Birkenhead, and this is certainly a family funeral. The song oddly echoes Keith West's weird single 'Excerpt From A Teenage Opera'.

'Sour Milk-Cow Blues' is a development of Sleepy John Estes 'Milk Cow Blues' covered by Presley on Sun, but the subject matter is again the death of marital love. Mary Costello became a well respected disc jockey, which might explain the line about breaking the hearts of "a million listeners". Lovers change, and the music – and Elvis's blues; phrasings – has a joy which counteracts the regretful lyrics. Pain can be a liberation.

In 'The Great Unknown', "infamous characters from celebrated songs have spiteful things done to them. I was having my doubts about being 'known'." 'Danny Boy' lies drowned, Tom Jones' 'Delilah' grows gruesome, and Elvis flees a wedding reception for a smoke outside. Even there he can hear his namesake's 'Wooden Heart' mangled, with the wrong tune. Elvis pictures himself as the Unknown Soldier, an unlikely concept, and the whole thing sounds suitably funereal.

'The Deportees Club' was "simply the wrong music for the right words". During the solo tour Elvis "found a tune more in keeping with an exile's lament". Christy Moore later recorded a fine cover version on *Voyage*. On a live radio broadcast in Philadelphia the line about "a piece of ass" was excised by the station censor. A descending organ chord, Elvis counts the band in, live in the studio, and the results sparkle. The same scream that opens 'Man Out Of Time' is interposed, just after a middle eight which – both musically and in its confiding, half whispered tone – is a dead ringer for The Who's 'I Can See For Miles'. This tale of Little Italy, in New York, even contains a good joke, about the "secret life of Frank Sinatra".

'Peace In Our Time' features Elvis banging an anvil, and brilliantly combines Euro-disco and Munich's earlier role, as the place where Chamberlain signed a peace treaty, a year before World War II. This has the same, conspiratorial atmosphere of *This Year's Model*, with Reagan as Number One. Elvis sounds truly anguished, singing with resigned sadness about the coming of nuclear war. The mournful sax and clanking anvil sound a death knell to the planet. *Goodbye Cruel World* began as a suicide note for a love affair, and has ended by destroying the whole earth.

The CD is not finished yet, and bonus tracks include some live performances from the solo tour – clearer and cleaner than the album – with a particularly heartfelt cover of The Boudleaux's 'Sleepless Nights', and 'Motel Matches', self accompanied on electric piano. Of the studio outtakes, 'Baby It's You' was the first duet on record with Nick Lowe, but Columbia deemed the track "too good", afraid that it would divert attention from the "real" singles.

There is a fascinating early version of 'I Hope You're Happy Now', "written during a brief summer trip to Italy", but rejected as an "instant single". 'Get Yourself Another Fool' was one of a "brace of R&B ballads" learned from a Sam Cooke record, and taped that summer. "All that I can do is pack up and run." If Elvis is faking the emotion here, he deserves an Oscar.

In June, Elvis and The Attractions made their debut at the Glastonbury Festival, headlining over the likes of Weather Report, The Smiths and Dr John. They bounced on stage at ten pm, to a huge cheer. Elvis announced, "Hello, we're The Grateful Dead." They rocked up The Byrds' 'So You Want To Be A Rock 'N' Roll Star', while 'New Lace Sleeves' mutated into a free-form version of Bowie's 'Fame'. Costello jetted off to appear alongside Van Dyke Parks, T-Bone Burnett, Jackson Browne, Warren Zevon, John Hiatt and Richard Thompson, all crammed onstage at the tenth anniversary of McCabe's guitar shop in Santa Monica. Thompson was to marry Nancy Covey, the shop's concert director, to whom the evening was dedicated. Costello duetted with Jackson Browne on 'Twist And Shout', and other rock classics. Laurel Canyon meets Crouch End. The evening's star was Burnett, backed by Ry Cooder, who had been recently dropped by WB, and responded with a set which evoked "a resonant sense of loss and yearning".

In August, 'The Only Flame In Town' appeared as a single, the matching twelve-inch labelled "version discotheque". The front cover was a cartoon of a lady of the night, lighting up. It was barely a hit, making UK Number Seventy-One, and US Number Fifty-Six. Speaking on the Richard Skinner show, Elvis reckoned that people would be convinced he was a midget, having appeared in the video with Daryl Hall, who was about nine feet tall! The same month saw Costello begin a full US tour with The Attractions, opening in Sunrise, Florida and ending in Los Angeles a month and a half later. The support act were old friends Nick Lowe's Cowboy Unit, featuring Martin Belmont and Paul Carrack. Elvis and band were booked at the last moment to open for Nick in Austin, Texas, and played a set of cover versions.

As headliners, they played high-energy, two-hour sets, dominated by recent songs. Mellowness went out of the window: The Attractions were once again the musical piledriver of the late Seventies, almost as if they knew that their time with Elvis was almost up. Elvis's guitar playing had been loosened up by his solo tour, and there was more jamming, with Elvis going upstage to play his breaks. These reworkings sometimes "obscured his pointed lyrics", but no-one could accuse Elvis of repeating himself. Nieve was now going under the stage name "Maurice Worm". Bruce Thomas was like a wild animal on bass, and performed a duck-walk during the band introductions. Part of the concert at Philadelphia's Tower Theatre was broadcast on American radio, and has since surfaced as the *Writing My Story* CD. It is a high energy, slightly chaotic show, with Barnacle used "sparingly" on sax, and the crowd singing along on the chorus of 'Alison'.

A review of a concert at Forest Hills spoke of the way the band tore songs apart, "turning rockers into ballads, ballads into funk tunes, adding crescendos and sudden hushes and shifty rhythms". At the Irvine Meadows Amphitheatre, he played the whole concert with a "decided Memphis R&B flavour: Elvis even threw in some flashy dance moves during an old James Brown tune." Another gig saw Sam Moore, of Sam And Dave, brought on for an encore of the song which Elvis had borrowed from his Sixties act. Elvis and band also appeared on the *Tonight* show. As well as chatting to hostess Joan Rivers, Elvis performed 'I Hope You're Happy Now' – Nieve had a muppet perched on his keyboards – and a solo version of 'Peace In Our Time'. The lyrics now said, of the White House spaceman, "What did you want to *re*-elect him for." Elvis seemed unrelaxed.

The rock industry was becoming increasingly corporate, with Stiff now part of the Island empire, and F-Beat under the umbrella of RCA. Major artists were given their own small labels to play with, like a grown up version of a toy train set, especially for a vinyl fanatic like Costello. "If a lot of things turn up, then I'll release a lot of good records," he said at the time. The IMP label reissued Costello's whole back catalogue, save the first album, which remained with Stiff. This paid further dividends a decade later, when the CD reissue programme – on Demon – came with comprehensive sleeve notes by Elvis himself, dozens of rare tracks, and careful remastering. Creative rock archaeology.

Meanwhile, the IMP label released Philip Chevron's version of 'The Captain And The Kings', taken from Brendan Behan's play *The Hostage*, and produced by Costello. Chevron had been lead singer with Irish punk band The Radiators From Space, and later joined The Pogues. Another IMP debut was by The Men They Couldn't Hang, blessed by the superb song-writing of Paul Simmonds, who alongside The Pogues and The Oyster Band were rocking the folk tradition ragged.

In October, Costello embarked on another British tour, his last with The Attractions for many years, augmented again by Gary Barnacle. Elvis followed, literally, in his father's footsteps by undertaking a Monday night residency at the Hammersmith Palais, for the whole month. The band matched the amphetamine rush of the American dates, so that even country smoochers like Johnny Cash's 'I Still Miss Someone' – given its own haunting reading by early Fairport – and the Burritos' 'Dark End Of The Street' were punked up and breathless. Ian Pye reported that Elvis's "sense of pace bordered on the insane", with his voice close to collapse. The only respite was a brief solo set, which "only served to underline how ugly this contemporary group sound".

Nick Kent found a lack of focus, although for virtually any other band the night would have been a triumph. There was a "calculated slickness" to The Attractions' sound. A solo rendition of 'End Of The

Rainbow' was the song "Costello seemed most vehemently in sync with throughout the night". As to his own material, "He tended to distance himself from the gut feelings of too many older songs, leaving them only marginally populated." How he resolves this dilemma is "an issue only he can answer with time". Time was running out all round. Hammersmith Palais – "the world's most famous nightspot" – was to close its doors for good in late 1997, with Rank Leisure set on turning it into more office space, just what London doesn't need.

Support act was The Pogues, featuring Cait O'Riordan, on electric bass. Her largely unsmiling onstage demeanour fitted in with the rough scowls of the rest of the band, exuding twisted charisma. Shane MacGowan's fearsome lack of teeth, and the band's rabid following – plus a name that meant "kiss my arse" in Irish – ensured that it was a brave man indeed who dared to heckle what was, in those days, largely a load of musical codswallop. After what Allan Jones described as a "jaded, uncharacteristically sloppy" show at the Dominion, The Attractions seemed to be following in their footsteps. It was the last night of the tour, and Elvis announced onstage that, "This is the last concert that we'll be playing for a very, very, very long time. Let me introduce you to the best band in the world."

In November Costello appeared as a "stone deaf A&R man" in the Comic Strip's *The Bullshitters*, in which Keith Allen and Peter Richardson drew out the homo-erotic elements of ITV's *The Professionals*, riotously. Elvis's character role is unctuous, suggests, "Let's do lunch, man," and is punched in the face. It was sweet revenge on some of the sleazier elements in the rock biz

November saw Costello undertake a solo tour of Britain and Europe, taking in premier league theatres, and with T-Bone Burnett as support. "He just called me up and asked me to open up for him on his tour," Burnett recalls. "I guess he wanted some meat to throw on stage before he came on." The only sour note was in Geneva, where the audience – expecting The Attractions – taunted the singer. He ground to a halt, after six songs, and one member of the audience threw a glass of wine full in his face. Nevertheless, he stayed onstage to complete a truncated set, which included The Pogues' 'The Boys From County Hell'.

Tom Morton was at the Edinburgh Playhouse, watching as Elvis "sauntered onstage, crushed velvet jacket rippling in the lights". There was "an almost awesome restraint", with Costello revelling in a "spacey minimalism". He made jokey introductions: "Elvis solo, or Napoleon Solo. This is called 'The Man From Uncle'." Of his illustrious namesake, "Five years in the army and they chopped off his bollocks and sent him to Hawaii. Music for lifts." Costello was concentrating back on *songs* again. A tape of that concert is one of my proudest possessions, and Elvis has his audience spellbound. 'Shipbuilding' has the added verse, "a small bunch of flowers is all you get/real marble letters and a box to bury your baby."

Allan Jones was at the Royal Festival Hall, and witnessed an epic performance, with some new songs, and a "knockabout half hour with T-Bone Burnett". They ran The Beatles' 'Baby's In Black' into Scott MacKenzie's hippie paeon 'San Francisco'. Burnett quipped that, "We'll probably do another tour when the money runs out." Not for a long time, then. Costello came back solo to sing the traditional song 'Month Of January', learnt from June Tabor, "a clutching 'Shipbuilding' and finally a darkly ironic 'Peace In Our Time'. Songs that had recently begun to sound exhausted, too familiar to move the spirit, were re-invested with a crucial emotional drama, a fierce pertinence." Finding Elvis back on this form was "like being reacquainted with greatness".

Costello's farewell onstage comment was more of a shock than his similar pronouncement at the Dominion. *We* was now *I*: "You won't see me for a long time." This time he really seemed to mean it, although none of the music papers seemed to pick up on its import. Maybe Costello was like the boy who had cried "wolf" once too often. He immediately disproved his words by taking part in two charity concerts back in Liverpool, in early December, for Ethiopian relief. Elvis was relaxed enough to perform for around half an hour, in his street clothes. Nevertheless, rumours began to circulate that he had disbanded The Attractions, was moving to New York, or had changed his name.

1985 began quietly, with Costello visiting the USA on a working holiday, attending concerts by George Jones and John Hiatt. As he told *Wight Venues*, "I'm going to take quite a long time off to do some writing. I don't know exactly what I am going to write yet. If it turns into a book, or a play, or just loads of songs, then that's what it will be." He resumed his lonely sojourn at the old F-Beat offices.

His first public appearance that year was on 9 March, when The Attractions rejoined Elvis for a benefit gig at London University. All proceeds went to help prolong the increasingly bitter Pit strike, of which this was the anniversary. It was to be another lost cause for Elvis, and another milestone for Mrs Thatcher, who having beaten the Argies was now looking for "enemies within" to confront. Elvis was definitely not "one of us".

Following fiery sets by Billy Bragg and The Men They Couldn't Hang, and a special appearance from the South Wales Striking Miners Choir, Elvis and his refound chums ran through a mix of songs old and new, all performed with ragged passion: "They appeared to have recovered all their old edge and brilliance. The set included Merle Haggard's 'No Reason To Quit' and 'Why Must You Throw Dirt In My Face', both ironic in the circumstances. This was to be The Attractions' only appearance with their former leader for that year and most of the next.

Eight days later, a St Patrick's Day concert at the Clarendon Ballroom saw Elvis sandwiched between Lash Lariat And The Long Riders, The Swamps and headliners The Pogues. David Quantick reported Elvis as wearing a "fetching pair of blue-rimmed spectacles, and a green rugby shirt emblazoned with a shamrock". He sang four numbers, three of them covers, one the new, country-flavoured 'The Big Light'.

Costello had just finished producing The Pogues' second album *Rum, Sodomy And The Lash*, in which their early punkish thrash began to mutate into music of startling power, with MacGowan proving himself to be one of the great rock poets. Elvis saw his job, as with The Specials, as being "to capture them in their dilapidated glory before some more professional producer fucked them up". After this album he called a halt on producing other people's records. "You can only marry the bass player once," was an indication of his own private life. Having appeared on the surrealistic video for 'A Pair Of Brown Eyes', Elvis was also seen, off set, with their bassist Caitlan, though enquiries by *The Sun* into quite what this relationship entailed was greeted with justified anger. The couple married the following year, and are still together. End of story.

April saw Elvis joining rubber-faced John Hiatt – the nearest thing to an American Costello – at the Duke of York's Theatre. They had enjoyed much the same kind of career trajectory. Hiatt had recorded two unsuccessful country-rock albums for Epic in the early Seventies, then punked up his backings and developed his image as a sardonic outsider. He was later to join Nick Lowe in the disappointing "supergroup" Little Village. He and Elvis duetted on Hiatt's 'She Loves The Jerk', a comic take on jealousy,and 'Living A Little, Laughing A Little', also released as a single, and originally recorded by The Detroit Spinners.

Another guest appearance, in a Paris studio, was on the new Eurythmics album, *Be Yourself Tonight*, where he sang with Annie Lennox on the song 'Adrian', joining a cast list which included Aretha Franklin and Stevie Wonder. This for a band which had started as a serious minded attempt to import the other-worldliness of Can into a British context.

He revealed to Mat Snow of the *NME* why he had gone to ground. "I just decided it'd been seven years without any longer than a month's break and two years with five days' holiday." The rock 'n' roll lifestyle had driven him to near exhaustion. "I was working on complete nervous energy for the last couple of months. It was a sort of hysterical energy you get when you're tired." He was characteristically spiky about the likes of Aztec Camera and Prefab Sprout: "They're responsible for their own failings . . I think the new record's a load of nonsense." Of his peers, he likes Billy Bragg, while, "Springsteen is a very sincere person who has had his life stolen from him by success."

On 25 April, Mary Costello opened her Choka Dobie nightclub in Great Portland Street. On the opening night, the main attraction was "The Pope Of Pop", and hard core fans queued for hours to witness a short set from Costello, which apart from a drastic re-working of 'The Deportees Club' contained only new songs. Elvis wore a jacket "made out of the entire cloth ration of the Swiss Guard". As *NME* discerned, in a confined space, he could use "the differing warbles and runways of his voice, be a bit more subtle in his inflections". One highlight was the opening line of 'Brilliant Mistake' – "Ronnie was the king of

America" – which makes the recorded version far more explicable.

In May, Elvis made two further guest appearances at London gigs, joining Los Lobos at the Electric Ballroom to sing 'I Got Loaded', and joining Ricky Scaggs – the rising star of new country – at the Dominion, for an energetic version of 'Don't Get Above Your Raising'. *NME* saw a "twitching, pallid, unshaven beatnik scruff" join the immaculate Scaggs: "They confer credibility on each other."

The lack of new "product" was temporarily filled by a TV-advertised compilation on the Telstar label, *The Best Of Elvis Costello – The Man*, which reached Number Eight in the UK album charts in May. The subtitle was a cheeky pinch from Van "The Man" Morrison. A matching collection of rock videos was released at the same time, taking in career highlights from 'Pump It Up' to 'The Only Flame In Town'. Most saw the band miming in the studio, but 'Accidents Will Happen' featured graphics by the creators of *Max Headroom* and 'Watching The Detectives' used stock footage from black and white examples of film noir.

The album had been preceded with the re-release of 'Green Shirt' as a single, which reached Number Sixty-Eight in Britain. It was packaged as "number one in a series of two", two of its five formats came in appropriate coloured vinyl, and the twelve-inch version featured Colin Fairey's remix of the same song, which added about ten extra drumbeats. Elvis poured scorn on this repackaging exercise, attacking "peace sign picture discs like the kind of crap they're doing now with 'Green Shirt'. It just devalues the song."

The IMP label was a practical demonstration by Elvis about how to do things properly. The label was "like a photocopier or an inflatable doll – you just get it out when you need it." Another new signing was the veteran night-club singer Agnes Bernelle. Half-Jewish, she had fled Germany just before the war, and broadcast counter-propaganda back to her homeland on Radio Atlantik. 'Radio, Radio', before the fact. Her broadcasts once caused a U-Boat captain to surrender his ship. IMP's first album release was her left-field *Father's Lying Dead On The Ironing Board*, settings of poems by Ringelnatz, the German counterpart of Edward Lear.

Mat Snow met the straw-hatted IMP supremo in a Soho cafe, before he and Cait rushed back to the studio. He declared, "Between forkfuls, eyes narrowing pointedly behind Dr Strangelove dark glasses, 'Music is the opium of the pencil. IMP isn't.'"

Elvis and his new signing appeared on that monument to low culture, the Terry Wogan show. As Wogan did his usual impression of a teddy bear with a concealed flickknife, his guest revealed that he was undertaking this interview as Declan MacManus, *not* Elvis Costello.

CHAPTER TEN

the king is dead,
long live the king

H e had formally changed his name by deed poll back to Declan
Patrick MacManus, adding the third name "Aloysius" in honour of
his years as Elvis Costello. Like Prince renaming himself as a squiggle,
such name changes confuse and annoy the public, and if Elton John
wished now to be called Reg Dwight, or Dylan Bob Zimmerman, or
Sting Gordon Sumner, it is simply too late: their stage name is their
brand name. After meeting his early idol Bruce Springsteen backstage
at Slane Castle, Elvis joined T-Bone in late June for an acoustic tour of
Australia and Japan which gave him a further chance to try out songs
from the forthcoming album, as well as retreads of Sixties classics like
'Satisfaction' and 'Substitute'. In early July, roles were reversed, and
Elvis turned up at T-Bone's gigs in Dublin while The Coward Brothers
took their "Second Comeback Tour" to London's Duke of York
Theatre. "These embittered characters made several unscheduled
appearances in my shows with T-Bone," Declan recalled. It was an idea
which The Traveling Wilburys were to follow.

Pete Thomas rejoined John Stewart for a short UK tour, and played
London pub gigs with Big Heat, featuring Bill Hurley from R&B band
The Inmates. 'Watch Me Catch Fire', their debut single, was produced
by Elvis. Nieve played sessions for The Damned and Madness, as well
as on Jagger and Bowie's charity single 'Dancing In The Street'. The
matching video was an outrageous (and tongue in cheek) ego battle,
with the two old troupers outcamping each other on the Martha And

The Vandellas song.

It was one of the highlights of Live Aid, Bob Geldof's extraordinary combination of a giant spectacle with a moral belief in the power of rock to change the world. Geldof was present at the third, and greatest, Isle of Wight Rock Festival in 1970, which left many of those attending with just such a sense of communal friendship. Costello had only just flown back from Russia after a disastrous holiday with his son Matthew.

At two pm on 13 July, Elvis strolled onstage, solo and bearded, to strum 'All You Need Is Love', hardly a mainstay of the punk repertoire. The Beatles' original, with Lennon's laconic declarations of togetherness, had also been broadcast live, seventeen years earlier, for *Our World*, the first global TV link up. Geldof borrowed the idea, with bands playing on two stages, on two continents, to a billion viewers, but he directed proceeds to famine relief. Elvis asked, "How are you? I want you to help me to sing this old Northern English folksong." And they did. Costello left with a wave and a smile, almost showbiz, leaving the stage to the likes of Dire Straits, Bowie and Queen.

July also saw his only new release of the year, a collaboration with T-Bone on 'The People's Limousine', issued as The Coward Brothers, and written after an Italian gig when the Marxist promoter ordered a stretch limo for them after the show. "It's a cultural clash between bluegrass and Italian Communism," Costello explains. "It's like the Louvin Brothers backed by The Pretty Things." The Mekons spent much of their post-punk career pursuing the same twisted vision, interpreted literally, with Dick Taylor of The Pretty Things on lead guitar.

A front page profile in *Melody Maker* did not notably augment the pitiful number of sales, or radio plays, but then the name or face of Costello does not appear either on the bag or the vinyl within. The whole thing is tongue in cheek: T-Bone is Henry Coward, Elvis plays Howard. They are first generation rockers, whose fans have grown old with them. "The problem with our audience is getting the stretcher space for them," Howard admits. "And the wheelchair access is always a problem." Bob Geldof asked them to reform, for Live Aid (which is perhaps a dig at Led Zeppelin, who really did). They claim *not* to be bitter. "Who cares that Paul McCartney has more money than he knows what to do with, and he made it all by stealing our songs?"

Things get weirder by the minute: their father Noel "wrote plays, kinda funny guy". Onstage, they would talk of their estrangement when they married the same woman, and claim that all the rock classics they were singing were self-written.

The single is reminiscent of The Everly Brothers, who are surely the chief butt of the whole exercise. The two take turns on the verses, and harmonise on the chorus. Burnett has always been a critic's favourite rather than a popular choice: his albums are full of verbal wit, but there is something whining about his voice which precludes huge sales. His real importance is as a behind the scenes manipulator, as which he was hugely beneficial to Elvis. They sing like angels on the flipside 'They'll Never Take Her Love From Me', written by Leon Payne, the man responsible for *Psycho*.

The duo jetted off to Los Angeles, to continue recording the new, as yet untitled, album. 'The People's Limousine' proved to be the template of a new way of working. "We recorded it in Hollywood and that became a blueprint for the way we made *King Of America*," Costello says. "I recorded a demo tape while I was there – unfortunately I drank a lot of whisky while I was doing it and it didn't turn out terribly well – but the songs were strong, so regardless of the shabbiness of the performances, we were able to start making a list of musicians we wanted to use." This early session took place at Sunset Sound, where Elvis laid down solo demos of all the songs he intended to use. The album was recorded "in a few sessions spread over a long period, because of other commitments, like Live Aid".

By now, Costello was in the middle of divorce proceedings, and he was accompanied on the trip to LA by Cait O'Riordan. The affair became more public at the year's end, when Costello joined The Pogues for their first European tour, depping on drums at a Swiss gig, which proved that he couldn't keep time to save his life. After that he was confined to the mixing desk, though he sang lead vocals at Malmo, when Shane was "unwell". The set list included 'Old Main Drag', 'Dirty Old Town' – an act of revenge on Ewan MacColl – and Eric Bogle's 'Band Played Waltzing Matilda', while Elvis and Cait duetted on 'A Pair Of Brown Eyes'. I attended a gig at the Dominion, when The Pogues barracked headliner Richard Thompson, and their green-clad army invaded the stage, waving banners and looking threatening. Costello was in one of the plush boxes, and I remember his glasses gleaming in the reflected light of Richard's fervent guitar playing, fuelled by the earlier, Shane-led chant of, "Who the fuck is Richard Thompson?" He was notably sparing in his thanks to them at the end.

On 3 August, Costello agreed at the last minute to play a solo set at a benefit gig, "Nicaragua Must Survive", at the Fridge, Brixton alongside The Pogues, Men They Couldn't Hang, and The Boothill Foot Tappers. Costello also appeared on BBC TV's *Saturday Review*, commemorating Joe Loss's fifty years as a professional musician. He joined his father for a "ragged but right" duet on 'Georgia On My Mind', by Ray Charles (another subtle apology).

Elvis was opening himself up to a more transatlantic style. Of course, his voice had always *sounded* American. He had been co-writing with John Doe, bassist of LA punks X (like Jefferson Airplane on speed). T-Bone had recently produced *How Will The Wolf Survive* by Los Lobos. No wonder that Elvis declared he could name "half a dozen bands in America that I think are really great, which I can't in England". Edsel, through their links with the US Zippo label, were to release many of the best albums of paisley pop and cow punk: guitar bands all, with attitude and musical muscle.

During the Far East tour, Burnett and Costello had planned which musicians to use. It was like Fantasy Football, choosing our dream team. Burnett recalls, "We had pages and pages of production notes. As the record was very much about America, I think he wanted to work with some American musicians on it. The songs leant themselves to those country players." Costello adds, "We did a cast list for every song. It was bit of an eye-opener because I'd never worked that way, calling people up."

As an exercise in transatlantic bonhomie, the album sessions succeeded where *Almost Blue* had failed. T-Bone found it heartening that musicians from such different genres were so compatible in the studio. "It didn't matter what your hairstyle was. If you couldn't bop to it, bombsville," he says.

One line-up was the heart of Presley's TCB band – it is odd that just as he was shedding Elvis's name, the singer was recording the album closest in spirit to the King. Drummer Ron Tutt, bassist Jerry Scheff and the legendary guitarist James Burton, who had first come to fame for his startling guitar breaks on Ricky Nelson B-sides had also worked with everyone from Gram Parsons to The Doors. The sessions were cut as live as possible, with Fifties-style reverb and a touch of echo on the vocals. Drummer Jim Keltner, jazz greats Ray Brown and Earl Palmer, and the Hall And Oates rhythm section, along with Marc Ribot from the Tom Waits band, all added a further American musical accent.

The Attractions seemed and felt redundant in this new order. Americans were far more into providing an accompaniment, not taking the lead. Sessions with The Confederates had gone so well that they cut half the album in three days. For Elvis, "Suddenly we had a bit of a problem. They played the worst they ever had done in the studio and it just blew us apart." In Burnett, Costello had a new buddy, helping him "see the potential of recording in a different way. Suddenly I was like a stranger to these three guys." This, in turn, drove a wedge between Costello and his band (T-Bone as Yoko, perhaps!). "It left my sullen and estranged band hanging around our hotel harbouring a grudge or honing an embittered anecdote." Or even a whole novel.

Pete Thomas puts the contrary view. "He should have just said, 'I'm going to make a solo album but don't worry about it.' The worst thing was that we were all there, day after day, *not* getting the call to go to the studio." After flying half way across the world, Bruce Thomas would have a cup of coffee with a guy "and say, 'Who are you?' and he'd say, 'I'm the bass player.'"

As to the new, more personal style in which Elvis was writing, one foretaste came with Nick Lowe's album *The Rose Of England*, with Elvis's as yet unrecorded 'Indoor Fireworks'. Providing uncredited backing vocals, it was as if Costello was teasing his audience, like a conjurer not yet ready to show off his full range of new tricks. 1986 would reveal all.

It was all a question of identity. In February 1986, Elvis's faithful remake of 'Don't Let Me Be Misunderstood' – a hit for The Animals, twenty-one years before – reached Number Thirty-Three in the UK charts. On the picture bag, Elvis is dressed entirely in black, save his straw hat, and a silver Celtic brooch. The flip side featured the non-album track 'Baby's Got A Brand New Hairdo', recorded with The Attractions, "a throwaway number that we could have played in our sleep. This steadied everybody's nerves, but we were not exactly having fun."

In May, the parent album, *The King Of America* was released, credited to the "Costello Show, featuring The Attractions and Confederates", though his original band appeared on only one track, 'Suit Of Lights'. In their absence, Elvis was exploring new musical directions – Irish traditional, cajun, Tex-mex, Forties swing – and this sense of freshness transferred itself to record buyers, who sent the album to Number Eleven in the UK, and Thirty-Nine in the USA.

The front cover photo is tightly focused on Elvis, in a pasteboard crown studded with rhinestones, and matching jacket. He looks sardonic and knowing on the front, more mischievous on the back, though Bruce Thomas came upon him one day in LA, surrounded by massive blow ups of the regal photo shoot. He thought Elvis had finally flipped, taking it all for real. The photographer is Terry Donovan, a doyen of the Sixties, who later took his own life. Sleeve consultant is Elvis's son Matthew.

Reviewers took their cue from the cover. For Sean O'Hagan, it was both "ridiculous *and* deadly serious", as was the whole, maverick album. He found not the expected "howl of desperation" but songs of "stoical calmness". Parts of the album recalled mid period Dylan, "that grey steely metallic sound", but at last Costello was speaking "with no-one's voice but his own". Conversely, the fully-named Nicholas Benedict Kent in *NME* thought Elvis looked "more like a mite than death warmed up (actually he resembles Dave Stewart on steroids)". He saw glazed eyes, and a rhinestone encrusted crown of thorns, but an artistic renaissance.

Burnett had achieved a cohesive, largely acoustic sound, with lyrics which "paces the listener through a remarkable shedding of skins". The new Elvis was "an older, wiser and more compassionate figure", mining his own family history. It was an album Kent would recommend "even the most poverty-stricken among you to purchase". I was at the time, read the review, and did. Mike Gardner in *Record Mirror* got his free, but still admired the mixture of "dramas, documentaries, current affairs, natural history, music, comedy and sport". *Sounds* was unsure whether "to forgive at once, or mourn for longer", and the pre-teenage *Smash Hits* doubted if it would win him any new fans. Looking back three years later, *Melody Maker* found it "laid the ghost of a confining persona".

'Brilliant Mistake' takes off from the re-election of Reagan, and portrays a civilisation in decline, to a slow beat. The first instrument we hear is string bass – shades of *Astral Weeks* – then Mitchell Froom's keyboards lay down textures as opposed to Nieve's lead lines. Froom has since worked with Crowded House, Richard Thompson, and Suzanne Vega, to whom he is married. Elvis is here "describing my ever-changing impressions of America": he sings with sad sweetness. Like so much of this album, a second look at what seems real reveals a sleight of hand, done with mirrors and with chemicals. The song becomes personal, as Elvis has taken his name and his voice from this shambles: "I was a fine idea at the time/now I'm a brilliant mistake."

'Loveable' has a Fifties sound, and co-written with Cait, who is possibly invoked as "Egyptian eyes/and a wicked look". The woman here, though, is also revealed as an illusion, "so lifelike" and therefore dead, or some kind of doll. David Hidalgo from Los Lobos comes in on harmony vocal, and the song features Elvis's only electric guitar playing on the LP. It is credited to the 'Little Hands Of Concrete', so dubbed by Nick Lowe after trashing yet another set of strings.

'Our Little Angel' is the first track to feature Presley's comeback band, and Costello's has the same intimate and pleading tone, though the original Elvis would never have sung a song as ambiguous as this. Impenetrable as well, in which a cabaret act turns sinister. The love object could well be Costello's muse, once "a chainsaw running through a dictionary", and now his "best mistake".

Costello described his take on 'Don't Let Me Be Misunderstood' as "a slow violent version", picking up the anguish of Eric Burdon's earlier cover, but the remit is wider. It could be seen as an apology for the excesses of the "angry young Elvis", just as Burdon's own song 'Good Times' was a bitter renunciation of drunken nights at the Club A Go Go. Where before Costello would have over-dramatised the song, here he is restrained and dignified, infinitely melancholic.

'Glitter Gulch' is "the tale of a game-show swindle", and starts off at a fair lick, like the tough side of Presley, and again using his band. The patsy here "was known by several different names", and to win a prize involves public humiliation. Costello would "rather be an outlaw" than grovel to the demands of the rock 'n' roll industry.

'Indoor Fireworks' is perhaps Elvis's tenderest song of warm love gone cold. The wonderful mastering image, worthy of a metaphysical poet, is again related to conjuring tricks and children's parties. It is again difficult not to read a personal meaning into the words here, divorce as "a broken effigy of you and me", especially given Costello's quiet, deeply emotional, rendition.

'Little Palaces' is accompanied only by Elvis himself, and Scheff's string bass, though the vocal is one of the most violent on the album. This saga of domestic violence, slum clearance and Catholic emblems is redolent of Costello's own family history. It is the down at heel England which the GI brides later flee, and which Elvis is himself to leave for the grander surroundings of Dublin. One thing about the rock star, globe-jetting lifestyle is that home looks all the shabbier when you come back.

'I'll Wear It Proudly' is a song of self-loathing, with Elvis as the "King of Fools". The tarot imagery and bad sex is heavily reminiscent of TS Eliot's *The Waste Land*, a huge influence on Dylan's similar dystopias, from 'Desolation Row' to 'Simple Twist Of Fate'. Like that poem, the song ends in redemption, a handful not of dust but "eagerness".

'American Without Tears' was "based on a chance meeting with a couple of former GI brides during a tour of Florida". He was drinking at the next table. "I added in a little of my own family history," Elvis explains. "It is as close as the record comes to having a theme." Rod Stewart's *Atlantic Crossing* was a crass take on the same thing, escape to a new land. Costello brings in memories of his grandfather, fleeing persecution. The whole thing has added jollity, thanks both to the accordion and something in Elvis's voice. It is one of his most positive sets of lyrics, even if its setting is (again) a slightly seedy cocktail bar, and he has come there to escape TV, and the modern world.

'Eisenhower Blues' is "an obscure JB Lenoir side", but nothing is for chance in Costello's world. It is a song from the cold war, Fifties America which can now seem a haven of innocence, though the song is about a will to escape. Elvis scats at the end, like a less growly Van Morrison. 'Poisoned Rose' uses the same line-up, of great jazz veterans, and Elvis found, "I just had to get my nervous voice under control." It is a song made for Sinatra, and Costello finds the right kind of torch singer's finessed emotion. Love as an illness.

'The Big Light' is "a fast, grim comedy" about a hangover. There is a quiet pun in the lyric sheet where his "Haggard face" is capitalised; Merle perhaps. Of course, being Elvis, the song has more than one meaning, and the big light he has to face could also be love, or fame, or death. The backing is prime Sun-era Presley, with that wicked combination of acoustic bass and electric guitar, and drums like horseshoes clattering down the road.

Elvis describes 'Jack Of All Parades' as "an unapologetic companion to 'I'll Wear It Proudly'", and though not as "simple" as claimed, the song is about true love entering when least expected. Nieve adds piano to a shuffle beat, led by Wolk's electric bass. Elvis's voice is endlessly echoed on the chorus. The odd reference to the "crimes of Paris" could either refer to a dirty French weekend, or the classical hero of Troy.

'Suit Of Lights' is "a song about work and respect, inspired by watching my father sing of experience and tenderness to an uncomprehending rabble of karaoke-trained dullards. The lessons I might have learned from my own words seem only to have dawned on me after the event." Costello is talking about his own career, and its literal resurrection. He sings from the back of his throat, with due menace, as befits a song in which an Ulster tarring and feathering becomes a work of art. The tensions running high in the studio made this one of Elvis's most passionate ever recordings with The Attractions, as well as perhaps their most restrained.

'Sleep Of The Just' is also set in Northern Ireland, and ends with soldiers raping a local girl. Modern details – the burning bus – meld in with memories passed down from Patrick MacManus. It is a sombre note on which to end an album which contains so many hints of cheerfulness breaking in, despite Elvis's best endeavours.

The CD adds more photos of Elvis in his crown, The Coward Brothers' single, and three outtakes. 'Shoes Without Heels' was "dashed off in solidarity with footsore waitresses everywhere", and falls in love with its subject. A limited edition of the CD adds a bonus disc of The Confederates playing later that year, live on Broadway. How appropriate! Largely covers, Elvis comes on like a more sprightly Van Morrison, even covering the same Mose Allison song. It all sounds like a bar band from heaven.

The album laid to rest some of the rumours surrounding Elvis, as did an appearance on *The Tube* "looking remarkably healthy, alert and upful". He underwent a whole series of media interviews, mostly saying much the same things. Danny Kelly met a man "bleakly regaled in a calf-length frock coat, a matching top hat on the table before him". Cait is a distinctly chilly presence in the corner. Why had he changed his name? "Elvis Costello became a character that I *played* because people wouldn't let him grow up." The name change is a way "to remind people that there was always a human being behind the funny glasses".

He tells Allan Jones the same, in almost identical words. "I saw very quickly the sound and limited vision of the first three albums as a straitjacket, and ever since I've been trying to get out of it." Richard Cook for *Sounds* was most struck by the "strange cluster of accents. Sentences end with the soft, fluted lilt of Ireland. A Liverpudlian rhythm breaks up his words. Most of the delivery is loud, assertive southerner, sometimes nearly a bark. An occasional Atlanticism peeks through."

If *King Of America* was the equivalent of a musical divorce from The Attractions – with many botched reconciliations in the years to follow – then Elvis made a new and permanent commitment when he married Caitlan O'Riordan in Dublin that summer. "Being happier, being with somebody nearly all of the time, the result was more outward looking. The songs could be more free from writing about tatty little affairs in code. Living the life and writing about other things." In May, he reassembled The Attractions to appear alongside The Pogues, U2 and Van Morrison at Dublin's "Self Aid", a concert aimed at reducing unemployment. Their version of 'Many Rivers To Cross' was "stirring stuff, as if they'd never been away".

Costello's "ridiculous canvas trousers" were singled out by *Melody Maker* as one of the lowlights of that year's Glastonbury Festival. He was backstage with The Pogues, "draped all over Cait as if just by letting her out of his sight for a moment, he might lose her forever". His solo appearance at the "Artists Against Apartheid" rally on Clapham Common was perfectly judged, with cover versions of 'Dark End Of The Street' and The Kinks' 'Tired Of Waiting'. "Costello has finally solved the argument between sentience and sentiment," was one verdict. He re-emerged with The Attractions, under canvas,as part of Denmark's Roskilde Festival. Lawrence Donegan reported that he seemed to have turned the clock back to 1977. "Coming across like amphetamine-crazed punks, they *raced* through a set that included most of the first two albums...it was as if the last few years had never happened."

Elvis had told Danny Baker that, "When I'm not working, people should keep their fucking noses out of my life," which did not prevent Mick St Michael from producing his "illustrated biography" that summer. Adrian Thrills found it "worthy but distant", leaving his private life well alone. Costello was involved in early sessions for Julian Temple's film of *Absolute Beginners*, "Though it's so out of control that it's hard to know what's in it. I disagreed with the director over whether I had telepathic powers or not." In August, he played a fifth-rate magician in Alan Bleasdale's film *No Surrender*, a characteristic mixture of tragedy and farce, when two parties of OAPs – one Catholic, one Protestant – arrive at a Liverpool nightclub, and much savagery ensues, especially when a party of the severely disabled join the fun.

As if in emotional sympathy, a new single, 'Tokyo Storm Warning', blew in from nowhere that same month, a hurricane of words and sound, with a cover made of tabloid headlines. *The Daily Mirror* reassembled by Jean Miro. Released on the IMP label, and reaching a lowly Seventy-Three in the UK charts – a disgrace on the part of record buyers of the time – The Attractions were back at their spiteful best, and Elvis sounded feral. "I was always surprised it wasn't a hit. But maybe releasing this and 'I Want You' – six-minute singles, back to back – wasn't the way to do it!"

If this was a foretaste, then the whole horror movie was released in October. *Blood And Chocolate* was exactly what no-one expected, a full-tilt revival of the original band, with Nick Lowe again setting the controls for the heart of the sun, and a ferocious live sound, taking the listener's breath away. Though the album reached Sixteen in the UK charts and Eighty-Four in the US, its reputation since has been that of inducing migraines, rather than aural balm. The Attractions' virtual exclusion from *King Of America* burst out here like a "rancid boil". "I'd agreed to do another record, but it was like, 'Let's do this one and see how far we can go on.'" The band were simply falling apart. "We'd seen too much of one another. Time had gone by so quickly." The new album captured just this sense of a musical unit in dissolution, like a final blazing of the light.

As he told *Record Collector,* "We set up and played as loud as we did on stage. It didn't really sound like *This Year's Model*, but the component parts were just the four of us, and we did very few overdubs. We played as much a combo sound as possible." The same technique was recaptured, almost a decade later, on *Brutal Youth*. "There were quite a few accounts – not scores – being settled on that record." The roughness of technique matched the raw emotions being unleashed, as on Neil Young's similar exercise in overload, *Tonight's The Night*.

Costello himself realised there was a danger in "using Nick Lowe again and going back with a very simplistic musical sound". He was writing songs using a table as accompaniment, beating it with his bare hands to get the rhythm. Some of the songs were "just like chants". Elvis had to get the agreement of the group "that we were going to approach it like this, that we wouldn't start losing our nerve", as with *Goodbye Cruel World*. Some engineers objected when the band wilfully tried to distort the sound, recorded as if for a live rehearsal. Nick Lowe did not think the album was entirely successful. It was a "much more uptight situation," he says. "There wasn't such a gang feeling." Mind you, the bile added to the music, and Lowe encouraged this. "As soon as it gets all cosy, you wind up like Chicago or Genesis, you can't make any decent music if you really like each other."

Costello confessed, "I probably annoyed the group more with that record than with any other. I wouldn't bend from the sound that I had in my head." He firmly instructed Nieve not to play any solos, and to confine his keyboard range to organ and piano, nothing too fancy and no overdubs. "There was just a big drone. That was the whole sound." Bruce Thomas thinks the album lacks heart, with Elvis's attempts at playing a psychopath not to his own taste. "I'll give him the address of a good analyst." Neurotic and attention grabbing, rather than self expressive. The musicians were separated as far apart as possible in the studio, with twenty-five feet between bass and drums.

It was hard for Pete to find the groove, but when it worked, as in 'I

Want You', you can almost hear him leaning over the drums. "The tension of that, of all these people straining, that is a great moment. You can tell that he's really going for it." For Elvis, "with 'Blood And Chocolate', we said, 'This is us truthfully, we're thirty-two, a couple of us have got divorced, we're pissed off and we've taken all the drugs and we've done all that stuff and we're still alive and this is what we sound like. And you know what? We're very much better at it now.' They didn't like it. They hated that record at Columbia."

Even the reviews were mixed. *MM*'s Simon Reynolds found the problem of "routine brilliance; it becomes steadily more difficult to argue that you *need* another Costello record." He has drifted far from the pop mainstream, to a world bounded by the John Peel programme and the rock music press, while his lyrics "increase in opacity", Reynolds comments with opacity.

Stuart Billie in *Record Mirror* finds an "academic exercise...buried in stylised self-absorption". *Sounds'* Richard Cook also finds a "trapped fellow", and an "endless, exhausting record from rock's outlaw bookworm". Costello's voice has become a bully in its own right. Nick Lowe's "dry mix seems to force that grimacing, infamous sneer right into your face". Mark Cooper, in the first issue of *Q*, finds Costello's noisiest album since *Get Happy!!*, and the usual "love stories that quickly turn to murder mysteries. Every time Elvis thinks he's found happiness, he turns up a third party hiding in the pillows." Yet the wordplay is often *too* clever. Costello has replaced emotion with skill, "full of sound and fury and signifying either nothing or too much".

Is this the same album which Adrian Thrills in *NME* describes as "impetuous and often violent" Costello's most bruisingly direct musical statement in years"? The returning Attractions "etch out a hard, abrasive edifice of noise-contortion", with Elvis as guitarist veering into "tangential, atonal pastures". Grunge, five years too early. Looking back, *Melody Maker* finds "a nightmarish description of love and loathing", with The Attractions at their peak, "claustrophobically intense, murderous and unhinged". It also points out that the album was a commercial disaster. As Costello painfully joked, the record company "buried it under a stone somewhere in Utah".

Blood And Chocolate takes a title from an incident back on the first Stiff tour, when Les Brown, the unpopular tour manager, was assaulted in his hotel room by some of the rowdier musicians, various Attractions in their midst. The sleeve painting is of "Napoleon Dynamite" – Costello's latest guise – by Eamonn Singer (say it aloud!). After a King, what next but an Emperor, albeit one who created himself, and ended in solitary exile in Elba. The back sleeve has Keith Morris's photos of the band, lit from the right, and looking like chocolate figures. The quickly withdrawn cassette version was actually packaged as a bar of Cadbury's Bourneville. The info is partly printed in Esperanto, that brave but failed attempt at a universal language, with "franko", "unu" and "du".

As the CD booklet explains, the album was recorded at Olympic, the historic site of sessions by Hendrix and the Stones. The band set up in the studio as they would when rehearsing, using speakers not headphones, and playing almost as loud as they would on stage. "This made for a booming, murky sound that made subtlety impossible," Elvis recalls. It also captured the brutish excitement of a live rock band, for good or ill. Many of the tracks were first takes, with Lowe joining in on acoustic rhythm, and Elvis on Telecaster, "Giving my parts a very harsh edge."

'Uncomplicated' was written quickly at home, in the kitchen, and opens the album with a wallop of drums and brutally struck guitar, mostly on one chord. "I don't know whether to some extent I was writing the band's story," which was hopeful, given the final line about this only being the beginning, though this is also a song of sexual fidelity, even if it is sung as if by a mass murderer. Like Crazy Horse with Neil Young, The Attractions will forever be on hold, waiting for their master to summon them when he has tired of more sophisticated partners.

'I Hope You're Happy Now' starts solo, then The Attractions crash in with a fairground swirl and Dylanesque menace. A song of jealousy, lovingly sung. A second cousin to 'She's Your Lover, Now', a song so vitriolic that Bob stumbles to a halt on the electric take, and with the same stabbing, accusing use of the word "you". A tea party, though, to the next track.

'Tokyo Storm Warning' was "little snapshots put together. It's a protest song too," and a drum riff leads into a groove which could go on forever. Words tumble down, like acid rain, and have that same trick as *Highway 61*, mixing and matching location, a catalogue of events which never quite cohere. "You can feel as if you've been taken to another planet," Costello explains. "Then I added in these other things, some of which are real – like the Heysel Stadium, the 'dead Italian tourists' and continuation of the theme of 'Pills And Soap'. It's mixed up, like a camera swirling round." One of Costello's best, circular guitar breaks gives his voice a brief respite, though you feel he could go on singing this forever.

This "thug's nightmare travelogue" uses the first take, "It borrows a Japanese folk song tune, and then goes somewhere very dark." "Purse" rhymes with "mercy" and Elvis almost shreds his throat at the end.

The slowly intoned "here comes Mr Misery" of the next song acts as a comment on what has gone before, and is thus almost comic, at first anyway. 'Home Is Anywhere You Hang Your Head' began as a "bright pop melody", but Costello recast in an "impossibly low register which made it sound as if I was either seething or gasping for breath". He describes this as "method singing", like the Brando of pop – he could have been a contender – but it is actually sung with lip-smacking relish, almost purring with self contentment towards the end. The backing track is a very Velvets-like drone, with bass rising up like a killer whale surfacing.

'I Want You' begins as a lullabye, and its passionate declaration provided a perfect backdrop to the most intense moment of Alan Bleasdale's 1997 retake on Francis Durbridge's *Melissa*, when the lovers first entwine in a luxury cabin. The song settles into a slow walk to Calvary, with Elvis half laughing, spiteful, desperate, lustful, jealous, murderous, soothing as he wipes down the blood. His voice intensifies as the instruments fall away, leaving him alone with his obsession like Norman Bates completely taken over by his mother in the final, dreadful scenes of *Psycho*. "Everything you hear for the last minute of that record is all from my vocal mic," he says. "That's the only thing in the mix. You can hear the band, but only when they're bleeding through onto my voice."

'Honey Are You Straight Or Are You Blind' is cheerful in comparison, back to Dylan in its drive and sexuality. Under its bright surface this is 'This Year's Girl' revisited, a doll you'd "like to pull to pieces", sex or death. 'Blue Chair' is even happier, sonically, with a double-tracked Elvis addressing a successful rival in love. The "blue chair" could be therapy, or drink, or drugged oblivion, but Costello sings with real warmth in his voice. One of three songs rescued from the *King Of America* sessions, the arrangement owes much to Prince's 'Manic Monday'.

Costello describes 'Battered Old Bird' as "a little bit of my childhood, based on the tenants of the house in which my family had the basement flat until I was five years old". This kitchen sink drama is like a song by Squeeze crossed with an Ian McEwan short story, and the young Elvis narrowly escapes dismemberment. This would explain a great deal. One thinks of Morrissey, and his nightmares of having been a victim of Brady and Hindley. Certainly Elvis sings in a mixture of confidentiality, nostalgia and anguish.

The song seems to go on longer than it should, because it is so personal. As the song contained so many "alarming childhood memories, I found it hard to make any cuts". The old maids, the alcoholic scriptwriter who kept Christmas trees in a cupboard, and presumably the suicide are all real. Elvis is the young swearer, though he actually was taught rude words in Welsh. He is also the marvellous boy, "who is going to do big things", and there is a sound collage after he is cut to pieces, in his own imagination. There is a noticeable jump, where two separate takes were spliced into one, which seems appropriate in the circumstances.

'Crimes Of Paris' expands a line from 'Suffering Face', though it is still unclear whether the setting is the Seine or Troy. Cait comes in on sweet harmony vocals, and there are bits here of The Kinks, Slade (back to those teenage gigs in Birkenhead) and Little Willie John's 'Leave My Kitten Alone', but nothing really adds up.

'Poor Napoleon' was originally covered in feedback. Elvis describes the subject as "a proud and vain character" who finds his love fatally compromised. Cait has a speaking role as "the voice of pity", and Costello sings either as a woman or transvestite: "When I take my stockings off." Like the previous song, it is as if Elvis is finally running out of creative steam, after ten albums of brutal originality. He sounds bored, and Nieve plays a perfect Procol Harum parody over plodding bass. In one of the rare flashes of poetry in his book, David Gouldstone describes this as sounding like "Val Doonican after taking an overdose".

In which case, the tune and sprightliness of 'Next Time Around' will have him back cheerful onto his rocking chair, even if the lyrics are about a love that kills. We're back in the lodging house, with Elvis overhearing his lover with her new boy, and predicting either a new romance or reincarnation. Like The Jam, he is going underground, and sounds none too displeased at the prospect. It could be a metaphor for escaping his public, who have proved so fickle. Elvis is right to comment that the song provides "a pretty good rave up finale for an album that stays mainly in the dark. There is a hint of the Californian sound, and on tour The Bangles improvised a Mamas And Papas vocal arrangement."

The (very) odd tracks which end the augmented CD are part too of this new reason to be cheerful. 'Seven Day Weekend' was co-written with Jimmy Cliff for the obscure movie *Club Paradise*. "I got to play a lot of loud guitar on the session," Elvis says, tremolo a speciality. Pop music, nothing more, nothing less.

The single version of 'Blue Chair' could almost be Cliff Richard, or Haircut 100. It is *not* great art, though it zips along at a fair old rate. 'Baby's Got A Brand New Hairdo' is so moronic that I had to check Elvis had written it. Fifties soda pop, which would fit well into *Back To The Future*, though a more careful listen reveals a spitefulness at the heart of the lyrics, like a Frank Zappa doo-wop parody. 'American Without Tears #2 (Twilight Version)' is a right mouthful, and a sequel to the original song. "The story is told from the perspective of the vanished husband. He tries to pluck up courage to return from his South American exile, but becomes cynical and loses his nerve." Same tune, with added marimbas, and a gangster who sings like Sammy Davis Jnr.

'A Town Called Big Nothing' was written in Spain during the shooting of Alex Cox's cult movie (without a cult), *Straight To Hell*. "This pastiche of a parody starred The Pogues, as a family of teetotal, non-smoking, coffee-addicted desperados," Elvis explains. "The film also featured Joe Strummer, Kathy Burke, Courtney Love and, rather briefly, Grace Jones and Dennis Hopper. I only went to visit Cait, and found myself playing the family butler, 'Hives', and toting a pump-action shotgun." Over a sub-Leone guitar-scape and mariachi trumpets (played by his dad), the narrative is spoken, eventually, by Sy Richardson, though, "The story that he tells has nothing to do with the movie, in fact it probably has more plot. I would not say that I wrote this with an entirely straight face." It is closer to The Comic Strip's own parody of the genre, *A Handful Of Travellers' Cheques*.

After *Blood And Chocolate*, Costello walked away from his Columbia contract, "owing them a million dollars. My relationship with The Attractions was that we were about to take an eight-year holiday from each other's company." Not before a quite extraordinary world tour…

That autumn's world tour, Costello Sings Again, was a bold if financially suicidal affair, in which he played brief residencies in upmarket theatres, presenting a different show every evening.

Elvis had abandoned his bizarre idea of playing the *King Of America* song on five successive nights, with five different bands – among them Los Lobos, ZZ Top and The Heartbreakers – in five different venues, for cable TV. This was the nearest he ever came to realising that mad dream. Song titles were printed onto a game show wheel, the "Spectacular Spinning Songbook", twelve-feet high, listing thirty-eight different titles. Members of the audience were invited onstage by "Xavier Valentine" – "your guide from your space in the stalls to your space in the stars", and in reality Elvis's bodyguard Paddy in a tuxedo – to give it a spin. The televising of the National Lottery would render this pallid and tasteful, in comparison. Even Elvis could never have dreamt up Mystic Meg.

As well as songs by Elvis, there were a few unexpected delights: 'Ferry 'Cross The Mersey', Tom Petty's 'American Girl', and Prince's 'Pop Life'. Contestants were quizzed by Elvis in the guise of Napoleon Dynamite, who entered up the centre aisle, and was thus able to "leer at the women and insult the men". Guest MCs included members of the Chicago Bears, Penn and Teller, and Tom Waits. Contestants were offered a choice of soft drinks, or a turn in the Go-Go cage, which was really no choice at all. "Our experience suggests that the world is full of frustrated Go-Go dancers."

The tour opened in Beverly Hills on 1 October, circled the USA, then visited France, Italy, Holland and Sweden before hitting the Royalty Theatre, London in late November. From there, on to Dublin,

Edinburgh and Liverpool. Shows would feature The Attractions, The Costello Show, The Confederates – James Burton, Jerry Scheff, Jim Keltner and Mitchell Froom – and The Coward Brothers, as well as Elvis solo, with a host of guest stars. In America, these included Tom Waits, The Bangles, Tom Petty, a coupling of Jules Shear and Aimee Mann (then still an "item"), and Buster Poindexter aka David Johansen of The New York Dolls, and now reborn as a night club comic.

David Fricke reported the Broadway Theatre, New York City show for *Melody Maker*. The first night he was "vintage aggro" with a reborn Attractions, recapturing the spitefulness of their early tours, as he kicked the PA stacks in apparent frustration. Night two saw Elvis solo, opening with an acoustic 'Tokyo Storm Warning', then The Coward Brothers concluding with 'Twist And Shout' and The Confederates, featuring James Burton's "diamond sharp lead guitar". Night three was a "ballad night", again with The Confederates, night four was a "three-hour blowout", featuring the big wheel. Steve and Pete wore brocade, Bruce a crushed velvet, bell-bottomed tuxedo. The resulting evening was "relentlessly funny", not a word usually associated with Elvis. The fifth evening was a special *Blood And Chocolate* affair, opening with a "volcanic blast" of the new single. The night, and residency, ended with 'Poor Napoleon', "a suicide mission of feedback, falling cinderblock rhythm, which ended with a police siren chorus of screaming amps as the band walked off". Somewhere during the melee, Costello begins shouting lines from John Lennon's 'Instant Karma'. This blast of apocalypse was worked up throughout the tour, with blinding strobe lights and Cait on spoken refrain. One critic compared it to a cross between The Velvet Underground and an EST therapy course, the late Sixties at full sensory overload.

Costello dedicated Dylan's 'I Threw It All Away' to Columbia Records: "Some friends of mine in a big black building uptown." During the US gigs, Cait played occasional bass, and was often to be found in the Go-Go cage as one "Kitten McCracken". Cover versions ranged from The Hollies' 'King Midas In Reverse' to 'Hit The Road Jack'. One-hundred-and-twenty-five different songs were performed in twenty-two shows. As a spokesman commented, "Catch it while you can. The tour is unlikely to be repeated, hard to surpass and impossible to duplicate." The critics' poll in *Rolling Stone* later voted it as the best rock tour of the year.

The European tour added odd delights. In Stockholm, Jackson Browne guested on 'Stay', 'Napoleon' entered playing an accordion, and after the show he jammed with The Fabulous Thunderbirds in a local nightclub. Elvis played a solo set in Paris at the Folies Bergere, and ran through a Gerry And The Pacemakers medley in Utrecht. In Milan, he indulged in a spot of tap dancing. Dublin saw him read his short story 'How Joe Soap Got Into Everything', and BP Fallon as guest host. Andrew Schofield from *Scully* was compere in Liverpool, and joined in on a spirited version of 'Twenty Flight Rock'.

Most memorable of all, though, was the-six night residency at London's Royalty Theatre, divided into *Blood And Chocolate*, solo and Spinning Songbook, and then the same again. The Confederates had not crossed the Atlantic. On one of the solo nights, Elvis returned the ticket money of one heckler, who was demanding to see The Attractions. Chris Difford and Nick Lowe joined in on the fun, and the other solo night opened with Costello's short story 'Getting Into Showbiz'.

David Quantick welcomed the "loosening of the reins", Jack Barron forms the opinion that, "Elvis is a very happy man," while for Allan Jones, "Costello filled these evenings with surprise." Here is a man who has come to terms with the "perverse impulses that threatened to engulf him". Personal highlights included Cait and Elvis duetting on 'Wild Mountain Thyme', 'The Deportees' as a heart-stopping ballad, and Nick Lowe frugging in the Go-Go cage.

In *Melody Maker*, Don Watson looked back over a year in which Costello had returned to what he had always done best, "being brilliantly miserable". His greatest skill now was at "balancing sentiment with bitterness", and over the past twelve months he had given us "two collections of bruised and beautiful songs, black of humour, blue of mood. Here's to Mr Misery." It would be three years before his next album.

In early 1987, Costello repeated his six-night extravaganza, this time at the Royal Albert Hall. The first three nights were with The Attractions and the Spinning Songbook retrospective. Reviewer David Stubbs seemed to be writing out of the Ian Penman lexicon: Costello is a "choked funnel of love", but what he most objected to was the singer's glasses, "outsize, as gogglingly obtrusive as The Residents' eyeballs, they signify his unendingly benign surveillance of us all". Stubbs presents Elvis as desperately eager to please, a "self-effacing buffoon" whose voice was "like wind blowing brokenly over a bottle, empty for want of the milk of human kindness". Bullshit, I say. *NME*'s Len Brown makes much the same initial point, that Elvis, his band and his audience are all "goons", but goes deeper: here is a man who exposes "all his weaknesses (and ours)". He could have done without The Attractions, though.

The second trio of nights was with The Confederates, making their first British appearance as Elvis's band, and the start of a short tour. Van Morrison duets on 'Jackie Wilson Said', then sings 'Help Me' with Elvis on harmonica. BP Fallon heard "some of the finest music it has been my pleasure to come across. *Ever*." Jim Keltner sits behind an unassuming drum kit and "flicks out the beat seemingly effortlessly". Tom Waits lookalike, T-Bone Wolk wears his porkpie hat backwards, while James Burton still wears the gold pendant that reads "Takin' Care of Business" given to him by Presley. The Attractions are in the audience, with no hard feelings. Later Nieve tells Jerry Scheff that Costello is the best, and Jerry simply nods in agreement.

'Blue Chair', together with two more outtakes from *King Of America*, was released as a single to tie in with The Confederates' visit. Elvis looks quizzical, brow deeply furrowed. Reviewing the Albert Hall gig, Terry Staunton found Burton in charge, the "silent authoritarian who keeps El in line". Buddy Holly's 'True Love Ways' is dedicated to Cait, while a relaxed Elvis even reads out latest scores from the FA Cup replays. Richard Cook, at the same gig, mourns the loss of the "chaotic energy" of The Attractions: "There was none of the scruffy abandon of the earlier shows." The Confederates performed their chores dutifully, but they remained backing musicians, not a band. David Stubbs is back, and finds Benny Hill's hairdresser on bass and Michael Gambon on lead guitar. Maybe he needs to borrow Elvis's oversized glasses. He also objects to Costello's saliva outtake. "If he showers any more phlegm on me, I'm going to catch pneumonia. He's worse than Roy Hattersley!"

A fine tape of the Manchester Apollo gig confirms both views. The Confederates are superbly professional, with not a note out of place, but the whole concert is oddly quiet, without the edge or danger The Attractions bring. There are fine solo versions of a singalong 'Radio Sweetheart', a tender 'Alison', and an urgent 'Tokyo Storm Warning' – he breaks off halfway, twice, with an anecdote about fish and chips, and an explanation of what a Japanese God Jesus robot is, reading out the instructions on the packet. He previewed one new song, 'Any King's Shilling', "about my grandfather". A chatty Elvis quips that, "This is the Mike Harding part of the show," and that Manchester has a psycho as a chief constable. The first encore is a solo 'I Want You', which blows the audience away. They finally rise to their feet on the fourth encore, 'Pay Day'. "We should have turned this into a dance hall earlier," chortles Costello.

A less enamoured reviewer at Newcastle describes The Confederates as a motley crew, with Scheff looking like Barry Cryer's long lost brother, and Burton "reminding me of my dad in his archetypal Christmas jumper". Young punks these were *not*, but that surely was the point of hiring them in the first place.

Always one to ring the musical changes, Elvis was billed as Declan MacManus as part of a Festival of Irish Culture, but this did not prevent a sell-out audience of 700 cracking the code and turning up at Brentford. He set off in April for an acoustic Almost Alone tour of America and the Far East, with only Nick Lowe for company, and playing mainly college gymnasiums. Tickets were at a premium. Highlights of his set included a Grateful Dead medley – 'Ship Of Fools' and 'It Must Have Been The Roses', preceded by a poem, 'The Day They Busted The Grateful Dead' – a beatbox-accompanied 'Uncomplicated' and the mini 36 title version of The Wheel. In LA, his voice was shot away, but he made a 5,000 seat arena "remarkably intimate" and battled through an eighty-minute set, focusing on his more obscure songs. At Duke University, he used a small TV set as a prop: "His voice was an instrument itself, going from a whisper to a scream." At Harvard, Elvis was presented with a mounted red shoe, and a student award for "Excellence in Contemporary Music", though he had to shout "shut the fuck up" at a noisy audience. At an after-show party, Elvis and Bono combined forces and attempted to write a country song together.

Forget psychedelic light shows, or Pink Floyd building a huge polystyrene wall, and then demolishing it, all in real time. Costello's latest on-stage distraction was to give his audience a slide show, with spoken commentary. This perhaps ties in with "EC Was Here", a printed history of his ten years in showbiz, full of anecdotes of Bill Monroe saying, "The good times, they're gone," of a decrepit Count Basie being patronised by a TV crew, and of his pride in working with the likes of Van Morrison or Johnny Cash.

There are memories of seedy gigs, of Ayr where the floor collapsed, of Merthyr Tydfyll where a gang of skinheads treated him to free lager, of Fishguard where plank-like beds were nailed to the floor. Was this a suitable career? Had he not been turned down because of his bad handwriting: "I might have got the first job I ever went for, and still be in that Dickensian office in Liverpool, going rapidly blind while correcting admiralty charts." By the same token, John Major might have become a bus conductor rather than prime minister. Costello sees the modern pop world as "like a cash-card advert. The guy who looks like he belongs in the Hitler Youth pops the card in the slot and suddenly all these cute cartoon squiggles come dancing out of the crowd and turn everybody pink, peach and purple, and Mel And Kim materialise through a brick wall and sing something about shopping and fucking." That last phrase was later "borrowed" as the title of a West End play.

In June, Elvis flew in from his new home in Dublin to headline the Glastonbury Festival, reunited with David Hidalgo of Los Lobos, and The Attractions. One between songs anecdote had George Michael, on the Jonathan Ross show, metamorphose into the slimy Cecil Parkinson, newly implicated in the Sara Keays affair. Both demand their right to party, and Elvis links Parkinson's return to the cabinet with Michael's song 'I Want Your Sex'. He also premiered 'Tramp The Dirt Down'. For David Stubbs, Elvis's acoustic guitar was "the largest in Britain": he played 'Suit Of Lights' "with dramatised, grandiloquent sweeps".

It was a performance of such epic proportions that, "It seemed at one point he was not going to leave the stage until he'd played every popular song ever written." They predated the craze for lounge music with a cover of Percy Faith's 'Theme From A Summer Place', and ended – exhausted -with the Plastic Ono Band's 'Instant Karma'. Elvis also joined Los Lobos for two encores, 'Slow Down' and 'I Got Loaded'. The Festival was now a more organised affair than the shambolic proceedings celebrated in *Glastonbury Fayre*, although isolated local protests forced the cancellation of the following year's event.

All was not well in The Attractions camp, either. Elvis's decision to take a year off had brought simmering resentments to the surface. "It was like realising that we weren't as close friends as you might have assumed," he explains. "We were never particularly friendly." To the others, the combo was a group, like The Rolling Stones, but to Elvis it was "me *with* a really great group, all better musicians than me technically speaking. It had to be my decision how it went, because it was me who was the mug out the front, that they threw stuff at. It's my name on the front of the marquee, I get blamed for everything."

Bruce Thomas saw things a little differently. He told Radio One, "Elvis went a bit peculiar, when he didn't know if he wanted to sack us or not, but after about twelve albums and forty odd tours, I thought this was a naff way to go on. He took us all out to Christmas lunch and I thought we were going to get a gold watch, and he said, 'If you thought it was you guys you were wrong. It was always down to me, it was always down to the songs. Thanks but no thanks and do as you're told.' Steve took it very, very badly, he was very affected by it. I sided with him, I thought Elvis was very much out of order."

Pete is more philosophical. "It was a fairly straightforward business decision, he needed to find a lot of money for other things suddenly, and was sick to death of touring with the same people all the time. We had been at it pretty hard. Below that, there was an enormous depth of love." It had been the best years of all their lives, whooping through their twenties, "So how could it not be like a marriage." Elvis told them that he was taking a year off, and could no longer afford to pay their salaries, but, "We couldn't see it clearly, I was still drinking, so you just get irrational about it. And it did hurt, it really hurt, but it seemed the best thing to do, for him."

That summer, another new pseudonym, The MacManus Gang, released the 'A Town Called Big Nothing' single, its sleeve a featureless photo of the Spanish badlands, to tie in with the movie release of *Straight To Hell*. This was described by its creator, Alex Cox, as "low down entertainment made for people who want to watch a bunch of unpleasant bastards behave unpleasantly until they finally get their come-uppance". For Elvis, "It was just another Pogues project" – a punk version of a *Carry On* movie which was quickly put together when a tour to war-torn Nicaragua had fallen through. His main memory was a lot of late night tequila drinking. In his own role as Hives the butler, with slicked-down hair like the elder Steptoe, he was "very tatty but well spoken", though he had been careful not to catch the "disease called 'Actor'. There's more bluffers and idiots in film than there are even in music. Than there are even in music journalism."

As one movie project (briefly) hit the multiplexes, Costello was writing the score for another, more serious, project, *The Courier*, a thriller filmed on location in Dublin and starring Cait. Elvis also appeared on Irish TV's *The Session* playing folk music with luminaries like Donal Lunny and Matt Malloy.

Elvis once described *Rolling Stone* as a magazine which he had watched go from "organ of the 'alternative society' to the *Playboy* of the cocaine generation, fostering the unhealthy notion of a rock 'n' roll pantheon by taking out the 'roll' and leaving the hard, cold immobile 'rock'." In August the same magazine had its twentieth anniversary, and listed its choice of the best 100 albums of the last twenty years. *This Year's Model* came in at Number Eleven, *My Aim Is True* at Twenty-Nine, and *Get Happy!!* at Sixty-Five.

Autumn saw Costello take part in *Roy Orbison And Friends*, an affectionate TV special filmed in black and white at Los Angeles' Coconut Grove, with famous guests Jackson Browne, kd lang, Linda Ronstadt and Bruce Springsteen. The musical director was T-Bone Burnett, and James Burton played lead guitar – with the likes of Billy Idol in the audience – though everyone left the spotlight to Orbison, fifty-one years old, and no longer in the best of health. He was to die of a heart attack the following year, but the grace and dignity of the televised proceedings still endures, as does his version of Elvis's ballad 'The Comedians'. It needed a second take on the night. "Even legends mess up," quipped T-Bone. Elvis doubled on harmonica during 'Candy Man', played keyboards on 'Mean Woman Blues' and guitar on 'In Dreams', newly famous due to its use in David Lynch's wonderfully twisted movie *Blue Velvet*. Elvis also joined in on harmony vocals for 'Oh Pretty Woman'. "You could imagine Springsteen and Costello, seated near each other and playing guitars, in a schoolroom, trying to please their favourite teacher as they nervously followed the notes."

There was a sense of history being made in the air that night. Less so, but still fun, was an evening in a tiny club in Mill Valley, that October. Elvis was in the audience for a gig featuring the musical talents of film star Harry Dean Stanton – about whom The Albion Band's Ashley Hutchings later wrote a song – when Maria Muldaur called him up on stage, and he banged hell out of a piano for Sam The Sham's nonsensical 1965 hit, 'Woolly Bully', ditto the Sir Douglas Quintet's 'She's About A Mover'. Punk music, first time around. Elvis then transformed 'Big Boss Man' into a ballad, growing "quieter and quieter on every stanza", until he sang in a whisper, "The prettiest treatment that old song has ever gotten."

In early November, he rejoined The Confederates for gigs in their own territory, the Deep South, for the South Of The Mason-Dixon Line Tour, which then crossed the Pacific for dates in Japan and Australia. Nick Lowe was solo support. Austin DeLone replaced Tench on keyboards, and Lowe joined on backing vocals, while Elvis opened each gig with 'Red Shoes', proudly showing off his new patent leather boots. There were new songs, including 'God's Comic', inspired by a recent, unspecified experience on Sunset Strip. The Confederates attempted 'Tokyo Storm Warning' twice on the tour, both failures. In Nashville, Denis from Dr Hook sang 'Lovable', and John Hiatt duetted on Jim Reeves' 'He'll Have To Go'.

Before the Tulsa gig, Elvis visited his namesake's home Graceland, and that night The Confederates played 'Let Him Dangle'. He followed this song about "killing people who kill people" with 'Mystery Dance', "about making people". Elvis strapped on his "trademark silver Fender Jazzmaster" for a distorted version of 'Uncomplicated'. At Austin, he added a new verse to 'Brilliant Mistake', which is presumably autobiographical. "He thought he was the king of every compromise/but it was just another very brilliant disguise", while in New Orleans, after sampling some native gumbo food, he ended proceedings on piano with yet another new song, 'That Day Is Done'.

'Last Boat Leaving', 'Pads, Paws And Claws' and 'Veronica' were held back for Japan, where Kyoto and Osaka heard them – and The Confederates – for the first time. In Australia, the scene of riots during an early tour, he banned bouncers from one concert, and encouraged the audience to dance. 'Pump It Up' now incorporated Prince's 'Sign O' The Times' and The Beatles' 'Revolution'. The concerts were well received, though one reviewer found at the Sydney gig that, "Costello tended to wander aimlessly from song to song, indifferent to mood, style or theme." Bring back the wheel!

November saw the release of *Out Of Our Idiot*, a second collection of outtakes, rare tracks and demos, credited to "Various Artists". Seven separate identities are emblazoned on the front cover, and the titles on the back, backed by pink and green stars which often fail to encompass them. The whole thing looks particularly cheap and cheerful – no photos inside or out – and a parody of a TV greatest hits album, just like his own *Elvis Costello – The Man*. The album was widely welcomed. John Wilde found the titles "irrational petulance" refreshing, though some its contents were instantly disposable, with "turn-ups on their Y-Fronts". Elvis had used "disguises, alter-egos and smokescreens" to put out second-rate material without harming his own name. As for the criminally neglected single 'From Head To Toe', though, it was like Jane Austen meeting Tamla Motown.

In *Sounds*, Mat Snow found that the album exemplified Costello's central dilemma. He dearly wants to write songs as moving as those that inspired him, but "can only express himself in the language of past pop itself". This gives his songs an "ironic playfulness" which preclude innocent enjoyment. Thus 'I Want You' can only strip away artifice, and unleash a torrent of jealousy, by paying homage to The Plastic Ono Band. As to the tracks actually under review, they showed Elvis has "the best ears in the country". *NME*'s Jonathan Romney finds, conversely, that "Elvis has a Midas-like way of making everything he touches unmistakably his own". A variable feast, but what was really wanted was a whole album of his cover versions. Meanwhile, "Our idiot, who art in Brentford, blessed be he."

To explain this arcane footnote, the album was issued by the Brentford based Demon, which had taken over the archive role of F-Beat, and of which Elvis was himself a director. *Blood And Chocolate* had destroyed the momentum of Elvis's career: since that album, "conforming to anyone else's expectations is low on the man's sense of priorities". In late 1987, he switched record labels, from minor to major, and signed a world-wide deal with American giant Warner Brothers. The days of being released by a small record label largely controlled by his manager were finally over, though Jake was to remain in the latter role for many years yet. Costello demanded a clause to be written into his new contract, forbidding the release of any of his material in South Africa, as long as apartheid remained.

Being part of the Warner Brothers empire for the next ten years meant confining himself to an international release schedule, roughly one new album every two years. Elvis confirmed this to *Record Collector*: "Their machinery isn't geared up for it to be your turn more often than that, though I've been working on other things. My output is higher. The main thing that altered my schedule after 1986 wasn't so much the record contract as the absence of a regular band. It meant that I toured less, because I either toured solo or had to put a band together – and to justify that expense, it had to be in support of a record."

Indeed, Costello was to adopt a low public profile for the next year or two, until the release of *Spike* in 1989. One press report had him turning down £30,000 for a one-off Christmas gig. As he later told an interviewer, "I went to Greenland." In his head, if not bodily.

Two of The Attractions became the house band on Jonathan Ross's aptly named *The Last Resort*, while the third, Bruce Thomas, planned literary revenge. Meanwhile, Paul McCartney contacted Costello, asking him if he would collaborate on some songs, taking over a half share in the sour and sweet chemistry between McCartney and John Lennon. For an ex-member of The Beatles' fan club, this was heaven indeed, especially for someone lucky enough to have met his heroes in various TV studios, while still barely more than a child. The first fruit of this collaboration – which has since enriched both men's careers while remaining a little peripheral in both cases – was 'Back On My Feet', the B-side of McCartney's 'Once Upon A Long Time Ago' hit single. Contacts continue up until the present day.

Both parties talked to Radio One. McCartney found that, "After all those years with John, it's lovely to have a collaborator. Just sitting down with a friend makes it twice as easy. Elvis is a John fan – I can tell in his whole stance, his whole attitude, his whole singing thing. That was very attractive for me." They sat on either side of a table, with notebooks and guitars.

Both came with half finished material. Paul thought, "What he was showing me was tending to ramble, a deep poem that's lovely at the fiftieth telling. Slam them a little hook." Elvis reckoned, "Paul made me very hard on the storytelling, he's hard on himself technically. He doesn't like false rhymes, or an uneven structure. Particularly on *Get Happy!!* I would change the structure on every verse." In turn, if Paul was "going up a bind alley, or using a word I didn't like", then Elvis pulled him up short. Paul sometimes felt shouted down. Elvis concurred. "Sometimes I annoyed him by being more outspoken than I need to be. He has a very high voice and if I sing in the same register my voice gets obnoxiously loud." Paul added, "He spits all over the place, you can't ignore him"

1988 saw only a handful of gigs, and Costello's sole new release the *Courier* soundtrack, with original songs by the likes of the Hothouse Flowers, Asia and U2, and incidental music by Declan MacManus. These ranged from "the Moroderesque chase sequence of 'Rat Poison' to the tranquillity of 'Painted Villain'". In February, Elvis took part in a charity gig at the Royal Albert Hall, for Bill Wyman's Wishing Well Appeal. He duetted with Chrissie Hynde on The Beatles' 'There's A Place', The Kinks' 'Days' and Burt Bacharach's 'Windows Of The World'.

He guested at the Shetland Folk Festival that spring. On the ferry over, he had run into an unofficial picket, enquired the reason, and agreed to play a benefit concert if he was allowed through. He was true to his word, and alongside other roots musicians, including The Albion Band, played a short solo set at Aberdeen Music Hall. "You read in the Tory press that they are madmen, but they are not," he said. "The Government are the swine, not these men." He also turned up at a Christy Moore concert in Dublin, and joined in two encores.

In a kind of twisted tribute, a band called Elvis Hitler, in reality Jim Leedy, was now making a name for itself. It was a more palatable tribute to the two original Elvises than Elton Motello, an Englishman responsible for the dreadful 1978 single 'Jet Boy, Jet Girl'.

That summer, Costello spent a month recording *Spike* in Dublin and New Orleans, and laid down final masters in Los Angeles. While in New Orleans, Costello immersed himself in the local ambience by recording with locals, The Dirty Dozen Brass Band. He also collaborated with Ruben Blades on his first English language album *Nothing But The Truth*, co-arranged a track for Was Not Was, and co-wrote the song 'Everything's Different Now' for Til Tuesday, featuring Aimee Mann on lead vocals.

Just in time for the Christmas market, Costello's back catalogue appeared on fourteen shiny new CDs, issued by IMP and Demon. In *Q*, Paul Du Noyer found their pristine soundscapes held a "seething cauldron of molten emotions". As to the new album, "Costello has the satisfaction of knowing that nobody else knows what the hell to expect."

Blue Velvet had helped revitalise Orbison's career – his quavering falsetto fitted perfectly into its sexual ambivalence. Like Costello, Lynch has been obsessed with revealing the violent and sexually predatory underlay of Sixties innocence. Orbison would have been a perfect visual image, corpse white skin and huge black glasses, gawky and menacing. And then he died. *Mystery Girl* was his vinyl obituary, released a month after he suffered a heart attack while visiting his mother, with songs by the likes of U2 and Jeff Lynne. Richard Cook of *Sounds* found it "a gentle record, a pleasing reminder that turned out to be a goodbye". His version of Costello's 'The Comedians' was a "cryptic obscurity which sounds like a Marty Robbins gunfighter ballad". The TV tribute, also screened in January 1989, took on the quality of a wake, its monochrome making it look as if it was filmed twenty years before. A freak accident had almost destroyed the original Cinemax print before anyone had a a chance to view it, which would have been a final irony. Orbison's life was dogged by spectacular ill luck.

Asked about Costello, Roy had revealed, "He's a terrifically hard worker. Just all business. We had some fun too, but he's very serious about it. He spoke to Bruce Springsteen, and they discussed me and how and what I would sing, and then he rewrote it for me. The song's about a guy who's running the ferris wheel, stops it at the top, and runs off with the girl."

Paul McCartney co-wrote 'Veronica', Elvis's first single release on Warner Brothers, its picture bag fronted by a Keith Morris photo of a gangster-like Elvis, in huge black shoes and with his fists clenched. This belies the song itself, a tender account of his grandmother, confined to a home with Alzheimer's. The video is much more appropriate to the song, and helped turn it into a Top Twenty single in the USA. "You want to believe that when people are 'senile', that there's some spirit or intelligence that they're unable to communicate," he said. The video was at first totally rejected by MTV because it had old people in it. "It had the old lady, and it had me. Then VH1, which is the older persons' MTV, that was the audience that the video appeared to hit. I was on aeroplanes and the steward would come up and be very emotional about the song: it paralleled something in their life. Then the record became a success, and MTV had to bow to it." Elvis was "a pop singer again".

Spike was released in early February, and produced by a consortium of Costello, T-Bone Burnett and Kevin Killen: it featured a range of guest stars, including McCartney, Roger McGuinn of The Byrds and Irish singer *par excellence* Christy Moore. It also rose to Number Five in the UK album charts, reflecting how badly Elvis had been missed by the great British public.

Columbia had pestered him to remake *Armed Forces*. "I said, 'Listen, I don't want to fuck around like this anymore. You tell me what record you want and I'll make it for you. You name the producer – I'll go with him. I'll fight with anybody. I'll pit my musical personality, voice and strength of will against his, if that's what it takes.'" Not surprisingly, Columbia backed down. "They said I could make any record I wanted. I said, 'I've got two or three different ideas. I want to make a sort of orchestrated record like Burt Bacharach used to make, using tuned percussion, and I'd like to do some stuff in New Orleans. I've got five other blueprints for records I can make.' As it turned out, I ended up on Warners with *Spike*, and combined all those ideas onto the same record."

Even so, "There were a couple of moments that hinted at the old sound: the bad guitar player's friend, the tremolo guitar, features through my career." He was attempting the uncluttered sound of The Attractions, with different musicians. "It was very rare for more than three instruments to be played simultaneously during the sessions. As a result the arrangements are very painterly, with little bits added here and there, and then you rub that bit out and add another bit – it was a very creative use of the studio. It frightened the hell out of people who were used to safer, combo-sounding arrangements."

Parts of the record now sound odd, even to its creator. "Sometimes when I put it on, I go, 'What on earth is going on there?', because I've played some of the songs in more concise, more organic band arrangements since I made the album. 'Deep Dark Truthful Mirror' has become a tough R&B song: when you hear the skeletal version on the record with two sets of piano and a tambourine for most of it, and then The Dirty Dozen Brass Band coming in, it's a very peculiar construction." The album has a wide emotional palate, from the playful 'Pads, Paws And Claws' to the vengeful 'Tramp The Dirt Down', "rawer" when he played it live, as on the memorable *Late Show* broadcast. Peter Doggett finds this song cheap, with Mrs Thatcher too obvious a target. Costello will not give an inch. "But she doesn't have a soul. She will burn in hell."

The reviews showed how much Costello had been missed. For *Q*'s Mark Cooper, he had found a voice "simple enough to wed his complex vision to the directness of delivery of his first records". The "tigerish irritant" had become a "good old boy, universally admired, but with his teeth blunted by approval". Now he was biting back.

For the adjectival Terry Staunton, the album exposed the world as "cruel, vindictive and heartless. *Spike* is an exciting, inspiring, bewildering and bloody frightening record." T-Bone Burnett saw Elvis as "entering into a new phase, getting harmonically much more complex. It was a very dark record. Almost every song was minor." In key, not scope. Elvis himself disclosed that some of the songs were written during his cruise to Greenland. "I don't think I'd ever do it again. It was a nightmare, the onboard bit, like a floating holiday camp." The time at sea took him out of "what we laughingly call civilisation, and opens your imagination to different kinds of stimulus".

The album sleeve is spectacularly disturbing. Elvis is a trophy on a wall, his head painted black and white, grinning disturbingly, and mounted on a heart-shaped board, set with blue velvet. The wallpaper behind is tartan. The "I" of the album title is indeed a spike, poised to strike through the hero's head, just like the scissors do in John Cale's sick story 'The Gift', on The Velvet Underground's second album. Underneath is the motto "The Beloved Entertainer", engraved on a gold plate.

Overleaf is a strange collage of a trumpet, a hideous porcelain ornament combining comedy and tragedy, and a bowl of wilting flowers. The missing words to the instrumental 'Stalin Malone' – told by a man who is, in turn, gangster, IRA bomber and jilted lover – are restored, credited like all the songs here to DPA MacManus. The album deals with a succession of forbidden subjects, the kind of stuff which editors usually "spike" ie refuse to print. Just as punk hairstyles were vaselined into spikes to simulate aggression, so Costello's songs are sharp and pointed. Right up the arse, in fact.

In an interview with the ECIS, Costello free associated about his new stage show, and a replacement for the wheel. "I'm having built a six-foot tall satin heart, labelled with the thirteen deadly sins I know of and six I haven't found. We're going to get people up on the stage and give them this spike, and blindfold them, and they stick the stake in the heart and whatever sin they hit they can either commit that sin on the stage, or they can elect a song. It's a moral challenge to the audience." He told another interviewer that the album title was inspired by Spike Jones, the gum-chewing madman who led The City Slickers, a big band on LSD before LSD was even invented. "Or it could be after the bulldog in *Tom And Jerry*. Or it could be a statement – spike the beloved entertainer. It's funny how everybody assumes spike is a noun."

'This Town' is deceptively bouncy and harmonic, with a three-pronged Rickenbacker attack: McCartney on bass, Roger McGuinn on twelve-string and Costello himself playing rhythm. Cait comes in on "lunge maracas". The song was inspired by John Pilger's TV exposure of the Australian Bicentennial, with Labour prime minister Bob Hawke seen hob-nobbing with corporate power brokers. Elvis provides three vignettes from the new capitalism, with the brilliant insight that "the corporation thief is the new Jesse James". It would have been a good theme song for the movie *Wall Street*. Most of us have since worked for creeps attracted by the false glamour of Gordon Gecko, even Elvis. It led to his eventually leaving WB.

Another kind of crime is the subject of 'Let Him Dangle', a Dylanesque tale of justice misdone. Nineteen years old and unarmed, Derek Bentley shouted, "Let him have it, Chris," and Christopher Craig shot a policeman dead, but was too young to himself hang. It was Bentley who dangled from the scaffold in his place, despite the ambiguities of the words he used. Elvis sings with an unsettling mixture of outrage and irony. The song is really a localised attack on the attitudes of the gutter press, from whom the song's title could almost be a headline.

In a bad tempered morning TV interview with Anne Diamond, Elvis joked about starting his own newspaper, *The Daily Miro*, "It's going to say let's kill the foreigner, and lets have more pictures of the Royal Family, that's going to make people feel much better about unemployment." Calls for the return of hanging come loudest when "the swine are under attack" though, as Elvis points out here, the policeman's widow never asked for vengeance. There is no ambiguity in *this* song, killing anyone – whether by gun or rope – is a "terrible crime". Odd then that Elvis sings so much about it.

'Deep Dark Truthful Mirror' features The Dirty Dozen Brass Band, and Allen Toussaint on steady rolling piano, on a song about self-delusion. The contrast between the traditional backing and the obscure, bizarre images, with butterflies feeding on a dead monkey's hand, is unsettling, especially given Costello's passionate delivery, as if all the words are technicolour camouflage for a personal hurt. Did anyone mention Bebe?

'Veronica' has a far more cheerful, Honeybus-like, sound, with sad words about how a lonely spinster waits for a man who left her sixty-five years before. McCartney's bass drives things along, and he has forced a concision which brings out the central ambiguity about the woman's name. 'Eleanor Rigby' revisited.

Elvis himself switches to Hofner bass on 'God's Comic', a song which even Lennon, let alone Paul, would have found bizarre. Elvis wrote it in Greenland, above the Arctic circle. "It is a comic afterlife song," he says. "God is sampling our wares. He's got an eight-track and a waterbed and Barry Manilow records: all the good stuff." He adds in another interview that, "We perceive God and Santa Claus as wise old men with white beards. It's about a drunken sleazebag priest dying and arriving in heaven which is God's MFI warehouse." One wonders if it inspired Channel 4's *Father Ted*; there is just the same sense of playful fantasy with darkness round the edges.

Costello sings with yet another new voice, oily and with a chuckle in the throat, like Bob Monkhouse. He deliberately trembles, as if with a shiver, on the word "cold", and the chorus sounds straight from hell. All part of the "unbelievable trash", and the backing could be by Joe Loss, though it actually comes c/o the Tom Waits sound system.

On this extravagantly varied album, 'Chewing Gum' comes on like a cross between Captain Beefheart's Magic Band and Waits' exercise in Americana, *Swordfishtrombones*. The words, about an unhappy, commercially arranged marriage, are almost secondary.

'Tramp The Dirt Down' borrows its tune from Stevie Wonder's 'Isn't She Lovely', and Elvis sings it with unsettling beauty, and iron determination. The song opens with Mrs Thatcher kissing a sick child. Costello needed to write "a real emotional response to events. It's getting the thing out of your head before it does you some damage." This is driven music, and it is the only Costello song that can still reduce me to tears. Davey Spillane and Donal Lunny from Moving Hearts bring a sweet sadness to the accompaniment, like an Irish lament, though never was a funeral so devoutly wished.

It is difficult now to remember how powerless many people felt during Thatcher's pomp. For good or ill, she changed the known world, and made it colder and more frightening, or less feather-bedded and freer for the enterprising individual, according to taste. Personally, I felt sickened by the sense of triumphalism and the violence of belief in what I regarded, then and now, as a con trick. Elvis's words were a shaft of light in that darkness, when even to offer a mild criticism was to invite a beating in some quarters. In turn, Mrs Thatcher inspired a cacophony of hatred among artists and writers which occasionally made one even feel sorry for her. As compared to Morrissey's imaginative exercise in putting her on a guillotine, Costello cuts about a million miles deeper, universalising the sentiments, with a genuine sense of tragedy.

Looking back, he continues this despairing view: "I don't think we'll ever see the back of it really. We've seen the back of her but she had become so ludicrous she was in danger of undoing a lot of the wickedness she had done, through her own belligerence. I think the things that she visited on society, we will never recover from. The dismantling of this invisible society is truly wicked, it's evil, it's beyond politics and into morality. I can only see things getting grimmer. People are much more at ease with themselves in Dublin than they are in England. That's why I don't live in England."

'Stalin Malone' is a punchy, jazzy instrumental, which gives the listener some mental space. Elvis is present only as composer. "You know Henry Street in Dublin? It came to me there. That is the most cacophonous street in the world. You can hear 800 fragmented conversations jabbering in your face. I tried for that – cuckoo clocks, saxophones, old nightmare movies. It's a daymare." As for the dismembered horses mentioned in the discarded lyrics, this is not a reference to *The Godfather*, but part of history. In Powder Lane, where his grandfather went to the Military School of Music, the powder mill blew up just as the King of Portugal was passing in his carriage, "and there were horses' heads up in the trees".

'Satellite' has aural colouring from Michael Blair, and Chrissie Hynde on second vocal. What sounds like a tender love ballad is in fact a prediction of Rupert Murdoch's Sky TV, which opened for business on the week after the album's release. "A woman goes into a photo booth which is really a blue screen where she can be superimposed on any TV special of her own choice. But in order to have this moment of glory, there's a big catch. She's got to be in a peep show. A techno peep show where the lights shine right through her dress, and she's revealed to this slimey, slobbering guy who's watching her on TV. And he's on TV being watched by a host of other voyeurs who haven't got the courage of his lust. They're afraid of the germs...It's very Philip K Dick." The problem is that only one in a million would work all this out from the song as it stands. It does develop the voyeuristic aspect of Elvis's work, from 'Alison' onwards. The watching eye is now universal, as the singer strains towards the top of his vocal range.

'Pads, Paws And Claws' is pure fun, aurally, with Elvis on sub-aqua guitar, and Marc Ribot playing "alligator" six string. Verbally, again McCartney cuts Elvis down to size, so that the song becomes a series of puns on domestic disharmony, a literal evocation of catwoman. 'Baby Plays Around' in sharp contrast has only Mitchell Froom on ("distant") organ interrupting Elvis's musical solitude as he sings a song of jealousy, straight. Not a word wasted, not a tear withheld.

'Miss Macbeth' combines native musicians from New Orleans and

Dublin, in a musical mix and match, which opens with a drone, and tries too hard for comfort. The words are based on "the old lady on the street that every child thinks is evil or witchy. So I thought, fuck it, what if she actually was." The song goes against the New Testament ideal that "the poor and crippled rise above their adversity and are ultimately good. But what if they're just bastards!?" A great idea on paper, but the actual song needed – and lacked – McCartney's little silver hammer to cut the words down to size.

'Any King's Shilling' is, on the other hand, as perfect as could be imagined. It centres on Elvis's grandfather. "He was wounded out of the First World War. He was a trumpet player in the army, and once he was out of combat he got stationed to Dublin. He was born in Birkenhead but his parents had come over a few years before, so it was like being sent back home, but he was on the wrong side. Although he wasn't in combat he was still in uniform. And he had Irish friends who told him, 'Keep your head down. Watch out, something's going to happen.'" The track opens with Irish harp plucked by Derek Bell from The Chieftains, and Elvis has never sounded so Celtic – the song is told from the point of view of the locals, and larded with a jumble of Irish voices – or so melancholic. Backing him is an Irish acoustic supergroup behind him – Lunny, Spillane, a silent Christy Moore on bodhran, and Frankie Gavin from the subtle De Danann on fiddle, all playing as quietly as can be.

The CD and cassette versions of the album add 'Coal Train Robberies' here, the B-side of 'Veronica', and a song about the celluloid fantasies peddled by Hollywood, hardly a new theme. Neither is 'Last Boat Leaving', in which a father is forced to leave home, surreptitiously, but Elvis invests it with pathos, and some beautiful acoustic guitar (along with ship's bell) singing with a choke in his voice. Cait plays snowbells. Costello multitracks his vocals, and replays family history. His grandfather worked the cruise ships, while Elvis must have himself often said goodbye to Ross, as he went off on tour, ditto Matthew to *his* dad. A musician's life…

Costello had flown to Australia to film the 'Veronica' video with Evan English. Lynden Barber interviewed him on Friday the thirteenth. He revealed that he and Cait had moved house to Dublin – house prices were cheaper and people friendlier – though he had kept on a flat in London. With unconscious irony, he then attacked "the opportunist, entrepreneurial instinct, at the expense of everything worthwhile. In England it's given a little window dressing. In Ireland it's bare-faced." It was the first of a series of promotional interviews.

Q's Paul Du Noyer met a slimline Elvis in "somewhat dashing in his black designer overcoat and fancy-clasped tie", striding across Hyde Park. He had taken a couple of holidays, one in Italy that Easter, and denied that he was a workaholic (as they always do). "I turn down a lot of things, high profile shows, big tours that I didn't think were right." The Attractions were on hold, because Steve Nieve still felt sore – "the door's open to him" – though he "plays with that idiot Jonathan Ross every Friday". It was ironic that he should end up producing The Pogues, when "for a long time I hated traditional music because I had to suffer the narrow-minded attitudes in the clubs, the woolly jumper folk".

He tells Sean O'Hagan of *NME* that *Spike* is a comedy record, though the future High Llama sees "disintegration as the central theme". Elvis agrees: "There is no future for the reasonable voice." Even his current listening is to jazz instrumentalists like Bill Frisell. Full marks to Costello for far-sightedness: his final remark is to sneer at Robert Maxwell (later branded a thief for stealing millions from Mirror Group pensioners) for making an official announcement "that he's retiring from charity. It's worn him out so much, he's wasting away, poor dear. Brilliant, utterly brilliant."

Costello chatted to Allan Jones over two editions of the *Melody Maker*, both with severe hangovers. Lowe once accused Costello of "*fighting* every drink or any drugs you take. You're trying to stay straight all the way through." He talks of his huge respect for Van Morrison and his "single-mindedness. He does it *his* way, and if you can't accept that then go somewhere else. I don't think he's gonna cry. There are only two or three people with this kind of singular identity in rock 'n' roll, like Lou Reed, Dylan..." As compared to that "facsimile of excitement", Michael Jackson, who would be forgotten fifty years from now, or Whitney Houston, who has "turned into this cabaret singer. The light's gone from her eyes. She's just another victim of the Pepsi generation." Elvis *does* admire interesting eccentrics like Morrissey, Michael Stipe or John Lydon. As to Sting, a long time *bête noir*, they had recently met at a benefit gig, and Elvis told him, 'Don't come around here with that serious artist shit. And, by the way, fire that fucking piano player.' He seemed to take it quite well."

The night before, Elvis had appeared with another hero, Christy Moore at the Irish Music Awards, and duetted on 'The Dark End Of The Street'. In *Sounds* he reveals a new musical passion. "Last week, I went to three concerts of string quartets, and I've never been to anything like that since I was a child. I looked in the paper and there were no rock 'n' roll concerts I wanted to see." His reason for this was particularly interesting. "I knew what anybody who was playing sounded like, so I wasn't gonna learn anything more." Most of us go to concerts precisely because we know what they are going to sound like. Costello is made of sterner stuff, and had thus discovered the music of Shostakovich, "complicated, strange and almost frightening". Meanwhile his son Matthew had graduated on to Public Enemy and Guns N'Roses, musical cartoons in Elvis's eyes.

To launch the album, Costello played a short – and free – set with a grey-haired Nick Lowe outside Tower Records in Piccadilly. A crowd of around 500 people had assembled to "meet Elvis at midnight", and after a twenty-minute set and some photo calls, Elvis – in leather jacket and cap – moved inside to sign copies of the new album. The crush was such that a window was broken, and Elvis had to go outside again with a loudhailer to instil order.

He felt that there was no way he could tour these new songs with a band. It would have been like The Beatles trying to tour *Sergeant Pepper*. "It was such an ambitious record in terms of instrumentation. In fact the first tour I did after *Spike* was solo. It was only after the record started to become a success that I assembled a band to go on the road."

In February, Elvis appeared on Swedish and Dutch TV, then flew to the States to promote the new album, where he guested on David Letterman's show. Roger McGuinn was playing a gig at Boston's Nightstage, and Costello joined him for an after-hours jam alongside Aimee Mann. They played three Dylan songs covered by The Byrds: 'My Back Pages', 'Mr Tambourine Man', 'You Ain't Going Nowhere'. Costello once had a strange meeting with Dylan with his sons in a parking lot in Minneapolis. "He lined them up like they were on parade, and I had to shake hands. He said, 'This is Jesse, he knows all the words to "Pump It Up".' Jesse was a punk fan. I think he thought his dad was a bit old fashioned."

While Costello was in the States, BBC2 broadcast his pre-recorded spot on *The Late Show*, complete with his verbal diatribe: "I'm thirty-five years old. I'm not a boy any more. Don't *patronise* me." *The Sun* claimed that he had sworn on a live TV show, whereas he had actually sworn on a recorded TV show. They also printed his reaction that he stood by every word: "Well, they must be fucking telepathic, because nobody spoke to me. But that's an accolade, to get that sort of thing printed about you in *The Sun*. It means you're getting up *somebody's* fucking nose."

In April, Elvis undertook the Surprise Attack solo tour of the United States, and those with long memories could not but help but compare the blitzkrieg kid of the late Seventies with a man who now "did everything but juggle to win over his audience", and was onstage for a minimum of two hours. Andy Smith in Kingston was particularly struck by the way his voice could rise to a howl on 'Let Him Dangle' then sink to an anguished tremor on 'I Want You': "His use of dynamics – sudden silences, tempo shifts, changed in volume, brief *a cappella* passages – was masterful." Dylan's 'Tangled Up In Blue' was incorporated into 'Brilliant Mistake'. "Here was a likable, funny Elvis Costello."

Elvis played a couple of duets with support act Nick Lowe – whose set had barely changed since his two previous tours with his old friend – and then wheeled on the giant red heart he had talked about to his unofficial Information Service. He had dropped the idea of wild dogs, and replaced them with a wolfman who shepherded women from the audience onstage. Elvis himself donned a red velveteen jacket, and wielded a pitchfork, as "Napoleon Dynamite", the game show host from hell (literally). Sins included "awesomeness", "girls, girls, girls", "doing lunch" and "getting caught again". "Sinners' choice" at Pittsburg included 'Almost Blue' and 'Oliver's Army'.

At Greenvale, Elvis proved that he took each concert as it came, making each one unique. 'Deep Dark Truthful Mirror' was "a series of crescendos that made every line tender and agonised": in 'God's Comic' he followed the line about giving the world to the monkeys with a medley of Monkees songs. On another night, Elvis played the tiny Sweetwater club, with a capacity of 125, to celebrate the twenty-first birthday of the Village Music shop, alongside James Burton and Jerry Garcia. Three generations' guiding spirits, rock 'n' roll, psychedelia and new wave. The shop's affable proprietor John Goddard bawled Costello out for only spending $70 at his record store today, though as he pointed out he had been there three weeks before. With a cheerful, "Good evening partygoers," Elvis tells the audience that this is "more nerve wracking" than playing for 7,000 people, and that it is "a very funny time in his life". He tells an anecdote about *The Brady Bunch*, and about his fantasy of five eighteen-year old girls playing his songs, which has happened now in the movie *Satisfaction*. In the words of Ed Ward, "He set about playing with a fury and a passion – and a sense of humour – I'd rarely seen in any performer." Complex songs like 'Deep Dark Truthful Mirror' blossom in their solo incarnation, while 'Mystery Dance' features blazing guitar. The little hands once made of concrete have now unfrozen.

Elvis tells a long shaggy dog story about a Swedish TV chat show he once appeared on, as a prelude to 'God's Comic'. In the middle of the song he breaks into a rap, with God's liking for Mickey Rourke, and his reading habits: Jackie Collins, Danielle Steel, and Brett Easton Ellis's *Less Than Zero*, a novel which not only takes an Elvis song as its title, but features a poster of the angry young Elvis as one of its central images. Costello quips that only God can get tickets for Andrew Lloyd Webber's shows. The audience fail to join in the "Now I'm dead" chorus, for obvious reasons. Strangely intimate and stately versions of 'Red Shoes' and 'New Lace Sleeves' follow. 'Pads, Paws And Claws' is introduced as being about a girl "who is so beautiful that she turns into a cat", and he shouts the last word, which does indeed sound much like "Cait", who is in the audience. One presumes a private meaning, here. During 'Radio Sweetheart', he reminisces about a crazy idea to have girl singers in cat costumes, but jokes that eventually thanks to lack of funds he and Nick Lowe had to wear the whiskers and tails themselves.

During his set, Elvis had been briefly reunited with Austin DeLone of pub rock pioneers Eggs Over Easy. The evening grew wilder and weirder, culminating with Commander Cody singing 'Riot In Cell Block #9' with Costello and Garcia on backing vocals. Elvis – but not Garcia! – even plays on the Grateful Dead favourite 'Turn On Your Lovelight', sung here by Bob Weir, and captured for eternity on *Live Dead*, which helps knock another nail into the coffin of punk. *NME* once carried out a hatchet job on Garcia because of the width of his trousers, not the magic encased in his nine good fingers. Their loss. A bootleg CD of the night has recently surfaced, which captures both Elvis's searing solo (ish) set, and the good-natured singalongs. A few days later, Elvis played a seven-song set at WB HQ in Burbank, and also appeared on *Saturday Night Live* with a band including GE Smith, long time Dylan cohort, on lead guitar.

In May UK, Costello brought his latest solo tour to the UK, with all dates sold out well in advance, and Nick Lowe still in support. Tying in with the tour was the twelve-inch single of 'Baby Plays Around' with two rare tracks and a cover shot of a half-shaved Elvis half in darkness, one eye staring. Three concerts were added at the Royal Albert Hall. Elvis played four successive Sundays at the London Palladium, haunt once of Bruce Forsyth and the famous revolving stage, and with a terrifying balcony high above the stage. It was billed, entertainingly, as "A Month Of Sundays".

For the hard core supporters, as assayed by the *ECIS*, this was the most disappointing Costello tour so far, with the shock of him being a solo act beginning to wear thin. A minority of supporters, however, thought it was the pinnacle of his career. Three "professionals" reviewed the Palladium gig. David Cavanagh noted that the weekday entertainment here was a stage version of *'Allo, 'Allo*, and heard "an often blisteringly violent set", culminating with "an almost demented 'Tramp The Dirt Down'. The piece is headlined "Good Year for the Oldies". Adam Sweeting finds a stand up comic, like a "novel fusion of Eric Morecambe and Ben Elton", but that the haphazard nature of some of the songs "begins to grate over such a long performance". By the time he concludes with 'Pump It Up' sung to a beatbox, a large number of the crowd has gone home. Barbara Ellen hears a "mad and remarkable solo set", which seems accidental, until you think of the "years of work" which led here.

Fans like Chris Lowe want The Attractions back, though. "Watching Elvis solo is getting to be like going to church, done as much out of sense of duty as much as anything else." John Foyle in Dublin found "no soul, man". There was only the briefest of applause. Costello broke the tour to fly to Holland for Pink Pop, delivering a "special guest solo performance" alongside REM, The Pixies and John Hiatt. The only disappointment was the lack of a special mystery guest, widely predicted to be McCartney.

The British solo tour ended at the Colston Hall, Bristol, where Mark Perry found Elvis with "bootlace tie and strange, fuzzy sideburns…he resembles a latter-day Teddy Boy." He opens with 'You Want Her Too', jumping to the other side of the mike to imitate an absent Paul. The verbals approach Monty Python in their inconsequence. Esther Rantzen interrogates God, Andrew Lloyd Webber has his new masterpiece labelled *Aspects Of Crap*, and Elvis breaks into 'Jesus Christ Superstar' at a key moment. When he sings about "out go the lights", so they do. The audience join in enthusiastically. For 'Pump It Up', a pre-recorded voice asks, "Have you ever seen a psychedelic circus? Those innocent fun games of the Hallucination Generation?" Elvis's addiction was to something else entirely. The *NME* revealed in May that on those unfortunate occasions when he is performing live during a Liverpool game, he has his roadies convey the score through an elaborate sequence of hand signals.

Back on the musical plane, he played the Glastonbury Festival in June, then set out on a European tour. It was his first solo appearance at Worthy Farm, and Alexei Sayle introduced the Festival headliner just after ten-thirty pm, on the Pyramid stage. He opened with 'Accidents Will Happen', then said, "I've got a lot of songs I want to sing for you tonight. It's just me and all of you." His dark-suited figure was illuminated by a psychedelic light show, posturing as a mock guitar hero during 'Pump It Up'. He ended with 'Tramp The Dirt Down' and alluded to the Labour Party's success at the recent European elections. Just nine more years to go…

NME thought him "hard pressed to fill the moonlit vastness" by himself, with "an acoustic guitar (which he can't play)". For *Melody Maker*, "Somehow the sheer span of his work and enormity of his presence have become oppressive. It's been three years, but it feels like a premature return." At least the sun blazed down. Costello also played Belgium's Tourhout Festival, alongside Nick Cave and Lou Reed, a waterlogged affair. "Chirpy and red faced", he ran through a crowd pleasing set. The European tour continued apace. In Torino he premiered 'So Like Candy'. At the Roskilde Festival he brought on Nick Lowe, Pete Thomas and Glen Tilbrook and busked through a set of standards, including 'Pretty Flamingo' and 'Let The Good Times Roll'. Then it was off to Japan for some solo dates in late July.

Interest in *Spike* was continuing, and Costello now bowed to the inevitable, touring the States for the second time that year, but now with a band, The Rude Five, a six-piece (perversely enough) with only Pete Thomas surviving from The Attractions. The others were all American: Steven Soles from The Alpha Band, Jerry Scheff, Larry Knetchel – who played piano on 'Bridge Over Troubled Water', Marc Ribot and Michael Blair. Most of the gigs were open air concerts: one even took place on a floating barge, which could easily have been swept out to sea, like a scene from a Marx Brothers film. The itinerary stretched from Pine Knob Music Theatre in early August to a mid September appearance, twenty-five gigs later, at the Concord Pavilion.

After a week's frantic rehearsal in an empty Chicago club, the set list rarely deviated, and contained few songs before *King Of America*: Costello covered earlier material in a twenty-five-minute solo set. The band radically reinterpreted any older songs, so that 'Watching The Detectives' now swung to an airy jazz tempo. The band, basically two guitarists, bass, drums, keyboards and percussionist was able to cover the sound palate of *Spike* adding tuba, E flat horn, trombone, accordion, marimba and mandolin to the mix. Steve Nieve's unique style was still hugely missed. Costello was obviously enjoying playing with a band again, though, and was increasingly free in his stage movements. "He seemed happiest at mid tempo, dropping it to straight blues and waltzes rather than kicking into overdrive." At the New York Palladium, the fervently vegetarian singer greatly objected to Burger King sponsoring the gig, and asked for their logo to be removed. In Los Angeles, Eric Burdon joined in for the final encore.

Harold DeMuir caught a "lean, mean two and a half hour show", with a band that "made up in depth and swing what it lacked in visceral punch". Costello himself was now both confident and commanding on stage. One fan at Colorado Springs – where a crowd of 5,000 sang along to virtually every song – shouted out, "Elvis, you're God." Even Gods, though, need to put their feet up occasionally. Elvis made only one further live appearance for the rest of the year.

That autumn, he won the award for Best Male Video at the sixth annual MTV beanfeast. In November, *Girls + £ – Girls = $ & Girls*, a formula which doubled up as a comprehensive career overview was released by Demon, and reached Sixty-Seven in the UK album chart. The order of tracks was not chronological, but "arranged so as to tell a number of stories", and a mystery was encoded in the album title. Michele Kirsch read it either as something to do with American rights, or "more dirtily, the easy access to American groupies"!

There were no outtakes, but Costello's seemingly endless variety was mirrored by the way that double album, double CD and twin cassette all carried radically different track listings, to each of which Elvis appended notes. We thus learnt that the screaming on 'Man Out Of Time' was "a tribute to 'free' alto players everywhere", and thus presumably played on saxophone. 'Sleep Of The Just' was an act of secret revenge following an encounter with a British soldier on the border between Ulster and the Irish Republic. As to 'Brilliant Mistake', "This might be called the title track of the collection." In *Q*, David Hepworth failed to solve the underlying puzzle (answers on a postcard to me c/o Sanctuary), but found that Costello was best when "dancing on the edge of the singles' chart. There is more fibre here than in just about any comparable diet, but the early showstoppers still stop the show."

Organisers of the annual *Christmas Rocks* at the Olympia Theatre, Dublin, held in aid of the Temple Street Children's Hospital, were amazed when Elvis appeared at the stage door and asked if he could play. They loaned him a guitar, and he performed 'Radio Sweetheart' and 'God's Comic', with a spoken section about Douglas Hurd and "acid, punk and Kylie". Alongside Mary Coughlan and The Pogues, he helped raise £22,000 for x-ray equipment. Proceeds of his two solo gigs at Liverpool earlier that year had already been donated, without any undue fuss, to the Hillsborough Fund.

Costello's first wife, Mary, still bearing his surname, was now making a name for herself as an eclectic DJ for GLR. Like Charlie

Gillett, she was busy booking bands and gigs, and broadcasting live sessions. "Other than that I'm just a Chiswick housewife," she says. "My house used to look clean and tidy. Now it looks like a record shop that's been burgled."

As *Record Collector* reckoned it, though, her one-time husband had lost focus with his supporters, particularly those who thought he should be frozen in time, "singing 'Oliver's Army' on stage at the Hammersmith Palais. Former pub rockers from the Hope & Anchor circuit weren't supposed to dress up in penguin suits and hang out with the local symphony." Early support from the rock music press was – as always happens – now turning sour. Here was no Ian Dury, (falsely) typecast as a cheeky chappy and indulged accordingly. Elvis was a man without frontiers and without limits, quite outside their control or patronage. "Without even a biographer in the last eight" – actually, now twelve – "years to attempt an explanation on his behalf, Costello's recent work can seem eccentric, to the point of self destruction."

Well, here goes! At this point in the story, the most extraordinary twists and turns in Elvis's career are still yet to come.

CHAPTER ELEVEN

the classical years

In March 1990, Costello was named Best Songwriter in *Rolling Stone*'s Critics' Awards. That same month, Christy Moore chatted about his new recording of 'The Deportees Club'. "He called round to the house with his wife, and we were just playing some songs round the fire, and he sang that song, and I really liked it," he said. The oral tradition, no less. Another tribute came from The Dirty Dozen Brass Band, who had outraged New Orleans by incorporating be-bop and R&B elements. Elvis took his mother to see the group at Sweet Basil's in New York. "He wanted us to create the horn parts and melodies that were to go with his music. It wasn't like he came in and said, 'I want you to play this.' We got to work as musicians instead of just sidemen."

Elvis had been touring and recording with much the same nucleus of American musicians, first as The Confederates and then as The Rude Five. "So then I recorded *Kojak Variety* in the Spring of 1990, as a kind of farewell to that band. I'd been working with them since 1985 in the studio and 1986 live and it was getting to be like a bunch of old friends. I thought, 'Well I won't see these guys for a couple of years – maybe not ever again if I get back going with The Attractions.'" In fact, he was to tour again with The Rude Five in 1991. "So we went and had some fun recording these cover versions. By then I had Larry Knetchel playing piano, who was the only person that I hadn't recorded with up to that point." The album was recorded at Blue Wave Studios in Barbados, then put on hold by Warner Brothers, concerned about its lack of commercial potential. Much bootlegged, it appeared officially five years later, when WB's suspicions were proved correct.

August saw another kind of kiss-off, when Bruce Thomas published *The Big Wheel*, a "novel" which drew heavily on his experiences as an Attraction. Its title comes from the cardboard song indicator used on stage, but this in turn becomes a rather heavy-handed metaphor for life itself, endlessly round. The book is highly readable, but more accurately described as a travel journal, with some of the names slightly altered. Relentlessly downbeat, it opens with the unnamed hero farting and picking one of his spots, and ends back home, walking the dog. The only respite comes in chapter ten, when Thomas remembers weird times in Suffolk, under what can only be the influence of LSD, by turns terrifying and lyrical. A rock 'n' roll *Dance To The Music Of Time*, in one volume, its code is not exactly difficult to crack. The band's Manager, for example, is called Johnny St Tropez, and Thomas declares his disinclination to write much about him. "Could I stand it waiting, breathless, for the knock that comes in the night?!"

Costello appears, not even thinly disguised, as "The Singer". He hates flying, is afraid of heights, dislikes the whole animal kingdom (though he doesn't eat it) and is a hypochondriac. He also changes his accent according to what town he is in, from "thick, nasal Scouse" in Liverpool to a "top o' the morning, bejabbers brogue" in Ireland, to Cheltenham cockney in London. The real thing was "a bit sad that he hadn't had more fun. But I didn't really give a shit." Which means that he did. He bemoaned the lack of any description or love of music emanating from these pages. "The overwhelming feeling was of sadness and bitterness."

Thomas agreed that he had attempted to "deflate" his former boss, by describing him as sweaty and overweight, though, "He's not the main character in the book anyway, I am." As to his new career as an author, he told Trevor Down on GLR that, "I think it was therapy": for years spent on the road, not any spitefulness towards Costello. After all, he had left The Sutherland Brothers and Quiver after a punch up with one of the singers. The former Attractions had now cleaned themselves up: the Keyboard Player – once given to violent mood swings – now went jogging, and the alcohol swilling Drummer was tee-total!

In the *NME*, Nicholas Wroe found Thomas "conveys convincingly the repetition that is touring as well as the institutionalising effect of band life, a world where self-indulgence has never been rationed". Thomas has since written a manual of unarmed combat, which he might have well needed after the publication of *The Big Wheel*.

Costello spent the summer of 1990 in Los Angeles, recording his next album, and returned that October to reunite in the studio with The Confederates. He found time to attend Tom Petty's fortieth birthday party, along with the likes of Springsteen and Jeff Lynne. Each autumn, Neil Young hosted a benefit gig for the Bridge School, which cared for "physically handicapped non-speaking children". Costello took part this year, at an acoustic evening held at the Shoreline Amphitheatre, Mountain View, California, alongside Young with Crazy Horse, Jackson Browne, Steve Miller and Edie Brickell. The compere was Cheech, out of Cheech And Chong. The greatest shock was in Elvis's new look, with a reddish, untrimmed beard, and shoulder length hair. Browne greets him with the words, "It's a whole *trip*."

'Veronica' blends into Young's 'The Ways Of Love'. Neil dances sidestage during 'Radio Sweetheart', and Elvis announces that he is retiring his Martin guitar. "Just before I came out tonight it spoke to me." One wag shouts out for 'Stairway To Heaven'. 'Tread The Dirt Down' predates Thatcher's sacking – by her own party – by just a few days. An encore of 'Alison' – which has since appeared on a compilation album of the finest performances from the Bridge concerts – is followed by 'My Aim Is True', with his host joining in on the chorus. Cheech announces that, "Elvis has left the Bay area." During Young's own set, Elvis was seen to be entwined with Cait, now with waist length hair, singing along and engaging in a beer or three. He then joins in with "great eccentric guitar solos" on 'Down By The River', "worth coming across a continent to hear".

Elvis was entering the big picture. In *The Godfather III* 'Less Than Zero' bursts out of cinema speakers during a love-making scene, set in 1979. Roger McGuinn's new album contained the scabrous 'You Bowed Down' commissioned specially. "Not only did he write me a song, but he sent me a letter telling me exactly how he wanted me to sing it, as a cross between 'My Back Pages' and 'Positively Fourth Street'," McGuinn recalls. At a McGuinn gig in February 1991 at London's Borderline, Elvis was too shy to come onstage, though invited. What did he have to hide?

As a taster for the new album, 'The Other Side Of Summer' was released as a single – which just about struggled into the Top Fifty – and featured a Nick Lowe song as a bonus on the twelve-inch. Its most startling aspect was the cover photo, with Elvis airborne by a wintry Brighton Pier, still holding onto his guitar. The real shock was his long untamed hair, and the inset photo of the new album cover, sporting full moustache and beard. The Californian look was here to stay, for a year or so anyway. Some fans almost rioted in the streets.

March 1991 saw Costello and Jerry Garcia sharing an interview for *Musician* magazine: the two looked like blood brothers. Elvis was now the antithesis of the young Stiff star, spiky haired and looking as if he'd never needed to shave in his life. As he told *Record Collector* about this drastic image change,"It's my life and my body, and if I want to fuck myself up and have a beard and wear my hair long, that's my business." He had his own reasons, "some of them personal, some of them just damn wilful". Looking back, "Some of the pictures with the beard I kinda like; others I see and think, 'God, you look terrible.'" Indeed, he looks more like a tramp than a trend setter.

As to Garcia, the epitome of hippie bonhomie, "I think he was a great musician, he had a big heart, he loved music, and I was delighted to be there with him. You don't always have to be scowling and trying to stare the camera down like I used to do – mainly out of defence, early on. I'm not that aggressive a person unless I'm pushed. Like most people, I just want to get on with what I do." That same year he contributed a stately 'Ship Of Fools' to *Deadicated*, alongside other unexpected acts Burning Spear, The Indigo Girls and Suzanne Vega, a choice of musicians which made this one of the finest tribute albums ever recorded. The Dead's move into country rock had been a vital influence on Flip City: thus did the big wheel turn.

In May, Costello released *Mighty Like A Rose*, which debuted at Number Five in the UK album charts, and Fifty-Five in the USA. Two songs were collaborations with Paul McCartney, while a classy production masterminded by Mitchell Froom gave it a luxuriance of sound most reminiscent of *Imperial Bedroom* and perfect for the CD revolution. The usual cast of top American session musicians was light years removed from Costello's early sound, though Pete Thomas and

Nick Lowe made cameo appearances. Bassist Rob Wasserman was the one new name involved.

Elvis agreed with *Record Collector* that the album had a more organic feel than its predecessor. "Maybe it's the presence of a band," he said, "even though it was a session band, so it didn't have the same we're-all-in-it-together-and-we're-all-on-the-same-payroll mentality about it as The Attractions." The original idea of reforming The Attractions had fallen through, largely due to Bruce Thomas's truculence. "So I went back to Hollywood. I tried to find the solutions to the questions inside a group of musicians, rather than using any instrumentation that flew into my head. That isn't to say that there weren't some quite bold arrangements."

Pet Sounds was a good role mode. As he told Radio One, he was trying not to copy Brian Wilson slavishly, but to adopt his technique. The way in which he would "take a keyboard line then copy it with a bass clarinet. So we'd put an unlikely orchestral instrument in the mix, it wouldn't be right in your face. There were songs that started out as spontaneous performances, but I just wanted to illuminate them a little." It was all part of Elvis's continuing attempts to push back the musical boundaries.

This applied equally to his lyrics, which were also growing more sophisticated. "But that just makes people even more furious," he says. "Pop singers aren't supposed to write allegorical songs. And in England, the album got some extremely hostile reviews – very much to do with the fact that I apparently let some people down who didn't want me to change my image. I'd successfully buried the geek guy for good."

Barbara Ellen's review for the *NME* certainly fits the bill, as suggested by its headline, "Imperial Boredom". The album is a "vinyl Pompeii", either "self indulgent and sour, or lazy and glutinously sweet. I rushed out to greet the cool surf, and found myself ankle-deep in snot." Ellen is virtually alone among the British rock press, though. The sheer verve of her invective must have overly depressed this "battered old bard".

MM's Chris Roberts came looking for a "glamourless righteous politico", but found "a bloodied love saint" instead. "The singing is gorgeous, *taunting* the edges of what's tender and what grates." Of the new breed of adult-orientated rock magazines, Mat Snow in *Q* thought it perhaps Costello's finest album yet for this "human jukebox", while

Shaun Phillips in *Vox* saw Elvis emerging here "older, wiser and still armed with a full set of incisors".

The cover of *Mighty Like A Rose* has a monochrome Elvis in huge spectacles – reflecting a city street – next to a red rose, blown up to the same size as his head. Produced by Froom, Killen and MacManus, it was recorded in Hollywood, with vocal and orchestral overdubs back in London. On the inside cover, a menacing Elvis has now swivelled his eyes towards the viewer, and the rose has grown hair. The album is dedicated, tongue in cheek, to "Cait, my unspeakable wife", while the CD reveals the source of the title, a lyric by E Nevin from the repertoire of John McCormack, the Irish balladeer honoured by the Pope.

'The Other Side Of Summer' has the clunking piano and harmonies of The Beach Boys – though not their laconic charm – and pours scorn on their dreams of endless surf "the same way Mozart did musical jokes. People took it far too seriously, I think its a beautiful track," Elvis insists. There is something smug here, though, with Elvis wallowing in pessimism. There is a sharp reference to Lennon, a millionaire asking us to imagine "no possessions". One can only agree with Barbara Ellen that this is "a malodorous lyrical gem wrecked by an irritating bubblegum chorus. If this evokes The Beach Boys then I'm a grain of sand up Brian Wilson's ringpiece." Catchy tune, though.

'Hurry Down Doomsday (The Bugs Are Taking Over)' is another piece of ecological agit-prop, though it seems to actually welcome Armageddon. It is a collection of great quotes, rather than a coherent song. The cluttered production shows Froom at his worst: he brought the same aural confusion to later Richard Thompson albums, and the reproof from one critic that the only bass he is aware of is a species of fish. It remains Elvis's favourite song on the album. "I still have days when I feel, 'Fuck this, let's get it over with.' It's the same impulse on a cosmic level as 'Tramp The Dirt Down' was on a personal level. It's fighting the negative, which comes upon all of us." His nasal vocal assault and the clattering, echoed backing is redolent of Lennon in his Plastic Ono Band phase, while Ribot adds avant-garde noise.

'How To Be Dumb' is a response to Bruce Thomas's novel, but unlike his former bassist's prose, it fails to universalise the experience: indeed all three songs so far are appallingly over-written, as if Costello has lost his usual quality control. Even *Goodbye Cruel World* had good songs ruined by sloppy performances. Here superb playing fails to rescue some dodgy songs. The odd line does cut through, like "you always had to dress up our bitterness in some half-remembered philosophy". Ouch! An update of 'Positively Fourth Street' with far less of a tune. I wonder if Thomas could sue for slander for some of the statements here!

'All Grown Up' is a haven of restfulness after that, beautifully orchestrated, and a kind of sequel to The Beatles' 'She's Leaving Home', when the girl has run back to daddy from her used car salesman. It is all surprisingly bitter, though sung with apparent tenderness. Costello has learned George Martin's tricks of underlaying an orchestra beneath vocal and drums, and this is simply gorgeous, a new direction for Elvis.

'Invasion Hit Parade' has mariachi trumpet from Elvis's dad, and the lad himself on "big stupid guitar and little foolish organ". It quotes from Roger Miller's 'King Of The Road', a hobo's lament, as part of a catalogue of betrayal. The lyrics update 'Less Than Zero', seen from the sourness of middle age, but set in a glorious soundscape, like a ten-million dollar movie. Another song which sounds better than it reads.

Harpers Bizarre were a vacuous US Sixties studio band, who covered 'Feelin' Groovy' and the bubbly charm of 'Anything Goes'. 'Harpies Bizarre' takes the same blend of harpsichord and French horn, but the song deals with a "naive girl seduced by a smarmy snob". Elvis's voice takes on the world-weary tones of the great Gary Brooker, and odd wisps of sound which make you think your speakers are malfunctioning. The woodwind arrangement is by Fiachra Trench, who provided a similar resuscitation act on the mid period albums of Van Morrison.

'After The Fall' is so redolent of Leonard Cohen, it has to be some kind of wind up. One reviewer discerned a sneering Spanish guitar and sickly sentimentality, so I must be particularly dim to actually like this, and find tenderness mixed in with the scorn. 'Georgia And Her Rival' is the story of a woman spurned on the telephone. Elvis thinks, "It's a beautiful melody, and we got far too tricky with the arrangement. It should have been about half the speed, and the story should have been much more tragic." It's fine anyway, infectious musically, with simple words and a clear-throated Elvis sounding pleased just to sing for the sheer joy of it. Like a bird.

'So Like Candy' is a collaboration with McCartney, and from a different musical planet to most of what has gone before. McCartney has again chopped Elvis down to size, and revealed a mountain. This is redolent of The Beatles circa the *Magical Mystery Tour*, with the same kind of trippy flute and post-psychedelic sadness as on 'Fool On The Hill'. The backing musicians are at their finest here, with Froom adding emotional colour, and Ribot a startling guitar solo. The subject, in Paul's words "about a sexy, model-y kind of girl", was a set exercise. This makes the calm desolation with which Costello sings, and the odd little details in the final verse (which he wrote alone, and unusually quickly) all the more strange, until one remembers that 'Candy' was one of his pet names for Bebe Buell, and everything then falls into place.

The brief 'Interlude' is played by The Dirty Dozen Brass Band, leading tunefully into the second McCartney collaboration, 'Playboy To A Man'. One reviewer thought that "Billy Joel has invaded the studio", and Costello certainly hardly sounds like himself, though his scream is back, at least. Filler. Which drags. Awfully.

'Sweet Pear' suffers from some over-obvious rhymes, but the way that Elvis's choirboy vocal soars against a brass backing lifts the hairs on the back of one's neck. It is the closest thing here to *Pet Sounds*, stately at first, then sweetly sad. Ribot's magnificent guitar break is the song's centrepiece, almost Thompsonesque, in the way it builds to a dying fall. The sense of profound melancholy – suddenly we are listening to a major album – continues into 'Broken', written by Cait. Costello's voice is at its best here when it leaves words behind, and takes on the bruised melancholy of David Accles on the mournful, dissonant 'His Name Is Andrew', of which there is no finer praise.

'Couldn't Call It Unexpected No 4' boasts a miraculous tune: one critic compared the cheerful thump of its backing to the hybrid of a colliery band and a banjo-driven New Orleans procession. Elvis sings with joy in his voice about the chills of love, and the tune leaps heavenwards, just as the words get genuinely spooky, Hitchcock on ice. Even the tune has been supposedly constructed from birds on a wire, reminding us of the scene when the junior school is under attack in *The Birds*. The song, and album, ends on a double negative, which resolves itself as positive. The musical backing is rich and antique, stuffed with calliopes and chamberlains, and clunks away into silence, like a departing circus.

That one Christine Fevret describes the closing, miraculous couplet here as "pompous and pondermost" does not auger well for her interview with Elvis in the *NME*. Neither does its title, "The Hirsute Of Excellence", over a picture of Elvis with hair receding at his temple, but sprouting everywhere else. The interview has been "bought in" from a continental magazine, but is fascinating. Elvis resents the fact he was never taught to read music, but now writes at the piano, and has a computer which "transcribes what I tape onto my four-track recorder as a score". The odd balance of *Mighty Like A Rose*, restricting each song to one emotion, was a deliberate policy, and moving from "despair, to cynicism to a fairly hopeful view".

In Ireland, in the wake of U2, there was now a school of thought that everybody born there "has some sort of mystical understanding of cosmic miracles. It's a lot of old bollocks really." Talking to Charles Shaar Murray in *Q*, Elvis admits that, "My main interest at the moment is in classical music. The problem is that the level of technique and complexity is such that in order to begin to express yourself, you have to study for twenty years. It's like being a Jesuit or a doctor." As to his own, more instinctual, working methods, "You have to trick yourself into singing, just as you have to trick yourself into writing." At the age of thirty-seven, he confided to *The Independent*'s Kevin Jackson that he was considering entitling his next album *Angry Old Man*.

Meanwhile, Elvis was off back to the States, appearing on NBC's *Saturday Night Live* and opening the Come Back In A Million Years tour with The Rude Five, now lacking Michael Blair. Support acts included Sixties revivalists The La's – whose bassist went on to form Cast – and Sam Phillips, on whose album *Cruel Inventions* Costello had made a guest appearance. Low key, two-hour sets from a man who now looked like Richie Havens, with the instrumental dexterity of Steve Winwood, trading lead guitar licks with Marc Ribot on 'Playboy To A Man' and playing piano to Larry Knetchel's organ on 'Couldn't Call It Unexpected'.

The venues were largely amusement parks, with audiences unfamiliar with the singer's past. Many thought him low on charisma: "He projects all the passion of a plate of cottage cheese. Elvis is dead." At Lake Compounce, he was alive enough to run through most of the cover versions from *Kojak Variety*, 'The Other Side Of Summer' in slow waltz time, and a "new, swinging" arrangement of 'Alison'. He seemed to be suffering from throat problems, made droll remarks between songs, taking a swan-like bow after each round of applause, and seldom played an encore after the show-stopper, 'Pump It Up'.

Other reviewers saw maturity rather than dissolution. "Like a latter-era Woody Allen movie, the ones without the jokes, Costello's show simmered with the kind of experienced, intelligent music that shows rock does not belong to the young and impetuous." The Rude Five were professional but unexciting – curiously "unanimated" – the one exception being Ribot, who could make his guitar "snarl and bite or laze around euphoniously".

In June, Elvis played New York's Madison Square Garden, and then recorded an edition of MTV's *Unplugged*. It was originally to have been shared with Jane's Addiction, who failed to show, but only twenty-four minutes were aired, and much of the best work was left on the cutting room floor. MTV also cut and pasted the songs, thus robbing the organic feel of the original run-through. His vocals were more of a rasp than a croon, but this somehow adds to the passion, while the format brings out the subtlety of The Rude Five: Knetchel's sumptuous piano on 'Deep Down Truthful Mirror' or Ribot's slide on 'Hurry Down Doomsday'. 'So Like Candy' segues into the last verse of 'I Want You'.

Elvis calls for a towel to wipe his sweaty brow, then says to no-one in particular, "Here's your chance for a shroud of Turin." This is cut from the broadcast, as is a startling take on The Louvin Brothers 'Why Must You Throw Dirt In My Face', and a beautiful 'Couldn't Call It Unexpected', with Elvis conducting The Rude Five, using his right arm like a baton. For Little Richard's 'Bama Lama Bama Loo', Costello straps on a light green hollow body Gibson, and announces, "Welcome to the first of a new series, MTV *Plugged Back In Again*."

Back in Britain in July, Elvis – with his throat restored to full working order – played six straight nights at the Hammersmith Odeon, as part of a UK tour, which attracted headlines like "The Imposter" and "This Year's Muddle". He had earlier played the rain-soaked Roskilde Festival, competing with a set by Iggy Pop, and slipping over, thus playing the last solo of 'Pump It Up' on his knees. One witness was shocked by what looked like David Crosby at his most addled.

At Hammersmith, 'Watching The Detectives' now incorporated 'Let

Him Dangle'. The band played loud, but looked like a session combo, stretched across the back of the stage in a straight line. The sound balance was poor – "marshmallow" one critic said – and there was a stunning lack of atmosphere, though a few brave souls got up from their seats and began dancing in the aisles. Max Bell, who had swapped the *NME* for *The Evening Standard* thought that Elvis now resembled an eccentric uncle, "maturing into a mellow version of his former ornery self", though The Rude Five were a "motley" group of has-beens.

This statement does not include Pete Thomas, who led the band from his elevated drum kit, and proved its driving force. At one point, one punter shouted out, "You're a genius." "Not yet I'm not," Elvis replied, "that's next week." The unexpected musical highlight was 'Sweet Pear', with Elvis's emotionally-charged vocal, and melodic guitar break drawing warm applause. Fanatics who attended all six nights reckoned that Elvis grew into the place, but were surprised by the lack of variety from show to show. The Attractions, with their huge repertoire, would never have restricted themselves in so limpet-like a way to the set list, or pre-planned arrangements. The most savage review was by Terry Staunton, who first scorned Elvis's beard – nine out of ten false ones looked more realistic – then his music, "fannying about" with his past while The Rude Five play like blind men. Costello had got "lazy, almost Las Vegas", with Pete Thomas playing his heart out, but the rest treating it as no more than a job. "At times the show is simply *horrendous*": could Elvis steer himself out of "the creative cul de sac he currently finds himself in"?

In Bristol, Elvis joked that 'Suit Of Lights' was full of backward messages, so anyone possessed by the devil should go to the chapel at the back of the hall. The play-out music was Vera Lynn's 'We'll Meet Again', which certainly cleared the hall in record time. In Glasgow, Sam Phillips played her half hour support set with her husband, one T-Bone Burnett. Elvis expressed the desire to strip off, paint himself blue and go berserk, but fortunately didn't. He did gain fervent applause when he declared himself pleased to have left England, making the point forcible with a string of four-letter words. In Edinburgh, T-Bone came out for the encores, the "fourteenth annual Coward Brothers reunion", and the two duetted on 'Ring Of Fire' and 'Lucille'.

Next it was off the beaten track to Lerwick in the Shetlands: Elvis's long-time production manager Milo Lewis has since reckoned it would have been cheaper to have given every Shetlander "a £10 note, a CD and a video of the last concert". Costello had first discovered the charms of this northern outcrop in 1981, when – escaping from a Norwegian cruise liner for a pint of Guinness – he found two of his singles on the jukebox. A near-capacity audience sat on hard chairs in the local leisure centre, with sporadic dancing breaking out at the back. Among those who had come over specially was Gary McVeigh, "a twenty-three-year-old instrument technician from Northampton", down from the oilfields, who had seen every one of Elvis's twenty British tours!

The "beard" tour continued into Europe, with a triumphant two am appearance at the Montreux Jazz Festival, and a ten-minute guitar duel on 'Pump It Up' in Stockholm. After a wild night in Hamburg, Elvis's BMW crashed into another car, and he had to take the tour bus, to a chorus of 'Accidents Will Happen'. Then it was back to the USA in August, then on to Japan and Australia. The absence of Marc Ribot – back recording in the States – stripped the backing band back to a three-piece: keyboards, bass and drums (Knetchel, Scheff and Pete Thomas), and a new nickname, the "Filthy Four". The club gigs in particular began to ring with the kind of intensity which many thought had gone for good. Shane Danielson in Sydney heard a "circuitous, almost sneaky return to the pub-rock approach of The Attractions". A wild night in Woolongong ended with Elvis singing Bulgarian folk tunes, while "the ghost of Jimi Hendrix kissed 'Alison' goodnight".

Costello also featured on BBC 2's *Bringing It All Back Home*, a palatable dollop of ethno-musicality, showing how Irish traditional music had infiltrated itself into everything from country and western to Broadway. Elvis sang 'Mischievous Ghost' with Mary Coughlan. In August he had taken part in the Feile 91 Festival at the Semple Stadium in County Tipperary, where Cait grew inebriated, and menaced the audience, themselves expressing annoyance at Costello's tardiness to come on stage.

The *NME* reckoned, bitchily, that EC had ordered the entire backstage area to be cleared before he walked the hundred yards to the stage. "It's pretty funny watching affronted VIP guests and pissed bands getting turfed out of their hiding places, but given Costello's mood that night, the order can hardly be put down to his sense of fun." Once onstage, and looking "like Van Morrison in a wig and beard", he stormed through his set, rearranging and stretching and resuscitating his repertoire. "On this form, Elvis should be drinking with The Manic Street Preachers, not playing Madonna backstage." Or even Elton John. Like his gradual reversion to his real name, it was all part of MacManus's rediscovery of his cultural heritage. Bringing it all back home, indeed. He also contributed a song, 'St Stephen's Murders' to *The Bells Of Dublin*, an album of seasonal songs by The Chieftains.

An indication as to another kind of musical influence came with the screening of Alan Bleasdale's Channel 4 drama *GBH*, starring Robert Lindsay in a hallucinogenic take on the Derek Hatton era of Liverpool City Council. The lead actor from *Scully* returned as a Militant Tendency activist, who suddenly drops his scouse accent and is revealed as a secret service agent, fomenting indiscipline. The incidental music had to refect the series' extraordinary energy, and range of set pieces, from scenes of childhood bullying, panic attacks, a terrifying assault on a junior school, sexual betrayal and the lead character's mental disintegration.

Costello and Richard Harvey, once of medieval rockers Gryphon, achieved this with aplomb, recycling some of Elvis's best tunes. The haunting title theme was 'Call It Unexpected No 4', without the words. As Elvis told *Record Collector*, "I was doing *GBH* at the same time as *Mighty Like A Rose* so some of the orchestral thinking transferred across." As he could neither read nor write music at the time, Richard Harvey would "take these themes and sometimes reorchestrate them quite radically away from the sense that I had". Costello had begun to listen to classical music, bringing to it the kind of close attention he once did to Stax, or Hank Williams or Abba. "I used to borrow a riff, the same way I used to from Howlin' Wolf, only now it was from Mozart," he admits. "It was a natural step from that to learn to write music down."

The *GBH* soundtrack was released by "Demon Soundtracks", its cover drawn from stills of the series, and the music now divided into twenty-two tracks, played by an twenty-strong studio orchestra. Titles included 'The Puppet Master's Work' and 'Prufrock Quartet: The Roaring Boy' which only made sense in the context of the plays. The music, though, stood on its own. The *NME*'s Andrew Collins praised its blend of Bernard Hermann and Vivaldi, "a remarkable and wonderful concept. Certainly the most useful thing Elvis Costello's tagged his name to in ages." It captures its subject perfectly; thus Michael Murray's breakdown is heralded by the play of "dainty xylophone and percussive tinkles over foreboding rumbles, and all the pomp and pantomime that heralds his presence".

Meanwhile, *My Aim Is True* finally went platinum, after a mere fourteen years in the record racks. It remains Costello's best selling album; commercially he has been going downhill, ever since. Undeterred, Elvis contributed his cover version of the Ray Davies song 'Days' to Wim Wenders' movie *Until The End Of The World*, and came along for part of the Dylan-Tom Petty-Roger McGuinn Temples In Flame tour. Though his particular *bête noir* Mrs Thatcher had fallen from power, she was neither forgotten nor forgiven. Live versions of 'Tramp The Dirt Down' refused to pity "the tragic, forlorn, vacant figure whose story is on sale", or John Major, who replaced her.

Elvis, not a monarchist despite once posing as the "King of America", looks forward to abolishing the House of Lords, "kicking the Royal cuckoos out of the nest/and placing the Queen Mother under arrest". The latter thought is about the closest thing to treason one can now utter in this country. The kind of thing that can still get your teeth punched out.

In February 1992, Radio One broadcast *Come In And Hear It* – the first of four weekly episodes in a series just called *Elvis Costello*. With help from the peerless Pete Frame, it was a brilliant piece of documentary radio, with lots of quotes from the likes of Jake Riviera and Bruce Thomas, but nothing from Steve Nieve. Everyone contacted exudes a kind of baffled respect. For Pete Thomas, Elvis's new passion for classical music is another example of his ability to totally immerse himself in a new style. "He's got a bag with about eight CDs and his nose in a book about 'Quite Good Pianists Of The Early 1730s' and it's about four inches thick." As to his talent – and Thomas is the only musician who has played on every Elvis album since 1978, "Basically, he writes great songs. What else are you going to do? Who else are you going to play with? Who writes songs anything like as good? And I'm sorry, I like good tunes."

As to Nick Lowe's thoughts on Costello, "Most people who are any good will go through periods of thinking – no, *knowing* – that they're useless, that they're frauds and charlatans. And they plunge to the depths of despair and the next minute they're so filled with their own talent they can practically bite it. Most of the greatest artists have this, and you try to grab a bit of it on the way up or down. It makes me think what a great artist he is. I haven't come in here just to be on the wireless. I'm here because I seriously believe that Elvis Costello is a great artist, and he'll get better."

Elvis himself felt, "I've got so many albums that I want to make. My responsibility is to put stuff out there. At the same time it's only records: if you don't like this one you might like the next one. They're not a series of red buses that are always the same. I'm always amused that people think that each record is an irredeemable step towards a pre-ordained fate. I might go on next to make the record that convinces everybody that I have really gone mad, or I might make it with a comb and tissue paper."

Or he could become a radio DJ. Costello had just appeared as the castaway on *Desert Island Discs*, and revealed that he once worked for the Midland Bank. Among the records he had chosen – to cheer himself up – was Beethoven's 'Opus 135', and other choices were his dad crooning with Joe Loss on 'At Last', Mozart's *The Marriage Of Figaro* and 'Blood Count' by Duke Ellington, with Johnny Hodges on alto. Cole Porter's 'I've Got You Under My Skin', sung by Sinatra who hits one note in a way he describes as "supernatural", was the first song he could remember hearing, in the cradle.

The only rock music chosen was The Beatles' cover version of Smokey Robinson's 'You Really Got A Hold On Me'. My own favourite, as it happens. At school teachers would twang imaginary elastic bands when they heard the name Declan MacManus. There was a "sort of dare element" in changing his name to Elvis. It also heightened his "contempt for parts of the media". He wants his island to be off Archangel, but hates the idea of having to kill animals to keep himself alive. He thinks his father is a better singer and his son a better guitarist.

Back in London, he lived with his father and "worked in branch banking: it was still quite Dickensian." During bullion deliveries, he had to stand outside the Putney branch with a whistle, in case there was a robbery. His mother had always been a classical buff, and while working as an usher at Liverpool's Philharmonic had heard most of the great conductors and soloists. His own particular discovery was the singer Anna Sofia von Otto, who here sings 'Dido's Lament', and who was a joint discovery by Elvis and Cait, who shared his new passion for classical sounds. He thought she had the same underlying sense of passion as Billie Holiday, though a radically different technique. As to his own musical self-development, he was now studying musical notation, twice a week. "Everyone has a voice, they just have to learn how to release it," he explained.

Costello feels neither wholly Irish nor wholly English. He comes from a long line of totally impractical people. Sue Lawley responds well, and says she thinks he sounds happy in himself, especially for a rock musician. He immediately lists all of his favourite miserable records, and makes a passionate declaration about the power of music. He considers Stravinsky, Ellington, Miles Davis and Charles Mingus as the greatest post-war composers, period. (One notices a corresponding lack of enthusiasm for Britten, or Lloyd Webber, or Zappa.) He would have liked private recordings of Cait singing, or Matthew playing guitar, but they might also make him unbearably sad. His favourite book is a selection from James Thurber, his luxury item an upright piano, decorated with an exact reproduction of the altar piece at St Barnabus by Botticelli. As it went out of tune, he could invent his own tonality, and people would have to rescue him to hear the entirely new music he had invented: "It would drift over the breeze, and people would hear it, and I would be rescued."

Costello paid his debt to Charles Mingus by appearing on the tribute album *Weird Nightmare*, singing the title song, with a house band including Bill Frisell and Marc Ribot. Others taking part included Keith Richards, Hubert Selby Jnr, Dr John and Robbie Robertson.

In summer 1989, Elvis had brought in some of his favourite records to the Andy Kershaw show on Radio One, mixing and matching Thelonious Monk and Leonard Cohen, Vladimir Horowitz, The Supremes, Maria Callas and the young Presley. On 1 July, 1992, he put this same sense of eclecticism into practice, when he was booked into the Amadeus Centre in London, to perform a work in progress with The Brodsky String Quartet. Mark Perry – now the English editor of *Beyond Belief* – remembers strolling across the canal at Little Venice, and grabbing a central table at the sold-out event, held in a converted Presbyterian chapel. A sheet of A4 paper announced that the ensemble would be performing seventeen completely new songs, unamplified. The musicians ask the audience to smoke, and wear designer casuals. Elvis has shaved off his beard, and now has short hair again.

Costello, looking slightly shy, stresses that the musicians have all joined in the compositions tonight. "I feel a bit of devilment coming on," he announces before the second half. The ensemble play with obvious enthusiasm, and receive a standing ovation for their pains, having premiered the whole of *The Juliet Letters*, a suite which always worked better live than on disc. Alan Bleasdale was in the audience, while Elvis walked unhurriedly through the audience, a holdall slung over his shoulder.

The same ensemble played songs from the same piece later that year in the 14C Great Hall, Dartington, where they were mid way through a residency. The Summer School's newsheet contained a reference to Elvis's prowess on the croquet field. This time, Elvis premiered a new song, 'Favourite Hour', written in situ. At the Gate Theatre, Dublin, Kevin Courtney noted Elvis's irreverence, "with many flicks of the eyebrow and some hilarious lyrics". He sang "in his recognisable dry, ironic tone, though he did stretch his range, just about reaching the required notes. He managed to plumb depths of feeling you wouldn't think possible with his limited voice."

Costello had introduced the evening with the expectation that, "These songs will thrive on a good, engaged, audience," and was proved correct. He declined an invitation to sing 'Oliver's Army' as an encore. "There's always one!" Elvis quipped. The concert was a complete run-through of the album, filmed in parts by the BBC, who captured the same musicians in Ardmore Studios, County Wicklow, miming to playbacks. Three American girls were heard to comment that Elvis was smaller than they had expected.

In September, he played at the same venue during a charity gala as part of the WB Yeats festival, with that most understated of traditional singers Andy Irvine and the poet John Montague. In October, he repeated the trick at the Chelsea Arts Ball, whose motto was "stuff the recession", alongside the Count Basie Orchestra, Shirley Bassey and Jools Holland.

That same month, Costello was expected to sing 'Positively Fourth Street' with Booker T And The MGs, and then introduce Lou Reed at Columbia's *Celebration Of The Music Of Bob Dylan* – to be headlined by the master himself – at Madison Square Garden. He did not appear, supposedly because he could not obtain a work permit, though a docket for the rehearsal has his name already crossed out, and Stevie Wonder in his place. Elvis has since expressed deep antipathy towards Sinead O'Connor, who disrupted the evening, and was booed offstage, and another view has him withdrawing in protest at her inclusion. He certainly issued a statement that, "Catholics, Catholic clergy and Catholic values have become the whipping post for every bigot in America."

Towards the end of 1992, Costello began work on a new album in the rock idiom, under the working title of *Idiophone*. As he told *Record Collector*, "I always have two or three vague ideas for titles when I'm working on something. When I wrote the notes for *The Juliet Letters* I put some red herrings in there – like I referred to 'my most recent touring ensemble, The Conquered Dogs' and there was no such band." The same applied with *Idiophone*, in which Elvis seemed to be feeling his way in the dark, especially after the critical mawling dished out to *Mighty Like A Rose*. In such circumstances, it is always best to go back to old familiar places or people, and this is exactly what Elvis did.

"Originally I went into Pathway Studio on my own, and cut several different songs," he explains. Still exhausted from the world tour, he ended up recording a few basic tracks, plus "the daft instrumental which I eventually called 'Idiophone'. There was also a heavy, distorted affair called 'Poison Letter' which I later carved up – the riff ended up being the foundation of 'My Science Fiction Twin' and words were 'All The Rage' with a completely different tune. So to some extent I was still writing the stuff."

He was using the recording studio as an electronic notebook, or a laboratory bench, and why not? Dylan had written some of his greatest mid sixties songs literally while the musicians sat waiting to record them. Times had changed, though, and Elvis himself needed more back-up. "Some songs needed a more considered approach than I was able to get at Pathway," he says. "And also a piano player, and probably a bass player as well, as opposed to me trying to do it all." Steve Nieve was the first of the old gang to get the call, and came in to play piano on '20% Amnesia'.

Nieve and Pete Thomas had spent the summer of 1992 touring the States with Squeeze. Steve's arm was in a sling throughout, but he filled the Jools Holland slot brilliantly. He also wrote the music for ITV's *The Monarchy* – perhaps an unconscious dig at the would-be King of America – and played some solo gigs, as Maurice Worm. One at McCabe's Guitar Shop opened with 'Fish Girl' which one reviewer mistook as an Elvis impersonation. While the evening proved diverting, "Nieve would do well to check his answering machine to see if Costello has called lately."

It was the beginning of a reunion, although The Attractions did not get a credit as such when much of this material was later re-recorded, and became the basis for *Brutal Youth*, released two years on.

The album that *did* emerge in January 1993 was *The Juliet Letters*, Costello's collaboration with The Brodsky Quartet. It was based on a short item in the morning paper, brought to Elvis's attention by Cait, and headlined "Juliet Of Verona Gets A Lot Of Letters From The Lovelorn". "We don't know how it started exactly," explains Giulio Tamassia, the bespectacled city spokesman for matters relating to Romeo and Juliet, "but one day in the Thirties, these letters started arriving. At a certain point, someone decided Juliet should write back." This year more than 1,000 letters from the lovelorn will arrive in Verona. "They tend to be sentimental." They come from all over – a teenage girl in Guatemala, a businessman in Boston, a high-school teacher in London. Some but not many are written by students in Shakespearean language. About 2% are addressed to Romeo, but Juliet replies.

"Writing the letter itself is really the first step towards solving the problem," says Mr Tamassia, a fifty-nine-year-old retired businessman who wants it known at the outset that he himself is *not* Juliet. He is more her correspondence secretary. "People express feelings that they would never admit to the person they love. Juliet's story inspires them." The immediate comparison I would myself make is with the Internet, barely in operation back then, with the same essential sense of anonymity. The gift which Elvis and his collaborators – two of them, ironically, surnamed Thomas – bring to this bizarre story, almost a hoax, is to invest it with strong narratives and with genuine emotion: it would have been easier to obtain some of the real letters, as found poetry, rather than write them from scratch. For such a complex project, the album's rise to Number Eighteen in the UK was a triumph, though it failed to penetrate the US Top 100.

As Elvis told *Record Collector*, "I went from being able to just write down a melody line, to doing piano music and four-part for strings in six months. Which is apparently pretty quick." He had first heard The Brodsky Quartet in 1989, playing Shostakovich, and for the next two years attended their concerts – playing the classical repertoire: Haydn, Schubert, Beethoven and Bartok. They in turn recognised him, and attended some of *his* concerts. The first formal meeting took part after a lunchtime concert in November 1991, and they "just talked and talked and...talked". Almost immediately he began to play and compose with them: it was like joining a musical family: "Started not to feel the cold so much. Got a haircut and a shave." *The Juliet Letters* was recorded "in a disturbingly tartan room" at Crouch End's Church Studios in late September 1992, having been tested out on selected live audiences. The Brodskys had by now been playing together for twenty years – since their cellist was eleven – and thus already had a shared respect and trust. Michael and Jacqueline are brother and sister: she then married Paul Cassidy. Jacqueline was the first female musician to appear on stage with Elvis on a regular basis; another taboo broken.

The whole experience deepened Costello, literally. "I sing a lot lower – I'm not covered up with a lot of low frequency instruments, so I can make more use of my speaking voice, which makes it sound more intimate. That's another reason why the people who hadn't closed their minds to it in advance realised that it was a very heartfelt piece, that has a lot of personal things in it as well as a lot of universal ideas. The entire piece is about people communicating, or failing to, which is a universal experience. Far from being an elitist or pretentious thing, it's incredibly down to earth."

All this has taught Elvis that he must continue to experiment, or die. "It's not about making everybody love me," he insists. "I don't care about that, I really don't. Not everybody that buys your records can be your friend. You don't love Michael Stipe because you buy his records. You admire him because he turns you on in some way, intellectually, sexually or whatever it is." Nobody is forced to listen. "They know where the door is. My life won't come to an end, and neither will theirs."

As to musical genres, they were creating a new one, all their own. "This is no more my stab at 'classical music' than it is The Brodsky Quartet's first rock 'n' roll album," Costello explains. "It does, however, employ the music which we believe touches whichever part of the being you care to mention." It is interesting that he chose the Brodskys. The Kronos Quartet, say, take a far more radical approach to the notion of a string section, orchestrating Jimi Hendrix tunes full on, and sometimes sounding like an avant-garde rock band with the power suddenly turned off. Elvis wanted something far more traditional.

Neither was this "song cycle" the first attempt to fuse rock and classical music. Van Dyke Parks took that description as a title for an early exercise in (over) ambition. Everyone from Presley and Buddy Holly onwards had orchestral parts added to the basic beat: Phil Spector made a whole career out of a Wagnerian sonic attack. George Martin's classical contacts brought in Dennis Brain for a Beatles session, and added everything from a string quartet on 'Eleanor Rigby', to piccolo on 'Penny Lane', and a huge orchestra portraying the end of the world on 'A Day In The Life'. They also acted as patrons: it was Apple that first brought John Taverner's religious epics to the attention of a mass audience. (Later, The Grateful Dead's charitable foundation was to fund experimental British composers, left to starve by the serialist obsessed Arts Council.)

There was a whole strata of baroque rock, led by the fragile purity of The Left Banke, while in Britain Denny Laine's 1967 era Electric String Band was a brave, failed attempt, which Jeff Lynne copied to huge commercial effect with The Electric Light Orchestra. The young Nick Drake played with a string orchestra while still a Cambridge undergraduate. Such "progressive" fusions gave the genre a bad press, though few would now dare sneer at the Harvest label alone using musical heavyweights like Malcolm Arnold – with Deep Purple – David Munrow – with Shirley And Dolly Collins – or David Bedford, with Roy Harper (and Mike Oldfield, and Kevin Ayers, and…). In turn, the marketing of Nigel Kennedy or even the execrable Liberace learnt much from the pop world, with its hype and disposability.

From Roxy Music and Can onwards, the main thrust of "classical" music into rock has come from the avant-garde: Brian Eno's "Obscure" label gathered some of the most interesting figures from both directions.

Costello is working in a far more traditional way, using musical textures for aural consolation, and irony, rather than trying for new sounds or concepts. As such, he is far closer to mavericks like The High Llamas or The Tindersticks, creating beautiful but troubling sounds.

The rock press had no idea of how to categorise the album. "It has a life of its own, aside from the ordinary way of promotion, and from whether or not somebody who writes for the *Melody Maker* likes it," Elvis admitted. "What does *that* matter. They should be writing about seventeen year olds, not me. I would much prefer it if none of them ever mentioned my name again. Frankly, they *don't* understand what I'm doing." This is unfair, as Allan Jones' piece in the *Melody Maker* is as literate and sympathetic as one would expect from Costello's longest-term champion.

Elvis, like Bob Dylan, like Neil Young, has always been willing to "test the patience of his audience", and rather than return to simple, acerbic pop songs, he has delivered the most uncompromising album of his career. It is daunting and intense, a series of unsent letters which tap into "the secret pathology of the way we communicate". Classical music and the tightness of the concept gives him the "authorial anonymity" he has always craved. It is good too to hear his voice recorded live, with no technical tricks. This is an album that will get better with time, that you can "live with down the years".

NME's Stuart Maconie similarly found "a clear and communicative change for the better", though Elvis's voice veered between "straight tenor, sneery Scouse, standard Americanese or Gilbert and Sullivan frivolity." *Vox*'s Patrick Humphries, though, finds a "farce", which makes you "want to cry for all the wrong reasons". For *The Independent* it is a battle which neither side wins, for *The Guardian*, Elvis's voice cannot cope, and he should have hired "a classical singer, or maybe two". To such criticism, Elvis replies, "I don't want to have my life wasted by that shit. I'm having too much fun."

The Juliet Letters is subtitled "a song sequence for string quartet and voice". The CD booklet features various posed photographs, in serious monochrome, of the quartet in their designer casuals, and Elvis the only one to wear a tie. They circle a draped chair, and look intensely serious, as befits the closing songs of death and resurrection. Elvis holds the score open in front of him.

Words and music are largely written collaboratively, with MacManus responsible for the bulk of the lyrics. They run through a gamut of styles and emotions. Three instrumentals serve as prelude and interludes. The conceptual nature of the whole, and its formal constraint, reminds me of some of Mike Westbrook's epics, or The Art Bears' *Winter Songs*, hugely ambitious, exuding gravitas, lyrically stiff. Whatever this is, it certainly isn't greasy kids' stuff.

'For Other Eyes' is told by a jealous woman, 'Swine' is carved on a gravestone. 'Expert Rites' reworks Juliet's story: Costello almost outdoes Pavarotti in the abandon of his singing. 'Dead Letter' is so called because it has no words: REM built a whole anthology of lost songs on much the same principle. 'I Almost Had A Weakness' is wonderfully rhythmic, and spoken by a bitter old aunt, who is leaving all her money to the RSPCA.

'Why' brings out Elvis's vibrato, in the voice of an abandoned child. 'Who Do You Think You Are' has some of the old Costello bile, in the guise of a jilted lover, but ends with a shiver. It was supposedly written by a "very, very affected man, sitting in a seaside cafe, and bored with life". 'Taking My Life In Your Hands' is an unsent letter, begging a reply, the lyrically crowded 'This Offer Is Unrepeatable' a chain letter, promising eternal life. Both songs take on a more sinister note in the light of the aptly mournful 'Dear Sweet Filthy World', a suicide letter. Juliet, after all, did the same.

In 'The Letter Home', an exile – a priest or nun, perhaps, judging from the address – writes about the death of a childhood friend from New South Wales between the wars. "They start to write a tender letter of condolence, but little by little they get haunted by it." It directly echoes David Accles' 'Montana Song', though without its epic sweep: both deal with pioneers in a new land. 'Jackson, Monk And Rowe' was the family nickname of the Brodskys' cellist, a private joke. It is here employed to describe a young girl grown up, and seeking a divorce, to a rock riff, and a great tune. If only the single version of this had reached the Top Twenty!

'This Sad Burlesque' was written on the eve of the General Election, to no-one in particular, with a PS admitting defeat. The sprightly 'Romeo's Seance' imagines that Romeo does not die, and tries to get in touch with Juliet on the psychic telephone. The lyric supposedly appears on the ouija board. In 'I Thought I'd Write To Juliet' "a very cynical writer, not anything like me, receives a sad and offending note which causes him to think again.. Elvis appears to quote direct from a letter *he* has received from a female soldier preparing for the Gulf War. Costello's singing takes on a manic note, with the strings playing a merry tune: Napoleon XIV, anyone? The Brodskys imitate an air raid alarm at the end, then straight into 'Last Post' a slow air, heavy with sadness.

The suite ends with three utterly devastating songs, composed by Costello alone. 'The First To Leave' could be written by Romeo to Juliet, or Eurydice to Orpheus; the intensity of the music and Costello's impassioned singing suggest far more than a lover's quarrel. It has the same taut simplicity as Romeo's dying speech: to "shake the yoke of inauspicious stars/from this world-wearied flesh."

'Damnation's Cellar' is 'Pills And Soap', set in Juliet's tomb, and sung cheekily. A time machine is being built, so the singer ponders whom to bring back. Shakespeare was adept at counterpointing tragedy with a comic wiseacre – Juilet's nurse or Macbeth's drunken porter – who echoed the main concerns of the play. Same here, as the underlying concern of the whole song cycle is death and resurrection. No Catholic ever escaped their training, and if the previous song was set in Purgatory, then this is Hell. By that token, 'The Birds Will Still Be Singing' is Heaven, or at least glimpses its possibility.

This song has the same unearthly atmosphere as the poems which close Ted Hughes strangest book, *Gaudete*, supposedly the work of a poet who has just returned from the underworld and emerged on the west coast of Ireland. Cello leads us in, then Elvis's voice soars over a shimmer of strings. If anyone ever says he can't sing, just play them this track. It is as if Romeo and Juliet are brought back to life for a second chance: "Banish all decay." In one sense they are, in every new love affair. Nature goes on anyway, whether or not the couple here get back together. In the fullness of time, it doesn't really matter.

Costello was aware of what he had achieved, with his new colleagues. The final song, at least, should endure over the centuries, so one can sympathise with his lack of concern about press reaction. For him, "*The Juliet Letters* has had an independent life which is completely free from the infinitely more conservative and conventional world of rock 'n' roll." It still had to be launched into the media world, however. Even Shakespeare had to endure hostile critics, and the opinions of his audience.

There was a small press gig on 6 January, a champagne buffet at the Orangery in Holland Park followed by selected pieces from the new album, played on a leaf-strewn stage. It was a grey wet day, and Elvis chatted nervously to the sixty industry figures who had turned up, while his wife – apparently unconcerned – read a newspaper. There were grins and warm applause after the performance. Strangely, Elvis's last public appearance in 1993 was in the same place, again with the Brodskys, to receive the Edison award for the best album of 1993, awarded by the MD of WB's Dutch operation.

On 6 February, Van Morrison was playing a gig at the Point Depot in Dublin. Superstars began to appear, like moths in the headlights of a car. Bono came on to sing 'Gloria', then Chrissie Hynde for 'It's All Over Now, Baby Blue', then its composer Bob Dylan, accompanied by Bono, Costello, Stevie Winwood and Kris Kristofferson, who stretched the song out for a good ten minutes. Bono and Elvis shared a mic.

Elvis and The Brodsky Quartet now hit the road for a series of upmarket venues, with ticket prices to match. In less than a calendar month, they played nineteen concerts in ten countries. Elvis's diary read: "In Barcelona perform in exquisite Palau de la Musica only days after appearing at Folies Bergere in Paris and a converted chocolate factory near Pisa. The piece turns out to be both funny and emotional in concert. Some folks bewildered by absence of electric guitars. Others tuning in for the very same reason."

Andrew Mueller took in the first date, at the Royal Concert Hall, Glasgow and found Elvis "caught in the spotlight, no guitar, no microphone". He does a little jig during the "madwoman's tirade" of 'I Almost Had A Weakness', while his vocal is "astonishing" on the show stopper, 'Taking My Life In Your Hands'. The best moments are the ones "that sound like great Elvis Costello ballads arranged for strings". Encores include 'Scarlet Ribbons' – which used to scare the boy Costello – and Kurt Weill's 'Lost In The Stars', but no new Costello numbers. Lights come up on a standing ovation.

Terry Staunton caught the same ensemble at the Theatre Royal, Drury Lane, and was startled to see Elvis holding a hardbound book, holding all the lyrics. The music, though, comes off even better in a live setting, with the "natural frailty" of Elvis's singing only enhancing the songs' drama. The biggest laugh comes during 'Damnation's Cellar', on the line about common humanity preferring the horse Nijinsky to the dancer of the same name. After all, you can bet on the former. A new encore is Jerome Kern's 'They'd Never Believe Me'.

Costello wore red shoes in Denmark, and Jacqueline explained the story behind 'Jacksons, Monk And Rowe'. A drunk shouted abuse from the balcony, and Costello directed the word "bastard" in 'I Almost Had A Weakness' to him. There was a new Costello/Thomas song, 'King Of The Unknown Sea'. The Paris gig reduced Martin Stone, for one, to tears. Robert Hilburn at UCLA's Royce Hall noted that the atmosphere at times was akin to British music hall, with Elvis prefacing each song with a jokey explanation. In Tokyo, they encored with 'God Only Knows', introduced as "a famous old Californian sea shanty".

Plans to release a seven-track live EP of songs performed during the encores drawn from these shows fell through, although a CD single of 'Jacksons, Monk And Rowe' had as an added bonus a fourteen-minute interview drawn from the official video release, itself drawn from the BBC documentary. Elvis describes the way that his voice intersects with the quartet as a "sonic fluke", but stresses that he is not the "leader". This is a quintet, with a human voice as one of the instruments. What comes across is Costello's creative generosity, making both songs and performances a genuine collaboration, and the sense of sudden freedom which the Brodskys feel, through this project. Elvis is amazed that so few classical composers have put a string quartet and singer together. As to the single, *NME* reckoned the strings would not disgrace a "Jim Webb epic", while the album is "everything that Paul McCartney's *Liverpool Oratorio* wasn't". As to the video, the "Brodsky Quartet come over as nice but characterless".

Costello found the English cultural mafia the problem here: "I blame the *Late Show*, that kind of sneering mentality." The programme was shut down soon after, with the musical interludes expanded into *Later*. Abroad was a different matter, with Elvis and the Brodskys making annual trips to this day to the Opera House in Valencia to perform the piece live. Swedish TV regularly repeats the matching video.

The relationship endured. "We've started to do mixed concerts, where we take some of *The Juliet Letters* songs out of context alongside some of my songs and pieces by Tom Waits and Brian Wilson and songs we've composed since the album," he explains. "At the Meltdown Festival, on the South Bank in June 1995, we did stuff with an eleven-piece ensemble, just to get different colours and moods, and to avoid being restricted to the quartet format. It was very much a high-wire act on the night, but it was very exciting." The *Later* special again featured the Brodskys, along with a brass section. Like fine wine, the songs improve with age.

Another spin-off was a commission from Opera For New Ears and the New York Metropolitan Opera, for Costello to write an opera for young people. Steve Nieve followed the same path in 1997, when he wrote music for a ballet, premiered in Paris.

Just as critics began to lock Costello into the pigeonhole of "serious musician", he sidestepped them with an insouciance that was little short of amazing. As lead singer of Transvision Vamp, "dumb blonde" Wendy James had represented the very cheapest form of pop fluff. Mindless crap, in fact, to most people over the age of thirteen. Her debut as a solo artist, the album, *Now Ain't The Time For Your Tears* – a straight steal from one of Dylan's most politicised songs – was revealed to have been completely written for her by Elvis.

The album even made Number Forty-Three in the UK charts. Elvis's lyrics proved to be bitterly ironic, a puppet girl singing about the machinations of the industry which controlled her, and not apparently even seeing the joke. As Allan Jones pointed out in *Melody Maker*, Wendy had only recently told that very paper that she would soon be one of the most popular celebrities in the world (so did Crispian St Peters, and whatever happened to *him*?). Becoming more famous than Madonna and winning an Oscar were merely two of her predictions, all this alongside publicity shots of her touching extremely intimate parts of herself.

Costello's lyrics told "a classic tale of ruthless ambition, betrayal, thwarted desires, manipulation, deceit, humiliation and eventual triumph", all in ten songs. A veritable rock opera, and one written in a few days, during the more serious enterprise of *The Juliet Letters*. Jones found songs that were uncanny echoes of *This Year's Model*, crossed with *Evita*, and not only because the mighty drums of Pete Thomas are again in the driving seat. Wendy James copes better than expected, bringing "an appropriate punky rasp" where required. Sian Pattenden was harsher, finding the singer can only express two emotions, "irritated" or "angry". It is a "sniffle of an album".

This is a little unfair. Wendy James does a perfectly adequate job, not least on the genuinely creepy 'The Nameless One', an abstract, almost avant-garde list of heroes and villains. The matching video features transvestites wearing "the skimpy little numbers" she was famous for wearing. 'Basement Kiss' is one of Costello's finest lyrics, set to a backing straight off *Blonde On Blonde*. A tale of town and country, its upper class heroine (or heroin) is closer to Marianne Faithfull than to Wendy, the whole song redolent of the mid Sixties Rolling Stones. Like Ray Davies' 'Waterloo Sunset', the album is Costello's love letter to London, its excitements and dangers, from Jack "The Hat" McVitie, murdered by the Krays, to high jinks in Belgravia. 'London's Brilliant' was too good a concept not to be recycled on Elvis's next album. If all else fails, play the album at a slower speed, and pretend it's Elvis.

Wendy James was *born* in 1966, the year in which '(I Don't Want To Go To) Chelsea' was set, and given away for adoption. She denied that she had once gone out with Jason Donovan. When Transvision Vamp folded, she sent Elvis a cry for help, asking if he could write her some songs. He agreed, though they had never met, and took his image of her from the media. "It was a challenge," he admits. "She was working with Pete Thomas, and asked him if he thought I'd write her one song to put among all this cartoon punk. I was up for writing a whole album of cartoon punk for her. In double quick time. It would give her a whole story – I always thought she was much more of an actress than a singer anyway. It was a fun way of spending the weekend. My wife and I wrote the words, I wrote all the tunes and it was done. That was the end of it, in more senses than one."

As he told *Record Collector*, he recorded the demos with a heavy cold, so he barely did them justice. "I tended to double-track my vocals so it took away the personality of the voice. It was a weekend's work on my part, well, two days to write the songs, two to record the demos. I had a lot of fun doing it."

Elvis only met Wendy James afterwards, when he went to a U2

concert at Earls Court. She was backstage "in this little tent, sitting across the way from Boris Becker. It was a funny scene. There were all these people who were individually quite well known in their field, but didn't appear to have any social glue. The only glue was the band." She came over to him, still bemused why he had agreed to the project.

"I just wished her luck with it: I knew she had a bit of a challenge on her hands, but that was the whole point. If you go around telling the world that you're going to win an Oscar, then when that doesn't come off, you've got to develop a sense of humour. I can't say she really got the joke all the time, but she did as creditable a job...you know, nobody ever said she was Maria Callas." The album's production, over which he had no say, pushed her vocals too far into the foreground. "If it had been hidden in a trashier sound, the thing might have come off better."

Costello extended his newly public enthusiasm for classical music when he guested that April on Channel 4's *Harry Enfield's Guide To Opera*. Less publicly, he had also been discussing the relicensing of his entire back catalogue. Demon records in the UK and Rykodisc in the US began a major reissue programme, opening with *2 1/2 Years*, an LP-sized, four-CD box which added the El Mocambo live set to his first three albums, all a fan's dream with multiple extra tracks and extensive sleeve notes.

Jeff Rougvie, the Rykodisc projects manager, was interviewed about the project for ECIS. He was delighted to get the job: "Elvis is probably the single most important artist today." He and Costello went through long lists of potential material, and argued their way to a compromise.

Elvis's name is die-cut out of the box lid, over a particularly bug-eyed photo from the years in question. His name gradually stencils itself onto the inner booklet, with dozens of pictures from the era, but not a word added, other than a dedication to the memory of Barney Bubbles. The box set led to all kinds of critical reassessment. Pete Doggett finds the packaging ephemeral, but the music it contains not "quite that easy to throw away". *MM*'s Chris Roberts found "his early grandiloquent emotion cracks like a whip" while Terry Staunton pointed out that two and a half years was now the average time gap between each release "in the lumbering, corporate Nineties". *Vox*'s Patrick Humphries "would have hoped for more". What exactly, the second coming of Jesus?

The wonderfully enthusiastic Andy Kershaw makes a rare appearance in print for *Mojo*, and it's worth the price of the whole magazine. He recalls his dad watching Elvis on TV and commenting, "He looks like he goes to a special school." Along with his mate, the trumpeter Dave Woodhead, Kershaw begins a life of fanaticism. "For five years, Elvis had to face us both, mouthing the words from the front row like a couple of theatre prompters. Our unfamiliarity with newer material could really bugger him up. Woodhead actually subscribed to a Dutch-based newsletter, disturbing in its obsessiveness." Still going to this day, as the ECIS, thanks to the determination of one man, Richard Groothuizen. "Together, we amassed and circulated an archive of bootlegs that could have caused the BPI a seizure."

Kershaw even had a walk-on role during the Wheel tour, bellowing for Hank Williams' 'You Win Again' from the back, but being called onstage once Elvis recognised his voice. He remembers, with embarrassment, introducing Elvis at Live Aid with the words "four eyes, one vision". On the *Old Grey Whistle Test*, Costello sneaked up behind him and placed the King of America's crown on his head: "That night, I was the proudest kid on the planet." By attending the sole English gig on the Almost Blue tour, Kershaw managed to flunk his degree, but it now seems a small price to pay.

After all this, Andy gets down to the box set in question. Here is the "finest songwriter of the age engaging triumphantly with his most accomplished band" seems to say it all.

CHAPTER TWELVE

crown strike

In January 1994, Elvis recorded 'Lost In The Stars' with the Brodskys in Toronto, for a movie score of the music of Kurt Weill, filmed in a derelict factory at twenty-seven degrees below zero. While attending a road show in February in Holland, Elvis's headphones blew up during the soundcheck, and he passed out for a while, though he recovered quickly enough to film two songs from the forthcoming album, solo and acoustic.

The man's rich past was resurrected, yet again, in *The Best Of Elvis Costello – The Man*, just nudging the Top Fifty. Of far greater interest was a new single, 'Sulky Girl', credited to Elvis Costello, but with an A-side featuring Pete Thomas, Steve Nieve and Bruce Thomas. (The lack of alphabetical order here speaks volumes). The cheapskate cover puts Elvis looking like a cat which had just got fed alongside a lipstick kiss, downturned. Backed by Costello shouting a WB Yeats' poem in the style of Tom Waits, and (on CD only) 'Idiophone' – drums clatter, then Zappa-esque horns – the single announced itself as a taster for the forthcoming album *Brutal Youth*, and powered straight into the UK Top Thirty.

Elvis appeared in the weekly "Diary" slot for *The Guardian* on 12 March. He gets a Monday morning phonecall to tell him of the summons to *Top Of The Pops*. "London bound, I torture myself with every report of mighty Tranmere Rovers' cruel cup defeat." You can always tell where someone's heart lies by their choice of football team, and these are the same south-of-the-Mersey strugglers beloved by Half-Man, Half-Biscuit. He plays out a goalless draw on Radio One – "the DJ, a Mr Campbell, affects a sort of matey rudeness and seems disappointed when I have the patience of a saint" – then off for press interviews in Paris. If it's Tuesday, it must be… "Imagine you are dead. What music would you have in your coffin?" is a sample question.

Wednesday brings the *Top Of The Pops* gig. "The greatest combo on the planet arrives to prove it – Steve Nieve from a Japanese tour, Bruce Thomas from his new home in LA, and Pete Thomas from…Sussex." They had previously been banned from the show when Pete played a drum solo on his head. "I get to sing with my voice these days." Afterwards, they roam the corridors of Elstree, searching for stills of Sylvia Sims.

Thursday it's a five-thirty am flight to Milan, for more interviews and a trip on Saturday to the Sistine Chapel. He has to lie down from the shock of its beauty, "Though the feeling remains that restoration gives the appearance of being coloured in by a Masters of the Universe cartoonist with a limited supply of crayons. Another corporate triumph." On Sunday he flies to Brussels, has some mussels and chips on the plane and feels a touch sick. Monday, it's on to Stockholm. 'Pump It Up', continued, except that press receptions and TV studios have replaced sweaty clubs. His overall advice is that singles are a waste of time, "You should save your money and buy this album, then play it until your ears drop off."

After all that effort, 'Sulky Girl' "didn't sell convincingly. Apart from cases of good luck or good timing, most of our sales are going to be on album these days. Then came 'Thirteen Steps Lead Down' for no better reason than there was a video for it." What purchasers *did* gain was a shot of a stern-faced Elvis in horn rims, and a special treat. The four surplus tracks – three on CD, one on vinyl – come from the demos for the Wendy James project. 'Puppet Girl' has an extra edge when sung by Elvis, and 'Basement Kiss' a stately grace, with a twelve-string guitar adding delicacy, just like the harpsichord on the Stones' 'Lady Jane'. 'We Despise You', made thick by his cold, has a surly menace.

Brutal Youth turned out to be a reunion with The Attractions in all but name, and exactly the kind of album which his record company had been waiting for. As Elvis told *Record Collector*, "It's a common way of selling anything." Record companies will always try to associate you with the time in your career when you were deemed to be market leaders. "It was a lazy way out. We were going through the corporate insanity at Warners, which gave the troops much less leeway to be creative. They grabbed hold of the one thing they saw as a saleable feature, which was, hey, the band is back, and they're rockin'. It's a bit of a simplification."

This attempted repositioning, as a kind of "godfather of Grunge", didn't fool anyone. "Magazines like *Spin* said it was a trick, and as a marketing device, it was *purely* a trick. It had nothing to do with us." Even a Warner's employee later asked for "less Guns N'Roses, more *Juliet Letters*"!

Elvis had cut his demos for Wendy James – "the Gwendolen letters" – back at the tiny Pathway Studio, where *My Aim Is True* had been recorded in such piecemeal fashion seventeen years before, and realised it was perfect for "a certain kind of violent music". He liked "the tiny room, the eight-track machine, the old perforated acoustic panels on the wall and the special drum sound". He taped 'Kinder Murder' and '20% Amnesia' there, with Pete Thomas, then, "I got excited" and returned to Dublin to write some new songs. The holy writ of the *Extreme Honey* sleeve notes give the official history, from Elvis's diary: "Six *Brutal Youth* melodies come to me in one day. Now I realise I will need real piano player so call up Steve Nieve, and a real bass player...calling Mr Nick Lowe...and a bigger studio for the extra musicians." Olympic fitted the bill here, and he called up a new production team, Mitchell Froom and Tchad Blake. In the summer of 1993, this line-up cut half the new album, then, "O happy day, bass player Bruce Thomas arrives. First Attractions sessions in over eight years complete the album."

The story told to *Record Collector* is slightly different, like an alternative gospel. Over Christmas, Costello had relistened to the tracks intended for *Idiophone*, then called in Mitchell Froom to lend fresh ears to what had at first been intended as a largely solo effort. "I brought in Nick Lowe to play bass on the tracks that suited him. And the extension of using Mitchell was that he'd been working with Bruce Thomas, and it smoothed the process of getting back with him. I probably wouldn't have made that call if it had been down to me."

They had met up again at a party hosted by Pete Thomas, always the diplomat of the group. "We got along fine, and it seemed the natural thing to use him." The ECIS tells a different story, with Froom pushing Elvis to give Bruce a chance on one track, which he nailed down first take. "Costello agreed that, personal differences aside, Thomas was the best man for the job."

Elvis mixed and matched. "Nick has this great pretence that he can't play anything with more than five chords in it. He prefers songs where he can get a groove figure that goes through all the chord changes. Bruce loves the challenge of trying to thread the same sort of line through a more complex set of changes. In between, I ended up playing bass on 'Kinder Murder' and the bridge of 'Just About Glad', just because the amateur approach seemed to be more appropriate."

Whatever the marketing, the album was far from a cynical move on Elvis's part to recreate the past. "We did *Brutal Youth* because it felt right," he insists. "I never thought any of it sounded remotely like our 1978 sound. It's less dark than *Blood And Chocolate* and much noisier than the earlier stuff. In England, people came to terms with the breadth of it, and it was the biggest selling record we'd ever had in Japan."

Costello found it "amazing that I've managed to be making records for seventeen years. But I have no desire to be seventeen again – I didn't particularly like it the first time. On the other hand, I think it's good to reflect upon the journey you might have taken from the time you were that age." He had tried throughout his career to write "one completely uplifting record about the positive side of life", and so far failed. The working title for the album had been *Crank*, thankfully changed at the last moment. "You don't want to leave people without hope. Let's say I'm suspicious of artificial optimism, although I quite enjoy the real thing."

The reviews bear out this hard-won maturity, though Pete Doggett sneered that the album "restored his favours with the Nick Hornby crowd", ie people of Costello (and presumably Doggett's) age, rather than a bunch of kids. *MM*'s Chris Roberts subbed his piece "Teen Rage Kicks". "The lovers in these deceptively shapely pop songs are exposed, stripped, dissected." Another "bitch of an album from the old dog", like

The Posies, scripted by Martin Amis: "lightning like this you grow into." Over at *NME*, David Quantick hears a man "shouting at you in the voice of Buddy Holly trapped in the larynx of a crow." He is returning to the amphetamined rock of his adolescence, but brings to that noise "something very close to maturity and wisdom". After three increasingly complex albums before, which felt like a slow crawl through molasses, here was a "throat-clearing, snot-spitting spring clean".

Vox's Patrick Humphries found "a humanity" which had gone AWOL, and "a man out of time, and back on track". For *Time Out* it was "emotionally fresh and cynically knowing at the same time", though for *The Sunday Times* he was trying too hard: "an impressive, but ultimately unnecessary, album." Maybe not, for those who don't get them free: I remember my own excitement at the freshness and vibrancy which the old gang could still muster.

The CD booklet, notably lacking a lyric sheet, has instead five photos of Elvis as a young boy – posing in cowboy uniform with a dinky holster, reading the *Dandy*, sunbathing, being cuddled by an older woman of at least eight, and with his arm around a young Jamaican boy, also in a cowboy hat. The grown man, clean shaven and with neat hair again, cradles his cheek onto a guitar, and outstares the camera. The album is dedicated to childhood friends: "It seems like yesterday."

Elvis embarked on a wide range of media interviews for the album, and his comments were sharp and to the point: for a full round up (and attributions) see ECIS 3/94. 'Pony Street' was sparked off by a seven-year-old girl's comment on Guns N'Roses: "I like Axl because he put a cucumber down his trousers." The scenario is the blurring of the generation gap, with fashion stripping teen rebellion of its meaning. "Come on, take your barbiturates, you've got to get into those Spandex trousers and go down to the Rainbow and act like a slut and don't you come back here trying to marry that accountant." Insect tinkling on the (slightly out of tune) ivories, and it's as if Nieve had never been away, with two-thirds of The Attractions wrapping themselves around Elvis's voice like a warm scarf. Matthew MacManus would be nineteen by now, perhaps inspiring this tale of teenage intransigence.

For 'Kinder Murder', Elvis had "this picture of a Norman Tebbit head, a sort of guy who believed any kind of liberal attitude was a disaster" then added to it the story of a soldier picking up a girl, leaving it deliberately unclear whether it is "a rape or just a seduction". The girl then kills the child which results. Sung with apparent indifference by Costello, doubling on bass and thick-toned lead guitar. He relishes the word "knickers" with a lustful chuckle.

'Thirteen Steps Lead Down' was "written after a visit to Escorial, where kings of Spain are buried at the foot of thirteen marble steps", near Franco but with more style. The song parodies the kind of book which promises you twelve steps to happiness: here it is any habit – sex, drugs, emotional blackmail – which repeatedly takes you to perdition. "The girl is in some cheap bondage scene in the first verse, and in the last she's in the bondage of luxury. And nothing really in between except unreliable lovers." The return of Bruce Thomas, and his bass ignites the musical explosion at the end: venomous guitar, fierce drums and psychedelic organ.

Of 'This Is Hell', Costello says, "I think you have to acknowledge that some people would really love hell." As so often, he locates it in a nightclub "when the lights come up and you realise that you've spilt ketchup on your lapel and you're trying to be so suave". A slow burn from the reunited Attractions, and Elvis croons knowingly and in a relaxed fashion about an eternity of *The Sound Of Music*. Bruce Thomas throws in a virtuoso flourish at the end, just to say hello.

'Clown Strike' is "really a very affectionate song", though others have attacked it for its emotional cruelty. "The girl is putting on this entire witchy act. She doesn't need to. She just doesn't have the confidence in her own attractions." Another song about dressing up, sung with exuberance and catchy backing vocals, and a guitar that almost talks. Costello had read a press account of a real clowns' strike at a circus though, this being Elvis, "strike" has a double meaning. Like so much of the album, there is a tunefulness and a sense of relaxation here – both in the music and the writing – which makes it so much more appealing and repeatable a listening experience than *Blood And Chocolate*.

'You Tripped At Every Step' is "about dealing with people who aren't in control of themselves. There's fighting and there's a drink involved but I think the tune tells you there's a lot of love in it." It starts with a wordless soul flourish, and a slowly-told tale of self-destruction, like *Get Happy!!* on valium.

A heavily echoed Elvis on 'Still Too Soon To Know' sounds like his namesake, and the pace has slowed down even further, with piano tinklings. Nashville self-pity, with Elvis's voice at its most dramatic like fingernails scraping down a window pane. "It is useful to look at things with a little bit of distance, but no less heartfelt. That maybe you didn't have the courage to say when you were supposed to be so confessional and so real." A song stripped of the usual irony and sense of verbal surprise, but still not plain enough to touch this listener's heart, for one.

'20% Amnesia' is "about how we've come to accept the unacceptable", and how the unemployed are swept away from view. (Nowadays, its called sickness benefit!) Musically, the pace has picked up to a sluggish anger, with Elvis's voice cracking like an overloaded hi-fi speaker. The band don't seem to have quite enough power to kick the song into overdrive, and sound almost toytown at the end. "I wrote it in little snapshots. It's an argument with somebody at the airport, a stupid pointless crime, somebody standing at the despatch with a brandy in his hand."

There are enough stories behind this song to fuel a novel, which is why it sounds so rushed. He had gone to the opera one night to see a posh version of *Cinderella*, and there was Gorbachev, who had come to Britain to beg for aid. It was a sick joke planned by the Foreign Office. On another occasion, he was trapped in an airport lounge with some heavy smokers while trying to protect his voice for a concert that night, and this led to a row with a security guard, who actually asked "what is your destiny", meaning destination. When asked whether the booby "in his bed-time boot-boy jersey/ringing up some fantasy tart" was David Mellor, Elvis refuses to comment, "with a devilish cackle".

'Sulky Girl' is about the "fantasy life of a Stuttgart schoolgirl who courts a scandalous reputation to test her powers". She is the polar opposite of the girl in 'Clown Strike', and the song continues the obsession with subterfuge and disguise which echoes throughout *Brutal Youth*. The Attractions are at their most musically seductive here, with massive bass guitar from Bruce, like a white rasta, and Elvis singing at half power (and thus all the more powerfully). Despite Costello's gloss, this sounds like a real encounter at a rock gig, with the pass-out stamp on her wrist glowing luminously.

'London's Brilliant Parade' was inspired by a moonlit stroll through the city streets with Cait. "If that's indulgent, I don't really care," he pouts. "That song is probably about as close as I'll ever get to writing a sentimental song about the town I was born in. I've never really regarded it as my home town." He sings with a mixture of contempt and nostalgia, with the line about "having the time of my life" particularly ambivalent. The Attractions blend into the aural scenery, there and not there at the same time.

The final verse is his "personal street map", but this is far more than a rhymed A-Z. "I wanted the idea of a guy falling asleep and dreaming about the London of all those groovy movies of the Sixties where everything's possible and everyone's fantastically attractive. Then he wakes up, and he's on Hungerford Bridge." The film is partly *Blow Up*, which features the brief incandescence of a Beck and Page-led Yardbirds having a smashing time in a nightclub built in the studio. The song itself is yet another example of Elvis's horrified regard for the Sixties, which he was just too young to enjoy.

'My Science Fiction Twin' provides a "comical look at the ideals you set yourself". It is about the imaginary friend many of us have as children, and satirises the grown up impulse to believe "there is another 'you' who can achieve anything. I could still have ended up living in Weybridge with a creation of the plastic surgeon." Or even *as* the same. After all that, the actual song is undistinguished, probably because it lacks a tune, simply running up and down the scale. There's a good riff, though, and some strange noises at the end.

'Rocking Horse Road' opens with stereo drums, and the kind of opening lines – sung in a high glide, like Marvin Gaye – which send chills right down your spine. The road in question is to be found in New Brighton, a peninsula near Christchurch in New Zealand. Elvis had been drawn there because it shared its name with the Liverpool resort where he spent his childhood summers. Sunstroke led to his stumbling through the local suburbs gripped by panic. "It just became the twilight zone. This perfectly benign suburban road became somehow really terrifying. People rode by on bicycles – then vanished.

Just my imagination probably."

Nieve captures this unease in his Hammer Horror keyboards – they break out suddenly in the middle section – and the song ends on a downward track, with Elvis doing a Van Morrison and endlessly repeating the same phrases. Indeed, this song – and album – has more than a touch of the charged recollections which fuel *Astral Weeks*. The song title suggests a return to childhood, though the situation is also possibly fuelled by Sixties cult TV like *The Avengers* where the most cosy of settings suddenly turn unusual. "That could have been the life I aspired to as a schoolboy, to have a nice house on a nice street." As if he doesn't!

'Just About Glad' has a Merseybeat swing to it, and deals with "a guy looking back at when he was twenty-one, when he thought he was a great lad." Much like young Declan MacManus, in fact. The music therefore mimes what he would have been listening to in the early Seventies, with Nick Lowe imitating Ronnie Lane's bass lines in The Faces, and Elvis himself Rod Stewart's cockiness. Not that Rod would ever confess to *not* having an affair. He would never have sung about "knickers" (for the second time on the album) with such lubricity, either, unless they were his own.

'All The Rage' is about "that function involving paper, ink and opinion", ie songwriting or – more likely – critical comment on the same. "Costello accuses himself of excessive anger" shock. Elvis counts in a Fifties-style smoocher, with words of bile and a good tune. The bridge is "the closest to a personal statement that this album has": "spare me the drone of your advice." But who is he talking to?

'Favourite Hour' deals on the surface about the gross details of a state execution, a subject which fuels Roy Harper's 'Hangman' for real: when in prison, Harper heard men being led to their appointed deaths. Oddly, Costello does not mention the ostensible subject, but says that the song is about "the options that have come up and gone away. One of them was college life: I never did that. When I was at Dartington, I saw a chapel which was now a music hall, beautiful trees and gardens with Henry Moore sculptures we stumbled on in the woods. I thought, 'This could have been the life I had.'" The final verse is deliberately trite, as if translated from German lieder: "It's all about babbling brooks and such."

An ominous piano chord, then Elvis comes in, and comes over all funereal, then builds to a climax. There is a well of sadness in his voice, but the words are too self-centred to be truly moving, though if this song isn't personal, I don't know what is. By containing the album's title, the song encapsulates *Brutal Youth*, a stuff that will not endure. Time drips away, like a Dali watch. We are all on death row.

Costello's media blitz that Spring was given extra impetus by public reaction to the album, "as vicious a state-of-the-decaying-nation address as anybody could hope for". He told *GQ*, one of the new men's style magazines, that he couldn't cross Hungerford footbridge on his own, "because heights put his equilibrium to flight". (The heroic character played by Michael Palin in *GBH* has the same problem: maybe Bleasdale based him on Elvis.) As to *GQ* itself, "How the fuck I get to be in it, I don't know."

Q is a different matter, part of his natural constituency. Maintaining steady eye contact, he tells Adrian Deevoy that he dislikes lyric sheets: "I much preferred REM before they started giving you the words." Ditto PJ Harvey. The albums he had most liked recently were all by women: "The guys are just boring at the moment, the young guys more boring than anyone." As for techno music, "I don't go to those places, why should I bother to buy the record. He certainly doesn't want to become a middle-aged trendy, "One of those people who turns up with the baseball hat on the wrong way round."

He submitted himself to *Wire*'s "Invisible Jukebox" slot in March, and successfully identifies the Brodskys, and Hank Williams after the first bar (from the "scrapy fiddle sound"). Like Billie Holiday, Hank had "next to no voice", with very little range and a one dimensional tone, but it acts like a "laser beam" on the listener: you cannot *not* listen. He only heard the *Basement Tapes* when they were commercially released – "I never bought bootlegs" – and had seen Dylan at the tail end of 1993. "I could not believe what I was hearing. Every line counted, every word seemed to be measured."

Costello went back into the studio to record some tracks for *Family*, a TV play written by Roddy Doyle, of *The Commitments* fame. These included a cover version of Cilla Black's hit single 'Step Inside Love'! *Get Happy!!* and *Trust* were the next albums in line for updating on CD, and drew high praise. Reviewers merely bickered about which was the better of the two, and noted how good The Attractions had been, "facilitative, tough and light."

No wonder, then, about the ecstatic reaction when on 1 April they got back together to play 'Thirteen Steps' live on the David Letterman show. It was the prelude to a seven-month world tour, "playing the violent end of *Brutal Youth* plus songs from previous seventeen years. Sometimes we play louder than you can think. Three months after the tour my ears stopped ringing." Rehearsals took place at the tiny Vogue Theatre in Vancouver, with the tour starting at the Orpheum, just down the road. Elvis had undergone some professional voice training, so his vocal pipes held out for the whole tour, this time round. Just as well, with thirty-three concerts – mainly "outdoor sheds" – in North America alone. The support act were Canadian band The Crash Test Dummies, outselling Costello at the time, but almost forgotten now.

Reviewers welcomed back the old, tough Elvis. He ripped straight into a fast-paced set – around thirty songs in two hours – mixing *Brutal Youth* with older songs, so that 'Thirteen Steps' segued into 'Radio Radio'. The effect was "at once reassuring and oddly nostalgic". Some found The Attractions "vibrant", others that the band had become "flasher and fussier", and the set "a greatest hits revue – and nothing more". All were agreed that Elvis himself was "relaxed, indefatigable: there wasn't a trace of archness or artiness in sight."

From the clutch of the CDs to emerge, I would describe the shows as showing routine brilliance. Girl punk band Bikini Kill were played over the PA, driving many punters to the bar: the band themselves designed a tour T-shirt, "More Than You Deserve", but this was now a vain hope rather than a boast. Elvis's mother was flown over for a Mother's Day show at Concord, when the band started to really fire. In Santa Barbara, some "obnoxious" students in the front row were thanked with an encore of 'This Is Hell'. The San Diego gig was interrupted every few minutes by the roar of jets landing at the adjacent airport! East coast gigs saw great music, but muted crowds. Elvis himself reckoned that Minneapolis was the best night of the tour so far, so it's just as well that it appears in its entirety on the *So Like Candy* double CD. In Maryland, he dedicated '*Dublin's* Brilliant Parade' to the Irish football team, doing well in the world cup.

While in the States, as his "buddy from Britain", and heavy on the vibrato, Elvis duetted with Tony Bennett – whose style was more closely associated with MacManus senior – on 'They Can't Take That Away From Me', for *MTV Unplugged*. "They'll be like brand-new records for the young people," the veteran crooner cannily explained. Elvis also sang 'Full Force Gale' on *No Prima Donna*, a tribute album to Van Morrison, with songs and guests *chosen* by Van Morrison.

Now that he had learnt to write music, and do his own orchestration, commissions like the recent one to compose a song for Robert Altman's movie *Short Cuts* were flooding in. He did remind *Q* that 'Accidents Will Happen' is on the soundtrack of *ET*: "One of the characters sings it for about eight seconds while opening the fridge door." He was much influenced by Nino Roto, who scored *La Dolce Vita* and *The Godfather*.

In the same issue, Radiohead's Thom Yorke named 'I'll Wear It Proudly' as the record that changed his life – "It's really upsetting, but I feel better afterwards, which is my ideal ingredient for a song." Elvis's contribution to the same item is David Accles' 'Down River'. When he was about fifteen, he used to play Accles' first two Electra albums in his room and listen "avidly" to their tales of men in prison, Vietnam vets handing out pornographic pictures to ruin children's lives, mainline saloons and other delights: "He had a very dark, deep, kind of older man's voice." Accles, crazily obscure to this day, makes Leonard Cohen sound like a sunbeam skipping through Disneyland.

There was no respite from the road. Before some heavy duty gigs in Europe, Costello and The Attractions played the Glastonbury Festival on 25 June, their first British gig for seven years. Elvis referred to them carefully as "these gentlemen on stage with me", never by their collective noun. He also told the audience they could take their clothes off, as the gig was not being televised. "If you come to Glastonbury, you have to be prepared to get sun on your head, and mud on your feet. This isn't for armchair hippies." Gavin Martin described his set as a "crowd pleasing carnival jukebox". The bootleg CDs boast a boomy sound, but added edge to the early American shows, with The Attractions interjecting more of their own personalities. The Kinks' mysterious 'See My Friends' is interjected into 'Man Out Of Time'.

Elvis played a speedy set at Roskilde – like "a hungry twenty-two-year-old, angry as on pills" – then came back for three concerts at the Royal Albert Hall. Reviewers saw a baggy-suited Elvis welcome everyone to "the first night of the Proms". *NME*'s Johnny Cigarettes was taken aback by "a mean, vein-rupturing Costello tearing his heart out"; now that his beard was on a barber's floor, "The orchestra have gone off touring Siberia, and the craggy Attractions have crawled out from under Ford Escorts." Steve Nieve played the grand RAH organ on 'Favourite Hour'.

The band then played much the same set for more dates in Europe, including Rome's Foro Italico, source of the magnificent soundboard bootleg *Buddy Holly On Acid*. A snatch of 'Wild Thing' prefaces 'Rockin Horse Road', and 'Less Than Zero' – of *all* songs – is now a singalong. Elvis chats away in fluent Italian, to polite applause. He also dedicates the show to Pete – "multo courageo" – who had ignored a doctor's advice and insisted on playing. Once he was recovered it was on to Japan for nine concerts, including Hiroshima. Costello inserted "string-breaking noise guitar solos", in the mould of Neil Young, and the light show glowed a different colour for each song. Perversely, the band had decided to play some songs never before attempted live – before an audience least likely to be able to translate them – so the likes of 'Human Hands' appear as if from nowhere.

As the tour wound down, in late September, Costello broke from his long-time manager Jake Riviera, after seventeen years, longer than most marriages. To fill the vacancy, he took things into his own hands, setting up his own *By Eleven* company. Rykodisc released yet another set of career highlights that autumn. *The Very Best Of Elvis Costello And The Attractions* peaked at a modest Number Fifty-Seven in the UK. A new CD single, 'London's Brilliant Parade', debuted at Forty-Eight in the singles chart, with a charming sleeve, a snaking row of children's toys.

Costello had wanted it released, without considering economics, in "much the same way that I wanted 'Tramp The Dirt Down' to come out of *Spike*, and was stopped by the record company because of the politics of it. Certain songs should be singles, just so they appear on the radio, however slight the possibility that they'll sell. I no longer have any vanity about whether records chart. The days of our consistent chart presence are long gone."

By late 1994, his on-stage grumpiness was the equal of the 1978 tour. "I got sick on the road. I'd just split from my manager, Jake Riviera, and I decided the healthiest thing was to prove I could still function professionally without him. Plus, I wanted to promote 'London's Brilliant Parade'. This he did with a twenty-one-gig British tour, with Cast as support act, plus four concerts at the Shepherd's Bush Empire, with Difford and Tilbrook. The tape on the PA this time around was a reading from the appalling *Princess In Love*. *MM* found Costello "roughly as predictable as a cornered mongoose". In an evening of bare-knuckled savagery, events open with 'I Want You', "a seething version which induces a feeling much like having your heart removed from your chest with a spoon, and ends with an apocalyptic assault on his fretboard."

NME's Paul Moody saw instead a man "barrel-chested and perspiring, bashing away at his Fender like some frustrated teenager in a suburban bedroom. As to the band, Pete is all spidery arms and machine gun rolls" and a long-haired Nieve ebbs "back and forth behind the organ, crunching out the melodies". The Attractions sound "as dark and desperate as ever". This is certainly borne out by the *I Never Talked To Jim Reeves* 2CD bootleg, which reveals a savagery and sense of dread missing from the earlier shows. 'I Want You' makes a good curtain raiser for this new mood, and Elvis interpolates a snatch of 'Say A Little Prayer For You', though the line about putting on makeup does not match hard man Jackie Leven's startling revival of the same song.

Elvis jokingly reminisces, about "those balmy afternoons, toasting an undergraduate on the fire". The version of '(I Don't Want To Go To) Chelsea' is as venomous as any version played in the late Seventies, winding down at the end like the last thrashings of a dying beast. Bruce Thomas looked "as miserable as sin" throughout, as he always had done, while Elvis was struggling with a heavy cold, which concentrated his voice down to its rough essence. After missing one gig, he explained at the next that he had left his sick bed, just in case Virginia Bottomley tried to close it! This was rapidly becoming the kind of tour you remember all your life, but as is usually the way with such, there were few "sold out" signs. Songs from the next album began to surface: 'Poor Fractured Atlas' and 'I Want To Vanish', accompanied only by Nieve. As to the average audience age, Mark Perry noted how "reflections of the purple stage lighting glowed from a liberal sprinkling of bald pates". And that was just the men.

Half-way through 'Clown Strike', Elvis talks through a strange narrative about a girl asking a man to come and see her trampolene. As she tapdances onto the window-sill, he shouts out, "Stop!" and tells her that she doesn't have to do all these things to make him love her. At the end he duels on guitar with Nieve, who then launches into a flight of "keyboard fancy", improvising on 'My Favourite Things' in the manner of Coltrane rather than Julie Andrews. His employer stands open mouthed. "What can you say to that?" he asks the crowd, when Nieve has worked himself to a dead stop, then they end the song on a brief snatch of The Doors' 'Break On Through'. Elvis later got into a rage when he failed to get the audience to its feet, changing the words of one encore to "you can't stand up for sitting down", and a final, half whispered, "God help you." And God help Elvis, who didn't have to face the same determined security guards, who threw anyone who attempted to dance right back in their seats.

The BBC broadcast a spirited *In Concert*, from the Barrowlands. Costello ended his world tour in Dublin, at the Point, "But it was like neither he nor his audience wanted it to stop." 'Pump It Up' brought the night – and Elvis's musical year – to a close "at fever pitch". Talking to Radio One's Simon Mayo in November, he suddenly remembers Sister Mary Cecilia, his old headmistress, and refuses to confess anything, other than that he recently shared a microphone with his father at a Joe Loss memorial show, and that Cait is a "cute redhead". He does reveal an unusual form of cross-marketing, with WB drawing on the same historical period for extra tracks on his CD singles as the relevant Demon reissue currently on new release.

Even more interesting was the CD single of 'You Tripped At Every Step', with otherwise unavailable versions of two Lennon/McCartney compositions, and Titus Turner's 'Sticks And Stones'. "We are our own little music supermarket for the next few weeks."

Next up on Demon were augmented retreads of *Imperial Bedroom* and *Almost Blue*. Michele Kirsch in *Vox* reckoned that both releases "collectively rubbish the notion that there can ever be too much of a good thing".

1995 opened with the centenary edition of *Q* magazine, and a guest interview with Elvis about his writing methods. On tour, he still writes songs "crouched in cupboards", and once had to buy a dictaphone to write down a tune that had come into his head. "There was muzak playing and I stood there with my fingers in my ears singing my bit of melody while they put the batteries in." He has also been known to stand in an open phone box, singing to his own answer-phone. A few months later, he wrote a song with Burt Bacharach "using fax and answer machine messages". Elvis starts a new song by writing phrases from his notebooks and rough jottings onto a large sketch pad, to see what pattern emerges. He enjoys life in Dublin, where, "I can make as much noise as I want to," and has finally learnt how to drive. As to being forty, he got fed up "with everybody ringing me up to ask what I was doing to celebrate". He doesn't drink milk, and he spent Christmas in the Caribbean.

January saw a working holiday, when he rejoined the Brodskys for five concerts in central Spain with *The Juliet Letters*. Two months later, his latest classical composition, 'Put Away Forbidden Playthings', was given its premiere by the countertenor Michael Chance and the viol consort Fretwork. It was part of a South Bank special, to mark the Purcell tercentenary, with contemporary composers asked to respond to the inventiveness of Purcell's 1680 viol *Fantasias*. Elvis's piece came at the end of a three-hour concert. The "loveliest" of these reinterpretations, it began with simple upward scales, with at its harmonic centre, "a ballad to lyrics of Costello's own, playing on words and alliterations in the manner of Purcell. This seemed a genuine homage."

On 23 March, Elvis and the Brodskys joined Paul McCartney for a benefit concert at St James Palace, "in front of alleged next king of England and flush pals", with all proceeds going to the Royal College of Music. Prince Charles had already been spoofed in the video for 'Everyday I Write The Book': the 300-strong audience had reputed each made a minimum donation of £250 to get in. McCartney introduced "another friend of mine", who sang 'I Almost Had a Weakness' and a particularly tender 'The Birds Will Still Be Singing', about characters "a picture or two short of a gallery". Costello then joined him for acoustic duets on 'Mistress And Maid' and 'One After 909', their first ever live appearance together. Elvis admitted that his own musical education came through listening to Paul, when he was still a Beatle.

The Brodskys also backed McCartney, reinterpreting such classics as 'Yesterday' and 'Eleanor Rigby': the evening had already seen the ex-Beatles' first classical work, *The Leaf*. Prince Charles unexpectedly wandered onto the stage to present Paul with a Fellowship of the Royal College of Music: fit reward for the smallest paying audience he had performed to for thirty years.

Over the next few weeks, Elvis appeared unannounced as the support act for Bob Dylan concerts in Paris, London and Dublin: forty-five minutes, around a dozen songs and an encore. This gave him the chance to air many of the songs from the forthcoming *All This Useless Beauty*. In the starkness of a live solo setting, the power of Costello's songs and voice come through at warp factor nine, as two live bootleg CDs attest. In Paris, 'Indoor Fireworks' was a highlight, "sung with the kind of voice Bob Dylan would like to recover". As to Dylan, for whom the Brixton concerts in particular marked the beginning of his artistic resurgence, "Him and Neil Young are people are I'm very encouraged by, they still make a huge effort. You know what it is? They haven't settled for a safe version of themselves the way a lot of artists have."

As he said on stage, "Isn't it great, I'm supporting *Bob Dylan.*"

John Harris reckoned that Costello, dressed in his usual poolhall red and black, "is the kind of figure who would have been unthinkable in a world that hadn't already played host to the headliner". Elvis later joined Bob for an encore of 'I Shall Be Released', which in Dublin saw the far-from-well Dylan accidentally send Carole King crashing eight feet into the orchestra pit, when he hugged her too tightly!

In May, Costello played 'Radio Sweetheart'/'Jackie Wilson Said' and 'Please Stay' to 350,000 people at the Primomaggio Festival in Rome, then joined his early hero Robbie Robertson to reprise 'I Shall Be Released'. As he commented, he "just happened" to know the words. The latest brace of Demon reissues appeared that same month. *Q* reviewed *Punch The Clock* and *Goodbye Cruel World* as "representing a time when his muse had largely deserted him", but praised the "generous portion" of extra tracks, and Elvis's honesty in his liner notes. Rykodisc's Jeff Rougvie was disappointed that the *Hello Cruel World* live bonus disc would not now be appearing. Augmented versions of *King Of America* and *Blood And Chocolate* would complete the reissue programme, as they did.

Elvis himself talked to Terry Staunton in May, having just appeared at half time as a guest celebrity on Channel 4's *Football Italia*. He talked largely about corporate politics – "With a major record company, it's a bit like circling over Heathrow waiting to land, sometimes it just isn't your turn to have a record out." He ends the interview smiling, though. A few hours later, he appears on *Fantasy Football League* alongside his old Liverpool hero Alan Hansen, "the only one on TV who talks any sense about football".

Despite – or because of – "too much advertising", Costello's five-year-old album of cover versions entered the UK charts at Number Twenty-One. *Kojak Variety* was the name of a department store in Barbados, close to the studio. The CD added two tracks to the most common bootleg in circulation, as well as scholarly footnotes from Professor Costello. "This is a record of some of my favourite songs performed with some of my favourite musicians." A fan's eye view of rock history, taking the byways rather than the main routes. He recalls with nostalgia his favoured record stores, from Potters Music in Richmond, to Probe "where I stumbled through a teenage crisis brought on by trying to like psychedelic music" on to Rock On in Camden Town, and Village Music, in Mill Valley, California. He looks forward to recording Volume Two "sometime in the next millennium".

The general consensus is that, like The Beatles' *Let It Be*, this album should have remained in the record company archives. It has the rough and ready sound of a bootleg, with a shouted intro and a false start into the opening track, 'Strange'. Pleasant as the record is, Elvis rarely transcends the originals. Considering the wealth of live material as yet unreleased, this seemed a strange choice to pick on, rather like CBS issuing outtakes from *Self Portrait* rather than Dylan at the Albert Hall in 1966. At least that can be taken as a threat to the errant superstar to sign a new contract, and it worked.

In *Melody Maker*, Andrew Mueller took a more charitable view. The album is an "engaging detour": the general effect "almost of random excerpts leaping from the pages of Costello's famously encyclopedic knowledge of music". At its best, as on 'I Threw It All Away', Elvis sings with "due impassioned tremble". The album falls flat on the faster tracks, where "Costello allows his pub-rock past to come back and haunt us". Rob Sheffield thought that, "Costello never lets himself have such a good time singing his own songs", while *The Guardian*, god forbid, that, "Elvis ought to do more covers and fewer of his own." *The Times* thundered that there is "a curiously reductive quality to Costello's performances…you hum it mate, he'll play it."

As he did in a showcase performance that same month at the Shepherd's Bush Empire, broadcast live via satellite TV to US alternative radio. The Attractions were joined by Marc Ribot and James Burton. Elvis writes of a "transatlantic radio disaster when voice departs in mid show, after stupidly singing 'Bama Lama Bama Loo' in front of Little Richard in Arctic TV studio conditions on the previous day". This is not too evident on the bootleg CD, but neither is any great excitement. Max Bell reported on the "samey quality of the delivery", delivered to a crowd who talked throughout, and pepped up only by Burton's guitar breaks. "A labour of love, accent on the word labour." The night only catches fire on an impassioned version of 'Alison'. *MM's Taylor* recoiled in horror. "I'm locked in with a couple of hundred music teachers in elephant cords and – ha ha ha – *I would rather be anywhere else than here today*. To take this man seriously would be to sink to his level."

And he got in free!

A few hours after the concert, Costello talked – or rather tapped – live on the Internet to American subscribers to *America On-Line* and *Compuserve*. How does he view his audience? "With a long telescope." What is your best advice to young musicians? "Speak loud, and carry a big stick." He claims to be "sexier than Bruce Willis", and would choose to change places with Madonna. Macbeth is his favourite Shakespeare character. What is more satisfying, a great night of making love, or a great night of making music? "Isn't it the same thing?"

Costello pursued this skein of thought on Radio Three, when he played some of his favourite classical recordings, taking culture to the citadel. He mixes in Miles Davis and Jeff Buckley, and reveals that his favourite recordings struggle to contain the music they carry. Of Stravinsky's 'Le Marche Royal', conducted by the composer himself, "It sounds as if the musicians are clinging on by the skin of their teeth." A few days later, he collected the award for "Outstanding Contemporary Song Collection" at the Ivor Novello Awards in London.

The young rebel was not at the heart of the musical establishment, and had been approached – in the way of such things – to direct that year's eight-day South Bank Meltdown Festival at the Royal Festival Hall. "You may hear things you've never heard before, and things you've heard before in an entirely different way," Elvis announced in the programme. Costello himself sang over fifty different songs "during numerous performances", including a short set with Bill Frisell, recorded for a subsequent live album. Frisell played "a very modern-looking guitar with hardly any body and no head". He also premiered a short orchestral overture, *Edge Of Ugly*.

As Elvis told *Record Collector*, "We did stuff with an eleven-piece ensemble, just to get different colours and moods, and to avoid being restricted to the quartet format. It was very much a high wire act on the night, but it was very exciting. You've got to be willing to take the risk, and not settle for the easy round of applause you'll get by doing a very popular song. At the Meltdown I did some well-known songs, but got away from relying on the fact that I automatically would be singing 'Good Year For The Roses' or 'Watching The Detectives' at the end of the night to a situation where I might not be singing any of those things." This was in the spirit of the whole Festival, breaking down the musical boundaries.

Elvis also hosted the Celluloid Meltdown at the National Film Theatre, showing some of his favourite movies from *A Hard Day's Night* to *This Is Spinal Tap*, the reggae thriller *The Harder They Come* to the Marx Brothers' most extreme flight of fancy, *Duck Soup*.

The guest list chosen by Elvis at the Festival and Queen Elizabeth Halls formed a kaleidoscope of different musics: old colleagues Steve Nieve, Marc Ribot and The Brodsky Quartet, ensembles – from The Rebirth Brass band to the London Philharmonic Composers' Ensemble, the Donal Lunny band to the London Saxophonic Orchestra – and future musical collaborators John Harle, The Fairfield Four and The Jazz Passengers with Debbie Harry. The Fairfield Four were particularly magical. They might have looked at first like a comedy act, but their *a cappella* singing would make "a cynical atheist sing hallelujah"! Their backing of Elvis on his "most personal song to date", 'That Day Is Done' (about his grandmother's funeral) was heart rending.

Costello seemed to single out musical mavericks: the blind street musician and symphonic composer Moondog, free range jazz pianist Keith Tippett, Danny Thompson – for so long exploring the gaps between folk, jazz and world music, and now working with mystical poet Aidan Dun – the chilling June Tabor and oddball steel guitarist BJ Cole. The greatest discovery was the brief flame of Jeff Buckley, a man whose voice – like his father's – could reduce a whole audience to tears with its sheer emotion.

Friday saw Gaelic band Anuna – their "cacophony" singing was among the week's highlights – supported by The All-Star Irish Band, with Elvis as guest vocalist and led by Donal Lunny. As an encore, Costello sang 'She Moved Through The Fair' with the headliners. "The Song", the final concert, did not end until one am: where else could one find Tabor, Buckley and opera singer Patricia Rozario on the same bill? The last named sang two Costello/Woolrich compositions, 'Punctured Dreams' and 'Malicious Observer', backed by the Composers' Ensemble, and preceded by Elvis reading the words. Like a small boy, he raced from concert to concert, appearing modestly as himself.

Later that same day, Elvis flew off to the Roskilde Festival, where he was the headlining act on the Green Stage, playing three songs with The Jazz Passengers featuring Debbie Harry – they duetted on 'One Way Or Another' – and a forty-five-minute set with The Brodsky Quartet. Luka Bloom – Christie Moore's brother – played a short set, then, with a hybrid of The Attractions, Mark Ribot and James Burton, Elvis performed songs old and new, including a short selection from *Kojak Variety* and the still forthcoming *Brutal Youth*, and culminating with 'Pump It Up'. Elvis seemed in a hurry to curtail to leave. "Fall down for two weeks," is the curt entry in his diary.

He now spent some time at home, rehearsing his new songs. His next public performance was at the Cambridge Folk Festival, at Cherry Hinton Hall. His set was "interesting but largely uneventful", in intense summer heat. He compared the place to a sauna, and played 'St Stephen's Day Murder', "a Christmas song to cool us all down". He was less successful in getting the somnambulant crowd to sing along on 'God's Comic", and finished bang on time, at eleven-thirty pm.

Early August saw Elvis reunited with The Attractions – "it's good to be back" was his first onstage comment – and playing a five-night residency at the Beacon Theatre in New York, with They Might Be Giants (which proved a false prophecy) in support. "See living artists at work" read the poster, and there was a definite sense of incompletion on stage, like a public rehearsal. "Tremble and thrill as they whip these tunes into shape like so many wicked lions." "Trapped in time, Costello is forced to reprise his past at the expense of his present," was one press comment, unfair in view of the number of new songs being previewed.

The set included 'God Give Me Strength', written for the soundtrack of Martin Scorsese's movie *Grace Of The Heart*, about the Brill Building songwriters. Live tracks from these shows were used as part of the recording process for the new album, recorded in Dublin over the next couple of months. Each night opened with 'Temptation', featuring Elvis on vocals and hand signals, and Steve Nieve's "lovely and sensitive piano arrangement". The band needed music stands and song sheets for some of the newer material. U2 and Allen Ginsberg were seen in the audience, while Marc Ribot joined in for the final encores. Jon Pareles wrote that Elvis remains a "fierce observer of humanity's failings, with songs that illuminate before they bite".

At the Edmonton Folk Festival, a few days later, Elvis was again solo, and played 'Ship Of Fools' as a tribute to the memory of Jerry Garcia. He really gave himself in a very emotional performance. He didn't say much about it, just, "That's one for the big man." Before the soundcheck he talked briefly to journalists, about how Garcia's songs would endure, "like Hoagy Carmichael, with that whole Americana feel that Robbie Robertson's best songs for The Band conjured up". When they finally met, Garcia was "exactly as I'd always hoped he'd be – full of positive feeling about music, very enthusiastic. Any dark side wasn't displayed to me." They had shared a common passion for jazz saxophonist Sidney Bechet and bluegrass. As to the Festival, he was playing because of the Guinness on offer!

In mid August, *Deep Dead Blue*, the Meltdown set with Bill Frisell, was released by Nonesuch records as a limited edition, a twenty-five-minute mini-album which unnaccountably left out 'Poisoned Rose'. It was certainly a shock to hear Elvis singing lounge jazz, and in particular 'Gigi': surely one of the least likely songs the angry young Stiff would have covered. The few reviews "confirmed that the rock establishment still found it hard to accept any Costello record that doesn't comprise three-minute Beatlesque pop songs", quite rightly in this case. A more comprehensive record of Meltdown would have been a better move, a box set even. What I would now give to hear Jeff Buckley's contributions, for starters.

Meanwhile, *King Of America* was reissued as part of Costello's continuing programme of sorting out his back catalogue. It made Seventy-One in the US. *Blood And Chocolate*, the final link in the chain, was described by *Q* as having "a weight and energy that was sorely lacking from much of the post-Attractions work that followed". It remained a testament to their "garage band" sound.

In November, Elvis joined the Brodskys at St George's in Bristol, with "new arrangements of works by Kurt Weill, Brian Wilson, Tom Waites (sic) and Costello originals", as well as *The Juliet Letters*, now part of the repertoire. The venue was a church converted into a concert hall. There were no musical surprises, but a chatty Elvis joked that, at St James Palace, Prince Charles had laughed "with ears flapping" half way through "I Almost Had A Weakness". Possibly he recognised in the song the eccentricities of his own family.

December saw Steve Nieve playing live at the Knitting Factory, in downtown Manhattan. Less than fifteen people turned up for the late show. Nieve was sporting short hair and a black pullover, looking "rather like an English professor". He began with a "sonorous expression", and opened with extended pieces of "pastoral music", much like Elvis and the Brodskys. At the end, he announced, "I've taken a couple of melodies from my friend Elvis and screwed them together." The result was called 'Shot With His Own Green Shirt'.

Elvis took a holiday, visiting St Petersburg to see the collection of art looted by the Red Army in 1945, and since kept hidden in a secret vault until *glasnost* allowed the current exhibition. "Every incident in 'My Dark Life' occurs during that short trip. The track was recorded in London in one furious fourteen-hour session with Brian Eno. I play piano, guitar and bass while Brian works gadgets and makes ample use of tape machine erase button." *Songs In The Key Of X*, a tribute album to the cult TV show *The X Files*, included this collaboration between Eno and Elvis, both fans. It was later collected on *Extreme Honey*.

On 6 January, 1996, the thirteenth day of Christmas, Sweden's Radio Symphony Orchestra played host to a capacity audience and two, radically different, vocalists: the mezzo-soprano Anne Sofie von Otter and Elvis. The compere announced that the latter had "no singing voice but boy, could he sing". A highly nervous Costello said "a few words to calm my nerves", about mixing together musical formats usually kept well apart.

He began with Bill Frisell's arrangement of *Upon A Veil Of Midnight Blue*, "with good backing from the orchestra", then 'The Birds Will Still Be Singing', newly arranged by Richard Harvey, far heavier than with the Brodskys. After the interval he duetted with von Otter on 'Autumn Leaves', each taking a verse in turn, and accompanied only by piano, as were the jokey 'Baby It's Cold Outside' and 'Without A Song'. Costello returned for a breathtaking 'Lost In The Stars', with a wonderful sustained vibrato note at the end. For encores, the orchestra and both guest singers combined on 'My Ship' – possibly the Walker Brothers classic – and 'Ev'ry Time We Say Goodbye'. Elvis dabbed at his eyes with a hanky: the audience refused to leave!

In January's *Mojo*, *Imperial Bedroom* was voted in at Seventy-Six in the poll of greatest albums of all time. The same issue saw Costello recommend Ron Sexsmith, as having produced the best album of the year: "You could all be listening to it for another twenty." Some old Elvis fans had meanwhile discovered the (minor) joys of John Wesley Harding. He was a Cambridge graduate who took his persona from a Dylan song title, and whose work Elvis was *not* a fan of, though Harding's first, totally solo album appeared on Demon. There, he namechecked the likes of David Blue and Phil Ochs as inspirations, but his first studio set featured both Pete and Bruce Thomas, and many reviewers drew the obvious conclusion.

In March, the *real* Elvis released the soundtrack album of Alan Bleasdale's *Jake's Progress*, again in collaboration with Richard Harvey. *Q* found "the dominant mood veers between melancholy and wistfulness". For 'Grave Dance', one of the characters literally dances on the grave of a man who sexually abused her and who she then bludgeoned to death. The soundtrack features Costello on electric guitar. "It's as if Jimi Hendrix has leapt into the orchestra pit." *Jake's Progress* itself was a genuinely shocking story about a curse foretold, scorned but eventually coming true, with a creepily assured acting debut by the boy playing Jake, the unwitting death-bringer. It also featured Bleasdale's usual repertory company, with Robert Lindsay playing an ex-rock singer, and Andrew Schofield a pretentious, grimy version of the author.

April saw Costello flying around Europe to promote his forthcoming album with some solo TV spots, and reuniting with The Brodsky Quartet at the Tivoli in Copenhagen. It was first announced that Elvis had bronchitis, and was appearing against his doctor's advice. He joked about "being on drugs", to keep him going. Despite claims that the concert would feature new songs from a forthcoming second album together, the only non-*Juliet Letters* material was 'Almost Blue', 'Pills And Soap', and some short instrumental pieces. 'God Only Knows' rounded off the evening.

Early May brought the much heralded release of *All This Useless Beauty*, another album put together conceptually. As Elvis told *Record Collector*, "The songs for this project have been recorded already by other artists, or I originally wrote them with people in mind – they have a history. In some cases, the artists didn't hear what I heard in the songs, and didn't record them." He compared his skills as a songwriter to those of a tailor: "You might have the style but you haven't quite got the cut."

Of the thirty songs originally considered, only four had been previously recorded, two of these by the same artist, June Tabor. "There is usually more than one way to sing a song." Here were the fruits of his maturity, songs he could not possibly have written during his first flash of fame. Reckless youth was not all that he was shedding. These performances "are probably our last performances as a band." If that has now become true, then it is a wonderful valediction.

All This Useless Beauty certainly drew some of the most thoughtful reviews of Elvis's career, generally taken as some kind of overview, though *Rolling Stone* reckoned it as the Nineties' answer to the "brilliance of the old Brill Building catalogue", a pointer to the future.

Roger Morton in *NME* found a "kind of stylist's catalogue, in which Elvis plays *Whose Tune Is It Anyway*, impersonating himself". His "scholastic songwriting formalism" had now dated, in an era of the "mad ramblings" of Shaun Rider, or Oasis's "couldn't give a shit sparkle". Elvis needs once again to step out from behind his disguises.

In *MM*, Daniel Booth found "the frustrated carpenter of rock". His songwriting divides between "a teardrop melancholy and a ramshackle vivacity", both lightened by occasional wit. Voyeurism is imbued with "a sense of playful ambivalence". In *Mojo* Mark Cooper discerned a "vocal *tour de force*: he has never sounded so intimate, so confiding or so contemptuous." The songs deal with issues of masculinity and sexual pride. "There is a newfound sense that Elvis's phrasing is now the equal of his lyrical genius."

The CD booklet spreads the lyrics over a montage of photographs of The Attractions posing in a Paris street, unsmiling, and a *bric a brac* of antiques, old musical instruments – including a curled serpent – china dogs, and a huge wrought iron devil, mouth wide open. The front cover is a wooden statue of a woman, chipped and half stripped: the picture disc has a putti, or cherub in almost blue, playing a stringed instrument. The whole evokes the title, beautiful fragments shored against our ruin.

Its songs share this quality, of briefly perceived delight. 'Other Side Of The Telescope' was co-written with Aimee Mann, "Someone I used to know." It is rich with Catholic imagery, and an *Alice In Wonderland*-like series of expansions and shrinkings. Elvis's voice is at its most abandoned, while Nieve doubles on piano and organ. Baroque, with a nod to Chopin, played in the tropics.

'Little Atoms' opens like Pink Floyd. The words are beyond comprehension, as is the musical quote from Haydn, now the German national anthem. The song seems to deal with St Paul's updated three commandments: hope, faith and charity, with chastity thrown in as an extra, and all four betrayed. The best part is when Elvis suddenly turns on the listener, and his voice suddenly leaps heavenward on the word "I".

'All This Useless Beauty' is – conversely – endlessly deep and lucid, with a classic tune, and subdued backing, sung with sad resolution. Written originally for the dour tones of June Tabor – she recorded it on *Angel Tiger*: all her albums begin with "A" – a woman wishes that her less than perfect husband could be more like the idealised figure in a Renaissance painting. From the reference to Christ, buoyed up by his mother, one supposes this to be a crucifixion scene. In Paris, Elvis once saw, and noted down in his ever present little black book, a woman studying classic art, then "looking at her unlovely late twentieth century specimen". In just the same way, modern politicians imagine they are classical gods, as they chew rump steaks. Modern "civilised" mankind has a brief attention-span: Elvis spent almost three hours admiring one painting by Botticelli. Others he gave one glance, then turned away.

In 'Complicated Shadows', Elvis's biblical attention has moved on to the Day of Judgement. Set in a graveyard, and in a Dylanesque sneer, it was written for Bob's friend Johnny Cash, and Elvis himself describes it as "Cash meeting Judge Dredd". Pete Thomas leads from the drum stool, and the final part comes live from the Beacon, cutting in just after Elvis's voice ends. The track has the same tough streak and vocal harmonies as the Stones' 'Street Fighting Man'.

'Why Can't A Man Stand Alone?' was written for Sam Moore of Sam And Dave, though he failed to record it. It's a bit wordy for straight-forward soul, though the lyrics have an intent steeliness, and a lovely Percy Sledge-like combination of crunchy piano and churchy organ. Elvis's voice zigzags up and down the scales: all that mixing with classical singers is obviously starting to rub off, or maybe like Pete Brown and Boy George he has had some singing lessons. Sin is again the keynote, and there is a Christ-like element to the hero here, standing alone, weighed down by his crown (of thorns?), just as the "tarnished" woman could likewise be Mary Magdalen.

'Distorted Angel' sets a tale of Catholic guilt (again!) to a backing redolent of the mellow side of Steely Dan. Young members of the faith are taught that we each have a personal angel, looking down on us. This is Elvis's *Satanic Verses* therefore, questioning whether this angel is the devil, and if Catholicism were as intolerant at Islam, this and other songs would have brought a fatwah down on his head. Laid-back jazz rock, and The Attractions *swing*. Elvis's falsetto near the end is truly lovely, and along with the keyboard flourishes seems to fly towards heaven.

'Shallow Grave' was co-written with Paul McCartney, and wakes the listener up after the slow luxuriance of the previous two songs. Warped rockabilly, this musical clattering would not be out of place on a Tom Waits album: "a kind of literary circle Cramps" as one reviewer had it. Coincidentally the film of the same name – a precursor of *Trainspotting* with the same Edinburgh setting, the same director and much the same cast – was released at much the same time. Yuppies descend into madness, cutting up the dead body of Keith Allen and turning on each other in a blood-soaked finale. As befits Elvis's resurfaced faith, this song is really more about martyrdom, from Christians in Rome's Arena to Joan of Arc onwards.

'Poor Fractured Atlas' opens with Elvis at his most vocally seductive, and what is almost a waltz, slow and stately. The words are a satire on the men's movement, fuelled by Robert Bly's book *Iron John*, fighting mock battles with paint guns in the woods. Costello turns this into an investigation as to what "man" has actually achieved, punching holes in the ozone layer. It is also a satire on its composer, "waving his withering pencil as if it were a pirate's cutlass". David Sinclair of *The Times* mentioned the musical quote from Beethoven's *Moonlight Sonata* played on Nieve's keyboards, as if an accident. Onstage, Elvis joked, "We thought it was from *Past, Present, Future* by The Shangri Las."

The story of a career girl gone mad, 'Starting To Come To Me' has echoes of 'People's Limousine', and was inspired by Mary Tyler Moore comedies. Steve found a button on his keyboard "that harmonised everything he played in a disgusting way". Again we have a reference to martyrdom, "the sweet smouldering scent". Jesus forgave the woman taken in adultery – "let him without sin cast the first stone" – but Elvis is of a more unforgiving hue.

'You Bowed Down' was written for Roger McGuinn, and is an affectionate tribute to The Byrds, twelve-string strumming and Elvis getting that half sneer, half folkie croon just right. The title sounds like an act of abasement to a king or God, but more likely refers to Elvis's problems with Warner Bros. The middle section is almost psychedelic, the kind of pastiche XTC mastered as the Dukes of Stratosphere, and a nod to Crosby drug excursions like 'Mind Gardens'.

'It's Time' opens with fake vinyl crackle. It's about a since regretted love affair (were this song fact, not fiction, one could guess the name), and designated for Bonnie Raitt. "Those LPs you scratched." The bass line leads, and a near hysterical Elvis follows. The high harmonies could almost be out of the early Kinks, 'Waterloo Sunset' and all, or Spooky Tooth.

Steve Nieve arranged 'I Want To Vanish' for the Brodskys, alongside tinkling piano and Elvis's emotive rendition. Like Christ he faces temptation in the wilderness. Strange lyrics for a rock star, but Costello has largely attained them since the final Attractions tour. He commented that the song might seem bleak on first hearing – or indeed the thousandth – "but the line 'as certain as a lost dog pondering a signpost' might be my motto". A lullabye, to end proceedings.

It was not The Attractions who toured America that May, but a slimmed down duo of Costello and Steve Nieve, on a nine-venue, ten-gig whistle stop tour across the nation. In between the major concerts, and radio interviews, they also played several "meet and greet" mini-events. Pete Thomas attended one at the Roosevelt Hotel, Hollywood – he was in town to record with Sheryl Crow – then the following night appeared for encores at the Troubadour, playing "bongos": a bass drum and a tom tom. Burt Bacharach, Tracey Ullman, Ray Davies and Suzanne Vega were in the audience: tickets had sold out to normal punters in thirty seconds. The duo premiered 'Passionate Fight', a joint composition, and gave the only version of 'Pills And Soap' on the tour, messing up the intro twice.

The previous evening's main show had been at the Ford Theatre, an open air amphitheatre where a deer and its fawn could be seen nibbling on some shrubs, seemingly unconcerned. Elvis played a Martin guitar, and Nieve a Steinway grand piano: Costello opened with a slowed down, solo 'Just About Glad', as if covered by John Lennon. The Fillmore West show has been captured on the *Ageing Gracefully* bootleg, but only those actually present took home a free poster. Bonnie Raitt and nouveau punks Green Day watched Elvis agree a request to play Garcia's 'Ship Of Fools' in *"his"* room. The light crew missed their cue during 'God's Comic', and Elvis quipped that they were trying "not to induce too many acid flashbacks". He also joked about being "interrogated" in Germany by a journalist with the body of Kate Moss and the voice of Laurence Olivier, asking him why he is destroying pop music.

Seattle featured a rare encore of 'Black Sails In The Sunset', and Elvis in a bright orange shirt. He jokingly invited a drunken reveller to, "Come up here while I kick your head in." Chicago premiered 'Unwanted Number', a song about incest. The Supper Club shows – the first of which was broadcast, and subsequently bootlegged as *Between Wisdom And Murder* – were marred by a noisy crowd of rock biz heavies at the bar, whom Elvis berated. He parodied his namesake, singing 'Heart Of Glass', and made even Nieve, who must have seen and heard *everything* laugh. The second show ended, appropriately with 'I Want To Vanish' at one-thirty am. The final show, at Long Island, featured four country numbers, and 'Indoor Fireworks'.

The unplugged setting allowed a chatty Elvis to emerge, and the same applies to an episode of VH1's *Storytellers* show, first aired in mid June. Again accompanied by Nieve, and recorded at the end of the tour, Costello gives priceless insights into the likes of 'Alison', inspired by a lovely young lady working in a supermarket. 'Temptation' was written about Bruce Springsteen in Nashville, 'All The Rage' about a drunken chat with Nick Kent. 'When Winter Comes' was the first song he ever wrote. Highlights from the tour concerts appeared on a subsequent limited edition 5CD set, *For The First Time In America* – adding up to a complete concert. In his notes to *Extreme Honey*, he suggests that this new pairing is far from played out. "Keep an eye on the new duo, I think they'll go far."

Paul Du Noyer interviewed Elvis for *Mojo* in June. He is no slouch at writing new songs, and "I don't plan on getting any more lackadaisical as I get older." He loves getting the details exactly right: something he admires in Jarvis Cocker of Pulp, lines like "there was woodchip on the wall". He is also thinking of deleting his whole back catalogue for the millennium, though surely by then everyone who wants it will already have got it! "I think after a while you've got to get rid of them, throw them away." He also resists fashion. "I hate these late twenties/thirties guys in the music press pretending they're age/class warriors, defending 'Us' against 'Them'. There is no Us and Them. We're all different."

At much the same time, he talked to Keith Cameron from *NME*. He now lives nine miles outside Dublin, satisfying his contrary needs of "peace and quiet or the freedom to make as much noise as I want in three in the morning". He had always lived in mixed communities, in Liverpool and West London, but England's "like wearing a crash helmet that's too small for you". Crushing and claustrophobic. At the age of forty-two, he retains a "novice's enthusiasm. I have no problem being the age I am. I hated being young, it was fucking terrible. I can say, 'Young man,' to people now, it's great."

Also that month, folk diva Norma Waterson – as great a singer as any opera star – covered 'The Birds Will Still Be Singing' on her award-winning, self-titled album. Norma brings out the vocal swoop and fractured rhythms, all translated into a down to earth Yorkshire accent, with Richard Thompson's miraculous acoustic solo adding a jazz tinge.

On 18 June, Elvis recorded the *Later* special – "A Career Review" as it was titled on the ticket, with the quote "don't start me talking, I could talk all night", and with musical support from The Attractions, The Brodsky Quartet and The White City Septet. The show was broadcast on BBC2 on 7 July, with an extended repeat on 12 July, then as a commercial video, *Live: A Case For Song*. Opening with the line "I just don't know how to begin" and closing with 'I Want To Vanish', Elvis sports a dark suit, open polka dot shirt and a scrubby beard. He holds his huge acoustic guitar then smaller electric with quiet authority, and The Attractions crash and clatter behind him.

They too wear dark clothes, bathed in blue light. Nieve crouches over his keyboards, and wears tiny dark glasses: Bruce Thomas doesn't. Elvis begins to sweat early, but what immediately impresses is the way he holds himself onstage. Like Paul Weller, he looks fully assured and at home, totally concentrated. Songs are largely drawn either from the new album or the early years. Clive Langer plays piano on 'Shipbuilding', along with everybody else, but what cuts deepest emotionally is a 'Veronica' with Nieve, and a totally solo 'Indoor Fireworks'. The whole thing is like a rock masterclass,

In July, Costello's newly heightened media profile was augmented with the weekly issue and deletion of four CD singles, each with a different title track from the new album, and featured a different colour negative of the original cover. All four also boasted the same studio take of the throwaway 'Almost Ideal Eyes', and a mixture of live takes, covers by Lush and Sleeper and remixes – one by the sinister, brilliant Tricky. Elvis's voice struggles to emerge from the kind of musical landscape last heard in the film *Eraserhead*, industrial bleeps and weird scrapings. The current craze for extended versions, through trickery in the studio, rather than any further input from the musicians, had arisen with the twelve-inch single, and was largely fuelled by the dance revolution. Not a phenomenon which hugely touched a man who danced onstage like a marionette with a few strings missing, and once wrote a song called 'No Dancing'!

Mojo took a backwards look when its key writers compiled a Top 100 albums (as its readers had done a few months before), and *This Year's Model* came in at Number Sixty-Nine. "We were full of the exports of Russia and Peru," Bruce Thomas now admits, "and full of ourselves." Vodka and cocaine sure beats blood and chocolate anytime.

Meanwhile, it was back on the road. "The last Attractions tour, in the summer of 1996, had many highlights, but I could feel us pulling apart again," the singer recalls. "So after six great nights in London, a rare old Parisian cabaret, the real Royal Court in Liverpool, our tragic Greek debut in Athens, one more time at Barrowlands in Glasgow, the Ryman Auditorium in Nashville, New York, Minneapolis, San Francisco, our first Portland date for over seventeen years, and Seattle it was over to Tokyo, and time to say…Nagoya and out."

The world tour opened close to home, at the National Stadium, Dublin on 26 June. ECIS correspondents were there with notebooks poised, and ready for every nuance. 'Pump It Up' saw Nieve on accordion: the set's rave up was now 'Complicated Shadows', ending literally with an explosion. The Attractions' sound has been redefined in terms of the new album, rockier than before. Elvis is in the finest voice of his career. The next concert was at La Cigale, near the Place Pigalle, the "rare old Parisian cabaret" mentioned by Elvis above. 'Thirteen Steps Lead Down' features a long guitar solo, and a "moods for moderns" rhythm. For some songs, the Thomas duo left the stage, leaving Costello and Nieve to resume their new role as a duo: they also played a handful of European gigs together during the tour.

In Amsterdam, the support act were The Beau Hunks, a kind of updated Bonzos with a repertoire of 1920s slapstick, who had appeared at Meltdown. 'Distorted Angel' segued into a slowed-down '(I Don't Want To Go To) Chelsea'. The main set was dominated by ballads, but he only agreed to come back for a second encore if the audience started dancing, and played some rockier material to suit. Only half the tickets had been sold for the Hamburg show, and Elvis missed out his usual story about being interrogated by a German rock hack.

Four nights in July at the Shepherd's Bush Empire saw well paced and mellow shows lasting for two hours plus, and with Ron Sexsmith as the support act for the final show, one of the greatest Elvis and The Attractions ever played. The crowd howled along with the chorus of an acoustic 'Motel Matches' and songs like 'You Bowed Down' "got the joint jumpin' in a way I haven't seen since 1983's Punch The Clock tour".

One of the two Roundhouse gigs was taped by Greater London Radio: Dele Fadele saw The Attractions as "functional, accomplished and disdainful" and Elvis as a slice of living history. The support act for much of the tour were Jub Jub, a scouse band much influenced by The Beatles: in Liverpool itself a sell-out crowd saw Costello play for a full three hours.

In between the London shows, Elvis jetted over to the Montreux Festival to perform separate sets with The Attractions, The Jazz Passengers and the Brodskys (no new songs, though). He also dashed off to the Dranouter Folk festival with Nieve, receiving "de warme respons van het publiek", and the Stockholm Water Festival the following day. Seeing some hot air balloons approaching during 'Radio Sweetheart', he said that he had always dreamed of having backing singers in sequined dresses – shades of his father – and here they were.

Elvis's mood began to darken during the American leg of the tour, with a growing rift between Bruce Thomas and Cait O'Riordan not helping matters. Lack of sales led to cancellation of two gigs, though their Nashville appearance – in a former church – was spectacular. On 'That Day', Elvis "threw his body into projecting each chorus". In Washington, as a *Beyond Belief* correspondent reported, "Elvis emerged from the smokey darkness like a beacon of light in his now familiar bright, blousey orange shirt and black leather vest." I think that this last garment needs to be translated from the American! A sell out gig at the actual Beacon had one wag shouting, "Elvis for President" and Costello replying he was unable to consume enough pizza.

In August, Elvis and The Attractions were playing live on the *Tonight Show*, when Elvis altered the refrain of 'You Bowed Down' to "I should have never walked back over the bridge that I burned", a reference either to his band or his record label. A new song of that title was the lead track on *Extreme Honey*. He told the show's host, Jay Leno, that, "This could be my last live performance. I'm gonna take a little break for a while and see what happens." And so he did, after a short tour of Japan.

In Tokyo, Elvis dropped in on John Harle, and the two rehearsed together in his hotel room. During the actual concert, Bruce Thomas poured his drink over an over-zealous security guard. A small earthquake preceded the next Tokyo appearance, and "thunderous sounds" marked the intro to 'Man Out Of Time'. It was like something out of *Anthony And Cleopatra*: a glory was departing the earth. In Nagoya, on 15 September, the show started with six songs run together, and a generally untalkative Costello. 'Human Hands' was "a request from Pete who is seventeen today". The third verse of the song was directed straight at Bruce, while Steve "danced a strange dance" as he played accordion on 'Pump It Up'.

After a "frenzied" set, with Elvis howling, "It's over," again and again, the night finished with 'This Year's Girl' and '(What's So Funny) 'Bout Peace, Love And Understanding'. A name check to all three Attractions, then, "Good night. God bless. Sayonara." Elvis appeared afterwards in the car park, dressed in a teddybear cap, and signed autographs. He said goodbye, got into his car, and waved. And that was that.

Autumn also saw the official release of *Never Before, Never Again*, a 5CD set which had already been available as a promo-only item. Both are already collectors' items. The last release with the full Attractions was the title track of the aptly named 'It's Time' CD single, which had a picture of a demented-looking Costello on its front cover, with huge spectacles. 'Life Shrinks' was a new song, with piccolo and drums beating out an extended end piece, like an Ulster rally. The third track featured Paul Riley on bass, so was presumably old stock: it was a cover of Bruce Springsteen's 'Brilliant Disguise'.

Elvis returned home to Dublin and completed work on 'Three Distracted Women': "A set of three songs written for The Brodsky Quartet and the beautiful voice of Anne Sofie von Otter. The piece was performed in Paris in November." His next move was typically unexpected. In late October, Costello was a special guest on tour with classical saxophonist John Harle. *Terror And Magnificence* drew on medieval and Tudor texts. Elvis sang Shakespeare, performing Harle's settings of three songs from *Twelfth Night*. Elvis was now in effect a session singer, like his dad with Joe Loss, though in a more rarefied setting. He even looked and sounded nervous, almost unbelievable after half a lifetime's experience of singing for his supper regularly, to a live audience.

Harle was a classical composer who had also written music for TV ads and the BBC drama series *Silent Witness*. He was also Michael Nyman's regular saxophonist, and played Harrison Birtwistle's sax concerto *Panic* on 1995's *Last Night Of The Proms*. A heavy orchestral dude, certainly, but he revered Elvis: "His voice comes from deep inside his personality. Every single thought that goes through his head is there in his voice."

Harle and Costello discussed their current project on Radio Three. For the composer, "Of all the singer songwriters I know, Declan is the one who has that mysterious kind of electric edge of intensity. The darkness in the words is associated, for me, with Declan's voice." Unlike classically trained singers, Elvis gets involved with the text. He agrees, "The lack of spontaneity that written music demands cuts them off from the spontaneous impulse to sing which must have been the reason they started to train in the first place." For Harle, "The current project could never have been written down, and that's where you have the magic."

The evening's biggest shock was Harle and young jazzer Andy Sheppard duelling saxophones on 'Hunting The Hare'. The thirteen-piece band also included trumpeter Henry Lowther, a particularly sensitive player present on the spirited early Keef Hartley albums, among much else. Costello, in a dark suit and striped tie, sang 'O

Mistress Mine', 'Come Away Death' and 'When I Was A Little Tiny Boy', sweating by the end. He came back for John Dowland's 'Flow My Teares' and – jumping 400 years – his own 'Shipbuilding'. He then sang Sir Philip Sidney's 'The Silent Ground' to a jazz rock accompaniment, and joined the "in the round" Irish singing of 'Rocky Road' with Harle and the other featured vocalist, Sarah Leonard. Elvis also appeared with the viol consort Fretwork, joining in on the song he wrote for them, 'Put Away Forbidden Playthings', and some more songs by John Dowland.

On a lower intellectual plane, *Q* arranged a meeting between Elvis and Justine Frischmann, of Elastica. Elvis was twenty-two when he first had his picture on the front cover of a magazine, Justine one year older. Elvis does reveal that he can't work on a typewriter, and doesn't like to see his words written down, even on an album sleeve. He sees his work aurally, not as words on a page (which is probably how he remembers so many different songs).

It certainly worked. In November, Elvis received the same magazine's Best Songwriter award at the Park Lane Hotel. He strolled up to the podium, fiddled with the microphone, and said, "Thank you." The jury included Eno, Joe Strummer, Sheryl Crow and Elton John. Also-rans this year included Sting, The Pet Shop Boys and John Martyn. His two-note solo on 'I Want You' made *Mojo* reader Peter Gale put him forward as a key instrumentalist. "The suspicion that the force of his playing has actually made the solo slightly out of tune merely adds to the prevailing sense of menace."

Francesco Calazzo interviewed Pete Thomas before the break-up, and *Beyond Belief* translated the results. Thomas admits to not understanding "lots of his songs". Matthew, Elvis's son, did "rhythm research" for 'It's Time' by going through his father's extensive collection of Detroit soul, and making a tape loop of the best riff. Elvis wouldn't allow anyone else to produce a tribute album of versions of his songs, and as to a live album, "Better not to talk about that." As for Elvis's next move, "He might go electro-pop, he might go jazz, he's crazy, completely crazy." Spoken with a mix of affection and puzzlement.

February 1997 saw the release of *Grace Of My Heart*, whose soundtrack included a collaboration between Costello and Bacharach.

In Allison Anders' movie, a young heiress – played by Ileana Douglas – reinvents herself as a Brill Building songwriter. Her rendition of 'God Give Me Strength', complete with "grape-treading march", is one of the film's highlights. When Anders first heard the song that she had commissioned, she drove through the San Fernando valley, crying with delight. Her heroine survives the reefs and shoals of psychedelia – one character is a parody of all the worst aspects of Brian Wilson, and emerges as a singer-songwriter, much like Carole King. Joni Mitchell also contributed to the soundtrack, but could only recreate her *Blue* period – I don't ever want to go back there, I don't ever want to be that vulnerable again – when one of her cats went missing.

As Bacharach said of Elvis, "He's a very unique talent. And a good survivor. He's still standing after all these years. It's been a while." That same month, Costello flew to the US to record an edition of the *Monday Concerts With Ricky Scaggs*, broadcast from the Ryman Auditorium. The evening saw him reunited with old friend and mentor George Jones. Scaggs and his six-piece band started the riff to Jones' 'One Woman Man', and its composer emerged stage right singing into a hand-held mic: a few seconds later, Elvis emerged stage left. He and Jones then duetted on 'Stranger In The House', with Costello on acoustic guitar, though Jones messed up the first take. "I haven't sung this since 1978."

Scaggs then joined them, and they sat on the edge of the stage, playing more songs by George, and reminiscing. Elvis chose some particularly obscure numbers and George remarked, "I can't believe he remembers them all." "That boy must have a computer chip in his head," was Ricky's assessment. The three ended by singing 'Why, Baby, Why'. A couple of days later, Costello returned to New York's Supper Club for an appearance with Deborah Harry and The Jazz Passengers. Joined for the evening by original member Marc Ribot and with Brad Jones on acoustic bass, "Elvin" Costello launched into 'Aubergine', a song he had co-written with Brad, but tonight introduced as 'Eggplant'. *Village Voice* described his relaxed vocals as "verbal fog". He and the former Blondie sang 'Don'cha Go 'Way Mad', their duet about cheating, and reprised this on the David Letterman show.

Twelve days later, Elvis was on the same show, this time with Burt

Bacharach on grand piano and the CBS Orchestra in support as he sang 'God Give Me Strength'. He and Burt also co-presented the thirty-ninth Grammy Awards at Madison Square Garden, broadcast live on CBS. "I am half way through composing a new album of songs with Burt, which I hope we will record by the end of 1997," Elvis told *Mojo*. Burt commented that when Elvis is working, "He almost becomes obsessed. That's right up my alley."

The next night it was back to the fringe, as Elvis sang 'Weird Nightmare' at the Fez Under Time cafe, as part of the regular Thursday night Charles Mingus Big Band Workshop. From country to spoof jazz, to MOR, to Fifties avant-garde, all in a few weeks. In addition, Elvis recorded tracks for tribute albums to two of his musical heroes, Joni Mitchell and Gram Parsons. Over in Paris, Steve Nieve premiered extracts from *Parasite*, his contemporary opera, at two concerts in Paris with a string quartet, two singers and a narrator, in the odd mould of Eric Satie.

In April, Costello's ten-year stretch on Warner Brothers came to an end. "I'd like to thank the good people at WB for the licence to record when and what I wanted to, even if, on occasions, it was for another label. My time at WB has had ups and downs. The good people know who they are. The bad people know where I live." A letter to *Q* from Terry Joynson, from Liverpool but obviously not a family friend, complained that "once again we get a big, fat rock star complaining about his record company not selling his records. In Elvis's bitter little world...a mouthy prat...foisting cold, calculating and deeply unlovable records on us." And so on. Elvis himself, like many a Tory ex-cabinet minister, decided to spend more time with his family.

His next appearance, "sporting severely cropped hair and wraparound shades", was a free event staged in Thames Chase, a "community forest" in Essex. This was the first ever public performance of Elvis's 'Tom Thumb', an orchestral piece for children – much like *Peter And The Wolf*, here narrated by Zoe Ball. In the programme notes, Elvis explained that the piece had been commissioned by "Rabbit Ears", who produced high grade cartoons. "Themes describe the fearless Tom and the carousing Knights of Camelot." As Tom is always trying to make himself bigger, his character is represented by a bassoon. John Cleese narrated the five surviving minutes of the film version, hard to locate, but shown at Meltdown. The audio version was broadcast on American public radio.

There was a moving tribute to the memory of Jeff Buckley in August's *Mojo*. Costello remembers him as "absolutely fucking fearless", taking on Purcell's 'Dido's Lament' at Meltdown, and just "*singing*, not doing it like a party piece, but doing something with it". His last memory was of the party afterwards, Jeff sitting with a viol group, a classical pianist and a jazz player, "all talking and laughing about music. He'd charmed everybody."

Elvis turned up in New York to sing Bacharach's 'Windows Of The World' with Ron Sexsmith on the *Sessions At West 54th* show. He also appeared at an all star concert in Nashville that October to launch The Fairfield Four's new album, featuring the Costello and McCartney song 'That Day Is Done'. Filmed at Caffe Milano, and broadcast by *Mountain Stage*, a select audience of 250 saw the five singers known as The Fairfield Four standing as ramrod straight as their age would permit. They were joined by Elvis – in black shirt and red tie – Kathy Matea and Steve Earle, among others. Costello introduced 'Deep Dark Truthful Mirror' as a "psychedelic gospel song". This by the same man who recently revealed that he saw The Grateful Dead at Bickershaw. Somehow, though, one cannot see even the young Declan in a headband.

He repeated 'That Day Is Done' at the Bottom Line, with Larry Knetchel on keyboards. Later, he bounded over to a watchful Lou Reed, who warmly shook his hand and drawled in admiration, "Elvis, how do you do the things you do!" While in New York, Elvis took in concerts by Toshi Reagon, mezzo-soprano Cecilia Bartoli, and the US premiere of McCartney's *Standing Stone*. Then, accompanied by "his trusty tour manager" Milo Lewis, he flew down to Brazil to appear with the Mingus Big Band at the Free Jazz Festival 97, alongside Neneh Cherry and Goldie. A further monument to Elvis's musical catholicism was his guest slot on Radio Ireland's *Eclectic Ballroom*. He chose tracks by Mel Torme, Ike And Tina Turner, Mingus, Al Green, Harpers Bizarre, The Verve, Blind Willie Johnson, Nina Simone, Genoese longshoremen, Anuna, Anita Carter, The Haimundos and himself, amongst others.

As a parting shot to their departing artist, WB issued *Extreme Honey: The Very Best Of The Warner Bros Years* in October. It included the previously unreleased 'The Bridge I Burned', featuring Elvis's son

Matthew on bass and Danny Goffey of Supergrass on drums. Prince had refused the use of a sample of 'Pop Life'. "I think he thought we were making fun of him. He is a very touchy man." The sample was replaced by a short rap by "MC MacManus", drawing on Ficino, a fifteenth Century Italian philosopher. "And remember to free faraway from the unbridled, the impudent, the malicious and the unlucky." Surely not Bruce Thomas. "For these being full of bad demons are maleficent and like lepers...they harm not only by touch but even by proximity and by sight."

The Eno collaboration 'My Dark Life', written for the *X Files* tribute was also included, though the likes of 'You Bowed Down' and 'God's Comic' were still missed out, as Elvis admitted in the extensive sleeve notes. An advert declared the album "both a history lesson and an astonishing reminder of Costello's vitality and importance", which for once was not hype but merely the truth.

In *Mojo*, Barney Hoskyns found the Warner Brothers years had produced "convoluted and opaque" music, with "knotty chamber arrangements". The new song, "queer fish of a hip hop ballad with a heartbreakingly lovely chorus" suggested that he was again taking off for pastures new, quite apart from changing record labels. WB's Steven Baker, who had indulged in a shouting match with Costello, and was probably stigmatised as one of these bad demons, would think to himself on the phone, "I'm talking to Elvis Costello, one of my all time favourite artists! This is a cool job." And then he dropped him. Baker also mentioned that there might be further Costello "product" from WB, involving unreleased material.

Elvis told the *Big Issue* that, "I was being told officially in this building [WB HQ] from the most senior levels that I was wasting my time." The head of music at the BBC told him the same. "He said I would have more hits if I took all the seventh chords and minor chords out of my songs." "Dumb it down or die, mate," Adam Sweeting commented in *The Guardian*. Elvis had been declared a has-been at the age of forty-three, not even ready yet for the revival tour. "All I'm trying to do is write how I feel. I may not be good looking, I may not be young, but I am curious. It is twenty years in, and I'm still doing things that are brand new – it can't be better than that." Whether or not his records still charted was "far less important". If he were ever to make an instrumental record "that's really, really moving and does the same thing as a record with songs on it, go immediately to the stone mason to buy my headstone, because that would be the end of it".

That aside, Nick Hasted saw *Extreme Honey* as "the album of the year", and it certainly has a flow which some of the albums it draws from lack. He talked to Elvis, and found him "as you'd expect…semi-shaven, trademark thick-rimmed glasses half swamping his face, half-masking his feelings". He was polite but distant, "filling every second he can with his own agenda". He describes Bruce Thomas as "that twattish bassist": the only picture of The Attractions which appears in the collage of images which grace the CD booklet, carefully crops Bruce out of the frame, and out of history. "I don't have any sentiment at all about The Attractions. You won't see them again. When someone is deliberately fucking it up, you have to get rid of them. It's as simple as that."

In the *Bangkok Post*, he personalised this: "Thomas couldn't concentrate any more and he was making a lot of embarrassing mistakes." Bruce told Marsh Gooch that The Attractions were far from over, though, and that they might back the likes of Suzanne Vega. "I think there might be quite a few people with The Attractions on their next album." But where does that leave Steve Nieve? As to the final tour of Japan, "It was just horrible."

As to Elvis, he left esotericism aside briefly to appear in the movie *Spice World*, popping up as a waiter to take Richard E Grant's order. He had come on side for The Spice Girls when they went up to receive an Ivor Novello award, and "there was this low grumpy rumble like you get in the House of Commons. And I thought, 'You bastards. It's only a bit of fun, it's only pop music.'" He also took part in an ad for the four-CD box set of *Pet Sounds*. "If all the record players would get broken tomorrow, these songs could be heard a hundred years from now." Part of the folk tradition, passed orally.

More acting came on several appearances on the spoof US chat show *Larry Sanders*. On one, the show host is too busy to attend properly to his special guest, Elvis Costello. Costello is friendly enough at first, but gradually realises that Sanders is far more interested in playing office politics. He also bans his crew – desperate for Elvis's autograph – from disturbing the limey star. After a splenetic version of 'Thirteen Steps Lead Down', with the reformed Attractions, which features a violent string-scrubbing guitar solo from our hero, Costello curtly gives Sanders a piece of his mind, and wrecks the hospitality room. Punk rools. Another appearance sees him sell a used sports car to the show's co-presenter. When the car breaks down immediately, the name of Elvis is dragged through the mud with explicit accuracy and he ends up having an hilariously foul-mouthed argument.

Elvis the pop star later confirmed that he had signed a new deal with Polygram, thus allowing him to release different kinds of records under affiliated labels. "I don't want to be put in a triple-A Box" – "Adult Album Alternative", in modern marketing terms – and be thus typecast. "I reached a place where I needed to be somewhere fresh," he told *Billboard*. His first project was for his song 'My Mood Swings' to be included in the soundtrack for the new Coen Brothers film, *The Big Lebowski*, a score orchestrated by old friend T-Bone Burnett, and a song written in a New York taxi.

Elvis found time to answer readers' questions in the February 1998 edition of *Q*. One was about teaching his music in college: "People should get marked down for doing my course. There must be something more improving than listening to my stuff." Did he celebrate New Year? "Which one? Jewish? Muslim? I'm a pagan." He denies that he doesn't really need spectacles, and explains that his songs won't fit on karaoke machines: "Too many words." As for The Attractions, putting them back together worked musically but not on a personal level. "There's bad blood."

His rule about live performance was if anything heavier than a paper cup was thrown, then he was off immediately. He would "need a lease on Jupiter to work with Andrew Lloyd Webber". As to "New Labour", "I don't know yet," but some of them were definitely dodgy. "I'm with Harry Enfield over Mendelssohn. I mean Mandelson…Mendelssohn! That's who they should have got." As to Mrs Thatcher, "I'd burn her in Parliament Square." Preferably alive.

Elvis's musical passions continued, reviewing Dylan's *Time Out Of Mind*, "the best record he's made", for *Mojo*. Dylan's songs derive partly from the Harry Smith archive of American folk music: "It's living tradition, and he's done it in such a smart way," taking the rural poetry from these songs and adding to it. Much as Costello himself has done, using the whole of popular music as his palette. Both are the playthings of forces quite beyond themselves. "Every kind of culture mixed up – I mean, what's Robert Zimmerman doing living in Duluth. That's in itself a story. His family had to get there from somewhere. There's folk music explained right there." Dylan's family were part of the Jewish diaspora, fleeing Russia.

Likewise, the young Declan MacManus landed up in West London, as part of the Irish emigrations. Meanwhile, Costello's four step-brothers – Kieran, Ronan, Rory and Liam – were gigging in the London area under the name Second Nature, including songs by their famous relative. The tradition continues.

Elvis also told *Mojo* about his favourite listening of the past year. The new U2 album, Radiohead and Toshi Reagon get the thumbs up, while Oasis doesn't move him, and he thinks that while Noel Gallagher "has written a few good songs" he has many years to go before he can outdo even The Bee Gees. "Elliot Smith is a very quiet, very sweetly voiced guy like John Sebastian, but the lyrics are really dark." His favourite musical memory of the year was a Bruce Springsteen concert in Nice. The circle is complete. "The Boss" played songs from last year, and twenty years before, "and they seamlessly sat in a narrative flow. He played with such power – very delicate at one point, very powerful the next – it was extremely impressive, something I could learn from."

While Elvis learns from others, so others owe him. One of the successes of recent years has been Nick Hornby, whose 1995 novel *High Fidelity* is sprinkled with references to Costello. The book tells the story of Rob Fleming, who runs a second-hand record shop, and begins with him being dumped by long-term girlfriend Laura: "I plug in the headphones and play every angry song about women by Bob Dylan and Elvis Costello I own." Hornby takes his title from an Elvis song and the singer looms large in the narrative. When Rob feels that life is passing him by, "Some days I'm afraid I'll go berserk and rip the Elvis Costello mobile down from the ceiling." Rob is a compulsive list-maker and at the end of one quiet day in the shop, "We list our top five Elvis Costello songs (I go for 'Alison', 'Little Triggers', 'Man Out Of Time', King Horse' and a Merseybeat-style version of 'Everyday I Write The Book' I've got on bootleg tape, the obscurity of the last cleverly counteracting the obviousness of the first)."

When Rob and Laura are talking things through, towards the end of the book, she turns the tables by quoting the singer back at him.

"So what happens if you get happy, and yes I know that's the title of an Elvis Costello album, I used the reference deliberately to catch your attention." By the end, Rob has come to realise that the "high fidelity" of a proper, sharing relationship is the best thing to aspire to (and he keeps the record shop too). It is a sunnier take on life than Costello's own appears to be most of the time.

Still, by 1998 Elvis was continuing to learn, by his own efforts. He won a "substantial commission fee" from National Lottery funds to write a piece of choral music for the Spring 1998 Norfolk and Norwich Festival, to be attended by its patron the Duchess of Kent, herself a keen classical singer. Other projects yet to see fruition were a second album with The Brodsky Quartet, and a song cycle with mezzo-soprano Annie Sofie van Otter.

A poll of *Beyond Belief* readers in 1996 voted that Elvis should produce albums by Ron Sexsmith, Jeff Buckley (sadly now too late) and Richard Thompson, and that he in turn should be produced by Brian Eno, Joe Boyd or George Martin. Rhino records released in May 1998 a compilation of previously unreleased covers of Elvis's songs. In 1994, Tasmin Archer released a four-track single of Costello compositions, led by 'Shipbuilding'. Of Jamaican parentage but born in Bradford, she was "torn musically between a love of Judy Garland and an aching to be Elvis Costello". Tasmin's need to create music could also apply to her role models: "Singing was an escape…it was a way in which I could get away from the life that was actually reality."

Elvis told a *Q* interrogator that he could host a weekly rock show, "no problem". A relaxed and chatty Elvis appeared on the Clive Anderson talk show in October 1997. It was great to see him close up, smaller than expected, scruffy in an open-necked orange shirt and blue suit. He came over as affable, musically literate, jokey about his many name changes, and Anderson did not resort to using his notorious verbal fangs. The show's regular theme tune is 'Let Them All Talk', appropriately enough.

Elvis took questions from the audience, and confirmed that yes, his father *was* the secret lemonade drinker. As to Declan MacManus, aka Elvis Costello, aka Napoleon Dynamite, aka The Little Hands Of Concrete, aka The Emotional Toothpaste, he looked just fine.

epilogue

I n *Love Is The Drug*, a collection of well known media folk recalling
their own heroes – "let them all talk!" – Stuart Maconie recalls first
seeing Elvis on *Granada Reports*, presented by a youthful Tony
Wilson. Costello "wore a pastel blue suit and horn rims and made ugly
faces throughout". He first saw him live at the RAR gig, in "red drape
jacket, brothel creepers, bootlace tie…dressed as a Ted, the kind of
stupid boozy reaction nitwit who thought that the fat Elvis was king.
What had gotten into him?" Maconie spent hours scouring Oxfam
shops for the more usual Elvis look, that of a "vengeful bookie's
runner turned Mod". He searched tirelessly for Trutex button-down
shirts, demob jackets and vented fifties suits, knitted ties "in
unpalatable hues of cerise and salmon pink", and Doc Marten boots.

At Liverpool University, a friend was working at the United Biscuits
factory in Huyton – Harold Wilson's old constituency – and claimed to
be working alongside Elvis's mum! Maconie meets Elvis backstage at
Stockport Floral Hall, and asks him to sign a packet of Bensons. "Well
all right, I'll sign it, but you have to promise to give up smoking."

Maconie's final homage to Elvis was to make a bee line for Worsley
Mesnes Labour Club, where Ross MacManus was performing. A pixie-
ish man in a white jacket came onstage promptly on time, played
trumpet on 'Georgia On My Mind', sang some standards, "and did a
weird little dance in a strobe light" during The Strawbs' 'Part Of The
Union'. In honour of his son's fans in the audience he even does an

Elvis set after the break, ending on 'Alison'. Backstage, he tells how his son once bought him a grand piano as a tax loss.

Stuart found new idols, finding Elvis's work after *Imperial Bedroom* first patchy and then "self-obsessed and charmless". Costello was becoming "a prize nana, piling on weight, dressing like James Robertson Justice and growing a crap beard". One afternoon, Maconie is gazing at Munch's painting "The Scream" when he notices Elvis doing the same, "He'd lost weight, cut his hair and he wore a rather smart leather jacket. He gives a look which said, quite clearly, 'Stop gawping, you arse,' then went back to listening to the commentary on his Walkman. It was nice to see him looking so well. It was nice to think that in the end we both got happy."

This is just one fan's personal trajectory, but it could be rewritten a million times, from near indifference to total adulation. Me, I come somewhere in the middle. Costello is a musician whom I respect rather than love, but that respect is boundless. As Clive Gregson once commented about his concerts, "You'll remember the songs thinking what a good band, but I've always ended up thinking about how unhappy Elvis looked." It is as if he is holding something back, "He's not really being himself." I would myself echo Thom Yorke of Radiohead: "He can be very emotional without being personal. That's his art." Conversely, at his greatest – in 'Alison' or 'I Want You' or 'Tramp The Dirt Down' – he can put aside intellect for the direct expression of jagged and naked emotion. When he reaches that kind of territory, there no-one else even comes close. The King of Pain.

Like another musical inhabitant of that bleak emotional terrain, Richard Thompson, Costello's more recent music reflects domestic contentment, though. Great for them, not so good for the vicarious listener, as only Jesse Colin Young – and perhaps the Dylan of *Nashville Skyline* – has really made great music about being happy with one's wife and family. John Goddard told *Beyond Belief* that Cait was "a big influence on Elvis because he's happy with her. It's obvious. They're very much in love." He remembers them together in his record store, dancing to a tune he was playing on the hi-fi. "They're really, really happy together. That's gotta have an effect on his writing, his career, everything. He's content with himself. He's not an angry young man anymore. He's more like a Jerry Garcia than a Joe

Strummer. You grow."

As Elvis himself told Mark Cooper in a *Guardian* interview in 1989, "Pop songs mention romance and attraction far more than they really care about it. Most love songs never mention the moment after. You know how it works – everybody does. The only people who don't are young enough to imagine that Kylie and Jason don't really do it, and that there's still a Santa Claus." He is not frustrated because of his low record sales as compared to a band like Pink Floyd, in whose live act every note is pre-ordained. "There's that kind of music and there's this: it's just different. Like the forty-eight flavours of Dayville's Ice Cream. I don't mind that as long as I don't get limited to vanilla. Life's just tutti frutti after all."

Elvis seems well aware both of his own historical importance, and of his place in the scheme of things. It is a harder and crueller world than the one in which he started his musical career, in every sense. "The measure of failure has become much more drastic, but I also know there are singers and bands who would be delighted by my smallest success. I am very proud to have had such a curious audience. I am the third in four generations of musicians in my family. I don't imagine I am going to stop now."

Just as I was completing this book, Bebe Buell phoned me from New York to put the record straight. She confirmed many of the conclusions which I had already drawn from Costello's music. Buell has not been in contact with Elvis since 1985, although since then she has accidentally run into him twice. Once was on the streets of New York near her current home: "I couldn't believe it," she recalls, "he and Cait were just walking towards me, so I hitched my glasses closer to my eyes, and kept on walking. Fast!" The other time was, of all things, at a football match in Italy: "Again, I couldn't believe it – to run into him in this dusty football arena. I only saw him from a distance – he was pointed out to me by an Italian official – and I'm not sure if he saw me. I was there with friends from one of my daughter Liv's films; Liv and I were working in Italy, researching for *Stealing Beauty*. Those occasions aside, Elvis and I are also sometimes at the same New York social events but we never speak to each other."

As she relived all this, her voice occasionally soared into laughter, and equally occasionally broke down into tears. Although herself now happily married, she clearly still loves him. It says something for Costello that he can retain her affection and respect as "a man of huge wit and intellect", though one who is also a loner. Bebe is clear eyed enough to see that his tempestuous personality will always force Costello to deny himself inner peace.

It was a love affair from the off. "Jake Riviera was worried about me from the very start," Buell insists. "He thought I would take 'angry Elvis' away and give him lots of babies. He built up this image of me as a temptress, and it's been repeated ever since. I'm looking to you to put the record straight." Even the *Mojo* interview with "extremely sympathetic" Mat Snow had been badly cut, and showed her in the wrong light. She admits now that, "It was wrong of me to break the news to Elvis" – about her termination of their unborn child – "in that way. It must have hurt him and his family very much. I never meant to hurt anyone and I now deeply wish that I had kept the baby.

"When I met Elvis after the Hollywood High concert, he had already left Mary, and was sharing a London apartment with Steve Nieve. I wasn't breaking up a marriage as people now try to say." What's more, despite popular myth, songs like 'This Year's Girl' had nothing to do with her (though one could also argue that they had partly been inspired by that chance first meeting in west London, which Bebe likens to being "struck by a lightning bolt"). Their relationship first came to light – lyrically – on *Get Happy!!*, though her vivid stories of a childhood partly spent as a "military brat" in Camp Lejeune entranced Elvis and Riviera, and may have partly inspired the gung-ho imagery of *Armed Forces* and the tour which followed. "They couldn't get enough of my stories of my life in that place," Buell says.

On the other hand, 'Party Girl' is not about her, Bebe insists. Neither is 'Girls Talk', which came about "after Elvis entered a room during a girls-only discussion of the size of various men's willies. Steve Nieve's girlfriend was comparing various acquaintances as Elvis came in, and he wrote the song within days."

Elvis's love of codes and mysteries has led him to refer to his (largely illicit) love affair with Bebe in asides and word play. As to specific clues – and here we enter the kind of territory explored by R Gary Patterson in his wonderful book *The Great Beatle Death Clues* – the word "blue" contains her first and last name and the cover of

Almost Blue can be read as "BE" – as in Bebe – with the "L" simply a tear and the "U" almost obscured by his weeping face. This further refers to Buell's own EP of cover versions, which had just appeared, "and whose sleeve shows me ripping up a record sleeve". Elvis expresses his feelings here through the words of others, just as he would give Bebe albums by the likes of Bob Dylan, to express his own feelings about her.

Many of Elvis's own lyrics of around this time derived from private poems and phrases written or said to Bebe. For example, "to murder my love is a crime" was "a phrase he used in a letter I still possess: later I heard it when I played his new album." Indeed, *Imperial Bedroom* is a maze of secret messages. Myth says if you listen closely, and turn the bass control down on your hi-fi, the lovelorn refrain "PPS I love you" on 'The Loved Ones' becomes quite clearly "BB, yes I love you". What's more, it is also rumoured that the tender, needy 'Human Hands', which follows immediately after, was about her: as Mat Snow pointed out in *Mojo*, her long digits seemed to entrance Costello. Even the intensely private 'Beyond Belief' starts to make more sense when one considers the song's initials.

On *Mighty Like A Rose*, 'So Like Candy' is already set in the past, before the CD revolution. The line about "records that you scratched" has a further resonance. "What really annoyed him was that when he was out and I wanted to leave him a message, I would tape it to a cover of an album and leave it out for him to see." He would then have to tear the sleeve to remove the sellotape, which drove him wild. The fact that this is one of the first fruits of his collaboration with McCartney introduces a further irony. "One time in 1978, Elvis and I ran into Paul and Linda when we all met by chance at Heathrow Airport, and he was just like an excited schoolboy. When we took a minicab afterwards to London, the driver was playing a Beatles tape, so we sang along. It was a marvellous moment."

It has been speculated that 'I Want You' was one of the last songs he would write about Bebe, but she is equally convinced that others take her as a subject. If all this is true, and there seems little reason to doubt it, then Bebe has continued to function as a muse for Elvis, endlessly provoking, mysterious, the path in life untaken.

Buell's daughter by the lead singer of Aerosmith, Liv Tyler, is now a famous film star. "Liv and I are very close; she's very curious about Matthew Costello, after all there's only a two-year gap between them." Bebe found Liv's starring role in the Bernardo Bertolucci movie *Stealing Beauty* particularly resonant, with Costello's *All This Useless Beauty* coming out in the same week in June 1996.

Bebe herself still treasures a choice string of pearls which Elvis gave her, with the throwaway comment that they were "the same colour as your teeth", another part of her anatomy whose perfection never ceased to amaze him. As to the path that Costello did choose to take, Buell remarks about how "young, tall and elfin-like Cait was when Elvis first met her thirteen years ago. She fulfilled his growing need to rediscover his Irish roots. Have you ever seen Elvis and his father together? They look so alike it's almost spooky." As if one were growing into the other – a pattern Matthew is presumably following.

As Costello once worked with Cait and The Pogues, *Cybersleaze* recently reported that Elvis had now dumped The Attractions to work with a band whose members were roughly half his own age, with Matthew on bass and Supergrass's Danny Goffey on drums. For all that, in February 1998, Costello and Nieve undertook a ten-city Italian tour, previewing a new song, 'Unfailing Welcome To The Voice', adopted from Steve's opera. A drunk man in a theatre watches the ghosts of his life pass in front of his eyes.

Billboard announced that the duo were recording an album together, lyrics by Elvis and tunes by Steve, for release sometime around the millennium. Meanwhile, Demon Records, part owned by Costello and Riviera, was sold to Crimson Productions, owners of Woolworth's. In March 1998, Elvis came in at Number Thirty-Eight, between Al Green and Miles Davis, in a poll compiled by VH-1, with the votes of 600 leading musicians, of the musicians' musicians. He outscored his collaborator Paul McCartney – although The Beatles topped the poll – and easily outdid the likes of Sting, Madonna and Nirvana. As vice-president Bill Flanagan commented, "Musicians are also big music fans, and I think the survey results show who their biggest influences are." Rock on…

Also in March 1998, Elvis returned to Irish radio's *Eclectic Ballroom*, playing guest DJ with a suitably eclectic choice, including Noel Coward, Dusty Springfield, Bette Davies, Dan Hicks and Victor

Jara. As to The Attractions, they were last seen in action recording with Zenji Magahata, a Japanese Costello sound-alike fanatical enough to have called his first album *Flip City.*

Elvis provided extensive sleeve notes for *Bespoke Songs, Lost Dogs, Detours And Rendezvous,* cover versions of his work by a bewildering variety of musicians, from wholesome Paul McCartney to the doomed Chet Baker. Where else would the post-modernist funk of Was (Not Was) meet the cool jazz of Annie Ross, Ronnie Drew of The Dubliners share a disc with the tortured croon of Roy Orbison, or revived rocker Dave Edmunds – from the Stiff tour – stand alongside folk diva June Tabor? *Q* was impressed: "The range of artists is as broad as Costello's songwriting acumen…a parallel-universe Elvisography," it raved. For *Beyond Belief,* Elvis's sleeve notes alone are worth the price of admission. Now, for example, we know that Orbison recorded a second version of 'The Comedians' with a Van Dyke Parks arrangement for small orchestra.

Another such snippet was in *Q*'s list of the hundred richest rock stars, with Elvis's publishing rights pushing him up to Number Sixty-Eight– tying with Liam Howlett of The Prodigy. Whereas Howlett has splashed out on an Essex farm with a home studio attached, a red Ferrari and snowboarding holidays in Colorado, Elvis is said to live simply: "His only addiction is to rare record shops." His one example of rock star extravagance, and a severely practical one at that, was to buy an American tour bus "and ship it back to England".

There is more insight in this one anecdote than in the whole of Tony Clayton-Lea's 1998 book on Elvis, laughably describing itself as "A Biography", and commissioned and written in four months. Big print, few pages and no index – the best that John Foyle of *Beyond Belief* could say of this "bland, toothless" tome was, "The book jacket is tastefully done, and the sturdy, flexible binding makes the publication easy to use." The book does convey one thing, namely that, "Elvis is an intensely private individual, as is his right."But *Q* missed "the thrills and the spills and the bellyaches".

Far better written, with knowledge and passion, is Elvis's own tribute to the memory of Frank Sinatra, published in *The Guardian* in May. He conjectures that Frank's decision to "sing low" was a conscious commitment made during "a short period without success and in vocal crisis in the early 1950s". One wonders if, like all the best critical insights, Elvis is also talking about himself, and those lost years on the pub-rock circuit.

It is the American crooner's sense of melancholy – and resilience – which Elvis most admires, though; his favourite of all the albums is *Only The Lonely*, a near-suicidal exercise in willed solitude (sung by a man whose sexual conquests were legion). This album shows Sinatra's ability to "build up the drama in a restrained way and then provide a wonderful knock-out blow in the last eight or sixteen bars". Costello has learnt from Frank this sense of dynamics, the "cunning boxer's technique" of how to pace himself on stage. Elvis grew up to the sound of Sinatra, and as soon as he was bringing home some wages, he invested in some of his classic albums, "and found they spoke very clearly about the adult things I was just beginning to understand".

This could also describe Elvis's respect for another American legend – and another musical father figure – Burt Bacharach. Unlike Sinatra, Elvis had the chance to actively collaborate with his hero, and grabbed it. His timing was immaculate.

Ian Dury, Costello's old rival as headliner on the Stiff tour, meanwhile, was becoming positively cuddly in his old age, with *Mr Love Pants*, a magnificent return to form with the reunited Blockheads. News that he was fighting cancer made Dury's 1998 tour a particularly emotional experience for all concerned, with what can only be described as love flowing across the footlights towards a man whose persona back with Kilburn and the High Roads can only be described as frighteningly hard.

Costello's distancing tactics, in contrast, inspired respect rather than affection. Any reunion with The Attractions looked increasingly unlikely, and a high-class collaboration with Burt Bacharach was taken by many as a final betrayal, as Elvis seemed to be embracing glossy pop, the tuxedo culture and songwriting by numbers. The critics could not have been more wrong, though some of my friends have confessed to listening to the resulting album behind closed doors, almost despite themselves, for enjoying something so uncool.

In fact, *Painted From Memory* proved to be as graceful and emotional a record as anything Costello had ever (co-)written. By cutting down on his usual wordplay, Elvis cuts deeper than ever before.

The album might be a careful and fictional construction —just like, say, even the wildest reaches of The Velvet Underground, or Nick Cave – but Brill Building discipline unleashed his most personal and affecting set of lyrics as he proved fiction can ring just as true as autobiography. *Painted From Memory* was as primal as Dylan's latest offering, and made Dury's fine album seem like nursery rhymes. Here was the adult pop Costello had spent half a lifetime learning how to contrive.

The eighteenth album in a twenty-two-year career, *Painted From Memory* was recorded at Los Angeles' Ocean Way Studios during two arduous weeks. As Elvis told *Details*, the project was carefully planned in advance, then "there were two days with a twenty-four-piece string orchestra; sessions for background voices, brass and woodwinds; and a day to add all kinds of tuned percussion instruments…much of the singing was done live at the rhythm section sessions, me taking cues from Burt as he conducted the band from the piano."

One of the new songs, 'This House Is Empty Now', was premiered at a concert in New York City's Hammersmith Ballroom, held on 8 April, 1998 in tribute to Bacharach's long career, and televised a week later. Costello appeared alongside a cast-list which spanned the history of post-war popular music, from Dionne Warwick to Sheryl Crow, Luther Vandross to All Saints. As to his latest partnership, Bacharach told the audience, "We've completed eleven or twelve songs together," then showed a brief clip of the two men composing. After an extremely emotive 'God Give Me Strength', Elvis came back on stage for the encores, and made a *Wayne's World* "We Are Not Worthy" bow to the camera. On the resulting album, *Q* noted that Elvis was "near histrionic"; impassioned would be a fairer description.

An even more fascinating slice of TV was the hour-long special shown on Channel 4 on Boxing Day 1998, which neatly mixed footage of a scruffy Elvis in rehearsal and chatting with Burt with a posh Elvis in tuxedo, black bow tie, shiny black shoes, cropped hair and cufflinks. The latter was like a man possessed, grasping the microphone as if for dear life, and acting out each song with hand gestures and vocal grimaces. Behind him, Bacharach sat at his piano in an open-necked shirt, intent with concentration – bending down to the notes in an oddly crab-like manner – while conducting an ensemble which combined a rock rhythm section, brass, strings and a three-girl chorus.

Between magnificent renditions of the new songs – some even better than the record, but performed in a noticeably different running order – Burt 'n' Elvis talked about their mutual admiration.

For Elvis, one of his first musical memories was hearing a DJ namechecking Bacharach as the composer of 'Anyone Who Had A Heart': "That was almost unique" for the time. The camera cuts to Elvis singing that very song, and completely expunging memories of Cilla Black's disgraceful assault on it some thirty years earlier. Bacharach describes the two first meeting – via fax and telephone – to compose 'God Give Me Strength'. "It was like a blind date," says Burt. "I knew where he was coming from, how he grew up and with his father, and how much music there was in that household. I think he wasn't just into *my* music, he was into all music. It just felt logical to do this again: we embarked on a plan to get together five, six times."

The two got together in Bacharach's music room, swapping between acoustic and electric piano, but set up one in front of the other, so that "he'd be staring at the back of my head. It would be quite comical if anyone saw it." Costello wants to put right the notion that Bacharach is "laid back, detached. I just hear deeply-felt songs." His work is "light-hearted, not light-weight", while his serious songs are "as deep as you get". "The surprise was his unbelievable energy and concentration," Elvis reveals. "In the studio it's a drive which moves other people, and gets thing out of people they couldn't imagine, playing things they had said were technically impossible." If you weren't there, you couldn't begin to imagine the "physicality" of his approach. Burt adds that in the studio comes the "moment of truth". A song will live or die depending on how it is executed.

One of Burt's greatest achievements was to get Elvis to sing "the quietest I've ever sung, but that means my voice sounded louder because I was trying much less to reach for intensity than to think and feel it. In the end, it's about the story, and I'm the messenger of all that. It's all about the voice serving the song. I'm using my voice in a different way, I never have before. I'm glad to be conducted, sometimes literally, or just in a word or two." Bacharach knows instinctively where his singer should hold back, not – as Elvis sometimes has before – "giving away everything, getting too far up in dynamic range, and leaving myself nowhere to go". Under Burt's direction, he says, "When I did get there, it was where the music wanted you to be, and it was so much better."

Bacharach knows "how obsessive" his own working methods are, "caring about each note. On one of our writing sessions, when I was awake at 3am", his mind spinning, he somehow knew that Costello was awake, worrying, too. As they sit together companionably, Elvis describes songwriting as "a pleasant torture", to which Burt responds that this would have been a good name for the album. He is very proud of the collaboration. "I think it's some of the best work I've done, and that hopefully Elvis feels the same way," he says. As to his new writing partner, "nobody writes lyrics like Elvis does. There's not one word in this album that's filler, that ever marks time. It's brilliance and it isn't ever common, ordinary, something you would expect." Not even from the Brill Building, he adds modestly.

Mercury's aggressive marketing campaign – "a new record like this comes along every ten years" – proved counter-productive. The first accounts I myself heard of the album, pre-release, was that it was a severe disappointment. Ian MacDonald in a review for *Uncut* spends most of his time recalling past glories of the seventy-year-old Bacharach, before condemning the new album as a failure, stemming from the "studious" quality of Costello's "ersatz" lyrics. Another review compares the female backing singers to Benny Hill's Ladybirds, and sees Elvis heading, like his illustrious namesake, for Las Vegas.

Even Dave Farr in *Beyond Belief* identifies a certain cheesiness in the backings, and Costello's occasional "overreaching" vocals. This was my own impression on a first, cursory listen. Farr then goes on to identify meticulously how the tension between "Bacharach's brilliant but sometimes too lush arrangements and EC's brilliant but sometimes too rough vocals" balances out.

After a few plays, I myself found the album hypnotic, the kind of thing you rush home from work to listen to again, and could only concur with *Neon* that the key was the way "Costello's sharp words begin to cut through Bacharach's warm envelope of sound". Dave Martino in *Mojo* talks of Costello's lyrics here as being "as perfect as modern pop music ever gets". Ian Macdonald is spot on about the range of subject matter: "regret, evanescence, solitude, yearning, twilight." Farr hits the nail on the head, for me at least, when he writes that there are moments here where "the vocal, or the music, or both, stir my heart, open my eyes, or take my breath away". It is as if, having heard Dylan's *Time Out Of Mind*, Costello had wanted to match that primal misery, of love denied. An *Only the Lonely,* for the *Friends* generation, the songs form a conceptual whole, about the bitterness of loss.

Typical, then, that the CD packaging should be quite the opposite, with the front cover emphasising two craftsmen at work – Elvis is studying sheet music, and listens while Burt makes a point. On the back cover, both men are grinning, as they do – more enigmatically – on the inside booklet. Elvis sports a straw hat and black leather jacket. As to the musical line-up, Steve Nieve trades keyboards with Burt, Elvis confines himself to vocals, and a rhythm section of Dean Parks, Greg Cohen and Jim Keltner provides the musical muscle to Bacharach's ornate arrangements. Baroque would be the best description, a touch of the *Left Banke.*

The album opens, literally, in 'The Darkest Place'. Muffled chords, and Elvis strains his throat muscles in self-pity. The way the girl singers interact – their sweet against his sour – and Elvis's aching voice at the end sounds like a trumpet which can wake the soul. Costello confides to the TV viewers, that he had "always imagined it would be the first song on the record". It was one of several titles which was considered as the overall title of the album, "although it would be cheating the listener to have gone with this one closed notion. And in fact the song is quite a different impulse." Note the deliberately impersonal terms he adopts here. "Somebody has just lost somebody, and they prefer to be in the place where no more bad things can happen, until they can get back together again." Themselves, one presumes, not the couple now split forever. It is just like when "you're in a dark room. You take a little time for your eyes to adjust, and you start to see, and you can find your way out." The album thus opens with a song about self-healing.

'Toledo' is a masterpiece of timing, particularly the way Elvis inserts "dream of" like a punctuation mark. The song is firmly in the mould of Bacharach/David travelogue pieces like 'Do You Know The Way To San Jose?', but also deals with a favourite Costello theme, betrayal. As he revealed on Channel 4, the song is "about someone coming home from being unfaithful, and seeing the light on the telephone going, knowing their lover has called them. The person they've cheated on has caught them out." Nevertheless, the song's protagonist thinks up "all kinds of alibis for their behaviour", but hears an insistent "how could you do that?" in their head. In a neat twist, "The vocal group comes in and says that in my ear as I'm singing."

Elvis's voice soars and ebbs on 'I Still Have That Other Girl', poignant as a kitten with a broken paw (but is the mention of "ugly rumours" a private joke on the name of Tony Blair's undergraduate pop group?). In concert, he acts the lyric out with his left hand, almost like a glove puppet. For Costello, this is a song which "has a musical dialogue running through it: the shortest song on the record and the most condensed. We wrote an equal part of the music." Elvis had nearly ruined the collaboration, though. Bacharach started to play the piano "in the most beautiful way" while Elvis was staring out of the window. "We've kept all the work tapes, it's good to capture the moment when a certain idea came up. I say, 'What's that?', his eyes are shut and he's actually writing it."

Dave Farr is spot on with 'This House Is Empty Now': "the out-of-breath way Elvis sings, so that it sounds the way one might talk while crying." The vocal just before the guitar break is like a man scratching angrily at a scab, sung over a backing track as tasteful as a jewel box. Bacharach has never written lyrics for his songs, but Costello reckons him over-modest about his contribution to the words which Elvis has then composed to match the music. Burt has a "very vocal sense", and his music points out underlying lyrical ideas to his songwriting partner.

He will even supply the odd word to work in progress, to indicate what theme the music should carry. The key word here was "remember", which formed the working title of this song. "I just knew it was about somebody walking through deserted rooms, maybe after a divorce, in not a sentimental but an angry way," he says. This is a song rich in experience, particularly the way that mutual friends of the one-time couple often have to decide which side to take, forever.

'Tears At The Birthday Party' is the first song on the album to try on one of Costello's extended metaphors for size. The adult protagonist's jealousy is backdated into childhood: a common theme with Elvis, 'Tears Before Bedtime' and the like. He inflicts real venom on "Now I see you share your cake with him", but whether or not he is being autobiographical, Costello the performer remains best at anger and hurt: the whole lyrical thrust of this record is really 'Alison' revisited. On the fade, Elvis duets with a saxophone. The piece's underlying narrative is "somebody that every year returns to a childish infatuation on the anniversary, thinking of all the years they didn't send a card", and how they never managed to impress on the other person how much they meant".

'Such Unlikely Lovers' parodies itself, but still leaves the listener with a catch in the throat. Love reborn. At the coda, Elvis comes in on soft falsetto, like Marvin Gaye, soaring above the female backing chorus. "The lyrical idea came into my head immediately upon hearing the music," he reveals. "It's something about people walking down the street, or a chance encounter. The most optimistic, romantic song on the record." Elvis's eyes swivel alarmingly as he sings this on TV.

'My Thief' is sophistication on a stick: Farr reckons it to be "in the league of Gershwin, with a melody that breaks your heart". The girl (literally) has the last word here, for a change. Costello is up to his old punning tricks on 'The Long Division', though the way he sings "it's a joke" is far from funny. John Donne, for the Brett Easton Ellis generation.

Feeling shades into nostalgia on the title track, with Costello starting quietly, rising to anguish, then ebbing back into meditation. Strings swirl moodily. Elvis later suggested, jokingly, that one of its lines – "because it's a lonely world" – could be given as the reason that he and Burt decided to work together. For world-class songwriters, it sure is. 'The Sweetest Punch' ups the tempo, and sounds much closer to mid-period Costello – lots of Steve Nieve – as do the ironic lyrics. Elvis's melody line is almost Arabic in its twists and turns. The song deals with a spot of emotional roughing-up visited on the singer.

'What's Her Name Today' does much the same to the listener. Elvis acts out – with gusto – the role of a rejected lover who accuses his rival of belittling and trapping his ex-girlfriend, "hung up like a chandelier", and ends up near-psychotic, coughing out the song title. This is followed by, in Farr's words, "a frightening cymbal sound that takes us out". Who mentioned David Accles? In the context of the full album, 'God Give Me Strength' acts as a prayer for redemption and release, bringing this song-cycle to its conclusion. Elvis's voice soars, aches, purrs, grates, sobs, then ends unresolved.

As Burt commented on TV, "All the songs are different," – but they join together to form a "theme of love that didn't work". The approach, though, is "never desperate, never too dark…there's still some hope". For Elvis, "The people in these songs are having the time of their lives, in the worst way that you can say that." He himself has had such times, "So I know what I'm talking about", as has Burt. In his usual sideswipe at the Laurel Canyon laureates of the early Seventies, neither Costello nor his new collaborator would "be so selfish as to make it like a diary". Elvis is obviously proud of his creation, but lets it go out into the marketplace. "In the long run, people will decide what use they make of it." For solace, in my own case, remembering the emotional turmoil of younger days, and that's just for starters…

Costello told Sean O'Hagan, "The shape of the melody, that's really Burt's bag. There's a suggestion in the music of something left unspoken in the actual lyric." As to *Painted From Memory*, it's "a record for people who luxuriate in melancholy, a celebration of heartbreak". It also failed to trouble *Q*'s Top Forty album Charts.

Bacharach and Elvis then embarked with a twenty-four-piece orchestra for a five-date tour, with one night each in New York, Washington, Chicago, Universal City and, finally, at London's Royal Festival Hall, on 29 October. The tour was a sell-out, even with ticket prices of £30 and £40; those less well-off were treated to an hour of highlights by Radio 2. Songs from the new album, and duets on the likes of 'I Just Don't Know What To Do With Myself' – an Elvis stage special back in the late Seventies – were interrupted by thirty minutes of Bacharach's greatest hits, and an Elvis solo spot. 'Accidents Will Happen' was given a two-minute orchestral coda, 'Veronica' became a mini-opera – "just a little something we knocked up at the soundcheck" – while 'Almost Blue' was played alone with Steve Nieve, and in Sam Taylor's words, "It made the ushers cry." Burt was dressed in a lounge suit and no tie: Elvis was in cropped hair and a tuxedo, like a slightly pudgy bouncer.

I couldn't get into the London show for love or money, though BBC2's *Late Review* team did – and sneered mercilessly. Pearls before swine. Serious critics took a longer view: Gavin Martin in *NME* found a mix of "harshness and delicacy, caution and fear", which was based on something far more substantial than showbiz convenience. In *The Observer*, Sam Taylor found that "Elvis has aged very gracefully indeed. Pretty soon, he'll be older than Burt."

In *The Guardian*, Michael Ellison described Elvis in New York, holding centre stage "like a slightly sleazy bingo caller". After twenty years of folk, country-rock, new wave, R&B, straight country, pop, rockabilly, AOR, contemporary classical and all points in-between (except acid-house and avant-garde jazz), Elvis is back home "where the family McManus started", a dead ringer for Ross fronting the Joe Loss Orchestra, grasping the mike like an old pro.

"He was bound to end up here. In short, Costello has turned into his dad."

Coventry University

discography

A ll songs by Elvis Costello, unless otherwise noted. PS = Picture sleeve. The Stiff material is credited to Elvis Costello, the Radar and early F-Beat material to Elvis Costello And The Attractions, and later material generally to Elvis Costello, or his various aliases. Whatever name his material appears under, though, Elvis's creative dominance is always beyond dispute.

Costello's discography would fill a whole book, indeed it already has. His career began at a time when the likes of Stiff records had been created largely to cater for the collector's market. Suddenly the Elvis fan was presented with a slew of special picture sleeves, alternate covers and mixes, the use of different formats etc: a desire for completeness closer to stamp collecting than trainspotting, but heavily addictive.

The fact that Elvis's work has been packaged so exquisitely, as well as having been stretched out over various record labels, and the wide range of musical genres he has covered mean that it is quite possible to collect and listen to Elvis and little else, without getting musical indigestion. Like Dylan, Van Morrison, Neil Young and few others, he has developed along a steady, if haphazard, curve, and has left a vast weight of vinyl, cassettes and CDs in his wake, far too much for the average fan to collect in full. You'd have to be almost as rich as Elvis to now buy up his complete oeuvre.

I have tried to sort out the wheat from the chaff, and have only listed reissues when they add something significantly new to the original release. Happy hunting!

uk singles

1977

Less Than Zero/Radio Sweetheart PS
Stiff BUY 11 March 77
Matrix notes: 'Elvis Is King' and 'Elvis Is King On This Side Too'
Alison/Welcome To The Working Week PS
Stiff BUY 14 May 77
Some copies accidentally pressed in white vinyl on A-side, black vinyl on B-side
Matrix notes: 'Elvis Joins The FBI' and 'Elvis Is King'
Red Shoes/Mystery Dance No UK picture sleeve
Stiff BUY 15 1977 July 77
Original copies have press out centre. Some have mispressing, with Max Wall's 'Dream Tobacco'
replacing 'Mystery Dance'
Matrix notes: 'Help Us Hype Elvis' and 'Larger Than life And More Fun Than People'. French
release *does* come in pic sleeve
Watching The Detectives/Blame It On Cain (live)/Mystery Dance (live) PS
Stiff BUY 20 October 77
There are two different picture sleeves, a picture of Elvis head-on and the more desirable
telephone directory shot, white on black, featuring literally a bunch of Stiffs. The B-side was
recorded in London, first credit to "Elvis Costello And The Attractions"
Watching The Detectives/Watching The Detectives (edit)/Blame It On Cain
(live)/Mystery Dance (live) Promo
Stiff BUY 20DJ October 77
Both tracks on B-side are different takes to the standard release

1978

(I Don't Want To Go To) Chelsea/You Belong To Me PS
Radar ADA 3 March 78
Stranger In The House/Neat, Neat, Neat (James) (live)
Radar SAM 83 March 78
Free with first 5000 copies of This Year's Model
Pump It Up/Big Tears PS
Radar ADA 10 June 78
B-side features Mick Jones of The Clash, on guitar
Radio, Radio/Tiny Steps PS
Radar ADA 24 October 78
Radio, Radio/Tiny Steps 12" PS
Radar ADA 24 October 78
Limited edition of 500
American Squirm/(What's So Funny 'Bout) Peace Love And Understanding (Lowe) PS
Radar ADA 26 October 78
A-side by Nick Lowe. Costello appears on B-side only, as part of 'Nick Lowe and his Sound' –
actually EC and The Attractions – and sings lead vocals
Talking In The Dark/Wednesday Week PS

Radar RG 1 December 78
given away free at London Dominion concert, Christmas 1978
Excerpts from Stiff's Greatest Hits
Stiff FREEB 2
Promo 33 rpm 7", with extracts from 'Alison', 'Red Shoes' and 'Watching The Detectives'

1979

Oliver's Army/My Funny Valentine (Rodgers & Hart) PS
Radar ADA 31 January 79
Live At The Hollywood High EP. Watching The Detectives (live)/Alison (live)/Accidents Will Happen (live) PS
Radar SAM 90 February 79
Came free with early copies of Armed Forces. 'Accidents' is spelt 'adcidents', on purpose
Accidents Will Happen/Talking In The Dark/Wednesday Week PS
Radar ADA 35 May 79
3 alternative sleeves: band posing in front of sign which reads "Fish is Brain Food!" /cartoon sleeve/cartoon sleeve reversed so that inner becomes outer (to illustrate the title song!)

1980

I Can't Stand Up For Falling Down (Homer Banks & Alan Jones)/Girls Talk
F-Beat XX1 March 80
Sleeve has title of 'b' with apostrophe, 'Girl's Talk'. First released on 2-Tone TT 7 January 80 PS, but withdrawn before release, and subsequently given away free at Rainbow gig. The first pressing does NOT have XX1 in run-off groove
High Fidelity/Getting Mighty Crowded (Van McCoy)
F-Beat XX3 April 80
Die cut sleeve, back and front, revealing two different labels, with and without red lettering in logo.
High Fidelity/Getting Mighty Crowded (Van McCoy)/Clowntime Is Over (Version 2) 12"
F-Beat XX3T April 80
Die cut sleeve front and back
Stranger In The House/A Drunk Can't Be A Man
Epic S-EPC 8560 April 80
With George Jones, Costello appears on A-side only, reissued in March 1982 in picture sleeve
New Amsterdam/Dr Luther's Assistant PS
F-Beat XX5 June 80
Budget priced companion to the EP, with 50p sticker
New Amsterdam EP: New Amsterdam, Dr Luther's Assistant, Ghost Train, Just A Memory PS
F-Beat XX5E June 80
New Amsterdam EP: New Amsterdam, Dr Luther's Assistant, Ghost Train, Just a Memory
Pic disc in transparent sleeve
F-Beat XX5P June 80
First 1,500 issued with black rim, all later copies with transparent rim
Five Tracks From Ten Bloody Mary's And Ten How's Your Fathers
F-Beat EL 1 November 1980
White label

Clubland/Clean Money/Hoover Factory PS
F-Beat XX12 December 80
'Hoover Factory' credited to Costello only

1981

Elvis Costello
Stiff GRAB 3 81
Reissue of four Stiff singles in plastic wallet. Copyrighted to Stiff Records, not Stiff Records Ltd, as on original pressings
Four Tracks From The 'Trust' LP. You'll Never Be A Man/Pretty Words/From A Whisper To A Scream/New Lace Sleeves 12"
F-Beat EL 2 January 81
White label
From A Whisper To A Scream/Luxembourg PS
F-Beat XX14 February 81
A-side features Glenn Tilbrook on guest vocals
Good Year For The Roses (Jerry Chesnutt)/Your Angel Steps Out Of Heaven
Jack Ripley
F-Beat XX17 September 81
PS version withdrawn in favour of a die-cut '45' sleeve
Good Year For The Roses (J Chestnut)/Colour Of The Blues (Williams/Jones)/Why Don't You Love Me (Like You Used To Do) (H Williams)/Sweet Dreams (D Gibson)
F-Beat EC 1 October 1981
Promo single
Sweet Dreams (Don Gibson)/Psycho (Leon Payne) (live) PS
F-Beat XX19 December 81
B-side recorded live at Palomino Club, North Hollywood, 16 February 1979

1982

I'm Your Toy (Ethridge/Parsons) (live)/Cry Cry Cry (J Cash)/Wondering (J Werner) PS
F-Beat XX21 April 82
A-side recorded live at the Royal Albert Hall on 7 January 1982, with the Royal Philharmonic Orchestra, arranged and conducted by Robert Kirby
I'm Your Toy (Ethridge/Parsons) (live)/My Shoes Keep Walking Back To You (Ross/Wills)/Blues Keep Calling (James Martin)/Honky Tonk Girl (Loretta Lynn) 12" PS
F-Beat XX21T April 82
Track 1 as above
You Little Fool/Big Sister/The Stamping Ground PS
F-Beat XX26 June 82
Early sleeves omit the credit to Nick Lowe as producer
Man Out Of Time/Town Cryer (alternate version) PS
F-Beat XX28 July 82
"Produced by Geoff Emerick from an original idea by Elvis Costello"
Man Out Of Time/Town Cryer (alternate version)/Imperial Bedroom 12" PS
F-Beat XX28T July 82
Track 3 credited to "Napoleon Dynamite and the Royal Guard"
Man Out Of Time (DJ edit)/Elvis Costello introduces 'Man Out Of Time'/Man Out Of Time

promo

F-Beat XX28DJ July 82

Taken from 'A Conversation With Elvis Costello' promo album

Beyond Belief/Man Out Of Time/Pidgin English/... And In Every Home

F-Beat EC 2 August 82

Promo single

From Head To Toe (Robinson)/The World Of Broken Hearts (Pomus & Shuman) PS

F-Beat XX30 September 82

Some copies came with a free copy of the Get Happy LP, thus causing a fracas about 'chart hype'

Party Party/Imperial Bedroom PS

A&M AMS 8267 November 82

With the Royal Guard Horns

Party Party/No Feelings (Matlock/Rotten/Cook/Jones) promo

A&M PARTY 5 November 82

B-side 'performed' by Banarama

1983

Tomorrow's Just Another Day/Blue Skinned Beast/Madness (Is All In The Mind)/Tomorrow's Just Another Day 12" PS

Stiff BUYIT 169 February 83

By Madness, track 4 by Madness & Elvis Costello

Pills And Soap/Extended Version No picture sleeve

IMP IMP 001 May 83

released as The Imposter

Everyday I Write The Book/Heathen Town PS

F-Beat XX32 July 83

Backing vocals by Afrodiziak

Everyday I Write The Book/Heathen Town/Night Time (Chambers) 12" PS

F-Beat XX32T July 83

Original release featured the 7" version of title track, but this was soon replaced by a "new extended mix" lasting 4'25"

Let Them All Talk/The Flirting Kind PS

F-Beat XX33 September 83

A-side with the TKO horns

Let Them All Talk (extended version)/The Flirting Kind 12" PS

F-Beat XX33T September 83

"Extended sleeve"! Track 1 extended 12" remix, 5'59"

1984

Peace In Our Time/Withered And Died (R Thompson) No picture sleeve

IMP TRUCE 1 April 84

Released as The Imposter

I Wanna Be Loved (Farnell & Jenkins)/Turning The Town Red PS

F Beat XX35 June 84

A-side, backing vocals by Green

I Wanna Be Loved (radio version) (Farnell & Jenkins)/Turning The Town Red/I Wanna Be Loved (extended smooch'n'runny version) 12" PS

F Beat XX35T June 84
LAFS/(Hey Big Mouth) Stand Up and Say That/Baby It's You (Bacharach/David/Williams) 12" PS
F-Beat XX 36T July 84
By Nick Lowe, track 3 by Elvis Costello & Nick Lowe
The Only Flame In Town/The Comedians PS
F-Beat XX 37 August 84
Special guests: Daryl Hall duet harmony, Gary Barnacle sax
The Only Flame In Town ('Version Discotheque')/The Comedians 12" PS
F-Beat XX 37T August 84
The Only Flame In Town ('Version Discotheque')/Pump It Up (1984 Dance Mix)/The Comedians 12" PS
F-Beat XX37Z August 84
Punch The Clock
F-Beat PUNCH 1 1984
Promo pack with 6 track EP and 2 singles

1985

Green Shirt/Beyond Belief PS
F-Beat ZB 40086 April 85
Some copies in green vinyl with PVC sleeve
Green Shirt/Beyond Belief/Green Shirt (extended mix) 12" PS
F-Beat ZT 40086 April 85
Some copies in green vinyl with PVC sleeve
Living A Little, Laughing A Little/I'm A Real Man PS
CBS A 6121 1985
With John Hiatt, B-side Hiatt only
Living A Little, Laughing A Little/I'm A Real Man/When We Rain/Everybody's Girl 12" PS
CBS TA 6121 1985
With John Hiatt, last three tracks Hiatt only
The People's Limousine ("Harry And Howard Coward")/They'll Never Take Her Love From Me (Leon Payne) PS, back sleeve die cut
Imp OO6 June 1985
Released as the Coward Brothers, with T-Bone Burnett
Green Shirt/Beyond Belief/The People's Limousine/They'll Never Take Her Love Away From Me last two by the 'Coward Brothers'
F-Beat ZB 40085/7
Shrinkwrapped double pack
Less Than Zero/Radio Sweetheart/Alison/Watching The Detectives 12"
Stiff BUYIT 239 November 85

1986

Don't Let Me Be Misunderstood (Benjamin/Marcus/Caldwell)/Baby's Got A Brand New Hairdo PS
RCA Z8 40555 January 86
Track 1 credited to the Costello Show featuring Confederates, track 2 to the Costello Show

featuring The Attractions
Don't Let Me Be Misunderstood (Benjamin/Marcus/Caldwell)/Baby's Got A Brand New Hairdo/Get Yourself Another Fool (Tucker/Haywood) 12" PS
RCA Z840555 January 86
Track 1 credited to the Costello Show featuring Confederates, tracks 2 to the Costello Show featuring The Attractions, track 3 to Elvis Costello and The Attractions
Tokyo Storm Warning Pt1/Pt 2 PS
Imp IMP 007 August 86
Tokyo Storm Warning Pts 1&2/Black Sails In The Sunset 12" PS
Imp IMP 007T August 86
Highlights from 'Blood And Chocolate': extracts from Blue Chair/Uncomplicated/Next Time Round/I Hope You're Happy Now
IMP CHOC 1 August 86
Promo, 1 sided red vinyl in plain sleeve
Uncomplicated (NME Version) flexi disc
NME Giv 3 September 86
With three other tracks, by Billy Bragg, Mantronix and Miles Davis, given away free with New Musical Express
I Want You Pt1/Pt2 PS
Imp IMP 008 October 86
I Want You Parts 1 and 2(McManus)/I Hope You're Happy Now 12" PS
Imp IMP 008T October 86

1987

Blue Chair/American Without Tears No 2 (Twilight Version) PS
Demon D 1047 January 87
As The Costello Show
Blue Chair/Shoes Without Heels/American Without Tears/American Without Tears # 2 (Twilight Version)
Demon D 1047T January 87
As The Costello Show/Elvis Costello on sleeve/songs credited to MacManus/track 4 a 'Napoleon Dynamite production
A Town Called Big Nothing/Return to Big Nothing PS
Demon D 1052 May 1987
As The MacManus Gang
A Town Called Big Nothing/Return to Big Nothing/A Town Called Big Nothing (The Long March) 12" PS
Demon D 1052T May 1987
As The MacManus Gang

1989

Veronica (McCartney/MacManus)/You're No Good (Clint Ballard Jnr) PS
WEA W7558 January 89
Veronica (McCartney/MacManus)/You're No Good (Clint Ballard Jnr)/The Room Nobody Lives In (John Sebastian)/Coal Train Robberies 12" PS
WEA W7558T January 89
Some copies available with poster

Veronica (McCartney/MacManus)/You're No Good (Clint Ballard Jnr)/The Room Nobody Lives In (John Sebastian)/Coal Train Robberies CD single
W 7558T January 89
Also released on picture disc
Baby Plays Around (MacManus/O'Riordan)/Poisoned Rose/Almost Blue/My Funny Valentine (Rodgers/Hart) PS
WEA W2949 May 1989
Baby Plays Around (MacManus/O'Riordan)/Point Of No Return (Goffin/King)/Almost Blue/My Funny Valentine (Rodgers/Hart) 10" PS
WEA W2949TE May 1989
Baby Plays Around (MacManus/O'Riordan)/Point Of No Return (Goffin/King)/Almost Blue/My Funny Valentine (Rodgers/Hart) 12" PS
WEA W2949T May 1989
Also available on cassette
Baby Plays Around (MacManus/O'Riordan)/Point Of No Return (Goffin/King)/Almost Blue/My Funny Valentine (Rodgers/Hart) CD single
WEA W2949CD May 1989

1991

The Other Side Of Summer/Couldn't Call It Unexpected No 4 PS
WB W0025 April 91
Also issued on cassette
The Other Side Of Summer/Couldn't Call It Unexpected No 4/The Ugly Things (Lowe) 12" PS
WB W0025T April 91
The Other Side Of Summer/Couldn't Call It Unexpected No 4/The Ugly Things (Lowe) CD single
WB W0025CD April 91
So Like Candy/Veronica (Original Demo)/Couldn't Call It Unexpected (live)/Hurry Down Doomsday (The Bugs Are Taking Over) PS
WB W0068 September 91
So Like Candy/Veronica (Original Demo)/Couldn't Call It Unexpected (live)/Hurry Down Doomsday (The Bugs Are Taking Over) 12" PS
WB W0068T September 91
So Like Candy/Veronica (Original Demo)/Couldn't Call It Unexpected (live)/Hurry Down Doomsday (The Bugs Are Taking Over) CD single
WB W0068CD September 91

1993

Jacksons, Monk & Rowe/This Sad Burlesque cassette
WB W0159C February 93
Jacksons, Monk & Rowe/Interviews CD single
WB WO159 CDX February 93

1994

Sulky Girl (single version)/A Drunken Man's Praise Of Sobriety (words by WB Yeats) PS
WB WO234 February 94
Also issued on cassette
Sulky Girl (single version)/Idiophone/A Drunken Man's Praise Of Sobriety (words by WB Yeats)/Sulky Girl (album version) CD single
WB WO234CD February 94
Thirteen Steps Lead Down/Do You Know What I'm Saying
Also issued on cassette
WB WO245 April 94
Thirteen Steps Lead Down/Puppet Girl (MacManus/O'Riordan)/Basement Kiss (MacManus/O'Riordan)/We Despise You (MacManus/O'Riordan) CD single
WB WO245 CD April 94
You Tripped At Every Step/You've Got To Hide At Every Step PS
WB WO251 July 94
Also issued on cassette
You Tripped At Every Step/Step Inside Love/You've Got To Hide Your Love Away/Sticks and Stones CD single
WB WO251C July 94
London's Brilliant Parade/London's Brilliant cassette
WB 0270C November 94
London's Brilliant Parade/My Resistance is Low/Congratulations/London's Brilliant 12" PS
WB 0270T November 94
London's Brilliant Parade/Sweet Dreams (Don Gibson)/The Loved Ones/From Head To Toe (William Robinson) CD single
WB WO272CD1 November 94
Limited and numbered ed
London's Brilliant Parade/New Amsterdam/Beyond Belief/Shipbuilding (Clive Langer/Elvis Costello) CD single
WB WO272CD2 November 94
Available as yellow CD in slipcase or red CD in jewel case

1996

It's Time/Life Shrinks/Brilliant Disguise (Bruce Springsteen) CD single
WB WO348 CD
Little Atoms/Almost Ideal Eyes/Just About Glad/Why Can't A Man Stand Alone? CD single
WB WO364CD
One of four, limited ed July 8 1996
The Other End Of the Telescope/Almost Ideal Eyes/Basement Kiss (Costello/O'Riordan)/Complicated Shadows (Cashbox Version) CD single
WB WO365CD
Two of four, Limited Ed July 15 1996
Distorted Angel/Almost Ideal Eyes/All This Useless Beauty (performed by Lush)/Little Atoms (DJ Food Rinse)/Little Atoms (Polished Glass Mix) CD single
WB WO366CD
Three of four, Limited Ed July 22 1996

All This Useless Beauty/Almost Ideal Eyes/The Other End of the Telescope (performed by Sleeper)/Distorted Angel (remix by Tricky) CD single
WB WO367 CD
Four of four, Limited Edition July 29 1996

uk albums

Costello's British album releases are spread over Stiff, Radar, F-Beat and Demon, with American pressings on Columbia and Warner Brothers. Between 1993 and 1995, Demon oversaw an exemplary reissue programme of remastered CD picture discs, with a generous helping of bonus tracks and invaluable comments from Elvis himself in the new info-packed booklets stuffed into the front cover.

MY AIM IS TRUE

Side One: Welcome To The Working Week, Miracle Man, No Dancing, Blame It on Cain, Alison, Sneaky Feelings
Side Two: (The Angels Wanna Wear My) Red Shoes, Less Than Zero, Mystery Dance, Pay It Back, I'm Not Angry, Waiting For The End Of The World
Backing musicians (uncredited) are Clover. The original pressing came in a variety of four different colour sleeves, with seven more variants later! The matrixes read 'Elvis Is King' and 'On This Side Too'. The US issue (Columbia AL 35037 March 78) adds 'Watching The Detectives'.
Stiff SEEZ July 77; Demon IMP FIEND 13 July 86; Demon IMP FIEND CD 13 July 86 CD issue; Demon DPAMI October 93. CD reissue, which adds 'Watching The Detectives', 'Radio Sweetheart', 'Stranger In The House', 'Imagination (Is A Powerful Deceiver), Mystery Dance, Cheap Reward', 'Jump Up', 'Wave A White Flag', 'Blame It On Cain' and 'Poison Moon'.

THIS YEAR'S MODEL

Side One: No Action, This Year's Girl, The Beat, Pump It Up, Little Triggers, You Belong To Me
Side Two: Hand In Hand, (I Don'tl Want To Go To) Chelsea, Lip Service, Living In Paradise, Lipstick Vogue, Night Rally
First 5,000 copies came shrinkwrapped and stickered, with a free single 'Stranger in The House'/'Neat, Neat, Neat'. Stiff's gimmick this time around was an off-centre sleeve, and an inner bag with avante-garde images. Matrix reads 'Special pressing 003. Ring Moira for your special prize'. The US issue (Columbia JC 35331 May 78) replaces '(I Don't Want To Go To) Chelsea' and 'Night Rally' with 'Radio Radio'. Original copies have Costello's not Columbia's logo on the label. Columbia also issued a picture disc which paired Costello's first two albums.
Radar RAD3 March 78; F-Beat XXLP 4 May 1980 *corrected sleeve*; Demon FIEND 18 January 86; IMP FIEND CD 18 January 86 CD issue; Demon DPAM2 October 93. CD reissue, which adds 'Radio, Radio', 'Big Tears', 'Crawling To The USA', 'Running Out Of Angels', 'Greenshirt' and 'Big Boys'.

LIVE AT THE EL MOCAMBO: 6 March 1978

Side One: Mystery Dance, Waiting For The End Of The World, Welcome To The Working Week, Less Than Zero, The Beat, Lip Service, (I Don't Want To Go To) Chelsea
Side Two: Little Triggers, Radio Radio, Lipstick Vogue, Watching The Detectives, Miracle Man/Band Introduction/You Belong To Me, Pump It Up
Canadian only promo issue, issued without permission, and limited to 500 copies. Much

counterfeited: fakes can be identified by the matrix number CDN-10, scratched not stamped into the run off grooves. My own copy has spoof inner labels, Buddy Love Sings About Girls, for Poverty Records, with song titles like 'Toiletta Simpson', 'A Piece Of Denise', 'My Favourite Enema Nurse', and 'Wild Woman Of Frenchtown'. I was almost disappointed to hear the actual album Columbia CDN-10C Canadian Issue; Demon DPAM3 October 93, as part of THE FIRST 2$^{1/2}$ YEARS (DPAM 4) a 4 CD box set with booklet. The CD reissue reproduces the original artwork, and is the first official – and British – release for this essential live document.

ARMED FORCES

Side One: Accidents Will Happen, Senior Service, Oliver's Army, Big Boys, Green Shirt, Party Girl
Side Two: Goon Squad, Busy Bodies, Sunday's Best, Moods For Moderns, Chemistry Class, Two Little Hitlers
With fold-out sleeve – like something from a kid's magic box – and post-modern inner bag: early copies also came with postcards and a free 'Live At Hollywood High' EP. A mispressing on some copies plays '(What's So Funny 'Bout) Peace, Love And Understanding' instead of 'Two Little Hitlers)'. The presence of a sticker proclaiming this fact suggests that though accidents can happen, so can sales gimmicks which appeal to the hardcore collector.
The US issue (Columbia JC 35709 February 79) replaces 'Sunday's Best' with '(What's So Funny 'Bout) Peace Love And Understanding' and has a different sleeve. It also includes the free EP. The French issue reverses the front and back covers
Radar RAD 15 February 79; Demon IMP FIEND 21 May 80; Demon IMP FIEND CD 21 January 86 CD issue; Demon DPAM3 October 93. CD reissue, which adds '(What's So Funny 'Bout) Peace, Love And Understanding?', 'My Funny Valentine', 'Tiny Steps', 'Clean Money', 'Talking In The Dark', 'Wednesday Week', 'Accidents Will Happen' (live), 'Alison' (live) and 'Watching The Detectives' (live).

GET HAPPY!!

Side One: Love For Tender, Opportunity, The Imposter, Secondary Modern, King Horse, Possession, Man Called Uncle, Clowntime Is Over, New Amsterdam, High Fidelity
Side Two: I Can't Stand Up For Falling Down (Banks/Jones), Black & White World, Five Gears In Reverse, B Movie, Motel Matches, Human Touch, Beaten To The Punch, Temptation, I Stand Accused (Colton/Smith), Riot Act
Pre-worn sleeve – an effect removed for non-British issues. A free poster comes with early pressings. The sleeve prints side 1 as side 2 and vice versa. There is also a very rare promo album (F-Beat XX Promo 1) consisting of two 45rpm 12" singles, each packaged separately in white covers with pasted-on info sheets and a poster and photo
F-Beat XXLP 1 March 80; Demon IMP FIEND 24 April 84; Demon IMP FIEND CD January 86 CD issue; Demon DPAM5 April 94. CD reissue, which follows the order of sides 1 and 2 as on the record rather than the LP sleeve, opening with 'Love For Tender', then adds 'Girls Talk', 'Clowntime Is Over No 2', 'Getting Mighty Crowded', 'So Young', 'Just A Memory', 'Hoover Factory', 'Ghost Train', 'Dr Luther's Assistant', 'Black & White World' and 'Riot Act'.

TEN BLOODY MARYS AND TEN HOW'S YOUR FATHERS

Side One: Clean Money, Girls Talk, Talking In The Dark, Radio Sweetheart, Big Tears, Crawling To The USA, Just A Memory, Watching The Detectives, Stranger In The House
Side Two: Getting Mighty Crowded, Hoover Factory, Tiny Steps, (What's So Funny 'Bout) Peace, Love and Understanding, Dr Luther's Assistant, Radio Radio, Black And White World, Wednesday Week, My Funny Valentine, Ghost Train
Originally a cassette in 'gold' case, which gathered up rare B-sides, promos, limited releases, Australian issues and one track previously unissued altogether, 'Black And White World'. Essential at the time, though many of these tracks have been recycled on the Demon CD release programme.

F-Beat XXC 6 October 80 *cassette only release*; Demon IMP FIEND 27 April 84 *first vinyl version*; Demon IMP FIEND CD 27 January 86 CD issue

TAKING LIBERTIES

Side One: Clean Money, Girls Talk, Talking In The Dark, Radio Sweetheart, Black and White World, Big Tears, Just A Memory, Night Rally, Stranger In The House, Clowntime Is Over
Side Two: Getting Mighty Crowded, Hoover Factory, Tiny Steps, (I Don't Want To Go To) Chelsea, Dr Luther's Assistant, Sunday's Best, Crawling To The USA, Wednesday Week, My Funny Valentine, Ghost Train
US version of the above, with antique record labels of the 'Costello' brand ("Viva-tonal recording, electrical process), and sleeve notes by Gregg Geller, Vice-President of Columbia Records. "Still in his early 20s, Elvis clearly demonstrates here that his potential and versatility are practically unlimited". The photo on the front cover is deliberately back to front: check out the 'phone' sign
Columbia BL 36839 November 80

TRUST

Side One: Clubland, Lovers Walk, You'll Never Be A Man, Pretty Words, Strict Time, Luxembourg, Watch Your Step
Side Two: New Lace Sleeves, From A Whisper To A Scream, Different Finger, White Knuckles, Shot With His Own Gun, Fish'N'Chip Paper, Big Sister's Clothes
The last of Elvis's first five LPs to be produced by Nick Lowe, here in association with Roger Bechirian. Glen Tilbrook adds vocals, and Martin Belmont guitar
F-Beat XXLP 11 January 81; Demon IMP FIEND 30 April 84; Demon IMP FIEND CD 30 January 86 CD issue; Demon DPAM6 April 94. CD reissue, which adds 'Black Sails In The Sunset', 'Big Sister', 'Sad About Girls', 'Twenty-Five To Twelve', 'Love For Sale', 'Weeper's Dream', 'Gloomy Sunday', 'Boy With A Problem' and 'Seconds Of Pleasure'.

ALMOST BLUE

Side One: Why Don't You Love Me Like You Used To Do (Hank Williams), Sweet Dreams (Don Gibson), Success (Mullins), I'm Your Toy (Chris Ethridge/Gram Parsons), Tonight The Bottle Let Me Down (Merle Haggard), Brown To Blue (Johnny Mathis)
Side Two: Good Year For The Roses (Jerry Chestnutt), Sittin' And Thinkin'' (Charlie Rich), Colour Of The Blues (Williams/Jones), Too Far Gone (Billy Sherrill), Honey Hush (Big Joe Turner), How Much I Lied (Gram Parsons/Pam Rifkin)
Recorded in CBS Studio A Nashville, 18-29 May 1981. Special guest John McFee. Produced by Billy Sherrill
F-Beat XXLP 13 October 81 issued in four differently coloured sleeves, all with blue as a base, originally with "warning" sticker: "This album contains country and western music and might produce radical reaction in narrow minded people"; Demon IMP FIEND 33 April 84; Demon IMP FIEND CD 33 January 86 CD issue; Demon DPAM 7 October 94. CD reissue, which adds five tracks live in Aberdeen – 'He's Got You' (Hank Cochran), 'Cry, Cry, Cry' (Johnny Cash), 'There Won't Be Anymore' (Charlie Rich), 'Sittin' and Thinkin' (Charlie Rich) and 'Honey Hush' – and 'I'm Your Toy' live with the RPO at the Royal Albert Hall. Further additions comprise the following studio outtakes: 'Psycho' (Leon Payne), 'Your Angel Steps Out Of Heaven' (Jack Ripley), 'Darling, You Know I Wouldn't Lie' (Wayne Kemp/Red Lane), 'My Shoes Keep Walking Back To You' (L.Ross/B Wills) and 'Tears Before Bedtime'. At last, an Elvis Costello song!

ELVIS COSTELLO INTRODUCES ... THE TRACKS FROM HIS NEW ALBUM 'ALMOST BLUE'

Signed and numbered promo item, in which Elvis explains all
F-Beat E.C.Chat 1 October 1981

ALMOST NEW

Side One: I'm Your Toy (Ethridge/Parsons) (live), Accidents Will Happen (live), Alison (live)
Side Two: I Can't Stand Up For Falling Down (Banks/Jones), Green Shirt, Pump It Up, (What's So Funny 'Bout) Peace Love And Understanding (Lowe)
Australian only mini-album compilation, released to tie in with 1982 tour 'down under' – the front cover looks like a map of Australia viewed by someone on LSD – and featuring a bewildering variety of tracks past and present. Weird
F-Beat ELVIS 82

IMPERIAL BEDROOM

Side One: Beyond Belief, Tears Before Bedtime, Shabby Doll, The Long Honeymoon, Man Out Of Time, Almost Blue, ... And In Every Home
Side Two: The Loved Ones, Human Hands, Kid About It, Little Savage, Boy With A Problem (lyrics by Chris Difford, additional lyrics EC), Pidgin English, You Little Fool, Town Crier
Lyrics spread over die-cut inner record bag and onto record label, in a torrent of words. Orchestrations by Steve Nieve. Produced by Geoff Emerick 'from an original idea by Elvis Costello'. Back cover photos by David Bailey. 1983 saw a US-release only half-speed master
F-Beat XXLP 17 July 82; Demon IMP FIEND 36 April 84; Demon IMP FIEND CD 36 January 86 CD issue; Demon DPAM 8 October 94. CD reissue, which adds 'From Head To Toe', 'The World Of Broken Hearts', 'Night Time', 'Really Mystified', 'I Turn Around', 'Seconds Of Pleasure', 'The Stamping Ground', 'Shabby Doll' and 'Imperial Bedroom'

A CONVERSATION WITH ELVIS COSTELLO

Double LP promo in single sleeve, containing the original music interspersed with an interview in which Costello explains the genesis of each track
F-Beat E.C. CHAT 2 June 82

PUNCH THE CLOCK

Side One: Let Them All Talk, Everyday I Write The Book, The Greatest Thing, The Element Within Her, Love Went Mad, Shipbuilding (Clive Langer/Elvis Costello)
Side Two: TKP (Boxing Day), Charm School, The Invisible Man, Mouth Almighty, King Of Thieves, Pills And Soap, The World And His Wife
The first of two albums to be produced by Clive Langer and Alan Winstanley. Features the TKO Horns and Afrodiziak, with string arrangements by David Bedford. Lyrics on inner sleeve come in various type sizes, while on the back cover the word 'invisible' becomes just that. The back cover photo adds a new dimension to the adjective 'unsmiling'
F-Beat XXLP 19 August 83; Demon IMP FIEND 72; F-Beat ZD 70026 September 84 CD issue; Demon DPAM 9 February 95. CD reissue, which adds 'Heathen Town', 'The Flirting Kind', 'Walking On Thin Ice' (Yoko Ono), 'Town Where Time Stood Still', 'Shatterproof', 'The World And His Wife' (live) and 'Everyday I Write The Book' (live)

GOODBYE CRUEL WORLD

Side One: The Only Flame In Town, Home Truth, Room With No Number, Inch By Inch, Worthless Thing, Love Field
Side Two: I Wanna Be Loved (Farnell/Jenkins), The Comedians, Joe Porterhouse, Sour Milk-Cow Blues, The Great Unknown (Costello/Langer), The Deportees Club, Peace In Our Time
Daryl Hall and Green, backing harmonies. Maurice Worm is credited with 'random racket'. Lyrics printed on inner sleeve
F-Beat ZL 70317 June 84; Demon IMP FIEND 75; F-Beat ZD 70317 March 86 CD issue
Demon DPAM 10 February 95. CD reissue, which adds 'Turning The Town Red', 'Baby It's You'

(David/Bacharach/Williams), 'Get Yourself Another Fool' (Tucker/Hayward), 'I Hope You're Happy Now', 'The Only Flame In Town' (live), 'Worthless Thing', 'Motel Matches', 'Sleepless Nights' (Felice and Boudleaux Bryant) – these last four live during Costello's first solo tour, all recorded in the US in Spring 1984 – and 'Deportee'

THE BEST OF ELVIS COSTELLO – THE MAN
Side One: Watching The Detectives, Oliver's Army, Alison, Accidents Wil Happen, Pump It Up, High Fidelity, Pills And Soap, (I Don't Want To Go To) Chelsea, New Lace Sleeves
Side Two: Good Year For The Roses (Jerry Chestnut), I Can't Stand Up For Falling Down (Banks/Jones), Clubland, Beyond Belief, New Amsterdam, Green Shirt, Everyday I Write The Book, I Wanna Be Loved (Farnell/Jenkins), Shipbuilding (Costello/Langer)
Telstar STAR 2247 April 85; Demon FIEND 52 May 86 *different sleeve*; IMP FIEND CD 52 May 85 CD issue choice of either sleeve

KING OF AMERICA
Face One: Brilliant Mistake, Lovable (MacManus/O'Riordan), Our Little Angel, Don't Let Me Be Misunderstood (Benjamin/Marcus/Caldwell), Glitter Gulch, Indoor Fireworks, Little Palaces, I'll Wear It Proudly
Face Two: American Without Tour, Eisenhower Blues (JB Lenoir), Poisoned Rose, The Big Light, Jack Of All Parades, Suit Of Lights, Sleep Of The Just
Issued as The Costello Show, featuring The Attractions and The Confederates, with Costello himself billed as 'the little hands of concrete' on guitar. Produced by T-Bone Burnett and Declan Patrick Aloysius MacManus (Just call him EC). Lyrics on inner sleeve
Demon IMP FIEND 78 April 86; F-Beat ZD 70946 March 86 CD issue; Demon DPAMLP 11 July 95 Limited edition double LP reissue, including the 'Live On Broadway' material: see below; Demon DPAM 12 September 95. CD reissue, which adds 'The People's Limousine' (Henry and Howard Coward aka Costello and T-Bone Burnett), 'They'll Never Take Her Love From Me' (Leon Payne), 'Suffering Face', 'Shoes Without Heels' and 'King Of Confidence'. Early copies come with a free live bonus disc, LIVE ON BROADWAY 1986, comprising six tracks, 'That's How You Got Killed Before' (Bartholemew), 'The Big Light', 'The Only Daddy That'll Walk The Line' (Penn/Oldham), 'Your Mind Is On Vacation' (Mose Allison)/'Your Funeral And My Trial' (Sonny Boy Williamson) and a reprise of the opening song

BLOOD AND CHOCOLATE
Flanko Uno: Uncomplicated, I Hope You're Happy Now, Tokyo Storm Warning (MacManus/O'Riordan), Home Is Anywhere You Hang Your Head, I Want You
Flanko Du: Honey Are You Straight Or Are You Blind?, Blue Chair, Battered Old Bird, Crimes Of Paris, Poor Napoleon, Next Time Round
Issued as Elvis Costello and The Attractions, with Elvis identifed as 'Napoleon Dynamite' on the back cover, and writing credits divided between Costello and MacManus. Produced by Nick Lowe and Colin Fairley. Lyrics reprinted on inner sleeve
Demon XFIEND 80 September 86; Demon XFIEND CASS 80 September 86 cassette release in withdrawn "chocolate" packaging; Demon IMP FIEND CD 80 September 86 CD issue; Demon DPAM 12 September 95. CD reissue, which adds 'Seven Day Weekend'(Costello/Cliff) – with Jimmy Cliff – 'Forgive Her Anything', 'Blue Chair' (single version), 'Baby's Got A Brand New Hairdo', 'American Without Tears No 2 (Twilight Version)' and 'A Town Called Big Nothing (Really Big Nothing)'. Early copies also include AN OVERVIEW DISC, a separate bonus interview CD, 78 minutes' worth between Elvis and *Record Collector*'s Peter Doggett, conducted in Dublin in July 1995

INTERVIEW PICTURE DISC

Baktabak BAK 2001 April 87

OUT OF OUR IDIOT

Side One: Seven Day Weekend (Costello/Cliff), Turning The Town Red, Heathen Town, The People's Limousine (Henry and Howard Coward), So Young (Camilleri/Faehse/Burstin), American Without Tears No 2 (Twilight Version), Get Yourself Another Fool (Tucker/Hayward), Walking On Thin Ice (Y Ono)
Side Two: Blue Chair, Baby It's You (Bacharach/David/Williams), From Head To Toe (W Robinson), Shoes Without Heels, Baby's Got A Brand New Hairdo, The Flirting Kind, Black Sails In The Sunset, Imperial Bedroom
The follow-up compilation of B-sides and rarities to 'Ten Bloody Maries ...' 'So Young' is previously unreleased, Jimmy Cliff is guest star on 'Seven Day Weekend' and Nick Lowe on 'Baby It's You'. The whole album is credited to 'Various Artists', including 'The Emotional Toothpaste' and 'Napoleon Dynamite & The Royal Guard'
Demon XFIEND 67 October 87

SPIKE

Side One: This Town, Let Him Dangle, Deep Dark Truthful Mirror, Veronica (McCartney/MacManus), God's Comic, Chewing Gum, Tramp The Dirt Down
Side Two: Stalin Malone, Satellite, Pads Paws And Claws (McCartney/MacManus), Baby Plays Around (O'Riordan/MacManus), Miss Macbeth, Any King's Shilling, Last Boat Leaving
Produced by Elvis Costello, Kevin Killen and T-Bone Burnett. Features the Dirty Dozen Brass Band, Chrissie Hynde, Derek Bell, Christy Moore, Benmont Tench and Paul McCartney. Lyrics are spread over back cover and inner sleeve, including those for 'Stalin Malone', which is present in instrumental form only
Warner Brothers WX 238 vinyl issue, January 89; Warner Brothers 925848-2 CD issue, January 89; Warner Brothers 7599-26575-2 In store promo, with 'rose' picture disc; Warner Brothers (details unknown) US only CD in fake leather photo-album, with black and white picture disc, May 91

GIRLS, GIRLS, GIRLS

CD One: Watching The Detectives, I Hope You're Happy Now, This Year's Girl, Lover's Walk, Pump It Up, Strict Time, Temptation, (I Don't Want To Go To) Chelsea, High Fidelity, Lovable (MacManus/O'Riordan), Mystery Dance, Big Tears, Uncomplicated, Lipstick Vogue, Man Out Of Time, Brilliant Mistake, New Lace Sleeves, Accidents Will Happen, Beyond Belief, Black And White World, Green Shirt, The Loved Ones, New Amsterdam, (The Angels Want To Wear My) Red Shoes, King Horse, Big Sister's Clothes
CD Two: Alison, Man Called Uncle, Party Girl, Shabby Doll, Motel Matches, Tiny Steps, Almost Blue, Riot Act, Love Field, Possession, Poisoned Rose, Indoor Fireworks, I Want You, Oliver's Army, Pills And Soap, Sunday's Best, Watch Your Step, Less Than Zero, Clubland, Tokyo Storm Warning (MacManus/O'Riordan), Shipbuiding (Costello/Langer)
Above is the CD track listing: from which the cassette, DAT and vinyl versions all slightly differ. The CD booklet contains some very insightful comments by Costello on each song, the whole thing "arranged in four parts so as to try and tell a number of different stories".
Demon DFIEND 160 Double LP, October 89; Demon FIENDCASS 160 Cassette, October 89; Demon FIENDDAT 160 DAT, October 89; Demon FIEND CD 160 CD, October 89

MIGHTY LIKE A ROSE

Side One: The Other Side Of Summer, Hurry Down Doomsday (The Bugs Are Taking Over) (Costello/Keltner), How To Be Dumb, All Grown Up, Invasion Hit Parade, Harpies Bizarre, After The Fall

Side Two: George And Her Rival, So Like Candy (McCartney/MacManus), Interlude: Couldn't Call It Unexpected No 2, Playboy To A Man (McCartney/MacManus), Sweet Pear, Broken (O'Riordan), Couldn't Call It Unexpected No 4
Produced by Mitchell Froom, Kevin Killen and DPA MacManus. Guests include Rob Wasserman, Nick Lowe, Fiachra Trench, Marc Ribot, Ross MacManus, and his son variously alluded to as playing "big stupid guitar", and as the "Mighty Corsican". The lyrics are printed on the inner sleeve, and the whole thing dedicated to "Cait, my unspeakable wife". Trusty sidekick Milo Lewis is given special thanks as "chief redcoat and keeper of the paperwork monolith"
Warner Brothers WX 419 LP version May 91; Warner Brothers WX 419CD CD version May 91

GBH-SOUNDTRACK
Side One: GBH Opening Titles: The Life And Times Of Michael Murray, "It Wasn't Me", Men Of Alloy, Lambs To The Slaughter, Bubbles, The 'Goldilocks' Theme, Perfume – The Honour Of Money, Barbara Douglas: Assassin, Pursuit Suite, Prufrock Quartet: The Roaring Boy
Side Two: "... So I Used Five!", Love From A Cold Land, In A Cemetery Garden, "Smack 'Im!", Woodlands – "Oh Joy", "It's Cold Up There", Going Home Service, Grave Music, The Puppet Masters' Work, "He's *So* Easy". Another Time, Another Place, Closing Titles
All music composed by Richard Harvey and Elvis Costello. Soundtrack to Channel 4 TV series by Alan Bleasdale
Demon Soundtrack DSLP 4 LP version, July 91; Demon S'tracks DSCD 4 CD version, August 91

THE JULIET LETTERS
Deliver Us, For Other Eyes, Swine, Expert Rites, Dead Letter, I Almost Had A Weakness, Why?, Who Do You Think You Are?, Taking My Life In Your Hands, This Offer Is Unrepeatable, Dear Sweet Filthy World, The Letter Home, Jackson Monk And Rowe, This Sad Business, Romeo's Seance, I Thought I'd Write To Juliet, Last Post, The First To Leave, Damnation's Cellar, The Birds Will Still Be Singing
All songs by Costello, some co-written with members of The Brodsky Quartet. Produced by Kevin Killen, Elvis Costello and The Brodsky Quartet. CD booklet carries full lyrics, and explanatory notes. "A song sequence for string quartet and voice"
Warner Brothers 9362 45180-2 CD issue January 93; Warner Brothers 9362-45180-1 Europe only vinyl edition, January 93

THE FIRST 2¹ᐟ² YEARS
4 CD box set with booklet, which issues the newly augmented and remastered versions of My Aim Is True, This Year's Model, Armed Forces *and* Live At The El Mocambo
Demon DPAM BOX 1 October 93

BRUTAL YOUTH
Pony Street, Kinder Murder, 13 Steps Lead Down, This Is Hell, Clown Strike, You Tripped At Every Step, Still Too Soon To Know, 20% Amnesia, Sulky Girl, London's Brilliant Parade, My Science Fiction Twin, Rocking Horse Rod, Just About Glad, All The Rage, Favourite Hour
Produced by Mitchell Froom and Elvis Costello. CD booklet includes photographs of the young MacManus, but no lyric sheet. Backing musicians are The Attractions, with Nick Lowe on bass for seven tracks
Warner Brothers 9362 45535 -2 CD issue, March 94

THE VERY BEST OF ELVIS COSTELLO AND THE ATTRACTIONS
Alison, Watching The Detectives, (I Don't Want To Go To) Chelsea, Pump It Up, Radio Radio, (What's So Funny) 'Bout) Peace Love And Understanding? (Lowe), Oliver's Army, Accidents Will

Happen, I Can't Stand Up For Falling Down, New Amsterdam, High Fidelity, Clubland, Watch Your Step, Good Year For The Roses (J.Chestnut), Beyond Belief, Man Out Of Time, Everyday I Write The Book, Shipbuilding (Costello/Langer), Love Field, Brilliant Mistake, Indoor Fireworks
CD booklet contains all the album and single sleeves from the period covered, 1977 to 1986
Demon DPAMLP 13 Double LP, October 94; Demon DPAM 13 CD issue, October 94

KOJAK VARIETY

Strange (Walter Hawkins), Hidden Charms (Willie Dixon), Remove This Doubt (Holland/Dozier/Holland), I Threw It All Away (Dylan), Leave My Kitten Alone (Little Willie John/Titus Turner), Everybody's Crying Mercy (Mose Allison), I've Been Wrong Before (Randy Newman), Bama Lama Bama Loo (R Penniman aka Little Richard), Must You Throw Dirt In My Face (Bill Anderson), Pouring Water On A Drowning Man (D.Baker/D.McCormick), The Very Thought Of You (Ray Noble), Payday (Jesse Winchester), Please Stay (Bacharach/David), Running Out Of Fools (K Rogers/R Ahlert), Days (Ray Davies)
"This is a record of some of my favourite songs performed with some of my favourite musicians".
*The CD is subtitled – or should that read 'file under' – Rhythm & Blues * Popular Ballads.*
Produced by Elvis Costello and Kevin Killen, featuring an all star cast of musicians: James Burton, Marc Ribot, Jim Keltner, Jerry Scheff, Larry Knechtel and Pete Thomas. Elvis provides notes about each song in the CD booklet
Warner Bros 9362-45903-2 CD issue, May 95

DEEP DEAD BLUE

Weird Nightmare (Charles Mingus), Love Field, Shamed Into Love (Costello/Ruben Blades), Gigi (Lerner/Loewe), Poor Napoleon, Baby Plays Around (Cait O'Riordan/MacManus), Deep Dead Blue (Costello/Frisell)
Mini album with Bill Frisell, live 25 June 95 at the MeltDown Festival, Queen Elizabeth Hall, London. The CD insert is one piece of thick cardboard, so no lyrics hereabouts
Warner Bros 9362-46073-2 CD issue, August 95

JAKE'S PROGRESS

Jake's Progress Opening Sequence, Map Of Africa, Julie's Pregnant Pause, Monica's Fortune Telling, Cisco Kid, Graveyard Waltz, Housewarming, Moving In, Howling At The Moon, Unhappy Home Service, Ursine Variations, Mrs Rampton Reminisces, A Friend In Need, Death Of Alex, Closing Titles Remembering Alex, Leaving Home, Eliot's Heartbreak And Flashback, Kate's Abuse, Grave Dance, Banquo, Fall From Grace, Play With Me Mummy
Music jointly composed by Elvis Costello and Richard Harvey
Demon S'tracks DSCD 14 CD issue, 1995

ALL THIS USELESS BEAUTY

The Other End Of The Telescope (Costello/Mann), Little Atoms, All This Useless Beauty, Complicated Shadows, Why Can't A Man Stand Alone?, Distorted Angel, Shallow Grave (McCartney/Costello), Poor Fractured Atlas, Starting To Come To Me, You Bowed Down, It's Time, I Want To Vanish
Produced by Geoff Emerick and Elvis Costello, and featuring The Attractions, as well as the Brodsky Quartet, Roy Babbington. Dedicated to "Dr O'Riordan". The CD booklet features the lyrics in various stages of legibility
Warner Bros 9362-46198-2 CD issue, 1996

FOR THE FIRST TIME IN AMERICA

1) Los Angeles: Live At The Troubadour 14 May 1996

Temptation, Poor Fractured Atlas, I Just Don't Know What To Do With Myself (Bacharach/David), It's Time, Man Out Of Time/Shallow Grave (McCartney/MacManus)
2) San Francisco: Live At The Fillmore 15 May 1996
Just About Glad, Why Can't A Man Stand Alone?, My Dark Life, All This Useless Beauty, Ship Of Fools (Garcia/Hunter)
3) Chicago: Live at The Park West, 18 May 1996
The Long Honeymoon, Starting To Come To Me, The Other End Of The Telescope (Costello/Mann), All The Rage, Watching The Detectives
4) Boston: Live At The Paradise, 20 May 1996
You Bowed Down, The Long Honeymoon, Distorted Angel, The Angels Want To Wear My Red Shoes, Little Atoms, My Funny Valentine (Hart/Rodgers)
5) New York: Live At The Supper Club, 22 May 1996
Black Sails In The Sunset, You'll Never Be A Man, Just A Memory, I Want To Vanish, Medley: Alison, Laughing A Little (Bell/Creed), Tracks Of My Tears (Tarplin/Moore/W Robinson), Tears Of A Clown (W Robinson/S Wonder/Cosby), No More Tearstained Make-up (W Robinson), Clowntime Is Over
Elvis Costello and Steve Nieve 'Live and acoustic. Five cities, five nights'. No producer credits
Warner Bros 9362 46469 2 5CD box, originally released as a promo, and subsequently in December 1996 as an 'extremely limited edition' by WB of New York

EXTREME HONEY: THE VERY BEST OF THE WARNER BROS YEARS

The Bridge I Burned, Veronica, Sulky Girl, So Like Candy, 13 Steps Lead Down, All This Useless Beauty, My Dark Life, The Other Side Of Summer, Kinder Murder, Deep Dark Truthful Mirror, Hurry Down Doomsday, Poor Fractured Atlas, The Birds Will Still Be Singing, London's Brilliant Parade, Tramp The Dirt Down, Couldn't Call It Unexpected #4, I Want To Vanish, All The Rage.
Warner Bros 9362 46801 2 CD issue, October 1997

PAINTED FROM MEMORY; THE SONGS OF BACHARACH AND COSTELLO

The Darkest Place, Toledo, I Still Have That Other Girl, This House Is Empty Now, Tears At The Birthday Party, Such Unlikely Lovers, My Thief, The Long Division, Painted From Memory, The Sweetest Punch, What's Her Name Today, God Give Me Strength.
Mercury 538 002-2 CD issue, September 1998
Steve Nieve plays keyboards.

missing in action

During his long career, some album projects have failed to come to fruition, or remain locked behind record company doors. The most tantalising include:

1) The Nashville shows in December 1977, recorded for a planned live album, for US ears only, but never released
2) 'Almost Almost Blue', a second volume of country and western standards
3) The January 7 1982 concert with the Royal Philarmonic Orchestra – of which only one track, 'I'm Your Toy', has seen the light of day – was videoed and recorded for release, but a contractual dispute with the Musicians Union ensued
Two projects, 'Encore' and 'Idiophone' were substantially reworked. 'Hello Cruel World' was to have been a variant of the album of almost the same name.

bootlegs: a chronological survey

When asked his views on bootlegs, Costello appeared relaxed on reproductions of music played live to a paying audience, but became angered about studio out-takes, as something never intended for public consumption. Fortunately, the vast bulk of Costello bootlegs dwell on live performances and, if nothing else, give an interesting overview of changing set lists over the years. The periods in Costello's ever changing live gigs best represented on bootleg are his first fiery years with The Attractions, and the mid 90s onwards. Not much seems to have surfaced between. Here are the most interesting items, the early listings of which come c/o *Hot Wacks*.

One warning: some of the titles below are – at the very best – speculative, often interpreted in another language from a dodgy tape. In all, vinyl bootlegs are more financially valuable nowadays, CD bootlegs – by and large – more musically fruitful, especially if the magic words "soundboard tape" appear on its packaging. Items not otherwise credited exist in good quality, but in cassette form only, and came into my own archive as part of that great ocean of tape trading which ebbs and flows between collectors the world over.

FLIP CITY DEMOS
Third Rate Romance (Amazing Rhythm Aces) (2 takes), Living In Paradise, Radio Soul (2 takes), Pay It Back, Imagination Is A Powerful Deceiver (3 takes), Knocking On Heaven's Door (Dylan), Packing Up (2 takes), Don't Stop The Band
OUR AIM IS TRUE LP (Stiff) *mono, with fake Stiff-style artwork*
AIM TO PLEASE/FLIP CITY DEMOS/STIFFED AGAIN CD (Conquer)
These mysterious demos have also been attributed to DP Costello, but they correspond more to the Flip City set list, as far as we know it, and can be fairly accurately traced back to the 1975 demos recorded at the Hope and Anchor Studios by Elvis's then band. 'Radio Soul' is an early version of 'Radio Radio'.

CAPITAL RADIO DEMOS, August 1976
Lip Service, Wave A White Flag, Blame It On Cain, Jump Up, Mystery Dance, Poison Moon
DANGER ZONE LP (Sherlock Holmes) limited and numbered ed
HONKY TONK DEMOS LP (Compact)
Recorded by Elvis at home on a 4 track tape recorder in his living room. All feature just voice and guitar. 'Cheap Reward' is a hybrid of the words of 'Lip Service' and the tune of 'Stranger In The House'. 'Mystery Dance' features an extra verse. 'Wave A White Flag', 'Poison Moon' and 'Jump Up' remain unreleased.

EARLY STUDIO OUTTAKES
Hoover Factory, You Belong To Me, Radio Radio
50,000,000 ELVIS FANS CAN'T BE WRONG
These three solo tracks are wrongly attributed on the sleeve to 'Radar Records Demo Tapes', and by

some experts to the Honky Tonk demos. They are, instead, most likely taken from the first demo – just voice and guitar – that Elvis quickly laid down at Pathway while Nick Lowe was getting a stiff drink down a highly nervous Wreckless Eric in a pub down the road. Elvis saw his chance, and took it.

The same bootleg also captures the first John Peel session ('Mystery Dance', 'Red Shoes', 'Less Than Zero' and 'Blame It On Cain') and a live 'Alison' from Granada TV. It further adds three songs live at Erics – '(I Don't Want To Go To) Chelsea', 'Watching The Detectives' and 'Lip Service' – a *Top Of The Pops* rendition of 'Watching The Detectives' and a couple of rare B-sides, as well as live material from the Ackers Club, New York, and the Agora, Cleveland.

The album is divided between 'The Elvis Outtakes' and 'The Elvis Live Show'

SWEDISH TV, 30 September 1977
Watching The Detectives, (Interview), Mystery Dance
SHAKEN, NOT STIRRED LP (Unfit) wonderful colour cover, a spoof of James Bond

OLD WALDORF THEATRE, SAN FRANCISCO, November 1977
Ist Show: Pump It Up, Welcome To The Working Week, Red Shoes, Blame It On Cain, Waiting FOr The End Of The World, The Beat, Less Than Zero, Alison, Miracle Man, You Belong To Me, Lipstick Vogue, Watching The Detectives
2nd Show; Mystery Dance, No Action, No Dancing, I'm Not Angry, Chelsea, Radio Radio, Less Than Zero, Living In Paradise, Alison, Miracle Man, Hand in Hand
RADIOACTIVITY CD (Gold Standard) *First US appearance*

CHICAGO, 3 December 1977
Welcome To The Working Week, Red Shoes, Waiting For The End Of The World, No Action, The Beat, Less Than Zero, Radio Radio, You Belong To Me, Lost In The Lipstick Vogue, Watching The Detectives, Pump It Up, Miracle Man, Mystery Dance, No Dancing
ARMED AND DANGEROUS LP (Impossible Recordworks) *WXRT stereo broadcast*
My copy is signed by all the band, especially surprising as they are credited on the back cover as Steve Naive: bass guitar, Pete Thomas: keyboards and Bruce Thomas: percussion

AGORA THEATRE, CLEVELAND, 5 December 1977
Welcome To The Working Week, (The Angels Wanna Wear My) Red Shoes, Hand In Hand, Waiting For The End Of The World, No Action, Less Than Zero, The Beat, No Dancing, Big Tears, Little Triggers, Radio Radio, You Belong To Me, Pump It Up, Lipstick Vogue, Watching The Detectives, Miracle Man, Mystery Dance
50,000,000 ELVIS FANS CAN'T BE WRONG 2LP (EL) *WMMS stereo broadcast*
This wonderful bootleg has a sleeve parodying the Elvis Presley album of (virtually) the same title.
NO DANCING CD (Joker)

HOT CLUB, PHILADELPHIA, 7 December 1977
Welcome To The Working Week, Red Shoes, Waiting For The End Of The World, No Action, Less Than Zero, The Beat, Roadette Song, Blame It On Cain, Little Triggers, Radio Radio

HIS FIRST KORNYPHONE RECORD LP (TAKL) WWMR stereo broadcast
Kilburn And The Highroads 'Roadette Song' is here mistitled as 'That's What It's All About'

FOUR ACKERS CLUB, UTICA, 15 December 1977
Living In Paradise, The Roadette Song, Little Triggers
50,000,000 ELVIS FANS CAN'T BE WRONG LP (EL)
'The Roadette Song' was written by Ian Dury, then of Kilburn And The High Roads, which makes

its misnaming on the sleeve here as 'I Wrote This Song' particularly ironic

The 1977 SHOW
Same track listing as Chicago 3.12 on CHARMED AND DANGEROUS
THE 1978 SHOW:
El Mocambo, Toronto 6 March 1978
EXIT LP (Toasted) 1980 Limited edition
Front cover is a young lady dressed in boxing kit, back cover a b&w shot of another younger girl in straps and armour. Last year's model?

SOMETHING NEW
Plain jacket, insert has b&w pic of Elvis on stage, *"featuring Girls Talk, Oliver's Army, Walk And Don't Look Back, You Lied To Me, Watching The Detectives, Pump It Up, plus more"*
Record is pressed as 'A Fool In Love' by the Regents
My copy signed by Elvis, Bruce Thomas and Pete Thomas

PARAMOUNT THEATRE, SEATTLE, 10 February 1978
Mystery Dance, Waiting For The End Of The World, Night Rally, No Action, Less Than Zero, The Beat, (I Don't Want To Go To) Chelsea, This Year's Girl, Little Triggers
WE'RE ALL CREEPS LP, *poor mono*
I'VE JUST COME FROM CALIFORNIA CD (Parrot) *perfect sound quality*

WARNER THEATRE, WASHINGTON DC, 28 February 1978 WHFS stereo broadcast
Pump It Up, Waiting For The End Of The World, No Action, Less Than Zero, The Beat, Red Shoes, (I Don't Want To Go To) Chelsea, Hand In Hand, Little Triggers, Radio Radio, You Belong To Me, Lipstick Vogue, Watching The Detectives, Mystery Dance, Miracle Man
IN THE DISTRICT OF COLUMBIA CD (Oh Boy)
ELVIS GOES TO WASHINGTON AND DAVE EDMUNDS AND ROCKPILE DON'T 2 LP (Pacifist). *This adds 'Blame It On Cain' and 'Chemistry Class' – here titled 'Final Solution'*

C.W. POST COLLEGE, GREENVALE, LONG ISLAND NEW YORK, 3 March 1978
Red Shoes, The Beat, Radio Radio, Less Than Zero, Waiting For The End Of The World, No Action, (I Don't Want To Go To) Chelsea, Pump It Up, You Belong To Me, Lipstick Vogue, Watching The Detectives, I'm Not Angry
CRAWLING THROUGH THE USA CD (Flashback)

EL MOCAMBO CLUB, TORONTO, 6 March 1978
A limited edition promo, and now officially released on CD, this superb CHUM FM broadcast was much bootlegged at the time
KORNYPHONE RADIO HOUR LP (TAKRL 901)
LAST YEAR'S MODEL LP (Time Warp)
RADIO RADIO ... LIVE AT EL MOCAMBO LP

ROUNDHOUSE, LONDON, April 1978
Stranger In The House, Oliver's Army, Accidents Will Happen, Waiting For The End Of The World, No Action, This Year's Girl, Lip Service, Less Than Zero, Big Tears, Hand In Hand, The Beat, Red Shoes, Alison, Miracle Man, (I Don't Want To Go To) Chelsea, Mystery Dance, Watching The Detectives, You Belong To Me, Pump It Up
ACCIDENTS 2LP (Impossible) *mono, low quality*
ELVIS COSTELLO LP (Toasted)

Nick Lowe on bass

ZELLERBACH HALL, BERKELEY CA, 2 June 1978 mistakenly given as 2 July
Mystery Dance, Red Shoes, Hand In Hand, Waiting For The End Of The World, (I Don't Want To Go To) Chelsea), Little Triggers, I'm Not Angry, This Year's Girl
CRAWLING THROUGH THE USA CD (Flashback)

SAN FRANCISCO, 7 June 1978
Goon Squad, Less Than Zero, Chelsea, Pump It Up, Radio Radio, Lipstick Vogue, Watching The Detectives, Party Girl, I'm Not Angry
THE LAST FOXTROT LP (Rubber Robot) *segues into a Nick Lowe concert*
LIKE BUDDY HOLLY ON ACID LP (Rubber Robot)

WDR STUDIOS, BREMEN, GERMANY, 15 June 1978
Mystery Dance, Waiting For The End Of The World, Lip Service, Two Little Hitlers, The Beat, Night Rally, This Year's Girl, No Action, (I Don't Want To Go To) Chelsea, Lipstick Vogue, Watching The Detectives, Pump It Up, You Belong To Me
SUPERLATIVE LIVE CD (Noria)
THE RISE AND RISE OF DECLAN MACMANUS CD (Tone 2)

OLD WALDORF THEATRE, SAN FRANCISCO, November 1978
Pump It Up, Welcome To The Working Week, Red Shoes, Blame It On Cain, Waiting For The End Of The World, The Beat, Less Than Zero, Alison, Miracle Man, You Belong To Me, Lipstick Vogue, Watching The Detectives, Mystery Dance, No Action, No Dancing, I'm Not Angry, (I Don't Want To Go To) Chelsea, Radio Radio, Less Than Zero, Living In Paradise, Alison, Miracle Man, Hand In Hand
RADIOACTIVITY CD (Gold Standard)

VARIOUS CONCERTS 1978/1979
Goon Squad, Big Opportunity, Oliver's Army, Busy Bodies, Two Little Hitlers, Green Shirt, Big Boys, Party Girl, Wednesday Week, Talking In The Dark, Stranger In The House, Neat Neat Neat, Radio Sweetheart, Night Rally, My Funny Valentine
HATE YOU LIVE LP (EC) *multi-coloured vinyl, good mono recordings taken from FM broadcasts*

PALOMINO CLUB, VAN NUYS, NORTH HOLLYWOOD, 16 February 1979
Big Boys, Hand In Hand, Opportunity, Accidents Will Happen, Goon Squad, Two Little Hitlers, The Beat, Green Shirt, I Stand Accused, Radio Radio, Stranger In The House, Psycho, If I Could Put Them All Together (I'd Have You), Motel Matches, He'll Have To Go, Girls Talk, Alison, Chelsea, Mystery Dance
LIVE AT THE PALOMINO LP (Centrifugal) good mono
6 tracks also turn up as Side 2 of SHAKEN NOT STIRRED (Unfit)
A legendary concert, with the original 'Psycho' – not the overdubbed studio B-side, and featuring some country influences, and John McFee from Clover on steel guitar

CANNES, December 1979, PARIS, June 1979, MONTPELLIER, December 1979
I Stand Accused, Hand In Hand, Opportunity, Green Shirt, Chelsea, B Movie, So Young, Oliver's Army, Stand Up For, Girls Talk, Five Gears, Clown Time Is Over, Watching The Detectives, Possession, Love For Tender, Gangster, I Need The Human Touch
BLITZKREIG 3 45rpm EP Box Set (Thunderbolt) Edition of 500, *blue vinyl*

HAMMERSMITH ODEON, CONCERTS FOR THE PEOPLE OF KAMPUCHEA, 29 December

1979
Elvis and The Attractions play 'The Imposter'
CONCERTS FOR THE PEOPLE OF KAMPUCHEA 2CD (Hammersmith)

VARIOUS CONCERTS, 1979
Opportunity, Moods For Moderns, Green Shirt, Party Girl, Girls Talk, Accidents Will Happen, Big
Boys, Goon Squad, Oliver's Army, (What's So Funny 'Bout) Peace, Love And Understanding, Radio
Radio
BIG OPPORTUNITY LP *multi-coloured vinyl*

JOHN PEEL SESSION, March 1980
B Movie, Possession, High Fidelity, Beaten To The Punch
RADIO BLAST EP (Bang)

HOPE AND ANCHOR, 14 May 1980
Guitarist Martin Belmont replaces Steve Nieve. An interesting run through of some of the Get
Happy!! *songs – and matching soul covers – the concert was recorded for the US King Biscuit
Flower Hour and BBC's Radio One In Concert*
Temptation, Help Me, I Stand Accused, One Fine Heartache, Secondary Modern, High Fidelity,
Lipstick Vogue, Waiting For The End Of The World, Walk And Don't Look Back, Girls Talk, Watching
The Detectives, You Belong To Me, Oliver's Army, Pump It Up
SOMETHING NEW LP (EC) *excellent mono*
From the same concert, 'Little Sister' appears on SHAKEN NOT STIRRED (Unfit), and other tracks
on HIDING UNDER COVERS

MONTREUX JAZZ FESTIVAL, 12 July 1980
Temptation, Walk And Don't Look Back, Clubland, From A Whisper To A Scream, Oliver's Army, I
Can't Stand Up, Pump It Up
SUPERLATIVE LIVE CD (Noriaa)

VENUE UNKNOWN, 23 August 1980
Alison, Clubland, Oliver's Army, Watching The Detectives, You Belong To Me, Lover's Walk, Less
Than Zero, Big Tears, High Fidelity, Radio Radio, Can't Stand Up For Falling Down, How Does It
Feel (?), Accidents Will Happen, The Beat, Temptation, (What's So Funny 'Bout) Peace Love And
Understanding, Mystery Man, Somebody, You'll Never Be A Man, Chelsea, Girl Don't, Pump It Up
HEATWAVE 2LP

APOLLO THEATRE, GLASGOW, 10 December 1980
Little Sister, Watching The Detectives, You Belong To Me, Oliver's Army, Don't Look Back, Girls
Talk
RED-SHOED IMPOSTER LP (Sphinx)

VARIOUS CONCERTS, 1980
Love For Tender, Human Touch, The Imposter, Secondary Modern, Girls Talk, King Horse,
Temptation, Opportunity, Five Gears In Reverse, I Can't Stand Up For Falling Down, Clowntime Is
Over, Possession, B-Movie, I Stand Accused, Motel Matches, High Fidelity
DELUXE LP (GHL) *Opening with a song made famous by the other Elvis, this has been put
together from various live sources to be a live counterpart to 'Get Happy', with Steve Nieve in
particularly good form. There are changes to the lyrics of 'Temptation', 'Five Gears In Reverse'
has an extra verse, and the second verse of 'Motel Matches' differs radically from the recorded*

version

LIVE 1981
Tonight The Bottle Let Me Down, He's Got You, Color Of The Blues, Sweet Dreams
DANGER ZONE LP (Sherlock Holmes)

LIVE 1982
Kid About It, Man Out Of Time
DANGER ZONE LP (Sherlock Holmes)

DINGWALLS, September 1983
Possession, High Fidelity, Town Cryer, Everyday I Write The Book, Backstabbers, King Horse, Say You Would've Cared, Watching The Detectives, Temptation, Clubland, World And His Wife, Man Out Of Time, Shipbuilding, Oliver's Army

GRUGAHALLE, ESSEN, WEST GERMANY, 15 October 1983
Let Them All Talk, Possession, Watching The Detectives, The Greatest Thing, Man Out Of Time, New Lace Sleeves, Mystery Dance, Shabby Doll, Kid About It, Big Sisters Clothes, Stand Down Margaret, Beyond Belief, Clubland, The World And His Wife, Alison, King Horse, Everyday I Write The Book, I Can't Stand Up For Falling Down, Pump It Up
RED-SHOWED IMPOSTER LP (Sphinx)

HAMMERSMITH, 17 October 1983 with Afrodiziac
Let Them All Talk, Possession, Watch Your Step, The Greatest Thing, Man Out Of Time, Shabby Doll, From Head To Toe, Charm School, Oliver's Army, Shipbuilding, The World And His Wife, Alison, Clowntime Is Over, Everyday I Write The Book, TKO (Boxing Day)
RIOT ACT CD (Postscript)

PIER 84, NYC, November 1983
Let Them All Talk, Possession, Watching The Detectives, Secondary Modern, The Greatest Thing, King Of Thieves, Mystery Dance, Shabby Doll, New Lace Sleeves, Every Day I Write The Book, Watch Your Step, King Horse, Clowntime Is Over, Tears Before Bedtime, High Fidelity, Alison, I Can't Stand Up For Falling Down, Pump It Up
ELVIS AT THE PIER 2CD (Bandido)

STUDIO OUTTAKES, 1983
Danger Zone, Big Sisters Clothes, Stand Down Margaret, Pills And Soap
DANGER ZONE LP (Sherlock Holmes)

TOWER THEATRE, PHILADELPHIA, PA SPRING 1984 TOUR with band
Let Them All Talk, Greatest Thing, Girls Talk, Lipstick Vogue, Watching The Detectives, Clubland, Everyday I Write The Book, The Only Flame In Town, Getting Mighty Crowded, Alison, Pump It Up
WRITING MY STORY CD (Beech Marten)

ROME, November 1984 solo
Girls Talk, The Invisible Man, Man Out Of Time, The Only Flame In Town, High Fidelity, Accidents Will Happen, Almost Blue, Worthless Thing, Little Triggers, Love Field, Every Day I Write The Book, Angels Wanna Wear My Red Shoes, Alison, Baby In Black
A MAN OUT OF TIME 2LP mono

PARIS, November 1984 solo
Almost Blue, Pills And Soap, Luxemburg, Hope You're Happy Now, In A Love Field, Nothing At The End Of The Rainbow, Alison/You Win Again, If You Give Me What I Want, Everyday I Write The Book, Image Of Me, Suffering Face, Baby's In Black, If You're Going To San Francisco, Soul Survivor, Rot Act
ELVIS COSTELLO GOES TO PARIS ... AND THE ATTRACTIONS DON'T CD (Archivio)

MINERS' STRIKE BENEFIT, LOGAN HALL, LONDON, 9 March 1985
Betrayal, No Action, Waiting For The End Of The World, Watching The Detectives, You Belong To Me, Less Than Zero, (I Don't Want To Go To) Chelsea, Brilliant Mistake, Why Don't We Try Anymore, Alison, You Win Again, High Fidelity, Sleep Of The Just, Beyond Belief, Clubland, Blue Chair, Why Must You Throw Dirt In My Face, No Reason To Quit, Big Sisters Clothes, Stand Down Margaret, Oliver's Army, Pump It Up, Shipbuilding
POLITICAL ACTION CD (Doberman)

VENUE UNKNOWN, 23 November 1986
THIS IS TOMORROW CD
ELVIS COSTELLO LIVE UNAPPROVED CD (Mojo)

ROYALTY THEATRE, LONDON, 28 November 1986
Suit Of Lights, Tokyo Storm Warning, Brilliant Mistake, Heathen Town, American Without Tears, King Of Confidence, Deportees Club, I'm Having It All, Pretty In Pink, You Little Fool, Our Little Angel, Crimes Of Paris/Wild Mountain Thyme
LITTLE HANDS OF CONCRETE 2 x CD (Doberman)
Acoustic solo performance

WATERMANS ARTS CENTRE, BRENTFORD, 29 March 1987
CD1: Introduction, Sally Sue Brown,Red Shoes, Green Shirt, Leave My Kitten Alone, Poisoned Rose, Inch By Inch, Only Flame In Town, Tonight The Bottle Let Me Down, Little Palaces, New Amsterdam/You've Got To Hide Your Love Away, King's Shilling, Radio Sweetheart, Jackie Wilson Said, Alison/You Win Again, Milk Of Human Kindness, Don't Let Me Be Misunderstood, Oliver's Army, Shipbuilding, (What's So Funny 'Bout)Peace, Love And Understanding
CD2: Introduction, Shamed Into Love, I Want You, Uncomplicated, Sleep Of The Just, True Love Ways, A Good Year For The Roses, Twist And Shout
LITTLE HANDS OF CONCRETE
Complete acoustic set

SWEETWATER, MILL VALLEY, 24 April 1989
Accidents Will Happen, Deep Dark Truthful Mirror, Mystery Dance, Poisoned Rose, God's Comic, Red Shoes, New Lace Sleeves, Pads Paws And Claws, Radio Sweetheart/Jackie Wilson Said, Peace Love And Understanding, Only Daddy'll Walk That Line, Leave My Kitten Alone, You Win Again, Tonight The Bottle Let Me Down, Why Don't You Love Me Like You Used To Do, CC Rider, Lovelight
SWEETWATER: ELVIS COSTELLO AND JERRY GARCIA CD (Moonlight)
Costello's solo show with guest appearances from some of The Confederates, and with Jerry Garcia

BBC LATE SHOW, 1989 solo
God's Comic, Let Him Dangle, Baby Plays Around, Tramp The Dirt Down
UNPLUGGED & UNSHAVED: A BEARD YEARS ANTHOLOGY CD (Smoking Crocodile)

MTV UNPLUGGED, 1991
Deep Down Truthful Mirror, Hurry Down Dooms Day, So Like Candy/I Want You, Other Side Of
Summer, Bama Laura Bama Lou
UNPLUGGED & UNSHAVED: A BEARD YEARS ANTHOLOGY CD (Smoking Crocodile)

RUDE 5 TOUR REHEARSALS, 1991
Strange, How To Be Dumb, Alison, My Hidden Shame, Watch Your Step, Georgie And Her Rival,
Home Is Anywhere You Hang Your Head, Suit Of Lights
UNPLUGGED & UNSHAVED: A BEARD YEARS ANTHOLOGY CD (Smoking Crocodile)

HOLLYWOOD, 13 May 1994
Intro/No Action, High Fidelity, The Beat, Pointer Street, Beyond Belief, London's Brilliant Parade,
You Tripped At Every Step, Amnesia, Clown Strike, Kinder Murder, Shadow Doll, Rocking Horse
Road, Still Too Soon To Know, Everyday I Write The Book, Watching The Detectives, You Belong To
Me, Just About Glad, Mystery Dance, 13 Steps Lead Down/Radio Radio
GOING STATESIDE CD (Hawk)

NORTHRUP AUDITORIUM, MINNEAPOLIS, 27 May 1994
CD 1: No Action, High Fidelity, The Beat, Beyond Belief, Sulky Girl, London's Brilliant Parade, Deep
Dark Truthful Mirror, You Tripped At Every Step, Pony Street, New Lace Sleeves, Clown Strike,
Kinder Murder, Shabby Doll, Rocking Horse Road,
CD 2: Still Too Soon To Know, So Like Candy, Man Out Of Time, Watching The Detectives, You
Belong To Me, 13 Steps Lead Down, Radio Radio, Lipstick Vogue, Party Girl, Alison, Tracks Of My
Tears, Accidents Will Happen, All The Rage, Pump It Up
SO LIKE CANDY 2CD (Rag Doll)

GLASTONBURY, June 1994
CD 1: No Action, The Beat, Waiting For The World, Beyond Belief, Sulky Girl, London's Brilliant
Parade, Deep Dark Truthful Mirror, Oliver's Army, Less Than Zero, Clown Strike, Kinder Murder,
Clubland, Rocking Horse Road,
CD 2: Man Out Of Time, Watching The Detectives, You Belong To Me, 13 Steps Lead Down/Radio
Radio, Lipstick Vogue, (I Don't Want To Go To) Chelsea/Lipstick Vogue, Alison, Tracks Of My
Tears/Tears Of A Clown/Clowntime Is Over, Accidents Will Happen, All The Rage, (What's So Funny
'Bout) Peace Love And Understanding, Pump It Up, Band Introduction, Sulky Girl, Rocking Horse
Road, 13 Steps Lead Down/Radio Radio
LIVE AT GLASTONBURY ENGLAND 2CD

THE FORUM, ROME, 19 July 1994
No Action, The Beat, Accidents Will Happen, Beyond Belief, Sulky Girl, London's Brilliant Parade,
Deep Dark Truthful Mirror, Everyday I Write The Book, Hand In Hand, Clown Strike, Kinder
Murder/Less Than Zero/Rocking Horse Road, Still Too Soon To Know, You Tripped At Every Step,
Shipbuilding/Mystery Dance/Watching The Detectives/You Belong To Me/13 Steps/Radio Radio
BUDDY HOLLY ON ACID CD (Kaleidoscope) *soundboard*
BRUTAL YOUTH TOUR 1994 CD
YOUTHFUL ELVIS CD (Home) *Audience tape of above*

KOSEI NEUKIN HALL, TOKYO, 22 September 1994
BRILLIANT PARADE CD (My Phoenix)

KOSEI NEUKIN HALL, TOKYO, 22 September 1994

CD1: Pony Street, Waiting For The End Of The World, Beyond Belief, Sulky Girl, London's Brilliant Parade, Deep Dark Truthful Mirror, Oliver's Army, You'll Never Be A Man, Temptation, New Lace Sleeves, Clown Strike, Kinder Murder, Shabby Doll, Rocking Horse Road, Brilliant Mistake
CD2: So Like Candy, This Year's Girl, Red Shoes, Mystery Dance, You Belong To Me, Thirteen Steps Lead Down, Radio Radio, Favourite Hour, Uncomplicated, Lipstick Vogue, Watching The Detectives, Little Triggers, Alison/You Win Again, (What's So Funny 'Bout) Peace, Love And Understanding, Pump It Up
TOKYO'S BRILLIANT PARADE
Soundboard recording

GLASGOW BARROWNLANDS, 16 November 1994

BBC FM broadcast
UNDER THE INFLUENCE CD (Kiss The Stone)

OXFORD APOLLO, 27 November 1994

Princess In Love (intro), I Want You, No Action, Accidents Will Happen, Watching The Detectives, Deep Dark Truthful Mirror, So Like Candy, London's Brilliant Parade, Pony Street, Honey Are You Straight Or Are You Blind, Clown Strike, Kinder Murder, (I Don't Want To Go To) Chelsea, Rockin' Horse Road, Shipbuilding, Lipstick Vogue, Beyond Belief, You Belong To Me, Good Year For The Roses, Can't Stand Up For Falling Down, This Is Hell, All The Rage, Pump It Up
I NEVER TALKED TO JIM REEVES

SHEPHERD'S BUSH EMPIRE, 4-11-25 November 1994

Girls Talk, Human Hands, Basement Kiss, Puppet Girl, Alison/You Win Again/He'll Have To Go, Complicated Shadows, You'll Never Be A Man, Dirty Rotten Shame, Poor Fractured Atlas, Green Shirt, Indecent Haste, The Other Side Of Summer, Man Out Of Time
I NEVER TALKED TO JIM REEVES

ROYAL COLLEGE OF MUSIC, 23 March 1995

I Almost Had A Weakness, The Birds Will Still Be Singing (both with Brodsky Quartet): One After 909, Mistress And Maid (both with Paul McCartney)
THE RISE AND RISE OF DECLAN MACMANUS CD (Tone)
A ROYAL PERFORMANCE CD (Yellow Dog) *soundboard, missing some tracks*

BRIXTON ACADEMY, 29-31 March 1995

Starting To Come Over, Clown Strike, Complicated Shadows, Let him Dangle, All This Useless Beauty, Crimes Of Paris, Indoor Fireworks, Little Atoms, If You Go, Deep Dark Truthful Mirror, Just About Glad, Tramp The Dirt Down, Riot Act, A Kind Of Murder, Poor Shallow Grave, Give Me My Rest, Rainy Day Women Ns 12 &35 (with Dylan), I Shall Be Released (with Dylan)
SUPPORTIVE MEASURES CD (Caucasian) *solo support slot to Dylan*
BRIXTON BLUES CD (Kiss The Stone) *duets only*

BRIXTON ACADEMY, March 1995

It's Starting To Come To Me, The Other End Of The Telescope, Complicated Shadows, Little Atoms, Poor Fractured Atlas, Discarded Angel, The Poison Rose, Man Out Of Time, Shipbuilding, Tramp The Dirt Down, Clown Strike, Let Him Dangle, All This Useless Beauty, The Crimes Of Paris, Indoor Fireworks, It's Time, Just About Glad, Riot Act, Kinder Murder, Shallow Grave, I Want To Vanish
I DID TALK TO BOB DYLAN CD *another audience tape, different tracks*

THE POINT, DUBLIN, 11 April 1995
Costello, Van Morrison and Carole King join in on 'I Shall Be Released' and 'Rainy Day Women'
DYLAN GETS TO THE POINT – DUBLIN '95 CD

SHEPHERD'S BUSH, 18 May 1995
Remove This Doubt, Hidden Charms, Everybody's Crying Merry, I've Been Wrong Before, Running Out; Of Fools, Leave My Kitten Alone, The Very Thought Of You, Pouring Water On A Drowning Man, Must You Throw Dirt In My Face, Bama Lama Bama Loo, Why Don't You Love Her, Medley: Tracks Of My Tears – Tears Of a Clown, Pump It Up
HIDDEN CHARMS CD (Little Big Man)
JESUS THIS IS ELVIS CD (KTS) *FM broadcast*

FILLMORE AUDITORIUM, 15 May 1996
CD1: Just About Glad, Starting To Come To Me, Red Shoes, Little Atoms, Temptation, You Bowed Down, Why Can't A Man Stand Alone, The Long Honeymoon, Poor Fractured Atlas, Complicated Shadows, Just A Memory, God Give Me Strength, God's Comic
CD2: Other End Of The Telescope, Accidents Will Happen, All This Useless Beauty, It's Time, My Dark Life, Ship Of Fools, Alison, Shallow Grave, Watching The Detectives, I Want To Vanish
AGING GRACEFULLY 2CD (DickyPoo) *KFOG-FM broadcast*

SUPPER CLUB, NEW YORK CITY, 22 May 1996: Early Show
CD1: Just About Glad, Starting To Come To Me, Red Shoes, Little Atoms, Temptation, You Bowed Down, Why Can't A Man Stand Alone, Long Honeymoon, Poor Fractured Atlas, Losing You Is Just A Memory, God Give Me Strength, God's Comic, Complicated Shadows
CD2: Other End Of The Telescope, Medley: Oliver's Army – Kid – Unchained Melody – If You Could Read My Name, Black Sails In The Sunset, All This Useless Beauty, It's Time, More Or Less Mine, My Funny Valentine, Distorted Angel, You'll Never Be A Man, Alison, Shallow Grave, Watching The Detectives, I Want To Vanish
BETWEEN WISDOM AND MURDER 2CD (Razor's Edge)

LATER SPECIAL, 18 June 1996, first broadcast 7 July
Accidents Will Happen, Little Atoms, Pump It Up, Why Can't A Man Stand Alone?, Riot Act, Veronica, Indoor Fireworks, Pills And Soap, The Birds Will Still Be Singing, Upon A Veil Of Midnight Blue, All This Useless Beauty, You Bowed Down, Complicated Shadows, Watching The Detectives, I Want To Vanish
LATER CD (Star) *recording of July 12th extended broadcast*
MAIN ATTRACTION CD (Kiss The Stone)
LATER SPECIAL WITH ELVIS COSTELLO CD (Diverse)

SHEPHERDS BUSH EMPIRE, LONDON, 26 July 1996
CD1: Opportunity, New Lace Sleeves, Thirteen Steps Lead Down, Why Can't A Man Stand Alone, Little Atoms, Still So Far From The Prize, Motel Matches, Veronica, A Passionate Fight, Almost Blue, My Funny Valentine, Oliver's Army, Brilliant Mistake, All This Useless Beauty, Man Out Of Time, Distorted Angel, (I Don't Want To) Go To Chelsea, Pump It Up
CD2: This Year's Girl, You Belong To Me, Riot Act, Accidents Will Happen, Complicated Shadows, Indoor Fireworks, The Other End Of The Telescope, Human Hands, Watching The Detectives, You Bowed Down, Red Shoes, No Action, Shipbuilding, I Want To Vanish, Shallow Grave, Alison, Rocking Horse Road, (What's So Funny 'Bout) Peace, Love And Understanding
BACK WITH A VENGEANCE VOLUME ONE 2CD (Doberman)

LONDON, July 1996

Twenty-nine more songs, performed at the other five London shows, including seventeen at the Roundhouse, alongside a final three songs from the Beacon Theatre, New York in August 1995
CD1: Clown Strike, Pills And Soap, The Long Honeymoon, Poor Fractured Atlas, Sulky Girl, Alison Medley – You Win Again, He'll Have To Go, Tracks Of My Tears, Tears Of A Clown, Clowntime Is Over, Honey Are You Straight Or Are You Blind, Just About Glad, I Just Don't Know What To Do With Myself, Beyond Belief, Clubland, It's Time, Possession, Just A Memory, King Horse, Miracle Man
CD2: Unwanted Number, I Can't Stand Up For Falling Down, Deep Dark Truthful Mirror, You'll Never Be A Man, Black Sails In The Sunset, Roundhouse Theme, Pump It Up/Slow Down, Lipstick Vogue, I Want You, London's Brilliant Parade, All The Rage, Mystery Dance, God's Comic, God Give Me Strength, Almost Ideal Eyes, Speak Darkly My Angel
BACK WITH A VENGEANCE VOLUME TWO 2 CD (Doberman)

Doberman have built up an extraordinary reputation as a CD-R series made for fans by fans: Name That Tune*, the most extreme example, is a mind-boggling double CD of Dylan at his considerable worst. The above, conversely, is Costello at something near to his best, despite being taken from audience tapes which mean that Elvis is sometimes drowned out by the audience backchat.*

This is the kind of release which would never be issued commercially, but remains essential stuff for hard-core collectors. It chronicles a glory departing this earth – The Attractions' last stand, complete with lots of accordions. It is as if Elvis is deliberately saying goodbye to one part of his career by singing virtually every song he ever performed with his one-time band (and some he didn't). Listening to it is a private pleasure, like sampling a rare and vintage bottle of wine, albeit slightly corked. Elvis is particularly chatty and inventive, and the range of material stretches belief, a complete career overview from 'Red Shoes' to 'God Give Me Strength'.

As a feat of memory it is as startling as the cover shot of Elvis madly staring. The concert tour these four CDs represent is a bran-tub of musical invention – caught on the cusp. As I said, a glory departing.

undated and various

PLUGGING THE GAPS CD (Tone 2)

Twenty-one tracks pirated from official releases, Elvis by himself and with George Jones, Ricky Scaggs, Madness, The Chieftains and Mary Coughlan. Gathering up the loose ends.

PLUGGING THE GAPS VOL 2 CD (Tone 2)

20 more of the same, again pirated rather than bootlegged. Includes tracks with the Dirty Dozen Brass Band, Rob Wasserman, Paul McCartney, Voice Squad, Eurythmics and live with The Brodsky Quartet.

compilations and outside projects on which costello appears

'Less Than Zero' (organ mix), A BUNCH OF STIFF RECORDS (Stiff) April 77
'Radio Sweetheart', HITS GREATEST STIFFS (Stiff) September 77
Live versions of 'I Just Don't Know What To Do With Myself' (Bacharach/David), 'Miracle Man' and
'Sex And Drugs And Rock and Roll (Dury), STIFFS LIVE STIFFS (Stiff) February 78
'(I Don't Want To Go To) Chelsea' and 'Crawling To The USA', AMERICATHON (Lorimar) October 79
GEORGE JONES: MY VERY SPECIAL GUESTS (Epic) 1979, LP *duets on 'Stranger In The House*
TWIST: THIS IS YOUR LIFE (Polydor) 1979. LP *backing vocals*
'Goon Squad', ROCK AGAINST RACISM'S GREATEST HITS (Virgin) 1980 *from RAR's Carnival 2,
Brixton, 24 September 1978*
'The Imposter' (live), CONCERTS FOR THE PEOPLE OF KAMPUCHEA (Atlantic) March 1981
'Psycho Song' (live), FUNDAMENTAL FROLICS (BBC) November 1981
'Big Sister', DANCIN' MASTER (NME) 1981, *mail order cassette*
SQUEEZE: EAST SIDE STORY (A&M) 1981, LP *backing vocals on 'Tempted' and 'There's No
Tomorrow'*
'Party Party', PARTY PARTY (A&M) December 82
PHILIP CHEVRON: THE CAPTAINS AND THE KINGS/FAITHFUL DEPARTED (Demon) 1982 7"
single *EC appears on the 'B3', whatever that means, on the B-side*
SQUEEZE: BLACK COFFEE IN BED (A&M) 1982, 7" single *backing vocals on A-side*
MADNESS: TOMORROW'S JUST ANOTHER DAY (Stiff) 1983 *backing vocals on reworked version
on B-side*
'Walking On Thin Ice' (Ono), EVERY MAN NEEDS A WOMAN (Polydor) September 84
Early demo of 'Really Mystified', SOMETIMES A GREAT NOTION (EMI) November 84 *in aid of the
British Deaf Association*
SPECIAL AKA: NELSON MANDELA (2 Tone) 1984 7" single *backing vocals*
EURYTHMICS: BE YOURSELF TONIGHT (RCA) 1985, LP *harmony vocal on 'Adrian'*
JOHN HIATT: LIVING A LITTLE, LAUGHING A LITTLE (CBS) 1985 7" single *backing vocal, song
later collected on Hiatt's album Warming Up The Ice Age*
RICKY SCAGGS: LIVE IN LONDON (CBS) 1985, LP *vocals on 'Don't Get Above Your Raisin'*
'The End Of The Rainbow' (Thompson), IT'S A LIVE-IN WORLD (EMI) 1986 *anti-heroin project*
'Your Funeral, My Trial' (Williamson) and 'Your Mind Is On Vacation', LIVE ON BROADWAY 1986
Demo of 'Watching The Detectives', POGO A GOGO (NME) 1986 *cassette*
'Big Nothing' *by The MacManus Gang*, STRAIGHT TO HELL (Hell) June 87
'Leave My Kitten Alone' (John/Turner), LIVE FOR IRELAND June 87, *Irish version*
'Many Rivers To Cross' (Cliff), LIVE FOR IRELAND (MCA) June 87, *UK version*
'Psycho' (Payne) – live – and 'They'll Never Take Her Love From Me' ("Coward Brothers"), FROM
HELL TO OBSCURITY (Blackmail) 1989 *mail order only*
CHRISTY MOORE: VOYAGE (WEA) 1989, LP *back-up vocals on 'Missing You'*
ROY ORBISON: A BLACK AND WHITE NIGHT (Virgin) 1989, LP *Costello is one of the many
celebrity guests in this aural record of the concert/TV extravaganza*
'That's How You Got Killed Before' on DIRTY DOZEN BRASS BAND: THE NEW ORLEANS ALBUM
(Sony) 1990
'The St Stephen's Day Murders' on CHIEFTAINS: THE BELLS OF DUBLIN (RCA) 1990
'Mischievous Ghost', BRINGING IT ALL BACK HOME (BBC) May 91
'Ship Of Fools' (Hunter/Garcia), DEADICATED (Arista) May 91
'Days' (Davies), UNTIL THE END OF THE WORLD (WB) December 91
SAM PHILLIPS: CRUEL INVENTIONS 1991, LP *includes Costello as a guest*
'Pump It Up' (BBC session), 1 AND ONLY 25 YEARS RADIO 1 (BBC) 1992
'Weird Nightmare', WEIRD NIGHTMARE (Columbia) September 92
'May 17', FERRINGTON GUITARS, J Cape, June 93, *CD attached to book*

'More Than Rain', 'God Only Knows (Wilson/Asher), 'They Didn't Believe Me' and 'I Always Had A Weakness', LIVE AT NEW YORK TOWN HALL 1993
'But Not For Me' (Gershwin), THE GLORY OF GERSHWIN (Mercury) July 94
'Full Force Gale' (Morrison), NO PRIMA DONNA (Exile) July 94
'Sally Sue Brown' (Alexander), ADIOS AMIGO, A TRIBUTE TO ARTHUR ALEXANDER (Demon) August 94
Live version of 'Deep Dark Truthful Mirror', MTV UNPLUGGED COLLECTION VOL I (WB) December 94
'Put Your Big Toe In The Milk Of Human Kindness', TRIOS WITH ROB WASSERMAN (MCA) 1994
'They Can't Take That Away From Me', TONY BENNETT: UNPLUGGED (Columbia) 1994
'My Dark Life' in SONGS IN THE KEY OF X 1996
'King Of Confidence', DOING IT RIGHT (Demon) 1996
'O Mistress Mine', 'Come Away Death' and 'When That I Was A Little Boy' – all songs from Shakespeare's plays – TERROR + MAGNIFICENCE 1996
AL ANDERSON: PAY BEFORE YOU PUMP (Imprint) 1996, CD
Costello and Ron Sexsmith add backing vocals on 'Bang Bang Bang'
JAZZ PASSENGERS: INDIVIDUALLY TWISTED (32 Records) 1997, CD *Elvis sings lead vocals on 'Aubergine' and duets with Debbie Harry on 'Don't You Go Away Mad'*

videos featuring elvis costello

THE JULIET LETTERS
With The Brodsky Quartet. 1993

THE VERY BEST OF ... ELVIS COSTELLO AND THE ATTRACTIONS 1977-86
(I Don't Want To Go To) Chelsea, Pump It Up, Radio Radio, (What's So Funny 'Bout) Peace, Love And Understanding (Lowe), Oliver's Army, Accidents Will Happen, Love For Tender, I Can't Stand Up For Falling Down, Possession, New Amsterdam, High Fidelity, Clubland, New Lace Sleeves, Good Year For The Roses, Sweet Dreams, You Little Fool, Everyday I Write The Book, Let Them All Talk, The Only Flame In Town, I Wanna Be Loved, Don't Let Me Be Misunderstood (Benjamin/Marcus/Caldwell)
Chronological parade of pop videos, mime-along-with-Elvis Demon 1994

LIVE, A CASE FOR SONG
With The Attractions Accidents Will Happen, Little Atoms, Pump It Up, Why Can't A Man Stand Alone, Riot Act,
With Steve Nieve Veronica (MacManus/McCartney),
Solo Indoor Fireworks,
With The Brodsky Quartet Pills And Soap, The Birds Will Still Be Singing, God Only Knows (Asher/Wilson),
With The Brodsky Quartet and White City Septet Upon A Veil Of Midnight Blue
With The Brodsky Quartet, the White City Septet, and The Attractions All This Useless Beauty,
With The Attractions You Bowed Down, Complicated Shadows, Watching The Detectives,
With Steve Nieve I Want To Vanish
Taken from the BBC Later *special, recorded on 18 June 1996 and broadcast on July 7 1996, then again on 12 July with 2 bonus tracks. Costello also played 'Temptation', 'I Almost Had A Weakness', 'Almost Blue', 'Shipbuilding' and 'Man Out Of Time', but none appeared either on TV, video or the matching radio broadcast*
Warner Music Vision 1996

records produced by elvis costello

BIG HEAT: WATCH ME CATCH FIRE (A&M) 1985, 7" single
BLUE AEROPLANES: BEATSONGS (Ensign) 1991, LP
co-produced by Elvis and Larry Hirsch
BLUEBELLS: AIM IN LIFE, B-side of FOREVERMORE (London) 1982, 7" single collected on mini-album THE BLUEBELLS (London) 1983
BLUEBELLS: EVERYBODY'S SOMEBODY'S FOOL (London) 1982 7" flexi single, on transparent vinyl, given away with initial copies of 'Forevermore'
PHILIP CHEVRON: THE CAPTAINS AND THE KINGS/FAITHFUL DEPARTED (Demon) 1982 7" single
co-produced by Costello – as The Imposter – and Clive Langer
CLIVE LANGER AND THE BOXES: SPLASH (F-Beat) 1980 LP
POGUES: RUM, SODOMY & THE LASH 1985 LP
SPECIALS: THE SPECIALS (2 Tone) 1979 LP
SPECIAL AKA: NELSON MANDELA/BREAK DOWN THE DOOR (2 Tone) 1984, 7" single
SQUEEZE: EAST SIDE STORY (A&M) 1981 LP *co-produced with Roger Bechirian*

acting roles

AMERICATHON

1979 movie, directed by Neil Israel, in which Elvis appears as a British pop star called Earl Manchester, and lip-syncs 'Crawling To The USA' in front of Buckingham Palace.

SCULLY

1984 Granada TV series set in Liverpool, and written by Alan Bleasdale, in which Elvis played the educationally challenged brother of the hero (played by Andrew Schofield). As befits the nature of the person he is playing, Costello's part is wordless apart from one line in the final episode. Costello also contributed the series' theme song, 'Turning The Town Red'.

THE BULLSHITTERS

A 1984 spin-off from Peter Richardson's Comedy Store Channel 4 series. This is a parody of hit TV series *The Professionals*, and has developed a life of its own, currently recycled as a TV advert for a new car. Elvis plays an A&R man.

NO SURRENDER

Costello, sans glasses, has a walk on role as Roscoe DeVille, a third rate magician in this 1985 movie, written by Alan Bleasdale.

STRAIGHT TO HELL

1986 movie directed in Spain by Alex Cox, of *Repo Man* fame, and starring Dennis Hopper, Joe Strummer of The Clash, The Pogues and Courtney Love. The disastrous results are a parody of a spaghetti western, in which Elvis plays the Butler Hives. Henceforth, his movie work would be confined to writing soundtracks, except for...

SPICE WORLD

Released in late 1997, Elvis, a bartender, is the visual punchline to a joke about the vagaries of fame.

LARRY SANDERS

Elvis has appeared twice on this spoof chat show, both as a performer and as "himself" selling a car to another character. (The car is a dud and the name Elvis Costello is roundly insulted.)

cover versions of songs written by costello: chronological order

In May 1998, Rhino released *Bespoke Songs, Lost Dogs Detours And Rendezvous: Songwriting By Elvis Costello*, a twenty-one-track collection hand-picked by Elvis, and with footnotes explaining how he wrote each song. All selections had been previously released. Costello waited years for a tribute album, having first to do the job himself on his four limited edition singles from July 1996, which include Lush's take on 'All This Useless Beauty' and Sleeper's 'The Other End Of The Telescope'.

Elvis was first taken on by Stiff as a songwriter, not a performer, and his work has been covered by a wide range of artists. Highlights and lowlights are listed below. For all that, his songs still seem to make the most sense in their own maker's voice. The greatest exeption is Robert Wyatt's 'Shipbuilding', which would have guaranteed Elvis rock immortality, even if he himself had never sung a word in anger.

BARRY CHRISTIAN: ALISON (Mercury) 1977, 7" single
DYAN DIAMOND: MYSTERY DANCE 7" single
Produced by Kim Fowley, this was released first as a single, and later on her album In The Dark
MCA 1978

LINDA RONSTADT: LIVING IN THE USA LP
Ronstadt pounces on 'Alison', like a cat on a juicy mouse. Like Rod Stewart, she could always spot a good song, the secret of a long career
Asylum 1978

HERMAN BROOD:
Apparently the German heavy rock king recorded a bizarre version of 'Watching The Detectives' among five cover versions on a 1978 LP

DAVE EDMUNDS: GIRLS TALK 7" single
Later recorded by Elvis himself on Get Happy!!. *A hit single for Edmunds, who subsequently included it on his Swan Song album* Repeat When Necessary
Swan Song 1979

GEORGIE FAME: THAT'S WHAT FRIENDS ARE FOR LP

Title song written by Costello. The lyrics are included in Costello's A Singing Dictionary *songbook*
Pye 1979

RACHEL SWEET: FOOL AROUND LP

Includes her version of 'Stranger In The House'
Stiff 1979

CARLENE CARTER: TWO SIDES TO EVERY WOMAN LP

With 'Radio Sweetheart'
WB 1979

OUTLAWS: IN THE EYE OF THE STORM LP

'Miracle Man' from a band the very antithesis of new wave, who repeated the song on a 1980 live sampler
Arista 1979

THE TREMBLERS: TWICE NIGHTLY LP

Weak power-pop for the one-time leader of Herman's Hermits, Peter Noone, who here gives a toothy treatment to 'Green Shirt'
CBS 1980

LINDA RONSTADT: MAD LOVE LP

Backed by The Cretones, she covers 'Party Girl', 'Girls Talk' and 'Talking In The Dark'. To Elvis's horror – though not, presumably, his accountant's – Ronstadt embraces the English new wave
Asylum 1980

HOT CHOCOLATE: CLASS LP

Contains 'Green Shirt'
RAK 1980

ROBERT WYATT: SHIPBUILDING 45 rpm single/12" single

Co-written by Costello and Clive Langer, recorded by Elvis himself on Punch The Clock. *Wyatt later included it on his album* Nothing Can Stop Us. *Costello makes a cameo appearance on the video promo for Wyatt's single, which hit 35 in the UK charts*
Rough Trade September 1982

SHAKIN' PYRAMIDS: CELTS AND COBRAS LP

Includes their rockabilly version of 'Just A Memory'
Virgin 1982

DUSTY SPRINGFIELD: WHITE HEAT LP

Costello supplies 'Losing You', a longer version of the song he records himself as 'Just A Memory' – see also above – and inspired by the English chanteuse. Apparently, he sang the lyrics over the phone to her, including the "I count the pages" verse, omitted on his own recording
Casablanca 1983

MATHILDE SANTING: HAND IN HAND 7" single

Dutch single, sung in English
Megadisc 1983

BILLY BREMNER: SHATTERPROOF 45 rpm single
Also to be found on Bremner's LP Bash: *Costello's original demo appears on the* Punch The Clock
reissue CD
Arista March 1984

TRACIE (YOUNG): I LOVE YOU (WHEN I SLEEP) 45 rpm single
Tracie Young was discovered by Paul Weller, and later included this track on her Respond LP Far
From The Hurting Kind. *Costello later adapted the song into 'Joe Porterhouse' on* Goodbye Cruel
World
Respond 1984

NICK LOWE: ROSE OF ENGLAND LP
'Indoor Fireworks' appears, a year ahead of Elvis's own version on King Of America
F-Beat 1985

MARTI JONES: UNSOPHISTICATED TIME LP
Includes 'The Element Within Her'
A&M 1985

MARTI JONES: MATCH GAME LP
*'Just A Memory' appears here, and Marti would often perform it in tandem with 'The Element
Within Her' as a Costello medley. Marty is the wife of Southern rocker Don Dixon. She reprised
the same song on her* Live At Sprit Square *album, released in 1996 on Sugar Hill*
A&M 1986

ALLAN MAYES: STUMBLING IN THE AISLE LP
Includes the song 'Maureen And Sam', co-written with Costello
STC 1986, *US issue only*

WINSTON REEDY: EVERYDAY I WRITE THE BOOK 12"
Reggae version of the Costello song
Priority Records 1986

PAUL McCARTNEY: ONCE UPON A LONG AGO 7" single
B-side, 'Back On My Feet', written by McCartney/Costello
Parlophone 1987

JOHNNY CASH: JOHNNY CASH IS COMING TO TOWN LP
Includes his version of 'The Big Light', premiered on the US TV show Austin City Limits
Mercury 1987

RUBEN BLADES: NOTHING BUT THE TRUTH LP
*'The Miranda Syndrome' and 'Shamed Into Love' co-written by Costello. Blades is a salsa star
who once stood for election as President of Panama. More prosaically, the first song owed much
to Costello's earlier 'The Town Where Time Stood Still'*
Electra 1988

THE COURIER LP
*6 tracks composed by Costello – under his real name – for a movie thriller set in Dublin, and
starring Cait O'Riordan. One of these instrumentals, used over the closing credits, was later*

given lyrics and became 'Last Boat Leaving', on Spike
Virgin 1988

WAS NOT WAS: WHAT'S UP DOG? LP
Co-wrote one song, 'Shadow And Jimmy', with David Was
Fontana 1988

EVERYTHING BUT THE GIRL: I ALWAYS WAS YOUR GIRL CD single
Contains their cover of 'Almost Blue'
Blanco y Negro 1988

JUSTINE BATEMAN & THE MYSTERY: SATISFACTION LP
Movie soundtrack, which includes cover of 'Mystery Dance'. Julia Roberts has an early role as bass player in the all female rock band around which the film is based. Hardly Cait O'Riordan
AJK 1988

PAUL MCCARTNEY: FLOWERS IN THE DIRT LP
Co-writing credits on 'My Brave Face', 'You Want It Too', 'Don't Be Careless Love' and 'That Day Is Done'
Parlophone 1989

ROY ORBISON: MYSTERY GIRL LP
Costello rewrites his song 'The Comedians' – from the 1984 album Goodbye Cruel World – *specifically for Orbison, who sang it on the 1987 video special. Here it appears posthumously*
Virgin 1989

TIL TUESDAY: EVERYTHING'S DIFFERENT NOW LP
Co-writing credit with lead singer Aimee Mann on 'The Other End (Of The Telescope)'
Epic 1989

CHRISTY MOORE: VOYAGE CD
Slightly reworked version of 'The Deportees Club'
Warners 1989

CHET BAKER: LETS GET LOST CD
Shortly before his death, Baker records 'Almost Blue'
BMG 1989

TODD RUNDGREN: NEARLY HUMAN
'Two Little Hitlers' appears as a bonus track on CD and cassette versions
WB 1989

JOHNNY CASH: BOOM CHICKA BOOM CD
Costello provides 'Hidden Shame' specially
Mercury 1990

ANNIE ROSS AND THE LOW NOTE QUINTET: SHORT CUTS
On the soundtrack of the Robert Altman movie, and subsequent LP , Ross sings 'Punishing Kiss', co written by Costello and Cait
Imago 1990

Q TIPS: BBC RADIO 1 IN CONCERT CD
Reissue of a 1981 concert tape, in which Paul Young's old band covers 'High Fidelity'
1991

ROGER MCGUINN: BACK FROM RIO CD
Costello has written 'You Bowed Down' for McGuinn, who provided 12-string guitar on the Spike
album
Arista 1991

THE RITZ, FEATURING CLARK TERRY: ALMOST BLUE CD
Title track is the Costello song
Denon 1991

HOUSE BAND: STONETOWN CD
Version of 'Sunday's Best', given a Celtic twist
Green Linnet 1991

CHARLES BROWN: SOMEONE TO LOVE CD
*'I Wonder How She Knows' – something which Costello had prepared earlier as 'Upon A Vale Of
Midnight Blue' – was reworked by Brown, who takes a co-composing credit. The legendary blues
singer shared a gig with Elvis at Mill Valley in 1989*
Bullseye Blues 1992

JUNE TABOR: ANGEL TIGER CD
Contains 'All This Useless Beauty', which will later give its name to one of Costello's finest albums
Cooking Vinyl 1992

T-BONE BURNETT: CRIMINAL UNDER MY OWN HAT CD
'It's Not Too Late' co-written with Costello and Bobby Neuwirth, Dylan's old sparring partner
Columbia 1992

ZUCCHERO: MISERERE CD
A writing collaboration between Elvis and Italy's answer to Joe Cocker, one of the stars of
Woodstock II
London 1992

EVERYTHING BUT THE GIRL: COVERS CD EP
Includes their take on 'Alison'
Blanco y Negro 1992

EXODUS: FORCE OF HABIT CD
The UK band cover 'Pump It Up'
Capitol 1992

MUDHONEY: FREEDOM OF CHOICE CD
*The same song, 'Pump It Up' is covered by the US grunge masters on this compilation, and later
on the soundtrack to the film* PCU
Caroline 1992

KATY MOFFAT AND THE GREAT UNKNOWN: INDOOR FIREWORKS CD
Title track is the Costello song
Red Moon 1992, Swiss release

MARY COUGHLAN: LOVE FOR SALE CD
Includes both 'Upon A Vale Of Midnight Blue', which Costello rewrote wth Charles Brown as 'I Wonder How She Knows', and 'Baby Plays Around'
Demon 1993

KAREN FARR: SISTINE CD
Karen performs 'Riot Act'
November 1993

WENDY JAMES: LONDON'S BRILLIANT/TO ALL BEGINNINGS/MY BALLAD TO 46 STREET 12" SINGLE, PS
Track 1 written by Costello/Riordan, tracks 2 & 3 by James/Taylor
MCA 1993

WENDY JAMES: NOW AIN'T THE TIME FOR YOUR TEARS CD
This Is A Test, London's Brilliant, Basement Kiss, Earthbound, Do You Know What I'm Saying, We Despise You, Fill In The Blanks, The Nameless One, I Want To Stand Forever
All songs written by Elvis Costello, 2, 3, 4, 5 and 7 with O'Riordan
MCA 1993

PAUL MCCARTNEY: OFF THE GROUND CD
'The Lovers That Never Were' and 'Mistress And Maid' co-written with Elvis
Parlophone 1993

PEACE TOGETHER CD
This compilation album includes two Costello covers, 'Peace In Our Time' by Carter USM and 'Oliver's Army' by Blur, pioneers of Brit Pop
Island 1993

TASMIN ARCHER: SHIPBUILDING EP
Shipbuilding, Deep Dark Truthful Mirror, All Grown Up, New Amsterdam
All songs by Costello. The Attractions later backed Archer on her debut album
EMI 1994

JUNE TABOR: AGAINST THE STREAMS CD
Costello wrote 'Against The Streams' specially for her
Cooking Vinyl 1994

THOSE DARN ACCORDIANS: SQUEEZE THIS CD
Accordion romp on 'Pump It Up', sans words
Flying Fish 1995

FITZ OF DEPRESSION: I'M THE MAN 7" single
Cover versions of Joe Jackson's song on the A-side, and Costello's 'Welcome To The Working Week' on the B-side, with a picture sleeve that mimics both artists. The Chicago based band have also covered 'Mystery Man'

1995

DURAN DURAN: THANK YOU CD
'Watching The Detectives' on their covers album
1995

GEORGIA: SOUNDTRACK ALBUM CD
Includes actress Jennifer Jason Leigh's version of 'Almost Blue' from the soundtrack
Discovery 1996

MARTY JONES: MY LONGHAIRED LIFE CD
Includes version of 'Sleep Of The Just'
Sugar Hill 1996

NORMA WATERSON CD
'The Birds Will Still Be Singing'
Hannibal/Rykodisc 1996

EDDIE GRUNDY: THE WORLD OF EDDIE GRUNDY CD
Actor Trevor Harrison sings songs in his Archers' persona, including 'The Big Light'
Demon 1996

WET WET WET: HIGH ON THE HAPPY SIDE CD
'Town Crier' appears on the bonus CD, issued under the name of 'Maggie Pie And The Imposters', which accompanied early copies of the above album. The same band feature 'Possession' on a live cassette

THE LOVED ONES: FIFTEEN MINUTES WITH THE LOVED ONES Cassette
Includes version of 'Green Shirt' from this New Jersey band, whose very name is inspired by a Costello song
Hedgehog 1997

CHRISTINE COLLISTER: THE DARK GIFT OF TIME CD
This wonderfully doomy set of songs includes Clive Gregson's former musical partner singing 'I Want To Vanish', with her usual air of subdued menace, and jazz legend John Surman on baritone sax

VARIOUS ARTISTS: SONGS OF ELVIS COSTELLO – BESPOKE SONGS, LOST DOGS, DETOURS & RENDEZVOUS CD
Dave Edmunds – Girls Talk, For Real – Unwanted Number, Paul McCartney – My Brave Face, Johnny Cash – Hidden Shame, Tasmin Archer – All Grown Up, Zucchero – Miss Mary, Was (Not Was) – Shadow and Jimmy, Mary Coughlan – Upon A Veil Of Midnight Blue, Anuna – Deep Dead Blue, Roy Orbison – The Comedians, Christy Moore – The Deportees Club, Annie Ross & The Low Note Quintet – Punishing Kiss, Ruben Blades – Shamed Into Love, Billy Bremner – Shatterproof, Ronnie Drew – Dirty Rotten Shame, Robert Wyatt – Shipbuilding, Norma Waterson – The Birds Will Still Be Singing, June Tabor – I Want To Vanish, Til Tuesday – The Other End Of The Telescope, Nick Lowe & His Cowboy Outfit – Indoor Fireworks, Chet Baker – Almost Blue
Rhino 275273 CD US only issue, May 1998

A useful bringing together of most of the best cover versions of Costello originals. The extensive sleeve notes are by Elvis himself, and are worth the price of admission alone.

Last, and definitely least ...

THE BEATLES COSTELLO: WASHING THE DEFECTIVES 45rpm single, PS
Despite 'Thanks To Declan' on the sleeve, no connection other than the name!
US Pious 1978, US issue only

A tribute album to Costello, using young turks rather than old lags, was planned by Mafia Money Records of Madison, Wisconsin, but seems to have fallen through. Among the twenty or so indie bands invited to take part were Ashtray Boy, Number One Cup, Hugh And The Ex-Action Figures

side projects by members of the attractions

ATTRACTIONS

Single Girl (Brain/Hart)/Slow Patience (B Thomas/P Thomas) 45rpm single PS
F-Beat XX7 July 80
Arms Race (Nieve)/Lonesome Little Town (B Thomas/P Thomas) 45rpm single
F-Beat XX10 September 80

MAD ABOUT THE WRONG BOY LP
Side One: Arms Race, Damage, Little Misunderstanding, Straight Jacket, Mad About The Wrong Boy, Motorworld, On The Third Stroke, Slow Patience
Side Two: La-La-La-La-La Loved You, Single Girl, Lomesome Little Town, Taste Of Poison, Highrise Housewife, Talk About Me, Sad About Girls, Camera Camera
Produced by Roger Bechirian, composing credits divided between Nieve, Brain & Hart and B Thomas/P Thomas. Title on back cover is (deliberately) misspelt as 'Mad AboutThe Rwong Boy'
F-Beat XXLP 8 September 80
FIEND 25, April 84

BLANKET OF SECRECY
Say You Will (extended version)/Feather In My Hand/In The Garden 12" PS
Written in turn by Tinker/Spy/Tinker/Taylor and Tinker/Tailor/Soldier
F-Beat XX24 T 1982

WALLS HAVE EARS LP
Side One: Say You Will, Young Heart, Love Me Too, Remember Me And You, Long Cool Glass, Photograph
Side Two: Yo Yo, Close To Me, Something I Don't Need, Tell Me Baby, Lovers, B.O.S. Theme
Rumoured to be The Attractions
F-Beat XXPL 16 1982

STEVE NIEVE

STEVE NIEVE PLAYS THEME MUSIC FROM 'OUTLINE OF A HAIRDO' 45rpm EP PS
Outline Of A Hairdo, Page One Of A Dead Girl's Diary, Sparrow Crap, The Tap Dancer
Composed and played by Steve Nieve, issued free with initial copies of The Attractions' Mad
About The Wrong Boy *LP. Track two seems to be a weird prefiguring of the plot of* Twin Peaks
F-Beat COMB 1 September 80

KEYBOARD JUNGLE LP
Side One: The Ethnic Erithian, Hooligans And Hula Girls, Al Green, Spanish Guitar, Man With A
Musical Lighter, Outline Of A Hairdo, End Of Side One
Side Two: Liquid Looks, Thought Of Being Dad, Pink Flamingoes On Coffee Pot Boulevard, The
Mystery And Majesty (Of A Banyan Tree), Couch Potato Rag, Page One Of A Dead Girl's Diary,
End Of An Era
Composed and played by Steve Nieve, sleeve notes by Chris Difford
Demon FIEND 11 December 83

PLAYBOY LP
Side One: Russians (Sting), Pictures From A Confiscated Camera, Once Upon A Time In South
America, Condition Of The Heart (Nelson), The Sword Fight, Ghost Town (Dammers), A Walk In
Monet's Back Garden, Life On Mars (Bowie), I'm Not In Love (Stewart/Gouldman)
Side Two: Shadows Of Paris, Love Boat, El Ray De Sol, The 9/4 Rag, Hands Of Orlac, Birdcage
Walk, White Girl (Doe/Cervenka), Divided Heart, Careless Whisper (Michael)
*All pieces played by Nieve, and composed by him unless otherwise noted. Produced by Steve
Nieve and Mark Stent. A press release with my copy states that Nieve is better known as "the
spindly dervish-like figure hunched over the workmanlike set of keyboards to Elvis's right
producing a never-ending cascade of solos, intricate three-second fills, and surging wall-of-
sound crescendos that shape The Attractions unique sound. Viewers of The Last Resort with
Jonathan Ross will know Steve in another guise; leading the programme's house band, Steve
Nieve and the Playboys"*
Demon FIEND 109 1987

IT'S RAINING SOMEWHERE CD
Before, The Time, The World, Black Is The Colour Of My True Love's Hair
*Released under the name STEVE NAIVE, an album of solo piano pieces recorded at the
Knitting Factory in December 1996. The music is described as "contemplative jazz" and "an
exploration of musical themes for an unstaged play of the same name"*
Knitting Factory KFW 198 1997
Steve Nieve also appears on the following records ...

The Twist: This Is Your Life (1979) LP
Howard Werth: Six Of One And Half A Dozen Of The Other (1982) LP
Carmel: Bad Day (1983) 45rpm single PS
JB's Allstars: One Minute Every Hour (1983) 45rpm single PS
JB's Allstars: Backfield In Motion (1984) 45rpm single PS

BRUCE THOMAS

Appears on the following records, before and after Elvis ...

Village: Man In The Moon (1969) *rare 45 rpm single on Head label*
Peter Bardens: The Answer (1970) LP
Quiver: Quiver (1971) LP
Quiver: Gone In The Morning (1972) LP
Ian Matthews: Tigers Will Survive (1972) LP
Marc Ellington: A Question Of Roads (1972) LP
Bridget St John: Thank You For (1972) LP
Al Stewart: Orange (1972) LP
Sutherland Brothers and Quiver: Dream Kid (1973) LP
Jonathan Kelly: Wait Til They Change The Backdrop (1973) LP
Billy Lawrie: Ship Imagination (1973) LP
Al Stewart: Past, Present And Future (1974) LP
Moonrider: Moonrider (1975) LP *with Keith West, of 'Teenage Opera' fame*
The Loftus Roadrunners: Queens Park Rangers (1977) 45 rpm single
Paul McCartney: Back To The Egg (1979) LP
Paul McCartney's Rockestra: Concerts For The People Of Kampuchea (1981) LP

PETE THOMAS

Chilli Willi and the Red Hot Peppers: Bongos Over Balham (1974) LP
Chilli Willi and the Red Hot Peppers: I'll Be Home (1996) CD
Various Artists: Stiff's Live Stiffs (1978) LP, *with Larry Wallis*
Sean Tyla & Tyla Gang: Just Popped Out (1980) LP
Richard Thompson: Mirror Blue (1994)
Richard Thompson: You? Me? Us? (1996)

IMPERIAL POMPADOURS

ERSATZ LP

Side One: The Crusher, See You Soon Baboon, Fu Manchu, Brand New Cadillac, Light Show, Little Black Egg, Moo-Goo-Gai-Pan, Gemini Spacecraft, I Want To Come Back From The World Of LSD, Chicken, There's A Fungus Among Us, King Bee, Black Leather Trousers And Motorcycle Boots
Side Two: Insolence Across The Nation
A bizarre and rare record, featuring (in disguise) the musical debut of Stiff/F Beat artist Barney Bubbles, with The Attractions supposedly in close support. Of course, it could just as well be a reformed Freddie And The Dreamers!
Pompadour Records POMP 001

selected bibliography

M any reviews not specifically listed here are acknowledged in the main text. Jim Perowne's *Elvis Costello: A Bio-Bibliography* was due from Greenwood Press in late 1998.

Amburn, Ellis	Dark Star: The Roy Orbison Story, NEL, 1990
Burchill, Julie and Parsons, Tony	The Boy Who Looked At Johnny: The Obituary Of Rock 'N' Roll, Pluto, 1978, p 93
Clifton, Piers	Elvis Costello: The Rough Guide, 1996, pp 194-6
Cooper, Mark	Review, *Q*, October 1986 'Scathing', *Q*, March 1989 Review, *Mojo*, June 1996
Clayton-Lea, Tony	Elvis Costello, A Biography, Andre Deutsch, 1998 *A scissors and paste job with colour photos and nice hard back sleeve, but no attempts to turn facts into a pattern, or give Costello the serious attention he deserves.*
Costello, Elvis	A Singing Dictionary, Plangent Visions, 1980 *Words and music for original songs from My Aim is True, This Year's Model, Armed Forces, Get Happy!! and Ten Bloody Marys and Ten How's Your Fathers, plus one unrecorded song.*

Everyday I Write The Song (Grumbling Appendix To The Singing Dictionary), Plangent Visions, 1983
Words and music for original songs from Trust, Imperial Bedroom and Punch The Clock.

'Musical Involvement In Films', *Mojo*, June 1994
Favourite LPs, *Q*, June 1994
'Best Thing I Heard All Year', *Mojo*, January 1996

Denselow, Robin   When The Music's Over: The Story Of Political Pop, Faber, 1989

Doggett, Peter   'Elvis Costello: The First 2½ Years', *Record Collector* 171, November 1993

Interview, *Record Collector* 193-4, September-October 1995

Eno, Brian   A Year With Swollen Appendices, Faber, 1996

Flanagan, Bill   Written In My Soul, Omnibus, 1990, pp 231-58

Frame, Pete   Family Tree, *Zigzag* 92, March 1979

Frith, Simon   Music For Pleasure: Essays In The Sociology Of Pop, Polity Press, 1988

Gale, Peter   'Costello As A Guitar Hero', *Mojo*, December 1996

Gimarc, George   Punk Diary 1970-79: An Eyewitness Record Of The Punk Decade, Vintage, 1997

Gouldstone, David   Elvis Costello – A Man Out Of Time, Sidgwick and Jackson, 1989

Gray, Marcus   Last Gang In Town: The Story And Myth Of The Clash, Fourth Estate, 1995, p 463

Groothuizen, Richard   Elvis Costello: So Far 1984. Privately printed
A special limited edition based on the fifteen Dutch editions of ECIS with additional material.

Groothuizen, Richard & Heyer, Kees den   Going Through The Motions: Elvis Costello 1982/1985, Privately printed 1986
Companion to above, 344 pages of information and rare memorabilia.

Guterman, Jimmy   Slipped Discs: The Worst Rock 'N' Roll Records Of All Time
Virgin, 1991, pp 126-7

Hillmore, Peter   The Greatest Show On Earth: Live Aid, Sidgwick and Jackson, 1985

Irwin, Colin   'Floor Singer's Revenge', *Folk Roots* 73, July 1989

Jackson, Richard   'Elvis Costello', *Record Collector* 16, December 1980

Jones, Allan,   'Songs Of Love And Hate', Classic Rock Interviews,
Mandarin, 1994, pp 234-46
1989 interview.

Kent, Nick   'Horn Rims From Hell', The Dark Stuff, Penguin 1994
pp 188-201

Kershaw, Andy   Review of $2^{1}/_{2}$ *Years*, *Mojo*, December 1993

Maconie, Stuart   'Get Happy', Love Is The Drug: Living As A Pop Fan,
ed John Aizlewood, Penguin 1994, pp 1-20

Marcus, Greil   'Elvis Costello Repents', *Rolling Stone* 377, 2 September 1982,
reprinted in The Rolling Stone Interviews: The
1980s, St Martin's Press (New York), 1989

In The Fascist Bathroom, Viking, 1993

Marsh, Dave (ed)   Rolling Stone Record Guide, Virgin, 1980, p 86

The Heart Of Rock And Soul: The 1001 Greatest Singles Ever
Made, NEL, 1989

O'Connor, Nuala   Bringing It All Back Home: The Influence Of Irish Music, BBC, 1991

Parkyn, Geoff   Elvis Costello – The Illustrated Disco/Biography,
Omnibus, 1984

Prendergast, Mark   Irish Rock: Roots, Personalities, Directions, O'Brien Press, 1987

Reese, Krista   Elvis Costello – A Completely False Biography Based
On Rumour, Innuendo And Lies, Proteus, 1981

St Michael, Mick   Elvis Costello – An Illustrated Biography,
Omnibus, 1986

Thomas, Bruce	The Big Wheel, Viking, 1990 *Fiction based on fact.*
White, Timothy	Rock Lives: Profiles And Interviews, Omnibus, 1991, pp 625-47 *1983 interview.*

Fanzines

Elvis has been particularly fortunate in the loyalty of his fans, and as well as the various sites posted on the internet, two fanzines have resulted, one in Holland and one jointly produced in Britain and America.

Elvis Costello Information Service, August 1979-
c/o Richard Groothuizen, Primulstraat 46, 1441 HC, Purmerend, Netherlands (SAEs and IRCs appreciated).

Groothuizen produced fifteen editions in both Dutch and English between August 1979 and December 1981 – the main information of which is collected in his long out-of-print Elvis Costello So Far *– and then the magazine started again, this time solely in English, from issue 1 in February 1982. It is still going strong.*

Beyond Belief
c/o Mark Perry, 6 Hillside Grove, Taunton, Somerset TA1 4LA or Mike Bodayle, 110 Granburg Circle, San Antonio, TX 78218, USA; email bb@perrys.prestel.co.uk

Mark Perry has been extremely helpful to me in compiling the present volume, and in turn I can highly recommend a subscription to this fanzine, published quarterly, and packed with facts and photographs.

Internet

Elvis Costello Home Page: http://east.isx.com/-schnitzi/elvis.html

Features lyrics, chords, a short biography, photographs and an exhaustive list of every public gig that Costello has ever played. There is also what Stuart Maconie of Q *describes as "a virtual jumble sale of Elvis paraphernalia", including a list of the musical and literary allusions in all his songs. "Drop by. You'll end up staying for hours."*

The internet at its best – mind-boggling detail lost in space.

index